D1244405

Price Competitiveness
in World Trade

NATIONAL BUREAU OF ECONOMIC RESEARCH
Studies in International Economic Relations

1. *Problems of the United States as World Trader and Banker*   HAL B. LARY
2. *Price and Quantity Trends in the Foreign Trade of the United States*
   ROBERT E. LIPSEY
3. *Measuring Transactions Between World Areas*   HERBERT B. WOOLLEY
4. *Imports of Manufactures from Less Developed Countries*   HAL B. LARY
5. *Demand-Policy Responsiveness to the Balance of Payments: The Postwar Pattern*   MICHAEL MICHAELY
6. *Price Competitiveness in World Trade*   IRVING B. KRAVIS AND ROBERT E. LIPSEY

Price Competitiveness in World Trade

IRVING B. KRAVIS
National Bureau of Economic Research and
University of Pennsylvania

AND

ROBERT E. LIPSEY
National Bureau of Economic Research and
Queens College

National Bureau of Economic Research

NEW YORK

1971

Distributed by Columbia University Press
NEW YORK AND LONDON

854528

Relation of the Directors to the Work and Publications
of the National Bureau of Economic Research

1. The object of the National Bureau of Economic Research is to ascertain and to present to the public important economic facts and their interpretation in a scientific and impartial manner. The Board of Directors is charged with the responsibility of ensuring that the work of the National Bureau is carried on in strict conformity with this object.

2. The President of the National Bureau shall submit to the Board of Directors, or to its Executive Committee, for their formal adoption all specific proposals for research to be instituted.

3. No research report shall be published until the President shall have submitted to each member of the Board the manuscript proposed for publication, and such information as will, in his opinion and in the opinion of the author, serve to determine the suitability of the report for publication in accordance with the principles of the National Bureau. Each manuscript shall contain a summary drawing attention to the nature and treatment of the problem studied, the character of the data and their utilization in the report, and the main conclusions reached.

4. For each manuscript so submitted, a special committee of the Board shall be appointed by majority agreement of the President and Vice Presidents (or by the Executive Committee in case of inability to decide on the part of the President and Vice Presidents), consisting of three directors selected as nearly as may be one from each general division of the Board. The names of the special manuscript committee shall be stated to each Director when the manuscript is submitted to him. It shall be the duty of each member of the special manuscript committee to read the manuscript. If each member of the manuscript committee signifies his approval within thirty days of the transmittal of the manuscript, the report may be published. If at the end of that period any member of the manuscript committee withholds his approval, the President shall then notify each member of the Board, requesting approval or disapproval of publication, and thirty days additional shall be granted for this purpose. The manuscript shall then not be published unless at least a majority of the entire Board who shall have voted on the proposal within the time fixed for the receipt of votes shall have approved.

5. No manuscript may be published, though approved by each member of the special manuscript committee, until forty-five days have elapsed from the transmittal of the report in manuscript form. The interval is allowed for the receipt of any memorandum of dissent or reservation, together with a brief statement of his reasons, that any member may wish to express; and such memorandum of dissent or reservation shall be published with the manuscript if he so desires. Publication does not, however, imply that each member of the Board has read the manuscript, or that either members of the Board in general or the special committee have passed on its validity in every detail.

6. Publications of the National Bureau issued for informational purposes concerning the work of the Bureau and its staff, or issued to inform the public of activities of Bureau staff, and volumes issued as a result of various conferences involving the National Bureau shall contain a specific disclaimer noting that such publication has not passed through the normal review procedures required in this resolution. The Executive Committee of the Board is charged with review of all such publications from time to time to ensure that they do not take on the character of formal research reports of the National Bureau, requiring formal Board approval.

7. Unless otherwise determined by the Board or exempted by the terms of paragraph 6, a copy of this resolution shall be printed in each National Bureau publication.

(Resolution adopted October 25, 1926, and revised February 6, 1933,
February 24, 1941, and April 20, 1968)

Foreword

The project described by this report, the fifth in the National Bureau's Studies in International Economic Relations, had two purposes. One was the development of methods of measuring relative prices and price movements in international trade. The other was the calculation, using these methods, of international price measures for the main exporting countries, covering machinery, transport equipment, metals, and metal products.

This study combines two strands of the National Bureau's earlier work, one devoted to the improvement of price measures and the other to the analysis of changes in the international economic position of the United States. The study of price measurement at the Bureau has a long history, but the most recent related work was the report on *The Price Statistics of the Federal Government* (New York, NBER, 1961). This included an appendix on "Export and Import Price Indexes" which reviewed the unit value indexes of the U.S. Department of Commerce; a staff paper by Zvi Griliches on "Hedonic Price Indexes for Automobiles: An Econometric Analysis of Quality Change"; and several papers on U.S. wholesale price indexes. A closer examination of the accuracy of the official U.S. wholesale price data has been performed recently in a report on *The Behavior of Industrial Prices* (New York, NBER, 1970), by George J. Stigler and James K. Kindahl, which also followed the practice of using reports from buyers, as the present study does to a substantial degree.

The National Bureau's recent analyses of international trade and payments began with Hal B. Lary's book on *Problems of the United States as World Trader and Banker* (New York, NBER, 1963). The genesis of the present study was a discussion in that volume of the inadequacy of the measures of international price relationships then available and of the need for better measures to aid in the analysis of changes in trade balances. The results of an effort to improve and interpret the historical record on the export and import prices of the United States were presented in *Price and Quantity Trends in the Foreign Trade of the United States* (Princeton University Press for NBER, 1963), by Robert E. Lipsey. The relation of price and quantity changes in foreign trade to those of the domestic economy was discussed there, and some comparisons between wholesale price and unit value data were included.

This report consists of five parts. Part One is a description of the scope of the study and a summary of the findings on method (Chapter 1) and the empirical results (Chapter 2). Part Two gives a more extended presentation of the methods used and the reasons for choosing them. Part Three gives the general empirical findings on price-quantity relationships and other aspects of international competitiveness, and compares the international price indexes derived here with wholesale price and unit value indexes. Part Four consists of more detailed reports for the main product groups covered in the study, particularly those for which there was information on nonprice factors or for which the analysis in some way went beyond the price collection itself. The basic data for the study are set out in the appendixes, of which A and B give the trade data; C, D, and E, the detailed indexes computed for the study; and F and G, indexes calculated from wholesale prices for several countries and from U.S. export unit value data.

IRVING B. KRAVIS
ROBERT E. LIPSEY

Acknowledgments

The collection of this large body of new price data required the assistance of many groups outside the National Bureau. Several hundred business firms, under a promise of anonymity, provided us with price data on products they bought or sold internationally and with insights into the peculiarities of individual markets. We are indebted to these companies and to the National Bureau directors, University of Pennsylvania trustees, and business organizations who arranged introductions to them. A number of American and foreign governmental and intergovernmental agencies and private groups supplied foreign data and particularly international bidding information which were a major source for us. Among those we can thank publicly are the U.S. Bureau of Labor Statistics, the Department of Defense, the Statistical Office of the Federal Republic of Germany, the IFO-Institut für Wirtschaftsforschung in Munich, and the Department of Economics of the Hebrew University in Jerusalem.

In the beginning of the study, Philip J. Bourque, of the University of Washington played a major role in the planning and data collection. Elizabeth Durbin, now of New York University, assisted in developing the price collection methods and was responsible for much of that work. At later stages, Marianne Tampier Lloris, Christine Mortensen, Doris Preston, and Zenaida Mata handled the major part of the assembly of data, machine calculation, and the checking of the manuscript. They were aided at various times, in the data collection and programing, by Jill Adler, Sultan Ahmad, Rita Bank, Betty Fishbein, Michelle Turnovsky, Lorenzo Perez, Joaquin Pujol, Jocelyn Coburn Whitmoyer, and Margot Zimmerman. Beatrice Grabiner managed the extensive data files and the other secretarial work of the project. Ester Moskowitz edited the volume, and H. Irving Forman drew the charts.

Among our colleagues, Hal Lary played a major part in initiating the study and in encouraging our efforts throughout its sometimes discouraging length. Ilse Mintz, Nancy Ruggles, and Raymond J. Struyk served on the staff reading committee, and David L. Grove, Douglass C. North, and Thomas A. Wilson were the directors' reading committee. We received numerous helpful comments from both groups and from other members of the staff and board of directors who read individual parts of the manuscript. We are also grateful for suggestions and criticisms from individuals outside the Bureau, including Phoebus J. Dhrymes, Lawrence R. Klein, Robert Summers, Paul R. Trumpler, and many of the suppliers of data who reviewed the product chapters to which they contributed.

The study was financed partly by two grants from the National Science Foundation and partly from the general funds of the National Bureau.

Contents

Foreword   vii

Acknowledgments   ix

PART ONE. INTRODUCTION AND SUMMARY

1. The Nature of the Study   3

The Need for New Measures   3
New Measures of International Prices   7
The Substantive Scope of the Study   11
Conclusions Regarding Method   15

2. Empirical Results   19

The Price Competitiveness of the United States, 1953–64   19
The Diffusion of the Changes   23
Categories Marked by Large Price Level Differences   26
Individual-country Weighting Systems   27
Effects of Price Changes on Trade Quantities   29
Nonprice Factors Affecting the Competitive Position of the United States   31
    Technological Leadership   32
    Large Size of the Domestic Market   33
    Quality of Product   33
    Speed of Delivery   35

PART TWO. METHODS

3. Conceptual Problems in Measuring the Role of Prices in International Competitiveness   39

The Index of Price Competitiveness as an Analytical Measure   39
    Relation of Price Competitiveness to Market Shares   40
    Prices and Costs as Alternative Approaches to Competitiveness   42
    The Interpretation of the Index of Price Competitiveness   43
Scope for International Differences in Prices   47
    Transfer Costs   48
    Restrictive Practices   55
    Product Differentiation   57
    Nonprice Factors   59

4. Methods of the Study   62

   Data Collection   62
     Method of Collection   62
     Sources of Price Data   63
     Selection of Items for the Sample   69
     Place of Reference of Prices   70
     Exclusion of Service Components of Prices   71
   Price Concepts   72
     The Comparability of Products and Prices   72
     The Quality Problem   72
     Unique Goods   74
     Use of Domestic Prices   75
     Use of Offer Prices   76
     The Problem of Intracompany Transactions   78
   Aggregation Methods   80
     The Problem of Weights   80
     Aggregation for Price Competitiveness Indexes   82
   Appendixes   89
     Copy of Instructions Left with Respondent Firms   89
     Form Used for Gathering Price Data   93

5. Measuring Price Differences by Regression Methods   94

   The Rationale of Regression Analysis in Price Comparisons   95
     Cost vs. Utility   96
     Use of Regression Coefficients for Price Measurement   97
     Specification Differences and Regression Strategies   98
   Automotive Diesel Engine Price Regressions   105
     Specification of the Relationship   105
     Mathematical Form   109
     Types of Regression   110
     Pooling with International Differences in Element Prices 111
     Other Types of Regression   115
     Conclusions   117
   Other Applications of Regression Methods   120

PART THREE. ASSESSING THE ROLE OF PRICES IN TRADE

6. Quantity-Price Relationships   127

   The Utility of the New Indexes   127
   The Price-Quantity Equations   130
   All Goods Treated as a Single Aggregate   132
   Two-digit Categories   134

Three- and Four-digit Groups 139
Earlier Estimates of Elasticities 141
Product Elasticities (1963 Cross-sectional Data) 144
Export Specialization and Price Trends 148

7. *Some Further Aspects of International Competitiveness* 151

The Relative Importance of Price and Nonprice Factors 151
Price Differentiation Between Domestic and Export Markets 157
Shipment Delay 158
Appendix: Copy of Form Used in Survey of Export Competitiveness 165

8. *Wholesale Prices and Unit Values as Measures of International Price Competitiveness* 169

Price Indexes from International and Wholesale Price Data 171
Price Competitiveness Indexes from International and Wholesale Price Data 182
Price Indexes from International Prices and Export Unit Values 186
Quantity-Price Relations Derived from Wholesale Price Indexes 191
Summary 194

PART FOUR. PRODUCT REPORTS

9. *Iron and Steel* 199

Trade 199
Nonprice Factors in Trade 203
Price Changes 207
Comparisons with Other International Price Data 211
Comparisons with Domestic Prices 215
Price Competitiveness 218
Price Levels 221
Summary 223

10. *Nonferrous Metals* 224

Nonferrous Metals as a Whole 227
International Price Indexes 227
Price Competitiveness 229
Price Levels 229
Comparisons with Wholesale Price and Unit Value Data 230
Factors Affecting Competitiveness in Individual Metal Groups 233
Geographical Influences 234
Institutional Influences 235
Copper 242

Aluminum   248
Other Nonferrous Metals   252
  Nickel   252
  Silver and Platinum Metals   254
  Zinc   256
  Tin   260
  Miscellaneous Nonferrous Metals   263
Conclusions   263

11. Metal Manufactures, n.e.s.   267

Trade   267
Price Trends   274
Price Competitiveness   275
Price Levels   276
Summary   280

12. Nonelectrical Machinery   281

Aircraft Engines and Parts   285
  Trade   285
  Price Changes   288
  Price Competitiveness   290
Internal Combustion Engines Other Than for Aircraft   292
  Trade   292
  Price Levels and Price Competitiveness   296
  Price Levels   297
Agricultural Machinery and Implements   299
  Trade   299
  Price Trends and Levels   303
Office Machines   307
  Trade   307
  International Price Indexes   309
  Price Competitiveness   312
  Price Levels   313
  Prices and the Pattern of Trade   315
  Summary   319
Metalworking Machine Tools   320
  Trade   320
  Price Trends   325
  Price Competitiveness   326
  Price Levels   328
Textile and Leather Machinery   331
  Trade   331
  Textile Machinery   331
  Machinery for Hides, Skins, and Leather   335

Sewing Machines ·   336
Textile and Leather Machinery as a Whole   338
Mechanical Handling Equipment   339
   Trade   339
   Price Trends   342
   Price Levels   343
   Price Competitiveness   345
Appendix: Price Estimates Based on Regression Analysis   346
   Aircraft Engines   346
   Outboard Motors   352
   U.S. Tractors   357

13. *Electrical Machinery, Apparatus, and Appliances*   362

Electric Power Machinery and Switchgear   367
   Trade   367
   Nonprice Influences on Trade   370
   Price Competitiveness   372
   Price Levels   375
   Price Trends   379
Electricity Distribution Equipment   382
   Trade   382
   Price Trends   384
   Price Levels   385
   Price Competitiveness   387
Telecommunications Equipment   388
   Trade   388
   Price Trends   393
   Price Competitiveness   395
   Price Levels   397
Household Electrical Equipment   400
   Trade   400
   Price Trends   403
   Price Competitiveness   405
   Price Levels   406
Appendix: Regression Analysis of Power Transformer Prices   408

14. *Transport Equipment*   422

Railway Vehicles   425
   Trade   425
   Nonprice Factors in Trade   429
   Price Trends   432
   International Price Levels   435
   Price Competitiveness   437
Road Motor Vehicles   439

Trade 439
Price Trends 445
Price Levels 449
Aircraft 453
Trade 453
Nonprice Factors in Trade 456
Price Trends 458
Price Levels 460
Price Competitiveness 462
Ships and Boats 463
Trade 463
Nonprice Factors in Trade 466
Prices 468
Appendixes 473
Comparisons Among Various Measures of Diesel Locomotive Price Trends 473
Regression-based International Price Index for Japanese Ships 478

15. *Passenger Motor Cars* 484

Background 484
Time-to-time Changes in Domestic Automobile Prices 486
Data 486
Independent Variables 492
Scope and Form of the Regressions 497
Time-to-time Movement of Domestic Automobile Prices 498
International Comparisons of Automobile Prices, 1964 508
Home Market Comparisons 508
Comparisons in Selected Markets 519
Summary of International Comparisons 529

PART FIVE. APPENDIXES

A. *Trade Data for 1963* 533

B. *OECD Exports, 1953–64* 568

C. *International Price Indexes* 599

D. *Indexes of Price Competitiveness* 640

E. *Price Level Indexes* 663

F. *Indexes from Wholesale Prices and Related Data* 691

G. *Indexes from U.S. Export Unit Value Data* 724

Index 727

Tables

1.1   OECD Exports of Machinery, Transport Equipment, Metals, and Metal Products, by Origin, Destination, and Commodity Division, 1963 and by Origin, 1953, 1957, 1961–64   13

2.1   International Prices, Price Competitiveness, and Price Levels of All Covered Commodities, 1953, 1957, 1961–64   20

Machinery, Transport Equipment, Metals, and Metal Products, 1953, 1957, 1961–64

2.2   International Prices   21

2.3   U.S. Price Competitiveness   22

2.4   Price Levels   24

2.5   Comparison of International Price Indexes Based on Various Country Weights, All Covered Commodities, 1953, 1957, 1961–64   28

3.1   Transport Costs for U.S. Imports of Metals, Metal Products, and Machinery, 1965   49

3.2   Average Tariff Rates, 1962   54

4.1   International Price Indexes Under Two Methods of Aggregation, All Covered Commodities, 1953, 1957, 1961–64   88

Automotive Diesel Engines

5.1   Summary of Data, 1962   106

5.2   Price Comparisons Based on Alternative Criteria for Pooling: Double Log Equations   113

Regression Coefficients for Automotive Diesel Engine Prices

5.3   Pooled Equations with No Allowance for Country Differences in Element Coefficients   116

5.4   Pooled and Individual Country Regressions   118

6.1   MacDougall's Estimates of Product Elasticities of Substitution, Selected Years, 1913–59   145

7.1   Distribution of U.S. Exports and Survey Data, 1964   152

7.2   Relative Importance of Factors Explaining U.S. Export Success   153

7.3   Alternative Test of Relative Importance   155

7.4   Factors Accounting for Factory Equipment Trade: German Imports vs. U.S. Exports, 1964   156

7.5   Relative Shipment Delay for Standard Specifications and Capacity Utilization, Europe, Japan, and the United States, 1953–64   160

7.6   Relative Delivery Time for Goods Offered in International Bidding, 1961–64   162

8.1   U.S. Wholesale Price Indexes Based on Domestic Weights vs. U.S. International Price Indexes Based on International Weights, 1953, 1957, 1961–64   172

8.2   Comparison of Price Indexes from International and Whole-
       sale Price Data, International Weights, 1953, 1957, 1961–
       64   174
8.3   Aggregation of Ratios of Wholesale to International Price
       Indexes, 1953, 1957, 1961–64   181

       U.S. Price Competitiveness, 1953, 1957, 1961–64
8.4   Comparison of Indexes from International and Wholesale
       Price Data   183
8.5   Aggregation of Ratios of Wholesale-price-based to Inter-
       national-price-based Indexes   185
8.6.   Comparison of U.S. Price Indexes from International Price
       and Export Unit Value Data, 1953, 1957, 1961–64   187
8.7   Aggregation of Ratios of Unit Value to International Price
       Indexes, United States, 1953, 1957, 1961–64   188
8.8   Machinery: NBER International Price Indexes vs. UN Ex-
       port Unit Value Indexes, 1953, 1957, 1961–64   190

       Iron and Steel (SITC 67)
9.1   OECD Exports, by Origin, Destination, and Commodity
       Group, 1963   200
9.2   OECD Exports, 1953, 1957, 1961–64   204
9.3   International Prices, 1953, 1957, 1961–64   208
9.4   Distribution of Year-to-year Percentage Price Changes in
       Subgroups, 1961–64   210
9.5   Price Indexes Based on Alternative Types of Price Data,
       1953, 1957, 1961–64   212
9.6   U.S. Price Competitiveness, 1953, 1957, 1961–64   218
9.7   U.S. Price Competitiveness Indexes Based on Alternative
       Types of Price Data, 1953, 1957, 1961–64   219
9.8   Price Levels, 1953, 1957, 1961–64   222

       Nonferrous Metals (SITC 68)
10.1   OECD Exports, by Origin, Destination, and Commodity
       Group, 1963   225
10.2   OECD Exports, 1953, 1957, 1961–64   228
10.3   International Prices, 1953, 1957, 1961–64   229
10.4   U.S. Price Competitiveness, 1953, 1957, 1961–64   229
10.5   Price Levels, 1953, 1957, 1961–64   230
10.6   Price Indexes: NBER, Domestic, and Unit Value, 1953,
       1957, 1961–64   231
10.7   Major Nonferrous Metals: Geographical Distribution of and
       Changes in Production and Consumption, 1954 and 1963   237

       *International Prices, Price Competitiveness, and Price Levels,
       1953, 1957, 1961–64*
10.8   Copper   246

10.9   Aluminum   251
10.10   Copper, Aluminum, and Lead: Ranking of Export Value and
           Price Ratios, United Kingdom to United States, EEC to
           United States, and United Kingdom to EEC   266

Metal Manufactures, n.e.s. (SITC 69)
11.1   OECD Exports, by Origin, Destination, and Commodity
           Group, 1963   268
11.2   Ratios of U.S. Exports to Manufacturers' Shipments and
           U.S. Imports to New Supply (Output plus Imports), 1964   270
11.3   OECD Exports, 1953, 1957, 1961–64   273
11.4   International Prices, 1953, 1957, 1961–64   274
11.5   U.S. Price Competitiveness, 1953, 1957, 1961–64   275
11.6   Price Levels, 1953, 1957, 1961–64   276

Nonelectrical Machinery (SITC 71)
12.1   OECD Exports, by Origin, Destination, and Commodity
           Group, 1963   282
12.2   OECD Exports, 1953, 1957, 1961–64   284
12.3   International Prices, Price Competitiveness, and Price Levels,
           1953, 1957, 1961–64   285

Aircraft Engines and Parts (SITC 711.4)
12.4   OECD Exports, by Origin and Destination, 1963   286
12.5   International Prices, 1953, 1957, 1961–64   289
12.6   U.S. Price Competitiveness Relative to the United Kingdom,
           1957, 1961–64   290
12.7   U.K. Price Level Relative to the United States, 1957,
           1961–64   292

Internal Combustion Engines Other Than for Aircraft (SITC 711.5)
12.8   OECD Exports, by Origin, Destination, and Type of En-
           gine, 1963   293
12.9   OECD Exports, 1953, 1957, 1961–64   296
12.10   International Prices and U.S. Price Competitiveness, 1953,
           1957, 1961–64   297
12.11   Price Levels, 1962   298

Agricultural Machinery and Implements (SITC 712)
12.12   OECD Exports, by Origin, Destination, and Commodity
           Subgroup, 1963   300
12.13   OECD Exports, 1961–64   303
12.14   International Prices, 1953, 1957, 1961–64   304
12.15   U.S. Price Competitiveness, 1953, 1957, 1961–64   305
12.16   International Price and Price Competitiveness Indexes Based
           on Wholesale Price Data, 1953, 1957, 1961–64   305

Office Machines (SITC 714)
12.17   OECD Exports, by Origin, Destination, and Commodity
         Subgroup, 1963   308
12.18   OECD Exports, 1953, 1957, 1961–64   310
12.19   International Prices, 1953, 1957, 1961–64   310
12.20   U.S. International Prices: NBER Index vs. Indexes from
         Wholesale Price and from Unit Value Data, 1953, 1957,
         1961–64   311
12.21   U.S. Price Competitiveness, 1953, 1957, 1961–64   313
12.22   Price Levels, 1953, 1957, 1961–64   314
12.23   Relation of Price Ratios to Export Shares and Export-
         Import Ratios, 1963   316

Metalworking Machine Tools (SITC 715.1)
12.24   OECD Exports, by Origin, Destination, and Type of Tool,
         1963   322
12.25   OECD Exports, 1953, 1957, 1961–64   324
12.26   International Prices, 1953, 1957, 1961–64   325
12.27   U.S. Price Competitiveness, 1953, 1957, 1961–64   327
12.28   Price Levels, 1953, 1957, 1961–64   329

Textile and Leather Machinery (SITC 717)
12.29   OECD Exports, by Origin, Destination, and Commodity
         Subgroup, 1963   332
12.30   OECD Exports, 1961–64   334
12.31   International Prices, Price Competitiveness, and Price Levels,
         Textile Machinery, 1953, 1957, 1961–64   334
12.32   U.S. Exports and Unit Values of Industrial Sewing Ma-
         chines, 1964   337
12.33   International Prices and Price Competitiveness, Sewing Ma-
         chines, 1953, 1957, 1961–64   337
12.34   International Prices, Price Competitiveness, and Price Levels,
         Textile and Leather Machinery, 1953, 1957, 1961–64   338

Mechanical Handling Equipment (SITC 719.3)
12.35   OECD Exports, by Origin, Destination, and Commodity
         Item, 1963   340
12.36   OECD Exports, 1961–64   341
12.37   International Prices, 1953, 1957, 1961–64   342
12.38   Price Levels, 1953, 1957, 1961–64   343
12.39   U.S. Price Competitiveness, 1953, 1957, 1961–64   346
12.40   Regression Analysis of Aircraft Engine Prices   350

Outboard Motors, 1962 and 1963
12.41   Number of Observations and Average Horsepower   353
12.42   Regressions   355
12.43   Comparative Prices, Based on Pooled Regressions   356

Tractors, 1953, 1957, 1961–64
12.44 Coefficients of Regressions 359
12.45 Price Indexes Derived from Regressions 359

Electrical Machinery, Apparatus, and Appliances (SITC 72)
13.1 OECD Exports, by Origin, Destination, and Commodity Group, 1963 363
13.2 OECD Exports, 1953, 1957, 1961–64 365
13.3 International Prices, Price Competitiveness, and Price Levels, 1953, 1957, 1961–64 366

Electric Power Machinery and Switchgear (SITC 722)
13.4 OECD Exports, by Origin, Destination, and Commodity Subgroup, 1963 368
13.5 OECD Exports, 1953, 1957, 1961–64 369
13.6 U.S. Price Competitiveness, 1957, 1961–64 373
13.7 Price Levels, 1957, 1961–64 376
13.8 International Prices, 1953, 1957, 1961–64 380

Electricity Distribution Equipment (SITC 723)
13.9 OECD Exports, by Origin, Destination, and Commodity Subgroup, 1963 383
13.10 OECD Exports, 1961–64 384
13.11 International Prices, 1953, 1957, 1961–64 384
13.12 Price Levels, 1957, 1961–64 385
13.13 U.S. Price Competitiveness, 1953, 1957, 1961–64 387

Telecommunications Equipment (SITC 724)
13.14 OECD Exports, by Origin, Destination, and Commodity Subgroup, 1963 389
13.15 OECD Exports, 1961–64 391
13.16 International Prices, 1953, 1957, 1961–64 393
13.17 U.S. Price Competitiveness, 1953, 1957, 1961–64 396
13.18 Price Levels, 1953, 1957, 1961–64 398

Household Electrical Equipment (SITC 725)
13.19 OECD Exports, by Origin, Destination, and Commodity Subgroup, 1963 401
13.20 OECD Exports, 1961–64 403
13.21 International Prices, 1953, 1957, 1961–64 404
13.22 U.S. Price Competitiveness, 1957, 1961–64 405
13.23 Price Levels, 1957, 1961–64 406

Prices of Power Transformers
13.24 Arithmetic Regression Equations, All Observations 411
13.25 Arithmetic Regression Equations, Excluding Large Transformers 412
13.26 Logarithmic Regression Equations, All Observations 413

13.27	Logarithmic Regression Equations, Excluding Large Transformers	416
13.28	U.S. Indexes from Regression Equations	418
13.29	Comparison of Several U.S. Price Indexes	419

Transport Equipment (SITC 73)

14.1	OECD Exports, by Origin, Destination, and Commodity Group, 1963	423
14.2	OECD Exports, 1953, 1957, 1961–64	424
14.3	International Prices, Price Competitiveness, and Price Levels, 1953, 1957, 1961–64	425

Railway Vehicles (SITC 731)

14.4	OECD Exports, by Origin, Destination, and Commodity Subgroup, 1963	427
14.5	OECD Exports, 1953, 1957, 1961–64	429
14.6	U.S. Exports of Diesel Locomotives, by Horsepower, 1953, 1957, 1961–64	430
14.7	International Prices, 1953, 1957, 1961–64	433
14.8	Price Levels, 1953, 1957, 1961–64	435
14.9	U.S. Price Competitiveness, 1953, 1957, 1961–64	437

Road Motor Vehicles (SITC 732)

14.10	OECD Exports, by Origin, Destination, and Commodity Subgroup, 1963	441
14.11	OECD Exports, 1953, 1957, 1961–64	443
14.12	International Prices, 1953, 1957, 1961–64	446
14.13	Official Wholesale and Export and NBER International Price Indexes, 1953, 1957, 1961–64	448
14.14	U.S. Price Competitiveness, 1953, 1957, 1961–64	450

Aircraft and Parts (SITC 734)

14.15	OECD Exports, by Subgroup, 1963, and by Year, 1953, 1957, 1961–64	454
14.16	International Prices, 1953, 1957, 1961–64	459
14.17	U.K. International Price Levels, 1957, 1961–64	461
14.18	U.S. Price Competitiveness, 1957, 1961–64	462

Ships and Boats (SITC 735)

14.19	OECD Exports, by Origin and Destination, 1963	464
14.20	Tonnage and Distribution of Ships Launched for Registration in Other Countries, 1953, 1957, 1961–64	466
14.21	International Prices, 1953, 1957, 1961–64	468
14.22	U.S. Price Competitiveness, 1953, 1957, 1961–64	470
14.23	Price Levels, 1953, 1957, 1961–64	471

Diesel Electric Locomotives

14.24	Comparison of U.S. Time-to-time Indexes from Various Sources, 1953, 1957, 1959, 1961–64	474

14.25   Comparison of Time-to-time Indexes from Bidding Data, 1959, 1961–64   477

14.26   Japanese Export Ship Contracts, Summary of Data, 1957, 1961–64   479

14.27   Ship Price Indexes Computed from Pooled Regressions, 1957, 1961–64   481

Passenger Cars
15.1   Output and Exports, 1953 and 1964   485
15.2   OECD Exports, by Origin and Destination, 1963   487
15.3   OECD Exports, 1953, 1957, 1961–64   488

Domestic Cars, 1953, 1957, 1961–64
15.4   Number of Models Included in Regressions Based on Domestic List Prices   489

15.5   Average Price and Characteristics of 1964 Models Included in Regressions   493

15.6   Price Relatives, Preferred Regressions   499
15.7   Price Indexes   500
15.8   Price Relatives, Comparison of Various Regression Estimates   501

15.9   Time-to-time Changes in Prices, NBER vs. Other Indexes   502

Changes in Standard Items Included in Car List Prices
15.10   Low-priced Four-door Chevrolet Sedan, 1953, 1956–64   504
15.11   Regular Four-door Buick Sedan, 1953, 1957, 1959–61   505
15.12   U.S. Price Competitiveness, Cars, 1953, 1957, 1961–64   507
15.13   International Comparisons of Domestic Car Price Levels, Based on Regression Analysis, 1964   509

Domestic Cars, Six OECD Countries, 1964
15.14   Regressions of Domestic Prices on Selected Characteristics   511
15.15   Number and Price per Horsepower Unit, by Horsepower Class   512

15.16   Number and Price per Pound, by Weight Class   513
15.17   Estimated Percentage Distribution of Car Production and NBER Sample, by Piston Displacement, Four European Countries, 1964   514

15.18   Specifications of Five Cars Taken as Representative of World Trade and Shares of Trade Represented   517

Price Comparisons for Five Makes of Car, 1964
15.19   Home-market Price Comparisons   518
15.20   Regression Comparisons of Home Prices and Prices on Four Other Markets   520

15.21   Export Price Level Comparisons Estimated from Regression Equations, Four Markets   523

15.22 Foreign-market as Percentage of Home-market Prices of Identical Cars, 1964 ... 526
15.23 Expected vs. Actual Foreign-market Prices of Cars, 1964 ... 528
15.24 Summary of Indicators of Relative Car Prices, 1964 ... 529

OECD Exports, by Country of Origin and Destination, 1963
A.1   All Covered Commodities ... 535
A.2   Iron and Steel (SITC 67) ... 537
A.3   Nonferrous Metals (SITC 68) ... 538
A.4   Metal Manufactures, n.e.s. (SITC 69) ... 539
A.5   Machinery Other than Electric (SITC 71) ... 540
A.6   Electrical Machinery, Apparatus, and Appliances (SITC 72) ... 542
A.7   Transport Equipment (SITC 73) ... 544

OECD Exports, Value by Country of Origin and Subgroup, 1963
A.8   Iron and Steel (SITC 67) ... 546
A.9   Nonferrous Metals (SITC 68) ... 549
A.10 Metal Manufactures, n.e.s. (SITC 69) ... 551
A.11 Machinery Other than Electric (SITC 71) ... 554
A.12 Electrical Machinery, Apparatus, and Appliances (SITC 72) ... 562
A.13 Transport Equipment (SITC 73) ... 565
A.14 Miscellaneous Manufactured Articles (Selected Items from SITC 8) ... 567

OECD Exports, by Country, for Two-digit SITC Divisions, 1953, 1957, 1961–64, and Three-digit Groups, 1961–64
B.1   Iron and Steel (SITC 67) ... 570
B.2   Pig Iron, Ferro-alloys, etc. (SITC 671) ... 570
B.3   Ingots and Other Primary Forms of Iron and Steel (SITC 672) ... 571
B.4   Iron and Steel Bars, Rods, Angles, Shapes, and Sections (SITC 673) ... 571
B.5   Universals, Plates, and Sheets of Iron or Steel (SITC 674) ... 572
B.6   Hoop and Strip of Iron or Steel (SITC 675) ... 572
B.7   Rails and Railway Track Construction Material of Iron and Steel (SITC 676) ... 573
B.8   Iron and Steel Wire, Excluding Wire Rod (SITC 677) ... 573
B.9   Tubes, Pipes, and Fittings of Iron or Steel (SITC 678) ... 574
B.10 Nonferrous Metals (SITC 68) ... 574
B.11 Silver, Platinum, and Other Metals of the Platinum Group (SITC 681) ... 575
B.12 Copper (SITC 682) ... 575
B.13 Nickel (SITC 683) ... 576
B.14 Aluminum (SITC 684) ... 576
B.15 Lead (SITC 685) ... 577

B.16 Zinc (SITC 686) 577
B.17 Tin (SITC 687) 578
B.18 Miscellaneous Nonferrous Base Metals Employed in Metallurgy (SITC 689) 578
B.19 Manufactures of Metals, n.e.s. (SITC 69) 579
B.20 Finished Structural Parts and Structures, n.e.s. (SITC 691) 579
B.21 Metal Containers for Storage and Transport (SITC 692) 580
B.22 Wire Products (Excluding Electric) and Fencing Grills (SITC 693) 580
B.23 Nails, Screws, Nuts, Bolts, Rivets, and Similar Articles of Iron, Steel, or Copper (SITC 694) 580
B.24 Tools for Use in the Hand or in Machines (SITC 695) 581
B.25 Cutlery (SITC 696) 581
B.26 Household Equipment of Base Metals (SITC 697) 581
B.27 Manufactures of Metals, n.e.s. (SITC 698) 582
B.28 Machinery Other than Electric (SITC 71) 582
B.29 Internal Combustion Engines Other than for Aircraft (SITC 711.5) 583
B.30 Agricultural Machinery and Implements (SITC 712) 583
B.31 Office Machines (SITC 714) 584
B.32 Metalworking Machine Tools (SITC 715.1) 584
B.33 Metalworking Machinery Other than Machine Tools (SITC 715.2) 585
B.34 Textile and Leather Machinery (SITC 717) 585
B.35 Machines for Special Industries (SITC 718) 586
B.36 Paper Mill and Pulp Mill Machinery, etc. (SITC 718.1) 586
B.37 Printing and Bookbinding Machinery (SITC 718.2) 586
B.38 Food-processing Machinery (SITC 718.3) 587
B.39 Construction and Mining Machinery, n.e.s. (SITC 718.4) 587
B.40 Mineral Crushing, Sorting, and Molding Machinery, etc. (SITC 718.5) 588
B.41 Pumps and Centrifuges (SITC 719.2) 588
B.42 Mechanical Handling Equipment (SITC 719.3) 589
B.43 Power Tools, n.e.s. (SITC 719.5) 589
B.44 Other Nonelectrical Machines (SITC 719.6 and 719.8) 590
B.45 Electrical Machinery, Apparatus, and Appliances (SITC 72) 590
B.46 Electric Power Machinery and Switchgear (SITC 722) 591
B.47 Equipment for Distributing Electricity (SITC 723) 591
B.48 Telecommunications Equipment (SITC 724) 592
B.49 Household Electrical Equipment (SITC 725) 593
B.50 Electrical Apparatus for Medical Purposes, etc. (SITC 726 and 729) 593
B.51 Transport Equipment (SITC 73) 593
B.52 Railway Vehicles (SITC 731) 594

B.53   Road Motor Vehicles (SITC 732)   595
B.54   Road Vehicles Other than Motor Vehicles (SITC 733)   596
B.55   Aircraft and Parts (SITC 734)   597
B.56   Ships and Boats (SITC 735)   597
B.57   Sanitary, Plumbing, Heating, and Lighting Fixtures and Fit-
        tings (SITC 812)   598

        International Price Indexes, 1953, 1957, 1961–64
C.1   Iron and Steel   600
C.2   Nonferrous Metals   608
C.3   Metal Manufactures, n.e.s.   610
C.4   Machinery Other than Electric   613
C.5   Electrical Machinery, Apparatus, and Appliances   626
C.6   Transport Equipment   632
C.7   Miscellaneous Manufactured Articles   637

        Indexes of U.S. Price Competitiveness, 1953, 1957, 1961–64
D.1   Iron and Steel   641
D.2   Nonferrous Metals   644
D.3   Miscellaneous Metal Manufactures, n.e.s.   645
D.4   Machinery Other than Electric   648
D.5   Electrical Machinery, Apparatus, and Appliances   655
D.6   Transport Equipment   659
D.7   Miscellaneous Manufactured Articles   662

        Price Level Indexes, 1953, 1957, 1961–64
E.1   Iron and Steel   664
E.2   Nonferrous Metals   668
E.3   Miscellaneous Metal Manufactures   669
E.4   Machinery Other than Electric   672
E.5   Electrical Machinery, Apparatus, and Appliances   683
E.6   Transport Equipment   687
E.7   Miscellaneous Manufactured Articles   689

        Indexes from Wholesale Prices, 1953, 1957, 1961–64
F.1   Iron and Steel   693
F.2   Nonferrous Metals   696
F.3   Metal Manufactures, n.e.s.   698
F.4   Machinery Other than Electric   700
F.5   Electrical Machinery, Apparatus, and Appliances   704
F.6   Transport Equipment   706
F.7   Miscellaneous Manufactured Articles   708

        Indexes of U.S. Price Competitiveness Computed from Domestic
        Wholesale Price Series, 1953, 1957, 1961–64
F.8   Iron and Steel   710
F.9   Nonferrous Metals   712
F.10   Metal Manufactures, n.e.s.   713

F.11   Machinery Other than Electric   715
F.12   Electrical Machinery, Apparatus, and Appliances   718
F.13   Transport Equipment   720
F.14   Miscellaneous Manufactured Articles   721
F.15   German Producers' Price Indexes, 1957, 1961–64   722
G.1   Indexes from U.S. Export Unit Value Data, 1953, 1957,
        1961–64   725

Charts

13.1   Indexes of U.S. Power Transformer Prices, 1953–64   418
14.1   Price Competitiveness and Export Shares in Locomotives, United
        States and Germany, 1957, 1961–64   438

PART ONE

INTRODUCTION AND SUMMARY

1

THE NATURE OF THE STUDY

THIS BOOK DESCRIBES new methods of measuring price competitiveness in the international trade of a developed industrial country and provides annual indexes of price changes and levels, calculated by these methods, for machinery, transport equipment, and metals and metal products. The indexes cover the United States, the United Kingdom, countries of the European Economic Community (EEC or Common Market), and Japan, for 1953, 1957, and 1961–64.

These are the main features of the methods: (1) Actual prices or price offers were used rather than unit values derived from trade statistics; (2) world trade weights were employed rather than the trade weights of the United States or some other single country; (3) country-to-country price relations for different points in time were used to help establish intertemporal movements in price competitiveness; (4) rather than prices gathered in terms of detailed, preselected specifications, pairs of prices were collected for specifications of the respondents' own choosing, each pair providing either a time-to-time or country-to-country price relative; and (5) regression techniques were employed to make international price comparisons for some commodity groups.

The price measures constructed for covered commodities and years are used in an exploratory way to analyze trade flows. The role of non-price factors in trade flows is also considered, although the chief focus of the work is on prices.

The Need for New Measures

This study was partly inspired by recent U.S. balance-of-payments difficulties. One explanation of these problems has been that the competitiveness of the United States economy has declined; that there has been a tendency for the United States to "price itself out of world markets."

While there has been disagreement over the causes of U.S. balance-of-payments deficits, few would deny that relative price movements should be examined in any analysis of balance-of-payment problems. Two measures of price change are usually used in assessing price competitiveness—foreign trade unit value indexes from customs data,[1] and wholesale and consumer price indexes for the domestic economy.[2]

Unit values are values per unit of quantity within detailed export or import classifications. However, since the classifications must in total cover every item of trade, they cannot be narrowly specified unless their number is increased far beyond any practical limit. As a result of the lack of close specification, there is never any certainty that a change in unit value represents a change in price; the unit value of a trade classification can change, even though all prices are constant, if there is a shift from one quality or type of item to another.

A few years ago, for example, foreign pressures to increase local production of components led to the reporting in export declarations of motor vehicles which contained smaller and smaller fractions of a complete car—some as little as 15 to 20 per cent by value.[3] The unit value series thus was biased downward as a measure of price movements. This problem may not be too serious for many crude or agricultural commodities, but exact specification is extremely important for finished manufactures, which have accounted for more than half of the value of U.S. exports for several decades and, recently, for half of its imports. The composition of manufactures at even a relatively early stage of fabrication may shift so as to produce spurious price movements, as the chapters on iron and steel and nonferrous metals indicate. In the former group, for example, the U.S. unit value series for tubular goods increased by 19 per cent between 1957 and 1961 because narrower and more specialized types of pipe were being exported, while

1 Export and import *price* indexes (as distinct from unit value indexes) are available for Germany and Japan but not for the United States or most other countries.

2 See, for example, Helen B. Junz and Rudolf R. Rhomberg, "Prices and Export Performance of Industrial Countries, 1953–63," *International Monetary Fund Staff Papers,* July 1965, pp. 230–239. Unit labor cost and productivity trends are also examined in that study.

3 See Stigler Committee Report, pp. 82–83 (Price Statistics Review Committee, *The Price Statistics of the Federal Government,* New York, National Bureau of Economic Research, 1961). The committee which compiled this report was established by the National Bureau at the request of the U.S. Bureau of the Budget.

export prices, holding quality constant, actually declined by 2 per cent. (See Chapter 8 for further analysis of U.S. unit value data.)

The existing export and import unit value indexes are defective not only because of the ambiguity of many of these unit value series but also because quantities are not reported at all for many manufactured products, and their unit values are therefore simply unavailable.[4] These faults, moreover, bias the corresponding quantity indexes in a direction opposite to that of the unit value series.[5]

Even if the unit value indexes accurately reflected the price movements of actual exports and imports, they would still be deficient indicators of price competitiveness in international trade. One disadvantage, which they share with export and import price indexes, is that the weights by which the different commodities are combined differ from one country to another, owing to the differing composition of export trade; therefore it is not possible to say whether an apparent change in price relations results from differences in price movements or from differences in the weighting of identical price movements. Second, each country's weights are themselves a function of its competitiveness in different products; commodities which encounter severe foreign competition tend to disappear from among a country's exports. In an index with changing weights, the weights of these commodities decline. Even if constant weights are used in the indexes, the worse the competitive position of a country in a commodity, the lower the weight of that commodity in that country's index.

Commodities produced domestically but not exported are omitted from export price indexes. Yet, as is pointed out below, these may have an important bearing on competitive strength. If the domestic price of a commodity falls, it may then be exported or may replace a foreign product previously imported. An index of export prices describes only one side of the story of a country's international price competitiveness; the competitiveness of its domestic products in comparison with imports, which is equally important, escapes notice.

These deficiencies have often led balance-of-payments analysts to

---

[4] In recent years from 23 to 35 per cent of finished manufactured imports and from 15 to 25 per cent of finished manufactured exports were covered in unit value index calculations (*Description of U.S. Foreign Trade Indexes,* International Trade Analysis Division, U.S. Dept. of Commerce, June 14, 1967).

[5] For a fuller discussion of unit value indexes, see Robert E. Lipsey, *Price and Quantity Trends in the Foreign Trade of the United States,* Princeton University Press for NBER, 1963, Chap. 4.

compare the movements of domestic wholesale and consumer prices. Other things equal, the consumer price indexes are less relevant to international competition than the wholesale price indexes, since the former include service items,[6] few of which can be traded, and refer to the retail level of distribution.

In contrast to unit value indexes, both types of domestic indexes are usually constructed from prices of carefully specified commodities. However, they too, for different reasons, are deficient measures of international price competitiveness. The indexes of the different countries vary widely in coverage, method of construction, and weighting, and reported prices include many list or other published figures which may not reflect transactions prices.[7] Most important of all, export prices may diverge from domestic prices for considerable periods. Differences between domestic and export price measures are discussed in Chapters 7 and 8, and several examples of variance are given in the chapters below dealing with individual commodities,[8] and even published examples can be found.[9] Nor can the direction of the differential movements of export and domestic prices be inferred simply from domestic economic conditions. In a booming domestic economy an industry may in some circumstances raise its home prices at times when keen international competition constrains it from increasing export prices. In other circumstances, especially where export trade is marginal, export prices may rise as home prices are kept constant or limited to smaller increases. Transportation costs; government interventions, such as tariffs and rebates on exports; and general market imperfections also make it possible for home prices to move differently from export prices.

If export unit value indexes were consistently in agreement with wholesale price indexes, most investigators might set aside these objections as valid in principle but of little quantitative significance. How-

[6] For example, services account for over one-third of the expenditure weights in the Bureau of Labor Statistics Consumer Price Index (see *Statistical Abstract of the United States, 1964*, U.S. Bureau of the Census, 1964, p. 358). Indexes of consumer commodity prices (excluding services) are available for the United States and for some, but not all, other countries.

[7] Stigler Committee Report, pp. 69–71, 373–458. See also George J. Stigler and James K. Kindahl, *The Behavior of Industrial Prices*, New York, NBER, 1970.

[8] See, for example, the chapters on iron and steel, nonferrous metals, agricultural machinery, automobiles, and equipment for distributing electricity.

[9] For example, see *Wholesale Price Index Annual*, Bank of Japan, for the differences between "wire rod of ordinary steel" and "wire rod of ordinary steel (for export)," between "sheets" and "sheets (for export)," and similar differences for "medium steel plates," "heavy thick steel plates," and "tin plates" in Japanese wholesale price data. See also *National Institute Economic Review* (London), February 1964, p. 48.

ever, the two sets of data have sometimes diverged substantially just at the times when there was the most concern over relative prices. For example, between 1959 and 1961, the U.S. wholesale price index, reweighted to reflect the composition of exports, fell slightly, while the total export unit value index rose by 3 per cent. For manufactures the reweighted wholesale price index fell by 0.2 per cent, while the export unit value index for finished manufactures increased by 5 per cent and that for finished manufactures and semimanufactures rose by 4 per cent.[10]

New Measures of International Prices

The deficiencies of the indexes we have described suggest a number of specifications for a more appropriate price index for internationally traded goods: (1) It should be based on actual prices or price offers, not unit values. (2) For goods which the country actually exports, the prices should refer to export rather than domestic transactions. (3) The indexes for different countries should refer to the same set of goods. (This requires that domestic prices should be taken for goods which a particular country does not export.) Our new price indexes for internationally traded goods, which we shall refer to as *international price indexes,* are designed to meet these requirements.

The basic point of departure for these indexes is that the universe of prices relevant to an evaluation of a country's price competitiveness is not limited to export and import prices. For an industrial country that produces the whole gamut of manufactures, such as the United States, the United Kingdom, Germany, or Japan, the relevant universe consists of prices of all those manufactured goods that enter world trade. For example, changes in the U.S. prices of *all* of these goods—whether they are imported, exported, or even produced but not imported or exported—affect the U.S. competitive position. If the U.S. price of a good neither imported nor exported rises sufficiently relative to foreign prices, the United States will begin to import the good; if the relative price falls enough, the product will be exported.

The selection of this universe of prices also leads to the choice of

---

[10] Hal B. Lary, *Problems of the United States as World Trader and Banker,* New York, NBER, 1963, pp. 62–63.

a weighting system based on the relative importance of commodities in world trade. As pointed out in Chapter 4, we may regard such weights as reflecting the importance of each commodity in consumption, adjusted for the different extent to which different commodities tend to be traded internationally.

We have taken as an approximation to world trade weights the aggregate 1963 exports of the countries belonging to the Organization for Economic Cooperation and Development (OECD), including trade among OECD countries. They are a close estimate of the total export trade of developed countries and, for most of the products in our study, of world trade as well.[11]

The new measures, prepared with the aid of these weights, are made up of three interrelated sets of index numbers.

1. *International price indexes.* These indexes, which we have already mentioned, are time-to-time indexes for each country. They were derived by applying 1963 world trade weights to each country's export price changes (or to its domestic price changes where exports of a particular category were nil or negligible). They measure the change in each country's prices of the bundle of goods that was exported by the industrial countries as a whole. The international price index for any one country such as the United States (S) is then:

$$ P_S = \frac{\sum \left(\frac{P_1}{P_0}\right)_S w_{63}}{\sum w_{63}} $$

where P_1 and P_0 represent U.S. prices in two different years and w_{63} represents the 1963 weights.

2. *The index of price competitiveness.* Our main interest in a country's international price index is in its movements relative to those of other countries. Did the U.K. price index rise by more or less than that of the United States in a given period, and by how much more or less? The comparisons of price movements can be presented systematically simply by dividing the international price index for one country by the corresponding index for another country. We call the result an index of price competitiveness. In calculating it, we place the foreign country's index in the numerator and the U.S. index in the denominator.

---

[11] The OECD includes eighteen European countries, and the United States, Canada, and Japan.

A rise in the index of U.S. price competitiveness, therefore, indicates that foreign prices of internationally traded goods have risen relative to U.S. prices and that U.S. price competitiveness has thus improved while that of the foreign country has declined. The index of price competitiveness for the United States vis-à-vis the United Kingdom, for example, is

$$P_{K/S} = P_K/P_S$$

where P_S is as defined above, and P_K is the corresponding index for the United Kingdom.

3. *Comparisons of price levels.* The index of price competitiveness can also be derived from country-to-country comparisons of price levels of internationally traded goods at a given moment in time.[12] Changes over time in these place-to-place indexes measure changes in price competitiveness in the same manner as comparisons of time series indexes. If we are comparing two countries, S and K, in two years, 0 and 1, the place-to-place comparisons for a single commodity can be described as

$$\frac{P_{K_0}}{P_{S_0}} \quad \text{and} \quad \frac{P_{K_1}}{P_{S_1}}$$

and the place-to-place index for year 0 as

$$\frac{\sum \frac{P_{K_0}}{P_{S_0}} w_{63}}{\sum w_{63}}$$

To compute the index of price competitiveness from the place-to-place price relatives, the ratio of foreign to U.S. prices for each year is taken as a percentage of the ratio for the base year. The index of price competitiveness derived in this way would be identical with that derived from the time-to-time data if, for each individual commodity specification for which we had place-to-place comparisons, we also had a set of time-to-time comparisons covering the same countries and years. In practice, of course, the data do not match perfectly. However, as we approach adequate coverage in both types of comparison, the two indexes of price competitiveness should converge. Both approaches

[12] Such country-to-country relatives measure the level of a country's price competitiveness and should explain, to some degree, the current pattern of trade in individual categories of products.

are used in this study since their feasibility and reliability vary from one type of commodity group to another.

For some commodities, only time-to-time data can be obtained; for example, two countries may produce machines which compete with each other but differ greatly in design or other characteristics. For other commodity groups—notably those sold on a "turnkey" basis (i.e., installed and ready to operate), such as large electrical generating equipment and communications systems—it is easier to obtain place-to-place than time-to-time price comparisons. Time-to-time price comparisons for such intricate, large, custom-made equipment are difficult because the specifications vary from one job to another.

In other indexes, this problem is often met by pricing major components of the equipment rather than the finished product itself. However, we were able to compute indexes directly, because this kind of equipment—heavy electrical installations and communications systems—is often purchased by public authorities under a system of bidding in which both domestic and foreign bids are made public at the time the award is announced. These bids, and similar bids received by private entities, when they can be obtained, provide a good basis for direct price comparisons between firms in different countries.

Each approach to the index of price competitiveness provides some information not given by the other. The country-to-country price relatives do not tell to what degree observed changes over time are attributable to price movements in one country or the other. The differential movements in the time-to-time indexes, on the other hand, tell us nothing about the absolute spread of prices between the two countries. This knowledge might help clarify nonprice aspects of competition, such as financing, servicing, and the like.

We have been able in a few product areas to compare results obtained from the two approaches. Such a comparison provides a significant test, of course, only in groups where the two types of data were derived from different sources.

Our place-to-place comparisons and indexes of price competitiveness in a way parallel the absolute and relative versions of the purchasing power parity concept. However, we have not sought to develop a measure suitable for the calculation of equilibrium exchange rates, and our system of weighting (world trade weights) does not correspond with those systems usually discussed in connection with purchasing power parities.[13]

The Substantive Scope of the Study

Since there is no centrally collected and publicly available body of price data for internationally traded goods, it was necessary to start with a program of data collection. Ways had to be found to fit this potentially formidable task into the resources available for the study. One means of reducing the volume of field work was to limit the commodity coverage. Since the study was largely methodological in objective, the proposed approach was put to the most rigorous test by applying it first to machinery and transport equipment, products that were likely to offer the greatest difficulty for the purpose at hand. In order to cover relatively homogeneous products as well as custom-designed ones, we included the whole range of manufactured metal products, beginning with pig iron and its nonferrous equivalents.

The precise commodity coverage of the study may be set out in terms of the Standard International Trade Classification,[14] which has been used as a framework for organizing the data collection and constructing the index numbers:

SITC Division		Weight
67	Iron and steel	13
68	Nonferrous metals	6
69	Manufactures of metals, n.e.s.	6
71	Machinery, other than electrical	32
72	Electrical machinery	13
73	Transport equipment	24
Selected items from section 8—		
Miscellaneous manufactured articles		7
Total		100

[13] For a recent discussion of purchasing power parity theory, see Bela Balassa, "The Purchasing Power Parity Doctrine," *Journal of Political Economy,* December 1964, pp. 584–596.

[14] *Standard International Trade Classification, Revised,* United Nations, Statistical Papers, Series M, No. 34, 1961.

These products accounted for 46 per cent of total exports by the OECD countries [15] in 1963, 45 per cent of total United States exports, and 64 and 69 per cent of the exports of products other than food and raw materials of the OECD countries and of the United States, respectively. We present indexes for all the two-digit SITC divisions included above, most of the three-digit groups contained in them, and many of the more important four-digit subgroups.

The dates of reference for price quotations are midyears 1953, 1957, and 1961 through 1964. It would have been preferable to construct the indexes for a longer period of time and for each year within the period. However, even these six years of data proved to be too much for many of our sources of price information, and it was felt that keeping the length of the period down and omitting some of the intervening years would improve the chances for getting the necessary cooperation.

Indexes for the covered commodity groups as a whole have been prepared for the United States, the United Kingdom, Germany, and the European Economic Community (which includes Germany, France, Italy, Belgium, the Netherlands, and Luxembourg). We chose these areas partly because of their importance in world metal and machinery trade and partly because we had access to price information there. We regret our inability to provide comprehensive indexes for Japan; for many of our respondents Japan emerged as an important competitor or alternative source of supply only near the end of our reference period. We are able to publish indexes for Japan for only three of the six SITC commodity divisions covered, and for a fair number of smaller commodity groups. Other countries such as France and the Netherlands also occasionally figure individually in the indexes presented for particular product classes.

The importance of the main countries and commodity divisions in the total trade covered by this study, and the main trends over time are displayed in Table 1.1, which shows the origin of the $45 billion of exports included and the main destinations for the exports of each country of origin.

[15] These countries accounted for 82 per cent of 1963 world exports in SITC section 7, divisions 67 and 68 (less group 681), and groups 691–695, 698, and 812 (*Monthly Bulletin of Statistics,* United Nations, March 1967, pp. xviii ff.).

Table 1.1
OECD Exports of Machinery, Transport Equipment, Metals, and Metal Products,
by Origin, Destination, and Commodity Division, 1963, and by Origin, 1953, 1957, 1961–64
(millions of dollars)

				Origin		
				EEC		
	Total OECD	U.S.	U.K.	Total	Germany	Japan
Total, all destinations (1963)	44,560	10,224	6,637	18,679	9,464	2,824
Destination						
U.S.	3,948		489	1,370	801	799
OECD Europe	20,257	2,378	2,431	11,992	6,222	329
U.K.	1,674	390		674	313	59
EEC total	11,724	1,385	1,300	7,460	3,395	141
Germany	2,957	384	300	1,576		44
Canada	2,726	2,177	277	157	98	54
Japan	698	373	67	183	123	
Latin America	3,563	1,669	280	1,009	462	229
Other	11,843	2,191	3,088	3,913	1,753	1,395
Unaccounted for	89		5	56	5	17
Special categories	1,436	1,436				

(continued)

Table 1.1 (concluded)

				Origin		
					EEC	
	Total OECD	U.S.	U.K.	Total	Germany	Japan
SITC commodity division (1963)						
Iron and steel (67)	5,693	514	573	3,166	1,146	702
Nonferrous metals (68)	2,725	449	348	837	256	43
Metal manufactures, n.e.s. (69)	2,519	500	371	1,146	570	200
Nonelectrical machinery (71)	14,164	4,046	2,404	5,492	3,299	351
Electrical machinery (72)	6,005	1,492	891	2,474	1,173	519
Transport equipment (73)	10,496	2,704	1,764	4,472	2,345	626
Selected items from SITC 8, miscellaneous manufactured articles	2,959	519	286	1,092	674	383
Year[a]						
1964	47,236	11,017	6,513	20,032	9,705	3,161
1963	41,557	9,661	6,351	17,587	8,789	2,441
1962	38,617	9,385	5,965	16,212	8,169	1,995
1961	36,088	8,500	5,855	15,379	7,820	1,695
1957	27,606	8,695	4,981	10,030	5,089	953
1953	17,353	6,092	3,513	5,548	2,363	381

Source: Appendix B and sources mentioned therein.
[a]These data do not include subgroups of SITC 8.

14

Conclusions Regarding Method

Since the development of methods of measurement was a main object of our study we list the conclusions we reached about method and about the direction that future work in this field should take.

Data gathering (Chapter 4). A major conclusion of our work is that it is feasible to collect many types of data relevant to the measurement of international price competitiveness that had never been collected before. Working with comparatively small price collection resources, we accumulated a large quantity of data. A well-financed official data gathering project should meet with even greater success.

An experiment we consider successful and more broadly applicable was the abandonment of the traditional method of using preselected specifications, in its stead placing on the respondent the burden of finding comparable products for two times or two places so that price comparisons could legitimately be made. For more complex products it would have been impossible to pick specifications applicable to any large number of respondents, and even for simpler products the efficiency of the price collection effort was greatly enhanced. The use of bidding data in a sense followed the same method, since each bid comparison was for a very particular product or set of products, and rarely were any two items identical in the degree required by prevailing price collection methods. No set of preselected specifications could have turned up more than a small fraction of the items appearing in these bids.

In examining the great number of bidding and selling arrangements, we were frequently reminded of the enormous variety of conditions attached to a sale, other than those usually subsumed under the heading of price. List prices were, of course, subject to many types of discounting, for cash payment, for size of order, or simply to meet expected competition. Often this discounting was ignored in sellers' reports and only revealed in buyers' reports and in bidding documents, and the prevalence of this discrepancy points strongly to the need for collecting data from buyers as well as from sellers.

Even the transaction price, however, should be regarded only as a reference base from which continual additions and subtractions are made through changes in such factors as credit terms, delivery time, and the provision of various services. All these features could conceivably be
York, NBER, 1963, pp. 62–63.

priced, but the information is difficult to obtain; lacking it we probably underestimate the real degree of price flexibility.

Use of regression methods (Chapter 5). For both producer and consumer durable goods we found that by using regression methods for international price comparisons we could cover many complex products that would defy comparison by conventional methods, which require identical specifications in two situations. For many such goods there are no cases of identical specifications from two countries or even, in some products, from two periods of time for the same country. We ran regressions on such products as locomotives, aircraft engines, automotive diesel engines, outboard motors, tractors, chemical reactors, automobiles, trucks, and ships, most of which would have been insurmountably difficult to compare if identical specifications had been required. The regression method essentially involves treating a commodity as a cluster of characteristics or quality elements and measuring the price of each characteristic through multiple regression of price against the amount of each element. The product samples and the regressions were in some cases limited to a single country in one year, but in others covered several countries, several years, or both. We applied it to numbers of models ranging from 20 to 1,000, using one to six physical characteristics of the product (but often experimenting with more), and we usually reached $\bar{R}^2$s of 0.9 or more in the best equations. Although we used regression methods mainly for international comparisons, our success in obtaining satisfactory results with such limited data augurs well for the use of these methods in domestic price index work as well.

Wholesale price and unit value indexes (Chapter 8). Neither wholesale price indexes nor indexes of export unit values can be relied upon to describe accurately changes in the international prices of the main industrial countries.

Wholesale price indexes do not adequately cover machinery classifications from the standpoint of international trade and are constructed by methods ill-suited to adjustment for quality changes. Also, to varying degrees from country to country and from time to time, the movements of domestic and of international prices of commodities diverge.

The discrepancies between the changes in wholesale prices and those in international prices were small during periods of little price change but became large, frequently five points or more, when there were larger changes in international prices.

In general, the use of wholesale price data for the 1953–64 period provides an unduly unfavorable view of the changes in the price competitiveness of the United States with respect to Germany. Between 1953 and 1957, for example, wholesale prices point to a 14 per cent decline in U.S. price competitiveness, but the international price indexes show only a 3 per cent decline. Although during the rest of the period the two indexes moved similarly at the aggregate level there were a number of major divergences, notably in iron and steel and in nonferrous metals.

The results for the two unit value indexes we could examine showed them to be even less reliable measures of international price competitiveness for metals and machinery than wholesale prices. An index of export unit values constructed from series used in the official U.S. index deviates from our U.S. international price index to a greater degree than did our reconstructed U.S. wholesale price series. It showed larger and more erratic time-to-time changes and tended to have a larger upward bias.

The other unit value series, a UN index for machinery as a whole (SITC 7) showed a 24 per cent increase between 1953 and 1964. The increase in the NBER international price series was 13 per cent.

Were we lacking international price indexes of the type presented here for 1953–64, we would choose wholesale price indexes rather than unit value indexes for analytical work on international trade. However, we would make them comparable for the various countries by recombining the components using a uniform set of weights.

Future directions of work. It seems clear that future efforts to collect international prices should be conducted in more than one country and preferably in many countries. Comparisons in any one market tend to be biased by trade barriers, consumer preferences, differences in the degree of competition and in the range of products purchased, and many other factors. The ideal arrangement would be for an international agency to act as a clearinghouse through which countries could exchange data derived from government purchasing activity and from firms operating in the individual countries, with each government and firm reporting on both its foreign and its domestic operations. It would be important to collect data from the less developed countries, since these are major markets for many products. However, even an exchange between any two or three countries could add greatly to the information available to each one on its competitive position.

We hope that the outcome of this investigation will encourage government and international agencies to pursue the measurement of international price relations on a more comprehensive basis. Such measurements would add to our understanding of trade patterns and of changes in the balance of payments of industrial countries and should also be useful in analyzing shifts in trade for specific groups of commodities. Our experience has persuaded us that indexes like these can be constructed on a regular basis and would be a great improvement over existing measures.

In related fields, much more could be learned about the relative roles of price and nonprice factors in various commodity classifications through survey methods. Until this is done even the best price measures will explain only incompletely the factors determining the composition and directions of trade flows and the changes in them.

2

EMPIRICAL RESULTS

The Price Competitiveness of the United States, 1953–64

PERHAPS THE MOST striking result of the study is that there was little change in U.S. price competitiveness relative to the European countries between 1953 and 1964 for our products as a group.[1] Relative to each foreign country, the index of price competitiveness—that is, the change in the ratio of foreign to U.S. prices—stayed within a range of five percentage points. Within that narrow range, U.S. price competitiveness tended to decline between 1953 and 1961 or 1962, and to recover afterward. The sharpest decline in the early period was relative to the EEC (Common Market) countries other than Germany, and this loss in position was not fully regained by 1964. The EEC countries also improved their position relative to the United Kingdom.

As this implies, there was a large degree of similarity of the extent and timing of the movement of the international price indexes of the United States, the United Kingdom, and the EEC countries. From 1953 to 1964 the prices of internationally traded goods, shown in Table 2.1 for the whole group of metal products and equipment we cover, rose by about 15 per cent in the United States and Germany, 18 per cent in the United Kingdom, and by 13 per cent in the EEC as a whole. In all three areas, the sharpest rises occurred between 1953 and 1957; there were smaller increases from 1957 to 1961 and again from 1963 to 1964.

When price levels are compared, U.S. prices were consistently higher. European price levels were between 7 and 11 per cent below U.S. prices

[1] The data for Japan are not adequate for the calculation of overall indexes.

Table 2.1

International Prices, Price Competitiveness, and Price Levels of All Covered
Commodities, 1953, 1957, 1961–64

	1953	1957	1961	1962	1963	1964
INTERNATIONAL PRICE INDEXES (1962 = 100)						
U.S.	88	97	99	100	100	101
U.K.	88	96	100	100	101	104
EEC	90	97	99	100	100	102
Germany	88	94	98	100	100	102
INDEXES OF U.S. PRICE COMPETITIVENESS (1962 = 100)						
Relative to						
U.K.	100	100	101	100	101	104
EEC	102	100	99	100	100	102
Germany	100	98	99	100	100	101
PRICE LEVEL INDEXES (U.S. FOR EACH YEAR = 100)						
U.S.	100	100	100	100	100	100
U.K.	90	89	90	90	91	93
EEC	93	91	90	91	91	92
Germany	91	89	90	91	91	92

Source: Aggregation of indexes shown in Appendixes C, D, and E, as described in
Chapter 4.

in all the years for which we have data, and ended the period 7 to 8
per cent below. The data do not suggest that there were very great
differences between the United Kingdom and Germany or the EEC.

The similarity of movements in the overall international price indexes
conceals a considerable variation among the countries in price movements for individual commodity divisions. This can be seen in Tables 2.2
and 2.3, which show the international price indexes and the indexes of
price competitiveness for the six major two-digit SITC categories included in our study.[2] The United States lost heavily in price competitiveness relative to all the other countries in iron and steel, even though
there was some improvement in the last year, 1964. In nonferrous metals
and in electrical equipment, on the other hand, the United States im-

[2] Some categories in SITC section 8, not shown separately in Tables 2.2, 2.3, and
2.4 are included in the figures of Table 2.1.

Table 2.2

International Prices: Machinery, Transport Equipment, Metals, and Metal
Products, 1953, 1957, 1961–64

(1962 = 100)

	1953	1957	1961	1962	1963	1964
IRON AND STEEL (SITC 67)						
U.S.	84	101	102	100	99	100
U.K.	99	110	102	100	96	104
EEC	101	118	104	100	96	104
Germany	94	111	104	100	96	104
Japan	NA	NA	110	100	99	100
NONFERROUS METALS (SITC 68)						
U.S.	96	100	101	100	100	108
U.K.	95	101	101	100	102	115
EEC	100	102	101	100	101	117
Germany	100	105	101	100	100	115
MANUFACTURES OF METAL, N.E.S. (SITC 69)						
U.S.	86	98	98	100	100	102
U.K.	90	101	103	100	99	103
EEC	87	99	100	100	97	98
Germany	84	93	98	100	99	101
Japan	NA	NA	98	100	93	101
MACHINERY OTHER THAN ELECTRIC (SITC 71)						
U.S.	81	92	99	100	101	102
U.K.	80	92	98	100	101	103
EEC	80	88	97	100	100	102
Germany	80	87	97	100	101	102
ELECTRICAL MACHINERY, APPARATUS, AND APPLIANCES (SITC 72)						
U.S.	102	108	104	100	97	97
U.K.	96	98	103	100	101	101
EEC	98	100	102	100	100	99
Germany	96	98	101	100	99	98
Japan	NA	124	106	100	97	99
TRANSPORT EQUIPMENT (SITC 73)						
U.S.	89	94	96	100	99	100
U.K.	87	94	100	100	102	107
EEC	94	98	97	100	101	102
Germany	90	95	96	100	101	101

Source: Appendix C (extrapolated indexes).

Table 2.3

U.S. Price Competitiveness: Machinery, Transport Equipment, Metals, and
Metal Products, 1953, 1957, 1961–64
(1962 = 100)

	1953	1957	1961	1962	1963	1964
IRON AND STEEL (SITC 67)						
Relative to						
U.K.	117	108	101	100	97	104
EEC	119	117	102	100	98	104
Germany	112	110	102	100	97	104
Japan	NA	NA	108	100	100	100
NONFERROUS METALS (SITC 68)						
Relative to						
U.K.	100	101	100	100	102	106
EEC	105	102	100	100	101	108
Germany	104	105	100	100	99	107
MANUFACTURES OF METAL, N.E.S. (SITC 69)						
Relative to						
U.K.	105	103	105	100	100	100
EEC	102	101	101	100	97	95
Germany	99	95	100	100	99	98
Japan	NA	NA	99	100	94	99
MACHINERY OTHER THAN ELECTRIC (SITC 71)						
Relative to						
U.K.	99	99	99	100	100	101
EEC	99	95	98	100	100	100
Germany	99	94	98	100	100	100
ELECTRICAL MACHINERY, APPARATUS, AND APPLIANCES (SITC 72)						
Relative to						
U.K.	94	91	99	100	105	103
EEC	96	92	97	100	103	101
Germany	94	91	97	100	102	101
Japan	NA	115	102	100	100	102
TRANSPORT EQUIPMENT (SITC 73)						
Relative to						
U.K.	98	100	104	100	103	107
EEC	107	105	101	100	101	102
Germany	102	101	100	100	102	101

Source: Appendix D.

proved its position relative to all the European countries. Nonelectrical machinery showed little or no trend. The same was true for miscellaneous metal manufactures except that U.S. price competitiveness declined relative to the EEC countries as a whole. In transport equipment the United States gained considerably on the United Kingdom but lost relative to the EEC countries.

In most of the divisions, Table 2.4 indicates, foreign prices were lower than U.S. prices in 1964, but the range was wide. The largest differences were in iron and steel, where European prices were about 20 per cent below those of the United States. In the other divisions the 1964 divergence was 10 per cent or less. In almost half of the other comparisons U.S. prices were lower or no more than 3 per cent higher than those of the other countries.

Japanese price data were insufficient for computation of a total index, but as can be seen from Tables 2.2–2.4 we are able to present Japanese indexes for three major divisions. In two of these, iron and steel and electrical machinery, the Japanese position improved greatly relative to all the other countries and in the third, miscellaneous metal manufactures, the Japanese price level was favorable throughout the period, but did not change substantially. We could not calculate price indexes for the other three major divisions, but in one of them, transport equipment, Japanese prices for two major components, automobiles and ships, clearly declined relative to those of other countries. Japanese price levels in 1964 were low not only in miscellaneous metal manufactures but also in iron and steel and electrical machinery, relative to both the United States and European prices.

The Diffusion of the Changes

The summary indexes presented in Tables 2.1–2.4 were built up from the much more detailed indexes on a three-, four-, and even five-digit level presented in appendixes C (international price indexes), D (indexes of price competitiveness), and E (indexes of price levels). The detailed indexes are interesting in their own right, since they represent price relationships for much more homogeneous groups of commodities than the summary indexes. Inferences derived from the detailed indexes

Table 2.4

Price Levels: Machinery, Transport Equipment, Metals, and Metal Products,
1953, 1957, 1961–64
(U.S. for each year = 100)

	1953	1957	1961	1962	1963	1964
IRON AND STEEL (SITC 67)						
U.S.	100	100	100	100	100	100
U.K.	92	85	79	78	76	82
EEC	88	87	76	74	72	78
Germany	85	83	77	76	73	78
Japan	NA	NA	75	70	70	70
NONFERROUS METALS (SITC 68)						
U.S.	100	100	100	100	100	100
U.K.	92	93	93	92	94	98
EEC	96	93	91	91	92	99
Germany	98	98	93	94	93	100
MANUFACTURES OF METAL, N.E.S. (SITC 69)						
U.S.	100	100	100	100	100	100
U.K.	97	95	97	92	92	92
EEC	97	96	97	96	93	91
Germany	90	87	92	92	91	90
Japan	NA	NA	74	74	69	73
MACHINERY OTHER THAN ELECTRIC (SITC 71)						
U.S.	100	100	100	100	100	100
U.K.	89	90	90	90	90	91
EEC	92	89	91	93	93	92
Germany	92	88	91	93	93	93
ELECTRICAL MACHINERY, APPARATUS, AND APPLIANCES (SITC 72)						
U.S.	100	100	100	100	100	100
U.K.	97	94	102	103	108	106
EEC	90	86	91	94	97	95
Germany	90	87	93	96	98	97
Japan	NA	103	91	89	90	91
TRANSPORT EQUIPMENT (SITC 73)						
U.S.	100	100	100	100	100	100
U.K.	85	87	90	87	89	93
EEC	102	100	96	96	97	98
Germany	94	94	92	93	94	93

Source: Appendix E.

about relationships between prices and trade movements and between prices and other variables are thus less subject to errors resulting from the aggregation of unlike commodities than those from summary data. However, these indexes are much more vulnerable to chance variation and to errors in individual observations. The individual categories to which they refer are analyzed in Part Four, but some general observations about their behavior relative to the summary indexes are in order at this point.

When the disaggregated indexes of price competitiveness are examined, most of the changes reported in the summary indexes seem to represent not only average changes for each group but also a large degree of consensus among the individual categories. In three-quarters of the cases, a majority of the component series within a two-digit SITC division moved in the same direction as the weighted average for the group as a whole.[3]

Although the direction of changes in prices and price competitiveness within each division is generally the same, in almost every instance, some subgroups move against the tide. Even within iron and steel, a division in which U.S. price competitiveness declined with monotonous regularity before 1964, there were in each period gains in U.S. price competitiveness relative to Germany and the United Kingdom in a quarter or more of the subgroups.

Also, the degree of diffusion of these changes in price competitiveness, that is, the proportion of the price competitiveness indexes moving in one direction, was not very closely related to the extent of changes in price competitiveness. A simple regression between the diffusion levels and the indexes of price competitiveness (taking the index of price competitiveness as a function of the proportion of subgroup indexes rising in that country for that division in that year) produces an $\bar{r}^2$ of only .57. However, the relationship is closer within all the SITC divisions except 69. The $\bar{r}^2$ for the other divisions ranges from .63 and .65 in electrical machinery (SITC 72), nonelectrical machinery (SITC 71), and transport equipment (SITC 73) to .84 and .85 in nonferrous

---

[3] Taking the price competitiveness indexes in each SITC division separately, there were 100 possible comparisons between a country's index for a commodity division in a particular time period and the corresponding diffusion measure (the latter being the proportion of series moving in the same direction as the group average). Eight cases in which the proportion was 50 per cent or in which there was no change in the index were counted as neither agreement nor disagreement.

metals (SITC 68) and iron and steel (SITC 67). For the international price indexes the corresponding $\bar{r}^2$ for all divisions was .59.

Categories Marked by Large Price Level Differences

The appendix tables also provide more details about relative price levels. Table 2.4, which presents some of these data, shows few examples of foreign price levels for major divisions more than 20 per cent below those of the United States, except in iron and steel, and none more than 10 per cent above. These did appear more frequently in the detailed price data, as we would expect, and the location of such observations points up some of the strengths and weaknesses of the U.S. position.

The U.S. competitive position, as measured by price levels, was clearly weakest in iron and steel. Subgroups in this division accounted for a disproportionate share of those showing foreign prices more than 20 per cent below U.S. prices in every year after 1957, particularly in 1962 and 1963 when almost half of the subgroups with these wide price disparities were in iron and steel.

Among nonferrous metals, zinc appeared on this list most frequently, but lead and worked aluminum also made several appearances. In miscellaneous metal manufactures, wire products (SITC 693), and fasteners (SITC 694) were most often in this category.

Among machinery subgroups these large price advantages for European and Japanese producers were less common. However, certain groups fell into that class in several years and relative to more than one country, particularly leather machinery among the nonelectrical machinery items and electricity distribution equipment among the electrical machinery ones. In transport equipment every competitor's prices for ships and boats were more than 20 per cent below U.S. prices in every year.

The group of products in which the U.S. showed price advantages of 10 per cent or more is in some ways more interesting because it is less well publicized, but it includes several important types of product. For example, agricultural machinery for preparing and cultivating the soil showed price levels strongly favorable to the United States. However, aircraft, which might be an even stronger case, are missing from the indexes because we lack price data on countries other than the United

Kingdom and the United States. The record of trade suggests that their price levels, if they could have been measured, would have shown that the United States held a position of unchallenged supremacy.

Individual-country Weighting Systems

One main difference between our indexes and those previously available is that we compare price levels and price movements for the same commodities in each country. We attain comparability by using weights derived from total exports of the OECD countries to aggregate all the individual-country prices. The question answered by the international price indexes is, for example: What have been the changes in each country's prices for the machinery and metal products exported by the OECD countries?

For other purposes one might wish to ask what changes have taken place in each country's prices for the products exported by the United States or by Japan. If we were interested in an index for the deflation of export values we might wish to measure each country's price changes for its own exports.

All of these and similar questions[4] can easily be answered by weighting our basic data in different ways. For example, Table 2.5 gives each country's total international price index based on OECD weights (those used in this study) and on the export weights of each country.

The logical expectation is that each country's price performance would appear most favorable in the index based on its own weighting system, because end-of-period weights for each country reflect the effects of shifts in its composition of exports toward those commodities in which its price competitiveness is improving. The results in Table 2.5 belie this expectation. The U.S. price index based on U.S. weights shows a larger rise in U.S. prices than U.S. indexes based on OECD, U.K., German, or Japanese weights. The U.K. index based on U.K. weights gives a less favorable picture of the development of U.K. price com-

---

[4] For example, at the request of the UN Commission on Trade and Development, price level indexes for machinery were calculated using as a weighting system the pattern of exports of developed countries to less developed ones, so as to measure the price differentials that might have been encountered in 1964 by countries receiving international aid, as a result of the tying of commodity purchases to the donor country. The results were incorporated in a report submitted to UNCTAD entitled "Some Evidence on Price Differentials Connected with Aid Tying," March 1968.

Table 2.5
Comparison of International Price Indexes Based on Various Country Weights, All Covered Commodities, 1953, 1957, 1961–64
(1962 = 100)

Weight Based on Exports of	1953	1957	1961	1962	1963	1964
U.S. INTERNATIONAL PRICE INDEX						
OECD	88	97	99	100	100	101
U.S.	86	95	99	100	100	102
U.K.	87	95	99	100	100	101
EEC	87	96	99	100	100	101
Germany	86	95	99	100	100	101
Japan	96	106	101	100	97	97
U.K. INTERNATIONAL PRICE INDEX						
OECD	87	97	100	100	100	104
U.S.	84	93	99	100	101	104
U.K.	86	95	99	100	101	104
EEC	88	97	100	100	100	104
Germany	87	96	100	100	101	104
Japan	96	106	101	100	98	101
EEC INTERNATIONAL PRICE INDEX						
OECD	90	97	99	100	100	102
U.S.	87	92	98	100	100	102
U.K.	89	95	98	100	100	102
EEC	91	98	99	100	100	103
Germany	89	96	98	100	100	103
Japan	95	104	100	100	98	101
GERMAN INTERNATIONAL PRICE INDEX						
OECD	86	94	98	100	100	102
U.S.	86	91	97	100	100	102
U.K.	87	93	98	100	100	102
EEC	89	95	98	100	100	102
Germany	87	94	98	100	100	102
Japan	93	101	99	100	98	101

Note: Each country's international price index based on OECD weights (those used in this study) is compared with indexes based on the export weights of each country. These OECD-weighted indexes, except those for the United States, differ from the ones in Table 2.1 because the latter are derived from the index of price competitiveness and the U.S. international price index (see Chapter 4 for explanation).

petitiveness than any of the others except that based on U.S. weights. The German index based on German export weights is more favorable than only the index based on U.S. weights.

One consistent feature of these indexes is the effect of the Japanese export structure in lowering prices. Every one of the four areas listed would have shown a smaller increase in prices if weighting had been by the composition of Japanese exports; and some of the differences are large. The United States would have shown almost no price increase, instead of the 15 per cent rise in the OECD-weighted index and the even larger gain in the U.S.-weighted index. One possible explanation for these differences is that Japan's successful entry into world markets, based to a large extent on price competition, tended to force down other countries' prices or restrain their price increases on the goods in which Japan was specializing. The U.S. export composition was related to prices in the opposite way; the United States, the United Kingdom, the EEC countries, and Germany all showed greater price increases in the indexes based on U.S. weights than in any other weighting system. The implication of this result is that the U.S. export bundle was heavily weighted, relative to those of other countries and particularly relative to Japan, toward goods that were rising in price.

We can only speculate about the implications of these differences in the relative importance of categories with rapidly rising prices in each country's exports. The differences might reflect differences in the rapidity with which entrepreneurs in different countries shift into products in which technological developments make price cuts possible. On the other hand, the products with declining prices might be in that category not as a result of technological change specific to that product but just because they are products in which Japan, with its high rate of productivity increase or possibly its aggressive export policy, is a leading exporter. For the United States, the explanation might lie in specialization in technologically advanced products that are price inelastic and income elastic.

Effects of Price Changes on Trade Quantities

Ideally, one should use these new indexes to measure the elasticity of substitution of trade, defined as the percentage change in relative quantities associated with a 1 per cent change in relative prices, holding constant such factors as income and the level of trade restrictions. We have in fact estimated elasticities from the equation

$$Q_{F/S} - 1 = a + b(P_{F/S} - 1)$$

where F represents a foreign country; S, the United States; Q, the index of relative export quantities;[5] P, the index of U.S. price competitiveness; b, the elasticity; and a, a constant.

The b in our equations must be regarded as descriptive of a particular historical relationship between quantity and price rather than as an estimate of one of the parameters of the international economy. The relationship we measure is a rather gross one since important nonprice influences have not been measured separately. Some of these factors, like market shares, are part and parcel of the functioning of a competitive economy and could be incorporated in a more thorough analysis than we have been able to make. Others, such as the progressive establishment of the Common Market, are not inherent in the operation of a competitive market but can be readily observed and could also be taken into account. In addition some among the wide variety of other influences, described in Scope for International Differences in Prices in the next chapter, limit the efficient operation of the market that is implicitly assumed in studies of quantity-price relations and are difficult to incorporate in a systematic analysis. Finally, to obtain the parameter b rather than an historically descriptive b, we would, for reasons described in Chapter 6, have to be more certain than we are that our observed changes in $Q_{F/S}$ were responsive to changes solely in supply conditions to the exclusion of influences arising from demand changes.

An additional difficulty is that the number of observations is fairly small. Almost every calculation therefore requires, for reaching a minimally adequate number of observations, the pooling of situations that we have reason to believe should not be pooled. In some cases these are different countries and in others, different commodity divisions. All our calculations suffer from the aggregation of markets, since we use data for the exports of each commodity to all destinations. Furthermore, the data exclude each exporter's own domestic market which is, however, counted in the exports of its competitors.

---

[5] Defined as the percentage change in the foreign country's exports divided by the percentage change in U.S. exports. For the method of measuring Q, see Chapter 6.

The elasticities we present incorporate the effects on quantity-price relationships of all these undesired factors. Because it cannot be assumed that the net effects will be unvarying from situation to situation, the elasticities we calculate should be taken very cautiously.

The historical elasticity of substitution for U.S. exports relative to those of two main foreign competitors, the United Kingdom and Germany, appears to have differed sharply between 1953–61 and 1961–64 for the products covered in this study. The data for large commodity divisions, pooled for all divisions and all countries, indicate that it was around −8 in the early period and around −1.25 in the later one. Quite possibly, nonprice factors, rather than a genuine shift in the degree of substitutability of U.S. and foreign goods, cause this difference. Data at a much more detailed commodity level are available only for 1961–64, and they yield results that are fairly consistent with those from the broader aggregates for the same period.

When we correlate relative quantities and relative prices between pairs of countries for the various categories of goods at a given moment in time (1963), we find, as MacDougall did earlier,[6] a significant inverse relationship: that is, a country tends to export relatively larger quantities of those product categories in which it has relatively lower prices. These "product" elasticities of substitution, calculated from fairly large numbers of observations for three- and four-digit SITC groups and subgroups in 1963, were larger than most of those estimated by earlier analysts. If the earlier data were subject to much larger errors of observation than ours, as we believe they were, we would expect our elasticity coefficients to be higher. We found coefficients for all three countries to be above 3.

Nonprice Factors Affecting the Competitive Position of the United States

Although we could not quantify nonprice factors in a way that could be used in econometric analysis, we did attempt to gather some information about nonprice factors that seemed to have a direct bearing on the U.S. competitive position. While our main objective in the study was the

[6] G. D. A. MacDougall, "British and American Exports: A Study Suggested by the Theory of Comparative Costs," *Economic Journal*, December 1951 and September 1952.

development of the price measures summarized in a preceding section, the broader motivation was to obtain an understanding of the factors at work determining the competitive position of the United States in world trade and changes therein. In our interviews,[7] therefore, businessmen were asked to discuss the sensitivity of their export sales to changes in relative prices and to comment on any nonprice factors that were deemed important.

With a few exceptions the generalizations we can make about these factors are nonquantitative and more impressionistic than the price indexes; they are not based, as the price indexes are, on many thousands of numbers which were gathered and summarized in an objective way. They are derived mainly from our interviews and also, to some extent, from trade publications, and they are therefore our generalizations of industry opinions. Some of the factors, like the role of technology, are well known and have received wide attention; others, like the part played by delivery time, have been less noted and appreciated.

We describe these factors more fully in Chapter 3, offer some limited quantification of one or two of them in Chapter 7, and link them to specific commodity groups in Part Four. Here we merely summarize them:

Technological Leadership

The strength of the U.S. trade position in machinery and related products rests to a large degree on the availability in the United States of products more sophisticated or technologically advanced than those produced abroad. In some products, such as computers and numerically controlled machine tools, the United States leads in knowledge. In others, such as machinery for the printing, baking, and pharmaceutical industries, the scale of the American economy makes the production of larger, faster, and more efficient machinery economical in this country before it is feasible abroad. Because of the greater technological sophistication of American industry, technological advances occur early in a given industry and the industry can find customers who are ready to use a more sophisticated product. In some of these cases American companies producing both at home and abroad recognize these differences by systematically lagging the production of new products abroad by one "product generation." We have found this to be true, for example, in the case of office machinery and construction machinery.

[7] See Chapter 4 for a description of the data sources.

Generally, products whose technology is well established and for which there are mass markets are cheaper abroad.[8]

Large Size of the Domestic Market

The large size of the market gives the U.S. economy an advantage not only in providing volume for new products more quickly, but also in making possible longer production runs and therefore lower costs. Of course the European and Japanese economies now also enjoy very large markets and are able to obtain the advantage of long production runs for many products, since the cost-reducing effects of larger and larger volumes are not limitless. However, the number of product variants for which economies of scale can be obtained is a continuous function of the size of the economy; in the American market a large volume of production is practicable even for relatively specialized variants of products which have only narrow markets in the smaller economies of U.S. competitors. In the anti-friction-bearing industry, for example, foreign firms were able to offer widely used types and sizes at half or less of the U.S. price during the study years, but the United States was still the largest exporter because it could supply specialized kinds of bearings requiring greater precision or resistance to heat, rust, radiation, or altitude. Even when such bearings were available abroad, they were usually produced in small quantities and at correspondingly high costs.

The economies of scale in this sense are not necessarily identified with large-scale enterprises. In the machine tool industry, for example, such economies tend to be achieved by a high degree of specialization by each of many small firms,[9] and the same tendency appears in other machinery industries such as textile machinery.

Quality of Product

No one country has a monopoly on reputation for quality, and product lines can be found in which each of the major industrial countries enjoys the reputation of quality leader. U.S. exports of machinery and equipment tend, however, to depend somewhat more frequently than those of

---

[8] Cf. Raymond Vernon, "International Investment and International Trade in the Product Cycle," *Quarterly Journal of Economics,* May 1966; and Irving B. Kravis, " 'Availability' and Other Influences on the Commodity Composition of Trade," *Journal of Political Economy,* April 1956.

[9] A few years ago it was reported that although there were over four hundred distinct types of machine tools, each plant typically produced a single or at most a few types. See Murray Brown and Nathan Rosenberg, "Prologue to a Study of Patent and Other Factors in the Machine Tool Industry," *Patent, Trademark, and Copyright Journal of Research and Education,* Spring 1960, p. 45.

other countries on the degree of confidence in the quality of American products established by technological leadership. Purchasers of a number of products reported to us that U.S. products (bearings and pumps, for example) were sometimes purchased, despite their higher prices, when critical uses were involved. The factor involved here was not only the average level of quality, but the confidence of the buyer in the consistency of the quality, or in the small risk of failure to meet the required standard.

In some cases (such as the bearings and pumps mentioned above), the main objective may be to avoid costly breakdowns that would be wasteful of both capital and labor, and the ability to meet this objective enhances the competitive position of the U.S. firms in all markets.

In other instances, the design of U.S. equipment, aimed at saving maintenance and other labor costs, is an adaptation to American conditions; Europeans, facing lower wage rates, may prefer to economize on capital rather than on labor. It was reported, for example, that European wire drawing machines were designed to operate at high speeds with one highly qualified operator while in the United States one man attended three slower-speed machines which "are designed so as to be virtually 'idiot proof' and to make the operator . . . a machine 'attendant.' " [10]

Foreign machinery is often adapted in other respects also to the different requirements prevailing abroad. Where markets are smaller, machines are designed for smaller volume, with lower speeds and, for industries such as printing, baking, and pharmaceuticals, for greater versatility. Occasionally, however, market conditions dictate the reverse directions of specialization. For example, in certain kinds of textile machinery the United States produces slower, more versatile varieties geared to rapid changes in style while Europe turns out high-speed machines that make standard styles (e.g., machines for sweaters).

Factors such as these account for most of the apparent cross-exporting that is observed in international trade (that is, country A both exports to and imports from country B goods in a given commodity classification). Putting aside the consequences of the fact that each country is not a single geographical point and each year is not a single point in

---

[10] From a letter of a U.S. machinery company attached to the brief of the Bethlehem Steel Company submitted to the Trade Information Committee, Office of the Special Representative for Trade Negotiations, Washington, D.C., February 3, 1964 (processed).

time, we have found only one clear-cut case of cross-exporting of a truly homogeneous product (see the section on aluminum in Part Four). The amount of cross-exporting can thus be regarded as an index to the heterogeneity of commodity classifications.[11]

Heterogeneity gives rise to trade because the national differences in machinery requirements such as those described in the previous paragraphs are only statements of central tendencies, and the dispersions around each mean are evidence of overlapping requirements. Thus, the United States exports large printing machines to Europe for high production in long runs, while it imports smaller and more versatile machines from Europe.

Speed of Delivery

In many cases speed of delivery was an important advantage for American firms during the study years. In almost all categories covered by our study, U.S. suppliers were able to offer shipment sooner after the placement of orders than their foreign competitors. This difference did not appear to have been a cyclical phenomenon, but one which persisted, although with fluctuating magnitude, over the whole period covered by this study. U.S. firms rather consistently offered earlier shipment not only on custom equipment such as is often called for in international bidding but also on standard machines and equipment and even supplies sold off the shelf. It is clear that buyers were often willing to pay premiums for early shipment by purchasing the higher-priced U.S. goods in preference to identical goods at lower prices from European or Japanese suppliers.

[11] For a discussion of the reasons for apparent cross-exporting, over a wide range of products, see Herbert G. Grubel, "Intra-Industry Specialization and the Pattern of Trade," *Canadian Journal of Economics and Political Science,* August 1967.

PART TWO

METHODS

3

CONCEPTUAL PROBLEMS IN
MEASURING THE ROLE OF PRICES IN
INTERNATIONAL COMPETITIVENESS

WHILE ECONOMIC THEORY stresses the role of prices in determining the directions and commodity composition of trade, the concepts involved in these relationships become elusive when we turn to the task of measurement. The theory is based on pretrade or pre-equilibrium comparisons, while the prices available for our measurement are posttrade prices drawn toward uniformity by international competition. It is thus difficult to formulate an empirical measure which will enable us to catch the causal influence of relative prices on relative quantities, or even the association between them. Hence, in this chapter, we review both the conceptual formulation of our index of price competitiveness and the reasons why we may expect to find systematic differences in export price levels and changes.

The Index of Price Competitiveness as an
Analytical Measure

In examining the index of price competitiveness as an analytical tool we begin with its relation to market shares, the most readily observed and frequently used measure of changes in competitiveness or in ability to export.[1]

---

[1] See, for example, *1964 Annual Report*, International Monetary Fund, pp. 123–130; and Anne Romanis, "Relative Growth of Exports of Manufactures of United States and Other Industrial Countries," *IMF Staff Papers*, May 1961. See also "Fast- and Slow-Growing Products in World Trade," *National Institute Economic Review*, August 1963, and the other studies mentioned there.

Both the concept of competitiveness and the share measure can be applied to total exports or to specific products or markets.

Relation of Price Competitiveness to Market Shares

Changes in shares are, of course, the product of changes in relative prices and in relative quantities. Competitiveness, in the sense of market shares, may rise or fall as a result of an increase in a country's relative prices, depending upon whether the elasticity of substitution between its exports and those of other countries is less or more than 1.

The changes in relative prices and relative quantities are influenced by both demand and supply factors. On the demand side, a country's export share might grow because importers' tastes shift toward its products, because its exports benefit from high income elasticities of demand in importing countries, or because its traditional markets enjoy a period of particularly rapid economic growth. On the supply side are changes in productivity and in monetary and fiscal policies which affect the level of prices and economic activity, government subsidies for exports, and many other developments, both internal and external to the firm and industry.[2]

The relative prices and relative quantities, and hence the market shares, that we observe for any period of time are, of course, the result of the interaction of all these demand and supply factors in the several countries. We therefore ask whether the changes in relative prices, which we measure through our index of price competitiveness, have any analytical significance beyond reflecting the changing points of intersection of supply and demand curves. If the answer to this question is negative, we cannot construct a measure of relative prices that will, in combination with other relevant variables account for changes in relative quantities.

Fortunately, there is a basis for thinking that our measure of the change in relative prices, our index of price competitiveness, reflects mainly influences that come from the supply side. The reason is that our index measures changes in the relative prices of a bundle of goods that is the same for all countries. An increase in world demand for a particular kind of good, such as ball bearings, for example, should raise the price of that good relative to others in all competing countries. Our index would remain unchanged if supply elasticities of exporting coun-

---

[2] In all these cases, it is the change in one exporting country relative to its competitors that is important.

tries were alike. In a comparison between conventional export price indexes, however, a country specializing in the favored good would appear to have lost in competitiveness, because the product rising in price is heavily weighted in that country's index. Our use of a single set of weights for all countries removes much of the influence of relative demand shifts from our index.

However, demand influences have not been completely eliminated. For example, the demand shift may favor a particular variant of a good produced in only one country. It is possible to imagine, for example, a rise in demand for one country's type of computer relative to another country's which could lead to an apparent decline in price competitiveness if the supply price increased. The more narrowly commodities and commodity groups are defined, the less important this phenomenon will be, but we cannot hope to eliminate it altogether. One remaining loophole is the effect of differences in proximity to a market in which demand is increasing. For example, an increase in Canadian demand may affect U.S. prices more than those of other sellers.

It is also true that a shift in world demand in favor of a particular good produced by a given country may have indirect effects on our index of price competitiveness, since the rise in demand for one commodity may tighten supply conditions and thus reduce the country's price competitiveness in other goods. Finally, an increase in world demand for a particular good, while it may have little impact on the relative prices of two exporting countries, may bring about a substantial change in their relative export quantities if their supply elasticities are markedly different.

Thus, we do not regard our index as a wholly adequate empirical counterpart of the notion of relative prices that plays such a prominent role in the explanation of trade flows found in trade theory. The most we can claim for it is that it comes closer than previous measures of relative price change.

There remain a number of other influences on relative quantities and market shares such as distance (transport costs),[3] trade restrictions,

---

[3] Linneman, in his study of trade flows, used distance itself as the variable to measure "the natural obstacles to trade," incorporating some, but not all, of the effect of transport cost, but also covering obstacles other than transport cost (Hans Linneman, *An Econometric Study of Trade Flows,* Amsterdam, 1966, pp. 25–30, 90–92, and 180–188). Differences among commodities in the importance of transport costs were ignored by Linneman, who was concerned solely with the aggregate trade of each country, but such differences would have to be taken into account in any effort to explain the commodity composition of a country's trade.

traditional commercial, industrial, and financial ties, credit terms, shipment delays, ease of order, and various types of service. Trade theory in its search for the main tendencies at work generally ignores the multifaceted aspects of each transaction, some of which represent "price" and others, "nonprice" factors, and subsumes under "price" all the net proceeds of the seller and net expenditures of the buyer per unit of the transaction. Some of these factors could, indeed, conceivably be translated into monetary terms and incorporated into the price of the product, but we have not undertaken the formidable task of making such calculations. In our empirical work we treat some of these nonprice factors separately, mainly in descriptive, nonquantitative terms.

Prices and Costs as Alternative Approaches to Competitiveness

Before returning to the index of price competitiveness to examine its interpretation more closely, we should, perhaps, recognize that prices are not the only possible focus for a study of international competitiveness. One could go farther back in the chain of causation toward costs, or beyond that to the factors affecting costs. Indeed, it has been suggested that the identification problems, in the interplay of demand and supply factors, discussed in the previous section, might be smaller when costs rather than prices are compared. The reason given is that export prices adjust to changed conditions more quickly than costs, and thus price comparisons may not reflect as clearly as cost comparisons the causes for shifts in the flows of trade.[4]

In general, the higher the elasticity of substitution between one country's products and another's, that is, the more completely buyers shift from one to the other in response to small relative price changes, the more likely will changes in competitiveness be observable only in quantity shifts and not in price movements. For example, if prices of all countries for certain standard raw materials move together, a loss of competitiveness by a given country will appear as a decline in the margin of price over costs. The result, sooner or later, is likely to be a fall in the country's export share without any unfavorable development appearing in relative prices. High supply elasticities contribute to this result.

This type of identical price change is much less likely to occur in

4 See, for example, Robert M. Stern, "British and American Productivity and Comparative Costs in International Trade," *Oxford Economic Papers*, October 1962. See also Robert M. Stern and Elliot Zupnick, "The Theory and Measurement of Elasticity of Substitution in International Trade," *Kyklos*, 1962, Fasc. 3.

manufactures, however, since substitutability is less perfect. Indeed, evidence already summarized indicates that in some sectors substantial price differences can exist between competing products. In manufactures, therefore, actual prices rather than costs may more adequately elucidate historical shifts in trade patterns.

Furthermore, prices have some decisive advantages over costs in an empirical study: (1) The concept of price, although not without its prickly aspects, is generally more objective and less likely to vary from one reporter to another. (2) Moreover, cost data can be built up only for whole plants, companies, or groups of commodities rather than for precisely specified individual commodities; international cost comparisons for individual products would be distorted by the diversity of methods of allocation of costs in different firms and countries. (3) Finally, it is easier to obtain information about prices than about costs, not only because many sellers are more willing to provide price than cost information, but also because price information can be supplied by buyers.

The Interpretation of the Index of Price Competitiveness

The implications of our index of price competitiveness may be better understood if it is contrasted with one that might be constructed from traditional indexes of export and import prices (or from unit value indexes, which are usually employed in lieu of export and import price indexes). Such an index of price competitiveness, P_T, would be

$$P_T = \frac{\Phi_{Mi}(P_{M2}, P_{M4}, P_{M6}, \ldots, P_{Mr})}{\Pi_{Xj}(P_{X1}, P_{X3}, P_{X5}, \ldots, P_{Xs})} \quad \begin{array}{l} i = 2, 4, 6, \ldots, r \\ j = 1, 3, 5, \ldots, s \end{array}$$

where M stands for import prices, X export prices, and each numerical subscript refers to a particular good: i includes even numbers from 2 to r and j, odd numbers from 1 to s.

As indicated by the choice of the subscripts, any one commodity is likely to appear among imports, but not exports, or among exports, but not imports, if the products are narrowly defined. P_T is more akin to a terms-of-trade index than to an index for measuring changes in price competitiveness. It may show changes in relative prices and in price competitiveness where none have taken place. A rise of 10 per cent in the import price of sugar accompanied by a 10 per cent rise in the domestic price does not imply a change in price competitiveness.

But it will appear as a change in price competitiveness because sugar has a weight in the import price index and little or no weight in the export price index. The same possibility exists for a manufactured product, such as home sewing machines.

Our index of price competitiveness, $P_{F/S}$, is

$$P_{F/S} = \Phi \left(\frac{P_{f1}}{P_{h1}}, \frac{P_{f2}}{P_{h2}}, \ldots, \frac{P_{fn}}{P_{hn}} \right) \quad n = 1, 2, 3, \ldots$$

where F represents any foreign country, S represents the United States, the f are foreign prices, h are U.S. prices, and each numerical subscript refers to a narrowly defined category of goods. (Both foreign and U.S. prices are export prices if the commodity is exported and home prices if it is not.)

The key difference between our index and the terms-of-trade index is our reliance upon *relative* (foreign to U.S.) prices. We consider that the impact of a foreign price cannot be defined except with reference to the movement of the *corresponding* U.S. price; similarly the impact of a change in a U.S. export price cannot be defined unless the movement of the *corresponding* foreign price is taken into account.

It is important to point out, however, that we do not try, in time-to-time price measurement, to match f_1 with h_1 in terms of detailed commodity specifications. What we do instead is to try to find for each country a sample of goods within each four- or five-digit SITC subgroup, or even within a narrower category if the subgroup is heterogeneous. For typewriters (SITC 714.1), for example, we prepared separate price indexes for electric, standard, and portable typewriters for each country, but the indexes were based on different brands and models in each country. Had we tried to match goods interspatially for time-to-time comparisons we would have embarked on an impossible task.

The $P_{F/S}$ index compares price movements of different countries within the four- or five-digit categories we use but not between them. The conventional export and import price indexes, on the other hand, compare price movements of largely different bundles of goods between which intercommodity substitutions are apt to be weak. Thus we compare price movements of U.S. and Italian portable typewriters and of U.S. and Italian electric typewriters; the comparison of export and import price indexes would, in effect, compare the price movements of

U.S. electric typewriters which we export with price movements of, say, transistor radios which we import.

The use of the $P_{F/S}$ index to explain changes in trade rests on the implicit assumption that international price competition takes place within the four- or five-digit groups but not between them. Of course, we are well aware that competition exists between commodities in different SITC items, subgroups, groups, and even major commodity divisions. Aluminum cable (SITC 693.13) competes with copper cable (SITC 693.12); electric locomotives (SITC 731.2), with diesel locomotives (SITC 731.3); aircraft (SITC 734), with ships (SITC 735); and electric motors (SITC 722.1) may soon compete with internal combustion engines (SITC 711.5).

Ideally one might wish to determine empirically which are actually the foreign goods that compete with each domestically produced good in the world and the home markets. A complete set of international price indexes would provide the information that would permit the insertion of the price of one commodity category in an equation explaining the exports of another.

It is evident from what has been said that the relations between price competitiveness and changes in a country's market share or in its trade balance cannot be expected to be simple and unvarying. For some categories, as we shall point out later, the nonprice factors play a large role, and if they move in an offsetting direction they may obscure the impact of relative prices upon the trade position. Even with nonprice factors constant, one can imagine a case in which a change in a country's price competitiveness index might not immediately be reflected in its trade balance. For example, suppose there were a rise in the U.S. price of a good produced but not exported by the United States, but which is exported by others. Since our index is weighted by the importance of each commodity in world trade, the U.S. index of price competitiveness would decline, although there might be no change in the U.S. balance of payments.

In fact, the index of price competitiveness would provide an important item of information. The rise in the price of the good would place it farther away from the export threshold and encourage more imports, or, if there were no imports before the change, move the good closer to the import threshold than it was before. It is possible that the margins of safety provided by differences in costs, transportation charges, and market imperfections might momentarily keep the price rise from affecting the trade balance, but sooner or later, the movements in the index of price competitiveness would be reflected in the trade statistics. For this not to happen would require that there be no import substitutes for the domestic good. Imperfect substitution doubtless is more common than perfect substitution, but commodities for which there is no foreign substitute are hard to find; in the marginal domestic use of the good, one would expect an imported good to replace a domestic good which has risen in price.

Furthermore, since our indexes are actually constructed from samples of items for four- or five-digit categories, it is even more unlikely that they will reflect price changes that are irrelevant to the trade balance of a major industrial country. Each of the countries for which we present indexes in this study, for example, is involved in every one of our four-digit categories as either an exporter or an importer.

With respect to policy implications, neither a rise nor a fall in the index of price competitiveness necessarily calls for remedial action. There is no unique share of world markets that represents the ideal share for a given country. Some declines in export shares for particular commodities are always occurring in every country as, in the course of economic development, comparative advantage moves from one type of production to another. For a nation as a whole, a decline in its export shares may be desirable or even necessary if it has had a long and persistent balance-of-payments surplus. In the longer run, if the underdeveloped countries are to gain relative to the developed ones in per capita and national income, they can be expected to gain in exports as well.[5]

As another example, a country which formerly concentrated on a single product might see its share of world exports decline if it reduced both import and export needs by diversifying its economy. A country which is beginning to reduce its rate of foreign investment and to repatriate income from past investments may well find that its export share is declining and its import share rising. The country may not, in a sense, be worse off; it is enjoying the fruits of its past frugality. Nevertheless, its competitiveness in the world economy has declined; the country's entrepreneurs find it more difficult to meet foreign competition. In this

[5] However, if grant aid and other capital flows to underdeveloped countries grow more rapidly than world exports, the share of these countries in world exports will fall.

case, the changes would represent the normal consequence of the shift in the country's overall relations with the rest of the world rather than an alarming development calling for corrective measures. A decline in price competitiveness is thus a warning signal only under circumstances which require a country to maintain or improve its trade balance.

Scope for International Differences in Prices

The tendency for international competition to equalize prices is subject to many frictions and interferences some of which tend to fragment markets or to isolate particular ones. Transport costs, including freight and insurance and sometimes extra packing costs, would create differences in f.a.s.[6] export prices even if competition worked perfectly to equalize prices of products from different national sources of supply at each destination.

In addition, tariffs and other restrictions on entry would create differences between f.a.s. export prices from foreign sources and f.o.b. prices from domestic suppliers, and in many cases also have a differential impact on alternative foreign sources.

Even without these transfer costs, observed f.a.s. export prices would differ for many manufactured prices because of product differenentiation. Such differentiation has both physical and service aspects, the former referring to real or reputed differences inherent in the appearance or performance of the product and the latter to nonprice factors such as presale advice, after-sale service, credit terms, and speed of delivery.

Other price differences represent disequilibrium situations in which some purchasers, particularly of complex products such as machinery, might take a considerable time to respond to price discrepancies. Even if a continuation of the price difference would eventually find the higher-priced seller with no customers, there may be a long interval in which sales are being made at both high and low prices. Lack of knowledge or the cost of obtaining it, uncertainty regarding the reliability of a supplier or the length of time he will remain in the market, reluctance to give up a satisfactory relationship with a supplier, commitment to one type of machine because of previous purchases or stocks of spare

---

[6] F.a.s. = free alongside ship, including export packing and inland freight; f.o.b. = free on board.

parts, and official or private buy-domestic policies may all prolong the adjustment.

Another reason for price differences in our data is that we include information on certain offer prices—i.e., the lowest price offered by each country other than the one actually making the sale. Thus some of the prices do not represent transactions but explain instead why transactions have not taken place. This is true of those data which consist of comparisons made by companies and governments before they decide where to purchase. All offers other than the one accepted are potential, but not actual, prices.

Many of the factors mentioned above also make possible divergent price movements among different national sources of supply. If transportation costs are important, for example, a rise in one country's f.a.s. price relative to that of other suppliers may cause the country to lose its more distant markets for a product while it retains the closer ones, reducing the geographical range of its sales but not eliminating them completely. Thus the investigator will be able to observe the relative rise in the f.a.s. price or in the domestic price if the export trade vanishes completely.

Differentiation in products such as machinery plays a role similar to that of transport costs in making differences in price movements visible to the investigator. When there is such differentiation, an increase in the f.a.s. price of a machine may reduce its sales in a particular area and narrow the machine's range of uses but will not drive it completely from the market.

Transfer Costs

Some notion of the possible magnitude of transport costs may be obtained from the data in Table 3.1 which show the estimated charges for U.S. imports in 1965. Average transport charges for the products covered in our study were around 9 or 10 per cent of the f.a.s. or foreign wholesale value; the range went from 1 per cent for products high in value relative to their bulk such as nickel and watches to 20, 30, or even 40 per cent for bulkier products such as containers and pleasure boats. The figures reflect not only the relative importance of the individual commodities within each category but also the distances from which they were shipped in the particular year.

The average rates shown in the table may not be typical for other

Table 3.1

Transport Costs for U.S. Imports of Metals, Metal Products, and Machinery, 1965
(dollars in millions)

Schedules, Parts, and Subparts of TSUS[a] (Abridged)	Value of U.S. Imports as Reported in Official Statistics	Estimated Freight and Insurance Charges as Per Cent of Reported Value
Schedule 6: Metals and metal products	$6,614	9
Part		
2. Metals, their alloys, and their basic shapes and forms:		
A. Precious metals	73	1
B. Iron or steel	1,236	13
C. Copper	377	4
D. Aluminum	266	4
E. Nickel	179	1
F. Tin	168	2
G. Lead	62	7
H. Zinc	44	9
J–K. Other base metals	58	3

(continued)

Table 3.1 (continued)

Schedules, Parts, and Subparts of TSUS^a (Abridged)	Value of U.S. Imports as Reported in Official Statistics	Estimated Freight and Insurance Charges as Per Cent of Reported Value
Part		
3. Metal products	6	21
A. Metallic containers	49	13
B. Wire cordage; wire screen, netting and fencing, bale ties	19	6
C. Metal leaf and foil; metallics		
D. Nails, screws, bolts, and other fasteners; locks, builders' hardware; furniture, luggage, and saddlery hardware	117	11
E. Tools, cutlery, forks, and spoons	80	2
F. Miscellaneous metal products	106	12
G. Metal products not specially provided for	33	9
Part		
4. Machinery and mechanical equipment		
A. Boilers, nonelectric motors and engines, and other general - purpose machinery	284	5
B. Elevators, winches, cranes, and related machinery; earthmoving and mining machinery	35	7
C. Agricultural and horticultural machinery; machinery for preparing food and drink	172	3
D. Pulp and paper machinery; bookbinding machinery; printing machinery	60	6
E. Textile machines, laundry and dry-cleaning machines; sewing machines	152	10
F. Machines for working metal, stone, and other materials	98	7

(continued)

Table 3.1 (continued)

Schedules, Parts, and Subparts of TSUS[a] (Abridged)	Value of U.S. Imports as Reported in Official Statistics	Estimated Freight and Insurance Charges as Per Cent of Reported Value
Part		
G. Office machines	133	4
H. Other machines	70	8
J. Parts of machines	65	2
Part		
5. Electrical machinery and equipment	686	6
Part		
6. Transportation equipment:		
B. Motor vehicles	1,045	11
C. Aircraft and spacecraft	139	40
D. Pleasure boats; floating structures	14	30
Schedule 7: Specified products; miscellaneous and nonenumerated products	1,462	10
Part		
2. Optical goods; scientific and professional instruments, watches, clocks, and timing devices; photographic goods; motion pictures; recordings and recording media		
A. Optical elements, spectacles, microscopes, and telescopes; optical goods not elsewhere provided for	63	6
B. Medical and surgical instruments and apparatus; X-ray apparatus	23	5

(continued)

51

Table 3.1 (concluded)

Schedules, Parts, and Subparts of TSUS[a] (Abridged)	Value of U.S. Imports as Reported in Official Statistics	Estimated Freight and Insurance Charges as Per Cent of Reported Value
Schedule 7 (continued)		
Part 2 (continued)		
C. Surveying, navigational, metereological, drawing, and mathematical calculating instruments; measuring and checking instruments not specially provided for	25	5
D. Measuring, testing, and controlling instruments	41	5
E. Watches, clocks, and timing apparatus	101	1
F. Photographic equipment and supplies	102	3
Part		
3. Musical instruments, part, and accessories		
A. Musical instruments	40	13
B. Musical instrument parts and accessories	10	9

Source: "C.I.F. Value of U.S. Imports," February 7, 1967 (mimeo).
[a]*Tariff Schedule of the United States*, U.S. Tariff Commission.

countries. Indeed, there is substantial evidence that U.S. outbound ocean freight rates in 1963 and 1964 exceeded inbound rates by 25 to 30 per cent on the average "with peaks in the Japanese trades reaching up to 50 per cent and beyond." [7] Whether the reason is that U.S. outbound rates are especially high or inbound rates especially low, such differences in freight rates may be expected to produce differences in f.a.s. export prices. However, even a difference of 30 per cent in transport charges amounting to 10 per cent of f.a.s. value would involve only a 3 per cent c.i.f.[8] price differential. For this reason much of the controversy over discriminatory freight rates has centered on comparatively low-valued products such as steel, for which the average ratio of freight to value in U.S. imports is shown in Table 3.1 to be 13 per cent. Several of the major steel products in international trade are characterized by still higher freight ratios.

Tariffs also make price level differences possible. Average 1962 tariffs on machinery and transport equipment (excluding automobiles) were 10.3 per cent in the United States, 11.7 per cent in the EEC, 17.0 per cent in the United Kingdom, and 17.1 per cent in Japan.[9] Data for some commodity groups included in our study are shown in Table 3.2. Even between these advanced countries the combination of transport costs and tariff can create substantial price differences.

The most important changes in tariffs affecting metal and machinery trade during the period of our study were those associated with the formation of the European Economic Community (EEC) and the European Free Trade Association (EFTA). Beginning in January 1959, the six EEC countries (France, Germany, Italy, and the Benelux countries) reduced internal tariffs in 10 per cent tranches; in the last year and a half of our period their internal tariffs were down to 40 per cent of the initial levels. The members also adjusted their tariffs to outside countries toward a common external tariff, 30 per cent of the way in January 1961 and another 30 per cent in July 1963. EFTA, formed in response to the EEC by the United Kingdom and six other European countries, reduced internal tariffs by 20 per cent in July 1960 and by a series of

[7] *Discriminatory Ocean Freight Rates and the Balance of Payments: A Report of the Subcommittee on Federal Procurement and Regulation,* Joint Economic Committee, 89th Cong., 2nd sess., August 1966, p. 8.

[8] C.i.f. = cost, insurance, and freight.

[9] Bela Balassa, *Trade Liberalization Among Industrial Countries,* New York, 1967, p. 56. The averages, which actually refer to investment goods, were computed by weighting individual duties by the combined imports of the above areas plus those of Sweden.

Table 3.2
Average Tariff Rates, 1962
(per cent)

	U.S.	U.K.	EEC	Japan
Pig iron and ferromanganese	1.8	3.3	4.0	10.0
Ingots and other primary steel	10.6	11.1	6.4	13.0
Rolling mill products	7.1	9.5	7.2	15.4
Other steel products	5.1	17.0	9.9	13.4
Nonferrous metals	5.0	6.6	2.4	9.3
Metal castings	6.6	16.0	12.4	20.0
Metal manufactures	14.4	19.0	14.0	18.1
Agricultural machinery	0.4	15.4	13.4	20.0
Nonelectrical machinery	11.0	16.1	10.3	16.8
Electrical machinery	12.2	19.7	14.5	18.1
Ships	5.5	2.9	0.4	13.1
Railway vehicles	7.0	21.1	11.1	15.0
Automobiles	6.8	23.1	19.5	35.9
Bicycles and motorcycles	14.4	22.4	20.9	25.0
Airplanes	9.2	15.6	10.5	15.0
Precision instruments	21.4	25.7	13.5	23.2
Sporting goods, toys, jewelry, etc.	25.0	22.3	17.9	21.6

Source: Bela Balassa, *Trade Liberalization Among Industrial Countries*, New York, 1967, pp. 180–181.

10 per cent cuts thereafter so that in the last year of our study, 1964, tariffs on intra-EFTA trade were down to 40 per cent of their original levels.[10] It is to be expected that the reductions in these intratrade tariffs not only decreased the extent of disparities in prices among the members of each group, but also lowered in each member country the delivered prices of imports from each fellow member relative to prices from the United States and other nonmember countries.

Preferential trade arrangements also extended beyond the membership of these two groups. The most extensive long-standing arrangements, those in the British Commonwealth, were of diminishing importance in the period, but the EEC was expanding its preferential associations with African and certain less developed European countries.[11]

[10] See Lawrence B. Krause, *European Economic Integration and the United States*, Washington, D.C., The Brookings Institution, 1968, p. 58.
[11] See *ibid.*, Chap. 6.

There was, on the other hand, some movement toward a single world market, as some of the restrictions of World War II continued to be dismantled. The most important was the reduction of import controls in the decade of the 1950s by western European countries under the Code of Liberalization adopted by the Organization for European Economic Cooperation.[12]

Quantitative restrictions, often imposed in addition to high tariffs, remained important in most developing countries. There were, as a result, instances of very large gaps between internal and world prices.[13] The existence of such varying restrictions made it possible for even the f.a.s. export prices of the same exporting firm in a developed country to vary from one destination to another.

It is difficult to make any broad generalization about alterations in the degree of market fragmentation in the world as a whole during 1953–64. International diplomacy was bent toward the reduction of barriers through negotiations under the General Agreement on Tariffs and Trade (GATT) and other means; but the Cold War, domestic pressures in the developed countries, and import substitution and related policies in developing countries worked in the other direction.[14] Although the average ad valorem tariff rate on dutiable imports has many defects as a general measure of protection, and although the United States is only one (albeit important) instance, it may not be without significance that for the United States this rate remained around 11 to 12 per cent despite GATT negotiations which reduced tariff levels on a large number of particular products.[15]

Restrictive Practices

Other factors which, like import quotas, fragment markets geographically include agreements among suppliers for each to avoid bidding in the others' markets or for each to take his turn offering low bids. Such

---

[12] See Irving B. Kravis, *Domestic Interests and International Obligations,* Philadelphia, 1963, Chap. 3.

[13] For example, in 1962 it was reported that prices of tin, lead, and zinc in India were about twice as high as prices being quoted in London (see Chapter 10).

[14] Despite the common view that trade barriers were diminishing, closer study of individual commodity sectors discloses some tendencies in the opposite direction. See, for example, the section on institutional influences in our discussion of nonferrous metals (Chapter 10).

[15] It actually fluctuated between 11.2 to 12.6 per cent from 1953 to 1964, according to a U.S. Tariff Commission tabulation (*Value of U.S. Imports for Consumption, Duties Collected, and Ratio of Duties to Values, Under the Tariff Act of 1930, 1930–69,* February 1970).

arrangements have been reported to prevail in the sale of pipe for use in oil fields, for example, but they are, of course, difficult to document. In some instances, it also appeared that firms would not bid against their licensees in a particular market, although there were also many cases in which they did compete.

Another factor which tends to weaken competitive forces in international markets are buy-domestic policies. Although the most widely publicized policy is that of the U.S. government, a similar practice appears to be just as widely applied by most foreign governments, through informal administrative means. Most governments were reported in the OECD study of government purchasing [16] to have few formal rules against purchasing foreign products. However, they do permit purchasing by selective tender, in which the invitation to bid is limited to selected suppliers, or by negotiation with suppliers, procedures which permit domestic suppliers to be favored without formal announcement of preferences.[17] Sometimes there are cumbersome administrative or excessive bonding requirements, or even regulations precluding foreign bidding on government contracts.[18] Buy-at-home policies of private firms, on both sides of the Atlantic, may have an even greater quantitative impact in fragmenting markets; in the case of electric power equipment, switchgear, and conductors it was U.S. government agencies that aggressively sought foreign bidding on major contracts, while private utilities, until recently, apparently maintained a firm policy against purchases from abroad.

In some cases, the domestic purchasing orientation of individual firms is abetted by reciprocity arrangements in which a firm buys from its own customers insofar as possible.

Reciprocity policies are not a monopoly of private firms. Similar agreements, sometimes formal, have been made between governments, or have been forced on private firms by their governments, and the

[16] *Government Purchasing in Europe, North America and Japan: Regulations and Procedures,* OECD, 1966.

[17] For examples of informal preferences in the United Kingdom, see the sections on electric power machinery and telecommunications equipment in Chapter 13. The OECD report nevertheless describes British purchasing procedures as follows: "No statutory requirements, nor any guidance of a formal or informal character issued to procuring officials stipulate that buying departments should give preference to United Kingdom supplies. . . . Foreign firms are not treated differently from domestic firms" (*ibid.,* p. 105).

[18] Robert E. Baldwin, "Nontariff Barriers: A Brief Study," *Compendium of Papers on Legislative Oversight Review of U.S. Trade Policies,* Senate Committee on Finance, 90th Cong., 2nd sess., February 7, 1968, Vol. 1, p. 339.

amounts involved may be larger than those involved in private arrangements. For example, a British agreement to purchase American military aircraft was accompanied by an American offer to facilitate the purchase of British defense equipment.[19] A Belgian decision to purchase French, rather than American, military aircraft, and German, rather than French, tanks was attributed to the inclusion in each of the products chosen of components made in Belgium and, in one case, to a commitment for the purchase of other unrelated products from Belgium. A Danish purchase of Swedish aircraft was attributed to similar offset contracts.[20]

For developing countries, import-substitution policies often result in a marked separation of domestic and world markets. The tying of aid also tends to shelter transactions from competitive forces and to result in higher prices for the purchaser from the source of aid than from other countries.[21]

Product Differentiation

Physical product differentiation ranges from almost incidental and accidental to purposeful and important differences in design. An example in the former category are price differences that arise from the use of 220-volt current in Europe and 110 volts in the United States. Although costs of production of bulbs adapted for either system would be about the same if they were produced in equal volume, bulbs for the 220 system are in fact mass produced in Europe and are relatively cheap there while 110 bulbs are relatively expensive, and the opposite is true in the United States. A similar situation applies, it was reported to us, to bolts with hexagonal heads (used more widely in Europe) vis-à-vis bolts with square heads. In the more deliberate category are differences in styling for consumer durables such as automobiles or in

[19] "America Expects Every Briton . . . ," *Economist* (London), January 13, 1968.
[20] "NATO Arms: Coordination Is a Mirage," *ibid.*, February 24, 1968.
[21] See Irving B. Kravis and Robert E. Lipsey, "Some Evidence on Price Differentials Connected with Aid Tying" (NBER, 1968 mimeo), in which data derived from the present study are used to compare the cost of buying various collections of goods entirely in the United States with the costs of buying entirely in each of several other countries or of buying each product from the cheapest source. A comprehensive analysis of the effects of aid tying is given in J. Bhagwati, "The Tying of Aid," UN Conference on Trade and Development, Second Session, New Delhi, Vol. IV, *Problems and Policies of Financing* (1968). Estimates of price differentials resulting from the tying of aid are given in that report as well as others in the same volume and in Mahbub ul Haq, "Tied Credits—A Qualitative Analysis," *Capital Movements and Economic Development*, Proceedings of a Conference held by the International Economic Association, London and New York, 1967.

specifications for electrical generating equipment which, it has been alleged, some countries have designed to exclude competing goods from foreign suppliers.

In some lines, notably in communications equipment, the initial installation locks the purchaser to the products of a particular supplier, and there may be substantial differences between prices offered for the original installation and those offered for expansion or replacement equipment.

Some differences in equipment design represent adaptations to different economic circumstances in the several producing countries. Detroit mass-produces automotive engines in the 150–400 horsepower range, built for heavy use over long distances, while in Europe, where distances are shorter and there are fewer miles of high-speed turnpikes, engines are built with 50 to 75 horsepower less than in the United States. Since food shopping in the United States involves large purchases with infrequent visits to the supermarket, larger refrigerators are in demand than in Europe where frequent small purchases are still more usual. European washing machines often contain water heaters, unnecessary in the United States where continuously available hot water from the tap is commonplace. High U.S. wages relative to those in Europe lead to the design of machinery that is directly laborsaving (such as heavy earth-moving machinery), through minimizing the need for maintenance (ball and roller bearings), or through providing for long continuous operation that avoids the setup costs of shifting to a different variety of product.

Knowledge and reputation for design capacity are often dominant elements in the award of contracts for industrial installations, such as petroleum refineries, chemical plants, paper and pulp mills, and steel mills. American engineering firms lead in some of these industries, notably in petroleum refining and certain branches of the chemical industry, but this does not necessarily mean that all procurement for the project will be in the United States. Indeed, some of these firms engage in systematic international price comparisons for standard items that enter into their work such as steel bars, electric motors, etc., so that they can make the most competitive bids on installations in any part of the world. In other equipment such as machinery for the generation of hydroelectricity and for the manufacture of paper and pulp, European firms have a strong position, and in still others, Japan has become a major factor in world markets, notably shipbuilding, including particularly the design and construction of large tankers.

Nonprice Factors

In the comparisons we made in this volume we tried by various means to make quality adjustments for those physical differences that are manifested in differences in size or performance. Yet even if we had been able to adjust the prices perfectly to take account of the physical differences in the products, there would still be, in addition to transport costs, other conditions of sale, which we have referred to as the nonprice factors, and which affect the balance of economic advantage to a buyer confronted with two quality-adjusted price offers. Each price may thus be regarded as part of a package which includes such nonprice factors as before-sale advice, speed of delivery, credit terms, ease of order, and quality of after-sale service. The importance of these nonprice factors varies from one line of trade to another, but they undoubtedly have substantial influence upon international competition.

We repeatedly came across illustrations in which these factors were reported to have played a determining role in decisions governing the flow of trade. A large American company, for example, applied a rule-of-thumb measure for the differential cost of placing a foreign order during the study years, and purchased at home whenever the size of the order was likely to fall below a certain dollar figure. Another cost of purchasing abroad is the greater uncertainty of delivery and consequently the need to maintain larger inventories. During the period of our study, for example, one large aluminum consumer reported switching to domestic aluminum, despite his ability to obtain European aluminum at a saving of 5 to 10 per cent in the delivered price, owing to the costs of maintaining adequate margins of safety in his stocks.

In many cases price is secondary to delivery date and, as will be discussed more fully below, the ability of U.S. firms to offer faster delivery is an important nonprice advantage. Under boom conditions it may lead to foreign purchases from the United States at quite high prices; in 1957, for example, foreign ship orders were placed with U.S. yards even though their prices were 50 per cent higher than those abroad.

Another very important nonprice factor is financing. In the machinery and equipment area most exports, particularly those destined for the developing countries, involve credit. Some firms have reported that the availability and terms of credit were sometimes more important to purchasers in developing countries than the nominal price; the amount that would have to be paid per annum was the critical factor in the decision. In some instances, a higher nominal price may simply conceal higher risk premiums on credit sales to a developing country; [22] in other cases the tying of credits from government sources may enable the seller to charge a higher price than he would get in world competition even though he may not bear any or much of the credit risk.

Important factors working to reduce the cost of credit to developing countries and also affecting the competitiveness of different countries are export credit insurance plans. Near the end of 1965, it was reported that the United States, Canada, Japan and sixteen western European governments were operating or supporting such systems. [23] The various arrangements, which evolved under competitive pressures, usually covered short- (up to 180 days) and medium-term (180 days to five years) credits extended by exporters to their customers or by banks to foreign importers and protected against both commercial risks (e.g., insolvency) and political risks (e.g., nonconvertibility, expropriation). The United States was the last major country to adopt a comprehensive insurance arrangement (in 1962) and was reported in 1965 to be insuring 5 per cent of its exports as compared to 25 per cent by the United Kingdom, 11 per cent by France, and 10 per cent by Germany. [24] The reason for the difference was the greater range and flexibility of coverage offered in the European countries, particularly for riskier and longer terms of credits. Comparisons of the costs of the insurance are difficult; according to one report in 1964, the U.K. plan had the lowest fees while U.S. fees were lower than those of France and Germany for the lowest risk markets. [25]

---

[22] The need to measure price and credit terms jointly has been discussed by Juster and Shay in connection with credit costs on U.S. automobile sales (see F. Thomas Juster and Robert Shay, *Consumer Sensitivity to Finance Rates: An Empirical and Analytical Investigation*, NBER Occasional Paper 88, 1964). In the nineteenth century U.S. purchases of rails from England were sometimes paid for with securities equivalent to 130 or 140 per cent of the nominal price (see Cleona Lewis, *America's Stake in International Investment*, Washington, D.C., The Brookings Institution, 1938, p. 38).

[23] Chase Manhattan Bank (New York), *Report on Western Europe*, No. 38, October–November 1965.

[24] *Ibid.*

[25] "Gains Scored in Financing of U.S. Exports," *Journal of Commerce* (New York), March 31, 1964.

More specific information on sources of international differences in prices beyond that which can be explained by transport costs may be found in the product chapters of Part Four. It will be seen there that even in categories such as nonferrous metals (Chapter 10) which consist of relatively simple standardized products, powerful forces tend to fragment markets and to prevent the operation of a single world market conforming to the competitive ideal.

4

METHODS OF THE STUDY

IN THIS CHAPTER we describe the nature and sources of the data used in our study. We seek to show also how we met the conceptual problems that arose in trying to translate the principles described in Chapter 1 into operating procedures for putting data together into index numbers. More detailed information about the application of these procedures to particular commodity groups will be found in the chapters in Part Four.

Data Collection

Method of Collection

An important technical feature of the study was the decision to abandon the usual practice of organizing the price collection effort around a set of product specifications selected in advance. In the area of machinery, which was the most important in our study, it would have been impossible in most commodity groups to select any specifications applicable to all or even to most sellers. Each firm buys or sells products with slightly different specifications, and it would not have been sensible, even if much greater price collection resources had been available, to discard relevant information because it did not refer to a particular set of predetermined specifications.

Our solution to this problem was to place the burden of determining comparability on the respondent, asking him to select the most important items in each group about which he had knowledge and to provide comparable quotations either over time or between exporting countries. With rare exceptions, we did not ourselves undertake to match two prices in order to compute a time-to-time or place-to-place price relative. In a sense it was the price relative itself that we were collecting in our field work, although we did obtain the actual prices as well. (In a few cases in which firms did nòt wish to divulge actual prices, we accepted price relatives without actual prices.)

Ideally, we would have wished to have both place-to-place and time-to-time comparisons for each individual commodity for all countries and all years. In practice, however, such complete comparisons were rarely possible. Even with a relatively simple commodity such as nails, we might find that a company bought one type of nail in 1953 and could compare U.S. and German prices for it, but bought a different type in 1957 and could compare the U.S. and German prices only for that type. A comparison of the United States and Japan might be possible only for a third type, and time-to-time price changes might be available only for a fourth. As was mentioned earlier, any unit of information was useful to us provided that it compared, for a precisely defined commodity, at least two countries' prices at one date or one country's prices for at least two dates. As a minimum, we required sufficient specification to assign each price relative to an appropriate five-digit SITC category. The price collection forms left with or sent to companies are reproduced in the appendix to this chapter.

Sources of Price Data

The comparative prices used in this study were gathered from a variety of sources. A major portion of the data came from more than 200 American firms, mainly large industrial companies, which in their aggregate account for a substantial fraction of American exports. About 375 firms of this type were approached for assistance in the study, and over 55 per cent provided some type of comparative price data. Most of the companies were among the 500 largest industrial corporations tabulated in the *Fortune* survey for 1963.[1] Almost half of the firms listed there were requested to assist in the study, and close to two-thirds of these cooperated. A high proportion of the largest companies on the list were approached (more than three-quarters of the 100 largest firms, of which 56 participated), and the proportion declined to less than one-quarter of the fifth hundred. In every group except the last hundred more than half of the firms from whom data were requested agreed to assist the study.

[1] "The *Fortune* Directory: The 500 Largest U.S. Industrial Corporations," *Fortune*, July 1963, pp. 177–196.

Aside from these large industrial firms about 150 other companies were asked to participate. These included a few foreign firms, a few large companies in such fields as transportation and merchandising, and a large number of smaller firms selected because the nature of their business suggested that they would be good sources of international price data, particularly for categories not covered by the large industrial firms in our sample. Most of these were machinery manufacturers and metals dealers; some were firms that we thought were likely to have bought in international markets. This second group of companies differed in a number of ways from those picked from the largest 500. The proportion cooperating was slightly under half, and most of them provided selling rather than buying prices.

Among the whole group of firms responding, the proportion reporting only selling prices was slightly greater than the proportion reporting only buying prices. Only $7\frac{1}{2}$ per cent of the firms reported both buying and selling prices. Among the firms picked from the 200 largest on the *Fortune* list, almost twice as many reported buying prices as selling prices. These proportions were almost reversed among those industrial firms drawn from the following 300, particularly among the smallest firms, of which about three-quarters reported only selling prices.

The characteristics of firms described here are not, of course, those of a random sample of U.S. corporations, but only of the particular sample used. Some of the characteristics stem from the way in which the sample was picked—particularly the fact that large firms were requested to help even when they were not engaged in machinery or metals products businesses. The assumption underlying this selection was that almost any large firm would have had some experience in purchasing metals and machinery even if it did not sell them. The smaller firms were selected mainly because of the nature of the products they sold and for that reason supplied mainly selling price data.

U.S. sellers of machinery and metal products were asked to provide their own export prices for our references dates and to compare these prices with those charged by foreign competitors or by their own foreign subsidiaries or licensees for identical or equivalent products. Companies involved in international markets through their purchasing activity were asked to compare offers from the United States and from foreign countries for specific items of equipment or metals, and also to trace the changes in the prices of such items over a period of years.

The extent of price data obtained from individual firms varied very widely. In one case a member of our staff spent many months digging out place-to-place and time-to-time price comparisons from the purchase records of a large international firm. A number of firms made extensive efforts to summarize their selling and/or purchasing experience for our benefit, giving us complete summaries of large numbers of export or purchasing transactions which, in a few cases, accounted for a significant fraction of world trade in the products covered.

A number of firms that operate on a worldwide basis provided extensive comparative price data originally gathered for their own internal use. In some instances the data were from market surveys in which export prices of competitors from different countries were gleaned from a variety of sources. More often they were gathered from suppliers in a systematic way in order to guide purchasing decisions or to provide the basis for the estimation of the costs of installing new plants in various parts of the world; in some instances the firm maintained records of the prices of fifty to one hundred items in the main producing countries. Other firms collected price comparisons in the course of more sporadic buying activity, like that involved in the building of a factory abroad for the firm's own use or in its role as consultant or adviser to a foreign or domestic firm building a factory abroad. In a large number of cases, of course, firms provided only a few sets of comparative prices relating to different points in time for a given country or to different national sources of supply.

Almost all the companies were visited at least once by a member of the staff and many two or more times. Follow-up inquiries were often necessary to clarify the nature of the price data, to gather additional information necessary to assign an item to its proper four- or five-digit SITC category, or to obtain information beyond that available in the trade statistics on the nature of international specialization in a particular SITC category. Respondents were assured that the information they provided would be kept confidential. Written instructions for price collection and a standard form for entry of the data, both reproduced in the appendix to this chapter, were often left with the firms at the initial interview.

In addition to information supplied by business firms, price data were obtained from a number of U.S. government agencies. Most of these data consisted of formal bids by U.S. and foreign firms to supply the government's needs for metals such as steel, aluminum, and copper, and for electrical equipment, scientific equipment, and so on. They were collected, with a great deal of help by the Bureau of Labor Statistics, from government-owned utilities, the military services, and other federal agencies. A small amount of data was obtained from local governments in the United States. All government data, which included bids probably numbering more than one thousand, represented purchase or offer prices.

The third major body of data was from foreign sources. Arrangements were made with several foreign research organizations for the collection of data in their own countries on U.S. and foreign prices. The most comprehensive time-to-time data were obtained from Germany through the aid of the IFO–Institut für Wirtschaftsforschung. These consisted of the official export price series broken down in considerable detail so as to provide, where available, information at the five-digit level, sometimes by destination. A considerable amount of data was also obtained on the movement of import prices, sometimes with breakdowns by country of origin. In addition to the time-to-time data taken from official sources, the German data included a limited number of direct place-to-place price comparisons gathered by the IFO–Institut. With the exception of the United Kingdom, where a private research organization supplied us with some comparisions based on selling prices, most other foreign data were based upon the purchasing experience of individual firms and public agencies. Some of this information came from agencies of the British and Canadian governments, but much more came from nonindustrialized countries. An extensive collection of comparative price information, involving both place-to-place comparisons and time-to-time data reflecting the development of prices from individual industrial countries, was obtained from Israel through arrangements made with members of the Department of Economics at the Hebrew University. The Israeli data provided both types of information for at least one product in virtually every one of the three-digit SITC categories included in our study. A more limited but significant body of data was obtained from Thailand; like the Israeli data, these reflected the purchasing experience of both private firms and public agencies.

In addition to the price data collected for the study by foreign research groups we were able to obtain additional information on bidding for contracts to supply foreign agencies, mostly governmental, with a wide variety of machinery and equipment, particularly the type required for development projects. More than thirteen hundred such bids, some of which ran into millions of dollars and provided international price comparisons for many items, were analyzed. Some of them, as in the case of railroad locomotives and construction equipment, were also used in comparisons over time where sufficiently detailed specifications were available.

We believe that those varied sources of price data provided good samples of the basic metals, metal products, and machinery included in our study. For some important commodity segments, particularly those usually purchased by the public authorities of developing countries, such as machinery for irrigation and electrical projects, the sample covers a substantial fraction of international trade. All in all at least some data are included for purchases of firms or public agencies in each of about fifty countries.

Much of our confidence in the results of the study rests not only on the large number of observations but also on the variety of sources. Data from each individual type of source may be subject to biases of unknown importance, but there was a good chance of overcoming most of these by including a large number of almost every type of transaction that involves world trade.

A number of biases affect particularly the place-to-place comparisons. It seems likely, for example, that data from U.S. purchasers show low prices for foreign products because the prospective buyers obtain quotations from abroad only when they think the offerings are likely to be at significantly lower prices compared to the domestically produced goods. Many items are purchased routinely in the United States without comparison with foreign prices because the foreign price is known to be higher than the U.S. price, and the purchaser will not have in his files the kind of precise comparison for these products that he has for those in which foreign suppliers are known to be competitive. A similar situation probably exists with respect to formal bidding data such as for U.S. government agencies. Foreign producers will simply not bid on many products for which they have little hope of winning orders. We would really like a foreign price for every bidding, but we tend to find them much more frequently on products often sold by foreign companies. This bias is exacerbated by any provisions, such as buy-American differentials, which favor U.S. companies. Their effect is presumably that foreign companies will limit their bidding to those products on which their advantage is great.

In bidding outside the United States the bias is not necessarily against the United States. The tendency is for the least competitive companies and countries to decline to bid, with the result that a number of the most unfavorable comparisons are omitted from every country's data. This bias is probably particularly strong for Japan and for the Common Market countries other than Germany, which tend to bid much less frequently than the United States, the United Kingdom, and Germany and, therefore, appear in an unduly favorable light. On the other hand, there are products on which U.S. companies do not try to win orders abroad, and in these cases the data are biased in favor of the United States.

This bias applies not only to particular commodities or to bidding against the buying country's own suppliers. The conditions of bidding in any particular country frequently tend to favor one supplier over another. Sometimes, for example, the specifications tend to resemble those of a traditional supplier, either deliberately or simply through the habits of the purchasers. A supplier in a neighboring country will be more likely to bid for a project than a supplier in a distant country, because the distant supplier knows that differences in transport cost may eliminate him. On the other hand, if a distant supplier does decide to bid on a project he is likely to offer lower f.a.s. prices (see footnote 4, below) than on a project closer to home, because he knows that he must overcome the difference in transport cost.

Another source of place-to-place data was information from U.S. firms whose foreign subsidiaries produced models identical to those manufactured in the United States by the parent companies. These data too seem likely to be biased against the United States because it is rare for a foreign subsidiary to produce the parent company's whole range of products, and the products selected for production abroad are presumably those in which foreign production has the greatest advantage. For the products produced more advantageously by the parent company there are no place-to-place comparisons. A possible example of this type of bias was found in the data on construction machinery. The intracompany comparisons on identical models were distinctly less favorable to the United States than the other intercountry comparisons for what the buyer considered equivalent products. A similar relationship was observed in railroad locomotives.

One type of differential pricing has a special interest. Companies are said to demand higher prices for goods sold under tied loans and grants than for those supplied under free international competition. In some commodity groups, in fact, U.S. companies say that they are able to sell abroad only to buyers using tied funds, because U.S. prices are higher than those of competitors. In practice, price offers under tied financing probably do not appear in our place-to-place comparisons since in such circumstances the buyer does not need to make international price comparisons. Sales under tied financing do, however, appear in our time-to-time data, but could not in most cases be distinguished from other sales.

The ideal solution, if the international market were completely separated from the tied fund market, would be to analyze the two markets separately, as if they involved different countries or different commodities. It is likely, however, that the two markets are not completely separated. Even under tied financing a buyer can exercise a choice among sources if several countries offer tied loans. In such cases the price of the product is one factor in a package that includes financing terms as well. It is not uncommon for countries operating under tied loans to switch purchases to other funds when the price differential between the offering under the tied financing and what is available elsewhere becomes too large. Countries that have tied loans or grants from more than one developed country naturally have wider opportunities to make given purchases from alternative sources.[2]

Because of these possibilities for bias, and others not mentioned, we considered it important to collect data from many different sources even if there was considerable duplication in commodity coverage and even when the cost per observation was much greater for some sources than for others. In this way we hoped to secure a representative sample of the world's purchases of internationally traded goods and to notice any serious biases in our data.

Selection of Items for the Sample

In some instances, respondents had to choose which price comparisons they would make for us from a great wealth of data on machinery and

[2] Cf. references on aid-tying cited in Chapter 3.

metal products. We suggested the following criteria of selection: (1) The items priced should be important in world trade (or else, as a second choice, in the exports or imports of the particular firm[3]); (2) the group of items selected taken together should be as representative as possible of world trade in the product category; and (3) preference should be given, as long as the first two criteria were met, to products which were produced in identical or comparable forms in different countries.

Since the selection of specific items was left to the respondents, additional firms were asked for information from time to time when it became apparent that those chosen earlier would not provide adequate data in certain product classifications. Instructions to the groups cooperating with us abroad were also adjusted to meet potential data deficencies.

Place of Reference of Prices

In order to focus on competitiveness as a feature of a country's own economy and to abstract from shifts in markets and differences in transport costs, we collected prices f.a.s. port of export wherever possible. Some data could only be secured on an f.o.b. factory basis, which we considered acceptable, and other information was available only c.i.f. destination. We accepted c.i.f. data but adjusted them to an f.a.s. or f.o.b. country-of-export basis before including them in the indexes.[4]

The alternative to this procedure would have been to measure price competitiveness in each different market of the world. The overall price competitiveness of each industrial country would then be determined by an averaging process in which each market would have a weight proportionate to its share in world consumption or imports. A more modest

---

[3] Where price data were available for a variety of sizes, quantity lots, and packagings (e.g., packaged versus bulk), the respondent was asked to supply data for his volume sales or purchases. In some product areas, quantity discounts or extras are quite significant and price relatives could have been distorted had not care been taken to ensure the comparability in this respect of the constituent prices of each relative.

[4] In order to make these adjustments for freight costs we collected information on freight rates, freight factors (ratios of freight to unit value), and f.o.b.-c.i.f. differentials from public bidding data and from the experience of some of the firms which supplied price data. Where these direct sources of information were not available we made use of some of the rates reported in congressional hearings on freight rates and from other governmental sources. See *Discriminatory Ocean Freight Rates and the Balance of Payments,* Hearings before the Joint Economic Committee, 88th Cong., 1st sess., Part 1, June 20 and 21, 1963; Part 2, October 9 and 10, 1963; and Part 3, November 19 and 20, 1963; and 88th Cong., 2nd sess., Part 4, March 25 and 26, 1964; and Part 5, Appendix; and *Steel Prices, Unit Costs, Profits, and Foreign Competition,* Hearings before the Joint Economic Committee, 88th Cong., 1st sess., April 23 to 29, May 2, 1963. "C.I.F. Value of U.S. Imports," U.S. Tariff Commission, February 7, 1967, mimeo.

alternative would have been to confine our attention to price competitiveness in one particular region of the world such as Latin America or in Europe. Our procedure is in a sense a compromise designed to provide a general measure of price competitiveness without entailing the enormous work of the first alternative and without limiting its geographical coverage as would the second alternative.

In collecting prices from exporters, our problems of measurement were sometimes complicated by the differences in f.a.s. prices that were charged for shipment to different markets. The ideal solution would perhaps have been to treat the shipments to each destination as a different product and to combine the price trends or international price comparisons for the different destinations according to the relative importance of the imports of each. In fact, however, firms were often loath to supply us with all of the necessary information, and we usually obtained relatives for a few of the chief markets.

Exclusion of Service Components of Prices

Since our interest is in commodity trade we tried to exclude service components from the prices we compared. In addition to transport costs, to which we referred earlier, the main service additions to "pure" commodity prices that we encountered were for erection and construction, distribution, and inspection. Erection costs were often included in bids on such products as storage tanks; and construction costs, in bidding on electrical and communication equipment. In almost all cases, however, the commodity cost was shown separately.

We excluded service costs if they represented transactions for which the price was independent of the price and characteristics of the commodity. An example might be a specification by the buyer that all tenders include two weeks of mechanics' time. However, if the service component was not independent of the commodity offer, and/or was substitutable for a part of the commodity price, it was included. The costs of special packing for export were, for example, included. So, too, were the costs for extra engineering time on a bid offer from one country where the product was being offered in a less advanced stage of assembly than other offers.

The costs of inspection created a special problem, particularly since buyers, in evaluating bids, sometimes estimated more extensive inspection costs for products from some sources of supply than from others.

In other cases buyers specified that the seller provide inspection services at the factory before the goods were shipped, or more often, at the point of delivery after arrival or at the time when the equipment was placed in operation. We chose finally to regard inspection services as the final step in commodity production, but we recognize that the case for their exclusion from our indexes is almost as strong as the case for their inclusion. In any event, the effect on the indexes is small since the charges were almost always well under 1 or 2 per cent of the total cost to the purchaser. Of course, only relative differences in inspection charges by producers in different countries would alter the place-to-place indexes. It is even less likely that the time-to-time indexes would be affected.

Generally, we rejected retail prices because they included the costs of internal distributive services that could not be expected to reflect the relative competitive strength of the supplying countries in the same direct way as f.a.s. export prices. However, retail prices of outboard motors and automobiles covered the range of models and the countries of origin and destination much more comprehensively than the f.a.s. export prices we really wanted. In these cases, we based our analyses on the retail prices and tried to adjust the results to the desired price basis. (See the discussions of product categories 711.5 and 732.1 in Chapters 12 and 15.)

Price Concepts

The Comparability of Products and Prices

The logic of our indexes required that the entire bundle of internationally traded goods be priced in each country for which the indexes were prepared. This requirement gave rise to two sets of problems. First, the quality of the goods exported often differed from one country to another. Secondly, there were cases in which a country did not export a good. The first of these difficulties often merged into the second, the distinction between the two depending in a given case on our definition of the commodity.

The Quality Problem

In making both the time-to-time and the place-to-place comparisons, primary responsibility for maintaining the comparability of the products was placed upon the respondent. In some cases, as in nonferrous metals, for example, this could be done rather straightforwardly, and only relatively minor problems arose. In such instances countries were exporting identical goods, usually to third countries, but not always to the same ones. In a few cases, such as aluminum, producing countries were actually exporting to each other's home markets. Usually, however, what appeared to be cross-exporting in the trade statistics turned out to involve different products traveling in the two directions.

Where there was less product homogeneity, the respondent had to determine what for his purposes were equivalent products. In some instances, as in the illustration relating to electric bulbs of 220 and 110 volts given in Chapter 3,[5] the equivalence was easy to establish. Where the differences in style or usage were not costless, the respondent, particularly if he was a purchaser, was frequently asked to evaluate the premiums or discounts which would be necessary to place him on the margin of indifference as between products of alternative design or quality among which he had to choose. Sometimes buyers felt unable to do this, and we could not obtain price relatives from them. We were not able, for example, to find buyers of typewriters who were very sure of their ability to make such estimates.

In still other instances, however, the assignment of such premiums or discounts was quite usual and even customary. Purchasers of textile machinery, for example, were often quite ready to estimate the worth for their purposes of one machine compared to another. Sometimes such comparisons are made systematically, as by many purchasers of heavy electrical generating equipment, although the methods used vary from one purchaser to another; the analyses of the bids made by the buyers or their advisers frequently include "leveled up prices" or "evaluated prices," which represent efforts to reduce the bids to comparable bases. In a few instances we even ran across fairly sophisticated methods involving multiple regression techniques making the price variable dependent upon weight and other physical or engineering characteristics.

In general, buyers were apt to be more helpful in making these quality adjustments in place-to-place comparisons, while sellers' records generally enabled them to be of greater assistance in time-to-time adjustments.

For certain products on which we could obtain enough data on physical and engineering variables and prices for a wide variety of makes, models, or countries to explain the variation in prices satisfactorily, we

[5] Page 57.

ourselves used regression methods. Our procedures are discussed in the next chapter.

Unique Goods

The methods just described often sufficed where the quality or end-use differences between the products of two countries were small enough to warrant treating them as variants of a single product. As the differences become more important, however, these cases merged into the situation of "unique" goods, that is, goods that are produced in only one country.

For unique goods and for goods produced in more than one country but in different qualities and for which there is no satisfactory way of evaluating quality differences we had two choices. One was to use import prices for the country that did not produce the particular good or quality. In the place-to-place comparisons this solution understates the price at which the importing country could produce the good. Its disadvantage for the time-to-time indexes is that a change in the price in the supplying country is offset, *ceteris paribus,* by an equal change in that of the importing country, so that the index of competitiveness does not change (as it should in order to reflect the altered ability of the supplying country to sell the good in the importing country).

The alternative we chose was to exclude unique goods from the place-to-place indexes but to include them in the time-to-time indexes of the producing country. We treated quality variations for which we could not find a basis for price comparison in the same way. In actual practice, since the sample of items which we used to trace time-to-time movements in each detailed classification varied anyway because of the method of data collection, we often did not know whether a particular product for which we had, say, U.S. but not other prices, was or was not unique.

The exclusion of unique products from the place-to-place comparisons, whether by design or owing to the nature of the sample, biases these comparisons against the country for which unique products are relatively important in exports. While we are not able to quantify the importance of these products, our field work has convinced us of the validity of the general view that unique goods play a larger role in U.S. exports than in those of other countries.[6]

The latest models in some product lines, such as (during the period

---

[6] Cf. Irving B. Kravis, " 'Availability' and Other Influences on the Commodity Composition of Trade," *Journal of Political Economy,* April 1956.

covered by our study) computers, crawler tractors, and large transport aircraft, were available only in the United States. Less frequently something that might be classified as a completely new product, such as television receivers or transistors, appeared. We do not know how pervasive such situations were or how much of each country's exports they accounted for, but it would be easy to exaggerate the distortion. Even unique goods usually have close substitutes, sometimes in the form of the older generation of models, which are likely to be produced in more than one country and which the large majority of customers may find satisfactory or even preferable, considering the price difference. Our view, therefore, is that if it were possible to estimate price differentials for unique goods which could then be averaged in with price differences for common goods (using world trade weights), the overall price level comparisons would show the United States in a more favorable position than our price level indexes (such as those in Table 2.1) but not by large amounts.

Use of Domestic Prices

In most cases international specialization among the countries that concern us was incomplete, and there was domestic production within each country even though not all of the countries exported the good. For example, the United States specializes in the export of crawler tractors and the United Kingdom in the export of wheel tractors, but each country produces both types. At an earlier date the crawler tractor may have been unique to the United States but at the beginning of our period only the very latest models of it were. With few exceptions a valid price could be found for each product even in countries which did not export it.

In such cases, the requirement that all international goods be priced was satisfied by taking the domestic price.[7] For place-to-place comparisons it was sometimes necessary to adjust the domestic prices for quality differences just as was done with export prices.

We used domestic prices in place of export prices not only where exports were nil but also where they were small or sporadic. The justification for their use is that the country would be willing to export at these prices if there were any market, and that they can therefore be regarded

---

[7] In principle the domestic prices should have been f.a.s. port of export, but we usually found it much easier to obtain f.o.b. factory prices and often used relatives based on these.

as equivalent to offer prices. In any case, domestic prices played only a minor role in our indexes.

Use of Offer Prices

We asked buyers and sellers to provide actual transactions prices, net of all discounts, rather than list prices. To the best of our knowledge most of our indexes are based on the prices at which goods were actually exchanged. It is, however, possible to view our use of offer prices in bid data as an exception.

Data arising from formal competitive bidding constitute a large and important body of information used in this study, particularly in categories, such as electric power machinery, in which custom-built equipment is the rule. The documents recording such bidding usually provide elaborate specifications in terms of physical characteristics or performance (particularly in the case of machinery), notations of any deviations from advertised specifications, and the prices quoted by each bidder. For certain kinds of equipment there often are evaluations of quality differences in monetary terms, ending in an explanation of the basis for the final choice by the purchaser.

In the place-to-place comparisons based on these bid data, the price used was the lowest offered by each country. Our main reason for discarding higher bids was that only the low bids influence the purchaser in his decision to buy from one country rather than another. The exclusion of higher bids also eliminated some which were obviously not seriously intended to win the order. Their purpose may have been to gain information on the prices offered by the other bidders or to insure that the company would continue to be invited to bid. Prices were as of the date of the bid; we used these prices even when they were subject to escalation and subsequent information about the actual price paid was available.[8]

Low bids rejected by the buyer because of doubts about the reliability of the supplier, the quality of the product, or the supplier's ability to supply the whole order or whole succession of orders were not used in our indexes.[9]

---

[8] We did not compare fixed prices with prices subject to escalation unless it was clear that the buyer regarded them as equivalent. In a few cases the comparison was made by assuming the maximum escalation permitted in the bid proposal.

[9] In some instances, one supplier was selected for further negotiation after the bids were opened. We did not take account of any price concessions that were obtained in this manner, since we could not know how far other bidders might have been willing to adjust their prices had they been confronted with a similar opportunity.

Place-to-place comparisons were thus made from bid data by comparing the lowest f.a.s. offer price from each country that had at least one bidding firm that met the specifications. Since only the winning bid could represent a price actually paid, the interpretation that may be placed on these comparisons deserves some comment.

The bidding data can be thought of as falling in a range between two types. One involves a highly detailed set of specifications, with the choice made on a price basis among bids meeting the specifications, with no consideration of bids not meeting them, and no allowance for performance beyond that specified. The second type is for a more standard product, such as a locomotive or electric generating equipment, for which some characteristics are specified but for which the customer evaluates positive or negative deviations from specifications, for example, efficiency in generating equipment.

In the first case the bid data supply not only a point along the supply function of the winning bidder, as would be the case for transactions prices, but also points on the supply functions of the losing bidders—points which might rarely or never show up in transactions prices because these companies would usually win bids for different combinations of characteristics. An example of this type might be U.S.-company bids on locomotives with diesel engines and hydraulic transmissions. International transactions prices for U.S. companies would show mainly or entirely data for locomotives with electric transmissions, but the use of unsuccessful bids supplies us with U.S. prices for the diesel-hydraulic combination as well—a characteristic of U.S. production relationships that we would otherwise miss.

The second type of bidding gives information on several points on the purchaser's consumption surface, as when a utility company evaluates various efficiency measures of electrical generating equipment in terms of the gain from greater output or the loss from possible failure to meet peak loads. Here again, the use of unsuccessful as well as winning bids in the price comparison greatly increases the amount of information available, because the unsuccessful bids would be excluded from an index based only on transactions prices. The inclusion of the unsuccessful bids means that a price comparison is contained in each purchasing decision rather than, as with transactions prices, only in the totality of purchase decisions.

One consequence of this type of price comparison may seem disturbing at first sight. The prices of two machines of similar function but different quality characteristics will be evaluated differently by different purchasers, even though the same nominal prices are offered to both purchasers. One may evaluate machine A as lower in price and the other may evaluate machine B as lower, because each is looking for a somewhat different mix of qualities in the product. The U.S. purchaser, for example, may be willing to pay a premium for a machine that will reduce breakdown time and maintenance man-hours; the European buyer may not value this quality so highly but may be willing to pay more for a machine that is adapted to short runs of a number of different variants of the end product. The same machines are available to both buyers but each has a different product mix in mind, and thus the price comparisons they make will differ.[10] Both comparisons will enter our interspatial indexes, and properly so since each reflects prices as seen by a purchaser and each determined a purchasing decision.

The Problem of Intracompany Transactions

A sizable part of international trade consists not of arms-length transactions between independent economic units but of intracompany movements of goods or sales to separate but affiliated companies.[11] The prices

[10] Price comparisons of this type are quite common in the analysis of such problems as choice among methods of transport. In comparing the price of two modes of travel the user will consider not only the nominal cost of each but also the time involved. Thus a price comparison by a laborer between a one-hour bus ride for 25 cents and a twenty-minute train ride for a dollar will differ from the same comparison made by a well-paid executive, because they will give different evaluations to the quality variable, i.e., time, associated with each price. If transactions prices alone were used, time would be evaluated at the single price of $1.25 per hour. Comparisons among modes of travel based on both time and money cost are discussed in Leon N. Moses and Harold F. Williamson, Jr., "Value of Time, Choice of Mode, and the Subsidy Issue in Urban Transportation," *Journal of Political Economy,* June 1963; and John F. Kain, "The Commuting and Residential Decisions of Central Business District Workers," *Transportation Economics,* New York, Universities–National Bureau Conference Series 17, 1965.

On a more general level, the role of time in purchase decisions is discussed in Jacob Mincer, "Market Prices, Opportunity Costs, and Income Effects," *Measurement in Economics: Studies in Mathematical Economics and Econometrics in Memory of Yehuda Grunfeld,* Stanford, Cal., 1963, and in Gary S. Becker, "A Theory of the Allocation of Time," *Economic Journal,* September 1965. Mincer suggests that the usual assumption that equal market or nominal prices represent equal opportunity costs to buyers often produces biased estimates of demand relationships, such as imputing price effects to the influence of income. He was mainly concerned with the omission of the cost of time in cross-sectional demand studies, but the outcome of his suggestions is a set of price comparisons which differ among purchasers even when the market prices are identical for all. The suggested comparisons are thus similar to those arrived at in this study through analysis of purchaser's evaluation of bids.

[11] Some data are available on the extent of exports by U.S. parent companies to affiliates in foreign countries during the period of our study. In 1963, more than three-quarters of the $5 billion of parent company exports to countries in which affiliates were established went through these affiliates. More than a third of all U.S. exports of manufactures of the type produced by U.S. companies abroad ($13.3 billion) were

and values attached to these goods in published trade data and in company records (and probably in most unit value indexes) are not necessarily market valuations. Frequently they may be determined by tax advantages or by bookkeeping convenience. The same kinds of problems affect data on exports of other industrial countries, but probably to a smaller extent, and data on exports by U.S. firms located in foreign countries.

We encountered the problem of intracompany trade in two types of situation. One is that of the U.S. company which exports to its own foreign subsidiary, which then assembles and/or distributes the product in the foreign country. Particularly for place-to-place comparisons it seemed inappropriate to compare the price at which the company sold to its subsidiary with a foreign wholesale price. In some cases it was impossible to make a comparison because the U.S. sale was not at the same level of completion (e.g., knocked-down cars) as the foreign product for which we could get data. However, even where the products were physically in the same state we were uncertain of the meaning of the price charged to the subsidiary. For example, the parent company might prefer to accumulate profits in a Swiss distributing subsidiary rather than in the U.S. parent company. In these cases we usually asked for the price at the first sale to an independent foreign purchaser, even though that was a domestic sale, rather than the price associated with the export movement.

The second type of problem was encountered where foreign sales of the U.S. company and its foreign subsidiaries were centralized in one trading company, and where export prices did not vary by country of manufacture. In such a case a buyer in any country purchases not from the local U.S. subsidiary but from the international company, which then decides whether to fill the order from local production or from the company's plants in other countries. Clearly there can be no relation between the prices paid by purchasers and the flow of trade, or between price movements and shifts in trade. The pattern of trade is determined by the decisions of the parent or international company rather than by those of the purchaser.

sold through foreign affiliates in that year, $3.4 billion through manufacturing affiliates and $1.2 billion through distribution affiliates. Of exports to manufacturing affiliates, $2.2 billion were to companies in primary and fabricated metals, machinery, and transport equipment, that is, the groups covered in this study (Samuel Pizer and Frederick Cutler, "U.S. Exports to Foreign Affiliates of U.S. Firms," *Survey of Current Business,* December 1965).

Since the international company makes the decisions which affect trade flows, the logical place to look for prices influencing trade flows is within the international company rather than the ultimate purchasers. Thus, we considered the final purchase as a domestic transaction between the purchaser and the local affiliate, and the purchase by the international company from its manufacturing affiliate as the international transaction. If the basis for the international company's decisions was the transfer prices it paid to different affiliates, we used these prices. If these were not the basis (e.g., if they were all identical), the best price measure was the cost of production in the various countries. This seemed closest to the idea of the price paid by the international company, and closest to the price which would determine the movement of trade. Accordingly, we have in a few cases used cost rather than price data in our indexes. (See, for example, the discussion of office machinery, SITC commodity group 714, in Chapter 12.)

Aggregation Methods

The Problem of Weights

Compared to other universes of commodities for which price indexes are desired, exports and imports are characterized by rapid changes in composition. Such changes, which reflect in part the sensitivity of trade flows to shifts in relative prices, occurred, for example, in the U.S. trade position in steel and textiles during the period of our study. The conventional export and import price indexes based on a single country's weights provide no satisfactory way of coping with such changes in the relative importance of goods in a single country's trade.

Even frequent changes in weights do not resolve the problem. A commodity characterized by rising prices and declining exports will be given progressively smaller weights with each revision and thus will have a diminishing influence on the measure of price competitiveness. The use of world trade weights and the concomitant expansion of commodity coverage beyond base-period exports and imports get around such difficulties.

More important, world manufactured exports represent the appropriate universe of prices for assessing the changing price competitiveness of a developed industrial economy such as that of the United States. The U.S.

economy—through its exports and imports and as a result of the comprehensive range of its manufacturing production—actually is confronted
by a potential market whose structure can best be adequately indicated
by the commodity composition of world trade. A change in the U.S.-
foreign price relationship of a four- or five-digit category of manufactured goods that looms large in world trade will be more likely to affect
the U.S. trade balance, whether or not the United States has been a big
factor in trade before or not, than if the price shift occurs for a good less
important in world trade.

It might be argued that the logic underlying the use of world trade
weights leads ultimately to the use of world production or consumption
as weights. After all, the potential market for the producers of a given
good in a given country is not merely the volume of that good which is
internationally traded, but includes all those markets currently being
supplied by home-produced goods. However, the disadvantage of using
world production or consumption weights is that the relative importance
of goods is often substantially different in world trade and in world
production. Some goods—because they are in universal demand, homogeneous, valuable in relation to their bulk, or available only from one or
a few sources—move more extensively in world trade than others. Thus
even if we take world production or consumption as a first approximation
to the proper weights, we must adjust these weights to allow for the
greater relevance of some products and prices to international trade. We
can define the degree of relevance as the probability that any particular
transaction in that product, chosen at random, will cross international
borders, and we can measure this probability as the ratio of exports (or
imports) of this commodity to total production (or consumption). The
weight for any commodity is thus

$$\frac{\text{value of exports}}{\text{value of production}} \text{ (value of production)}$$

which reduces to the value of exports as a weight.

If these differences in the "tradability" of goods change only slowly,
world trade weights will yield a more sensitive indicator of price competitiveness in international trade than world consumption or production,
and one more closely related to changes in trade flows.

On a more practical level, we point out that at present there are no
world consumption or production data sufficiently detailed for weighting

fairly narrow commodity groups. Accordingly, the weights for our new indexes have been derived in principle from world trade data, and in practice from exports of the OECD countries. The advantages and disadvantages of this weighting scheme, which permits the measures of a country's price competitiveness to be affected by prices of goods no longer important in its trade, have been discussed earlier.[12]

For any uses that require measures based on individual-country or other weights, it is a simple matter to reweight our subgroup or item indexes, as we have done for U.S. and other countries' export weights and for weights based on different years (see Chapter 2). The essential characteristic of the data, for all of these purposes, is that prices be collected for each country for the same commodities or commodity groups.

Aggregation for Price Competitiveness Indexes

The time-to-time and place-to-place indexes for the most detailed classifications employed in the study—generally four-digit categories, but sometimes more detailed breakdowns—were based on simple averages of price relatives.[13] The weights discussed in the preceding section were applied to these four-digit or more detailed categories to build up indexes for the two- and three-digit groups.

There are several possible alternative methods of aggregating the indexes for four-digit or smaller subgroups to reach the estimates of price competitiveness for three-digit or larger groups. Our method was to calculate indexes of price competitiveness at the lowest level, usually four-digit, and to aggregate these. At this detailed level, the index of price competitiveness ($P_{F/S}$) for a period was calculated from either time-to-time or place-to-place observations, the choice depending on our judgment as to which was superior in terms of the number of observations and the reliability of the data.

The summary international price indexes and the summary international price levels presented in Chapter 2 are derived from $P_{F/S}$ indexes and are consistent with them. The international price indexes for each

---

[12] See Chapter 3.

[13] There are technical grounds for preferring a geometric over an arithmetic mean (the former meets the time reversal test and the latter does not). However, the extra burden of computing geometric means would have been great because the calculations at this level of detail were not done by computer, and the difference in result would probably have been slight.

country other than the United States are derived from the U.S. international price index (based on time-to-time data) and the $P_{F/S}$ indexes relating U.S. price movements to those of the other country. The international price levels are the levels for the best year, in terms of the availability of data, extrapolated to other years by the $P_{F/S}$ indexes.

These summary indexes provide the most consistent comparisons among countries and over time that we can extract from our data, but they are not necessarily the best international price indexes for any one country or the best international price level estimates for any one year. For example, the summary international price index for Germany is the best for comparison with the movements of the U.S. price index, but it may omit certain subgroups because data on them were not available for the United States. For estimating the price movement for Germany or the United States separately, the summary international price indexes may be less appropriate than the indexes aggregated directly from time-to-time data,[14] which often include some time-to-time data not incorporated into the summary indexes. However, the summary international price indexes do incorporate some place-to-place observations which, when combined with a time-to-time index for any one country, provide estimates of international price movements for the foreign countries which might otherwise be unavailable. In some products this advantage outweighs the omission of some time series data, and the summary index is superior to the one calculated exclusively from time-to-time data even as an estimate of the one country's price movements.

Instead of casting the basic aggregation in terms of the price competitiveness index, we could have aggregated the international price indexes for each country and calculated price competitiveness from the aggregate country price indexes, or we could have aggregated the place-to-place price level comparisons and calculated price competitiveness by comparing aggregate price levels in different years.

The preference for aggregating the price competitiveness indexes is based on some purely technical advantages, on sampling advantages, and on certain economic considerations as well. The technical advantage of aggregating the subgroup indexes of price competitiveness is that we can then combine time-to-time and place-to-place data in one group index. Were we to aggregate either type by itself we would lose any subgroups

---

[14] These are the ones described in Chapter 1. They are given, along with the summary indexes, in Appendix C.

for which only the other type of data was available, or we would have to use some subgroup indexes that were inferior to those of the other type. This was an important practical consideration since the availability of each type of data varied widely from one commodity sector to another.

Some further considerations, revolving around the problem of bias in sampling, suggest the advantages of using the same set of commodities in both countries being compared rather than the best price index for each country, which might include some commodities in each not covered in the other country. This comparability of commodity coverage is characteristic of aggregates of price competitiveness indexes but could also be achieved by calculating price indexes for each country confined to those product groups covered in the index for the country being compared with it.

The advantage of using comparable commodity coverage can be analyzed by thinking of each commodity price movement in a given country as being composed of several elements. The first is the change in the general price level for the country (C) which is attributable to such variables as the stage of the business cycle or monetary developments. The second is the change in price for that commodity or its industry (I) throughout the world as a whole, attributable to factors such as the rate of growth of the industry, the development of new technology in the production of the commodity, or shifts in world demand for the commodity, as from changes in income or the development of substitutes. The third element is a residual (R) incorporating all other factors which operate on the price of the commodity in a particular country. These might include restrictions or trade barriers which insulate a country's prices for a particular product from the influence of developments abroad, or innovations in production which have not yet spread to other countries. Factor C does not account for any sampling variability in estimating, for a group of commodities, either price movements in one country or price competitiveness between two, because it is assumed to be constant within each country. Factor R contributes to variability in the estimates of both price and price competitiveness. Factor I contributes to sampling variability in price indexes and therefore also to sampling variability in price competitiveness indexes calculated from aggregates of price movements, if prices in the two countries are sampled separately. It does not contribute to variability in an index calculated directly from individual observations on price competitiveness or in one calculated from aggregates of identical price series in both countries because in those cases the I factor affects both countries' price movements in the same way. In any one country's price index, however, the I factor does contribute to sampling variability because the index calculated will reflect the characteristics of the industries that enter the sample.

The sample of commodities in each country's best international price index can be thought of as containing two parts: one consisting of commodities also included in the other country's index and one of those not covered. If the sampling in each country had been random, the advantage of a larger sample in each country, and therefore of a better estimate of each country's price, might outweigh the addition of variability from the I factor. Whether it does or not will depend on the importance of the I factor relative to the R factors. The evidence of the nonelectrical machinery items suggests that the I factor is relatively large, i.e., that the worldwide differences among industry price movements may often outweigh the country differences. This is indicated by the greater similarity of price competitiveness indexes than of price indexes for different commodity groups.

In fact, the selection of commodities is not random, and we cannot, therefore, be certain that the expected value of the price changes for the group of commodities not common to both countries is the same as for the common set. It may be much easier to find data on office machines in one country and on agricultural equipment in another. In such a case, the addition of noncommon commodities may involve adding, to a set of comparisons between corresponding commodity groups, a comparison between one country's prices of adding machines and another country's prices of plows.

The aggregation of subgroup indexes of price competitiveness rather than of the international price indexes is based also on the design of the study of comparative prices. We made all comparisons on a set of world trade weights at the finest level of detail available, four-digit or five-digit SITC codes. Two aircraft engines, for example, are compared with each other, even though they are not identical in specification, since they are in the same four-digit subgroup, which is not further subdivided. The aircraft engines are not compared with automobile engines, since they are in a different subgroup. This is clearly a sensible separation but one could argue that some of the smallest groups we use should be further subdivided. The aircraft engines, for example, should probably be divided into rough size categories, since large engines for transport aircraft do not compete with small engines for business or private aircraft. On the other hand, none of these comparisons is relevant to competition across subgroup lines, as between copper and aluminum, or aluminum and steel.

Finally, aggregation of the price competitiveness indexes is more appropriate to the analysis of price-quantity relationships in international trade. If competition takes place only within the finest subdivisions, the price influences on trade movements may be represented by the subgroup indexes of price competitiveness and the elasticities of substitution between different countries' exports of these subgroups.[15] For each subgroup the price competitiveness index is the denominator of the formula for the elasticity of substitution, plus 1. That is, for commodity X exported by countries F (foreign) and S (United States) in years 0 and 1, the elasticity of substitution (ES) will be

$$ES_{F/S} = \frac{\% \text{ change in relative quantities}}{\% \text{ change in relative prices}} \tag{1}$$

In terms of the index of price competitiveness (see Chapter 1) and a corresponding index of relative quantity change we can rewrite (1) as

$$ES_{F/S} = \frac{Q_{F/S} - 1}{P_{F/S} - 1} \tag{2}$$

There is, of course, a necessary relationship among relative prices, quantities, and proceeds. In this notation it is:

$$TC_{F/S} = P_{F/S} \times Q_{F/S} \tag{3}$$

where TC is an index of relative export revenues (R).

For any subgroup consisting of a single commodity, any one of the terms, $TC_{F/S}$, $P_{F/S}$, and $Q_{F/S}$ may be readily derived from the other two. Where some aggregation is involved, however, matters are somewhat more complicated. Assume, for example, that we wish to derive a rela-

---

[15] For simplicity we are ignoring here that part of international competition which takes place on the domestic markets of the two countries being compared.

tive quantity index between countries A and B for two equally weighted commodities, X and Y. The overall relative quantity index taking $\bar{Q}$ as the average of the Q's, is

$$\bar{Q}_{F/S} = \frac{(Q_{F/S})_x + (Q_{F/S})_y}{2} \tag{4}$$

In terms of ES and P, this is

$$\bar{Q}_{F/S} = \frac{\{ES_x[(P_{F/S})_x - 1] + 1\} + \{ES_y[(P_{F/S})_y - 1] + 1\}}{2} \tag{5}$$

It is apparent from (5) that the relative quantity index ($\bar{Q}_{A/B}$) cannot be derived from any aggregate price competitiveness index because the quantity index depends on the covariance between elasticity of substitution and change in price competitiveness ($P_{F/S} - 1$). Only if these two are assumed to be uncorrelated can the aggregate relative quantity change be calculated from the average price competitiveness and the average substitution elasticity within the aggregate.

No such calculation can be made from price competitiveness indexes derived from aggregates of international price indexes because it is difficult to define any relationship between these and any average of substitution elasticities. We are thus led to the aggregation of price competitiveness indexes as having more economic content than price competitiveness measured from aggregated international price indexes.

The decision to aggregate primarily in terms of indexes of price competitiveness gives us two alternative international price indexes for each country except the United States in each group and division: a preferred one, obtained for each three- and two-digit group by using the U.S. international price index based on time-to-time data together with the U.S. index of price competitiveness relative to each country; and a second one based on the aggregation of the time-to-time international price indexes themselves. The results of the two aggregation methods are presented in the tables of Appendix C, the former as the extrapolated (E) indexes, the latter as the aggregated (A) indexes. We can see there that the differences are minor for the study as a whole and even for the two-digit divisions, but that they are of considerable importance in some of the three-digit groups.

Differences between the extrapolated and aggregated international price indexes occur for two reasons. One is that the international price index number formula implied by the aggregation of price competitiveness indexes and estimation from the U.S. international price index is different from that implied by straight aggregation of the foreign international price indexes. The second is that the extrapolated price indexes for foreign countries were derived from place-to-place data in a number of groups for which the time series data were inadequate for use in the international price indexes. This was the case most frequently among the indexes for iron and steel.

We cannot leave the question of aggregation without referring to our methods of treating subgroups for which no price data were available.

Table 4.1

International Price Indexes Under Two Methods of Aggregation;
All Covered Commodities, 1953, 1957, 1961−64

(1962 = 100)

	1953	1957	1961	1962	1963	1964
United States						
Full value	87.9	97.0	99.4	100.0	99.5	101.0
Covered value	88.5	97.2	99.4	100.0	99.5	100.9
United Kingdom						
Full value	87.4	96.7	99.9	100.0	100.4	104.1
Covered value	88.0	97.0	99.8	100.0	100.5	104.3
EEC						
Full value	89.3	96.4	98.6	100.0	99.9	102.6
Covered value	89.3	96.6	98.6	100.0	99.9	102.5
Germany						
Full value	87.4	94.3	98.0	100.0	99.6	102.0
Covered value	87.4	94.3	98.0	100.0	99.6	102.0
Japan						
Full value			101.6	100.0	95.9	101.1
Covered value			101.1	100.0	96.2	100.5

Note: In the full-value indexes, each three-digit SITC group is weighted by the importance of that group in OECD exports. In the covered-value indexes, each three-digit SITC group is weighted by the importance in OECD exports of the subgroups in that group for which price indexes were computed.

Each method involved some assumptions regarding the universe of prices being sampled and the characteristics of the sampling method. The principles involved have been discussed elsewhere,[16] but the practical issue here was to decide whether to give each two-digit division and each three-digit group its full weight in world, or OECD, trade in aggregating or to give it only the weight of the commodity items within it for which price data were collected.

Giving each group its full weight implies that the commodity stratification was a good one and that price changes, price competitiveness, or the price level of any commodity for which we do not have data is more likely to resemble that of other commodities in its group than the average of all commodities. The considerable agreement between the proportion of price and price competitiveness series changing in a given direction and the direction of movements of the indexes suggests that our stratification of commodities was a meaningful one and that the aggregations using full group weights are appropriate.

In fact, as can be seen in Table 4.1, the differences between the two weighting systems are very small, mainly because coverage levels are so high. In the international price indexes for all machinery, transport equipment, metals, and metal products, the difference was greater than one-half of one percentage point in only four out of thirty cases and greater than one percentage point in only one case. Three out of the four largest discrepancies were in 1953, when the data were weakest. In half the cases there were no discrepancies at all between the two methods.

Appendixes

Copy of Instructions Left with Respondent Firms

International Price Comparison Study

Instructions for Collection of Purchase Prices and Price Offers

The purpose of this study is to compare the prices at which U.S. sellers offer machinery, vehicles, and metal products with prices at which U.K., Common Market, and Japanese companies offer the same products. The products included in the study are those covered by the following parts of the Standard International Trade Classification (SITC):

[16] See Robert E. Lipsey, *Price and Quantity Trends in the Foreign Trade of the United States,* Princeton University Press for NBER, 1963, Chap. 5.

Division 67   Iron and steel
Division 68   Nonferrous metals
Division 69   Manufactures of metals, n.e.s.
Section 7   Machinery and transport equipment
Division 81   Sanitary, plumbing, heating and lighting fixtures and fittings
Group 861   Scientific, medical, optical, and controlling instruments
Group 864   Watches and clocks
Group 891   Musical instruments, sound recorders, and reproducers and
               parts and accessories thereof
Group 894   Perambulators, toys, games, and sporting goods
Group 897   Jewelry and goldsmiths' and silversmiths' wares

The National Bureau has not selected any standard list of commodities
for all respondents to use. We ask each cooperating company or government agency to pick out several items in each three-digit SITC group and,
if possible, in the more important four-digit groups with which it has had
purchasing experience. The essential characteristic of each item selected
is that the respondent be able to make a precise comparison, either place
to place or time to time. To make a place-to-place comparison, he must
know the price at which a U.S. seller is offering the product at a given
time and the price at which a seller in the United Kingdom, the Common
Market, or Japan is offering the identical or a comparable product at
the same time. To make a time-to-time comparison he must know the
price at which a particular product is offered by one country at two
different times.

Ideally we would wish to have both place-to-place and time-to-time
comparisons for each individual commodity for all countries and all
years, such as would fill out the following table completely:

Product: 100 lbs. of 8d common bright steel nails

	USA	UK	Germany	France	Other EEC	Japan
1953						
1957						
1961						
1962						
1963						
1964						

In practice, however, such complete comparisons are rarely possible. The company may have bought one type of nail in 1953 and be able to compare U.S. and German prices for it, but it may have bought a different type in 1957 and be able to compare the United States with Germany for that type. The company may have a U.S.-Japanese comparison for a third type of nail and might have consistently purchased a fourth type from the United States over a period of years and thus be able to supply time-to-time data only for that. Any unit of information is useful to us provided that it compares at least two countries' prices at one date or one country's prices for at least two dates.

Other criteria for selection of products are that they be important in international trade and, preferably, typical of the SITC groups they are in.

In the case of complex machinery, of course, it is almost never possible to find absolutely identical products offered from two countries. Our aim is to get as close as possible to the criteria used by the purchaser in deciding which product to buy. In some cases, such as electrical generating equipment and transformers, specific measures of differences in quality are often calculated, and these can be added to the base prices to make comparisons. If there is formal competitive bidding, a set of requirements is imposed by the buyer, and only the offers meeting the specifications should be considered. Sometimes the buyer can make a judgment as to the value to him of specific features present in one machine and not in another. Even qualitative comparisons which can be expressed only roughly in value terms are of interest to us. In all cases it is important that precise specifications be included with the prices collected and that qualitative differences which enter into the purchaser's decision be described to help us classify the commodity and, in some instances, to help us understand the price relationships.

The time periods covered by the study are midyears 1953, 1957, 1961, 1962, 1963, and 1964. If data are not available for these midyears, prices for other nearby dates can be used. The date of each price and each offer should be listed.

F.a.s. prices are preferred, but f.o.b. prices are also acceptable. Even delivered prices can be used if necessary, but in that case it should be carefully noted whether tariffs and other costs are included. If possible, estimates of transportation and insurance cost should be collected.

Where both unit price and total value of a bid or contract are available they should be collected. In any case, the size of the total order in quantity terms should be indicated. In some cases, one order or bid contains many specific items (such as different sizes of the same product). If quantities or values are available on each item individually they should be recorded, as well as the prices, if they are given. The quantities or values are useful for estimating the relative importance of the various items included.

The specifications supplied should be detailed enough to permit classication into five-digit SITC codes. That means, for example, that electrical machinery must always be distinguished from nonelectrical, that the particular metal used in metal products (other than machinery and vehicles) must be specified, that insulated wire be separated from noninsulated. Measures of capacity or average output of a machine should be given if they are available, as well as weight, speed of operation, efficiency, and, in general, whatever qualitative factors the purchasing agency considers important.

Information about nonprice factors in the selection of products is also of great interest. Delivery periods offered by various sellers should be recorded, where they are given, and other factors such as financing arrangements, tied loans, compatibility with existing equipment, service facilities, experience of producer, should be noted whenever they have played an important role in the choice of supplier.

Form Used for Gathering Price Data

CONFIDENTIAL

NATIONAL BUREAU OF ECONOMIC RESEARCH
INTERNATIONAL PRICE COMPARISON STUDY

Product (Identify briefly and attach description or specification circular
    if available)

_____

_____

_____

_____

Unit_____
(each, dozen, etc.)

Country of origin	1964	1963	1962	1961	1957	1953
United States	___	___	___	___	___	___
_____	___	___	___	___	___	___
_____	___	___	___	___	___	___
_____	___	___	___	___	___	___
_____	___	___	___	___	___	___

1. Please indicate net U.S. and net foreign selling price for products of comparable quality.
2. If quality differs between countries or over time indicate in space below.
3. F.a.s. price is preferred; please note if f.o.b. or other basis is used.
4. Subject to the condition that comparable quality be maintained over time, the lowest price quoted by a satisfactory source of supply is desired, both for U.S. and for the foreign price.
5. Please return this report even if partially complete.

5

MEASURING PRICE DIFFERENCES
BY REGRESSION METHODS

IN THIS CHAPTER we set out the rationale for the use of regression methods in international price comparisons and discuss the problems encountered in using this technique. The bulk of the chapter is devoted to the development in considerable detail of regression-based index numbers for automotive diesel engines as an illustration of the problems and alternative solutions. The use of regressions for other commodities in the study as a whole is also summarized.

Regression methods of price measurement are applicable to many commodities that are difficult or impossible to price by traditional methods, and can be used for time-to-time as well as place-to-place comparisons. They were first applied to domestic price indexes, and we used them for intertemporal international price indexes in a number of commodity classifications. We also extended their use to international price comparisons where they had not been used before, and we dwell on this application in the present chapter. However, our tests of the effect of alternative techniques on the final price measurement should be relevant to domestic price measurement as well.

The basic problem in international price comparisons, whether their purpose is to compare the purchasing power of currencies or to measure price competitiveness in international trade, arises from international differences in product specifications. Not only are many products highly differentiated among the producers within each country, but there are often significant international differences in the characteristics of products that serve the same general purpose. As a result, it is frequently

Note: A shorter version of this chapter was published in the *International Economic Review*, June 1969.

impossible to find identical products in two countries, even though products performing the same function are manufactured in both countries.

A similar problem of comparability over time has troubled compilers of domestic price indexes. In recent years the main problem has been a suspected upward bias in price indexes due to insufficient accounting for improvements in quality. It has been suggested that the failure to measure quality change adequately is the most important defect in existing price indexes.[1]

The construction of "hedonic" price indexes, using multiple regression, was suggested by Andrew Court in an article in 1938,[2] but the idea was neglected for many years and only recently revived by Richard Stone, Zvi Griliches, and others.[3] The method has now been applied not only to automobiles, as originally proposed by Court, but also to farm tractors, electrical generating and transmission equipment, and single-family house prices.

The Rationale of Regression Analysis in Price Comparisons

The application of regression analysis to price measurement rests on the hypothesis that price differences among variants of a product in a particular market can be accounted for by identifiable characteristics of these variants.[4] Each of these characteristics is regarded as an element of a complex product; variations in the mix of the elements produces product differentiation at a moment in time and changes in product quality over time. By fitting a regression equation to observations on the price and characteristics of commodity variants, typically in a cross section of the market at a given time, the characteristics associated with the price of the commodity and their relationship to the price can be determined. If the relevant characteristics have been correctly identified, the coef-

---

[1] Stigler Committee Report, p. 35 (Price Statistics Review Committee, *The Price Statistics of the Federal Government*, New York, NBER, 1961).

[2] "Hedonic Price Indexes with Automotive Examples," *The Dynamics of Automobile Demand*, New York, General Motors Corp., 1939.

[3] For a bibliography of such studies see Zvi Griliches, "Hedonic Price Indexes Revisited: Some Notes on the State of the Art," *Proceedings of the Business and Economics Section, American Statistical Association*, December 1967.

[4] Cf. Richard Stone, *Quantity and Price Indexes in National Accounts*, Paris, 1956, Chap. 4. For the extension of the theory of consumption to deal with the conception of goods as bundles of characteristics see K. Lancaster, "A New Approach to Consumer Theory," *Journal of Political Economy*, April 1966.

ficients of the equation can be interpreted as prices for the characteristics. These prices are then used in comparisons among markets or time periods in which the commodity differs in quality (i.e., has different specifications or combinations of elements). Court, for example, computed regressions of automobile prices against weight, wheelbase, and horsepower in order to measure price changes over time.

Cost vs. Utility

Most discussions of the meaning of price indexes derived by regression methods, and the very name, "hedonic," applied to them, have stressed measures of utility to the consumer. Court, for example, spoke of "the potential contribution of any commodity . . . to the welfare and happiness of its purchasers and the community" and of ". . . establishing an objective composite measure of usefulness and desirability. . . ." [5]

The Bureau of Labor Statistics and other producers of major price indexes rely on production relationships rather than on consumption relationships. The BLS "finds equivalence of quality in equal production cost. . . ." [6] The adoption of production cost rather than utility as a measure of quality does not preclude the use of regression methods, since valuation in terms of production cost and valuation in terms of utility may be viewed as alternative means of assessing the relative qualities and hence the relative prices of variants of a complex product each having a different mix of elements.[7] On a single market in competitive equilibrium, the two valuations should be identical. As Adelman and Griliches have pointed out, if the ratio of the marginal rates of substitution between two quality dimensions is smaller than the ratio of the costs exacted for them, both price and consumer purchases will adjust until

[5] *Op. cit.*, p. 107.
[6] Stigler Committee Report, p. 37.
[7] Cf. in *loc. cit.* the Stigler Committee position on producers' goods. Regression analysis, it may be added, can be regarded as a means of inferring statistically the prices of elements of a product for which the total price is determined by what is sometimes referred to as unit or component pricing. In component pricing, which may be found in industries as different as men's apparel and residential construction, the costs (assumed constant) of particular units of work (such as making a buttonhole or providing and installing a window frame) are used to build up the cost and price of a particular product (such as a suit or house).
It would, however, be unduly confining to restrict regression analysis to the variables that form the building blocks used in industrial price formation. These are sometimes difficult to discover, and in any case performance characteristics may sometimes better explain price differences, particularly where different producers achieve given performance by using different physical components.

equilibrium is reached, provided that price is not administered. If prices are administered, and therefore not free to vary, equilibrium between the marginal rates of substitution and the cost of the quality dimensions will be reached by a change in the ratios of quantities purchased.[8]

Thus, in the regression analysis of prices, we may formulate the elements entering into a complex product either in terms of the cost of characteristics such as horsepower and fuel economy or in terms of their utility to consumers at a particular place and time.

Use of Regression Coefficients for Price Measurement

In a regression in which price is taken as the dependent variable, the coefficient of each element (that is, each independent variable) shows its price (that is, the cost per unit for additional units) in the mix of elements included in the complex product.[9] These regression coefficients may tend to change over time. To the extent that such changes reflect economic rather than statistical factors, they may be interpreted in the same way as the changes shown by other kinds of prices. For example, the lowering of the price of power over time accompanied by a shift toward more powerful machines that we have found in regressions for such products as railway locomotives and aircraft engines may be interpreted either as supply-based changes or as demand changes under conditions of decreasing supply price.[10]

International differences in the regression coefficients may also be expected, particularly if each country's market is isolated from the others. They could arise, for example, from differences in relative factor prices which would produce interspatial differences in the relative prices of the

8 Irma Adelman and Zvi Griliches, "On an Index of Quality Change," *Journal of the American Statistical Association,* September 1961, p. 547. As between two situations at different times, however, the cost and utility approaches, as they are sometimes defined, will yield different results when there are cost-free improvements in the second situation that were not present in the first. This outcome depends on the assumption that costs may be defined in terms of the physical characteristics of a product independently of the utility the product yields. The issues raised in this connection are not a special problem connected with regression methods and will not be pursued here.

9 The existence of the constant term presumably indicates that the assumption of linearity in element prices, even where it is satisfactory within the range of observation, does not apply outside it, particularly near the zero level. The explanation might be that there are elements in the product (including overhead costs) which we do not try to account for in the equation.

10 An illustration of a supply-based change is the lower price of horsepower in automobile engines which has been attributed to engine redesign (F. Fisher, Z. Griliches, and C. Kaysen, "The Costs of Automobile Model Changes Since 1949," *Journal of Political Economy,* October 1962, pp. 441 f.).

elements unless the factor mix required for increments in each quality element did not vary from one element to another in any of the countries.

In the case of diesel engines, for example, additions to weight (taken either as an element of cost or as a proxy for durability and/or reliability) might require a high materials content while additions to horsepower might require a relatively high labor content. In these circumstances the ratio of the U.S.-to-U.K. coefficient or "price" for weight would be smaller than the ratio for horsepower. If, on the other hand, it took more labor to build a sturdier engine and high weight were achieved through high labor content, the difference might be in the opposite direction. Or, again, the relative prices might differ if one country's industry specialized in a narrow range of the product (e.g., low horsepower) while another produced a wide range.

If there were truly competitive and frictionless international markets, we would not expect to find international differences in product prices, and if quality elements could be varied independently of each other, with no interdependence in utilities or costs, we would not expect to find international differences in their prices either. Any price that was out of line would bring a fall or rise in market share, changing cost and price until price equality was established.

International markets for most products probably fall between the extremes of complete national isolation and complete international integration. For many products, transport costs, tariffs, and other isolating factors are sufficiently strong to permit the production in different countries of the same products or elements of products at different costs, and their sale at different prices.

Specification Differences and Regression Strategies

Some of the problems encountered in comparing prices in two situations are set out in a series of pictorial cases below. The examples are very simple, involving only one quality variable, and omit the complexities arising from the use of several variables, such as those from intercorrelations among quality characteristics and interactions between them. However, these illustrations introduce and catalog some of the problems referred to later.[11]

[11] For an exploration of these problems in a different context see James N. Morgan and John A. Sonquist, "Problems in the Analysis of Survey Data and a Proposal," *Journal of the American Statistical Association,* June 1963.

In the simplest price measurement case, the price of the product is uniformly higher or lower in situation II than in situation I, over the whole range of the quality characteristic (Figure 5.1). The slope of line II, in other words, is equal to that of line I.

If there are observations at the same level of the characteristic, say horsepower (*HP*), in both situations, the price difference can be measured in the traditional way by comparing identical engines in the two places or two years.

If the same range of engines is produced in both situations, but no pair is identical in horsepower, the conventional method, relying on identical specifications, is useless, because there are no comparable items produced in both situations. Producers of index numbers probably meet this difficulty (if they do not drop the commodity from their indexes) by interpolating between two observations in situation I, for example, to estimate a price for the item produced in situation II. The method is a very crude version of the regression technique, involving fitting equations to individual pairs of points rather than to the whole set. It could give erratic results if the points were scattered around the line instead of being on one line as in Figure 5.1.

In the more typical case, particularly if the years are some distance apart or the places very different, the bulk of the observations of the characteristic fall in different ranges in the two situations. Although the *HP* observations of the two situations usually overlap, let us consider for the moment the extreme case shown on Figure 5.2 in which

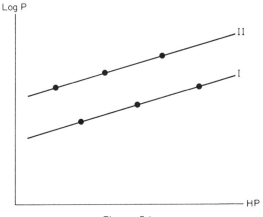

Figure 5.1

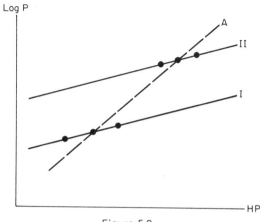

Figure 5.2

they do not. Here again, no index could be calculated by conventional methods, because there are no identical products to compare.

If a regression equation were fitted to each set of observations the regression line for II would be above that for I, and we would calculate that prices were higher in II. The same result would follow from fitting a line to pooled data for I and II, with a dummy variable for II.

If we fitted a single equation to pooled data (A) and measured the price level in each situation by comparing actual prices with the equation, we would calculate that there was much less price difference. In the extreme case, when the line passed through the means of the two groups, we would make a finding of no price difference ($P_{II}/P_I = 1.00$).

All the examples up to this point have had one characteristic in common: In the two situations being compared the slope was the same. There is no index number problem, since all prices have changed, or differ, by the same amount. Thus if there are any overlapping observations, both conventional methods and regression analysis can easily cope with the measurement problem.

If the slopes differ in the two situations, an index number must be calculated by selecting particular points within the range of the characteristic and measuring the price relationship for those points. The simplest case to picture is that of Figure 5.3, where the range of observations is the same for both countries but the slopes differ.

In this case, if the data were pooled and a single regression line were

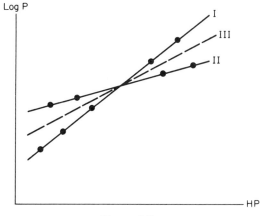

Figure 5.3

fitted, its graph would look like curve III. The conclusion would be that situation I and situation II do not differ in price if an index were calculated from the coefficient of a dummy variable representing one of the countries, since neither country is consistently above or below line III. The same inference would be drawn, provided each observation were given equal weight, if the equation were fitted without dummy variables and the index measured from each country's residuals, or if the price difference were estimated from separate equations for I and II. However, the result from an index calculated by weighting each price comparison by the importance of the engine to which it referred would depend upon the product mix.[12] If smaller engines were more important, situation I would be considered lower in price; if larger ones predominated, situation II would be lower. For measuring export price competitiveness, for example, the weights would be determined by the relative importance in international trade of engines of different horsepower.

The same results as from separate equations for I and II could be obtained from a single equation pooling the data for the two situations but adding variables to differentiate for the level (i.e., intercept) and slope of situation II as compared to the level and slope of I.[13]

---

[12] Assuming that the regression were not also weighted.

[13] This method is discussed further below. Other examples of this technique are given in S. Ben-David and W. G. Tomek, "Allowing for Slope and Intercept Changes in Regression Analysis," Department of Agricultural Economics, Cornell University, A. E. Res. 179, November 1965, mimeo.

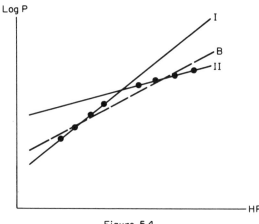

Figure 5.4

Figures 5.4 and 5.5 represent more difficult cases, in which the fitting of the equation or equations involves additional assumptions about the nature of underlying, but incompletely observed, relationships.

One assumption, represented by Figure 5.4, is that there are two price-horsepower relationships for the two situations, as I and II in Figure 5.3, but that all the engines for which prices are known for situation I are below the mean *HP* and all those for situation II are above. Such a case might evolve from Figure 5.3 if each country specialized in that *HP* range in which it was superior, and drove the other from the market in that range.[14] The outcome of the calculation here would again depend on the weighting of the different *HP* sizes. In a weighting based on that of one of the two situations (one country's exports or production, for example) that situation would be found to have the lower prices.

If a single equation (*B*) were fitted to the data of the case represented by Figure 5.4, with price indexes calculated from residuals or from country dummy variables, but with no country-slope interaction terms, the conclusion would be biased toward finding that there was no price difference between situations I and II. This would be true even if the price comparisons used only the horsepowers observed in one of the two situations, because the regression line would tend to pass near the means of the observations of each of the situations. However, the intro-

[14] Note that the collection of offer prices, in addition to transactions prices, might fill out the other end of the range for each country.

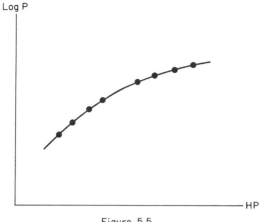

Figure 5.5

duction of an intercept and a slope interaction term would restore the conclusions derived from I and II.

As long as we restrict our consideration to linear functions, the estimation of separate equations or the use of country and slope interaction terms seems clearly superior to the fitting of a single function. Once we lift this restriction, we must consider the possibility that the two situations lie on the same price-horsepower function. If such were the case, as in Figure 5.5, we would have to conclude that the prices of I and II are the same, whether we compared prices on I's products, II's products, or a combination of both of them. However, when there is no overlapping, the data do not show us whether one function (as in Figure 5.5) or two functions (as in Figure 5.4) should be fitted. In these circumstances, we would need other information about the nature of the shape of these functions. Fortunately, we have not had to face such extreme cases in which there were no overlapping observations.

We are thus left with the alternatives of estimating separate equations or, what will yield the same price comparisons, using pooled regressions with situation (intercept) and slope dummies. A compromise between these two alternatives, which retains advantages of each, is "flexible pooling." In this technique we begin by estimating an equation in which there is a dummy variable for each situation [15] and a situation-interaction

[15] Actually, a dummy variable is used for each situation except the base. See D. B. Suits, "Use of Dummy Variables in Regression Equations," *Journal of the American Statistical Association*, December 1957, pp. 548–551.

term for each combination of situation and characteristic. If situation I is taken as the base, the situation dummy variable distinguishes the intercept of situation II from that of situation I; the interaction term distinguishes the slope in situation II from the slope in the base situation. By dropping the dummy and interaction terms that do not prove to be significant and retaining those that do, we use the whole size and range of the combined sample for the two situations to estimate the coefficients which seem to be common to them while permitting the estimation of separate coefficients for the two situations where these appear to be warranted.

In order to simplify the foregoing outline of alternative regression strategies, we posed the pricing problem in terms of a single independent variable. In fact, of course, it is necessary to take into account more than one product element in explaining the price differences between two situations. Indeed, for a complex product such as an automobile or even a diesel engine, product differentiation between models, brands, times, and places turns upon a very large number of elements. However, most of these tend to be highly intercorrelated, so that it is frequently possible to account for 90 per cent or more of the price variation by including as few as three or four elements as independent variables.

It should be mentioned that both our purpose and the price data we employ differ in several ways from the simple examples described above and from those of other experiments with regression techniques. One difference is that the data relate to several different markets connected, to some degree, by international trade. They can, therefore, contain price differences for whole commodities and for particular quality characteristics which we would not expect to find within a single market. Another point is that the list of specifications could not be enlarged to take account of the regression results. Ideally, such an analysis should provide opportunities to test more thoroughly the effects on price measurements of alternative combinations of independent variables. We could also have examined more closely the cases in which such results as negative coefficients for features apparently useful and costly to produce suggested that the variables were acting as proxies for others not covered. However, since the data were originally collected for conventional price comparisons we were obliged to do as well as we could with the variables that seemed important in advance.

It should be emphasized that our main purpose has not been to analyze the economic factors underlying price changes or to account for differences in price levels. For that reason we had no real interest in the element coefficients themselves. The price indexes, and therefore the country dummy variables from which they were derived, were the object of the experiment. The other coefficients were important only as they affected the price estimates.[16] Our major question in using regression methods was whether the price indexes which they produce would be sensitive to choices among equally justifiable alternative equation forms and explanatory variables. Indexes computed by more traditional methods are not immune to similar problems, but the ranges of indeterminacy involved in the two approaches have not been compared.

Automotive Diesel Engine Price Regressions

Data on 1962 price, horsepower, revolutions per minute, engine displacement, and weight were obtained for seventy-three automotive diesel engines produced in four countries (see Table 5.1). What we refer to as the "average" engine has the mean specifications (unweighted) of the seventy-three engines. The specifications of the "export" engine were derived by weighting each country average by the relative importance of that country in automotive diesel engine exports.

The American firm that was the main source of information had gathered the data in a market survey, presumably including the variables considered important. We had no opportunity to enlarge the list of specifications, even though a longer list would have been desirable for our purposes.

Specification of the Relationship

The main utility sought by the purchaser of a diesel engine is power. The concomitant considerations include durability, frequency and ease of repair, fuel economy, and smoothness of operation. These qualities

---

[16] Since we are not interested in the coefficients themselves it has been suggested that factor analysis or principal components analysis would have been appropriate techniques for dealing with the problem of multicollinearity. The drawback of these methods is that the independent variables lose their identity. It is then impossible to impose any criteria for the reasonableness of the relationships. For an application of principal components analysis see Phoebus J. Dhrymes, "On the Measurement of Price and Quality Change in Some Consumer Capital Goods," *Discussion Paper No. 67*, Department of Economics, University of Pennsylvania, September 1967.

Table 5.1
Summary of Data for Automotive Diesel Engines, 1962

	U.S.	U.K.	Ger-many	France[a]	Total or Average	"Export" Engines[b]
No. of producers	4	6	5	1	16	
No. of engines	22	22	23	6	73	
Averages:						
Price (dollars)	3,470	1,593	2,023	2,394	2,360	2,250
Horsepower	190	147	163	184	168	164
RPM	2,182	2,191	2,367	2,050	2,232	2,217
Displacement						
(cu. in.)	517	539	488	590	520	524
Weight (lbs.)	2,117	1,531	1,509	2,123	1,749	1,715

Note: The U.K., German, and French data were supplied by an American firm; the U.S. data came from that firm and three others. Prices are mainly those charged to distributors in the country of manufacture but include also some on sales directly to truck manufacturers.

[a]In addition, information was available on price, horsepower, and revolutions per minute but not on weight and displacement for five engines of two other French producers. The averages for all eleven French engines were: price, $2,147; horsepower, 166; and rpm, 2,273. Only the six engines for which complete information was available were included in the pooled regressions; all eleven were included in the separate regressions for France.

[b]The "export" engine is the average of country-type engines weighted by the estimated share of each country in automotive diesel exports. The weights used were: United Kingdom, 50 per cent; United States, 30 per cent; Germany, 18 per cent; and France, 2 per cent.

may also be viewed as being related to components of the total cost per unit of freight delivered (for a truck) such as driver time, repair and fuel costs, and costs of delayed delivery.

The variables at our disposal—horsepower (H), displacement (D), revolutions per minute (R), and weight (W)—are summary variables in the sense that they are determined by other elements such as the number and size of cylinders, inlet pressure and temperature, fuel-air ratio, and spark advance. Neither our summary variables nor the more detailed specifications behind them directly measure the various facets of delivery costs which may be important to the buyer. Indeed, only H is a direct measure of a major utility to the diesel engine consumer. The other variables are proxies for performance characteristics we are unable to measure.

Three of the variables—*H, D,* and R—are parts of an engineering relationship that may be expressed as follows:

$$H = \frac{M \times D \times R}{k}$$

where *M* is mean effective pressure (the amount of pressure that operates on each cylinder) and *k* is a constant.[17] While *M* was not specifically included in our data, it is obvious that we can easily calculate it, since we know the values of the other variables in the relationship.

The relationship indicates that a given horsepower can be achieved by means of different combinations of *M, D,* and *R*. Each has its advantages and disadvantages. For example, as between two engine designs with the same *H*, the one with the higher *R* will be smaller and may cost less because it uses less materials. On the other hand, it may vibrate more, thus requiring more servicing, and may have poorer combustion, thus consuming more fuel.

The relation of weight to the other variables is more difficult to specify. On the one hand an engine that is too light may not be durable; indeed, one industry source suggested that in a cross section of engines at any one time weight could be taken as a rough guide to the reliability and durability of an engine. On the other hand, weight per se is a disadvantage, and costly effort such as more careful casting may be undertaken to keep down weight.[18] Furthermore, since *W* is highly correlated with *D* and (inversely) with *R*, it may be expected to add little to the explanation of price variation. In fact $\bar{R}^2$ was substantially reduced when weight was eliminated, and there were some large differences in the price relatives. Since weight may contribute to the durability of an engine, and is statistically significant in the explanation of price variation, equations that include it are clearly preferable.

To explain the variation in diesel engine prices, *W* and any three among *M, H, D,* and *R* can be taken, because any three of them

[17] The constant is 792,000 for a four-stroke-cycle engine and 396,000 for a two-stroke-cycle engine. See A. R. Rogowski, *Elements of Internal-Combustion Engines,* New York, 1953, p. 53; and B. H. Jennings and E. F. Obert, *Internal Combustion Engines,* Scranton, Pa., 1944, p. 40. All of the engines in our sample are, to the best of our knowledge, four-stroke-cycle engines.

[18] The relationship of weight to utility may be positive across models at a given time but negative over time.

determine the fourth. We chose to eliminate H, partly because it is more highly correlated than M with the other variables and partly because the coefficients of the other variables make more sense when M is used. H is the one variable we are certain represents a utility to the purchaser of diesel engines. Leaving it out of the function permits us to measure the value of additions to the other elements when they result in additions to horsepower. Including H produces coefficients of the other variables whose meaning is ambiguous because an addition to any other variable, holding H constant, involves a subtraction from whichever variable is omitted (M, D, or R). For example, if H is used, the coefficient for D represents the price of an addition to displacement that does not add to horsepower, and therefore involves a reduction in M. It is difficult to say what sign such a coefficient should logically have. On the other hand, if M is used, the coefficient for D represents the price of an addition to displacement which does add to horsepower, clearly implying a positive sign.

The relation between an equation in M, D, and R and one in H, D, and R can be expressed as follows:

$$P = aH^bD^cR^d$$

implies, given $H = MDR/k$, that

$$P = \frac{a}{k^b} M^bD^{b+c}R^{b+d}$$

The coefficients in this formula represent the price of additions to horsepower through additions to each of the other variables. Since weight is not included in the function, the addition to displacement and horsepower will probably involve an increase in weight, too, and thus represent essentially the value of a larger engine minus the drawbacks attendant on increased size. However, if weight is included in the function the D coefficient represents the price of increased horsepower through greater size without any weight penalty, presumably through the use of lighter materials or other engineering changes. We would expect this D coefficient to be larger than the one which allows for increased weight, since higher power is more desirable if it does not bring greater weight.

Alternative formulations might involve including both H and M but excluding D or R. If R were excluded, the H coefficient would represent the price of increased horsepower achieved by raising R, the M coefficient would represent the price of substituting M for R at a given horsepower, and the D coefficient would measure the price of substituting D for R.

The results presented below are based on regressions in which W, M, D, and R are the main independent variables,[19] but these, it should be remembered, only imperfectly and incompletely represent the desired performance characteristics of a diesel engine. Because we do not know how the missing factors are related to the proxies used, we can only speculate as to whether the coefficients are logical. We must depend on the assumption that their relation to the true utility elements does not differ substantially among the countries or on the assumption that if it does, the differences do not affect the price comparisons.

Mathematical Form

Linear, semilog, inverse semilog, and double log regressions were fitted to the data in all the alternative combinations of variables and regression methods we tried. However, the double log regressions were preferred for several reasons. The arithmetic and semilog forms were rejected because the factors that underlie the international differences in price—whether profit margins, labor or material costs, better technology, or more skillful management in one country as compared with another— are more likely to result in a fixed percentage difference between prices for all variants of an engine—large and small, weak and powerful, etc. —than in a fixed absolute dollar difference.[20]

The inverse semilog and double log forms estimate percentage rather than absolute price differences between countries, and it is percentage differences that we wish to express by index numbers. Each of the other forms yields a single absolute difference in price between each pair of countries for all engines, small or large, cheap or expensive.

The choice between the inverse semilog and double log forms was not as clear. The double log form was preferred because it incorporated the character of the technical relationships among the independent vari-

[19] The statistical results of using other combinations of independent variables, including $(D \times R)$ as a composite variable, were generally inferior to those of the $MDRW$ equation.

[20] A related factor is that the equations in which arithmetic price is the dependent variable are fitted by minimizing squares of absolute deviations from actual prices while the inverse semilog and double log forms are fitted in terms of percentage deviations. The latter seems more desirable because a larger absolute error is acceptable in estimating the price of a $5,000 engine than in estimating the price of a $1,000 engine.

ables described in the previous section—a multiplicative rather than an additive relationship.

Types of Regression

Three types of regression analysis were tried, each in several variants differing in the choice of variables and mathematical form. One type involved pooling all data under the assumption of equal element prices in all countries (additive dummy variables). The equation was

$$P = \Phi(M, D, W, R, k, g, f)$$

where P = price of engine
M = mean effective pressure
D = displacement
W = weight
R = number of revolutions per minute (rpm)
k = dummy variable for U.K. engine
g = dummy variable for German engine
f = dummy variable for French engine

A second approach was to fit a separate regression for each country:

$$P_u = \Phi_u(M, D, W, R)$$

$$P_k = \Phi_k(M, D, W, R)$$

$$P_g = \Phi_g(M, D, W, R)$$

$$P_f = \Phi_f(M, D, W, R)$$

where P_u is the U.S. price; P_k, the U.K. price; P_g, the German price; and P_f, the French price.

A third technique was to pool all data but to allow for international differences in the prices of quality elements (additive and multiplicative dummy variables):

$$P = \Phi'(M, D, W, R, k, g, f, kM, kD, kW, kR, gM, gD,$$
$$gW, gR, fM, fD, fW, fR)$$

We chose this last method of "flexible pooling" as the most appropriate: Where there were no significant differences in element prices among countries, the size of the sample and its range were enlarged. On the other hand, it did allow for differences in element prices where they appeared to be statistically significant.

In pooling without allowances for differences in element prices, the assumption is that the relative prices of the different elements making up the product mix are the same in the different situations involved in the price comparison. This may be a questionable assumption even when the situations involve two different points in time referring to the same country; it seems quite unlikely when prices are being compared for two or more different countries. There are obvious and important differences in relative factor prices from one country to another, and these may affect the prices of the elements in our equations for diesel engines. U.S. labor costs are high relative to those of Europe, but the prices of alloys or certain castings requiring advanced technology are low. Since we did not know what factor mix was required to produce the various elements that made up the product mix and we could not assume that it was identical in each country from element to element, we chose a regression method which did not impose the requirement that all price differences be summarized by a single intercept dummy.

We present, first, the results from our application of flexible pooling, since we used them in the larger price study. These are then compared with the outcomes of the other two methods.

Pooling with International Differences in Element Prices

The pooled regression, in this approach, includes as independent variables not only the several engine characteristics and the dummy variable for each foreign country, but also a dummy for each foreign country for the slope of each continuous variable. In the case of the weight variable, for example, this is accomplished by retaining a basic weight variable and adding a weight slope variable for each foreign country that reflects the country-weight interaction. If the relationship between price and weight in a foreign country is the same as in the United States, the weight *slope* coefficient will be zero or at least insignificantly different from zero. If intercept and slope dummies were included for all variables the results would be the same as those obtained by fitting a separate regression for each country, using the same mathematical form and the same independent variables.

These regressions are based on sixty-seven observations for the United States, the United Kingdom, and Germany, and contain fourteen independent variables.[21] In view of our earlier discussion, we confine ourselves to the inverse semilog and double log forms.

The following rules were adopted to govern the retention and elimination of dummy variables from the equation finally used to compare prices:

1. The slope dummy coefficient for a country was not retained unless the coefficients for both that country and the base country conformed to a priori economic and technical considerations. For example, the slope dummy for U.K. mean effective pressure taken in conjunction with the base coefficient implied a negative relationship between price and pressure in the United Kingdom and was therefore rejected.

2. No intercept or slope dummy was retained unless it was at least as large as its standard error. This choice of a 1-standard-error test in preference to the frequently used 2-standard-error test raises the issue of priority among the independent variables. We preferred to assign priority to quality characteristics in partitioning the observed variation in international prices into quality differences on the one hand and country-to-country differences in prices (for given qualities) on the other. This might imply that the variables which measure price differences (the country and slope dummies) should be retained only when highly significant—i.e., when they met the 2-*S.E.* test. However, this policy would rule out an observed difference in international prices unless the odds were overwhelming (20 to 1) that the difference would not be produced by chance. At the other extreme, by retaining all slope coefficients, however insignificant, we would forego the advantages of pooling.[22]

3. Even if significant in these terms, a slope dummy variable was not retained if its addition to the equation caused the corresponding element variable to lose its statistical significance.[23] The retention of

---

[21] If we included all four countries in such a regression there would be nineteen independent variables, four basic ones for the engine characteristic, and one intercept and four slope dummies for each of the three foreign countries. Since we have only six complete observations for France, there is little point in including France in a regression in which it would require five additional independent variables.

[22] The criterion of one standard error, if carried through consistently, would produce the highest level of $\bar{R}^2$. See Yoel Haitovsky, "A Note on the Maximization of $\bar{R}^2$," *American Statistician,* February 1969.

[23] If the *t*-ratio for the basic variable was 2 or more prior to the addition of the slope dummy, the dummy was not retained if with its presence the *t*-ratio of the basic variable was less than 2. If the original *t*-ratio was between 1 and 2, the dummy was retained if its addition was not accompanied by a reduction in the *t*-ratio to a level below 1.

the dummy variable under these circumstances would have had the effect of depriving the base situation of the advantages of pooling in cases in which the unpooled coefficient for that variable was not significant in the base situation.

4. When more than one equation (each with a different set of dummy variables) satisfied these three conditions, the one with the highest $\bar{R}^2$ was chosen.

5. If, for a given foreign country, no combination of dummy variables met the above conditions, all the slope dummy variables were dropped. Rather than read the result as representing no price difference, the coefficients of the intercept dummies were taken as the best measure of the price difference.

The "best" double log equation selected by these criteria has an intercept dummy for the United Kingdom and has German slope dummies for displacement and weight; it yields U.K.-U.S. and German-U.S. price relatives of 70 and 85, respectively. In Table 5.2, these results are compared with those based on alternative criteria for the retention of dummy variables. The U.K.-U.S. relatives range from 68 to 70 and the German-U.S. relatives, from 83 to 85 in those equations which do not contain negative coefficients for pressure.

Table 5.2

Automotive Diesel Engine Price Comparisons Based on Alternative
Criteria for Pooling: Double Log Equations

Criteria Met[a]	Dummy Variables[b]	$\bar{R}^2$	U.K./U.S.[c]	Ger./U.S.[c]
All, using 1 S.E.	k, g_d, g_w	.911	70	85
All (1 S.E.) excl. No. 3[d]	k, k_d, g_w	.914	69	83
All, using 2 S.E.	k, g	.909	68	85
All (2 S.E.) excl. No. 3	k, k_d, g	.913	69	84

S.E. = standard error.

[a]See accompanying text for list.

[b]The letters k and g without subscripts refer to country (intercept) dummies for the United Kingdom and Germany, respectively. With the subscripts d and w they refer to slope dummies for displacement and weight, respectively.

[c]Dropping criterion 1 produced price level indexes of 61 and 62 for the United Kingdom and 81–84 for Germany.

[d]See text.

The "best" inverse semilog equation yields U.K.-U.S. and German-U.S. price comparisons of 81 and 93, respectively.[24] There is thus a notable difference between the results from the two forms. Statistical criteria such as the $\bar{R}^2$'s and tests for heteroscedasticity [25] do not point to a decisive advantage of one form over the other, but we opt for the double log form on the grounds mentioned earlier.

There is one other complication in taking double log results of the flexible pooling approach. An equation yields different price indexes for each engine specification whenever one or more slope dummies is retained. One way of dealing with such situations is by pricing the "export" engine, for each of the four countries.[26] Averages obtained in this manner for displacement and weight enter, for example, into the computation of the estimate of 85 for the German-U.S. price relative selected as the preferred result of flexible pooling.

An alternative approach to averaging is to make a series of binary price comparisons, one for each country's average engine, and then to average the estimates with the use of export weights. Thus we set out below the German-U.S. price comparisons based on the average specifications of each country (rows 1–4) and export-weighted averages of the relatives in row 7.[27]

	Engines with Specifications of	German-U.S. Relative
1.	United States	81
2.	United Kingdom	87
3.	Germany	85
4.	France	82
5.	Average	84
6.	Export	85
7.	Weighted average of relatives	85

[24] Unlike the case of the double log form in which only one set of dummy variables met all of the first three conditions given in the text, seven different sets of dummy variables satisfied these conditions in the inverse semilog form. They produced U.K.-U.S. price relatives ranging from 76 to 84 and German-U.S. relatives ranging from 90 to 94.

[25] Each form meets the test performed.

[26] The average specifications for each country are shown in Table 5.1. These averages refer only to the engines in our sample, and we do not know precisely what the true averages are for each country's exports.

[27] The preferred equation contained no slope dummies and only a country dummy for the United Kingdom. The U.K.-U.S. relative thus is 70 for all specifications of engines. See Table 5.1 for specifications for rows 1–6. Row 7 is an average of rows 1–4 weighted by the relative importance of each country in exports.

The rationale for the export-weighted average of relatives is that the average engine of each country is regarded as representing a particular product variant whose importance in international trade is proportionate to the country's share in diesel exports. However, the alternative methods of averaging (rows 5–7) do not, in this and in other cases we have examined, produce very different answers.

A troublesome feature of these data is that in some instances the U.S.-type engine seems to be relatively cheaper in Germany than any of the European-type engines. Either the German producers are foregoing a significant market opportunity, or, what is more probable, if they actually began to make engines with U.S. specifications in larger volume, the coefficients of the German regression would shift so as to make the U.S.-type engine relatively more expensive, compared to U.S. prices, than the average-type engines now being produced in Germany. Actually our estimates of German prices of U.S.-type engines are based on relatively few observations and are probably misleading. Under these circumstances the smaller price differences suggested by the comparisons based on German-type engines might be a better approximation to the true relationship. Another possibility is that we have overlooked some quality elements which make U.S. engines more desirable at the larger end of the scale. In any case, the low German-U.S. ratio for U.S.-type engines shows there is a defect in our analysis. Fortunately, the lighter and lower horsepower German- and U.K.-type engines take up most of the weight, and the export-weighted averages would not be very different if the U.S.-type engine were excluded.

Other Types of Regression

In order to test the extent to which our choice of flexible pooling as a method determined our relative price estimates we ran regressions based on the two other methods described earlier.

Pooling the data without allowance for differences in element prices produced equations which fitted the data well in inverse semilog and double log forms (Table 5.3) and considerably less well in arithmetic and semilog forms. The price comparisons calculated from equations in the two preferred forms were (U.S. = 100):

Form of Equation	France	Germany	U.K.
Inverse semilog (log-arithmetic)	79	93	77
Double log (log-log)	72	85	68

Table 5.3

Regression Coefficients for Automotive Diesel Engine Prices:
Pooled Equations with No Allowance for Country
Differences in Element Coefficients
(figures in parentheses are standard errors)

	Inverse Semilog[a]	Double Log[a]
Pressure (M)	.4418	.9110
	(.0773)	(.1444)
Displacement (D)	.00059	.5045
	(.00021)	(.1260)
Weight (W)	.00038	.4856
	(.00006)	(.1297)
Revolutions per minute (R)	-.00021	-.2831
	(.00010)	(.2111)
France	-.2414	-.3243
	(.0805)	(.0794)
Germany	-.0681	-.1676
	(.0578)	(.0567)
United Kingdom	-.2663	-.3802
	(.0620)	(.0611)
Constant	6.5312	2.9133
	(0.3348)	(1.9512)
Standard error as per cent of mean	3.18	3.16
$\bar{R}^2$	.910	.912
$\bar{R}^2$ (transformed data[b])	.919	.911

Note: Price in dollars, displacement in cubic inches, rpm in units, weight in pounds. Mean effective pressure obtained by dividing horsepower by product of displacement and rpm and multiplying by 10,000. The logs are natural.

[a]In the inverse semilog equation the dependent variable (price) is logarithmic and the independent variables are arithmetic; in the double log equation all variables are logarithmic.

[b]Correlation between antilogs of actual and predicted prices.

At the opposite extreme from this pooling are separate country regressions, which use no information from one country in the estimate for another of the relation of price to quality characteristics.

The difficulty of basing each comparison on a set of identical elements is that elements which explain a very high percentage of price variation in one country may explain only a low percentage in another. If we use, for each country, all the variables that are significant for any country, the $\bar{R}^2$ for a particular country, corrected for degrees of freedom, may be less than with a smaller number of variables. A frequent concomitant of this defect will be the presence of regression coefficients which seem unlikely on economic grounds. The use of such a coefficient would imply that an element which has a positive value in one country has a negative value in another.

This difficulty is illustrated by the equations for each country using M, D, R, and W in Table 5.4, where the separate regressions produce some striking differences in the coefficients.[28] In particular, the U.K. coefficient for pressure is negative and not significantly different from zero while those of the other two countries are positive and significant (at the .05 level) in both the inverse semilog and double log equations. The most likely explanation for the negative U.K. coefficient is the extent of multicollinearity among the four engine characteristic variables.

A major difference between the United Kingdom and the other two countries is in the narrower range of observation of mean effective pressure [29] and, to a smaller degree, of displacement. Because the U.K. coefficients of M and D are calculated over relatively narrow ranges, we can place less confidence in their values than in those for other countries. Similar problems arise when other combinations of independent variables are employed in U.K. regressions.[30]

Conclusions

The preferred results from double log equations produced by each method can be summarized as follows (U.S. = 100):

[28] We drop further reference to French prices in this section since we decided against computing separate regressions for the six engines for which complete information was available. It would greatly add to the number of alternative results (all of them inferior) that we would have to present for the other countries if we based comparisons on equations including only H and R, the two variables for which there are eleven French observations.

[29] The ranges for the United Kingdom, the United States, and Germany for $(H/DR) \times 10,000$ were 1.14–1.48, 1.20–2.48, and 1.07–2.64, respectively.

[30] One way to deal with these country differences would be to base the comparisons on *unlike* equations; that is, to fit a different equation for each country, using those variables and that mathematical form which produced the closest explanation of price. Prices for engines of given specifications could then be estimated from each country's "best" equation and compared.

The derivation of indexes from unlike equations is based on the assumption that we are warranted in comparing the prices of diesels in terms of a different set of elements in each country. It involves the questionable assumption that a variable not significant over the range of variation present in the sample for country A would not be significant—that is, would have a zero price—over the wider range found in country B, if country A produced that wider range of products.

Table 5.4
Regression Coefficients for Automotive Diesel Engine Prices: Pooled and Individual Country Regressions
(figures in parentheses are standard errors)

	Mean Effective Pressure	Displacement	RPM	Weight	Constant
Inverse semilog (log-arith)					
Pooled	.4418 (.0773)	.00059 (.00021)	-.00021 (.00010)	.00038 (.00006)	6.5312 (0.3348)
U.S.	.5282 (.1066)	.00076 (.00027)	.00047 (.00031)	.00046 (.00008)	4.6334 (0.8105)
U.K.	-.2795 (.3664)	.00165 (.00075)	-.00046 (.00013)	-.00007 (.00027)	7.8716 (0.7290)
Germany	.6469 (.1808)	.00165 (.00063)	-.00016 (.00020)	-.00006 (.00022)	6.1799 (0.7605)
Double log (log-log)					
Pooled	.9110 (.1445)	.5045 (.1260)	-.2832 (.2111)	.4856 (.1297)	2.9134 (1.9512)
U.S.	.9973 (.2598)	.4649 (.1780)	.2033 (.7250)	.5652 (.2149)	-1.2311 (6.2515)
U.K.	-.2622 (.4706)	.7988 (.4294)	-.6544 (.2954)	.2635 (.4644)	5.4689 (3.2322)
Germany	1.4020 (0.3338)	1.1116 (0.3287)	.1523 (.5605)	-.1172 (.3024)	-0.1592 (5.3910)

Note: Prices in dollars, displacement in cubic inches, rpm (revolutions per minute) in units, weight in pounds. Mean effective pressure obtained by dividing horsepower by product of displacement and rpm, and multiplying by 10,000.

	U.K.	Germany
Flexible pooling (4 types)	68–70	83–85
Pooled regressions	68	85
Separate country regressions		
MDRW		81
HDRW		81

Depending upon the choice of independent variables, the specifications to be priced, and the extent of pooling—but leaving aside regressions rejected for poor fit, unreasonable coefficients (such as some zero or negative coefficients), or heteroscedasticity in the residuals— the U.K.-U.S. price relatives ranged from 68 to 70 and the German-U.S. relatives from 81 to 85. We do not list the U.K.-U.S. coefficients for separate country regressions because they contained negative coefficients for variables which had significant positive coefficients in equations of other countries.

Use of the inverse semilog form yielded a range of 77–81 for the United Kingdom and 87–93 for Germany, the range being wider and the level higher than the results from the preferred double log equations.

The application of regression analysis to diesel engine prices in this chapter was necessarily along simple lines in keeping with the resources of our study and its need to cover a very broad range of products. An obvious extension would be to take account of more engine characteristics, some of which might be continuous variables and others, such as power transmission, on an included-or-not basis (i.e., represented by dummy variables).

A more difficult extension of the work would be to aim at variables which reflect utilities to the consumer. The proxies we have been obliged to use represent these performance characteristics very imperfectly. We are therefore unable in many instances to judge whether the coefficients obtained are logical from an economic standpoint. Indeed, we cannot be certain that we have not omitted some key characteristic that accounts for a significant part of the observed difference in price in the two situations. Thus, it has been suggested to us that in the case of diesel engines the "quality" of the U.S. diesels is higher than that of European makes so that the real difference in price is smaller than our estimates indicate. We cannot rule this possibility out, even though the industry itself competes in world markets with specifications set out mainly in terms of the elements we have used.

Other Applications of Regression Methods

The regression analysis of automotive diesel engine prices is only one of several used in the study. Regression methods for a number of commodity groups in which conventional measures based on common specifications would have been impossible to calculate provided both place-to-place and time-to-time comparisons. These applications are described in the product chapters, but for the convenience of the reader they are summarized here.

In the case of aircraft engines, for example (Appendix to Chapter 12), it was not possible to find American and British engines of identical characteristics, from which conventional price comparisons could be made, although the two countries produced engines in the same weight and power range. Regression equations were fitted to data on twenty engines, relating their prices to take-off thrust, weight, and country of origin. The resulting price comparisons varied within a range of four percentage points, and $\bar{R}^2$ ranged from .85 to .95. The regressions we ran were a simpler version of one performed by a leading aerospace company, on essentially the same data, for predicting the price of new engines.

Another set of place-to-place comparisons was performed by multiple regression for outboard motors (Appendix to Chapter 12). About 100 observations from six countries were available for each of two years, all gathered in a market survey by a large producer. The equations related price to horsepower, country of origin, market of sale, and the presence of an electric starter. The equations produced high levels of $\bar{R}^2$, and the price level indexes were similar (mostly within five percentage points) as between arithmetic and logarithmic forms.

A U.S. price index for tractors, 1953–64, was constructed from data for sixty-one tractor prices, obtained from six U.S. manufacturers. Information for all years was pooled, and the price index was estimated from year dummy variables. Price was related to horsepower, weight, and a dummy variable for type of tractor, as well as the year of sale. The $\bar{R}^2$ were extremely high for both arithmetic and logarithmic equations but lower for mixed equations. The logarithmic equations, however, showed a more rapid price increase in both types of tractors, by nine to twelve percentage points over the eleven years. Almost all the difference was accounted for by the first period, when the sample was extremely thin; the 1957–64 period showed differences of only three percentage points.

In the case of power transformers (Appendix to Chapter 13), there were virtually no time series data on prices. Our prices were from reports by buyers, who would rarely purchase the same product twice, and from bidding documents, which were usually for unique products. We chose to calculate price changes over time by fitting regressions to the lowest prices bid by U.S. companies on approximately 150 power transformers. We used only capacity as a quality variable, and included as dummy variables the year in which the bidding took place and the location of the project (United States or foreign). Slope dummy variables allowed for differences among the years in the slope of the price-capacity relationship. All the logarithmic equations produced high levels of $\bar{R}^2$ but there were some substantial differences in price movement, particularly in 1963–64 when the significant dummy variable for foreign projects was dropped. The price change was taken directly from the equations except for 1963–64, where the change in slope meant that the price movements differed by size of transformer.

The regression, crude as it was, produced price indexes quite similar to others for U.S. domestic prices which were derived by much more elaborate regressions and by other methods involving the use of a greater number of variables. The price change was calculated for several different sizes, and these were then weighted by the importance of each, as estimated from the bidding data.

For railway locomotives a regression-based index was calculated for the U.S. time-to-time index but was used only as a check on the conventionally calculated one (Appendix to Chapter 14). The number of categories available for equation fitting was small, and there were some erratic changes in the coefficients. The method used in this case was to fit a separate regression for each year and to price the 1963 set of locomotives produced in the United States in each year's equation, to produce what was essentially a Laspeyres price index with 1963 weights for locomotive types.

A Japanese ship price index was computed from data for 205 contracts for ships built in Japanese yards. The logarithmic equation finally selected included continuous variables for the tonnage and horsepower of ships, and dummy variables for type of ship (bulk carrier, cargo vessel, or tanker) and for the year of purchase, using pooled data for all years. The indexes computed from this logarithmic equation were similar to those from a semilogarithmic equation and from an arithmetic equation using 1963 ship specifications. The logarithmic equation also produced the best fit, and the price indexes calculated from it were not sensitive to the addition of other marginal variables to the equation.

Regression-based index numbers were used in place-to-place comparisons for truck prices in the United States and the United Kingdom (Chapter 14). Separate regressions were computed for diesel and gasoline-powered trucks. Gross vehicle weight, wheelbase, and displacement were used as continuous variables in both cases with the addition of dummy variables for cowl and forward control.

Both time-to-time and place-to-place indexes for automobiles were derived by regression techniques (Chapter 15). Only in this group was such extensive use made of this method and virtually none of conventional price indexes. The basic data consisted of over 1,000 domestic list price observations for the U.S. and 700 for five foreign countries, covering all six years of the study. The listed makes of car included in the comparisons accounted for 95 per cent or more of national output in every case. The specifications included weight, length, horsepower, engine displacement, number of cylinders, the presence of automatic transmission, number of doors, and volume of production, but not all of them were used in the final regression equations.

The regression equations were calculated by pooling data for pairs of years, permitting coefficients for the two years to differ where the difference was statistically significant (the method of flexible pooling described earlier in this chapter). The price index was derived from a time dummy variable or that variable in combination with others in cases where the characteristic coefficients differed between the two years.

The average $\bar{R}^2$ for the whole period, based on various combinations of explanatory variables, ranged from .85–.88 for the United States and Japan (the lowest proportions explained) to .94–.97 for Italy and Germany. The range of variation in the alternative estimates of price movements was highest in 1953–57, when there were several instances of five and six percentage point differences. After that there were only three cases out of twenty-four in which the range among the price changes calculated from the variants of the equation was greater than three percentage points.

The place-to-place indexes for 1964 were calculated in two ways. The same domestic price data as in the time-to-time indexes were used to calculate equations matching pairs of countries (United States with each other country) instead of pairs of years. The $\bar{R}^2$ ranged from .892 to .967 but the price relatives, in every case, differed widely by type of car, with foreign prices always very high for U.S.-type cars and comparatively low for foreign-type cars. Wide differences in the type of car produced in different countries created serious problems in these price level comparisons. U.S. cars were, of course, larger and more powerful than European cars, and the ranges for some variables hardly even overlapped. The worst instance is the comparison of the United States with France. Because of these wide differences, price comparisons were made for five classes of cars and then averaged on the basis of estimates of the importance of each type in world trade.

In addition to these comparisons of home market prices, comparisons were made of prices in four specific markets, based on a total of over four hundred observations and using the same method of flexible pooling. The pattern of comparative advantage appeared much the same as in the comparison of home market prices, with the United States the lowest-priced seller of large cars and the highest-priced seller of small cars.

In this chapter, we particularly stressed the dependence of the estimates of price change and price differences on the choice of independent variables, mathematical form, and mode of pooling. Regression-based indexes have been criticized because of the indeterminacy caused by this variety of possible methods. However, it is important to realize that the range of indeterminacy in results based on regression methods is not inherently different from that which is embedded in the results of more traditional methods. The difference is that in more conventional methods, indeterminacy is neither avoided nor eliminated but concealed, whereas in regression methods it is made explicit.

Indeed, the former often turn out to be the equivalent of crude regression techniques such as the arithmetic interpolation of prices for a few models on the basis of one or two independent variables. In such cases, many decisions about alternative methods or assumptions are made at disaggregated levels in ways that are difficult, if not impossible, to summarize and present to the index user. An important advantage of the regression technique is that the choices among methods and their results can be described and presented clearly and systematically.

Aside from making explicit the methods and the unavoidable indeterminacy of the results, regression techniques also permit the use of a much wider range of product varieties in price measurement, and make possible price comparisons between different times and places for complex, differentiated products which are usually omitted from price indexes because of the difficulty of applying traditional methods of price measurement to them.

Thus, although much experimentation is still needed to put price measurement by regression methods on anything like a routine basis, even in the present embryonic stage they provide an important and useful tool in the making of price indexes.

PART THREE

ASSESSING THE ROLE OF PRICES IN TRADE

6

QUANTITY-PRICE RELATIONSHIPS

The Utility of the New Indexes

Indexes of the type we have developed should be superior to previously available measures as the price variable in trade models which incorporate other important influences such as incomes in exporting and importing countries, tariffs and other restrictive or preferential arrangements, and transport costs. We would have liked to test the indexes in this role, but such an undertaking would have required the extension of our work far beyond our original purpose into virtually a new study of its own. One reason is that the assessment of the role of price and of the success of our indexes in measuring that role requires knowledge of the underlying supply and demand functions, and some way of taking account of the influences of the prices of import-competing goods and of income changes and other nonprice factors. Another and practical reason is that to test our indexes we would need an extensive body of matching trade data, much of it not readily available.

For both reasons, therefore, we attempt a more modest goal. We assume, first, that we have a group of countries producing exports that are more or less competitive. What we would like to measure in our quantity-price studies is the impact of a change in relative prices, attributable to a change in supply conditions in one or both of a pair of these countries, upon their relative export quantities, all other influences held constant. If the exports from the two countries were perfect substitutes in all uses and locations, the quantity response of buyers to a small change in relative prices would be infinite. In fact, substitutability is limited by transport costs and market preference for the goods from one source of supply over another as a result of custom or of real or fancied differences in product quality or design. It is because these limitations upon substitutability exist that the extent of substitution is measurable and worth measuring.

To estimate properly the extent to which the exports of different countries are substitutable we would have to be able to isolate the effects of demand and supply in our data. In the price indexes, as we argued earlier (Chapter 3), our use of a common set of weights reduces, but does not eliminate, the possibility that our indexes will show relative price changes induced by changes in demand for a product. If the demand effects had been eliminated, the effects of relative supply changes could be gauged from the price shifts, and the response produced from existing (and unchanging) demand conditions could be measured from the quantity shifts.

Unfortunately, this identification of the effects of demand and supply would be valid only if it could be assumed that the elasticity of supply of each of the pair of countries being compared was the same. If this is not the case, then a rise or fall in demand will bring a larger quantity response from one country than the other, even though neither country's supply curve has shifted, and we can no longer be sure to what extent the correlation between relative prices and relative quantities reflects changes originating from supply or changes traceable to demand factors. As we suggested earlier (see Chapter 2), there is reason to believe that U.S. supply elasticities are higher than those of Europe and Japan. Thus the relative quantity changes that we observe are the results not only of changes in supply conditions in one or both trading countries, which are what we would like to observe, but also, to some extent, in shifts of sources of supply (without a change in the country's supply curve) in response to changes in total market demand. The upshot is that even though we would like to estimate the basic parameters of the international economy, all we can be sure we are measuring falls in the category of historical description.

An additional deficiency of our calculations is that we cannot allow for the possibility of lagged reactions of quantity to price, because the period we cover is too short and because we have gaps in both time and commodity coverage of the price series for the early years.

With further work it should be possible to deal with some of these problems more adequately than we have done here. It would be useful, for example, to experiment with measures of determinants of export supply, possibly including the relationship between export and domestic

prices and data on the movement of domestic costs. This would, however, require trade data we do not now possess, a fact which leads up
to the second major limitation on our ability to use our new indexes
to explain trade flows.

We would like to compare our new price series with trade data that
include information on each covered country's exports over the whole
period of the study, 1953–64, subdivided by destination and commodity
class, with the commodity division comparable among all countries and
aligned to the classification used for the price indexes. Some of the
obstacles to the fulfillment of this goal cannot be surmounted completely. Particularly important in this regard are the difficulties arising
from the change in the Standard International Trade Classification in
1961, which makes the assembly of comparable time series on a detailed
commodity level difficult. Another problem is that data for even
ostensibly identical SITC classes have had to be drawn from differing
national statistical systems. Unfortunately, the set of products included
in a given international trade classification may vary from country to
country. The U.S. data are particularly troublesome in this respect for
three reasons. One is the presence of "special-category" export classes
which conceal destinations of shipments and, often, the exact commodity
description as well. The second is that the U.S. trade classification before
the 1960s was not based on the Brussels Tariff Nomenclature (BTN),
the basis for the SITC. The third, partly a result of the second, is that
the published attempts to fit U.S. trade data into the SITC contained
many serious classification errors, and official corrections to the data
have been made only for 1962 and later years. There may, of course,
be similar defects in the figures for other countries that we are not
aware of because we are not as familiar with the data.

At present, we have two-digit data for 1953 and 1957, and more
detailed data only for 1961–64, except for a small number of commodity
groups. Unfortunately, 1961–64 are analytically unsatisfactory because
they were years of comparatively small price changes for most commodity groups. Furthermore, our present data collection gives destinations
of exports only for 1963, the year shown in the trade data of Appendix A.

Given the lack of detailed trade data for 1953 and 1957, we have had
to restrict our examination of the relation between price changes and

trade flows for the whole period to highly aggregated totals (all commodities and two-digit categories), and to confine our examination of three- and four-digit data to 1961–64. We are able, in addition, to use some cross-sectional data comparing relative exports and relative price levels for 1963.

Our inability at this stage to distinguish each country's exports according to destination may be a serious defect because Germany's exports were concentrated in the Common Market countries, and therefore most strongly influenced by developments there, while the United States had a particularly large stake in Canada and Latin America; and Japan, in the United States.

We hope, in subsequent work, to fill some of the gaps described in the preceding paragraphs. For a first step in this direction, see "The Elasticity of Substitution as a Variable in World Trade," to be published in a forthcoming volume of Studies in Income and Wealth.

The Price-Quantity Equations

The basic form we used in estimating quantity-price relationships relates the percentage change in relative exports (foreign to United States) during a period to the percentage change in relative prices (foreign to United States), i.e., to the percentage change in U.S. price competitiveness, including a constant term. That is,

$$V_{F/S} - 1 = a + b(P_{F/S} - 1) \qquad (1)$$

or

$$Q_{F/S} - 1 = a' + b'(P_{F/S} - 1) \qquad (2)$$

where F represents a foreign country; S, the United States; V, the index of relative export values;[1] $P_{F/S}$, the index of U.S. price competitiveness,[2] that is, the ratio of foreign to U.S. prices; and Q, the index of relative export quantities.[3]

---

[1] $V_{F/S} = V_F/V_S$, where $V_F = V_{F(t)}/V_{F(t-1)}$ and $V_S = V_{S(t)}/V_{S(t-1)}$. V_F represents foreign and V_S, U.S. exports in dollars; t represents a reference year and $t - 1$, a preceding reference year.

[2] $P_{F/S} = P_F/P_S$, where $P_S = \Sigma[(P_1/P_0)_S w_{63}]/\Sigma w_{63}$ and P_F is the corresponding index for the foreign country. See Chapter 1 for discussion of these measures.

[3] $Q_{F/S} = V_{F/S} \div P_{F/S}$.

The coefficient of the price variable in equation (2), the quantity-price regression, is the familiar elasticity of substitution.[4] In the double log form, this coefficient is equal to the coefficient in equation (1), the export value–price regression, minus one.[5] In the arithmetic form which we employed, the substitution elasticity in terms of quantity cannot be inferred exactly from the elasticity in terms of value. Whatever the mathematical form used, a higher coefficient of correlation was obtained when the dependent variable was relative export quantities rather than relative export values.

Elasticities of substitution derived from the regression of relative quantities on relative prices are subject to several types of measurement problems. If the relative prices and quantities reflect demand as well as supply changes, the elasticities will typically be biased toward zero. If quantity change is derived from value and price changes, as is almost universally the case, errors in value measurement bias the elasticity toward zero, and errors in price measurement, probably more frequent and larger, bias it toward one.[6]

The elasticity measure is also affected by the choice of index number and base period. A fixed base-price index, such as we use, implies a quantity index with given-year weights. A base year near the end of the period produces results different from those of an early-year base (see footnote fourteen, below).

Another foreign trade parameter used frequently in analytical work, the price elasticity of demand for a country's exports of a product, can be derived as a weighted average of the elasticities of substitution with respect to each rival exporter. Harberger [7] gives this relationship as $E_x = \Sigma_i s_i b'_{xi}$ where E_x is the elasticity of demand for exports of country x; i, one of the countries for which elasticities of substitution with

---

[4] It is really only an approximation to the true point elasticity, since the price changes are finite. Arc elasticity measures yield similar results and are therefore not shown separately.

[5] $Q = aP^b$ or $\log Q = \log a + b \log P$
$PQ = aP^{b+1}$ or $\log V = \log a + (b + 1) \log P$.

[6] Cf. Guy H. Orcutt, "Measurement of Elasticities in International Trade," *Review of Economics and Statistics,* May 1950; G. D. A. MacDougall, "British and American Exports: A Study Suggested by the Theory of Comparative Costs, Part II," *Economic Journal,* September 1952; and Raymond E. Zelder, "Estimates of Elasticities of Demand for Exports of the United Kingdom and the United States, 1921–1938," *Manchester School of Economic and Social Studies,* January 1958, p. 34.

[7] Arnold C. Harberger, "Some Evidence on the International Price Mechanism," *Journal of Political Economy,* December 1957. The formula underestimates E_x if some of the commodities exported by x can be substituted for commodities not covered by the b'_{xi}.

respect to x are available; and s_i, the share of country i in the total exports of x and the other included countries.

All Goods Treated as a Single Aggregate

We begin with the price-quantity relationship for the total of machinery, transport equipment, metals, and metal products. We have a total of ten observations, consisting of five time-to-time comparisons (1957/1953, 1961/1957, 1962/1961, 1963/1962, and 1964/1963) for the United Kingdom/United States and five for Germany/United States. Given the small number of observations, an obvious approach is to pool all of the observations, regardless of country and period.[8] The changes first in the value and secondly in the quantity of relative exports associated with changes in relative prices are as follows, with the subscript KG/S representing pooled data for the U.K.-U.S. and Germany-U.S. comparisons: [9]

$$V_{KG/S} - 1 = .14 - 6.34(P_{KG/S} - 1) \qquad \bar{r}^2 = .03 \qquad (3)$$
$$(1.12)$$

$$Q_{KG/S} - 1 = .14 - 7.56(P_{KG/S} - 1) \qquad \bar{r}^2 = .08 \qquad (4)$$
$$(1.33)$$

The price elasticity for the value of trade is around $-6\frac{1}{3}$ and the price elasticity of substitution around $-7\frac{1}{2}$. The positive constant term may be interpreted as a rising trend in foreign exports relative to those of the United States that is attributable to factors other than relative prices. These nonprice factors include changes in commercial policies, buyer preferences, supply availabilities (at fixed prices), and different rates of growth in various geographical markets, all of which may favor one country or another. They also include any effects on relative exports of the covered countries that are attributable to price changes in excluded countries or for excluded products.

If the constant term is interpreted as a trend, it must be trend per period. Since some of the periods were four years long and others only one year, we tried inserting a specific time variable to take account of

---

[8] As will be seen later, there is evidence against the propriety of both types of pooling.

[9] The figures in parentheses under the coefficients are t-ratios.

this difference. The time variable, a 4 or a 1, in combination with the
constant term, can produce any combination of trends per year before
and after 1961 that will best fit the data. Of course, the effects of any
change in trend over time still cannot be distinguished from the effects
of differences between one-year and four-year periods in general, since
the two four-year periods make up the period before 1961. However,
even if the cause of the differences cannot be fully explained, it is clearly
preferable to take account of them rather than to ignore them as in
equations comparable to (3) and (4).

When the time variable (T) is added, the equations corresponding to
(3) and (4) are as follows:

$$V_{KG/S} - 1 = -.12 + 0.11T - 2.07(P_{KG/S} - 1) \qquad \bar{R}^2 = .44 \qquad (5)$$
$$\phantom{V_{KG/S} - 1 = } (2.63) \quad (0.45)$$

$$Q_{KG/S} - 1 = -.12 + 0.11T - 3.32(P_{KG/S} - 1) \qquad \bar{R}^2 = .47 \qquad (6)$$
$$\phantom{Q_{KG/S} - 1 = } (2.61) \quad (0.72)$$

The time coefficient is significant but the elasticities and the t-ratios
are smaller than those of equations 1 and 2, and not statistically significant. This implies that the elasticities in the earlier equations were biased
upward because they included part of the effects of nonprice trends
against the exports of the United States, a country which also had adverse (relatively rising) price movements, particularly in the two four-
year periods before 1961. The combination of the constant and the T
coefficient in equations 5 and 6 tells us that the trade and quantity ratios
of the United Kingdom and Germany to the United States tended to
rise, owing to nonprice factors, by 8 per cent per annum $\{[-0.12 +$
$(.11 \times 4)] \div 4\}$ before 1961 and to fall by 1 per cent per annum
$[-0.12 + (.11 \times 1)]$ after 1961.

Alternatively, it may be that the elasticities differed before and after
1961. There is, indeed, some evidence that the elasticity was higher
before 1961. However, when a slope dummy was added for the two
four-year periods, the coefficient, with or without the time variable, was
not significant. For example,

$$Q_{KG/S} - 1 = -.13 + 0.11T - 2.10(P_{KG/S} - 1) - 2.03D_4$$
$$\phantom{Q_{KG/S} - 1 = } (2.35) \quad (0.27) \qquad\qquad\qquad (0.20)$$
$$\bar{R}^2 = .38 \qquad (7)$$

where D_4 is the slope dummy for the two four-year periods.

Two-digit Categories

The use of the total of covered commodities involves a very small number of observations, and the relationships should be tested with large numbers. This can be done by relating relative exports and price competitiveness for two-digit SITC divisions. If all countries and commodities are pooled, under the implied assumption that elasticity is not correlated with commodity or country characteristics, 68 observations are obtained: 29 for the U.K.-U.S. comparison (5 time periods and six two-digit categories) [10] plus 29 for Germany/United States, plus 10 for Japan/United States. The resulting equations are:

$$V_{F/8} - 1 = -.14 + 0.13T - 4.58(P_{F/8} - 1) \qquad \bar{R}^2 = .37 \qquad (8)$$
$$(4.06) \quad (3.34)$$

$$Q_{F/8} - 1 = -.15 + 0.14T - 6.22(P_{F/8} - 1) \qquad \bar{R}^2 = .42 \qquad (9)$$
$$(4.03) \quad (4.18)$$

A comparison with the previous set of equations shows that disaggregation into commodity groups reduces the $\bar{R}^2$'s and raises the elasticities. However, if we had confined these calculations to the United Kingdom and Germany, as in the equations for the aggregate, the price elasticities would have risen only to -2.34 and -3.67.

The larger number of observations provides an opportunity to determine whether the elasticities differ systematically from one country to another, from one time period to another, by product category, or by size of the change in the index of price competitiveness. For brevity, we present only the equations in which relative quantity is the dependent variable and time and relative price are independent.

The equations for the individual binary comparisons are as follows:

$$Q_{K/8} - 1 = -.10 + 0.04T - 2.66(P_{K/8} - 1) \qquad \bar{R}^2 = .41 \qquad (10)$$
$$(2.14) \quad (3.04)$$

$$Q_{G/8} - 1 = -.35 + 0.26T - 4.73(P_{G/8} - 1) \qquad \bar{R}^2 = .59 \qquad (11)$$
$$(5.04) \quad (2.49)$$

$$Q_{J/8} - 1 = -.77 + 0.89T - 3.24(P_{J/8} - 1) \qquad \bar{R}^2 = .99 \qquad (12)$$
$$(15.88) \quad (3.12)$$

[10] SITC 67, 68, 69, 71, 72, and 73. For SITC 67 comparisons were made for 1961/1953 rather than 1957/1953 and 1961/1957 to avoid the distorting effects of the Suez Crisis upon 1957 data.

where K stands for the United Kingdom; S, the United States; G, Germany; and J, Japan. The German elasticity is higher than that of the United Kingdom and also Japan, which is based on a subset of years and commodity divisions. The increasingly favored position of Germany vis-à-vis the other countries in the rapidly expanding markets of its EEC partners may have increased the size of its T coefficient. When the U.K. and German comparisons are based solely on the subset of ten observations available for the Japanese-U.S. comparison, they produce elasticities of -1.26 for the United Kingdom vs. the United States and -1.79 for Germany vs. the United States.[11]

The combination of the constants and time coefficients in equations 10–12 implies the following percentage changes per annum in the relative quantity ratios attributable to nonprice factors: [12]

Country	1953–61	1961–64
U.K.-U.S.	+1.71	−6
German-U.S.	+18.0	−9
Japan-U.S.	NA	+12

The substantial difference in the elasticities for the U.K.-U.S. and German-U.S. comparisons between those based on ten and those based on twenty-nine observations suggests that the elasticities may vary according to time period or product category. This possibility can best be explored by examining the two comparisons for which we have virtually complete coverage for each of the five periods and each of the six commodity groups. To avoid erratic results attributable to small numbers, we pooled the U.K-U.S. and German-U.S. data and consolidated the periods and groups.

For the time periods, we compare 1957/1953 and 1961/1957 on the one hand with 1964/1963, 1963/1962, and 1962/1961 ratios on the other:

$$(Q_{KG/S} - 1)_4 = .32 - 8.03(P_{KG/S} - 1)_4 \qquad \bar{r}^2 = .20 \qquad (13)$$
$$(3.18)$$

$$(Q_{KG/S} - 1)_1 = -.03 - 1.23(P_{KG/S} - 1)_1 \qquad \bar{r}^2 = .15 \qquad (14)$$
$$(2.66)$$

[11] The Japanese comparison is omitted for 1957/1953, when the other two countries had large price changes and high elasticity coefficients. However, it may be the size of the price changes rather than the time period that is relevant here. Japanese prices for 1957–64 have as wide a range of changes as European prices for 1953–64.

[12] The Japanese coefficient is not shown for 1953–61, because the number of observations is too small.

where the numerical subscripts refer to the early four- and the later one-year periods, respectively.[13] The difference between -8.03 and -1.23 can be regarded either as a difference between one-year and four-year elasticities of substitution or as a decline in the elasticity between earlier and later periods. Since a high elasticity does not characterize 1961–64 as a whole, the latter view is supported. Indeed no correlation was found between changes in relative quantities and relative prices between 1961 and 1964; the elasticity for the pooled U.K.-U.S. and German-U.S. data was virtually zero.

Somewhat different results are obtained when the Japanese-U.S. observations are included; the elasticity coefficient for the three-year period (-5) is significant and lies between the high coefficient for the four-year periods (-11) and the lower one for the one-year periods (-2). This result suggests that the length of the period may explain part, but not all of the difference between the elasticity coefficients for the earlier and later periods.

Our method of computing the elasticities tends to increase the difference between two periods over the result that might be obtained from other procedures. The reason is that the elasticities are computed not from individual prices but from price indexes with end-of-period weights. Such indexes probably tended to produce larger elasticities, particularly for the early periods when there were relatively large price changes, than those that would have been obtained from indexes with beginning-of-period weights.[14] It seems unlikely, however, that the large difference

[13] In equation 13, SITC 67 is taken for the 1961/1953 ratio. Japan is omitted because the observations were concentrated in the one-year periods.

[14] The difference between an index with end-of-period weights (P_e) and one with beginning-of-period weights (P_b) depends on the covariance of price and quantity changes for individual commodities, as follows:

$$\frac{P_e}{P_b} = \frac{V}{V - \mathrm{cov}_W}$$

where V is the value index, and cov_W is the weighted (by value) covariance of price and quantity relatives (cf. Robert E. Lipsey, *Price and Quantity Trends in the Foreign Trade of the United States*, Princeton University Press for NBER, 1963, pp. 88–89). If the covariance is negative, as we expect, and large, then P_e will be substantially smaller than P_b, and the price index based on end-of-period weights will imply larger quantity changes, and therefore a higher price elasticity, than an index with beginning-of-period weights. How different the index will be depends on the covariance. The covariance, in turn, is related to the price elasticities and the extent of price changes for individual commodities; if both are high the covariance will be high. Thus, if individual commodities have high elasticities, an end-weighted price index will usually yield a higher group elasticity than a beginning-weighted one. Furthermore, large price changes will also contribute to such a difference.

Therefore, some of the higher elasticities in 1953–61 relative to 1961–64 may be attributable to the use of end-of-period weights, since price changes were compara-

in the elasticities for the two periods can be explained entirely on these grounds.

The equations described thus far involve the assumption that the substitution elasticities and constant terms could, and obviously did, differ among countries and perhaps from period to period, but not among commodity groups, or that if they did, such differences were not correlated with country, time periods, or price changes. Since the commodities range from standardized metals to complex machinery, with probably different price behavior and different degrees of response to price change, the assumption that elasticities do not vary for different commodities is hazardous. However, it is not clear how the substitution elasticities of various groups should differ. One would expect that where there is product differentiation along national lines, as is at least partially true, for example, of U.S. and German automobiles, the elasticities will not be as high as, say, in metal products, which are more standardized. It is conceivable, however, that the true elasticities may be unobservable for highly standardized products because similar export price changes are imposed in all the countries by market forces. We have some evidence (see Chapter 8) that export price movements are more alike than domestic ones, and trade shifts for standardized goods could come about principally through the operation of domestic supply elasticities in countries with declining competitiveness.[15]

The number of observations of two-digit commodity groups is small. However, we divided the commodities into "metals" (M) and "equipment" (E). The former includes iron and steel (SITC 67) and nonferrous metals (SITC 68); the latter, metal manufactures (SITC 69), nonelectrical machinery (SITC 71), electrical machinery (SITC 72), and transport equipment (SITC 73). The results, based on eighteen and forty observations, respectively, are:

$$(Q_{KG/S} - 1)_M = -.35 + 0.19T - 3.30(P_{KG/S} - 1)_M \qquad \bar{R}^2 = .40$$
$$\phantom{(Q_{KG/S} - 1)_M = -.35 + } (1.98) \quad\ (.77) \hspace{4.5cm} (15)$$

$$(Q_{KG/S} - 1)_E = -.13 + 0.11T - 2.34(P_{KG/S} - 1)_E \qquad \bar{R}^2 = .29$$
$$\phantom{(Q_{KG/S} - 1)_E = -.13 + } (3.97) \quad (1.70) \hspace{4.3cm} (16)$$

tively large in the early years. Similarly, the weighting may account for some of the high Japanese elasticity estimates, since Japanese price changes were, for the most part, larger than those of other countries.

[15] See Robert M. Stern and Elliot Zupnick, "The Theory and Measurement of Elasticity of Substitution in International Trade," *Kyklos*, 1962, Fasc. 3.

The metals elasticity is higher, but the difference is not statistically significant.

Another possibility is that relative export changes (value or quantities) may not be a continuous function of relative price changes but may be different for large price changes and small ones or different for relative price changes of opposite directions. Accordingly, we estimated the coefficients for relative declines in foreign prices of 2 per cent or more, for changes in either direction of less than 2 per cent, and for relative increases in foreign prices of 2 per cent or more:

Change in $P_{F/S}$	No. of Obser- vations	$\bar{R}^2$	Constant	Time	Coefficient of $P_{F/S}$ (elasticity)
Decline $\geqq 2\%$	15	.43	−.71	0.18 (1.50)	−14.17 (1.66)
Change $< 2\%$	36	.07	−.02	0.03 (0.94)	−10.18 (1.96)
Increase $\geqq 2\%$	17	.63	−.03	0.10 (5.30)	−3.56 (2.72)

This set of figures indicates that relative declines in foreign prices were associated with substantial increases in foreign export quantities relative to the United States, while relative increases in foreign prices were associated with smaller gains in U.S. exports. The evidence is, however, too slight to accept without further investigation.

In general, then, we found that price competitiveness was a significant but far from exclusive factor in accounting for shifts in trade shares. The data suggest that trade shares were more sensitive to price changes before 1961 than afterward. The trend in trade shares, which presumably reflects the effects of factors other than price, also ran against the United States during the years from 1953 to 1961. After 1961 only Japan still gained at the expense of the United States, aside from the effect of price changes.

Some of the further exploration suggested by these results requires larger numbers of observations. We cannot add to the time or country coverage for this purpose but can raise the number of observations by splitting the large and heterogeneous two-digit divisions into smaller and more homogeneous groups and subgroups.

Three- and Four-digit Groups

As already noted, the detailed trade data necessary to match our three- and four-digit price indexes are available at present only from 1961 on. Taking relative quantities as the dependent variable, the results for the completely pooled data for 1964/1963, 1963/1962, and 1962/1961 for all countries (161 observations) and for the United Kingdom and Germany combined (147 observations) are as follows:

$$Q_{F/S} - 1 = -.017 - 1.47(P_{F/S} - 1) \qquad \bar{r}^2 = .06 \qquad (17)$$
$$(3.98)$$

$$Q_{KG/S} - 1 = -.008 - 1.04(P_{KG/S} - 1) \qquad \bar{r}^2 = .03 \qquad (18)$$
$$(2.71)$$

The elasticity in (18) is very similar to that in (14), which is for two-digit groups over the same periods. The results for individual-country comparisons are:

Country Compared with U.S.	Constant	Elasticity Coefficient	$\bar{r}^2$	Number of Observations
U.K.	−0.006	−1.55 (2.60)	.06	91
Germany	−0.010	−0.54 (1.11)	.002	99
Japan	−0.17	−2.81 (2.84)	.20	29

Only the price coefficients for the United Kingdom and Japan are significant, while that for Germany, which showed the highest coefficient in the two-digit data, almost vanishes.

Although we experimented with several ways of classifying the data, we were unable to improve substantially upon these results. For metals (SITC 67 and 68) all the $\bar{r}^2$'s were slightly higher, and the equations pointed to higher (though not significantly higher) elasticities except for Japan. When elasticities for different ranges of price change were examined, the results for all countries for all three periods (1964/1963, 1963/1962, 1962/1961) pooled were as follows:

Change in $P_{F/S}$	Elasticity
Decline $\geqq 2\%$	−4.04
	(2.58)
Change $< 2\%$	−1.37
	(0.56)
Increase $\geqq 2\%$	−0.97
	(1.43)

The results are somewhat surprising, for we would have expected the disaggregated data to produce higher elasticities of substitution than the two-digit data for the same countries and periods on the hypothesis that the substitutability of U.S. and foreign goods would be greater within three- and four-digit SITC categories than within two-digit ones. Indeed, the implicit assumption underlying these calculations is that substitution occurs only within the four-digit subgroups and that there are no cross elasticities operating beyond these boundaries, or at least that if there are significant cross elasticities between products, they affect the two countries equally. As we compare quantities and prices at ever higher levels of aggregation, the results become more subject to the operation of price-induced substitutions in relative exports across detailed SITC classifications. For example, suppose a rise in the German-U.S. price ratio for copper leads to a decrease not in that ratio but in the German-U.S. export ratio for aluminum. Quantities and prices in the two-digit data, in which copper and aluminum are combined in the nonferrous metals division (SITC 68), would move in opposite directions. However, the three-digit data, in which copper and aluminum are in separate categories, would not reveal such a negative association in either category. We do not in fact consider it likely that such cross elasticities are very important, and their impact would be offset or more than offset by reductions in the measured substitution elasticities resulting from the combination into two-digit categories of goods having low cross elasticities.

Grunfeld and Griliches's "synchronization" or "grouping" effect of aggregation may explain the higher coefficients of correlation of the one- and two-digit data compared to the three- and four-digit grouping.[16] In our data, we find an intercorrelation for our main independent vari-

16 Y. Grunfeld, and Zvi Griliches, "Is Aggregation Necessarily Bad?" *Review of Economics and Statistics,* February 1960.

able (the index of price competitiveness) for the detailed categories we combine into more aggregative ones.[17] In addition, we may expect that the residuals arising out of the use of only one (price competitiveness) or two (prices and length of period) independent variables in the estimating equation will be offsetting for the detailed categories that are consolidated into more aggregative groups. As long as the intercorrelation of the independent variable is larger than that of the residuals, the correlation coefficient based on more aggregative data will be higher.

The very tentative conclusions that emerge from this preliminary use of our new indexes, if we ignore the possible biases arising from aggregation and omission of important variables, is that the historical elasticity of substitution between U.S. exports and those of its main foreign competitors was around -8 for the period 1953–61 and about -1 to -1.5 for the period 1961–64. The many questions raised by these findings can be investigated only after the additional data, noted at the beginning of this chapter, have been assembled. The low correlation coefficients between relative quantities and relative prices make it clear that factors omitted in our analysis, including income, capacity utilization, and nonprice elements of competitiveness, had significant influences on export shares. A possibility that is difficult to check on is that the elasticities for the early period are exaggerated because prices were not permitted to reflect tight European and Japanese supply conditions. If that were the case, the easing of supply would not result in large price declines, as in a free market. It would instead appear as a large increase in exports with little change in price and, therefore, a high price elasticity.

Earlier Estimates of Elasticities

These estimates add to a long series of calculations of foreign trade elasticities beginning with Tinbergen's pioneering article in 1946.[18] All except a few of the previous estimates were derived from aggregative export and price data. Among the small number of studies that were based on quantity and price data for individual commodities or groups of commodities, those of Zelder and of Ginsburg and Stern may be

---

[17] That is, changes in the index of price competitiveness tend to be similar for categories in the same two-digit group.

[18] Jan Tinbergen, "Some Measurements of Elasticities of Substitution," *Review of Economic Statistics,* August 1946.

cited.[19] Both studies used unit values for prices and both derived elasticities of substitution between the United Kingdom and the United States, the former for 1921–38 and the latter for 1922–38 and 1948–59. Zelder computed elasticities for 27 commodity groups and 12 subgroups through a regression of relative quantities against relative prices based (usually) on one observation relating to each of the eighteen years he covered.[20] Elasticities of −1 to −3 characterized 17 of the 27 groups; the others were about evenly divided on either side of this spectrum.[21] Elasticities for the subcategories were higher; 7 out of the 12 were over −3. The distribution of elasticities for the 16 groups and 8 subcategories that fell in the metal and machinery classifications covered by our study was not substantially different.

Ginsburg and Stern worked with 60 to 70 commodities, and in each of the two periods they pooled the data for all years and all commodities using dummy variables to distinguish the intercept terms for different years. In one formulation they assumed that the elasticity of substitution was the same for all commodities; the coefficient was −1.59 for 1922–38 and −1.49 for 1948–59. However, a statistical test led them to reject the hypothesis that all commodities had the same elasticity of substitution, and in a second formulation they permitted each commodity to have its own elasticity (retaining the same intercept dummies as before). The resulting elasticities were somewhat more dispersed than Zelder's, with about one-fifth positive in each period and 21 out of 50 negative

[19] Zelder, op. cit., and Alan L. Ginsburg and Robert M. Stern, "The Determination of the Factors Affecting American and British Exports in the Inter-War and Post-War Periods," Oxford Economic Papers, July 1965. Mention may be made also of Z. Kubinski, "The Elasticity of Substitution between Sources of British Imports, 1921–38," Yorkshire Bulletin of Economic and Social Research, January 1950. Kubinski calculated 289 elasticities of substitution between various pairs of countries, modifying the basic regression of relative quantities against relative prices in over half the cases by inserting a time lag, distinguishing different subperiods, eliminating trend, or transforming the variables into deviations from moving averages. Ignoring the 24 cases in which a positive coefficient was obtained for relative prices, the averages of his coefficients were as follows:

	Mean	Median	No. of Cases
Food, drink, and tobacco	−6.3	−3.4	63
Raw materials and articles mainly unmanufactured	−2.4	−2.2	52
Articles wholly or mainly manufactured	−4.5	−2.2	150
All	−4.5	−2.4	265

[20] Zelder also presents the elasticities derived by regressing prices against quantities and elasticities based on the division of the coefficient of variation of the quantity ratios by the coefficient of variation of the price ratios. The elasticities obtained from the coefficients of variation represent geometric means of those derived from the two regression forms (op. cit., pp. 35–36).

[21] Two were positive, four were between zero and −1, and four were above −3.

ones in the −1 to −3 range in 1922–38 and 24 out of 53 in 1948–59. (The other negative coefficients were divided about evenly on either side of this range in both periods.) In general, Ginsburg and Stern worked with more narrowly defined categories than Zelder, and only about a fifth of them fell within the scope of the present study.[22] For those categories which appear both in the Zelder and in the Ginsburg and Stern study (1922–38 data),[23] the elasticities compare as follows:

	Zelder	Ginsburg and Stern
Ammonium sulphate	−3.11	−3.10
Sodium hydroxide	−1.22	−2.52
Pig iron	−3.10	−4.36
Iron and steel sheets, galvanized	−1.85	−1.90
Motorcycles	−5.52	−4.02
Copper wire, uninsulated	−3.83	−1.59
Cement	−2.61	−1.42
Glass, plate and sheet	+2.10	+2.48
Cotton cloth	−1.45	−3.72

While the differences between the two sets of estimates are not inconsequential there are important elements of agreement also; the extreme estimates apply to the same products in the two lists, the range and medians are very similar, and for several of the items the elasticities are very close. If this small sample of overlapping subsets can be relied upon, the more sophisticated methods used by Ginsburg and Stern do not produce results that differ, for similar sets of data, in their general contours from the results of Zelder's simpler approach.

It is difficult to assess the significance of the apparent agreement between the U.K.-U.S. substitution elasticity of −1.55 for 1953–64 produced by our disaggregated data and the elasticity of −1.49 for 1948–59 calculated by Ginsburg and Stern. Only one of our time periods falls in their time span, we cover more complicated types of

[22] They used data originally selected by MacDougall with the idea of avoiding categories for which a wide product mix would make changes in unit values a poor proxy for price changes. A number of Zelder's categories such as, for example, "automobiles and chassis," "pipes, tubes, and fittings," and "electricity generators," are quite suspect from this standpoint.

[23] Aluminum sulphate has been omitted since the large difference between Zelder's −2.02 and Ginsburg and Stern's +1.96 may have been due to Zelder's exclusion of data for 1921–24.

goods, and we base our analysis on categories of goods that are some-what broader than those for which they used unit values.

Product Elasticities (1963 Cross-sectional Data)

Another approach to the measurement of elasticities of substitution was offered by MacDougall in his famous study dealing with British and American exports.[24] He calculated what he called "product" elasticities of substitution from cross-sectional data; the product elasticity of substitution is the percentage variation in two countries' relative exports from one category of goods to another, associated, at a moment in time, with a 1 per cent difference in relative prices as between the categories. It is calculated from a regression, across commodity groups, of export ratios against price ratios. This formula—log $(Q_F/Q_S)_t = a + b \log (P_F/P_S)_t + e_t$—assumes that quantity-price relationships are determined by common factors operating across commodities. The more usual time series formulations assume that there are differences in the factors affecting different commodities but that these differences remain constant over time and are eliminated in equations like those discussed in the previous section.

Opinion is divided on the economic significance of product elasticities. MacDougall argued that, with suitable corrections for errors in the price and quantity data and with adjustments to take account of differences in the trade patterns of the two areas introduced by an aggregation bias that makes the actual or "total" elasticity of substitution smaller than the product elasticity, the latter provides a useful basis for order-of-magnitude estimates of the true elasticity of substitution. Mac-Dougall estimated that his product elasticity of −3.6 for U.S.-U.K. exports of manufactures for 1934–38 should be adjusted to −4 or −4.5 on the first account and then downward to −2.5 to −2.8 on the second account, and finally perhaps raised to −3 to allow for the impact of price changes on the quantity of both countries' exports.[25]

Others, including Nicholson [26] and Bhagwati,[27] have questioned the

---

[24] MacDougall, *op. cit.*, Part I, December 1951, Part II, September 1952.

[25] *Ibid.*, December 1951, p. 720 and September 1952, p. 495.

[26] R. J. Nicholson, " 'Product-Elasticities of Substitution' in International Trade," *Economic Journal*, September 1955. See also MacDougall's rejoinder in the same issue.

[27] J. Bhagwati, "The Pure Theory of International Trade," *Economic Journal*, March 1964, p. 11.

Table 6.1
MacDougall's Estimates of Product Elasticities of Substitution,
Selected Years, 1913–59

	Number of Commodities	r	Product Elasticity
U.S./U.K.			
1913	32	-0.54	-3.2
1922–38[a]	86 to 109	-0.40 to 0.68	-1.8 to -3.2
1934–38[b]	109	-0.73	-3.6
1948–59[a]	90 to 95	-0.36 to 0.62	-1.9 to -3.0
1929	109	-0.57	-2.6
U.S./Germany, 1929	51	-0.60	-2.4
U.S./France, 1929	56	-0.54	-2.4
U.S./Japan, 1929	41	-0.62	-2.8
U.K./Germany, 1929	77	-0.43	-1.6
U.K./France, 1929	58	-0.48	-2.2
U.K./Japan, 1929	44	-0.61	-1.6

Source: G. D. A. MacDougall, "British and American Exports: A Study Suggested by the Theory of Comparative Costs, Part I," *Economic Journal,* December 1951; and D. MacDougall, M. Dowley, P. Fox, and S. Pugh, "British and American Productivity, Prices and Exports: An Addendum," *Oxford Economic Papers,* October 1962.

[a]Ranges of data for individual years given in source.

[b]Based on quantities and average values for the period as a whole.

relevance of a measure based on instantaneous price and quantity comparisons for various categories of goods to a concept such as the elasticity of substitution which is designed to gauge *changes over time* in the quantity ratios associated with changes in the price ratios.

It requires, as MacDougall himself observes, a bold step to draw conclusions about the elasticity of substitution from the product elasticities. On the other hand, the strength and persistence of the inverse association between relative exports and relative prices found by MacDougall calls for some explanation.[28] It can be seen from Table 6.1 that MacDougall found product elasticities mainly in the −1.5 to −3.5 range for the U.S.-U.K. comparisons at dates spread over nearly fifty years and for half a dozen other pairs of countries in 1929.

For 1963, the year selected for weighting purposes in this study, we

[28] Bhagwati is "astonished" at the results (*op. cit.,* p. 12n). The relative "prices" used by MacDougall were unit values. Relative exports were relative quantities exported to third countries.

collected trade data showing the origin of exports for the classifications for which we produced price indexes—almost all three-digit and many four-digit categories.[29] With these data and our 1963 price level comparisons, we can estimate product elasticities. When, for example, we pool the U.K.-U.S., German-U.S., and Japanese-U.S. comparisons for 1963, we obtain a product elasticity of substitution, i.e., a coefficient of relative price levels, of −3.6. The equation, based on 96 observations covering 59 different product categories, is:

$$\log \frac{Q_F}{Q_S} = -0.46 - \underset{(7.23)}{3.59} \log \frac{P_F}{P_S} \qquad \bar{r}^2 = .35 \qquad (19)$$

Our own results confirm and even strengthen the earlier findings. For individual binary comparisons we obtain:

Country	Number of Categories	$\bar{r}^2$	Constant	Product Elasticity
U.K.-U.S.	43	0.39	−0.64	−3.75 (5.28)
Germany-U.S.	37	0.48	−0.07	−3.63 (5.91)
Japan-U.S.	16	0.31	−1.28	−4.83 (2.78)

Our U.K.-U.S. elasticity is higher than those obtained by MacDougall and well above his results for 1953–59 (the period which overlaps our study) which varied between −1.9 and −2.6. An upward shift in the elasticity between the 1950s and 1963 may cause the difference, but it may be due also to the smaller bias in our coefficient if, as we think, the errors in our price comparisons are smaller and less systematically correlated (inversely) with the errors in the quantity comparisons than was true of MacDougall's "prices" based on unit values.[30]

Also, less clearly, our estimate may be higher because of the difference in commodity coverage. When manufactured foods were omitted from

[29] However, we restrict analysis of the data in this section to the categories for which we give price indexes in the appendixes. The proportion of total exports of metal, metal products, and machinery covered by these categories is less than one-half for Japan, two-thirds for the United Kingdom, three-quarters for Germany, and four-fifths for the United States.

[30] For a discussion of the bias imparted by errors of observation in the price and quantity ratios, see MacDougall, op. cit., Part I, pp. 721 f.

MacDougall's regressions, the elasticities were changed by amounts ranging from −0.1 to −0.4 in the years 1953–59. These changes suggest that his results are sensitive to the nature of the categories included.

Our own data are not very helpful in determining whether elasticities tend to be associated in any systematic way with the degree of processing.[31] The following figures compare the product elasticities of our three- and four-digit categories within two-digit SITC divisions, with U.K.-U.S., Germany-U.S. and Japanese-U.S. comparisons being pooled to build up the number of observations:

SITC		Number of Observations	$\bar{r}^2$	Constant	Product Elasticity
67	Iron and steel	18	.00	0.47	−1.34 (1.00)
68	Nonferrous metals	2		Not calculated	
69	Metal manufactures, n.e.s.	14	.14	−0.41	−2.75 (1.77)
71	Machinery, nonelectric	32	.19	−0.60	−3.53 (2.87)
72	Electrical machinery	17	−.02	−0.18	−1.30 (0.82)
73	Transport equipment	8	.76	−0.68	−5.39 (4.84)

Our findings offer independent confirmation that there tends to be a significant inverse correlation between relative quantities and relative prices in the exports of pairs of industrial countries. Perhaps the best interpretation of this finding is to regard it as the outcome of the comparative advantages of each of the pair of countries as manifested in an imperfectly competitive world.[32] Under perfect competition and with

[31] Ginsburg and Stern found wide variations in elasticities among the products they examined. For 1948–59, for example, the largest negative coefficients were for barbed wire (−9.19), fertilizers (−7.92), and ferromolybdenum (−6.51). Positive coefficients included those for finished cotton thread, railway spikes, and box cameras. Their results suggest higher elasticities for more standardized products, as might be expected.

[32] Cf. Nicholson, op. cit., and MacDougall, op. cit. Note that the existence of transport costs also tends to produce inverse quantity-price relationships.

no transport costs, P_F/P_S would always equal unity and the quantity ratios would deviate much farther from unity than they actually do.

Export Specialization and Price Trends

The quantity-price relationships may also be examined in terms of the changes in relative quantities for goods characterized by different types of price movement. It may be interesting to know, for example, whether some countries have tended to gain relative to others in exports of types of goods marked by rising prices.

Some evidence on this question was offered earlier (Chapter 2) when the detailed international price indexes were aggregated with the export weights of each country in turn. To investigate the matter more directly, we calculated "average" international price indexes for 1964/1953 for each three- or four-digit level, weighting each country's price change for a category over the whole period from 1953 to 1964 by that country's exports of the category in 1963. The value of each country's 1963 exports of each three- or four-digit category was then taken as the dependent variable in a regression in which the average international price index was the independent variable. The regression coefficients [33] and their t-values (in parentheses) are:

U.S.	2.07	(1.44)
U.K.	0.02	(0.02)
Germany	−0.14	(0.08)
Japan	−1.62	(2.81)

The positive U.S. coefficient indicates that U.S. exports were larger in groups with relatively rising prices, and the negative Japanese coefficient indicates that exports were larger in groups with declining world prices. A U.S. export product mix weighted in the direction of relatively rising prices, and the opposite for Japan, conform with the earlier finding based on the reweighting of international price indexes by various country weights (Table 2.5).

One possible explanation of this finding is that the impetus to the relative price increases comes from the demand side and that the U.S.

[33] The regression coefficients were the b's in each country equation, in the form $E_j = a + bP_j$, where E_j is the value of exports by the country of commodity j in 1963, and P_j is the average price change for that commodity in all countries from 1953 to 1964.

economy has more elastic supply conditions. The United States, on this hypothesis, is more flexible than others in shifting production into lines of growing demand; the lack of adequate supply response in other countries causes prices to rise, and the United States enjoys large market shares for these products. If in fact rising quantities were correlated with rising prices, an explanation along these lines would be plausible, but our lack of detailed trade and quantity data prior to 1961 prevents us from ascertaining this.

An alternative is to seek explanations based on the assumption that the impetus to the price change comes from the supply side. A country such as Japan may be catching up technologically with cost-reducing methods developed elsewhere, or rapid growth at home may provide it with economies of scale that can be extended to exports. The leader in price reduction would also gain in export shares, and world prices of the commodities in which that country specialized would decline. The facts fit this hypothesis, but further investigation would be required to eliminate alternative hypotheses that might also be consistent with the observed behavior of trade and prices, such as the role of technological leadership in producing the observed changes.

It would be useful to have a measure of technological progress in the various commodity groups with which to compare the export performance of the different countries. We do not have such a measure, but insofar as technological progress takes the form of cost reduction in the production of a particular commodity (rather than the development of new product variants) it should result in a fall in price relative to the prices of commodities enjoying slower technological gains. If we use, as a proxy for cost-reducing technological development, the average price change for that commodity,[34] described above, the conclusion would be that Japan leads in the technological race and the United States is last.

A more likely reading of the technological implications of the U.S. concentration on products with relatively rising prices takes account of the introduction of new product variants and of their subsequent diffusion and price behavior. The United States might be specializing in the earliest stage of innovations in product type—the introduction of new,

---

[34] The average price change seems preferable to the largest price decline in any country as a measure, because the latter would include some cases that represent only a catching-up by a backward country, rather than a characteristic of the commodity in general. Countries in the early stages of production of a commodity, when the catching-up process produces very steep price declines, will be given little or no weight in the average.

more sophisticated products, perhaps products still in the experimental stage. The possibly low price elasticity for the new product at this stage, might account for the price behavior of U.S. exports. Following this may be a second stage of rapidly rising production of a now more standardized product with falling cost and prices.[35] Production may then shift to overseas plants of U.S. companies, or to countries such as Japan, specializing in low-cost production rather than innovation. As noted in Chapter 12, we observed industries in which something like this may occur systematically; U.S. parent firms in these industries typically develop and introduce new models in the United States and begin production in their plants abroad only at a later stage of product acceptance.[36]

Finally, we may not have been uniformly successful in removing the effect of quality improvement in different groups, and U.S. exports, concentrated in high-technology or rapidly changing products, may be more affected by this upward bias than those of other countries. The large predominance of price rises over declines in the nonelectrical machinery division suggests that this explanation cannot be entirely dismissed.

[35] See Raymond Vernon, "International Investment and International Trade in the Product Cycle," *Quarterly Journal of Economics,* May 1966.

[36] For some recent discussions of the role of technology in international trade see the papers by Gary C. Hufbauer and Seev Hirsch in *The Technology Factor in International Trade,* New York, Universities–National Bureau Conference Series 22, 1970.

7

SOME FURTHER ASPECTS OF
INTERNATIONAL COMPETITIVENESS

OUR FOCUS on measuring price competitiveness kept us from exploring the broader aspects of price and nonprice competition in world trade as thoroughly as we would have liked. We cannot therefore attempt to present a well-rounded discussion of factors other than price changes and differences, but on a few points we gathered enough information for a worthwhile report.

The Relative Importance of Price and Nonprice Factors

The relative importance of price and nonprice factors can probably best be studied through statistical or econometric analysis, and in the previous chapter we reported some work along these lines. It is, however, very difficult to quantify the nonprice factors, and even for prices we have the relevant data for only six years. An alternative approach, which has obvious disadvantages of its own, is to ask firms engaged in international trade to assess the various factors that enable them to export or that cause them to import.

A pilot survey was made in 1964 to determine the feasibility of using a mail questionnaire to gain information about the role of prices in U.S. exports as this role was seen by large U.S. industrial firms. A questionnaire we prepared (see appendix to this chapter) was sent out on our behalf by the National Association of Business Economists to a selected list of its members in over 100 firms. Of 64 responses, only 26 provided useful information and, considering our small staff and heavy price collection burden, we decided against a wider survey along these lines. A brief report on the answers is worthwhile, however. The 26 firms that did provide data were responsible for a wide range of exports amounting to over half a billion dollars out of a 1964 total of $22 billion in the sectors they covered and an overall total of U.S. exports of $26 billion. At the three-digit SITC level, they provided 69 reports on 43 different categories. The distribution of firms reporting and of their exports by one-digit SITC sections is compared with total U.S. exports in Table 7.1.

For those SITC sections for which we had at least five different firms reporting and for the aggregate of all products, we show, in Table 7.2

Table 7.1

Distribution of U.S. Exports and Survey Data, 1964

(dollars in millions)

SITC No.	Section	Exports Total (1)	Sample (2)	No. of Firms Reporting (3)
2	Crude materials, inedible, except fuels	$2,951	$92.5	5
3	Mineral fuels, lubricants, and related materials	911	12.4	3
4	Animal and vegetable fats and oils	434	[a]	1
5	Chemicals	2,375	33.7[b]	6
6	Manufactures, classified by material	3,201	97.8[b]	10
7	Machinery and transport equipment	9,350	307.3[b]	10
8	Misc. manufactured articles	1,715	[a]	1
9	Commodities not classified according to kind	611	[a]	1
	Total	21,548	556.1	37[c]
Total U.S. exports[d]		26,086		

Source: Col. 1: *United States Exports of Domestic and Foreign Merchandise; Commodity by Country of Destination,* 1964 Annual, U.S. Dept. of Commerce, Report FT 410, June 1965; cols. 2 and 3: NBER survey.

[a]Not available or not given because only one firm reported.

[b]Figure excludes at least one major firm which gave responses to questionnaire but did not report dollar amount of exports. In these categories therefore the sample covers substantially more exports than are given in column 2.

[c]Unduplicated number of firms was 26.

[d]U.S. exports in SITC sections for which none of the sample firms reported any exports were: SITC section 0, food and live animals, $3,983 million; SITC section 1, beverages and tobacco, $554 million.

Table 7.2

Relative Importance of Factors Explaining U.S. Export Success[a]

(per cent)

Factor Underlying Ability to Export	Crude Materials (SITC 2)	Chemicals (SITC 5)	Mfrs. Classified by Material (SITC 6)	Mach. & Transp. Equip. (SITC 7)	All Products
1. *Prices equal or below foreign*	*43*	*56*	*18*	*14*	*28*
2. *Product more expensive, but:*	*42*	*30*	*66*	*70*	*57*
a. Product custom built; sales depend on engineering skill	5	1	11	10	9
b. Produce for stock, but product is superior	12	2	9	29	13
c. U.S. goods in general or company's brand command(s) premium	7	14	11	15	12
d. Faster delivery	2	3	7	5	5
e. Better after-sale service	15	10	13	8	12
f. Tied grants or loans			6	2	3
g. Other			8	3	3
3. *Unique product; no close foreign substitute*	*6*	*5*	*10*	*14*	*10*
4. *Other*	*10*	*8*	*6*	*3*	*5*
Total	*100*	*100*	*100*	*100*	*100*
Addendum: No. of firms reporting	5	6	10	10	26

Note: Percentages may not add to totals because of rounding.
[a]Twenty-six U.S. firms are covered. They reported relative importance in percentage terms, and the figures in the table are averages of the reported percentages.

the relative importance assigned by the firms to different factors accounting for their success in exporting. Low prices received only 28 per cent of the weight on the average. At the other extreme, firms did not feel that they could rely very heavily on the uniqueness of their goods: Uniqueness received only a 10 per cent weight. The greatest importance (57 per cent) was assigned to factors that enabled the U.S. firms to sell abroad even though their products were more expensive than those of foreign competitors; product superiority in one form or another (a, b, and c) accounted for the largest part (34 per cent out of the 57 per cent), with better after-sales service the leading runner-up (12 per cent). There was, as would be expected, a greater emphasis on relative price in basic products (SITC 2 and 5) than in manufactured goods (SITC 6 and 7). Indeed, over half the firms reporting upon manufactured goods in SITC 6 and 7 did not attribute any of their export success to their ability to match foreign prices. This does not mean, of course, that they were unconcerned about the size of the price differentials between their products and those of their foreign competitors. Firms selling transportation equipment, the returns suggested, placed more emphasis on relative prices than did other machinery producers.

The general nature of the responses of the twenty-six firms is little changed if, instead of averaging their percentage responses, we count the number of times each factor was mentioned (Table 7.3). Uniqueness of product and miscellaneous factors (items 3 and 4),[1] were mentioned relatively often but not assigned a great deal of weight.

We compared these results with more extensive surveys into reasons for imports conducted by the IFO Institute of Germany [2] and by the National Economic Development Council in the United Kingdom.[3]

In the German survey, which was limited to imports of factory equipment in 1964, the responding firms [4] reported they made 63 per cent of their purchases because the desired equipment was produced only abroad and another 12 per cent, because of the superiority of foreign equipment; only 7 per cent was purchased abroad for price advantages.

---

[1] Effective foreign sales or distributive organizations were the most frequently mentioned items in the miscellaneous category.

[2] "Warum kauft die Industrie ausländische Ausrüstungsgüter?" IFO *Schnelldienst*, July 8, 1966.

[3] *Imported Manufactures; An Inquiry into Competitiveness*, 1965.

[4] The survey went to 3,000 firms of which 27 per cent responded. The goods included in the survey covered 41 per cent of German machinery imports in 1964. Motor vehicles and office and farm machinery were excluded.

Table 7.3

Relative Importance of Factors Explaining U.S. Export Success,
Alternative Test

	References to Each Factor		Per Cent Distribution of Importance[a]
	No.	Per Cent	
1. *Price*	*35*	*29*	*28*
2. *More expensive but*	*57*[b]	*47*[c]	*57*
a. Engineering skill	19	5	9
b. Superior product	28	8	13
c. Preference for U.S. goods or brand	36	10	12
d. Faster delivery	23	6	5
e. Better after-sales service	42	12	12
f. Tied grants or loans	14	4	3
g. Other	9	2	3
3. *Unique product*	*20*	*16*	*10*
4. *Other*	*10*	*18*	*5*
Total	*122*	*100*	*100*

[a]From Table 7.2.

[b]Number of times one or more items in group 2 was referred to in a company report on a three-digit SITC category. Since in most replies reference was made to more than one of these items the number of references to 2a–2g totals 171.

[c]Percentages in lines 2a–2g (which sum to 47) show distribution of 171 references mentioned in previous note.

The full distribution of reasons, when tabulated and compared with our returns covering the same products, agrees remarkably with it (see Table 7.4). About three-fourths of German imports (from all sources) and of U.S. exports (to all destinations) are attributable to some degree of product differentiation. Under this general rubric there are substantial differences between the relative importance assigned by German importers and U.S. exporters to uniqueness versus types of product differentiation involving higher degrees of substitutability between domestic and foreign goods. To some degree the greater weight given by German importers to uniqueness may reflect differences in definition or judgment, but the direction of the differences is plausible. One would expect German importers to find the products they buy from the rest of the world unique compared with what is produced only in Germany more

Table 7.4
Factors Accounting for Factory Equipment Trade:
German Imports vs. U.S. Exports, 1964
(per cent)

	German Imports	U.S. Exports
Price	7	7
Product differentiation	77	73
Unique goods	63	22[a]
Superior goods	14	51[b]
Technical features	(10)	
Quality	(5)	
Service and other factors	16	20
Better service	3	9
Delivery time	9	8
Miscellaneous	4	3[c]
Total	100	100

Source: "Warum kauft die Industrie ausländische Ausrüstungsgüter?" IFO *Schnelldienst,* July 8, 1966. NBER survey: machinery and equipment, excluding motor vehicles, office machinery, and farm machinery. Parts do not always add to totals because of rounding. U.S. coverage differs from Table 7.2 to provide comparability with Germany.

[a]Questionnaire, sum of lines 2a and 3.
[b]Questionnaire, sum of lines 2b and 2c.
[c]Questionnaire, sum of lines 2f, 2g, and 4.

frequently than U.S. exporters would find the goods they sell as unique compared with the whole range of products available abroad.[5]

The results of the U.K. study, which covered manufactured goods,[6] were not summarized quantitatively. The findings, based on surveys of opinions of users, consumers, and competing manufacturers, indicated that the relative importance of price differences varied from one product to another. For machinery: "The crucial factor [determining the choice between a domestic and foreign purchase] is what a machine can do or

[5] It is also possible that an exporter is inclined to perceive products of other exporters as competitive with his, while the firm purchasing foreign equipment tends to think of the item it has decided to import as being unique relative to domestically available goods.

[6] Chiefly chemicals, paper and paperboard, textiles and apparel, iron and steel, machinery and transport equipment, instruments, photographic and optical goods, and watches and clocks.

how economically and reliably it can do it; superiority in this sense out-weighs quite large differences in price." [7] Price was, however, a "cru-cial" [8] factor in paper and paperboard, textiles and clothing, some con-sumer durables (refrigerators and motorcycles), and iron and steel; but it was not clear that quality-adjusted price comparisons were the basis for these conclusions. Shortage of capacity also played a role in 1964 imports, particularly in chemicals.

Price Differentiation Between Domestic and Export Markets

One result of the importance of product differentiation, of nonprice factors, and of the separation of markets by transfer costs, aid-tying, and the like is that sellers have considerable discretion to vary their pricing policies from one market to another.

Although we did not seek to investigate the extent to which firms did in fact differentiate between markets, such policies often came to our attention directly or indirectly. The evidence points clearly to the con-clusion that prices of a substantial fraction of international trade in manufactured metal products and machinery differ from those in domestic markets.

The most direct evidence to support this view came from sellers. Although we explicitly stated that our interest was not in domestic but in export prices, about half of the 121 U.S. sellers who gave us prices nevertheless indicated their pricing policies. Of these, about half stated their foreign and domestic prices differed. [9]

The information from these and other sellers and from buyers, some from abroad, suggests that price differentiation between various markets is more widely practiced by European and particularly Japanese export-ers than by U.S. ones. The probable reasons are the greater relative importance of the domestic market for U.S. firms and the greater extent to which they export differentiated products less exposed to price competition.

More specific references to price differentiation will be found in a number of the product chapters, including those dealing with aluminum,

---

[7] *Ibid.*, p. 18.

[8] *Ibid.*, p. 28.

[9] We included among the "same-price" firms some which charged higher prices to foreign customers to cover higher packaging expenses encountered in preparing goods for overseas shipment.

steel, aircraft, power transformers, electricity distribution equipment, and agricultural machinery.

Shipment Delay

An offset to the often lower and generally more flexible pricing of Europe and Japan is U.S. speed in shipment from factory after receipt of order. This U.S. advantage emerges clearly from two bodies of data we gathered in our study and accords with conclusions reached for a narrower commodity sector by another group of investigators using a completely different type of data.[10]

One source of information, which consisted of periodic surveys of the supply outlook and shipment delays, was conducted by the purchasing department of a large international firm with procurement activities in many countries to support worldwide production and distribution operations. These reports, which were sent to the company's requisitioning officers in various parts of the world, were generally prepared at irregular intervals depending upon the extent of variation in supply conditions; in some years only one report was issued, in others as many as four. The reports were concerned with standard specifications of products rather than with special-purpose variants that had to be custom made. There were some changes in the form and content of the reports over the years. In general they became somewhat more comprehensive, so that more comparisons can be made for the recent dates than for the early ones. The coverage of the reports was very stable over the years, although in a few instances the specific variant of a product differed from one report to another. In addition, some items appeared only sporadically. Nevertheless, U.S. and foreign sources of supply could be compared over time for enough items to enable us to construct indexes of relative shipment delays for metals and metal products (SITC 67, 68, and 69) and for machinery and transport equipment (SITC 7).

One report was selected for analysis for each year—the one nearest the midyear when there was a choice. Most of the reports relating to shipments from foreign plants referred to the European area as a whole. One or two reports, however, dealt with the U.K. and European coun-

---

[10] M. D. Steuer, R. J. Ball, and J. R. Eaton, "The Effect of Waiting Times on Foreign Orders for Machine Tools," *Economica*, November 1966.

tries separately; in these instances, the shortest European shipment time was taken for comparison with the United States. Japan was introduced only in 1963, and it is treated separately in our calculations. The reports gave the time required between the date of the order and shipment from the factory; requisitioning sources were to add to this time the necessary period for the shipment of the goods to the desired point of use. The times were usually expressed in ranges such as "stock" to 2 weeks, 6 to 8 weeks, or 1 to 2 months. The midpoint of these ranges was used in the calculations. "Stock" or "immediate delivery," given without any range, was taken as one week.

All times and time ranges for each year were converted into weeks and classified into appropriate four-digit SITC categories. Place-to-place ratios were then calculated for each item. The first step in averaging these ratios was to obtain an unweighted average of all ratios in a specific four-digit SITC category in a specific year. The four-digit averages were then combined into weighted three-, two-, and one-digit and overall averages by using 1963 OECD trade weights. Thus in these indexes, the composition of items in the comparisons changes somewhat from year to year. The results are shown in Table 7.5.

The figures suggest that fast shipment is a structural characteristic of the U.S. metal and machinery industries relative to those of Europe and perhaps Japan. Only in 1956 was European delivery time shorter than that of the United States: Our indexes fell in the quarter marked by a five-week U.S. steel strike. There is, however, no trend over this eleven-year period in the relative European-U.S. times.[11]

---

[11] Substantially the same results were obtained when the data used for the computation of the indexes were restricted to those items for which corresponding ratios were available in adjacent years. In these calculations we obtained two four-digit averages for each year, one comparable with the preceding year and the other with the succeeding year. For each pair of years, matching four-digit averages were then combined into three-, two-, and one-digit and overall averages, using 1963 trade weights as above. For all categories of product, these indexes are compared, below, with those in Table 7.5 by converting them to a 1962 base:

Europe/United States
(1962 = 100)

	All Items	Over-lapping Items		All Items	Over-lapping Items
1953	52	59	1959	81	90
1954	37	43	1960	70	78
1955	63	66	1961	71	79
1956	28	33	1962	100	100
1957	63	70	1963	63	63
1958	78	87	1964	59	57

Table 7.5

Relative Shipment Delay for Standard Specifications and Capacity Utilization,
Europe, Japan, and the United States, 1953–64

(U.S. for each year = 100)

Year and Quarter	Total		Metals and Metal Products		Machinery and Transport Equipment		Indexes of Capacity Utilization		
	No. of Observations (1)	Relative (2)	No. of Observations (3)	Relative (4)	No. of Observations (5)	Relative (6)	U.S. (7)	Western Europe (8)	Europe/U.S. (9)
Europe/United States									
1953-IV	85	154	56	141	29	159	88		
1954-IV	113	110	70	115	43	108	81		
1955-III	114	187	72	122	42	210	91	99	109
1956-III	106	84	72	80	34	85	90	95	105
1957-III[a]	112	188	72	223	40	175	89	91	103
1958-III	114	232	74	225	40	234	73	90	123
1959-I	115	240	75	207	40	251	79	88	111
1960-III[b]	111	207	73	221	38	203	80	96	120
1961-I	110	210	72	228	38	204	72	96	134
1962-II	121	295	69	336	52	281	80	95	119
1963-III	122	185	69	278	53	153	81	94	117
1964-I	128	175	68	239	60	153	81	96	118
Japan/United States									
1963-III	120	215	66	295	54	187			
1964-I	85	164	38	220	47	145			

Source: Cols. 1–6: Derived from procurement data of large international company by the method described in the text; cols. 3 and 4 include SITC 67, 68, and 69; cols. 5 and 6 cover SITC 7, and cols. 1 and 2 are a combination of SITC 67, 68, 69, and 7. Cols 7 and 8: Based on disaggregation of capacity indexes presented in *Wharton Economic Newsletter*, Spring 1968, p. 18. Include fabricated metal product, machinery, motor vehicle, aircraft, and instrument industries.

[a] 1957-IV for Europe.
[b] 1960-II for Europe.

Our second body of data was based on international bidding on projects in developing countries. In this case, the time given in the bidding was the length of the period between placement of the order and delivery (including transport time). Large machinery, sometimes custom built, was frequently involved, but some data were also available for steel structures and other metal products and smaller or standardized types of machinery or transport equipment. There was very little consistency over time: The specifications and quantities of even the few comparable items, on which data were available in adjacent years, varied greatly. Thus year-to-year comparisons are often based on quite different items. The place-to-place comparisons, however, are presumably exact: Bids not substantially meeting specifications were excluded. The countries consistently competing on these projects, besides the United States, were the United Kingdom, Germany, other EEC countries, and Japan. When several bids were submitted by the same country, the delivery time of the acceptable bid with the lowest f.o.b. price was chosen for comparison. Similarly, the delivery time chosen to represent the EEC (excluding Germany) was that of the country offering the lowest f.o.b. price.

Data before 1961 were too scattered and insufficient for us to derive reliable comparisons. Within the years for which we did attempt to compute indexes, the months in which the bids fell varied greatly. However, bids on many different items often came together at a particular date during the year because a purchasing country often asked for bids on a variety of items needed for one installation (such as a complete electrical power plant). The delivery time on most bids is given in months or days. The methods used in preparing the index numbers were similar to those described above for the first set of data.

The results, set out in Table 7.6, confirm the earlier finding that U.S. firms have consistently been faster in filling orders. Beyond this, few inferences can be drawn from the data; the sample is apparently too thin to produce reliable indicators of changing relative delivery speeds.

Both cyclical and structural factors may be involved in producing the differences we have observed between the United States and Europe in both sets of data. It is reasonable to suppose, for example, that shipment delays will expand and contract with cyclical conditions, and that relative shipment times will be affected by the different cyclical timing and amplitude in the two regions. With this possibility in mind, we added to Table 7.5 some indexes of capacity utilization as cyclical indicators,

Table 7.6

Relative Delivery Time for Goods Offered in International Bidding, 1961–64

(U.S. for each year = 100)

Year	United Kingdom		Germany		Other EEC		Japan	
	No. of Observations	Relative	No. of Observations	Relative	No. of Observations	Relative	No. of Observations	Relative
MACHINERY OTHER THAN ELECTRIC (SITC 71)								
1961	3	141	2	114	3	174		
1962	24	202	19	134	25	268	14	106
1963	33	155	17	119	29	168	20	132
1964	13	154	12	206	13	390	5	118
ELECTRICAL MACHINERY, APPARATUS, AND APPLIANCES (SITC 72)								
1961	11	199	14	152	10	229	6	246
1962	23	127	26	363	21	223	15	124
1963	26	253	50	150	36	183	30	210
1964	21	103	27	110	19	106	39	212
MACHINERY AND TRANSPORT EQUIPMENT (SITC 7)								
1961	18	165	19	206	17	193	8	217
1962	57	131	50	232	54	266	35	111
1963	65	155	70	125	68	176	59	147
1964	35	251	39	178	33	235	44	146
METALS, METAL PRODUCTS, AND MACHINERY (SITC 67, 68, 69, AND 7)								
1961	21	210	24	197	20	229	10	303
1962	63	131	56	222	61	244	43	126
1963	71	149	86	123	75	156	72	146
1964	41	248	45	204	37	225	48	155

Source: Derived from international bids.

but no clear relationship between the shipment date and the capacity indexes emerged. Perhaps the relationship is too complex to be revealed by matching the ratios for one quarter of each year as we did. Another factor is that the European level of capacity utilization observed in this period was relatively high and the range narrow (all the indexes fall between 88 and 99); the U.S. levels were relatively low and the range broad (indexes between 72 and 91). Perhaps for this reason, average shipment times in the underlying data vary less for Europe (11–17 weeks) than for the United States (7–17 weeks). However, the U.S. range is not greater than the European one if the steel strike period is excluded.[12]

Average U.S. shipment periods exceeded 10 weeks during 1955, 1956, and 1957,[13] when the U.S. capacity utilization index was around 90. In the other seven years, when the capacity index was never higher than 81, the averages were around 7 weeks. While this suggests that the faster shipment time of the United States may conceivably be related to the greater slack in its capacity utilization, U.S. shipment delays were shorter than in Europe even in 1957 when capacity utilization in the two areas was nearly alike.

The overall relationship showing higher U.S. prices and faster U.S. delivery is logical, since a long delivery period increases purchaser's cost; and fast shipment, the seller's. However, a superficial analysis of the material underlying Table 7.6 did not reveal a strong inverse relationship between price and shipment delays either within countries or for offers of different countries for given pieces of equipment. The explanation may be that the trade-off between price and speed of shipment exists along an indifference curve or isoquant for an individual seller or buyer, and our data give us information about only one observation on this trade-off curve for each seller. A losing bid involving

[12] Average number of weeks between receipt of order and shipment for all metals, metal products, machinery, and transport equipment:

	U.S.	Europe		U.S.	Europe
1955	10.8	15.8	1960	7.7	14.3
1956	18.2	13.7	1961	8.0	14.4
1957	11.0	17.5	1962	6.8	15.1
1958	7.5	14.6	1963	7.2	10.9
1959	7.5	14.5	1964	8.3	13.9

[13] In the period from 1955 to 1964 when capacity indexes were available for both Europe and the United States.

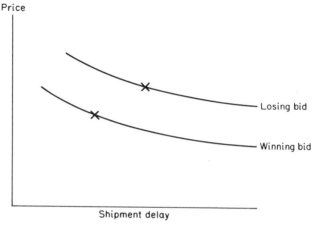

Figure 7.1

a higher price and slower shipment may have been on a higher price-shipment delay indifference curve (Figure 7.1): [14]

Faster delivery may be explained by the relatively large size of the U.S. market and of the average U.S. firm. Though we can only speculate on this effect, it seems reasonable to suppose that volume makes it relatively cheaper to maintain more complete inventories not only of a greater variety of sizes and styles of standard items, but also of items for which the holding of stocks in a smaller market would be costly or risky. In connection with the latter categories, Zarnowitz, in a study of the relationship between order backlogs and price changes within the United States,[15] mentioned long "lead times" in machine tools because they must often be made to order, and in steel rails because the demand is so sporadic. Perhaps the size of the U.S. economy reduces the risk of producing relatively specialized supplies and even whole machines or their components to stock, rather than to order, and the United States as a result has shorter shipment periods than other countries. This may be the case even for products made to order if the manufacturers

[14] A further step, which was not taken, would be to compare price-delivery combinations on actual transactions. Such a comparison is difficult because we are dealing with nonstandard products and therefore have no simple way of comparing one transaction with another. The analysis could be performed if we had a regression relating price to the physical quality variables, in which case the delivery periods could be compared with the residuals from the equation or could be included in the equation as an additional explanatory variable.

[15] Victor Zarnowitz, "Unfilled Orders, Price Changes, and Business Fluctuations," *Review of Economics and Statistics*, November 1962; reprinted as NBER Occasional Paper 84.

are able to produce the main components to stock and then simply combine them to order in different ways. Finally, larger volume makes it more worthwhile for management to expend greater effort on inventory control, and faster handling of incoming orders may be a concomitant gain in efficiency.

The materials considered in this chapter illustrate some of the factors, other than pure price competition, that influence trade flows. A number of other influences, such as financing costs, are also reported to be important, but we were not able to collect data on them. It seems clear that more systematic research into such factors could greatly increase our understanding of the operation of international markets.

Appendix: Copy of Form Used in Survey of Export Competitiveness

NATIONAL BUREAU OF ECONOMIC RESEARCH

March 1964

Pilot Survey of Competitiveness of U.S. Exports of Manufactures

The National Bureau of Economic Research is engaged in a major research project designed to determine to what extent the United States is competitive in world trade in manufactures with respect to prices and other facets of competition.

The study is centered on the role of prices, and the price experience of a substantial number of firms buying and selling in world markets has been canvassed through direct interviews. In these interviews, businessmen have often stressed the importance of non-price factors, which are, in many respects, more difficult to assess than the relative price position. The purpose of the attached questionnaire is to make a trial effort at identifying and, in at least some respects, quantifying the non-price factors that are important in explaining our manufactured exports.

The questionnaire is concerned mainly with your firm's 3 most important export products in 1963 or some other recent 12 month period. Ideally, we would like each "product" to correspond in coverage to one of the 3-digit categories of the Standard International Trade Classifica-

NBER Export Survey

I. Name your company's three most important exports from the U.S.

Product		Annual Exports ($ million)

1. _____
2. _____
3. _____

These three products accounted for approximately _____ percent of our exports.

* Canada, Latin America, U.K., Common Market, other Europe, Japan, other Asia, Africa.

II. We would like to know what underlies your success in exporting. As nearly as you can, assign approximate percentages to the factors listed below to indicate the degree to which you regard each as playing a part in your company's ability to sell abroad.

*Three most important destinations ***

	Product 1 Destination			Product 2 Destination			Product 3 Destination		
	(a)	(b)	(c)	(a)	(b)	(c)	(a)	(b)	(c)
1. Our prices are as low as or lower than foreign prices.									
2. Our product may be more expensive than foreign substitutes but we can meet foreign competition because:									
a. Our product is custom built; our sales depend on our engineering skill.									
b. We produce for stock but our product is superior to those available abroad.									
c. U.S. goods in general or our brand in particular command(s) a premium.									
d. We can deliver good more promptly.									
e. We provide better service after sale.									
f. Our exports are based on tied grants or loans.									
g. Other (Explain below).									
3. Our product is unique; no close substitutes are available abroad (Explain below).									
4. Other reasons (Explain below).									
Total (sum of 1, 2, 3 and 4 should add to 100)									

Explanations

166

III. Do you have a foreign subsidiary or licensee producing any of the three products mentioned above? _____
If so, please indicate the approximate percentage of your exports from the U.S. that fall in the following classifications:

	Product 1	Product 2	Product 3
1. U.S. exports are to areas other than those served by foreign subsidiary.			
2. A different type, variety, or brand of product is exported from the U.S.			

IV. The obstacles to our exporting more of the things we produce in the U.S. to each of the areas mentioned below may be ranked in order of importance as follows:

	Canada	Europe	Latin America	Other
a. Foreign firms sell similar products at lower prices.				
b. Foreign competitors extend more favorable financing.				
c. Tariff barriers.				
d. Quantitative restrictions.				
e. Specifications or procurement practices favor national (or other non-U.S.) suppliers.				
f. Other government rules or regulations.				
g. We are not in position to match the sales efforts of our competitors.				
h. Other (please specify). _____				

V. Would your firm be willing to supply prices for a few internationally traded machines or metal products based on either your selling or your purchasing experience?
Selling _____   Purchasing _____   Both _____

Name of Company _____
Name of Respondent _____
Date _____   Address _____

Note: — We should be grateful for any comments which you may wish to attach amplifying your responses to the foregoing questions.

167

tion (SITC). A list of these [omitted here] is attached. We realize, however, that it will be necessary for you to select the product classifications in terms of your firm's accounting records. Please tell us enough about each "product" you select to enable us to assign it to its proper place in the SITC.

For each of the 3 products, we would like to know the operative factor accounting for your firm's ability to export the product. We realize that the factors underlying export ability are often very complicated and that more than one element in our list in paragraph II may be involved. However, you are asked to allocate the dollar volume of exports (in percentage terms) among the various rows afforded in paragraph II as well as you can. We would be pleased to have any additional comments you wish to make.

The response of any individual company will be kept confidential. Indeed, the names of the participating firms will not be made public. Furthermore, care will be taken to publish the results in a way that will avoid the disclosure of information pertaining to an individual firm.

We have asked the cooperation of the National Association of Business Economists in sending out this questionnaire to its members as a pilot study to test the feasibility of collecting this information. We hope that you will be willing to cooperate by supplying answers to these questions and by offering suggestions as to ways of improving the form of the questionnaire.

Irving B. Kravis (signed)
Robert E. Lipsey (signed)

8

WHOLESALE PRICES AND UNIT VALUES AS MEASURES OF INTERNATIONAL PRICE COMPETITIVENESS

IN THE ABSENCE of adequate international price data for measuring changes in international price competitiveness, economists have turned to the closest available approximations, domestic wholesale price indexes, implicit price indexes from national accounts, and export and import unit value indexes.[1] For many reasons these variables may, as we mentioned earlier, fail to represent international price changes satisfactorily.[2] Without international price data with which to compare the proxy measures it was difficult, we noted, to say how important the defects were. When the various proxies moved differently, it was clear that at least some were giving a misleading picture of international price movements, but there was little basis for saying which, if any, were correct, and it was even difficult to account for the divergent movements.

The calculation of our international price indexes provides a standard of comparison for these proxy variables and should permit us to measure differences in behavior of the various types of price series. We would

---

[1] See, for example, Hal B. Lary, *The United States as World Trader and Banker,* New York, NBER, 1963, pp. 56–68; Walter S. Salant *et al., The United States Balance of Payments in 1968,* Washington, D.C., The Brookings Institution, 1963, pp. 70–80; and Bela Balassa, "Recent Developments in the Competitiveness of American Industry and Prospects for the Future," *Factors Affecting the U.S. Balance of Payments,* Joint Economic Committee, 87th Cong., 2nd sess., 1962; in which wholesale and consumer prices, implicit price deflators, and export and import unit values were all examined for the light they can shed on U.S. international competitiveness; and Hans Neisser and Franco Modigliani, *National Incomes and International Trade,* Urbana, Ill., 1953, in which price variables constructed from wholesale price and unit value data were used in constructing a model of world commodity trade. An article by Helen B. Junz and Rudolf R. Rhomberg, "Prices and Export Performance of Industrial Countries, 1953–63," *IMF Staff Papers,* July 1965, used comparisons of export unit values, wholesale prices, unit labor costs, and productivity as measures of international competitiveness.

[2] See Chapter 1 and Lary, *op. cit.,* pp. 56–57.

not argue that a discrepancy between one of our indexes and a proxy series, resulting from differences in the base year or in the index number formula, implies that the proxy is defective or inappropriate. We do assume in the following discussion that a discrepancy attributable to a difference in price movements on the commodity or subgroup level, or to a lack of data for the proxy series on a subgroup ostensibly covered, reflects error in the proxy variable as a measure of international price change. That is not to say that a particular series, such as a wholesale price, incorrectly measures the domestic price it is intended to represent, although we suspect that is often the case, particularly in the machinery area, in which conventional price index methods do not cope adequately with quality improvement. Our conclusions refer only to its accuracy in international price measurement, and it could be in error for that purpose even if it were a perfectly accurate domestic price measure.

We have made two types of comparison between our indexes and others. One method is to compare our aggregate indexes with frequently used indexes published by others (as in Table 8.8) or with indexes derived from published data but arranged by us in the SITC classification system (Table 8.1). In one sense, this comparison of the conclusions that would be reached by using our indexes with those that have been reached using the various proxy variables is the most important. The results of the comparison are inevitably ambiguous, however. Some part of the discrepancy will be due to the previously mentioned differences in base-year or index-number type. Other discrepancies will reflect such factors as the failure on the part of some users to adjust domestic price indexes to international weights or to insure the comparability of coverage of different indexes; that is, they will be only a measure of the carelessness of users.

We attempted to eliminate some of this ambiguity in our second method of comparison. For this, we constructed new international price and price competitiveness indexes from the basic wholesale price and unit value series for individual commodities, weighting these by the 1963 OECD international trade values used in weighting the NBER subgroup indexes (Tables 8.2, 8.4, and 8.6). Any differences between these and the NBER international price indexes can then be attributed either to differences in the behavior of the underlying basic prices or to differences in coverage, usually inadequate coverage in the domestic index. We can test for the role of coverage differences by comparing the several types of index on the three- and four-digit levels and aggregating the comparisons (Tables 8.3, 8.5, and 8.7). Differences between these and the previously described results are attributed to differences in coverage, and the remaining changes in proxy series relative to international prices are attributed to errors in the measurement of individual prices, including coverage differences within four-digit subgroups. Deficiencies in coverage can be just as serious as defects in the basic price data, and as likely to lead to incorrect conclusions, but the task of correcting for them may be simpler.

In addition to these comparisons of the indexes themselves, we estimated quantity-price relationships using indexes derived from our wholesale price data and compared them with those obtained from international price indexes. This exercise was not repeated for unit value indexes, partly because the very detailed series necessary to convert the foreign unit value series into world-trade-weighted indexes were not available.

Price Indexes from International and Wholesale Price Data

For the United States, we have sufficiently detailed information on individual-commodity wholesale prices and weights to compare domestic price indexes with domestic weights and international price indexes with international weights. The detail is needed to avoid the finding of apparent discrepancies which reflect merely differences in the definitions of product classifications, and we have been able to eliminate at least some of the more obvious of these.

The comparison of the two sets of indexes, in terms of SITC categories, reveals larger discrepancies in 1953–57 than in the later years (Table 8.1). In every case the wholesale prices overstated the initial-period price increases and, in every case but one, the increases for the period as a whole. Electrical machinery and iron and steel were the divisions with the most persistent and substantial bias. In these two cases, it continued through 1963, but the relationship between the two indexes was then reversed in 1964.

In making these comparisons we have gone some distance toward providing comparability in coverage between the domestic and international data by applying the same commodity classification system to the

Table 8.1

U.S. Wholesale Price Indexes Based on Domestic Weights vs. U.S. International
Price Indexes Based on International Weights, 1953, 1957, 1961–64

Weighting Basis	$\frac{1957}{1953}$	$\frac{1961}{1957}$	$\frac{1962}{1961}$	$\frac{1963}{1962}$	$\frac{1964}{1963}$	$\frac{1964}{1953}$
TOTAL MACHINERY, TRANSPORT EQUIPMENT, METALS, AND METAL PRODUCTS						
International	110	103	101	100	102	115
Wholesale	117	104	100	100	101	122
METALS (SITC 67, 68, AND 69)						
International	115	101	99	100	103	118
Wholesale	118	103	100	100	102	124
IRON AND STEEL (SITC 67)						
International	120	100	98	99	101	118
Wholesale	126	103	100	100	100	131
NONFERROUS METALS (SITC 68)						
International	104	101	99	100	108	113
Wholesale	108	102	98	99	106	113
METAL MANUFACTURES, N.E.S. (SITC 69)						
International	114	100	102	100	103	120
Wholesale	117	102	101	100	102	123
MACHINERY AND TRANSPORT EQUIPMENT (SITC 7)						
International	110	103	101	100	101	115
Wholesale	116	104	100	100	101	122
MACHINERY OTHER THAN ELECTRIC (SITC 71)						
International	114	107	101	101	101	126
Wholesale	120	108	101	101	102	135
ELECTRICAL MACHINERY, APPARATUS, AND APPLIANCES (SITC 72)						
International	106	96	96	97	101	95
Wholesale	115	100	98	99	99	110
TRANSPORT EQUIPMENT (SITC 73)						
International	106	102	104	99	100	113
Wholesale	114	104	100	98	102	119

Notes to Table 8.1

Note: The international price index here is an aggregation of indexes for subgroups and groups using 1963 OECD export values as weights. The index from wholesale prices is an aggregation of domestic series using the weights of the BLS wholesale price index. The differences between them stem from differences both in individual price series (including coverage) and in weighting.

Source: Appendixes C and F.

two sets of data. The discrepancies would have been considerably larger in some of the product areas of our study if we had used the BLS series as published. In electrical machinery, for example, the published BLS series shows a 19 per cent rise from 1953 to 1964, as compared to the 12 per cent rise in the series adjusted for comparability by adding domestic appliances, television sets, etc., and the 5 per cent decline in the international price index. This discrepancy illustrates the need for careful attention to commodity coverage, even aside from weighting differences, in judging international price movements.

A comparison between international and wholesale prices for the total of products covered by our study, weighted identically so as to remove the effect of weighting differences, can be performed for the United States and Germany (Table 8.2). We did not compute an aggregate international price index for Japan or an aggregate index from wholesale prices for the United Kingdom because the data had too many gaps.

In the United States the international price index rose considerably less than the index derived from wholesale prices between 1953 and 1961—13 per cent as compared to 21 per cent (Table 8.2). The main difference in the German figures was that international prices apparently rose more than domestic ones in response to the Suez crisis in 1956, but the effect of this divergence was short-lived. After 1961 the two indexes moved closely together in both the United States and Germany.

In general, the international price indexes for the two countries were much more similar to each other than the wholesale price indexes. The largest range between the total U.S. and German international price indexes in Table 8.2 for any one period was three percentage points, while the range between the wholesale price series was as high as twelve percentage points.

The index from wholesale price data was usually biased upward relative to the index from international price data. We can see this rela-

Table 8.2

Comparison of Price Indexes from International and Wholesale Price Data,
International Weights, 1953, 1957, 1961–64

Type of Price Data	1957 / 1953	1961 / 1957	1962 / 1961	1963 / 1962	1964 / 1963	1964 / 1953
TOTAL MACHINERY, TRANSPORT EQUIPMENT, METALS, AND METAL PRODUCTS						
United States						
International	110	103	101	100	102	115
Wholesale	116	104	100	100	101	122
Germany						
International	107	104	102	100	102	116
Wholesale	104	111	103	100	102	120
IRON AND STEEL (SITC 67)						
United States						
International	120	100	98	99	101	118
Wholesale	127	102	100	100	101	130
United Kingdom						
International	113	94	97	97	108	108
Wholesale	127	103	103	100	100	135
Germany						
International	117	93	96	96	109	110
Wholesale	106	110	101	98	100	116
Japan						
International	NA	NA	90	101	100	NA
Wholesale	124	98	92	100	100	112
NONFERROUS METALS (SITC 68)						
United States						
International	104	101	99	100	108	113
Wholesale	113	106	97	98	105	120
United Kingdom						
International	106	100	99	102	112	120
Wholesale	114	108	98	101	111	137

(continued)

Table 8.2 (continued)

Type of Price Data	1957 / 1953	1961 / 1957	1962 / 1961	1963 / 1962	1964 / 1963	1964 / 1953
NONFERROUS METALS (continued)						
Germany						
International	105	96	99	100	116	116
Wholesale	97	105	96	98	109	104
METAL MANUFACTURES, N.E.S. (SITC 69)						
United States						
International	114	100	102	100	103	120
Wholesale	121	105	101	101	103	133
United Kingdom						
International	113	102	104	100	104	122
Wholesale	117	110	103	102	104	142
Germany						
International	108	106	102	100	101	117
Wholesale	106	110	104	100	101	122
Japan						
International	NA	NA	92	86	104	NA
Wholesale	115	100	97	98	103	114
MACHINERY OTHER THAN ELECTRICAL (SITC 71)						
United States						
International	114	107	101	101	101	126
Wholesale	119	107	101	101	101	131
United Kingdom						
International	114	107	102	100	102	127
Wholesale	NA	NA	NA	NA	NA	NA
Germany						
International	109	111	103	101	101	127
Wholesale	110	114	105	101	102	137
ELECTRICAL MACHINERY, APPARATUS, AND APPLIANCES (SITC 72)						
United States						
International	106	96	96	97	101	95
Wholesale	110	100	97	98	100	105

(continued)

Table 8.2 (concluded)

Type of Price Data	$\frac{1957}{1953}$	$\frac{1961}{1957}$	$\frac{1962}{1961}$	$\frac{1963}{1962}$	$\frac{1964}{1963}$	$\frac{1964}{1953}$
ELECTRICAL MACHINERY, APPARATUS, AND APPLIANCES (continued)						
Germany						
International	102	104	98	99	99	103
Wholesale	NA	NA	101	99	100	NA
Japan						
International	NA	98	92	86	104	NA
Wholesale	105	100	97	97	99	97
TRANSPORT EQUIPMENT (SITC 73)						
United States						
International	106	102	104	99	100	113
Wholesale	112	105	100	100	99	116
United Kingdom						
International	106	107	101	102	104	121
Wholesale	NA	NA	NA	NA	NA	NA
Germany						
International	104	100	106	100	99	108
Wholesale	94	108	102	101	100	105

Note: The indexes from wholesale prices are aggregated using the same weighting, at the four-digit SITC level, as those based on international prices. Differences between the two indexes in this table therefore reflect differences in individual price movements but not in weighting. The index based on U.S. wholesale prices in Table 8.1 differs from this one solely in weighting.

tionship by taking each country (i.e., the United States, the United Kingdom, Germany, and Japan), for one SITC division [3] in one period as the unit of observation: [4]

	Number of Cases
Index from wholesale prices rises relatively	47
No relative change	12
Index from wholesale prices falls relatively	24

[3] The SITC divisions included are 67, 68, 69, 71, 72, 73.
[4] The source of the figures is Table 8.2.

This apparent bias in the wholesale price measures was evident in all the years through 1963, but the direction of the bias was then reversed. From 1963 to 1964 the indexes from wholesale prices fell relative to the international price indexes in more cases than they rose:

	Number of Cases				
	1953–57	1957–61	1961–62	1962–63	1963–64
Index from wholesale prices rises relatively	10	14	10	10	3
No relative change	0	1	1	4	6
Index from wholesale prices falls relatively	4	0	7	4	9

The wholesale price indexes seemed to perform better as international price measures during 1962 and 1963, when international price changes were small, than in 1953–57, when they were large. In general, the large discrepancies between wholesale and international price indexes, at this level of aggregation, were associated with periods of large price changes, as can be seen in the following cross tabulation of discrepancies against the size of international price changes:

Wholesale Price Index Minus International Price Index (percentage points)	Change in International Price Index				
		3 and 4%	2%	1 and 0%	Total
	≧5%				
≧5	17	6	0	4	27
3 and 4	6	3	2	1	12
2	2	2	4	5	13
0 and 1	3	6	2	20	31

Of 39 discrepancies of three percentage points or more, 32 took place during periods of international price changes of 3 per cent or more. Among the 31 discrepancies of zero or one percentage point, on the other hand, only 9 were during such periods, and 20 involved years of little or no international price change.

The relationship between wholesale and international price indexes seems to vary with the direction of change in international prices. When international prices increased substantially wholesale prices sometimes rose more and sometimes less. When there were large international price decreases, however, wholesale prices declined less, if at all. In other words, compared with the international prices collected for the present study, the prices used in the official wholesale price indexes tended to understate price increases about as often as they overstated them, but they almost always understated price decreases. This relationship between wholesale and international prices is similar to that found by Stigler and Kindahl between transactions prices and U.S. wholesale prices reported by the BLS.[5] The similarity of the two findings suggests that the differences occur because wholesale prices are mainly list (instead of transactions) prices rather than because they are domestic (instead of international) prices.

A comparison of Table 8.1 with Table 8.2 makes clear that, at least for the United States, the major discrepancies between domestically weighted wholesale price indexes and the corresponding international price indexes with international weights are not mainly the result of weighting differences but rather of differences in the price movements reported for individual commodities and in the samples of commodities. Taking the 1964/1953 price ratios, for example, we find that the three indexes compare as follows:

	Wholesale Price Indexes		
	Domestic Weights	*International Weights*	*International Price Indexes*
Total	122	122	115
Iron and steel	131	130	118
Nonferrous metals	113	120	113
Nonelectrical machinery	135	131	126
Electrical machinery	110	105	95

For iron and steel the internationally weighted wholesale price indexes are hardly closer to the international price indexes than the domestically weighted wholesale price indexes. For nonferrous metals they are even further away. In the machinery groups, weighting seems to be more important, but it still accounts for less than half of the difference between domestic and international price indexes.

The comparisons to this point have been based on consistent classification and on the best coverage available in each source of data. It is conceivable that the upward drift of wholesale prices relative to inter-

---

[5] George J. Stigler and James K. Kindahl, *The Behavior of Industrial Prices*, New York, NBER, 1970.

national prices, evident in Table 8.2, could be the result of differences in commodity coverage, even when the same weights are used for both indexes, because there are many gaps, particularly among the wholesale price data.

Most countries had fairly good coverage of iron and steel in their wholesale price indexes, the main exception being Germany, for which several important groups were completely unrepresented. In nonferrous metals the number of series was much lower, but all of the countries did include copper and aluminum in either wrought or unwrought forms or both. Only the United States and Japan had reasonably good coverage in metal manufactures not elsewhere specified. Two groups were omitted from the U.K. index and the number of series in the other groups was small. The German index was even weaker, including at its peak only seven series for this whole SITC division.

The worst coverage deficiencies appear in the wholesale price indexes for the machinery division. The U.S. data for nonelectrical machinery were by far the most complete, but they omitted such important trade items as aircraft engines and computers. We could not even compute an index for the United Kingdom because no detailed price series are published. Only an aggregate index for all engineering and allied industries and indexes for a few broad subgroups are available. The German index omits all internal combustion engines, office machinery, and most of the miscellaneous machinery groups of SITC 719. The Japanese index is somewhat better, although inferior in coverage to that of the United States.

For electrical machinery our British index could cover virtually none of the major items because of the aggregation mentioned above. The other countries' indexes contain important gaps but are not hopelessly thin. However, even the covered groups contain some serious deficiencies, as can be seen in Chapter 13, where several detailed comparisons are made between wholesale prices and international prices.

All the wholesale price indexes for transport equipment omit two principal export products, aircraft and ships, both of which were characterized by major technological developments. The German and Japanese indexes do not include locomotive prices, and all the automobile and truck prices are subject to problems of unmeasured quality changes (see Chapters 14 and 15).

Since the coverage deficiencies of the wholesale price indexes are concentrated in the machinery groups, probably being worst in those types of machinery that are most complex and those undergoing the most rapid technological change, we may expect them to be biased upward relative to the more comprehensive international price indexes regardless of the relationship for specific commodities.

The effects of coverage differences at the four-digit level and above are eliminated in Table 8.3. The ratios of wholesale to international price indexes, for all four-digit SITC subgroups for which both were available, were aggregated, using our OECD trade weights, to the two-digit and to the total levels. The relative upward trend of the wholesale price indexes remains strong for the United States, but not for Germany, in the total for all covered commodities. In the individual two-digit divisions for the United States, the United Kingdom, and Japan, the upward drift of the wholesale price series (stemming mainly from the first two periods) ranged between 4 and 26 per cent over the period as a whole.

The aggregated ratios of Table 8.3 are compared with ratios of wholesale to international price indexes derived from Table 8.2 for those indexes covering the whole time period, in the table below. For each country, column 1 shows the results with identical weighting (from Table 8.2); column 2, the results with identical weighting and coverage (from Table 8.3).

	United States		United Kingdom		Germany	
	(1)	(2)	(1)	(2)	(1)	(2)
Total covered commodities	106	107	not available		103	101
Iron and steel (SITC 67)	110	110	125	126	115	100
Nonferrous metals (SITC 68)	106	106	114	123	90	97
Metal manufactures (SITC 69)	111	112	116	116	104	105
Nonelectrical machinery (SITC 71)	104	104	not available		108	102
Electrical machinery (SITC 72)	111	109	not available		not available	
Transport equipment (SITC 73)	103	106	not available		97	94

For the United States, the two indexes are close; the largest difference is three percentage points. This similarity indicates that coverage

Table 8.3

Aggregation of Ratios of Wholesale to International Price Indexes, 1953, 1957, 1961–64

	$\dfrac{1957}{1953}$	$\dfrac{1961}{1957}$	$\dfrac{1962}{1961}$	$\dfrac{1963}{1962}$	$\dfrac{1964}{1963}$	$\dfrac{1964}{1953}$
TOTAL MACHINERY, TRANSPORT EQUIPMENT, METALS, AND METAL PRODUCTS						
United States	106	102	98	100	100	107
Germany	95	106	101	100	99	101
IRON AND STEEL (SITC 67)						
United States	107	102	101	100	100	110
United Kingdom	110	110	106	104	93	126
Germany	84	118	108	102	90	100
Japan	NA	NA	103	99	99	NA
NONFERROUS METALS (SITC 68)						
United States	107	104	99	99	98	106
United Kingdom	110	108	100	101	101	123
Germany	94	111	99	101	94	97
METAL MANUFACTURES, N.E.S. (SITC 69)						
United States	107	105	99	101	100	112
United Kingdom	105	108	99	103	100	116
Germany	99	104	102	101	100	105
Japan	NA	NA	108	115	100	NA
MACHINERY OTHER THAN ELECTRIC (SITC 71)						
United States	104	99	100	100	100	104
Germany	99	102	101	100	101	102
ELECTRICAL MACHINERY, APPARATUS, AND APPLIANCES (SITC 72)						
United States	105	105	100	100	99	109
Germany	NA	NA	103	101	101	NA
Japan	NA	102	104	102	94	NA
TRANSPORT EQUIPMENT (SITC 73)						
United States	111	101	94	101	100	106
Germany	93	103	97	100	101	94

differences at or above the four-digit level were not a major factor in the relative increase in wholesale prices. Since weighting differences have also been eliminated, there are only two possible explanations. One would be a rise in reported domestic prices compared to export prices for identical products. The other would be a systematically biased selection within four-digit groups, either of products declining relatively in price in our study, or of products rising relatively in price in the domestic indexes. Both are plausible, since export products are more likely to be those enjoying productivity gains while the domestic indexes, based on fixed specifications, may be biased toward older products.

The German data give quite different results. There are much larger differences between the two ratios, as we would expect in view of the poor coverage of the German wholesale price series. The difference is not consistent in direction, but what there is suggests that some of the relative increase in wholesale relative to international prices in the German case does arise from differences in coverage.

Price Competitiveness Indexes from International and Wholesale Price Data

Biases in price indexes based on wholesale price data would not be serious for our main purpose, the comparison of international price movements, if they were uniform among countries. There was some indication in the previous section that they were not, but that question can be examined more directly by comparing our measures of international price competitiveness with those derived from wholesale price data. These results (Table 8.4) are not completely consistent with Table 8.2 because the total price competitiveness indexes are aggregates of subgroup price competitiveness indexes rather than ratios of aggregate price indexes (see Chapter 4). However, the results are sufficiently similar to the previous ones that we need not comment in detail.

If ratios of price competitiveness of wholesale to international data for the four-digit subgroups are aggregated for subgroups for which both sets of data are available, the effects of differences in coverage can be separated from those of differences in price movements.

In the table below, we show, in column 1 for each country, ratios based on identical weighting (from Table 8.4) and, in column 2, ratios based on both identical weighting and identical coverage (from Table

Table 8.4

Comparison of Indexes of U.S. Price Competitiveness from International
and Wholesale Price Data, 1953, 1957, 1961—64

	$\dfrac{1957}{1953}$	$\dfrac{1961}{1957}$	$\dfrac{1962}{1961}$	$\dfrac{1963}{1962}$	$\dfrac{1964}{1963}$	$\dfrac{1964}{1953}$
TOTAL MACHINERY, TRANSPORT EQUIPMENT, METALS, AND METAL PRODUCTS						
Relative to Germany						
International	97	101	101	100	101	101
Wholesale	86	104	103	100	101	93
IRON AND STEEL (SITC 67)						
Relative to U.K.						
International	93	93	99	97	107	89
Wholesale	100	100	103	100	100	103
Relative to Germany						
International	98	93	98	97	107	93
Wholesale	83	107	101	100	98	87
Relative to Japan						
International	NA	NA	92	100	100	NA
Wholesale	96	96	92	100	100	85
NONFERROUS METALS (SITC 68)						
Relative to U.K.						
International	101	99	100	102	104	107
Wholesale	102	103	102	105	106	119
Relative to Germany						
International	101	95	100	99	108	103
Wholesale	89	100	99	101	103	91
METAL MANUFACTURES, N.E.S. (SITC 69)						
Relative to U.K.						
International	98	102	95	100	101	96
Wholesale	96	105	103	101	101	107
Relative to Germany						
International	96	105	100	99	99	100
Wholesale	89	103	102	98	98	90
Relative to Japan						
International	NA	NA	101	94	105	NA
Wholesale	96	96	97	97	101	87

(continued)

Table 8.4 (concluded)

	$\frac{1957}{1953}$	$\frac{1961}{1957}$	$\frac{1962}{1961}$	$\frac{1963}{1962}$	$\frac{1964}{1963}$	$\frac{1964}{1953}$
MACHINERY OTHER THAN ELECTRIC (SITC 71)						
Relative to Germany						
International	95	104	102	100	100	101
Wholesale	89	105	104	100	101	98
ELECTRICAL MACHINERY, APPARATUS, AND APPLIANCES (SITC 72)						
Relative to Germany						
International	96	107	103	102	98	108
Wholesale	NA	NA	104	100	100	NA
Relative to Japan						
International	NA	88	98	100	101	NA
Wholesale	88	90	98	98	98	75
TRANSPORT EQUIPMENT (SITC 73)						
Relative to Germany						
International	99	98	100	102	99	99
Wholesale	81	102	104	100	101	87

Note: These indexes were calculated by aggregating all the available four-digit subgroup indexes of each type in each two-digit division. The indexes from international price data do not necessarily include only those subgroups covered also by wholesale price data.

8.5). Comparing the ratios, we conclude that coverage deficiencies were rarely responsible for the difference between international price and wholesale price measures of competitiveness.

	United States Relative to			
	United Kingdom		*Germany*	
	(1)	*(2)*	*(1)*	*(2)*
Total covered commodities	not available		92	94
Iron and steel (SITC 67)	116	121	94	96
Nonferrous metals (SITC 68)	111	114	88	92
Metal manufactures (SITC 69)	111	118	90	94
Nonelectrical machinery (SITC 71)	not available		97	97
Electrical machinery (SITC 72)	not available		not available	
Transport equipment (SITC 73)	not available		88	87

Table 8.5

U.S. Price Competitiveness: Aggregation of Ratios of Wholesale-price-based
to International-price-based Indexes, 1953, 1957, 1961–64

	$\frac{1957}{1953}$	$\frac{1961}{1957}$	$\frac{1962}{1961}$	$\frac{1963}{1962}$	$\frac{1964}{1963}$	$\frac{1964}{1953}$
TOTAL MACHINERY, TRANSPORT EQUIPMENT, METALS, AND METAL PRODUCTS						
Relative to Germany	88	105	103	99	100	94
IRON AND STEEL (SITC 67)						
Relative to						
U.K.	108	109	104	106	93	121
Germany	82	118	108	101	92	96
Japan	NA	NA	101	98	99	NA
NONFERROUS METALS (SITC 68)						
Relative to						
U.K.	102	103	102	103	103	114
Germany	88	106	101	102	96	92
METAL MANUFACTURES, N.E.S. (SITC 69)						
Relative to						
U.K.	100	102	115	101	99	118
Germany	89	103	103	99	101	94
Japan	NA	NA	99	105	99	NA
MACHINERY OTHER THAN ELECTRIC (SITC 71)						
Relative to Germany	94	101	101	99	101	97
ELECTRICAL MACHINERY, APPARATUS, AND APPLIANCES (SITC 72)						
Relative to						
Germany	NA	NA	102	98	99	NA
Japan	NA	102	104	99	97	99
TRANSPORT EQUIPMENT (SITC 73)						
Relative to Germany	81	103	104	98	102	87

Note: These are aggregates of ratios, calculated at the four-digit level, of wholesale price competitiveness to international price competitiveness indexes. They therefore include only those subgroups for which both types of data are available.

In several cases the discrepancies were larger when coverage differences were removed, and in no case was as much as half of the apparent error in the measurement of price competitiveness from wholesale prices due to coverage differences.

Price Indexes from International Prices and Export Unit Values

Most of the price indexes now used as measures of international price competitiveness are based on what are called unit value data, and the indexes themselves are frequently referred to as unit value rather than price indexes.[6] For most countries we cannot explain differences between these indexes and ours because we do not know what portion of any discrepancy should be attributed to differences in index number formulas, in choice of base years, in the sample of commodities, or in weighting. For the United States, however, we were able to go back to the original commodity observations and combine them by our own weighting system and methods of aggregation; we can thus make a useful comparison with the NBER indexes. The U.S. unit value indexes presented here, it should be clear, are not those constructed and published by the Department of Commerce. The component series we used do enter into the Commerce indexes, but we combined them using weights similar to those employed for the NBER indexes in order to facilitate comparisons with the latter.

For the total of all the commodity groups covered in our study, the export unit value index showed a substantially greater rise in U.S. prices than the NBER index: 22 per cent instead of 15 per cent (Table 8.6), mainly because the underlying unit value index rose much more than the international price index from 1953 to 1957 and from 1957 to 1961.

The two series for iron and steel show a similar relationship, with the unit value index rising 31 per cent from 1953 to 1961 while the international price index increased by only 20 per cent. In nonferrous metals the unit value index was no higher in 1964 than in 1962, despite the widely publicized price increases in 1964. These did appear to affect the international price index.

---

[6] See Chapter 1 for a brief discussion of the deficiencies of unit value indexes as measures of international prices and price competitiveness.

Table 8.6

Comparison of U.S. Price Indexes from International Price and Export
Unit Value Data, 1953, 1957, 1961–64

Index Basis	1957 / 1953	1961 / 1957	1962 / 1961	1963 / 1962	1964 / 1963	1964 / 1953
TOTAL MACHINERY, TRANSPORT EQUIPMENT, METALS, AND METAL PRODUCTS						
International prices	110	103	101	100	102	115
Export unit values	116	106	100	100	99	122
IRON AND STEEL (SITC 67)						
International prices	120	100	98	99	101	118
Export unit values	126	104	101	99	101	133
NONFERROUS METALS (SITC 68)						
International prices	104	101	99	100	108	113
Export unit values	122	90	101	98	102	111
METAL MANUFACTURES, N.E.S. (SITC 69)						
International prices	114	100	102	100	103	120
Export unit values	116	104	98	103	105	129
MACHINERY OTHER THAN ELECTRIC (SITC 71)						
International prices	114	107	101	101	101	126
Export unit values	116	112	100	104	104	141
ELECTRICAL MACHINERY, APPARATUS, AND APPLIANCES (SITC 72)						
International prices	106	96	96	97	101	95
Export unit values	104	102	99	104	96	104
TRANSPORT EQUIPMENT (SITC 73)						
International prices	106	102	104	99	100	113
Export unit values	115	107	97	94	94	105

Note: These indexes were calculated by aggregating all the available four-digit
subgroup indexes of each type in each two-digit division. The indexes from international
price data do not necessarily include only those subgroups covered also by unit value
data.

Source: International prices: unlinked indexes underlying Appendix C; export unit
values: unlinked indexes underlying Appendix G.

In both machinery groups and in metal manufactures, n.e.s., unit value series showed a strong upward bias relative to the international price indexes. For electrical machinery the result was a rise in prices over the period as a whole instead of the decline shown by the international price series.

The unit value index for transport equipment showed wide year-to-year differences from the international price index but no consistent bias. However, the coverage is so poor that it could be said that this group was not really included in the official unit value index during these years.

During the first two periods unit value increases were typically greater than international price increases at this two-digit level. The export unit values rose relatively in 10 out of 12 cases. After that relative increases did not predominate. Throughout the whole period, however, the unit values fluctuated more widely. The change in the unit value indexes was greater than that in the international price indexes in 18 cases, equal in 2, and smaller in 10.

The results from aggregating ratios of unit value to international price indexes for the United States are given in Table 8.7. The aggregation of these ratios eliminates the effects of lack of comparability in coverage by comparing only those subgroups for which we have both unit value and international price data. There are still large discrepancies, compared with international prices for the aggregate in the 1957/1953 and 1961/1957 ratios. In several instances there were greater departures

Table 8.7

Aggregation of Ratios of Unit Value to International Price Indexes, United States, 1953, 1957, 1961–64

	$\dfrac{1957}{1953}$	$\dfrac{1961}{1957}$	$\dfrac{1962}{1961}$	$\dfrac{1963}{1962}$	$\dfrac{1964}{1963}$	$\dfrac{1964}{1953}$
All covered commodities	108	107	99	101	98	113
Iron and steel (SITC 67)	106	104	103	100	100	112
Nonferrous metals (SITC 68)	119	90	102	99	96	104
Metal manufactures, n.e.s., (SITC 69)	104	108	95	102	102	111
Nonelectrical machinery (SITC 71)	106	107	100	103	102	120
Electrical machinery (SITC 72)	100	121	105	108	98	134
Transport equipment (SITC 73)	114	103	90	94	95	94

from international prices than in the comparisons of Table 8.6, which were not corrected for coverage differences. They also show larger divergences from international prices than did the wholesale price data; in the two-digit divisions their deviations from the international indexes were larger than those of the wholesale price indexes in 24 out of 30 cases (compare Tables 8.7 and 8.3). The unit values were erratically related to international prices, rising much faster in 1953–57, declining sharply in some cases in later years, and rising rapidly at other times relative to the international prices.

Since the export unit value index is the closest the United States comes to an official international price index it is worth commenting on the coverage in these commodity groups. The iron and steel division boasts the best coverage. Although several items are missing, including wire rods, the main groups are represented and the number of series is sub-stantial—thirty-five in the best year. In nonferrous metals the unit value data are confined to copper and aluminum. All the other metals are unrepresented. The manufactures of metal, n.e.s. (SITC 69) are repre-sented by no more than five unit value series, even though the division is heterogeneous, and before 1961 only two of the eight groups are cov-ered at all for the whole eight years.

The lack of data is even more serious in nonelectrical machinery because this division is so important in U.S. and in world trade. Only agricultural equipment can be claimed to be at all well covered, and that coverage is confined to two subgroups. There are no data on such important products as aircraft engines, computers, machine tools and other metalworking machinery, textile machinery other than sewing machines, or most special industry machinery. Even the few series that are included show many instances of erratic changes in unit values that are unlikely to represent price changes, as is pointed out in several of the chapters in Part Four.

Electrical equipment is almost equally ill-covered and includes a similar number of unit value changes that are unbelievable as price movements. Coverage of transport equipment is confined to road motor vehicles, excluding all railway equipment, aircraft, and ships.

On the face of it, then, the U.S. export unit value data for at least the machinery portion of the index are so inadequate that one could not expect them to provide a good representation of international price movements even if the individual series were highly accurate. In addition, many of the individual series that are used are poor approximations of prices even for the specific products they are supposed to represent.

The only comprehensive unit value index that has been available in the past for this range of commodities is the one published by the United Nations for machinery as a whole (SITC 7). This index, for exports of all developed countries, is compared with a combination of our indexes for the United States, the United Kingdom, the EEC countries, and Japan in Table 8.8.

The relation between the two series is similar to that between the NBER and reweighted U.S. export unit value indexes. In particular, the unit value series seems to have a strong upward bias relative to the international price series over the period as a whole, and the bias in the UN series, an increase of 24 per cent as compared with 13 per cent in the NBER series, is similar to that we found above for the U.S. export unit values for all commodities covered. The major discrepancy between the two series was in the second period. The two indexes remained close together in the next three years of comparatively stable prices, as they had been in the first period when prices rose rapidly.

There are a number of possible explanations for divergence between these two series, aside from deficiencies in the basic unit value data, which have been discussed earlier. The country coverage of the UN series is

Table 8.8
Machinery: NBER International Price Indexes vs. UN Export
Unit Value Indexes, 1953, 1957, 1961–64
(each year on earlier year as 100)

	NBER[a]	UN[b]
1957/1953	108	109
1961/1957	103	109
1962/1961	101	102
1963/1962	100	101
1964/1963	101	101

[a]Indexes for the United States, the United Kingdom, the EEC countries, and Japan combined, using each country's exports of machinery in 1963 as weights.

[b]Source: *Monthly Bulletin of Statistics,* United Nations, November 1965, p. xxv. Developed area exports to developed and underdeveloped areas. Developed area comprises the United States, Canada, western Europe, Australia, New Zealand, South Africa, and Japan.

slightly broader, including western European countries other than the United Kingdom and members of the EEC, Australia, New Zealand, and South Africa. However, the weight of the countries covered in the NBER index is so large that this factor could not account for the divergent movement of the two indexes.

Another difference is that the NBER international price index is a Laspeyres index on a 1963 base while the UN index consists of Paasche indexes on a 1953 base through 1956 and a 1959 base, 1956 through 1964, linked at 1956. On this account we might expect the UN index to rise more rapidly than the NBER index, if we can assume a shift in the value of trade toward those commodities with relatively falling prices. The NBER index should weight these more heavily in the early years because the weights of the NBER index are based on a later year's trade.

This difference in index number formula appears unlikely to account for all or most of the apparent upward bias in the unit value index. The U.S. machinery unit value indexes, which must account for a large share of the weight of the UN index, show very similar biases even when put into the same weighting and index number formulation as the NBER international price indexes (Tables 8.6 and 8.7). This fact suggests strongly that the bias in the UN export unit value index, like that in the U.S. export unit value index, is attributable to deficiencies in the basic data or in coverage. Whichever is the reason, the unit value indexes appear to be seriously biased as measures of international prices of machinery and metals.[7]

Quantity-Price Relations Derived from Wholesale Price Indexes

Of the two generally available types of price series, wholesale prices offer a more promising basis than unit values for analyzing changes in international price competitiveness in the absence of indexes of international prices such as we constructed for 1953–64. Their behavior is less erratic, and for the period we studied they came closer to the results of the international price indexes.

However, wholesale prices intended for these purposes should not be

---

[7] Unless there are offsetting errors in the other commodity components, the UN unit value series overstate the deterioration in the terms of trade of developing countries, a deterioration for which these series have often provided the main documentation.

taken ready-made from the official or other standard source without any attention to country-to-country differences in commodity coverage and weighting. In the absence of international price data, the concordance of the wholesale price series of the countries being compared should, at the very minimum, be improved by reweighting and by adding or eliminating commodities so that coverage will be more nearly similar. Adjustments of this kind, which we made in using the wholesale price indexes discussed above (see also Appendix F), do not require new data collection as do international price indexes, and they should be feasible for any serious analyst of quantity-price relations in international trade. Even so, adjusted wholesale price indexes are still apt to be deficient because of inadequate coverage and, more basically, because they refer to domestic rather than international prices.

In view of these considerations, we compare the quantity-price relationships derived from our international price indexes with those derived from our adjusted wholesale price indexes. We begin our comparisons with two-digit categories for which we had both the index based on wholesale prices and the one based on NBER international price data.[8]

The first pair of equations shows the comparisons when data for U.K.-U.S., German-U.S. and Japanese-U.S. ratios are pooled (51 observations), and the second pair when only U.K.-U.S. and German-U.S. ratios are pooled (41 observations):

$$(Q_{F/S} - 1)_W = -.17 + 0.15T - 6.45(P_{F/S} - 1)_W \quad \bar{R}^2 = .45 \quad (1)$$
$$(3.34) \quad (3.92)$$

$$(Q_{F/S} - 1)_N = -.14 + 0.15T - 6.85(P_{F/S} - 1)_N \quad \bar{R}^2 = .43 \quad (2)$$
$$(3.03) \quad (3.38)$$

$$(Q_{KG/S} - 1)_W = -.21 + 0.15T - 4.83(P_{KG/S} - 1)_W \quad \bar{R}^2 = .45 \quad (3)$$
$$(3.32) \quad (2.92)$$

$$(Q_{KG/S} - 1)_N = -.25 + 0.17T - 3.51(P_{KG/S} - 1)_N \quad \bar{R}^2 = .40 \quad (4)$$
$$(3.47) \quad (1.54)$$

where the subscripts W and N stand for wholesale and NBER international prices, respectively, and where the other symbols have the same meanings as in Chapter 6.

There is little basis in these equations for preferring one source of

---

[8] Equations based on international prices in this chapter differ from those in Chapter 6 because the latter include some groups for which there are no matching wholesale data.

price data over the other. However, our earlier results (described in Chapter 6) indicate that we are not warranted in assuming, as we do in pooling the data in these equations, that the relationships are the same for all countries. When we compare the relationships derived from wholesale and international prices separately for each foreign-U.S. comparison, a different picture emerges. The following comparisons are based on 14 observations for the U.K./U.S., 27 for Germany/U.S., and 10 for Japan/U.S.

$$(Q_{K/S} - 1)_W = -.14 + 0.04T - 1.62(P_{K/S} - 1)_W \qquad \bar{R}^2 = .07$$
$$\qquad\qquad (1.39) \quad (.58) \qquad\qquad\qquad (5)$$

$$(Q_{K/S} - 1)_N = -.06 - .001T - 5.25(P_{K/S} - 1)_N \qquad \bar{R}^2 = .59$$
$$\qquad\qquad (.04) \quad (3.55) \qquad\qquad\qquad (6)$$

$$(Q_{G/S} - 1)_W = -.41 + 0.29T - 2.34(P_{G/S} - 1)_W \qquad \bar{R}^2 = .56$$
$$\qquad\qquad (4.06) \quad (1.09) \qquad\qquad\qquad (7)$$

$$(Q_{G/S} - 1)_N = -.36 + 0.26T - 4.27(P_{G/S} - 1)_N \qquad \bar{R}^2 = .57$$
$$\qquad\qquad (4.53) \quad (1.45) \qquad\qquad\qquad (8)$$

$$(Q_{J/S} - 1)_W = -.80 + 0.85T - 4.98(P_{J/S} - 1)_W \qquad \bar{R}^2 = .99$$
$$\qquad\qquad (15.74) \quad (3.24) \qquad\qquad\qquad (9)$$

$$(Q_{J/S} - 1)_N = -.77 + 0.89T - 3.24(P_{J/S} - 1)_N \qquad \bar{R}^2 = .99$$
$$\qquad\qquad (15.88) \quad (3.12) \qquad\qquad\qquad (10)$$

In the case of the United Kingdom, the equation based on international price data is clearly superior to that from wholesale price data. The elasticity coefficient and $\bar{R}^2$ are higher, and the coefficient is statistically significant whereas it is not significant in the wholesale price equation and $\bar{R}^2$ is low. With respect to the other two countries, the coefficients themselves give us little guidance for choice.

At the three- and four-digit level the elasticities based on overlapping observations (29 for the U.K./U.S., 57 for Germany/U.S., and 22 for Japan/U.S.) have negative signs whether wholesale or international prices are used. However, the elasticities derived from wholesale price data are small and not statistically significant while those derived from international price data are in the -1 to -2 range and are statistically significant for the United Kingdom and Japan. The comparisons, which are based on pooled data for 1962/1961, 1963/1962 and 1964/1963, are shown below.

Ratio	Constant	Elasticity	$\bar{r}^2$
U.K.-U.S.			
Wholesale prices	−0.05	−0.49	0
		(0.58)	
International prices	−0.02	−2.15	.27
		(3.37)	
Germany-U.S.			
Wholesale prices	−0.001	−0.95	0
		(0.97)	
International prices	0.001	−1.15	.02
		(1.61)	
Japan-U.S.			
Wholesale prices	0.11	−1.39	.02
		(1.24)	
International prices	0.12	2.21	.19
		(2.41)	

Thus in those cases where the levels of the coefficients and their *t*-values provide some basis for choosing between the two sources of price data, they seem to support the use of international rather than wholesale prices. This reason for our preference is in addition to those set forth in the earlier parts of this chapter, and is buttressed by the implausible behavior of some of the price series themselves, as described in the various product chapters of Part Four.

Summary

We found that neither existing wholesale price indexes nor indexes of export unit values can be relied upon to describe accurately changes in the international prices of the main industrial countries.

The difficulties in the wholesale price index arise because its coverage of machinery classifications is inadequate from the standpoint of international trade and because it uses methods that do not lend themselves to making allowances for quality change. More adequate measures of domestic price change and adjustments to allow for the importance of goods in international trade would help, but the fact remains that to varying degrees from country to country and from time to time, the domestic and international prices of commodities have diverged, and not entirely because of failures to measure domestic prices adequately.

During the years covered by our study the wholesale price indexes tended to overstate the increase in international prices not only for all the covered commodities as a whole but quite often for the major subgroups as well. The wholesale price indexes tended to miss the shading of prices during periods of price decline and to fail to catch price increases adequately when demand conditions improved. The discrepancies between the changes shown by the wholesale price indexes and those shown by the international price indexes were small during periods of little price change but became large, frequently five points or more, when there were larger changes in international prices.

In view of the deficiencies of conventional wholesale price indexes as measures of international price movements, it is to be expected that they will sometimes give misleading indications of relative price changes for pairs of countries. In general, wholesale price data for 1953–64 provide an unduly unfavorable view of the changes in the price competitiveness of the United States with respect to Germany. Between 1953 and 1957, for example, wholesale prices point to a 14 per cent decline in U.S. price competitiveness, but the international price indexes show only a 2 or 3 per cent decline. Although during the rest of the period the two indexes moved similarly at the aggregative level there were a number of major divergences, notably in iron and steel and in nonferrous metals.

We were able to examine only two unit value indexes, but the results indicate that they are even less reliable as measures of international price competitiveness for metals and machinery than wholesale prices.

An index of export unit values constructed from series used in the official U.S. index deviates from our U.S. international price index to a greater degree than did our reconstructed U.S. wholesale price series. The unit value indexes show larger and more erratic time-to-time changes and tend to have more upward bias than the wholesale price series. For electrical machinery, the unit value series rose 4 per cent during 1953–64, while the international price index fell 5 per cent. In iron and steel and nonelectrical machinery the index from unit values exaggerates the price increase by about fifteen percentage points, almost doubling the rise shown by our international price indexes in the first of these divisions. The better agreement in the nonferrous metals division over the whole period is probably a fortuitous result of large offsetting discrepancies in the shorter periods. These unit value figures are our calculations from series used in the official index by the Department of Commerce, which does not publish indexes at this level of disaggregation. The deficiencies, which apparently stem from inadequate coverage and the erratic behavior of included series, are to some extent inevitable in unit value series, particularly those that aim to cover complex commodities.

The other unit value index we compared with our international price indexes is a UN index for machinery as a whole (SITC 7). Between 1953 and 1964 this index shows a 24 per cent increase. The increase in the NBER international price series was 13 per cent.

In the absence of true indexes of international prices such as those constructed in this study for 1953–64, wholesale price indexes, adjusted for differences in classification, weights, and coverage, provide a better second-best measure of relative price changes for the analysis of international trade than unit value indexes even though they, too, have ineradicable defects.

PART FOUR

PRODUCT REPORTS

9

IRON AND STEEL

Trade

The iron and steel division is one of two mainly semimanufactured product groups included in the study, the other being nonferrous metals (Chapter 10). It thus covers items at an earlier stage of processing, and includes a much higher proportion of standardized products than most other groups. Some of the results and subjects discussed here reflect this characteristic of iron and steel.

Germany was the leading exporter of iron and steel in 1963, followed by Belgium-Luxembourg, France, and Japan. The United Kingdom and the United States were the fifth- and sixth-ranking exporters (Table 9.1) instead of being two of the first three, as was the case in most commodity divisions. More than two-thirds of EEC exports went to OECD Europe (almost 50 per cent to other EEC countries); the proportion was much smaller for the three main non-EEC exporters. In markets outside Europe, on the other hand, the EEC countries were far less important. Japan was the leader by a wide margin, and both the United States and the United Kingdom sold more than Germany.

The bulk of exports—about 75 per cent—is accounted for by three of the nine iron and steel groups. These are bars, rods, angles, shapes, and sections (SITC 673); universals, plates, and sheets (SITC 674); and tubes, pipes, and fittings (SITC 678).

An unusual aspect of this commodity division, as contrasted with most machinery, was that a good deal of the competition for markets involved the U.S. market. U.S. imports of iron and steel were consider-

Note: SITC 67. *Value of OECD exports in 1963:* $5.7 billions; 13 per cent of study total. *Coverage:* Pig iron and ferro-alloys; ingots, bars, rods, plates, sheets, hoops, strips, and other semimanufactures; wire, rails, tubes, pipes, and fittings.

Table 9.1
OECD Exports of Iron and Steel (SITC 67), by Origin, Destination, and Commodity Group, 1963
(dollars in millions)

	Value of Exports	Per Cent of OECD Exports in 67	Share in OECD Exports (per cent)			EEC				
			OECD	U.S.	U.K.	Total	Germany	France	Belgium-Luxembourg	Japan
Total, all destinations and groups	$5,693	100.0	100.0[a]	9.0	10.1	55.6	20.1	13.3	15.5	12.3
Destination										
U.S.	631	11.1	100.0		8.2	36.8	10.6	7.6	17.9	33.8
OECD Europe	2,910	51.1	100.0	3.0	7.1	73.6	28.2	16.5	21.3	2.1
U.K.	148	2.6	100.0	5.4		45.9	6.1	9.5	10.8	1.4
EEC total	1,941	34.1	100.0	2.7	4.5	78.3	28.7	17.7	25.2	2.4
Germany	586	10.3	100.0	2.6	3.6	72.5		31.4	31.4	0.2
France	464	8.2	100.0	1.5	2.8	90.9	52.2		33.6	
Belgium-Luxembourg	148	2.6	100.0	6.8	7.4	75.7	32.4	25.7		0.1
Canada	188	3.3	100.0	60.6	13.3	16.0	6.9	2.7	6.4	7.4
Japan	14	0.2	100.0	28.6	7.1	42.9	35.7	0.7	c	
Latin America	364	6.4	100.0	25.5	8.2	39.3	11.5	7.7	8.0	17.0
Other	1,586	27.9	100.0	13.6	16.3	38.7	12.5	12.3	6.9	22.1

SITC commodity group										
Pig iron, ferro alloys, etc. (671)	251	4.4	100.0[a]	3.6	4.0	43.4[b]	21.1	16.7	c	2.8
Ingots and other primary forms (672)	415	7.3	100.0	6.0	1.2	64.3	30.1	c	14.7	6.5
Bars, rods, angles, shapes, and sections (673)	1,299	22.8	100.0	4.2	7.4	67.1	23.1	14.3	27.4	11.9
Universals, plates, and sheets (674)	2,057	36.1	100.0	10.5	13.2	50.8	13.9	15.2	13.8	15.5
Hoop and strip (675)	291	5.1	100.0	10.0	10.7	60.8	22.7	11.0	23.4	4.5
Rails and railway track construction materials (676)	111	1.9	100.0[d]	15.3	9.9	45.0	18.9	13.5	10.8	7.2
Wire, excluding wire rod (677)	233	4.1	100.0	6.4	12.0	51.1	18.5	c	22.7	18.5
Tubes, pipes, and fittings (678)	968	17.0	100.0	13.3	11.9	52.0	25.2	12.0	c	13.6
Castings and forgings (679)	61	1.1	100.0[e]	31.9	8.3	27.9	12.7	c	10.4	

Source: Appendix A.
[a] Including Norway, 20.3 per cent; and Canada, 10.8 per cent.
[b] Excluding Netherlands exports of SITC 671.2.
[c] Not shown separately; less than 10 per cent.
[d] Including Canada, 14.4 per cent.
[e] Including Canada, 23.8 per cent.

ably greater than exports, particularly in the first three groups and in iron and steel wire. The main U.S. trade deficits were in bars, rods, etc. (SITC 673), which contained two products, wire rod and reinforcing bars, in which foreign inroads into the U.S. market were important.

Despite the amount of controversy engendered by steel imports the ratios of the value of imports to U.S. new supply (output plus imports) were still, at the end of our period, 5 per cent or less for all but one of the five-digit Standard Industrial Classification (SIC) codes included in this division, the sole exception being steel wire, at 10 per cent. The ratio for the main aggregate—blast furnace, steel mill, electrometallurgical products—was 4 per cent.[1]

These ratios are much lower than many quoted elsewhere, for two reasons. One is that the categories are fairly broad, and therefore do not distinguish individual items such as wire rod and reinforcing bars, which were meeting severe foreign competition. The second reason is that the ratios are frequently given in terms of tonnage rather than value. The imports are usually items that are less fabricated or of lower quality than most of the domestic products in the same group, and the tonnage data therefore tend to exaggerate the importance of imports. Some of the tonnage ratios for specific products in this division in 1964 are shown below: [2]

Ingots, blooms, billets, slabs, etc.	13.8%
Wire rods	45.1
Structural shapes	10.4
Plates	5.3
Reinforcing bars	11.5
Other bars and tool steel	7.2
Pipes and tubing	9.1
Drawn wire	13.5
Sheets and strip	3.4

While the tonnage data presumably exaggerate the impact of imports, the value data probably understate it, because the prices are lower for imports than for the competing American products.

[1] *U.S. Commodity Exports and Imports as Related to Output, 1965 and 1964*, U.S. Bureau of the Census, 1967. Data are given in this publication for all the four- and five-digit product codes of the Standard Industrial Classification that could be matched with export and import trade categories.

[2] *Foreign Trade Trends: Iron and Steel, 1967*, American Iron and Steel Institute, 1967, p. 67.

The severe competition encountered by U.S. producers in the U.S. market had its counterpart in Europe. European producers suffered inroads by imports into their domestic markets, and the degree of competition appeared to increase during the period covered by this study. The OECD observed a change in the international market for iron and steel during the early 1960s which it described as ". . . the increasing interpenetration of the industrialized countries' markets." To some extent this may have been a response to low demand levels in home markets even at low prices. However, the OECD report pointed out that the trend continued even in 1964 when most member countries' home markets were expanding.[3] This increasing trade may, therefore, represent a trend, rather than a cyclical phenomenon.

The outstanding change in export shares during the period of our study (Table 9.2) was the decline of the U.S. share from 22 per cent to 9 per cent between 1957 and the early 1960s. Although it recovered somewhat after 1962 it did not rise above 10 per cent. The main beneficiaries of the U.S. decline were at first the Common Market countries, whose share rose by over ten percentage points between 1957 and 1961 but then receded to the earlier level. Within the EEC, Germany replaced France as the main exporter. After 1961 the main development was the growth of Japanese exports. The Japanese growth began before 1961, although at a slower rate.

Nonprice Factors in Trade

Price competition, on which our measurement is focused, was only one of the influences determining the flow of iron and steel trade. Some large changes in trade were the result of strikes, government actions on tariffs and other restrictions, and various other factors which our price indexes do not encompass.

In the case of several strikes, for example, foreign sellers were able to win part of the domestic market of the country in which the strike had taken place and also some of that country's usual export markets. Illustrations are provided by the strikes in the United States in 1959 and in the United Kingdom in 1963–64.[4]

---

[3] *The Iron and Steel Industry in 1964 and Trends in 1965,* OECD, 1965, p. 29.

[4] The British strike was said to have resulted in large imports of steel coil from the United States, and even the prospect of the U.S. strikes in 1959 and 1965 stimulated

Table 9.2
OECD Exports of Iron and Steel, 1953, 1957, 1961–64
(dollars in millions)

| | Value of OECD Exports | Share in OECD Exports (per cent) | | | EEC | | | | |
		OECD	U.S.	U.K.	Total	Germany	France	Belgium-Luxembourg	Japan
				INCLUDING SWITZERLAND AND SPAIN					
1964	$6,680	100.0	10.0	9.1	54.2	18.5	13.3	15.5	13.6
1963	5,693	100.0	9.0	10.1	55.6	20.1	13.3	15.5	12.3
1962	5,471	100.0	8.6	10.3	59.0	22.8	14.0	16.2	9.7
1961	5,148	100.0	9.4	11.5	65.3	25.0	17.2	16.6	7.4
				EXCLUDING SWITZERLAND AND SPAIN					
1961	5,097	100.0	9.5	11.7	65.9	25.3	17.3	16.7	7.5
1957	4,955	100.0	22.4	12.1	55.0	19.0	14.3	16.6	4.2
1953	2,577	100.0	20.0	14.7	54.4	13.0	18.5	19.3	5.4

Source: Appendix B.

Another influence on the flow of trade was the existence of capacity limitations for specific products in some of the countries outside of the United States. Some types of steel plates and sheets (SITC 674) were in short supply in the earlier years of our period, and exports of British firms were held down by an informal limit on sheet exports until 1961. Over part of the period British capacity was inadequate for the demand, and there were, in addition, some quality advantages in foreign steel, but both of these reasons for U.K. imports diminished in importance by the end of the period.[5] The issue of capacity arises in the case of steel pipe (SITC 678) because demand for pipe sometimes comes in large lumps, and few countries find it economical to have enough capacity on hand for these peak demands.

More broadly, however, the growth of capacity, protected by tariffs and quotas, in countries that were formerly net importers slowed the growth of trade in iron and steel. This was reflected in a reduction in the proportion of iron and steel trade which the United Nations has described as "deficit covering" from almost 80 per cent in 1950 to only 54 per cent in 1964.[6]

Aside from these commercial considerations, trade in iron and steel has been influenced by a variety of governmental policies and interventions. For example, exports of pipes, tubes, etc. (SITC 678) have been affected by political and military considerations. A Russian order for large-diameter pipe was turned down by Germany in 1963 under pressure from NATO, on the ground that they were strategic material. The NATO restrictions were helpful to non-NATO countries in the competition for such orders. In a number of instances, large amounts

inventory accumulation and brought into the market for foreign steel American firms which had usually confined their buying to domestic sources. "United Kingdom: SCW Buys U.S. Coil," *Metal Bulletin*, January 28, 1964; "Steel Strike in Britain Leads 2 Auto Makers to Order Foreign Steel," *Wall Street Journal*, January 2, 1964; "Scramble for Steel: More Metal Users Turn to Warehouses, Imports to Build Strike Hedge," *ibid.*, Febuary 5, 1965; *The Iron and Steel Industry in Europe, 1958–1959*, OEEC, 1960, pp. 81–83; "U.S. Steel Strike: A Long and Bitter Struggle Expected," *Metal Bulletin*, July 21, 1959.

[5] "A Hollow Warning? The Complexities of Supply and Demand in Steel Sheets," *Metal Bulletin*, October 12, 1964; "Wanted—A Fourth Wide Strip Mill," *ibid.*, March 8, 1955; "Sir Julian Talks Horsesense," *ibid.*, March 27, 1962; *Imported Manufactures: An Inquiry into Competitiveness*, U.K. National Economic Development Council, London, 1965; "Steel Imports: Non-issues," *Economist*, August 13, 1966.

[6] *World Trade in Steel and Steel Demand in Developing Countries*, United Nations, Economic Commission for Europe, 1968, pp. 13, 47–49, 121–122. "Deficit-covering trade" is equal to the net imports of those countries that are net importers and is contrasted with "exchange trade," the rest of trade which represents mainly trade among the iron and steel exporters.

of steel pipe were sold in barter for other commodities, directly or under general understandings about reciprocal orders. In some of these trades political or balance-of-payments motivations were primary, and price, or at least nominal price, was a secondary consideration.[7]

Another governmental influence on the direction of the international steel trade was the formation of the European Coal and Steel Community (ECSC) under which a common market in steel began operations in 1953. Effects of the common market in the form of increased price competition would be captured by our indexes, but the changes in delivered prices that resulted from tariff reductions would be missing, because we used only f.a.s. or f.o.b. prices. In addition, other aspects of the common market, such as the reduction of nonprice barriers to trade, would influence the flow of trade even if they were not reflected in price changes.

At times the major steel producers have attempted through agreements among the sellers to curb the price cutting which was eroding their domestic price structures. One report stated that "a gentlemen's agreement between Germany and Japan prohibits the export of products freely available in the respective home markets." Similar agreements between the ECSC and U.K. mills were reported ". . . whereby each side undertakes not to undercut the other's home prices . . ." on steel pipe. One of the most specific reports described a purported agreement on small-diameter steel tubes in which European and Japanese firms divided up the North American market, the former taking the area roughly as far inland as Chicago and New Orleans and the latter taking the western half of the country. The cartel was to regulate prices and sales quotas.[8]

Part of the competition in the steel producers' own markets involved purchases of foreign steel by nonintegrated processors, who used imports to escape the price structure imposed by integrated producers. The processors alleged that they were being squeezed by artificially low margins between semimanufactured and finished product prices maintained by domestic integrated producers. An example of the conflict

---

[7] "Israel Orders Steel from West Germans," *New York Times,* December 23, 1967; "Austria Agreeable on Soviet Pipeline," *ibid.,* March 3, 1967; "Russian-Italian Talks on National Gas Pipeline Reach 'Advanced Stage,' " *Wall Street Journal,* October 25, 1966; "Tubes: Reactions to NATO Pressure," *Metal Bulletin,* January 8, 1963; "NATO Lifts Embargo on Oil Pipe to Reds," *Wall Street Journal,* November 11, 1966.

[8] "Japan-Europe Tube Cartel," *Metal Bulletin,* April 19, 1963; "ECSC-UK Rebar Agreement?" *ibid.,* July 5, 1963; "Steel Price Truce?" *ibid.,* January 25, 1963; "A Ruthless World Market," *ibid.,* May 7, 1963; "The Japanese Scene: More Hot Coil Sales," *ibid.,* May 22, 1964.

between integrated and nonintegrated firms was the claim that in times of high demand the integrated British producers met their own needs and forced rerollers to buy overseas at premium prices, and that in times of slack demand the British mills kept up their prices of semi-finished steel even when the market for finished products was weak. The nonintegrated producers were then forced to buy lower-priced steel from abroad in order to survive. A number of other examples can be found of claims by nonintegrated producers that the domestic price spread discriminated against them and that only overseas purchases permitted them to escape this discrimination. Independent wire manufacturers both in Britain and the United States purchased wire rod abroad on these grounds. In the United States independent wire drawers charged that the integrated producers kept the price of wire rod high and stable between 1959 and 1963 (after raising it rapidly before then) while the price of welded wire mesh was falling. The price differential between domestic wire rod and finished products declined so far (even to zero) they claimed, as to leave no room for profitable production using American steel, and only the import of foreign wire rod, mainly from continental Europe and Japan, permitted them to survive. An attempt by the major integrated steel companies to bring action against wire rod imports was rejected by the Tariff Commission in 1963.[9]

Price Changes

The major price developments in iron and steel were the large increases in U.S. and European prices between 1953 and 1957, the sharp de-

[9] "The Steel Billet Controversy," *Metal Bulletin,* December 4, 1962; U.K. Iron and Steel Board, *Steel Imports,* August 26, 1964; "Steel Imports and Dual Distribution: The Plight of the Independent Wire Drawer and Fabricator," *Congressional Record,* Appendix, April 28, 1965; "Imports of Steel Rods Necessary, Say Wire Producers at Hearing," *New York Times,* May 8, 1963; "Steel Men Lose Case on Dumping," *ibid.,* May 7, 1963. See also U.S. Tariff Commission, *Hot-rolled Carbon Steel Wire Rods from Belgium,* T.C. Pub. 93, June 19, 1963; *Hot-rolled Carbon Steel Wire Rods from West Germany,* T.C. Pub. 95, June 21, 1963; *Hot-rolled Carbon Steel Wire Rods from Luxembourg,* T.C. Pub. 94, June 19, 1963; and *Hot-rolled Carbon Steel Wire Rods from France,* T.C. Pub. 99, July 15, 1963.

For an analysis of competition on the U.S. market for wire rods and wire products see Walter Adams and Joel B. Dirlam, "Steel Imports and Vertical Oligopoly Power," *American Economic Review,* September 1964. Lawrence B. Krause has suggested that for several reasons, including fear of antitrust action, the integrated domestic firms in the United States might not make use of this method of undermining the independent nonintegrated producers. See Lawrence B. Krause, "Import Discipline: The Case of the United States Steel Industry," *Journal of Industrial Economics,* November 1962.

Table 9.3

International Prices of Iron and Steel, 1953, 1957, 1961–64

(1962 = 100)

	1953	1957	1961	1962	1963	1964
U.S.	84	101	102	100	99	100
U.K.	99	110	102	100	96	104
EEC	101	118	104	100	96	104
Germany	94	111	104	100	96	104
Japan	NA	NA	110	100	99	100

Source: Appendix C (extrapolated indexes).

cline in European, but not U.S., prices between 1957 and 1963, and in Japanese prices (not available for earlier years) from 1961 to 1963, and then the jump in European prices in 1964 while U.S. and Japanese prices were almost stable (Table 9.3). In four of the five time intervals, price movements were in the same direction in all the countries listed, the exception being the period from 1957 through 1961, when European prices declined substantially from their Suez highs, while U.S. prices rose slightly.

It has been suggested that some of the apparent upward trend in U.S. domestic steel price indexes up to 1957 or 1958 and, presumably, in some of our international prices as well, reflected only an upward bias in them caused by the neglect of quality improvements: ". . . thickness tolerances have become much more stringent, although the AISI [American Iron and Steel Institute] standards have not been changed. . . . In many other respects, such as strength, hardness, surface characteristics and flatness, customers' requirements have become more strict without any change resulting in charges for 'extras.' " [10]

The declining price trends shown by our indexes during the early 1960s were related in the OECD annual reviews of the industry to the entry of new producers and ". . . the resulting fierce and often cutthroat competition," with mention being made specifically of rising sales by Eastern bloc countries and ". . . strong Japanese price competition on export markets. . . ." [11]

[10] Harleston R. Wood, "The Measurement of Employment Cost and Prices in the Steel Industry," *Review of Economics and Statistics,* November 1959.

[11] *The Iron and Steel Industry, 1961,* OECD, 1961, pp. 75, 79–80; *The Iron and Steel Industry in 1962 and Trends in 1963,* OECD, 1964, p. 74.

Sharpening international competition led to an increase in ECSC tariffs on most iron and steel products to the Italian level early in 1964, and to a specific duty on pig iron imports, most of which came from outside the ECSC.[12]

OECD reports for the first half of 1964 agreed with our indexes in describing a strong recovery in most steel prices, although the dating of our observations at midyear may have caused them to represent a maximum for the year rather than an average.[13]

European and Japanese international prices appear in these indexes to have been more flexible than U.S. prices after 1957, varying over a much wider range with changes in economic circumstances. This picture is confirmed by a good deal of nonquantitative comment about export price policies in the different countries. The OEEC Iron and Steel Committee suggested in 1960 that

> . . . there is a fundamental difference in the export price policy pursued by producers in the various exporting areas . . . ; the producers in the E.C.S.C. and Japan seem to adopt a much more flexible policy than others, such as those in the United Kingdom and the United States . . . ; producers in the E.C.S.C. and in Japan . . . seem to be prepared to try to expand their share of the export market by making price sacrifices in order to keep their plant in operation. This policy is in marked contrast to that followed in the United States, and, it would seem, in the United Kingdom, where the steel industries seem less disposed to offer heavy cuts in prices to overseas consumers.[14]

Our indexes do show smaller fluctuations in U.K. prices than in EEC prices but the difference is not as great as this quotation suggests, and the range of U.K. price movements after 1957 seems closer to that of the EEC than of the United States.

It is conceivable that the apparent differences in price flexibility for iron and steel as a group among the steel-exporting countries might not reflect differences on an individual product level. Even if price fluctuations for individual products were of equal size in Europe and the United States, the European aggregate indexes might swing more widely if European price movements for different products were closely synchronized while those for the various American products were unsynchronized and therefore offsetting. This possibility can be tested with

---

[12] *The Iron and Steel Industry in 1963 and Trends in 1964,* OECD, 1964, p. 69, and *Steel Pricing Policies,* London, PEP, December 1964, pp. 354–59.

[13] *The Iron and Steel Industry in 1964 and Trends in 1965,* OECD, 1965, pp. 50–52.

[14] *The Iron and Steel Industry in Europe, 1958–59,* OEEC, 1960, p. 97.

data for the individual subgroups (four-digit SITC). Using the data for 1961–64 (excluding 1953 and 1957 because the effect of the Suez crisis was not of equal importance to each country), we find that the frequency of very small price changes among the detailed subgroup indexes was greatest in the United States and the frequency of large price changes greatest in Japan (Table 9.4). The average and median price changes also show the United States to have had the most stable prices. The U.K. prices showed larger fluctuations, the German prices still larger, and Japanese and other EEC countries the largest of all. In other words, the greater flexibility of European and Japanese prices does reflect the movement of individual series and is not simply an aggregation phenomenon.

To some extent, the frequency of price changes represents trend rather than cyclical movements. That seems to be the case with Japan in particular, since its prices were declining relative to those of the other countries over the period as a whole. A confirmation of the Japanese trend element is that its price changes were largest of all in 1962, a year of generally declining prices, but smallest of all in 1964, a year of rising prices. There is a bias in the opposite direction, however, because we have no Japanese price data for SITC group 671, which accounted for some of the largest price changes in other countries.

These data do not confirm the idea that price flexibility in the United

Table 9.4

Distribution of Year-to-year Percentage Price Changes in Iron
and Steel Subgroups, 1961–64

Price Change	Per Cent of Subgroup				
	U.S.	U.K.	Germany	EEC	Japan
15% and over	2	2	5	5	11
10% but < 15%	11	10	10	15	11
5% but < 10%	9	31	28	30	22
2% but < 5%	28	24	28	17	33
< 2%	50	33	29	33	22
Average % change	3.6	4.9	5.4	5.6	6.0
Median % change	2.0	4.1	4.2	5.0	4.5

Source: Appendix C.

Kingdom was similar to that in the United States, as is suggested by the earlier quotation from the OEEC. Although the fluctuations in U.K. prices were somewhat smaller than those in Continental or Japanese prices, they were closer to them in size than to the U.S. average.

A similar conclusion that the United States stood alone in the degree of price inflexibility in iron and steel products was reached in a study covering approximately the first half of our period. For four important types of steel products it was found that ". . . U.S. export prices of steel increased in both the 1954 and the 1958 recession, and decreased in the 1954–57 expansion, relative to the export prices of steel of the other major producing countries." [15] There was also some indication that Japanese prices fluctuated over a wider range than British prices.

Comparisons with Other International Price Data

The relationship for all machinery and metals between our international price indexes and indexes derived from wholesale price and unit value data is discussed in Chapter 8. The iron and steel group, however, is particularly interesting in this respect because it consists of comparatively standardized products, because there is considerable contemporary comment about price changes, and because there are published export as well as domestic prices. Export price information on iron and steel is published in leading trade journals, particularly the *Metal Bulletin*, published in London, and the *American Metal Market*. The former especially is widely cited in discussions of export price movements. The most important alternative indexes are shown in Table 9.5.

The coverage of U.K. export prices in these sources was too limited for the computation of group indexes, but we were able to compute fairly broad indexes for EEC iron and steel export prices (from the *Metal Bulletin*) and for U.S. export prices (from the *American Metal Market*). In Table 9.5 these indexes are called published export price data. It should be stressed that the publications cited are not the authors of the indexes but are sources for the specific price series which we

[15] Hang Sheng Cheng, "Relative Movements in the Prices of Exports of Manufactures: United States Versus Other Industrial Countries, 1953–59," *IMF Staff Papers*, March 1962, p. 94.

Table 9.5

Iron and Steel Price Indexes Based on Alternative Types of Price Data,
1953, 1957, 1961—64

	$\frac{1957}{1953}$	$\frac{1961}{1957}$	$\frac{1962}{1961}$	$\frac{1963}{1962}$	$\frac{1964}{1963}$	$\frac{1964}{1953}$
NBER international prices[a]						
United States	120	100	98	99	101	118
United Kingdom	113	94	97	97	108	108
EEC	119	88	95	96	109	105
Germany	117	93	96	96	109	110
Japan	NA	NA	90	101	100	NA
Published export prices						
U.S.: *American Metal Market*	121	101	100	101	102	124
EEC: *Metal Bulletin*	118	78	93	95	118	97
U.S. export unit values	126	104	101	99	101	133
Official data on domestic wholesale prices						
United States	127	102	100	100	101	130
United Kingdom	127	103	103	100	100	135
Germany	106	110	101	98	100	116
Japan	123	98	92	100	100	112
U.K. Iron and Steel Board data on domestic prices						
United States	NA	104	100	101	102	106[b]
United Kingdom	NA	97	104	100	100	102[b]
Germany	NA	105	99	100	100	104[b]
France	NA	89	104	100	100	92[b]

Source: NBER prices: See notes to Appendix C.

American Metal Market: Prices for 35—65 items each year were taken from the issue closest to July 1. They appear to be posted prices, and there is no indication that any deviation of market prices from posted prices would be recorded. No prices are listed for SITC 671, 672, and 679. Data for SITC 678 are given only at the end of the period.

Metal Bulletin: Prices for 10—20 products, collected from issues closest to July 1. They purport to represent actual market conditions rather than posted prices. Unfortunately, very few items are listed, and only four of the three-digit SITC groups in division 67 are covered at all. These groups do, however, account for two-thirds of the value of trade in the division. The chief group omitted is tubes, pipes, fittings, etc. (SITC 678).

Unit value data: See notes to Appendix G. About half of the commodities included are semi-manufactures, and half are finished manufactures. The major gaps, from the point of view of our OECD trade weights, are ingots, bars, billets, slabs, etc. (SITC 672), and wire rods (SITC 673.1).

Wholesale price data: See notes to Appendix F.

U.K. Iron and Steel Board: Prices, covering 30–40 products, are confined to the first five three-digit groups in division 67 (see Table 9.1). These account for over three-quarters of the trade in the division but exclude the more highly manufactured products: wire, rail, pipe, and tubing. We combined the published prices into unweighted indexes for four-digit SITC subgroups and aggregated these into three-digit groups and the total index for iron and steel, using the OECD trade weights described earlier.

[a]These price indexes are calculated directly from time-to-time data for all countries, and therefore do not correspond precisely with those in Table 9.3.

[b]For 1964/1957.

combined, using our international trade weights, for comparison with the NBER international price indexes.

For the United States, the NBER international price indexes follow those computed from published export prices very closely. The discrepancies, although small, are all in one direction, and therefore cumulate through the period, with the NBER indexes declining slowly, but consistently, with respect to the *American Metal Market* data. Over the period as a whole, therefore, the difference is more substantial—about six percentage points. The differences, which are slightly larger in 1961–63 than in the other years, suggest that the published series may have missed some of the shading of prices by American companies in those years in reaction to European and Japanese competition. The apparent bias in the published series was widespread throughout the various groups of iron and steel products, and it is unlikely, therefore, that the difference, small as it is, can be attributed to chance. A revealing fact about the published U.S. prices is that reinforcing bars, subjected to intense foreign competition, were dropped from the published indexes after 1961, when published prices were withdrawn by U.S. companies. Thus the international price index from published export prices does not reflect the subsequent behavior of this price. We have some indication of the ensuing events from the BLS reports of a fall of 4 per cent from 1961 to 1962 and a further 11 per cent from 1962 to 1963 in the domestic price of reinforcing bars.[16]

[16] *Wholesale Prices and Price Indexes,* U.S. Bureau of Labor Statistics, various issues. The figures are averages of June and July.

The relation between NBER and *Metal Bulletin* prices for EEC exports was of a different nature. There was no consistent difference in one direction, but the index from published prices showed more violent fluctuations. It is possible that the index derived from *Metal Bulletin* prices is more volatile than EEC export prices in general because of the small number of commodities covered. These tended to be the ones most important in trade and include several, such as wire rods and concrete reinforcing bars, that were subject to particularly severe international competition. Products of alloy steels or those incorporating other special features, not as standardized as the items in the *Metal Bulletin* list, or those playing a less important role in international competition, may have undergone less violent price fluctuations. The NBER price collection, taken in large part from the purchase experience of private companies, includes more of these items.

The third section of Table 9.5 gives an index derived from U.S. export unit values, constructed, as far as possible, from data for the commodities used by the U.S. Department of Commerce in its official export value index (for which no separate iron and steel component is published). No effort was made to pass judgment on the quality of the individual unit value series used. Our main alteration in the unit value data was the use of single-year OECD trade weights in place of the Commerce Department's shifting U.S. export weights.

The largest difference between the unit value and NBER indexes is in 1953–57, when the unit value index rose by six percentage points more than the NBER one. The unit value index again outpaced the international price index in the next two periods, but the differences were smaller in the later years when price changes were smaller. Over the whole time span we cover, however, the export unit value index exaggerates the rise in U.S. prices by a considerable amount.

Comparisons of the unit value and NBER price indexes for the individual SITC groups show wider differences and more frequent cases of movements in opposite direction. The unit values for tubular goods (SITC 678) exhibit particularly erratic behavior (see Appendix G). Between 1957 and 1961, for example, they increased by 19 per cent while the NBER index declined by 1 per cent, and the wholesale price index showed virtually no change. This discrepancy cannot be explained as a vagary of the unit value series for one or two commodities, since it is based on fourteen relatives, of which twelve showed increases of more than 11 per cent. Apparently the tightness of supplies in Europe following the Suez crisis led, in 1957, to the purchase from American suppliers, especially for Venezuela and Canada, of large quantities of cheaper types of pipe not ordinarily bought in the United States. By 1961 U.S. exports again consisted of the smaller, more specialized, and therefore more expensive types of pipe. Because the system of pipe classification in U.S. trade statistics omits some critical price factors, such as diameter, the unit value index is vulnerable to this kind of error.

The unsatisfactory performance of unit value indexes in this category casts them in a dubious light, since steel products present fewer problems for the construction of unit value indexes than most other kinds of manufactured goods. Physical quantity data are given in the trade statistics, and the degree of commodity detail is substantial: Over 100 separate commodity numbers are available in Schedule B (the U.S. export trade commodity classification) for products in SITC 67. Furthermore, steel products are comparatively homogeneous, certainly more so than the machinery or transport equipment discussed in later chapters. The size of discrepancies in this division, therefore, suggests that the unit values from customs data are not useful for the construction of price indexes over a wide range of products.

Comparisons with Domestic Prices

From 1953 to 1957 our index of U.S. domestic prices of iron and steel based on BLS data rose substantially relative to international prices, and there was a similar, but smaller, difference in the following three periods. From 1963 to 1964, the two indexes showed the same price movement. The U.S. index based on U.K. Iron and Steel Board data showed a stronger and more persistent upward bias as a measure of international price movements.

The differences between domestic and international price movements were larger in the case of the United Kingdom. Domestic prices rose by twice as much as international prices in 1953–57, and then, if we judge by the wholesale price data, continued to rise in 1957–61 and 1962, when international prices fell. The Iron and Steel Board data were a little closer to the international price index in 1957–61. However, both domestic series were stable in 1963 in the face of a further decline in international prices. In each of these cases we can say that the domestic price index was biased upward, using the word "bias" to describe any movement different from that of the international price index. In 1964, however, the domestic price index, in both versions, was stable in a year when international prices rose sharply. Overall, the wholesale price index described a rise of 35 per cent from 1953 through 1964, and the international prices only an 8 per cent increase.

Except in 1953–57, the relationship was similar for Germany: an upward bias in the index from domestic prices until 1963, and then stability in domestic prices accompanying a large rise in international prices. In the first period, however, domestic prices, presumably less influenced by the Suez crisis, rose much less than international prices.

Since domestic prices are often used as proxies for international prices, these differences in movement are important. They were noted in published reports on the iron and steel industry as well.[17]

The differences in movement between the indexes of home and export prices reflect not only the behavior of the two types of prices but also differences in the degree to which the reported prices correspond to actual transactions prices. The 1958–59 report of the OEEC stated that ". . . the export prices used correspond in general to transactions actually carried out, while the home price quotations, at least in the E.C.S.C. . . . do not necessarily reflect the prices consumers actually had to pay for their steel. . . ." The point was made specifically in the report for 1962, one of the years in which the domestic price index appeared to be biased upward. The OECD reported that list prices of Luxembourg and German firms, except for those of one company, had remained constant during the year and French list prices had risen at a time when real prices were declining. Consequently, ". . . the effect that this sometimes unrestrained competition had on prices is not clearly discernible from the published price lists." The same remarks were made about both EEC and U.K. prices in 1963, and are in accordance with the results in Table 9.5. Similarly, the OECD reported that the movement of home market list prices in 1964 failed to reflect the improvement in prices that occurred in the first half of that year. One reflection

---

[17] The OEEC report for 1955–56 stated that ". . . export prices, being directly subject to the fluctuations and pressure of demand, rose more sharply than certain home prices" (*The Iron and Steel Industry in Europe,* Iron and Steel Committee, OEEC, 1957, p. 43). The 1958–59 report, in the same vein, stated that ". . . export prices were again more flexible than home prices from July 1958 to the end of 1959" (*ibid., 1958–59,* p. 95).

of the change was that the volume of ECSC sales aligned on offers from third countries, which had increased in 1962 and 1963, when we found home list prices to be biased upward, fell off by almost half in 1964, a year in which we found home prices to be biased downward in comparison to international prices.[18]

For the United States, these differences between international and domestic prices of iron and steel apparently cannot be attributed to the use of list rather than transactions prices in domestic indexes. Stigler and Kindahl found that in this industry transactions prices moved very closely with the BLS indexes.[19]

The difference in trend between home and international price indexes partly reflects a major change in the relationship between the absolute levels of home and export prices which accompanied a shift from a sellers' to a buyers' market. At the beginning of our period export prices were higher than home prices, in some cases by substantial amounts, particularly in the United Kingdom. That relationship, at least in the United Kingdom, was still maintained in 1956. By the 1960s, however, the United States was complaining about dumping of some products by the United Kingdom, the EEC countries, and Japan, and these charges implied export sales at prices below those of home sales. Similar price-cutting was reported in intra-European trade, one article pointing out in 1963 that ". . . British mills, like those in the ECSC and elsewhere, are selling steel overseas at prices below national market levels, have been doing it for years, and sometimes recently have quoted virtually dumping prices." [20]

The shift in the relationship between export and domestic prices was paralleled by a corresponding change in the relationship between actual export prices charged by ECSC countries and the "Brussels Convention" official minimum prices. ". . . In the sellers' market from 1953 to 1958, effective export prices were significantly higher than the official minimum prices. In the recession of 1958, on the other hand, effective export prices fell well below the official minimum prices, despite severe reductions in the latter." [21]

---

[18] *Ibid.,* p. 96; *ibid., 1962,* p. 73; *ibid., 1963,* pp. 71–72; *ibid., 1964,* p. 49.

[19] George J. Stigler and James K. Kindahl, *The Behavior of Industrial Prices,* New York, NBER, 1970, Chap. 6.

[20] "The Export Market: Re-Rolled Steel Prices Reduced," *Metal Bulletin,* July 24, 1953; "Steel Prices on the March," *ibid.,* November 6, 1956; "Imports: U.S. Gets Tougher," *ibid.,* January 1, 1963; "Limiting the Steel War," *ibid.,* July 2, 1963; "Steel Consumers in Revolt," *ibid.,* July 20, 1963.

[21] Hang Sheng Cheng, *op. cit.*

Price Competitiveness

The price competitiveness of the United States in iron and steel relative to each of its main competitors declined sharply between 1953 and
1962 (Table 9.6). There was no change in 1963 relative to Japan, but
a continued decline relative to the EEC countries and the United
Kingdom. In 1964 the movement of the price relationships was reversed,
with the United States gaining on all the countries except Japan. Over
1961–64 U.S. price competitiveness declined relative to Japan but
gained slightly relative to the EEC and United Kingdom. But, over the
whole period after 1953 the United States lost heavily in comparison
to all the other countries. No Japanese index is shown for the years
before 1961 but the few fragments of data available for universals,
plates, and sheets (SITC 674) suggest a large improvement between
1953 and 1957 in Japanese price competitiveness relative to all the
listed countries.

Data for individual groups within iron and steel, given in Appendix
D, spell out much the same story of U.S. decline until 1962 or 1963
followed by a recovery in 1964. The main exceptions to the pattern
were tubes and pipes, in which 1961 was the low point in U.S. price
competitiveness, and some groups and subgroups in which the U.S.
position improved temporarily in 1957, as a consequence of the rapid
rise in EEC prices which resulted from the Suez crisis. But this brief
gain was quickly erased, and the period after 1957 showed a decline

Table 9.6
U.S. Price Competitiveness, Iron and Steel, 1953, 1957, 1961–64
(1962 = 100)

	1953	1957	1961	1962	1963	1964
Relative to						
U.K.	117	108	101	100	97	104
EEC	119	117	102	100	98	104
Germany	111	109	102	100	97	104
Japan	NA	NA	108	100	100	100

Source: Appendix D.

in U.S. price competitiveness throughout the range of iron and steel products.

The published export and domestic price data discussed earlier imply alternative indexes of U.S. international price competitiveness, which are compared with the NBER indexes in Table 9.7. The differences are sometimes large, but vary from one index to another. The index relative to the EEC countries that is based on published export prices magnifies the fluctuations shown in the NBER index. The declines are larger in each period between 1957 and 1963, and the rise is much larger in 1964. The former index shows not only larger fluctuations than the latter, but also a greater deterioration in U.S. price competitiveness over the whole span of years: 22 per cent instead of the NBER estimate of

Table 9.7
U.S. Price Competitiveness in Iron and Steel: Indexes Based on
Alternative Types of Price Data,
1953, 1957, 1961–64

	$\dfrac{1957}{1953}$	$\dfrac{1961}{1957}$	$\dfrac{1962}{1961}$	$\dfrac{1963}{1962}$	$\dfrac{1964}{1963}$	$\dfrac{1964}{1953}$
NBER international prices						
United Kingdom	93	93	99	97	107	89
EEC	98	88	98	98	107	88
Germany	98	93	98	97	107	93
Japan	NA	NA	92	100	100	NA
Published export prices						
EEC	98	77	94	95	116	78
Official data on domestic wholesale prices						
United Kingdom	100	100	103	100	100	103
Germany	83	107	101	100	98	87
Japan	96	96	92	100	99	85
U.K. Iron and Steel Board data on domestic prices						
United Kingdom	NA	94	104	99	99	96[a]
Germany	NA	102	99	99	98	98[a]
France	NA	85	105	99	98	87[a]

Source: Table 9.5.
[a]For 1964/1957.

12 per cent after 1953, and 20 per cent instead of 10 per cent after 1957.

The indexes from published export price series, although they seemed to exaggerate movements in price competitiveness, generally changed in the same direction as the NBER series. The indexes derived from domestic price data, on the other hand, frequently moved oppositely to the NBER indexes or were stable in the face of large changes in the price competitiveness measures based on international prices. The wholesale price data showed a slight gain in U.S. price competitiveness relative to the United Kingdom over the whole period while the international price data showed a substantial loss. Relative to Germany, the wholesale price data index moved opposite to the international price data index in 1957–61, 1962, and 1964. These comparisons clearly show that domestic prices frequently give highly misleading indications of the extent and direction of changes in international price competitiveness in iron and steel.

Comparisons between changes in price competitiveness and in export shares are hindered by the effect of the Suez crisis in 1957. If we compare 1953 to 1961, ignoring 1957, the indexes show large declines in U.S. price competitiveness relative to both the U.K. and EEC countries, with the decline relative to Germany not as large as that relative to other European countries (Table 9.6). The U.S. decline is reflected in a sharp cut in the U.S. share of exports—from 20 to less than 10 per cent (Table 9.2). The German price record, apparently less impressive than that of the United Kingdom or other European countries, was associated with an excellent export performance—almost doubling Germany's share of OECD steel exports.

From 1961 through 1963 the main development in price competitiveness was the improvement in Japan's position, and this gain was matched by a major gain in export share. The continuing deterioration in U.S. price competitiveness relative to the United Kingdom and the EEC countries did not have any apparent effect on export shares.

In 1964, both Japan and the United States improved their price competitiveness relative to the United Kingdom and the EEC countries, and both Japan and the United States increased their export shares at the expense of the United Kingdom and the EEC countries. The deterioration in price competitiveness was slightly larger for Germany than for the other EEC members, and it was Germany that accounted for the fall in the EEC's export share.[22]

We have discussed the effects of changes in price competitiveness in terms of the share of export markets. In several items of this group, however, much of the competition has been on the U.S. domestic market between imports from abroad, which appear in our export data, and U.S. domestic sales, which do not. The extent to which exports by Japan and the European countries replace U.S. domestic rather than export sales is not revealed in our tables here. However, it has been the focus of much of the recent discussion of the declining competitiveness of the American steel industry, and our indexes should relate to this competition as well as to that on foreign markets.

Adams and Dirlam, in a study concentrating on wire rod and wire prices, found a large decline in U.S. price competitiveness in wire rods on the U.S. market between 1958 and 1962.[23]

This fits the pattern of our price data although we do not find U.S. prices quite as stable as the published domestic prices they use. The consequence of the decline in U.S. price competitiveness was a rise in the ratio of imports to U.S. production of wire rods from 1 per cent in 1957 to almost 15 per cent in 1962, and a rise in the ratio of imports to non-captive production from 5 per cent to 39 per cent in the same period.[24]

Price Levels

Despite the considerable improvement in the U.S. price position in iron and steel in 1964, price level differences between the United States and the competing European and Japanese producers at the end of our period were larger than for any other commodity division for which we

[22] Hang Sheng Cheng (*ibid.*), examining changes in exports over shorter periods than ours for the early years, concluded that ". . . a significant part of these changes in the U.S. share can be attributed to changes in U.S. export prices of steel relative to those of other exporting countries. . . ." He found that relative U.S. prices increased in the 1954 and 1958 recessions and decreased in the 1954–57 expansion, and that the U.S. export share fell during the recessions and rose between 1954 and 1957.

[23] Walter Adams and Joel B. Dirlam, "Steel Imports and Vertical Oligopoly Power," *American Economic Review*, September 1964, p. 636.

[24] *Ibid.*, p. 631. Adams and Dirlam have suggested that since independent wire fabricators continued, for reasons of safety among others, to purchase part of their requirements at the high domestic price, the integrated companies found it more profitable to keep the price structure at the cost of losing part of their market than to risk a widening of price competition among domestic firms (*ibid.*, pp. 638 ff.).

Table 9.8
Price Levels, Iron and Steel, 1953, 1957, 1961–64
(U.S. for each year = 100)

	1953	1957	1961	1962	1963	1964
U.S.	100	100	100	100	100	100
U.K.	92	85	79	78	76	82
EEC	88	87	76	74	72	78
Germany	85	83	77	76	73	78
Japan	NA	NA	75	70	70	70

Source: Appendix E.

had data. The United Kingdom was the highest priced of the competitors listed, followed by the EEC countries, at 22 per cent below the U.S. level, and Japan at 30 per cent lower (Table 9.8). The gap was largest in 1963, when the European countries' prices were approximately 25 per cent below the U.S. level. The EEC price level was below that of the United Kingdom in every one of the years except 1957, when the Suez crisis led to larger fluctuations in EEC than in U.K. prices. Japan's positions as the lowest-priced exporter was clear by 1962, but it may have been reached earlier. However, Japanese export prices were probably fairly high at the beginning of the period. The data in Hang Sheng Cheng's article, referred to earlier, imply large gains between 1953 and 1959 in Japanese price competitiveness relative to the United States in bars, plates, sheets, and structural steel, and relative to the United Kingdom and the ECSC countries in all except plates.[25] Since the Japanese levels were similar to those of the United Kingdom and the ECSC countries in 1961, these gains in price competitiveness suggest that the Japanese prices were probably above European levels before 1961.

The large price level differences ran consistently through the individual groups of iron and steel products. All the EEC price levels for three-digit SITC groups were 20 per cent or more below the U.S. level in 1962 and 1963 (see Appendix E). Japanese price levels were generally lowest of all in the later years; they were below those of the European countries in 1964 in all four of the groups for which we could calculate them.

[25] Hang Sheng Cheng, *op. cit.*, p. 92.

Summary

U.S. prices of iron and steel products increased relative to those of the European countries and Japan before 1963 but held even with Japan and gained on the other countries in 1964. The main price changes seem to have been at least roughly reflected in shifts in trade shares: large losses for the United States and large gains for Japan.

Published export price data appear to distort the size, but not the direction, of changes in price competitiveness, while domestic prices are often misleading even as to direction. The U.S. unit value data appear to exaggerate the rise in U.S. export prices seriously and also to incorporate changes in average values which clearly do not represent price changes even in some of the more narrowly defined commodity groups.

The U.S. price level for iron and steel relative to that of other countries was higher than that of any other commodity division in 1964. Japan was the lowest-priced seller, but even the European countries were undercutting U.S. prices by about 20 per cent.

10

NONFERROUS METALS

SEVEN METALS—copper, aluminum, nickel, silver, zinc, tin, and lead—accounted for over 90 per cent of the nonferrous metals exports of the developed countries in 1963; copper and aluminum each constituted about one-third of the nonferrous exports, and nickel one-eighth (see Table 10.1). Over two-thirds of the exports consisted of "unwrought" forms such as ingots, billets, anodes, cathodes, and pellets; and the rest consisted of "worked" metals, which are rolled, extruded, drawn, or forged into plates and sheets, foil, tubes, pipes, and fittings.[1] These proportions, however, understate the importance to the economies of the OECD countries of exports of worked metals relative to exports of unwrought metals. The reason is that, for most of the countries we cover, value added by the country itself represents a much higher fraction of the export proceeds from worked metals than from unwrought metals, for which the value added is mainly in the smelting and refining processes.[2] The United States and Canada, which are important producers of some of the ores, are the main exceptions to this generalization. We have not tried to adjust our weights to a value-added basis, particularly since the problem is negligible in other parts of our study.

Note: SITC 68. Value of OECD exports in 1963: $2.7 billion; 6.1 per cent of study total. Coverage: Silver and platinum, copper, nickel, aluminum, zinc, tin. Uranium and thorium (SITC 688), which accounted for a little under 1 per cent of nonferrous trade in 1963, has been omitted. Ores are excluded since they are not regarded as manufactured products (they are in SITC 28). Gold is excluded from the trade classification and from our study, since gold transactions predominantly involve monetary settlements rather than ordinary merchandise transactions.

[1] We use the terms "unwrought" and "worked" in this report even though they do not appear to be widely used in the nonferrous metal trades of the United States, because they are used in the SITC, which we follow in this study. Those that are in wider use, such as "ingot," "semis," and "fabricated," would not correctly convey the precise coverage of the SITC categories.

[2] Conceptually, the prices for processing ores into metals would be more appropriate measures for our purposes than the prices of the metals, but these could not have been obtained without a much more intensive field effort, and perhaps not even then.

Table 10.1

OECD Exports of Nonferrous Metals (SITC 68), by Origin, Destination, and Commodity Group, 1963

(dollars in millions)

| | Value of Exports | Per Cent of OECD Exports in 68 | Share in OECD Exports (per cent) | | | | | | | | |
| | | | | | | EEC | | | | | |
			OECD	U.S.	U.K.	Total	Germany	France	Belg.-Lux.	Canada	Japan
Total, all destinations and groups	$2,725	100.0	100.0	16.5	12.8	30.7	9.4	5.3	13.1	26.0	1.6
Destination											
U.S.	587	21.5	100.0		6.5	16.7	6.0	3.6	6.1	63.4	2.6
OECD Europe	1,540	56.5	100.0	17.1	12.4	39.2	10.6	6.2	18.6	16.0	0.3
U.K.	314	11.5	100.0	22.0		8.9	2.9	1.0	3.8	55.1	0.3
EEC total	897	32.9	100.0	19.3	15.1	47.5	8.8	8.6	25.3	4.8	0.2
Germany	329	12.1	100.0	20.1	12.5	37.4		6.1	23.7	6.7	0.1
France	189	6.9	100.0	21.2	13.2	57.1	11.1		42.3	3.2	0.5
Belgium-Luxembourg	100	3.7	100.0	6.0	21.0	65.0	17.0	47.0		3.0	
Canada	83	3.0	100.0	71.1	25.3	2.4	1.2	a	1.2		0.4
Japan	47	1.7	100.0	38.3	19.1	14.9	4.3	2.1	8.5	25.5	
Latin America	84	3.1	100.0	39.3	6.0	19.0	8.3	4.8	3.6	27.4	2.4
Other	384	14.1	100.0	19.8	22.1	28.9	12.5	6.2	7.0	14.1	5.7

(continued)

225

Table 10.1 (concluded)

SITC commodity group or subgroup[c]	Value of Exports	Per Cent of OECD Exports in 68	Share in OECD Exports (per cent)			EEC					
			OECD	U.S.	U.K.	Total	Germany	France	Belg.-Lux.	Canada	Japan
Silver (681)	$226	8.3	100.0	19.5	35.0	28.8	17.3	2.7	6.6	12.8	0.1
Copper (682)	932	34.2	100.0	22.7	11.2	40.0	12.9	2.9	22.2	16.6	1.6
Unwrought copper (682.1)	621	22.8	100.0	30.3	8.2	35.7	7.7	1.6	26.1	20.5	0.2
Worked copper (682.2)	312	11.4	100.0	7.7	17.0	48.4	23.1	5.4	14.4	9.0	4.5
Nickel (683)	327	12.0	100.0	6.7	18.3	7.6	3.4	3.7	0.1	53.2	0.1
Aluminum (684)	853	31.3	100.0[b]	14.2	6.1	25.1	7.0	10.0	5.4	32.9	2.0
Unwrought aluminum (684.1)	527	19.3	100.0	12.5	0.6	12.3	1.3	10.8	0.1	50.5	1.1
Worked aluminum (684.2)	326	12.0	100.0	16.9	14.7	45.7	16.6	8.6	14.1	4.6	3.4
Lead (685)	60	2.2	100.0	1.7	16.7	46.7	10.0	8.3	23.3	25.0	0.6
Zinc (686)	120	4.4	100.0	9.2	3.3	42.5	6.7	3.3	26.7	32.5	0.8
Tin (687)	67	2.4	100.0	7.5	40.3	49.3	6.0	0.6	25.4		0.5
Miscellaneous (689)	137	5.0	100.0	24.4	8.9	35.6	5.9	3.4	19.3	10.4	6.7

Source: Appendix A.
[a] Less than 0.05 per cent.
[b] Including Norway, 13 per cent of SITC 683, 11 per cent of SITC 684, and 10 per cent of SITC 689.
[c] SITC 688, uranium and thorium, was omitted from the table. Total OECD exports were less than $1 million.

In any event, the price movements of worked metals are often closely related to those of unwrought metals.

Nonferrous Metals as a Whole

Canada was the leading OECD exporter of nonferrous metals, having a pre-eminent position in nickel and aluminum and being a significant source of other metals as well (see Table 10.1). Among the other major OECD exporters, the United States was important in copper and aluminum, while Belgium and the United Kingdom were significant factors in a wider range of metals. The special elements affecting the roles of the individual countries in the more important nonferrous metals are considered below.

The share of the United States in nonferrous metal exports more than doubled between 1953 and 1961 (Table 10.2), and declined slightly after that. Export shares of the United Kingdom, the EEC countries as a group, and Canada all declined over the whole period.

International Price Indexes

The prices of nonferrous metals relevant to international trade have usually moved in the same direction in the different countries, but often in different degrees (Table 10.3). The main changes over time were price increases between 1953 and 1957 and again, larger ones this time, between 1963 and 1964.[3] The U.K. and German indexes reflect greater price variability over time than does the U.S. index. The smaller U.S. price increases in the face of booming metal markets in 1964 are the clearest indication of this difference.

The temporal variability of prices was also great for Belgium, the most important nonferrous exporter in the Common Market.[4] However, this variability cannot be seen in the EEC index because the fluctuations were damped when Belgian price changes were averaged with those of other member countries to calculate the EEC index as a whole.

[3] Price changes within the period 1953 to 1961 were larger than is suggested by our reference years. See, for example, our discussion of copper prices further on in this chapter.

[4] Although Belgium is a more important factor in nonferrous metals than any of the other EEC countries, the data are more adequate for the larger EEC countries, particularly Germany, because the effort made to collect prices was in accordance with the relative importance of the various countries in aggregate exports of metals, metal products, and machinery.

Table 10.2

OECD Exports of Nonferrous Metals, 1953, 1957, 1961–64

(dollars in millions)

	Value of OECD Exports	Share in OECD Exports (per cent)							
						EEC			
		OECD	U.S.	U.K.	Total	Germany	Belgium-Luxembourg	Canada	Japan
INCLUDING SPAIN AND SWITZERLAND									
1964	$3,232	100.0	15.4	12.0	32.7	9.2	13.0	24.7	1.8
1963	2,685[a]	100.0	15.3	13.0	31.2	9.5	13.3	26.4	1.6
1962	2,629	100.0	15.6	14.0	29.8	10.0	12.1	26.7	1.3
1961	2,625	100.0	16.5	13.0	30.6	10.0	11.9	26.6	1.1
EXCLUDING SPAIN AND SWITZERLAND									
1961	2,574	100.0	16.8	13.2	31.2	10.2	12.1	27.1	1.1
1957[b]	2,321	100.0	13.5	15.0	25.5	8.4	9.8	30.1	1.1
1953[b]	1,418	100.0	7.9	15.0	35.5	9.0	14.4	31.0	1.1

Source: Appendix B.

[a]The figure here is $40 million less than that given in Table 10.1. The reason is that, for that table, U.S. and OECD exports were increased by this amount to take account of the failure of the United States to report silver, platinum, and other metals of the platinum group (SITC 68.1) or copper foil (682.23). These adjustments were not made for the other years, and the country-of-origin distribution above is based on unadjusted data for all years.

[b]In 1953 and 1957 the division includes waste and sweeping of silver (285.02) copper matte (283.12), nickel matte and speiss, etc. (283.22), and zinc dust (284.08).

Table 10.3
International Prices of Nonferrous Metals, 1953, 1957, 1961–64
(1962 = 100)

	1953	1957	1961	1962	1963	1964
U.S.	96	100	101	100	100	108
U.K.	95	101	101	100	102	115
EEC	100	102	101	100	101	117
Germany	100	105	101	100	100	115

Source: Appendix C.

Price Competitiveness

The price competitiveness of the United States in nonferrous metals was about the same relative to the United Kingdom every year until the last two, when it improved (Table 10.4). In 1964 U.K. prices had risen 6 per cent more from the 1962 base than U.S. prices. U.S. price competitiveness vis-à-vis Germany and the Common Market as a whole was lower in 1961–63 than in earlier years, but there was a sharp improvement in 1964.

Price Levels

European price levels were almost always somewhat below those of the United States, as can be seen in Table 10.5. The difference in 1964 can probably be considered negligible, given the possible margins of error in these calculations, but the earlier price differences do appear to have been significant, particularly in 1961–63.

Table 10.4
U.S. Price Competitiveness, Nonferrous Metals, 1953, 1957, 1961–64
(1962 = 100)

	1953	1957	1961	1962	1963	1964
Relative to						
U.K.	100	101	100	100	102	106
EEC	105	102	100	100	101	108
Germany	104	105	100	100	99	107

Source: Appendix D.

Table 10.5
Price Levels, Nonferrous Metals, 1953, 1957, 1961–64
(U.S. for each year = 100)

	1953	1957	1961	1962	1963	1964
U.S.	100	100	100	100	100	100
U.K.	92	93	93	92	94	98
EEC	96	93	91	91	92	99
Germany	98	98	93	94	93	100

Source: Appendix E.

These price differences, however, do not necessarily indicate that the United States was able to export at prices 8 or 10 per cent above those prevailing in Europe. In certain cases the United States did sell at prices above those in Europe, as will be pointed out later for specific commodities. However, some of the data reflect unsuccessful bidding by U.S. companies, especially on certain fabricated or semifabricated products which the United States did not export to any substantial degree.

Comparisons with Wholesale Price and Unit Value Data

In Table 10.6, the NBER indexes of international prices, presented as percentage changes for individual periods, are compared with wholesale price series and, in the case of the United States, with export unit value series also. To minimize gaps in coverage, official wholesale price series were supplemented by price series from trade journals. Both the wholesale prices and the export unit values are weighted by the same world trade weights used in making the NBER indexes. As is to be expected, the wholesale prices of each country show more country-to-country differences in the direction and amount of movement than the export prices, since the latter refer more nearly to a common market than the former. Thus, the four international price index series are more alike than either set of the corresponding four wholesale price indexes except when export prices responded differentially to boom conditions in 1964.

The figures suggest that, in periods of price instability, the wholesale price indexes are not reliable indicators of international price competitiveness. There are larger differences between the wholesale and NBER indexes for 1957/1953, 1961/1957, and 1964/1963 (all intervals of relatively large price changes) than for 1962/1961 and 1963/1962

Table 10.6
Nonferrous Metals Price Indexes: NBER, Domestic, and Unit Value,
1953, 1957, 1961−64

	$\dfrac{1957}{1953}$	$\dfrac{1961}{1957}$	$\dfrac{1962}{1961}$	$\dfrac{1963}{1962}$	$\dfrac{1964}{1963}$
NBER INTERNATIONAL PRICE INDEXES					
U.S.	104	101	99	100	108
U.K.	106	100	99	102	112
EEC	101	99	99	101	116
Germany	105	96	99	99	116
WHOLESALE PRICE INDEXES[a]					
U.S.	111	103	99	99	106
U.K.	110	101	99	103	112
EEC	100	88	98	101	107
Germany	96	105	95	100	111
WHOLESALE PRICE INDEXES[b]					
U.S.	113	106	97	98	105
U.K.	114	108	98	101	111
Japan	100	102	97	100	107
EEC	103	84	98	100	105
Germany	97	105	96	98	109
France	107	97	99	102	110
U.S. EXPORT UNIT VALUE INDEXES					
Total	122	90	101	98	102
Copper	111	96	103	101	104
Aluminum	135	84	99	94	100

Note: The NBER series are derived from Table 10.3; the index from wholesale prices, from Appendix F and notes; and from Irving B. Kravis and Robert E. Lipsey, *Comparative Prices of Nonferrous Metals in International Trade, 1953−64*, NBER Occasional Paper 98, 1966, Table 5; and the unit value series, from Appendix G.

[a]Official series and trade journal prices.

[b]Official series only.

(intervals of relative price stability). The largest discrepancy between the two sets of data is for the change between 1953 and 1957 in U.S. price competitiveness relative to Germany; according to the wholesale indexes, the U.S. position deteriorated by 14 per cent,[5] while the NBER indexes indicate a slight improvement.[6] In this case, the German wholesale price index is probably at fault, since it comprises only five series.

That narrow commodity coverage may be responsible for other differences between the two sets of indexes is suggested by the closer conformance to the NBER indexes of the wholesale price indexes when supplemented by trade journal prices. However, while many of the discrepancies between the NBER and wholesale price series may be explicable in these terms, it should not be forgotten that the latter are based on formally quoted prices which may differ from actual transactions prices, particularly when prices are changing.[7] Indeed, sometimes, it has been alleged, a published price has been maintained at one level by the firms reporting the price to the trade journal or other publisher while different prices were in effect for selling.[8] In addition, as will be indicated in the discussions of particular metal markets, actual transactions prices sometimes differ for domestic sales and exports.

We included a series on Japanese wholesale prices of nonferrous metals, although we were unable to gather enough primary data to construct our own indexes for Japan. The Japanese wholesale price indexes show less variation in these years than any other price series in the table. In view of the great dependence of Japan upon foreign supplies of many nonferrous metals, it would be surprising if the Japanese index of international prices for nonferrous metals—if it could have been constructed—would have shown such stability relative to the United States and Europe.

[5] $(96 \div 111) \times 100 = 86.$

[6] $(105 \div 104) \times 100 = 101.$

[7] George J. Stigler and James K. Kindahl found, for the United States, larger discrepancies between list and transactions prices in nonferrous metals than in iron and steel. Transactions prices fell more rapidly during periods of declining prices and rose more rapidly during periods of rising prices. The largest discrepancy was at the end of their period, when there was a large rise in prices (*The Behavior of Industrial Prices*, New York, NBER, 1970).

[8] "Perhaps the most insidious evil of all inherent in current trends in pricing practice is the way in which, in certain markets, a price can be kept running on a certain basis —of historical validity—while the trade contrives to effect much of its business at lower prices, the effect of which is, however, not allowed to reflect back on the published price, because the basis on which it is concluded is different from the basis on which the published price is fixed" (*Metal Bulletin*, October 6, 1961, p. 12). See also *Engineering and Mining Journal, Metal and Mineral Markets*, June 24, 1963; *Metal Bulletin*, July 19, 1963, p. 21; and *Engineering and Mining Journal*, February 1965, p. 94.

The NBER international price index for U.S. nonferrous metals has also been compared in Table 10.6 with an index of U.S. export unit values weighted by our standard foreign trade weights. The unit value index is based on eight series of export unit values chosen to conform to those used by the Department of Commerce in its official unit value indexes. Four of the series are unit values for copper, three for aluminum, and one is for pipe fittings of copper or other nonferrous alloys.

There are sometimes wide discrepancies between the unit value index and the NBER international price index, which seem to us to cast serious doubt upon the reliability of unit value indexes—even when the underlying series are carefully selected—even in so relatively simple a product area as nonferrous metals.[9]

The large differences between the U.S. export unit value index and the NBER international price index are not due primarily to the fact that the unit value index covers only copper and aluminum. The differences between the separate unit value indexes for those two metals and the corresponding international price indexes of Tables 10.8 and 10.9 are as great as those for nonferrous metals as a group, and the discrepancy between the two total indexes is almost an average of those for the two main components. There could, of course, be differences in coverage within the individual metals, but these are not likely to be important, since the unit value data cover both unwrought and worked metals in both groups. The main differences probably come about because the commodity composition of the trade classifications used for computing unit value indexes may change markedly, particularly when there are significant changes in demand and supply relationships that cause prices to change.

Factors Affecting Competitiveness in Individual Metal Groups

In considering nonferrous metals, an observer is likely to think that they fall into the category of highly standardized commodities in universal

---

[9] Part of the smaller range of price movements in the NBER international price indexes may be attributed to the inclusion of a much larger number of series. However, it would probably be difficult to increase substantially the number of unit value series included in the calculations because most of those available are characterized by erratic fluctuations due to wide variability in the product mix of the trade classifications to which they refer.

demand, for which prices will act to localize production at the cheapest source. This view may be fundamentally correct as a description of the long-run tendencies at work, but to understand the actual role of prices in the real world, it is necessary to consider some of the geographical and institutional factors that influence or interfere with the operation of the price mechanism in nonferrous metal markets.

Geographical Influences

A conspicuous influence on the direction of trade in nonferrous metals is the location of ores in relation to markets. Among the major metals mentioned above, copper, silver, lead, and zinc ores are relatively common, while deposits of tin and nickel ores are less widespread. Lead and zinc ores are found, for example, both in the United States and in western Europe. In most cases, however, the advanced industrial countries do not possess sufficient quantities of these ores to meet their needs. This is true even for the United States, which is one of the world's greatest sources of each of these metals. The pressure of demand and the exhaustion of the cheaper sources have forced recourse to less desirable ores and thus have tended to make the domestic metals expensive compared with those available from Canada, Latin America, Africa, and elsewhere. In many instances, the absolute volume of output in these places is smaller than in the United States, but much or all of it is exported because domestic demand is small. Thus the net exports of a country depend not merely upon access to ore supplies; the supplies must be in quantities that are abundant relative to its home needs. The possession of domestic ore supplies may not be an advantage in the nonferrous metals trade, however, if they can be exploited only at a relatively high cost. A high-cost domestic mining industry frequently demands protective policies that result in high domestic prices which put domestic metal refining and fabricating industries at a competitive disadvantage. Many of the price differences between the United States and Europe are attributable, in part, to the relative freedom of Europe to acquire ore supplies from the cheapest sources.

Some countries without domestic ore supplies, notably Great Britain and Belgium, have been important metal-refining and metal-exporting countries because they have had access to foreign sources of ores and because their metal-refining industries have been close to great markets. The history of the exploration and settlement of the Americas, Africa, and Oceania, the search for ores, and the financing of mining operations has left its mark on today's trade flows. Thus, the United States obtains copper from Chile and lead from Mexico; Britain gets tin from Malaya and lead from Australia; Belgium imports copper from the Congo; and France relies upon New Caledonia for nickel ore. New forces of nationalism and development are weakening many of these trading and financial ties. Many underdeveloped countries are encouraging the processing of their ores at home and even the fabrication of refined metal into semifinished or finished products. The smelting of tin, for example, has been declining in the United Kingdom and Benelux and rising in Malaya and other ore-producing areas.

Another important factor determining the location of some nonferrous metal industries, particularly those dependent upon electrolytic refining, is the availability of cheap power. This appears to be the chief explanation for the development in Canada of an aluminum industry second in the free world only to that of the United States, even though Canada must rely on bauxite supplies from the Caribbean area. Cheap power is the basis also for the Norwegian aluminum industry, whose capacity is exceeded in western Europe only by the French. To a smaller degree, abundant power is helpful in nickel refining also. In this metal, however, Canada's position as the world's leading producer depends mainly on the possession of rich and extensive ore deposits. The location of a nickel refinery in Norway, even though it has to use Canadian raw material, is due to the availablity of low-cost power.

Institutional Influences

In assessing the role that price may play in international competition in nonferrous metals, it is necessary to take account not only of the way in which geographical factors affect trade patterns but also of the manner in which the structure of the metal-refining industries and the organization of metal markets make it possible for differences in price levels to exist. In these respects there are, as might be expected, important differences from one nonferrous metal to another, but there are also some striking similarities. We shall deal with the similarities first.

1. The two main markets for most of the major nonferrous metals in their unwrought form are New York and London. The importance of the New York market for some metals, such as copper, lead, and zinc, arises in part from the large volume of United States output. However, the more basic factor, one which applies to all the nonferrous

metals, is the role of the United States as a consumer. In 1963, for example, the United States accounted for about one-third of total free world consumption of copper, lead, zinc, and tin and for around half of the consumption of nickel and aluminum (see Table 10.7). The London market is important because it is the great world trading center where the forces of supply and demand can meet without the restrictions on metal trade that have been imposed in the United States to protect domestic mines. The London Metal Exchange is the world's most important organized metal market, and substantial quantities of copper, lead, zinc, and tin that are not actually sold through the market are transferred at prices prevailing on the market.

2. As is implied in the foregoing, government laws and regulations tend to separate metal markets along national boundaries, each market having its own price level. The most common justifications for these interferences are defense, foreign currency shortages, and economic development, although the element of protection is usually large and clearly visible. Contrary to the common impression that trade barriers are being eroded, government impediments to free trade in unwrought nonferrous metals were probably increasing in the period covered by this study.[10] Certainly, this is true of the United States for a number of important metals, although not for aluminum; within the period covered by this study, the United States reimposed a 1.7 cents per pound duty on copper and placed imports of lead and zinc under quota. The effects of such restrictions can be seen in copper, for which the U.S. price tended to be a cent or two a pound higher than the London price in these years. In other countries that protect domestic mining operations, such as Australia, Japan, and Spain, copper prices were 3 to 6 cents above the London price.[11] One of the most extreme illustrations was a report from India that domestic prices of tin, lead, and zinc were about twice as high as those being quoted on the London market.[12]

Tariffs and quotas are not, however, the only ways in which governments have affected metal markets. One of the most important influences on nonferrous metal markets was the building up and then dimin-

[10] See the statement of an official of a U.S. metal-refining company quoted in the *Metal Bulletin*, July 5, 1963, p. 29. Since 1964, the terminal year of this study, the United States, faced with sharply rising metal prices, has eased some of its protective measures on imports, but has placed controls on certain exports and intervened vigorously in the domestic pricing of several metals.

[11] J. L. Chender, "Copper," in *Engineering and Mining Journal*, February 1965, p. 114.

[12] *Metal Bulletin*, July 17, 1962, p. 10.

Table 10.7
Major Nonferrous Metals: Geographical Distribution of and Changes in
Production and Consumption, 1954 and 1963
(per cent)

Metal[a]	Share in World Production					U.S. Share in Consumption	
	U.S.	Europe[b]	Eastern Bloc[c]	Rest of World	Total World	World Excl. Eastern Bloc	World
1954 Shares							
Copper	37	22	14	27	100		
Aluminum	47	18	15	20	100		
Nickel	16	22	20	43	100		
Zinc	32	30	16	22	100		
Tin	14	36	9	41	100		
Lead	25	28	13	34	100		
1963 Shares							
Copper	32	19	18	31	100	36	29
Aluminum	39	20	22	20	100	54	42
Nickel	6	23	24	48	100	48	33
Zinc	24	26	23	27	100	34	27
Tin	1	18	26	55	100	34	26
Lead	16	31	23	29	100	31	25

	Changes in Production or Consumption		
	1963 Production as Per Cent of 1954 Production		1963 U.S. Consumption as Per Cent of 1954 U.S. Consumption
	U.S.	World	
Copper	134	154	136
Aluminum	158	193	186
Nickel	59	160	132
Zinc	110	146	122
Tin	4	99	101
Lead	82	125	104

Notes to Table 10.7

Source: Computed from data in *Metal Statistics, 1954–1963*, Metallgesellschaft Aktiengesellschaft, Frankfurt, 1964. Some figures, especially those for centrally planned economies, are necessarily rough estimates.

[a]Refinery production for copper and lead; smelting output for nickel, zinc, and tin.

[b]Europe includes Finland, Yugoslavia, and all European OECD countries except Turkey.

[c]Eastern block includes all countries in the Soviet sphere in Europe and all countries in the Chinese sphere in Asia.

ishing of its stockpiles by the U.S. government. During a four-year period beginning in the middle of 1954, for example, the U.S. government bought up the equivalent of 20 to 25 per cent of the domestic production of lead and zinc and acquired substantial quantities of foreign lead and zinc in exchange for agricultural surpluses. The program buoyed up prices, and production also, but when it ended, prices slumped. At the end of the period covered by this study, when there were supply shortages, U.S. disposals served to curb the tendency for prices to rise.

Government intervention may also have other motives. Illustrations are provided by two U.S. regulations on silver. A U.S. prohibition against dealing in silver originating in mainland China led to a premium for non-Chinese silver on the London market which was sometimes greater than half a cent an ounce.[13] U.S. law also prevented the export of silver purchased from the Treasury, with the result that in 1959–61, when Treasury sales were an important source of silver for industrial uses, New York silver prices were slightly lower than those in London.[14] Perhaps government neutrality is impossible in the market for a monetary metal, but neither of these regulations appears to have been necessitated by the monetary use of silver.

3. Another common characteristic of nonferrous metals is their susceptibility to alternating phases of overcapacity and extreme shortage. Mining capacity cannot be altered rapidly, and even changes in the rate of utilization of existing capacity apparently cannot be made quickly.[15] The impact of cyclical and secular changes on the demand for a given

[13] *The Silver Market in 1962*, New York, Handy and Harman, 1963, p. 8.

[14] *The Silver Market in 1959*, p. 9; *The Silver Market in 1960*, p. 8; and *The Silver Market in 1961*, p. 7. Dependence on Treasury silver was attributable in part to a widespread strike in the nonferrous refinery industry during the last half of 1959.

[15] For example, the manager of a large lead and zinc company was quoted as saying that "... a decision today to change the rate of mine production in Australia would probably take six months or longer to be reflected in the physical metal available in the large consuming markets" (*Metal Bulletin*, May 3, 1963, p. 14).

metal is difficult to foretell, as can be readily ascertained from past forecasts in the trade journals. In these circumstances, nonferrous metal prices are almost inevitably subject to sharp fluctuations; within the dozen years covered by this study, for example, there have been year-to-year upswings and downswings in the annual average price in excess of 25 per cent for copper, 20 per cent for lead, and 15 per cent for zinc.[16] As is pointed out below in connection with copper prices, many of these fluctuations, because of their timing, are not reflected in the indexes published here.

Many of the differences among the markets for the various nonferrous metals stem from differences in the number of producers and other facets of the structure of those industries. For none of the nonferrous metals can the number of primary producers outside the centrally planned countries be counted in terms of hundreds, and for most not even in tens. However, the degree of concentration varies from one metal to another, and the same degree of concentration does not always have the same market significance. The number of producers of worked metals is larger, but the big primary producers are often also producers of worked metals. Their pricing policies thus affect worked metal prices directly and also indirectly, since worked metals such as sheet are often priced in terms of a margin over the prevailing primary price. Producers of the major unwrought metals have generally integrated backward into ore production, although to varying degrees. In aluminum, for example, important producers of the metal typically control their own bauxite sources. In tin, on the other hand, the market in ore concentrates is more independent, although ties between smelters and ore producers are quite common.

The production of nickel is perhaps the most concentrated among the nonferrous metals. One producer—a Canadian firm which has its own ore supply—accounts for over half of the free world output, and the world price of nickel follows closely the price set by this firm.[17] The policy of the company has been to seek stable prices, making price changes at relatively long intervals.[18]

The organization of the world aluminum industry has been in flux

[16] Based on data in *Engineering and Mining Journal,* February 1965, p. 83.

[17] *Inquiry into the Strategic and Critical Material Stockpiles of the United States, Hearings,* Senate Committee on Armed Services, 87th Cong., 2nd sess., 1962, Part 8, pp. 2591 and 2647.

[18] Statement of the company president, quoted in *Metal Bulletin,* September 4, 1964, p. 11.

during the past decade. For few, if any, other metals was the prospect for rapid growth in consumption so clear: New companies entered the industry, and existing ones tried to break into new geographical markets.[19] In the United States the number of primary producers rose from three in 1953 to seven in 1963; in 1963 the largest of these accounted for 34 per cent of U.S. capacity and the top three for 86 per cent. In Canada, the leading producer had 85 to 90 per cent of the nation's capacity, and in almost all the other aluminum-producing countries of the free world primary production was limited to two to four firms, with the largest usually accounting for somewhere between 50 and 80 per cent of output.[20] Most of these firms are integrated into the worked metals stage; in the United States, for example, producers consume around two-thirds of the ingot they make.[21]

There has been a growing internationalization of the aluminum industry, which has involved the United States as both a capital importer and a capital exporter. By the end of 1964 aluminum metal was being produced in the United States by a subsidiary of a Swiss company, and subsidiaries of French and Canadian companies were producing worked aluminum products. However, U.S. residents owned a large part of the shares of the leading Canadian producer. Elsewhere, one or more of a half-dozen large U.S., Canadian, Swiss, or French producers were to be found with interests in almost every aluminum-producing country of the non-Communist world.[22] In the struggle for new markets, production has often been established in new countries to gain or retain access to markets in the face of protective measures or subsidies.

The structure of the world copper industry has been relatively stable during the period of our study. In each of the major producing areas of the free world, the bulk of refinery output is accounted for by a few firms—five in the United States, three in Africa (two are British, and one is Belgian), and two in Canada. Two of the American firms are also responsible for a large fraction of copper output in Chile, by far the most important of the Latin American copper-producing countries, and U.S. firms also have interests in African production. In addition, some smaller producers market their copper through one of the

19 Aluminum was also pushed into new uses by the aggressive research and promotion of its producers.
20 *Minerals Yearbook, 1963* and *1953*, U.S. Bureau of Mines, 1964 and 1956.
21 *Aluminum Factbook*, U.S. Dept. of Commerce, 1963, pp. 16–17.
22 *Minerals Yearbook, 1963*.

large firms. Thus, there are perhaps ten sellers who market 80 to 90 per cent of the free world production of primary copper.[23]

Among the other major nonferrous metals, the production of tin is most highly concentrated: Two smelting companies in Malaya and Singapore supply a major share of the metal consumed outside the Eastern bloc.[24] The smelting and refining of silver, lead, and zinc are much less concentrated partly because these metals are mined and refined in a larger number of countries. Within individual countries, however, the number of producers is usually small. In the United States, for example, at the end of 1964 there were only five firms which smelted or refined primary lead.[25]

Several factors, however, limit the market power that small numbers may confer upon the producers. In aluminum, very rapid growth in consumption has stimulated competitive expansion in which the leading firms have struggled to keep their market position. More generally, an important restraint is imposed by intermetal competition (including steel) and by the availability of nonmetallic materials, especially plastics, as substitutes. The expansion of aluminum, in particular, has sometimes occurred in uses formerly served by copper, notably in the electrical and automotive industries. While overlapping financial interests in different metals exist—particularly in lead and zinc but also in copper and other metals—by and large the interests which have large stakes in aluminum differ from those involved in copper, and the same tends to be true of other pairs of major nonferrous metals.

Another limitation which varies in importance from one metal to another and, for a given metal, from one country to another is the availability of metal recovered from scrap.[26] This source of metal appears to be most important compared to primary production in the case of lead; in the United States, for example, it accounts for about one-half of total production.[27] The production of secondary metal tends to be

[23] The statements in this paragraph are based in part upon information in the *Minerals Yearbook, 1963,* and in part upon information obtained from trade sources.

[24] *Minerals Yearbook, 1963.* See also *Inquiry into the Strategic and Critical Material Stockpiles,* Part 5, p. 1740. The extraction of ore in Malaya is much more dispersed.

[25] *Lead and Zinc: Report to the President,* U.S. Tariff Commission, 1965.

[26] The impact of scrap is affected also by its spectrum of uses, which varies from one metal to another; in some cases, such as aluminum, scrap can be used for fabricating a wide range of products and thus competes directly with the primary metal, while in others, such as copper, it may compete with the primary metal in a more limited range of uses.

[27] Based on data in *Minerals Yearbook, 1963.* About 40 per cent of primary production has been from foreign ore supplies.

less concentrated than that of primary metals; again taking lead in the United States as an example, there are over a score of major secondary smelting firms excluding the six primary producers, some of which also produce secondary metal.

A different aspect of the organization of the metal industries that must be considered in analyzing price competitiveness is the practice of treating metals on a toll or conversion basis. Much of the copper, lead, and zinc exported by Belguim and Germany represents metal smelted or refined in those countries for a fee paid by the foreign owner, usually the sales organization of a mining company. It is true that comparative costs of conversion in different countries may influence the owner's choice of country of conversion, but the determining factor may be the availability of capacity and of the technical skill and facilities required to obtain maximum recovery of the metal content, including subsidiary elements such as silver, cadmium, and others. To measure the price competitiveness of the processing country, we would have to know the toll charges; the prices of the smelted or refined metal may reflect the price competitiveness of the country of the owner of the metal to a greater degree than that of the processing country.

Another factor at times, particularly in aluminum, zinc, tin, and silver, has been sales in Western markets by the Soviet Union, other eastern European countries, and China. As may be seen from the figures in Table 10.7, production of nonferrous metals expanded more rapidly in the centrally planned countries than in the free world; these countries probably account for close to one-fourth of the world output. The U.S.S.R. is by far the most important producer in the bloc, accounting for the bulk of output and particularly for sales of aluminum in Western markets. China has been a sporadic source of exports of tin and silver to the West.

Copper

The United States is the world's leading producer of mine copper (23 per cent of world production), followed by the U.S.S.R., Zambia (Northern Rhodesia) and Chile (12 to 15 per cent each), Canada (9 per cent), and the Congo Republic (6 per cent).[28] Very little ore moves in

[28] F. L. Wideman, "Copper," *Minerals Yearbook, 1963,* Table 44.

world trade; it is generally more economical to ship copper after it has been extracted from the ore by concentration, roasting, or, most commonly, by smelting. Latin American copper exports have been divided in roughly equal proportions between Europe and the United States. A good part of the Latin American copper reaching the United States is refined and re-exported to Europe, and this copper accounts for the bulk of U.S. exports. Canada has shipped more copper to Europe than to the United States. African copper has gone mainly to Europe, with the United Kingdom receiving over 40 per cent of Zambia's output; and Belgium, about two-thirds of the Congo's production. African and Latin American exports of unwrought copper were more than one and a half times greater than the exports of the advanced countries (shown in Appendix A).[29]

While the United States used to be an important exporter of copper, it has generally been a net importer in recent years. Most of its imports have consisted of blister copper (the unwrought product obtained by smelting the ore), mainly from Chile and to a lesser extent from Peru and Mexico. At the same time the United States has been importing refined copper; most of these imports, mainly from Canada, have apparently been absorbed domestically. Exports of refined copper in the form of cathodes, ingots, and wire bars to western Europe, India, and Japan, and other destinations have not been large enough to offset all the imports of copper.

OECD countries' exports of worked copper, such as sheet and tube, have been about half the dollar volume of their exports of unwrought copper. Germany and Belgium are the leading exporters of worked copper, and European destinations account for most of the shipments.

While the large producers of primary copper have generally preferred to sell directly to fabricators, some copper, chiefly secondary metal, is traded on the London Metal Exchange (LME). The prices established on the LME are free market prices. The 1961 turnover on the LME amounted to only 16.6 per cent of estimated world consumption, and, as a result of speculation and hedging, only a fraction of the copper traded was for actual consumption.[30] The price of copper on the LME, however, has a significance (which varies at different times) beyond that

[29] See *Metal Bulletin,* September 24, 1963, pp. ii–iii.

[30] According to one source, deliveries amounted to about 20 per cent of the trading volume (*Economist,* February 22, 1964, p. 733). The estimate of trading turnover as a share of world consumption was reported in *Metal Bulletin,* March 20, 1962, p. 8.

indicated by the amount of metal traded. At times, the large producers sold copper to markets outside the United States under long-term contracts setting minimum and maximum quantities, with the price for each lot to be determined by the quotation on the LME at the time of shipment or delivery. However, the LME tends to be very sensitive to changes in supply and demand conditions and to produce sharp fluctuations in price. In 1956, for example, the price of copper was driven up to £437 per ton only to fall back by the end of the year to £240. Such fluctuations led the European producers to abandon the system of pricing based on freely determined LME prices. They controlled the LME price through open market operations while simultaneously curtailing production and accumulating stocks. From the latter part of 1961 to the beginning of 1964, the producers succeeded in stabilizing the LME price of copper at £234 per ton (29.25 cents per pound).[31] In the United States the price remained at 30.6 cents per pound (31.0 cents delivered) during this period. It was reported that the producers had disposed of the surplus stocks they had acquired in their price support operations through cut-rate sales to eastern Europe, Japan, and India.[32] A new, and apparently unanticipated, surge of demand in 1964, coupled with strikes in the United States and Chile, caught the producers without the stocks necessary to prevent price increases. The Chilean government also was pressing for price increases.[33] In January 1964, the producers abandoned their efforts to control the LME price, and toward the end of the year they were rationing supplies to their customers at £260 per ton while the LME price was £520.

The producers made these determined efforts to keep prices down for fear that high copper prices would, beyond a certain point, encourage the long-run substitution of aluminum and plastics and thus adversely affect the value of their ore deposits. Price instability was also thought to encourage such substitution, particularly because aluminum prices were very stable until the last few years of the period.[34] Finally, the

[31] Altogether about 160,000 tons of copper (worth over $100 million) were purchased in this operation (*Metal Bulletin,* June 19, 1964, p. 12). According to one estimate, the 1962 price might have been about £220 per ton (27.5 cents per pound) without producer support (J. Zimmerman, "Copper," *Engineering and Mining Journal,* February 1963, p. 101). For a brief assessment of the copper price operations of the producers, see the *Economist,* October 9, 1965, pp. 185–187.

[32] See *Metal Bulletin,* June 19, 1964, p. 12, and *Engineering and Mining Journal,* February 1964, p. 115.

[33] *New York Times,* October 6, 1964.

[34] It was reported, for example, that aluminum was substituted for copper in making lamp bulb bases when the price of copper soared to 46 cents a pound in 1956 and that

producers feared that the high temporary profits created by high prices would have a ratchet effect on wages, leaving copper less able in the long run to compete with other materials.

Although these motives were common to all the major producers, it does not mean that they always acted together. The U.S. producers were enjoined by law from collaborating to fix prices,[35] and the European producers did not always agree on the proper course. In 1955–56, for example, one British firm, in an effort to keep prices from rising, sold its copper at prices lower than the LME prices which were used by the other major producers. On the other hand, the U.S. and the European-based primary producers apparently have not competed in each others' home markets. For example, one large U.S. buyer of unwrought copper stated in the course of an interview that his company could never obtain foreign copper at a price lower than the domestic price. In general, the United States producers appear to have been better able than European-based ones to curtail and expand production to meet the swings in demand, with the result that the producers' price in the United States tended to be more stable than that in Europe. The U.S. producers' price also tended, within the period covered by this study, to be slightly higher, the main exceptions being in the years 1953–55. The reimposition of the 1.7 cents per pound duty by the United States in July 1958 helped to maintain a differential between the European and U.S. producers' prices.[36]

Merchants were critical of the pricing policies followed by the producers in 1961–64. They argued that the producer-controlled prices did not permit the price mechanism to provide guidance to consumers and producers. The producers, on the other hand, felt that the merchants

bulb makers feared to switch back to copper even after the price fell to 25 cents (*New York Times,* March 15, 1964).

[35] See the *New York Times,* December 29, 1963, for a report that describes one U.S. copper mining official as resenting the notion of U.S. collaboration in price maintenance; the official referred to the attitude of U.S. producers as one of "benevolent neutrality" toward the price stabilization efforts of foreign producers. The U.S. producers could hardly avoid taking account of the pricing policies of the foreign producers and the impact that their own production policies would have on the world-wide copper situation. Thus, as was pointed out by a copper merchant, the U.S. producers cut their production by 5 to 10 per cent in July 1962 when foreign firms were supporting the LME prices even though U.S. consumption exceeded U.S. production. See Zimmerman, *op. cit.,* p. 102.

[36] The statements about prices in this paragraph are based largely on the *Engineering and Mining Journal* average prices for copper sales in the United States and abroad. The prices are taken from reports of producers accounting for 80 to 85 per cent of the copper trade (*E & MJ Metal and Mineral Markets,* June 24, 1963).

Table 10.8

International Prices, Price Competitiveness, and Price Levels, Copper,
1953, 1957, 1961–64

	1953	1957	1961	1962	1963	1964
INTERNATIONAL PRICE INDEXES (1962 = 100)						
U.S.	98	95	100	100	100	107
U.K.	98	94	99	100	100	112
EEC	100	96	101	100	100	119
INDEXES OF U.S. PRICE COMPETITIVENESS (1962 = 100)						
Relative to						
U.K.	100	99	99	100	100	105
EEC	102	102	101	100	100	111
INTERNATIONAL PRICE LEVELS (U.S. FOR EACH YEAR = 100)						
U.S.	100	100	100	100	100	100
U.K.	94	93	93	94	94	99
EEC	96	96	95	94	94	105

Source: International price indexes from Appendix C; price competitiveness indexes, Appendix D; price levels, Appendix E.

were more interested in the active trading that would come with frequent price changes than in the long-run trend of copper consumption.

In any case, producer pricing led to a multiple price system for copper. In periods of slack, consumers in the United States and Europe were able to obtain merchant copper at prices lower than those maintained by producers, and in periods of tightness they had to pay higher prices for a part of their supplies. According to one estimate, for example, about 25 per cent of free world copper was purchased at premium prices in 1964; in the United States about 20 per cent was exchanged at premium prices.[37] In markets outside the United States and Europe, the producers themselves were reported sometimes to have departed from their regular prices, particularly, as we have aleaday noted, in the case of occasional sales to eastern Europe, Russia, and Japan.

The price relationships produced by these structural and market features of the world copper industry are shown in Table 10.8. The

[37] J. L. Chender, "Copper," *Engineering and Mining Journal,* February 1965, p. 113.

time-to-time indexes indicate that the levels of world copper prices were not very different at the various dates of reference used in our study, except for the last one (see top panel). While this is true, it gives a misleading impression of the stability of copper prices over the twelve-year period; prices soared to high levels between 1953 and 1957 and sank to low levels between 1957 and 1961.[38] Using the midyear prices of U.S. producers to indicate the magnitude of the changes, we find that the price of primary copper was between 28.5 and 32 cents a pound at every one of our reference dates, but it was over 45 cents in 1956 and less than 25 cents in 1958.

For our reference years, movements in U.S. and U.K. prices corresponded closely, and until the very last year U.K. prices were 6 or 7 per cent lower than those of the United States (see bottom panel of Table 10.8). The Common Market, where Belgian prices were the most important, was characterized by the same relationship in 1962 and 1963, but EEC prices were a little closer to U.S. levels at the beginning of the period and higher than U.S. prices in the final year. Germany, with less direct access to primary copper, was sometimes in a less favored position relative to the United States than were the United Kingdom and Belgium.

The European export prices of worked copper products, such as sheet and pipe, tended to be lower relative to the United States prices than those of unwrought copper; this was particularly true of brass products. U.K. export prices were only a few percentage points below those of the United States for unwrought copper, but around 12 per cent lower for worked copper in 1962, for example. However, unwrought copper was about twice as important as worked copper in the exports of the advanced countries, and this relationship is reflected in the weights used in preparing the indexes.

Until the final year of our period, the price position of the United Kingdom and the Common Market as a whole relative to that of the United States hardly changed (see middle panel). There is some evidence, on the other hand, that the German position relative to the United States improved; this improvement appears to reflect the movement of German prices, initially high, to levels closer to those prevailing in Belgium, the other important Common Market exporter (see Appendix A).

---

[38] See, for example, the price reports in the *Metal Bulletin*.

The indexes for 1964 are subject to additional margins of error because, while in general we had rather comprehensive information, there was a key piece missing. For 1964 as for other recent years, we have extensive data covering sellers' prices of unwrought copper abroad, as well as a good sample of prices of worked copper products. We also have good information about the premium prices that were paid for unwrought copper; these varied widely during the year and from market to market, but the mean premium seems to have been in the range of 25 to 40 per cent above the producers' price. What we do not know is the fraction of each country's exports of unwrought copper that was sold at premium prices. On the basis of information gleaned from trade journals [39] and from conversations with people in the trade, we have taken the premium-priced exports to be 10 per cent for the United States, 25 per cent for the United Kingdom, 100 per cent for Germany, and 50 per cent for the Common Market as a whole. The possible margins of error introduced by this assumption may be indicated by applying the alternative assumption that premium-priced exports constituted 10 per cent of the unwrought copper exports of each country. The results in 1964 are price levels lower by two points for the United Kingdom and four points for the EEC than the figures shown in Table 10.8 (bottom panel). Corresponding adjustments in the indexes of price competitiveness would affect the magnitude but not the existence of a relative improvement in the competitive position of the United States between 1963 and 1964.[40]

Aluminum

The United States, the U.S.S.R., and Canada accounted for about 68 per cent (38, 18, and 12 per cent, respectively) of primary aluminum production in 1962–63. World production has been expanding rapidly, and has become more dispersed. In 1953–54, for example, world output was only about half of the 1962–63 level, and the three leading countries accounted for about 78 per cent of production (47, 12, and 19 per cent, respectively). Production has been rising most rapidly in Japan,

[39] See, for example, *Metal Bulletin*, October 6, 1964, p. 15, and Chender, *op. cit.*, p. 113.

[40] Actually, the figures in the table probably understate slightly the improvement in the U.S. position, since the 10 per cent estimate is more likely to be too high than too low.

India, and the Soviet sphere. The number of producers has tended to expand within each country, although it still remains small.[41]

About 20 per cent of unwrought aluminum production enters world trade. The pattern of trade differs substantially from the pattern of production. The United States, with its high absorptive capacity for metals, has played a smaller role in world trade than might be inferred from its importance in world production. In recent years, U.S. exports of primary aluminum have been less than 15 per cent of the free world total, with the United Kingdom, Germany, and Latin America the main destinations. U.S. exports have been equivalent to 7 or 8 per cent of domestic production; imports, to 17 or 18 per cent, well over half from Canada, and the rest almost entirely from Norway and France.

Canada, which consumes about 15 per cent of its own production of unwrought aluminum, supplies about half of the world's exports. Norway and France are also important exporters; the former, like Canada, sells most of its output abroad.[42] A limited number of destinations tend to account for a large share of each country's exports. Over half of French exports are to the Common Market and over a quarter to the United States; about two-thirds of Canadian exports are sent to the United States and the United Kingdom; and about three-quarters of Norwegian exports are shipped to the United Kingdom, the United States, and Germany. U.S. exports, however, have a more varied list of destinations.

The smaller trade in worked aluminum is more dispersed. Canada and Norway are smaller factors; and Germany, Belgium, the United Kingdom, and the United States (with about equal export volumes) furnish about two-thirds of the exports of the advanced countries. Germany and Belgium send their exports largely to European destinations; the United Kingdom and the United States to more varied markets.

Aluminum was not traded on any metal exchange during the period

[41] The data in this and the following paragraphs are based mainly on *Minerals Yearbook, 1963,* and earlier editions, and *Metal Statistics, 1954–1963,* and other issues (Frankfurt am Main, Germany, Metallgesellschaft Aktiengesellschaft). These sources also show the patterns of production and trade in bauxite. The U.S. imports over 80 per cent of its bauxite requirements; the U.S.S.R., less than one-fourth. France alone of the major aluminum producers is a net exporter of bauxite; most others, like Canada and Norway, import virtually all they use. Almost half of the world's supply of bauxite is produced in the Caribbean area, particularly in Jamaica, Surinam, and British Guiana. In Europe, Hungary, Yugoslavia, and Greece follow the U.S.S.R. and France in production. (Production data for the centrally planned economies are necessarily rough estimates made in the sources cited.)

[42] The U.S.S.R. is also a significant exporter, with the bulk of its shipments going to other Communist countries.

of this study and hence was producer priced. The price leadership of the major Canadian producer appears to have been widely accepted at least for nominal purposes in world trade. The Canadian firm has generally avoided any challenge to other price leaders in their domestic markets (as in the United States); [43] the existence of tariffs and transport costs has permitted small differences between prices in different countries. While changes in the posted world prices of aluminum ingot— the key item in the price structure—have not been frequent,[44] sales below the nominal world price have been common, especially in the last few years of our study when the struggle among the major producers for the growing world market seems to have intensified. Sales of Russian aluminum added to the competitive pressures. Price cutting appears to have been common in sales made by major producers of one country in the markets of other major producing countries. Large buyers in these markets, willing to follow aggressive purchasing policies and not setting a high premium on the continuity of their sources of supply, could usually find aluminum at 1 or 2 cents below the list price.[45] As a result there was cross shipping of identical products between the United States and Europe; indeed, more than one reliable source reported occasional purchases of U.S. aluminum in Europe for reshipment to the United States. The market for European aluminum in the United States appears to have been confined largely to the coastal areas, particularly the eastern seaboard, and the Great Lakes region. The aluminum industry is more highly integrated vertically than the copper industry, and competition sometimes focused on worked aluminum products as well as on ingot.[46]

The dispersion of prices makes the average relationships shown in Table 10.9 less representative than others in this volume. Furthermore,

[43] On price leadership, see the *Metal Bulletin*, April 1, 1958, p. 13; February 16, 1962, p. 13; and December 13, 1963, p. 13. See also Carl M. Loeb, Rhoades & Co., *Aluminum Industry*, September 1965, p. 10.

[44] Although the ingot price changed three times in 1964, there were only twenty changes in the previous eighteen years (Irving Lipkowitz, in *Engineering and Mining Journal*, February 1965, p. 98).

[45] Public statements about these practices are naturally infrequent, but the head of the largest French aluminum firm was quoted in the press near the end of 1962 as acknowledging that French aluminum was being offered in the United States at 22.5 cents a pound at a time when the U.S. list price was 24 cents. (The U.S. duty of 1.25 cents and freight were apparently paid by the seller.) He was also cited as saying that foreign aluminum—U.S., Canadian, or Japanese—was being offered in France at less than the French domestic price of 22.5 cents despite a duty of 15 per cent (*New York Times*, November 16, 1962).

[46] *Metal Bulletin*, January 1, 1963, p. 18.

Table 10.9
International Prices, Price Competitiveness, and Price Levels, Aluminum,
1953, 1957, 1961–64

	1953	1957	1961	1962	1963	1964
INTERNATIONAL PRICE INDEXES (1962 = 100)						
U.S.						
Aluminum	99	108	103	100	97	103
Unwrought	104	109	103	100	94	103
Worked	92	107	102	100	101	103
U.K.	98	111	105	100	100	107
EEC	107	109	103	100	97	104
INDEXES OF U.S. PRICE COMPETITIVENESS (1962 = 100)						
Relative to						
U.K.	99	103	102	100	104	104
EEC	108	101	101	100	100	101
INTERNATIONAL PRICE LEVELS (U.S. FOR EACH YEAR = 100)						
U.S.	100	100	100	100	100	100
U.K.	90	94	94	92	95	95
EEC	96	90	90	89	90	90

Source: Same as Table 10.8

the time-to-time figures for the United Kingdom and the underlying figures for some of the Common Market countries are not based on a broad enough sample of prices to produce reliable averages.[47] The figures for the United States and Germany, on the other hand, are believed to be reliable. The former are based on producers' data that represent a high fraction of U.S. exports, as well as on buyers' information of more limited scope; and the latter, on both purchasers' data and on more than a score of export price series.

The time-to-time indexes of the United States, the United Kingdom, and the EEC (top panel) show similar directions of change for the most part, although there are sufficient differences to cause variations in relative price levels. In general, the European prices have been 5 to 10 per cent

[47] However, the place-to-place comparisons for the Common Market and the United States in 1961 and 1962 are reliable, each being based on several hundred observations.

lower than those of the United States (see bottom panel). Within Europe, EEC prices have generally been lower than U.K. ones.

The differences between U.S. and European prices have generally been significantly smaller for ingot and other forms of unwrought aluminum; indeed, European export prices have in some instances been higher than those of the United States. For worked aluminum, however, European prices have in many cases been 15 to 20 per cent lower than those of the United States. In 1962, a year for which there was a substantial number of observations, the international price levels were as follows (U.S. = 100):

		EEC	
	U.K.	Total	Germany
Aluminum (684)	92	89	94
Unwrought aluminum (684.1)	95	95	101
Worked aluminum (684.2)	86	80	82

Within the EEC, French prices have tended to be relatively low for unwrought aluminum, while German and Belgian prices have been relatively low for worked aluminum. As in the case of copper, where a similar situation prevailed between U.S. and European prices, trade in the more highly fabricated stage is only half as important as trade in the less processed material, and the indexes are weighted accordingly. The overall changes in price competitiveness (middle panel) have been relatively small and, with the exception of the improvement of the EEC and German positions after the earlier years, there does not seem to have been any trend.

Other Nonferrous Metals

For the one-third of world nonferrous trade that does not consist of aluminum and copper, we do not present separate indexes. However, our comments on the more important of these metals follow.

Nickel

Canada accounted for 58 per cent of the world's mine production of nickel in 1962–63; about 80 per cent of Canadian output came from one company. The other major producing countries are the U.S.S.R.

(23 per cent), and New Caledonia (8 per cent).[48] The sole U.S. producer accounted for only about 3 per cent of the world's supply of mine nickel. The United States, which uses over a third of all the nickel consumed in the world, imports about 90 per cent of its requirements.

As might be expected from this situation, Canada is by far the most important factor in world nickel trade; it accounts for about two-thirds of free world exports of unwrought nickel and its alloys. Most of the rest of the export trade is carried on by Norway and the United Kingdom, which rely almost entirely on Canadian ore. Canada exports little ore to the United States, but around 75 to 85 per cent of her exports of unwrought metal have gone there. The United States also gets some unwrought nickel—about 20 per cent of its imports—from Norway, France, and the United Kingdom. In European and other markets outside North America, the United Kingdom and Norway often match and sometimes exceed Canadian sales. France, using New Caledonian ore, is a smaller exporter.

The countries with the most advanced metallurgical industries— the United States, the United Kingdom, and Germany—accounted for about 75 per cent of 1963 trade in worked nickel and nickel alloys in such forms as bars, sections, wire, plates, sheets, and tubes. The main destinations were other industrial countries. Canada and France, mentioned above as exporters of unwrought nickel, were net importers of worked nickel.

As already noted, the Canadian firm that is the world's largest producer acts as a price leader and has followed a policy of stable prices. During the early part of the period covered by this study, nickel was in short supply owing in large measure to the impact of the Korean War upon U.S. government demands for current use (jet engines, among others) and stockpiling. During these years of shortage (1953–57), the posted price of nickel rose only by 20–25 per cent, but smaller producers sometimes got higher prices, and free market sales at extremely high prices were reported.[49] By 1957 free world output was

---

[48] These figures are based on data in G. C. Ware, "Nickel," *Minerals Yearbook, 1963*. Metallgesellschaft Aktiengesellschaft data (*Metal Statistics*), give a little higher share for Canada and a somewhat lower share for the U.S.S.R. The latter source also indicates that both the Canadian and U.S.S.R. shares have fallen in the period since 1953–54 while the successive editions of the *Minerals Yearbook* indicates a sharper drop for Canada (from 67 per cent) and a slight rise for the U.S.S.R. (from 20 per cent).

[49] *Metal Bulletin*, May 29, 1962, p. 9. The *Engineering and Mining Journal* reported free market prices of $3 a pound when the producers' price was 64.5 cents (February 1963, p. 142).

50 per cent higher than in 1953, and U.S. government demands had eased. The producers' price remained constant for a period of four and a half years beginning in December 1956. At the end of June 1961, there was a 10 per cent price increase, but because of lagging demand small producers were reported to be shading the official price.[50] The price was reduced by about 2.75 per cent in May 1962, but even at this level production had to be cut in the latter part of the year. Demand strengthened in 1963 and even more markedly in 1964, but no further price changes were made that year.

The evidence we have, from a half dozen sources, mainly foreign, suggests that European export prices have been slightly lower than those of the United States. The differences are more marked for worked nickel products, but these were only about one-fourth as important as unwrought nickel, for which price differences appeared to be small. Prices seem to have moved largely along parallel lines in the different countries.

Silver and Platinum Metals

At least small amounts of silver are produced in a large number of countries, but the Americas (chiefly Mexico, Peru, the United States, and Canada) accounted for about three-quarters of free world output in 1963.[51]

In most years the United States consumes more silver than it produces, and it imports significant quantities from Canada, Mexico, and Peru. Germany and Belgium have also been important in the world silver markets (mainly as re-exporters), and China disposed of large quantities in 1960–62 (probably in large part from the demonetization of coins) although the United States was not, of course, a buyer of silver from this source. Until recently, consumption of silver for coinage and for industrial uses had been expanding at about equal rates, with coinage absorbing between 20 and 35 per cent of world silver consumption. The enormous increase in U.S. coin requirements in the last few years covered by our study greatly altered the world silver market; the *increase* in silver absorbed for U.S. coinage in 1964

[50] *Metal Bulletin*, May 29, 1962, p. 9.

[51] J. P. Ryan, "Silver," *Minerals Yearbook, 1963*, Table 14. According to estimates given in this source, the main producer in the Soviet bloc is the U.S.S.R. with more than 10 per cent of world output.

compared with 1962 was equivalent to more than one-third of all world silver consumption in 1962. In addition, world consumption of silver for industrial uses alone, for some years, exceeded world production.[52]

Despite the homogeneity of silver and its worldwide use, its prices in different places are not always equal, even allowing for transfer costs. Some U.S. regulations causing price differences have already been mentioned, but other illustrations may easily be found. The difference between the Indian price and others—the result of strict controls over imports and exports—has been one of the largest. The lowest Indian price during 1964, for example, was $1.58 an ounce compared to a U.S. high of $1.293 and an English high of $1.302.[53]

Silver prices in New York and London rose from around 83 cents an ounce in 1953 to 85 cents in 1954–55 and then to an 89–91 cent range in 1956–61. The suspension by the U.S. Treasury of sales of nonmonetized silver at the end of 1961, an action related to growing coinage requirements, led to a sharp increase in prices to $1.293 (in September 1963), a ceiling established by the availability of Treasury silver at this price through the redemption of silver certificates.

London and New York silver prices have moved in close accord, with the London price usually slightly higher. Prices have moved somewhat more independently on the Continent, apparently at a higher level than U.S. or U.K. prices. The only deviation from published prices that was reported to us referred to silver originating in the Soviet bloc.

Of the platinum metals grouped with silver in the SITC, platinum and palladium are the most important; iridium, osmium, rhodium, and ruthenium are also included. These metals have properties of chemical inertness, hardness, and ability to withstand heat that make them useful as catalysts in chemical processes, as refractory materials, and as durable electrical contacts in communications switchgear.[54]

The U.S.S.R., Canada, and South Africa are the major sources of supply. The United States, which accounts for half to two-thirds of free world consumption, has obtained its platinum metals chiefly from Canada and the United Kingdom, with smaller supplies coming from

[52] *The Silver Market in 1964*, p. 19. Beginning in 1965, however, U.S. coinage requirements were sharply curtailed by a shift to the use of filler materials in "silver" coins.
[53] *Ibid.*, pp. 12, 16, and 22.
[54] G. C. Ware, "Platinum Group Metals," *Minerals Yearbook, 1963*, pp. 4–5.

the U.S.S.R. and Switzerland.[55] The United Kingdom is by far the most important exporter of these metals, supplying not only the United States but also the Common Market, Japan, and even Canada.

Platinum metals have been exported from the United Kingdom at prices slightly below those of the United States, and Continental prices have been only a shade above those of the United Kingdom. There was, however, a relatively sharp rise in the German price of platinum between 1963 and 1964, and, as a result, the German and EEC indexes of price competitiveness for SITC 681 as a whole moved favorably for the United States.

The NBER indexes for this group are based in part on prices published by trade sources and in part on information from about a score of other sources.

Zinc

Lead and zinc are linked together because they are frequently found in the same ores. Since zinc is more important in trade, it will be discussed first.

About 40 per cent of the mine production of zinc is accounted for by the New World and about one-third by Europe; the United States is responsible for about one-third of the output of the Americas, and the U.S.S.R. for a similar share of European output. Australia is the third most important producer, providing about 10 per cent of the world supply. U.S. production plummeted from high Korean War levels, and the gradual comeback since the 1958 low had not, by 1964, restored output to its former level. World production, on the other hand, showed a more persistent expansion; 1963 output was 30 per cent above 1954.[56]

Most of the ore-producing countries also export unwrought zinc, particularly Canada, the U.S.S.R., and Australia. However, as with lead, smelter production tends to be located in industrialized areas. The United States and Europe account for over two-thirds of world smelter output, with the United States and the U.S.S.R. accounting for

---

[55] The United Kingdom refines ores from South Africa and the U.S.S.R., and Switzerland is a trading center for metals primarily of U.S.S.R. origin.

[56] *Metal Statistics*, p. 21. Belgium, the United States, France, the United Kingdom, and Germany were the big importers of zinc ores and concentrates. In general, the United States relied heavily on Canada and Latin America for supplies while the European importers drew upon European as well as Latin American and Canadian supplies. The United Kingdom obtained over three-quarters of its raw material from Australia.

23 and 13 per cent, respectively. The shares of Japan, Canada, Belgium, France, Poland, and Australia fall in the 5 to 8 per cent range.[57] Belgium, without ore supplies of its own, is a major factor in the world zinc trade. The leading importers are the United Kingdom, the United States, and Germany.

U.S. government intervention has been a more important factor in the lead and zinc markets than in other metals. Although at times, especially in wartime, the United States has adopted measures to stimulate exploration and production, during most of the past decade U.S. policy has been faced with a high-cost domestic industry in a world in which other sources of supply were capable of substantial expansion in output. The basic fact is that U.S. deposits of high-grade ores have been so depleted that in recent years the domestic mining industry has been working ores that are only half as rich in metal content as ores mined in foreign countries.[58] The U.S. industry thus has required higher prices than foreign producers. In the slump after the Korean War boom, the U.S. government rejected the domestic producers' application for additional protection against imports and embarked upon a stockpiling program that absorbed the equivalent of one-fifth to one-fourth of the domestic mine production of lead and zinc in the four years beginning in mid-1954.[59] A still larger quantity of lead was acquired from foreign producers in 1956–61 by bartering surplus agricultural commodities. Zinc was also acquired from foreign sources through barter in 1956–57 in an amount equal to a little more than 70 per cent of the quantity acquired from domestic producers in 1954–58.[60] This program was accompanied by efforts to induce foreign producers to restrict production.

It seems likely, however, that the net effect of government stockpiling was not only to push up prices but also to stimulate lead and zinc production, especially in the United States, where acquisitions from domestic sources were confined almost entirely to metal from newly mined ore.[61] As long as the government was absorbing substantial quantities of lead and zinc, the excess of production over consumption

[57] H. J. Schroeder, "Zinc," *Minerals Yearbook, 1963*, p. 29.

[58] *Lead and Zinc: Report to the President on Escape-Clause Investigation No. 65*, U.S. Tariff Commission, 1958, p. 18.

[59] Based on data in *Inquiry into the Strategic and Critical Material Stockpiles*, Part 4, p. 1240.

[60] *Ibid.*, pp. 1264–1265.

[61] *Lead and Zinc: Report to the President*, 1958, p. 29.

did not depress prices. When the government announced the curtailment of its procurement programs in 1957, there was a worldwide decline in lead and zinc prices. Indeed, foreign prices fell below those in the United States by more than the cost of freight and insurance, with the result that foreign refined pig lead and slab zinc were sold in the United States at substantial discounts below the U.S. producers' prices.[62]

In these circumstances, the United States abandoned its effort to avoid protective measures in the course of aiding its domestic producers. Effective in October 1958, the U.S. limited imports of unmanufactured lead and zinc to 80 per cent of the average annual commercial imports in 1953–57. The effect was to raise U.S. prices and to increase the difference between the U.S. and foreign prices.[63]

The demand for zinc was stronger than that for lead, and the operation of market forces outside the United States changed the price relationship of the two metals earlier than in the United States; the price of zinc, which had been 2 or 3 cents lower per pound than the price of lead for a number of years, first exceeded the lead price in London at the end of 1958, whereas the price crossover did not occur in the United States until a year later. The resumption of a notable upward trend in the free world consumption of lead and zinc began in 1959, but the expansion in zinc was greater.[64]

The recovery of metal markets in early 1964 caused first a narrowing of the differential between New York and London zinc prices and then a reversal of the historical pattern, in which the London price had been lower than the New York price.

In July 1964 zinc producers outside the United States, fearful of the adverse effect of rising London Metal Exchange zinc quotations upon the competitive position of the metal, began an effort to maintain a producers' price as in copper. The United States released 75,000 tons— equivalent to about 7 per cent of a year's domestic production—from its stockpile to alleviate the shortage.[65]

As a result of these developments the U.K.-to-U.S. index of com-

[62] *Ibid.*, pp. 39–42. The duty on lead has been 1.0625 cents per pound and on zinc 0.7 cents per pound since 1951. Freight and insurance costs have of course varied but they have generally been less than 1 cent per pound.

[63] See *Lead and Zinc: Report to the President,* 1960, Tables 10 and 11; and 1965, p. 26, and Tables 11 and 12.

[64] *Metal Statistics, 1954–1963,* pp. 11 and 23.

[65] F. R. Jeffrey, "Zinc," *Engineering and Mining Journal,* February 1965, p. 108.

petitiveness fluctuated more than the indexes for other nonferrous metals; it wound up in 1964 in a position reflecting much higher relative U.K. prices than in any former year. Zinc export prices from the Continent tended to conform to the U.K. pattern of changes over time.

Lead

The Americas account for about one-fourth of the world's mine production of lead; the centrally planned economies, for one-fourth; Australia accounts for one-sixth, and non-Soviet Europe, for one-seventh. U.S. mine output, which still makes up over one-third of the New World production, declined by nearly 25 per cent from 1953–54 to 1962–63. World output increased by about the same percentage, expansion being most rapid in the Soviet bloc.

Belgium, Germany, the United States, and France import large quantities of the ore from Canada, Latin America (especially Peru and Bolivia), and Australia. The European countries also rely upon closer sources such as Sweden, Bulgaria, and Morocco. Belgium and the United States obtain substantial supplies from southern Africa. There has been a growing tendency to process ores in the countries in which the mines are located.

The geographical distribution of smelter lead production nevertheless is still dominated by the pattern of industrialization. The Americas and non-Soviet Europe each produce one-third of the world total, and the Soviet bloc produces one-fourth. The United States accounts for half of the New World output, its production having declined in absolute as well as relative terms during the past decade.

The most marked increases in the consumption of lead have been in the Soviet bloc and non-Soviet Europe; U.S. consumption has hardly increased over the past decade. In the United States, over half of current consumption is supplied by recovered scrap.

Manufactured lead is traded predominantly in unwrought form. The chief exporters are Australia, Mexico, the U.S.S.R., and Canada. Belgium, without ores of its own, is a significant net exporter of lead. Germany and the United Kingdom also export small quantities, but they are net importers by a substantial margin. The United States, an important net exporter of lead before World War II, is the largest importer, followed at some distance by the United Kingdom and Germany.

With only brief exceptions at the very end of the period, the New

York price of lead exceeded the London price during the period covered by this study. In the early years the difference between lead prices in New York and London fluctuated around the transfer costs of approximately 2 cents a pound (1.0625 cents duty plus freight and insurance). With the announcement of the end of stockpile purchases, in 1957, and the subsequent imposition of quotas by the U.S. government, the differential tended to be larger—around 3 or 4 cents a pound—and more variable. It shrank again with the recovery of metal markets in 1964 as U.S. producers restrained the extent of price increases in the face of tightening supplies; in the latter part of the year it actually reversed direction for a time. The United States released 50,000 tons of lead from its stockpile in 1964.

As in the case of zinc, official prices tend to reflect actual transactions prices more fully when supply and demand are in balance and prices are stable. In periods of excess supply, a number of export transactions take place at lower prices, and in periods of shortage, some exports are sold at premium prices. Even where producers attempt to maintain the published quotations, secondary metal is readily sold at a discount or premium. Thus, in the case of the U.S. price movement for lead exports between mid-1963 and mid-1964, for example, we have estimated the export price increase at 26 per cent, although the several publicly available wholesale and producers' price series show increases ranging from 18 to 22 per cent.

Our indexes show that European prices were lowest relative to the United States in 1961 and 1962 when there was a differential of about 20 per cent, with U.K. prices slightly lower than those of Germany and the EEC. Differences were much smaller in 1964 and, in the case of the EEC, prices were almost up to the U.S. level.

Tin

Tin is one of the few important metals which were not marked by rising world production during the period under review. Mine production of tin in 1962–63 was within 1 per cent of the 1953–54 level. The major sources of supply in the terminal years were Malaya (32 per cent), China (15 per cent), Bolivia (12 per cent), the U.S.S.R. (10 per cent), and Indonesia and Thailand (8 per cent each). Increases in output in China, the U.S.S.R., and Thailand were offset by declines in Indonesia, Bolivia, and the Republic of the Congo. Only as the period drew to an end did it appear that serious supply shortages and premium prices might begin to stimulate a new surge in output.

In some cases, such as Malaya and the U.S.S.R., tin concentrates are smelted, and only tin metal is exported. In others, particularly Bolivia and Indonesia, tin concentrates are exported. Bolivian concentrates have gone mainly to the United Kingdom, while the destination of Indonesian concentrates has varied with political circumstances including, at times, the Netherlands, Malaya, and the United States, among others. Toward the end of the study period some developing countries which exported concentrates, such as Nigeria, began to establish local smelting facilities. The result of these changes, already noted, was that the share of the United States and western Europe in world tin smelting declined from more than 50 per cent in 1953–54 to around 20 per cent in 1962–63.

Malaya has been the world's major exporter of unwrought tin, probably accounting for more than 75 per cent of world trade. The United Kingdom, the Netherlands, Belgium, the U.S.S.R., China, and Germany accounted for most of the balance. A large part of the tin consumed in the United States and western Europe is used to make tinplate (SITC subgroup 674.7), which is five times more important in international trade than tin itself.

The price of tin has been influenced by the International Tin Agreement, which came into effect in 1956. A buffer stock financed by the producer countries was established, and its manager was required to buy tin when the price was below the floor (successively raised from £640 per long ton in 1956 to £1,000 near the end of 1964) and to sell when the price was over the ceiling (£800 in 1956 and £1,200 by the end of 1964). When the price was between the floor and ceiling but near one or the other, the manager could buy or sell (according to the case) at his discretion, but when the price was in a middle £50 or £100 range between the floor and ceiling he could not come into the market. Export quotas were also assigned to the six producing member countries from December 1957 to October 1960; quotas were curtailed during 1958 but expanded in 1959–60.

In the first few years of the period covered in this study, U.S. stockpile purchases buoyed up the world tin market.[66] By 1957, these pur-

---

[66] Deliveries to the United States under stockpile contracts in 1953–56 were equivalent to more than one year's world production (*Inquiry into the Strategic and Critical Material Stockpiles,* Part 5, pp. 1724–1725).

chases had been ended; and this shift, combined with low tin demand due to recession conditions and with Russian sales, forced the buffer stock manager to buy tin to keep the price from falling below the floor. Nevertheless, the producer members insisted upon raising the floor price in 1958, and the buffer stock manager ran out of money. In the final years of the period, the opposite difficulty appeared; the buffer stock manager had no tin to sell. This situation first appeared in mid-1961, when it was attributed to speculation.[67] Prices subsequently declined partly because of a U.S. decision to release 50,000 long tons (nearly a third of a year's world production) from its stockpile, and the buffer stock manager was led to buy tin again in the latter part of 1962. However, the basic situation was one of shortage, since consumption had exceeded production for several years; and prices began to climb again. In October 1963 the buffer stock of tin ran out once more, and prices rose, first moderately and then at an accelerating rate, reaching a peak in October 1964 that was about twice the October 1963 level. The price increases came despite U.S. stockpile releases of 6,000 tons in 1963 and 22,000 tons in 1964.[68]

The three major tin markets are the London Metal Exchange, which includes both spot and future transactions and which is the focus of consumers, traders, and speculators from all over the world; the Penang market (Singapore before May 1964), which deals in tin for physical delivery; and the New York market, which caters chiefly to U.S. consumers. All three markets are closely related, but short-run divergent price movements are possible within narrow limits, since it takes four to six weeks to move tin from Malaya to London or New York and one or two weeks between London and New York. Transfer costs usually ensure that the London and New York prices will be higher than the Malayan price; the New York price, in turn, has tended to run slightly higher than the London price. The index of price competitiveness has thus not varied very much from year to year.

We had to rely on published prices to a considerable extent in making up our indexes for this group, as we had independent data only from a few U.S. and German sources, all buyers. However, our U.S. sources rather consistently showed smaller fluctuations than the published prices, and we based our indexes for the United States mainly on these private data.

---

[67] *Engineering and Mining Journal*, February 1963, p. 111.
[68] K. Friedlander, "Tin," *Engineering and Mining Journal*, February 1965, p. 93.

Miscellaneous Nonferrous Metals

This category covers about a score of nonferrous metals. Belgium is the largest exporter, followed by the United States, the United Kingdom, Japan, and Germany. Our time-to-time indexes are based on the more important metals in the group such as magnesium, tungsten, molybdenum, antimony, cobalt, chromium, cadmium, titanium, and manganese. We used wholesale price data more extensively here than in any other nonferrous group. For example, five of the seventeen series used in preparing the U.S. index represent published wholesale price data. The German indexes are based on the smallest number of series, six, although in this case none of them represents a published series. The indexes for all of the areas (the United States, the United Kingdom, Germany, and the EEC) reveal a sharp drop in prices between 1953 and 1957. Aside from a further decline in the United States between 1957 and 1961, prices tended to remain stable through 1961 and 1962, only to rise again in 1963 and more sharply in 1964. The rise in these recent years carried European prices beyond the levels that had prevailed in 1953, whereas the same was not true of the U.S. prices. Thus, European miscellaneous nonferrous metal prices, which had often been 15 to 20 per cent below U.S. prices, were about the same as U.S. prices in 1964 (U.K. prices were actually still a little lower, while German prices were a little higher, than U.S. prices).

Conclusions

During most of the years covered by this study, European international prices of nonferrous metals were 5 to 10 per cent below U.S. prices, taking the bundle of nonferrous metals exported by the advanced countries as a whole. The gap between American and European prices was widest in 1961 and 1962, but had diminished substantially, to only a couple of percentage points, by 1964. Among the European countries, Germany appeared to have less of a price advantage over the United States than either the United Kingdom or the EEC countries as a group. In both copper and aluminum, the two most important nonferrous metals in the exports of developed countries, the difference between U.S. and foreign price levels was larger for worked than for unwrought metals. In some instances, such as lead in 1962, European international prices were as much as 20 per cent below those of the United States, and in other, less frequent cases European prices were higher. The latter was true, for example, of EEC copper prices in 1964, German prices of primary aluminum in 1962, European silver prices more often than not, and U.K. zinc prices in 1964. Quite generally the United States was least price competitive in 1961–62, and its position in 1964 was more favorable than at any other time except, possibly, the very beginning of our period.

For primary metal products, direct price competition in the sense of cutting prices in order to enter new markets including the home markets of rival producers, appears to have been confined to the aluminum industry. For worked metals, price competition has been somewhat more common.

In a number of the other major nonferrous metals, U.S. prices have often been maintained at comparatively stable levels, usually higher than those abroad. In slack markets the U.S. producers have not been completely immune to pressures from lower foreign prices because, when the price difference becomes large enough, foreign primary metal is brought into markets ordinarily served by U.S. producers, and, more frequently, because products fabricated out of foreign metals begin to displace those produced from U.S. metals. Pricing policies, particularly in copper, have been influenced by the threat of price competition from rival metals and other substitute products.

The pricing policies followed in Europe tend to differ from those of the United States. The tendency in Europe is to differentiate between home and foreign markets and to export metals at prices reflecting current world supply and demand conditions, although by the end of the period under study both primary copper and primary zinc were being sold in Europe at prices established by producers rather than at those set on the free market. Concentration in the nonferrous metal industries is high in both the United States and Europe, particularly at the primary stage, and cannot account therefore for the differences in pricing policies between the two. They are more likely the natural outcome of the difference in the capacity of the nonferrous metal industries relative to home demand in the two areas. The home market is of overwhelming importance to U.S. producers, and since it is protected— always by transport cost and time, and frequently by trade restrictions as well—it is only sensible to gear price policies to it. Of course, separate pricing policies can be applied to exports, and sometimes they have been.

The nonferrous industries of the European countries, on the other hand, are built to serve external markets; in some extreme cases such as Belgian copper and Norwegian aluminum, for example, the domestic market absorbs only a small part of output. The pressure on firms in this position to meet world supply and demand condition is, of course, much greater. This situation also leads to differential pricing for various markets.

Thus, the imperfections and fragmentation of world nonferrous metal markets are greater than might have been expected for goods which, in their homogeneity and ubiquity of use, conform so well to the stereotype of standardized internationally traded goods. Tariffs and quotas, the division of markets, the tendency to maintain customary trade channels, technical know-how, and other factors operate to varying degrees, not so much in the dynamic aluminum industry as in the slower-growing copper industry, to reduce the impact of price differences on trade flows.

Although, as noted, the direction of trade in nonferrous metals is influenced by a great variety of nonprice factors, probably to a greater extent than in other products included in this study, much of the trade pattern is consistent with price relationships. For example, the ranks of the 1963 ratios of U.K. and EEC exports to U.S. exports, for the five categories of metals for which price ratios were considered at least partially publishable, were, as expected, inversely related to the price ratios (Table 10.10).

An element of chance may be involved, since the data are somewhat rough and the differences between some of the price ratios are quite small; but there is, in any case, considerable consistency between the prices and export movements of these metals.

One result of the computation of these indexes of international prices is to show that for nonferrous metals, as for iron and steel, the existing wholesale price and export unit value indexes are at times seriously misleading as measures of international price movements and of international price competitiveness.

Some of the deficiencies of the official data are due to the inadequacy of commodity coverage. The improvement of coverage through the addition of trade journal prices for commodities not in the official

Table 10.10
Copper, Aluminum, and Lead: Ranking of Export Value and Price Ratios,
United Kingdom to United States, EEC to United States, and
United Kingdom to EEC
(value ratios ranked from high to low; price ratios from low to high)

	U.K./U.S.		EEC/U.S.		U.K./EEC	
	V	P	V	P	V	P
682.1 Copper, unwrought	4	4	4	4	4	4
682.2 Copper, worked	2	3	2	3	2	1
684.1 Aluminum, unwrought	5	5	5	5	5	3
684.2 Aluminum, worked	3	2	3	1	3	5
685 Lead	1	1	1	2	1	2

V = ranking of value ratios.
P = ranking of price ratios.
Note: Price ratios are from detailed data underlying Appendix E. Values are from
Appendix A.

series moves the index of U.S. wholesale prices closer to the NBER index in every period, and the effect is usually, although not always, the same for foreign-country indexes.

The unit value index differs more from the NBER index than the wholesale price indexes in most years. Part of this discrepancy may again reflect coverage differences, since the unit value data used for the index cover only copper and aluminum. However, NBER and unit value indexes even within copper and aluminum show large differences, apparently the result of defects in the basic unit value data for individual commodities.

We conclude, therefore, that even in a relatively uncomplicated group such as nonferrous metals, the existing official wholesale price and unit value measures give inadequate or misleading impressions of international price competitiveness.

11

METAL MANUFACTURES, N.E.S.

Trade

Germany was the leading exporter in the miscellaneous metal manufactures division as a whole, followed by the United States, the United Kingdom, France, and Japan, in that order (Table 11.1). The United States maintained a lead in several subgroups, however, particularly in finished structural parts and structures (SITC 691) and in containers (SITC 692). France accounted for more than 10 per cent of exports in these two groups and in household equipment of base metal (SITC 697), and Belgium-Luxembourg was the largest exporter of all in wire products (SITC 693) at $48 million, leading Germany, the next in importance, by more than 30 per cent.

For the most part, this division, which is a miscellany of products not closely related in use or manufacture, consists of commodities which have not undergone major innovations in either design or production methods during the years covered here. A possible exception might be the finished structural parts group, in which some of the items, such as oil drilling structures and prefabricated buildings, underwent considerable improvements in design.

Aside from the price data, discussed later in this chapter, and the trade data, which show the United States to have been a net importer in several of the groups, the weakness of the U.S. competitive position in division 69 is suggested by the many complaints of injury from imports and demands for escape-clause investigations made by U.S. companies, on such products as wood screws (SITC 694), axes and

Note: SITC 69. *Value of OECD exports in 1963:* $2.5 billion; 5.7 per cent of study total. *Coverage:* Finished structural parts and structures, containers, wire products and fasteners, tools, cutlery, and miscellaneous manufactures of metal.

Table 11.1

OECD Exports of Metal Manufactures, n.e.s. (SITC 69),
by Origin, Destination, and Commodity Group, 1963

(dollars in millions)

| | Value of Exports | Per Cent of OECD Exports in 69 | Share in OECD Exports (per cent) | | | | | |
			OECD	U.S.	U.K.	EEC Total	EEC Germany	Japan
Total, all destinations and groups	$2,519	100.0	100.0	19.8	14.7	45.5[a]	22.6	7.9
Destination								
U.S.	252	10.0	100.0		9.1	38.1	15.9	37.3
OECD Europe	1,067	42.4	100.0	9.1	10.5	63.4	36.2	1.5
U.K.	71	2.8	100.0	21.1		42.3	26.8	4.2
EEC total	621	24.7	100.0	6.0	8.7	68.1	34.5	1.3
Germany	126	5.0	100.0	11.1	9.5	49.2		3.2
Canada	205	8.1	100.0	79.5	8.8	5.4	3.4	3.9
Japan	15	0.6	100.0	53.3	13.3	20.0	13.3	
Latin America	218	8.7	100.0	46.8	6.4	33.9	16.1	6.0
Other	762	30.3	100.0	17.1	26.8	37.4	13.1	9.7

(continued)

Table 11.1 (concluded)

SITC commodity group	Value of Exports	Per Cent of OECD Exports in 69	Share in OECD Exports (per cent)			EEC		Japan
			OECD	U.S.	U.K.	Total	Germany	
Finished structural parts & structures (691)	$317	12.6	100.0	24.3	14.8	46.4[b]	18.3	4.4
Metal containers for storage & transport (692)	176	7.0	100.0	22.2	15.3	49.4[c]	17.6	2.8
Wire products (excl. elect.) & fencing grills (693)	205	8.1	100.0	7.9	15.6	56.1[d]	17.1	10.2
Nails, screws, nuts, bolts, rivets, etc. (694)	214	8.5	100.0	14.5	9.8	39.3	18.7	22.9
Tools for use in hand or machine (695)	505	20.0	100.0	22.6	14.7	40.2	27.1	5.3
Cutlery (696)	160	6.4	100.0	5.0	22.5	43.1	28.1	20.6
Household equipment of base metal (697)	235	9.3	100.0	13.6	10.6	56.6[e]	21.3	6.4
Manufactures of metal, n.e.s. (698)	707	28.1	100.0	25.5	15.6	43.4	24.6	5.1

Source: Appendix A.
[a] Of which France, 8.3 per cent.
[b] Of which France, 11.7 per cent.
[c] Of which France, 15.3 per cent.
[d] Of which Belgium-Luxembourg, 23.4 per cent.
[e] Of which France, 11.5 per cent.

Table 11.2

Ratios of U.S. Exports to Manufacturers' Shipments and U.S. Imports to New Supply (Output plus Imports), Metal Manufactures, n.e.s., 1964 (per cent)

			Ratio	
SITC	SIC-based Product Code	Title	Exports to Manufacturers' Shipments	Imports to New Supply
691		*Finished structural parts and structures, n.e.s.*		
	3441	Fabricated structural iron and steel	3	NA[a]
	34492	Prefabricated and portable metal buildings and parts	3	NA[a]
692		*Metal containers for storage and transport*		
	3411	Metal cans	1	NA[a]
	3491	Metal shipping barrels, drums, kegs, and pails	2[b]	NA[a]
	34434	Gas cylinders	15[b]	c
	34435, --37, --38, --39	Metal tanks	4	
693		*Wire products (excluding electric) and fencing grills*		
	34811, 33151	Noninsulated ferrous wire rope, cable, strand	3	7
	34814, 33157	Iron and steel woven wire products	3	
	34815, 33575	Nonferrous woven wire products	2	4
	34816, 33156	Fencing and fence gates		
	34812, --13	Wire springs	1	NA
	34819, 33159	Other fabricated wire products		3
	33571, 33521	Aluminum and alloy wire and cable, not insulated	4	1
	33572, 33511	Copper and alloy wire and cable, not insulated	2	1

(continued)

Table 11.2 (concluded)

SITC	SIC-based Product Code	Title	Ratio	
			Exports to Manufacturers' Shipments	Imports to New Supply
694		*Nails, screws, nuts, bolts, rivets, and similar articles*		
	33152	Steel nails and spikes	3	22
	34521	Standard industrial fasteners	3	4
695		*Tools for use in the hand or in machines*		
	3544, —45	Special dies, jigs, and fixtures, and machine tool accessories	2[b]	1
	3425	Hand saws and saw blades and accessories	8	4
696		*Cutlery*		
	34211	Cutlery, scissors, shears, etc.	4	15
	34212	Razor blades and razors, excl. electric	4	4
697.1		*Domestic stoves, boilers, cookers, etc.*		
	34334	Domestic heating stoves	5	NA[a]

Source: *U.S. Commodity Exports and Imports as Related to Output*, 1965 and 1964, U.S. Bureau of the Census, 1967.
[a]Group total ratio less than 0.5 per cent.
[b]1965 ratio.
[c]Less than 0.5 per cent.

271

axheads (SITC 695), stainless-steel table flatware, scissors and shears (SITC 696), straight pins, and safety pins (SITC 698).[1]

Another view of the U.S. trade position in this group is given by data on the ratios of exports and imports to output. Some of the latter ratios were substantial, as can be seen in Table 11.2. The matching of trade to output data is not perfect and does not cover all the products in this division but does include most of the important ones. In two of the items frequently mentioned as being subject to severe foreign competition on the U.S. market, steel nails and spikes and some cutlery, imports supplied 15 per cent or more of the domestic market, but in wire products, a frequent subject for complaint, the ratios of imports to output plus imports were below 8 per cent.

As was pointed out in Chapter 9, the import ratios that are usually quoted are larger than those of Table 11.2 because the commodity breakdown is finer and the items most subject to foreign competition are therefore more clearly pinpointed and because the data usually cited are based on tonnage rather than value. The use of tonnage exaggerates the importance of imports because the imports tend to be of lower average value per ton than U.S. production; that is, they consist mainly of the least fabricated types of steel products.[2] Some idea of the overall effect of using tonnage rather than value is given by the comparison of ratios for the total of steel mill products. The tonnage ratio for steel mill products as a whole was 7.3 per cent in 1964,[3] while the value ratio for total blast furnace, steel mill, and electrometallurgical products plus fabricated wire products was about 4 per cent (see source to Table 11.2). The value ratio, it should be added, tends to understate the importance

---

[1] U.S. Tariff Commission, *Wood Screws of Iron or Steel: Report to the President on Escape-Clause Investigation No. 34* . . . , October 1954; *Axes and Axe-Heads: Report on Escape-Clause Investigation No. 76* . . . , May 1959; *Stainless-Steel Table Flatware: Report to the President on Escape-Clause Investigation No. 61* . . . , January 1958, and later reports on the same product; *Scissors and Shears, and Manicure and Pedicure Nippers, and Parts Thereof: Report to the President on Investigation No. 24* . . . , March 1954, and later reports on the same products; *Straight (Dressmakers' or Common) Pins: Report to the President on Escape-Clause Investigation No. 7-109* . . . , T.C. Pub. 52, February 1962; *Safety Pins: Report to the President (1962) under Executive Order 10401*, T.C. Pub. 46, January 1962, and later reports on the same product.

[2] Tonnage data for wire products (U.S. imports as a percentage of apparent consumption, 1964) often cited as examples of import competition are:

Wire nails and staples	48.8%
Barbed wire	47.9
Woven wire fence	27.9

The data are taken from *Foreign Trade Trends, Iron and Steel,* American Iron and Steel Institute, 1967, p. 67.

[3] *Ibid.,* p. 65.

Table 11.3

OECD Exports of Metal Manufactures, n.e.s., 1953, 1957, 1961—64

(dollars in millions)

	Value of OECD Exports	Share in OECD Exports (per cent)					
		OECD	U.S.	U.K.	EEC Total	Germany	Japan
INCLUDING SWITZERLAND AND SPAIN							
1964	$2,828	100.0	19.1	14.3	45.6	22.7	8.3
1963	2,514	100.0	19.7	14.8	45.6	22.7	8.0
1962	2,358	100.0	20.4	16.1	45.0	22.6	7.5
1961	2,217	100.0	19.6	16.6	46.2	23.6	6.9
EXCLUDING SWITZERLAND AND SPAIN							
1961	2,166	100.0	20.0	16.9	47.3	24.2	7.1
1957	1,747	100.0	22.3	20.6	43.1	22.4	4.1
1953	1,144	100.0	23.0	24.9	40.5	19.8	2.5

Source: Appendix B.

of imports, to the extent that the lower value per ton of the imports is a consequence of lower prices rather than lower quality or product mix.

Exports of metal manufactures, n.e.s. (that is, SITC division 69 as a whole) more than doubled between 1953 and 1964 (Table 11.3). The United States almost held its share of the export market after 1961 following losses in the earlier years, while the U.K. share declined throughout the period. Germany gained sharply before 1961, and Japan increased its share of OECD exports in every year. The most pervasive shifts in export shares among the individual commodity groups within division 69 were the losses by the United States and the United Kingdom and gains by Japan and Canada. Germany and France lost ground in more cases than they gained, while Sweden, and the EEC countries other than Germany and France showed more gains than losses.

Some of these shifts resulted from nonprice factors. For example, in metal containers (SITC 692), one obstacle to international trade and competition was the existence of safety regulations, such as those of the Interstate Commerce Commission in the United States. In some cases, products that were acceptable to the purchaser could not be bought for the United States or for countries adopting U.S. standards because the regulatory agencies were slow to accept new technological

Table 11.4
International Prices, Metal Manufactures, n.e.s., 1953, 1957, 1961–64
(1962 = 100)

	1953	1957	1961	1962	1963	1964
U.S.	86	98	98	100	100	102
U.K.	90	101	103	100	99	103
EEC	87	99	100	100	97	98
Germany	84	93	98	100	99	101
Japan	NA	NA	98	100	93	101

Source: Appendix C.

developments which would eventually lower prices substantially. In other cases, products which met physical requirements fully were not acceptable for lack of a stamp attesting to inspection and testing in the United States. Internal company rules, geared toward American-manufactured products, had to be amended so that advantage could be taken of lower foreign prices for products of equal quality.

In electric wire and cable (SITC 693), Japan's gains in export share were due, according to one report, both to increases in Asia's share of world building of electric power installations and to Japan's success, by the end of the period, in overcoming its previous handicap of producing only a limited range of cable sizes to the point where its range was equal to that of the European exporters.[4]

Price Trends

Prices of miscellaneous metal manufactures in the United States moved almost completely in step with those of European countries over the whole period of our study. They rose in each period shown until 1962, remained constant or almost constant in 1963, and then rose slightly in 1964 (Table 11.4). Only Japan showed some sharply different price trends, with a large decline in 1963, and then a larger rise in 1964 than in any other country.

Price indexes constructed from domestic wholesale price data, using

[4] "Electric Wire, Cable Exports Running High," *Journal of Commerce,* September 29, 1965.

international trade weights, rose relative to the international price indexes for every country listed (see Appendix F). Except for Japan, this meant a larger rise in the indexes from wholesale prices. In other words, if the international price indexes are at all reliable, wholesale prices of these metal products were biased estimators of international price movements for most countries, and the bias was consistently upward. Japanese wholesale prices, in contrast, declined, while the international price index rose. This may have been a consequence of a weakness in our data (the international price index constructed entirely from Japanese time series data, listed in Appendix C, fell even more than the wholesale price index) or of the restrictions imposed by the United States on imports of some of these products.

Price Competitiveness

The price competitiveness of the United States in this division relative to Germany and Japan was quite stable during the period for which we have indexes (Table 11.5). Relative to the United Kingdom and the EEC countries other than Germany, however, the U.S. price position deteriorated.

U.S. price competitiveness indexes built up from wholesale price data for the individual groups show a substantial improvement in the U.S. position relative to Britain between 1957 and 1964, at a time when the index based on international prices showed a decline (see Appendix F). Relative to Germany, however, the two price competitiveness indexes show virtually identical developments from 1957 to 1964. An index

Table 11.5
U.S. Price Competitiveness, Metal Manufactures, n.e.s., 1953, 1957, 1961–64
(1962 = 100)

	1953	1957	1961	1962	1963	1964
Relative to						
U.K.	105	103	105	100	100	100
EEC	102	101	101	100	97	95
Germany	99	95	100	100	99	98
Japan	NA	NA	99	100	94	99

Source: Appendix D.

of U.S. price competitiveness based on U.S. and Japanese wholesale price series shows a decline from 1953 to 1963 and then a leveling off in 1964.

In the individual groups, the indexes of U.S. price competitiveness from wholesale price data do not show any consistent relationship to those from international prices. However, in three out of four cases of very large divergence between the two, listed below (data from Appendixes D and F and underlying data), the change in price relationships implied by international price data was less favorable to the United States than that implied by the wholesale price data.

| | | | Change in U.S. International Price Competitiveness | |
SITC	Country	Dates	From Domestic Wholesale Prices	From International Prices
692	U.K.	1957–64	+26%	−17%
693	Japan	1961–64	+4	−14
695	Germany	1953–64	−8	+9
696	Germany	1953–64	+3	−14

Price Levels

European price levels for metal manufactures, n.e.s., ranged between 3 and 13 per cent below U.S. prices in all the years covered in the study (Table 11.6). The gap between American prices and those of the United

Table 11.6

Price Levels, Metal Manufactures, n.e.s., 1953, 1957, 1961–64

(U.S. for each year = 100)

	1953	1957	1961	1962	1963	1964
U.S.	100	100	100	100	100	100
U.K.	97	95	97	92	92	92
EEC	97	96	97	96	93	91
Germany	90	87	92	92	91	90
Japan	NA	NA	74	74	69	73

Source: Appendix E.

Kingdom, and EEC (except Germany) widened considerably between 1953 and 1964. Japanese prices were far lower than those of the other countries, 25 to 30 per cent below the U.S. level in all the years for which we have data.

Price levels among the individual groups varied considerably (see Appendix E). Fragmentary data indicate a fairly favorable U.S. position in SITC 691, finished structural parts and structures which covers a wide range of degrees of fabrication. At the lower end it includes slightly fabricated structural steel products akin to the iron and steel bars, rods, plates, and sheets of SITC 673 or 674, with only the addition of minor adaptations to fit them for particular jobs. At the higher end it covers complete prefabricated structures. At least at the beginning of the period British firms bidding on construction projects abroad were said to be at a disadvantage relative to Continental producers in terms of the range and quality of structural steel products available to them. Italian firms showed particular strength in markets for electrical transmission towers, winning a considerable number of bidding contests in foreign countries. After the end of the period covered by this study there were accusations by American companies that Italian successes in this country were due to subsidies from the Italian government, and the U.S. Treasury eventually imposed a countervailing duty against steel transmission towers from Italy on that ground.[5]

In cable manufacturing (part of SITC 693), Japan was still considered a newcomer even after the end of our period and was accused by some of selling at a loss to break into the international market.[6] In copper cable, the existence of price differences among copper markets at times favored one cable producer over another (see Chapter 10). This type of case occurred during the wide price swings of 1966, when British cable producers, purchasing copper at producers' prices, were said to have a considerable advantage over German producers who had to buy half of their copper requirements at prices 40 per cent or more above the producers' price level.[7]

A British wire rope producer was accused of dumping its products in the United States at the end of our period, but the Treasury Department

[5] "Steel: Beams for the Builder," *Economist,* November 2, 1957; "Italy Firm Low Bidder on Peace River Job," *Journal of Commerce,* August 24, 1965; "Bite for Steel," *Economist,* April 29, 1967.

[6] "Electric Cable: Current Setback," *Economist,* December 24, 1966.

[7] "BICC: A Real Cost Squeeze," *ibid.,* April 23, 1966.

dropped the case after the company agreed to raise its prices, which were found to have been below its home market prices.[8]

Both the United Kingdom and the EEC countries substantially undersold the United States in nails, screws, nuts, etc. (SITC 694) by the end of the period. The weakness of the United States in this group was reflected in the difficulties of U.S. companies in even staying in some parts of this business in the face of foreign competition. The problems of the U.S. steel industry in the market for nails came into the open after the period covered by the study, but they probably began before 1964. In 1966, one large steel company announced that it was withdrawing published prices for several sizes of nails in favor of negotiated prices in view of the inroads of foreign competition, exemplified by the fact that half of the nails sold in the United States in 1965 had been imported. Another American steel company announced two days later that it was abandoning nail production entirely as a result of foreign competition. One report quoted a price difference in the United States of about 30 per cent early in 1966, very close to our margin of 31 per cent relative to the EEC in 1964.[9]

Only Germany showed much lower prices than the United States in tools (SITC 695), while U.K. prices were at about the American level. One part of the U.S. industry, in a brief opposing tariff reductions, stated that foreign competition, at least in the United States, was confined to high-volume metal cutting tools.[10] The American producers seemed safe on some special items within the United States for security reasons, and were said also to have a strong competitive position in some high-quality tools.

In cutlery (SITC 696) the fragmentary data available, which were not adequate for publication, indicated that European prices were close to those of the United States. Only Japan had ever enjoyed a large price advantage over the United States.

[8] "Treasury Study Finds Britons Not 'Dumping' Wire Rope in the U.S.," *Wall Street Journal*, September 24, 1964.

[9] "U.S. Steel Sets Major Revision of Prices, Including Boosts, Cuts, Dropping of Quotes," *Wall Street Journal*, March 1, 1966; "Jones & Laughlin Is Pulling Out of Nail Business," *ibid.*, March 3, 1966; "Jones & Laughlin Ends Nails Making," *New York Times*, March 3, 1966; "Some Rivals Expect to Follow U.S. Steel on Prices; Changes Called a Slight Net Rise," *Wall Street Journal*, March 2, 1966.

[10] "Statement of the Metal Cutting Tool Institute in Opposition to Possible Further Tariff Concessions on Metal Cutting Tools by the Government of the United States," New York, February 3, 1964, mimeo.

Several Tariff Commission investigations of cutlery were made because of complaints by U.S. producers that they were being seriously injured by imports. The Tariff Commission found injury to U.S. producers in imports of stainless-steel tableware and recommended withdrawal of some GATT (General Agreements on Tariffs and Trade) concessions by the United States. The report described considerable differences in the foreign exports. Japanese exports were at the low end of the quality scale and were made to order for U.S. importers on the basis of designs furnished by them; the European products, on the other hand, were frequently higher in quality than the U.S. products and sold on the basis of distinctive design and superior finish. One U.S. manufacturer explained his imports from Europe on the basis that high-quality tableware was uneconomical to produce in this country because of the high labor content involved.

As a result of these investigations, both the United States and Japan took measures to reduce the volume of Japanese exports to the United States. The United States withdrew the GATT concessions, and Japan imposed its own limitation on exports. A sharp reduction in U.S. imports then took place.[11]

In scissors and shears also, a Tariff Commission investigation pointed to a U.S. disadvantage in the higher-quality products, but not in lower-quality ones, which required a smaller proportion of labor cost.[12]

In miscellaneous metal products (SITC 698) all the countries listed had price levels more than 10 per cent below the U.S. level in 1964, with Japan the lowest.

The price level relationships clearly do not explain all the differences in country export shares from one group to another. For the United Kingdom in particular, the price ratios seem to be unrelated to the export ratios of Table 11.1. The United Kingdom does better as an exporter of wire than one would expect from the price data but less well in manufactures of metal n.e.s. Of course the latter group is so heterogeneous that the price level index may well be unrepresentative.

The relationship between German and U.S. export shares fits the price relatives much better, that is, the ratio of German exports to U.S. exports is high where the ratio of German prices to U.S. prices is low, and vice versa.

[11] See reference in footnote 1.
[12] See reference in footnote 1.

Summary

In this group, which contains several items in which foreign competition affected the U.S. as well as foreign markets, the U.S. price position worsened by comparison with the United Kingdom and EEC countries other than Germany, but showed little or no deterioration relative to Germany and Japan. However, Japanese prices for most items and other countries' prices for some were far below the U.S. level, and some of the problems of American firms may have been a consequence of this large price differential (that is, a delayed reaction to earlier price changes) rather than of contemporaneous changes in price competitiveness.

Disagreements between international and wholesale price data were extensive in this division, with wholesale prices usually biased upward and frequently showing price competitiveness movements opposite to those in our international price data.

12

NONELECTRICAL MACHINERY

NONELECTRICAL MACHINERY is by far the largest division of those included in this study, encompassing almost a third of OECD exports in the products covered. Aside from a brief description of the division as a whole, we have chosen seven groups and subgroups for more detailed discussion. These are aircraft engines, other internal combustion engines, agricultural machinery, office machinery, metalworking machine tools, textile and leather machinery, and mechanical handling equipment.

The United States was the leading exporter of nonelectrical machinery, followed by Germany and the United Kingdom, with Japan a comparatively minor factor (Table 12.1). Germany dominated the market in the European OECD countries, which were the destination of almost half of OECD exports in 1963. The United States accounted for more than half of imports into Canada, Japan, and Latin America, and the United Kingdom was the strongest exporter to "other destinations," mainly Africa and Asia. The United Kingdom was not the largest exporter in any of the individual SITC groups. It was second to the United States and far ahead of Germany in power generating and agricultural machinery. Germany was the largest source of exports in metalworking and textile and leather machinery, with a long lead over both the United States and the United Kingdom. The United States accounted for almost a third or more of OECD exports of power generating, agricultural, office, and special industry machinery and was substantially ahead of its nearest rival in each. Japan's share was over 2

Note: SITC 71. *Value of OECD exports in 1963:* $14.2 billion; 31.8 per cent of study total. *Coverage:* Power generating machinery; agricultural machinery; office machines; metalworking machinery; textile and leather machinery; other nonelectrical machinery.

Table 12.1
OECD Exports of Nonelectrical Machinery (SITC 71),
by Origin, Destination, and Commodity Group, 1963
(dollars in millions)

	Value of Exports	Per Cent of OECD Exports in 71	Share in OECD Exports (per cent)				EEC		Japan
			OECD	U.S.	U.K.	Total	Germany		
Total, all destinations and groups	$14,164	100.0	100.0	28.6	17.0	38.8	23.3		2.5
Destination									
U.S.	715	5.0	100.0		16.9	31.2	18.7		7.7
OECD Europe	6,502	45.9	100.0	17.1	14.3	53.3	34.0		0.1
U.K.	568	4.0	100.0	31.5		47.4	28.9		0.1
EEC total	3,739	26.4	100.0	17.4	14.5	53.6	32.1		0.5
Germany	822	5.8	100.0	20.7	16.8	35.3			0.9
Canada	1,044	7.4	100.0	83.0	10.7	3.8	2.3		0.4
Japan	432	3.0	100.0	52.5	8.6	29.9	21.3		
Latin America	1,299	9.2	100.0	50.3	8.9	29.3	15.3		1.8
Other	3,892	27.5	100.0	23.3	28.1	32.2	16.4		6.1
Unaccounted for	280	2.0	100.0	99.6					0.4

(continued)

Table 12.1 (concluded)

	Value of Exports	Per Cent of OECD Exports in 71	Share in OECD Exports (per cent)			EEC		Japan
			OECD	U.S.	U.K.	Total	Germany	
SITC commodity group								
Power generating machinery (711)	$2,024	14.3	100.0	32.7	23.9	29.3	14.8	2.0
Agricultural machinery (712)	1,398	9.9	100.0	34.5	28.0	23.5	12.7	0.5
Office machinery (714)	1,024	7.2	100.0	35.4	10.8	40.0	16.0	0.8
Metalworking machinery (715)	1,370	9.7	100.0	25.3	12.1	49.3	35.5	1.7
Textile and leather machinery (717)	1,296	9.1	100.0	14.7	17.5	42.9	27.5	9.2
Machines for special industries (718)	2,015	14.2	100.0	35.1	16.5	35.5	24.5	1.8
Machinery, appliances, and machine parts, n.e.s. (719)	5,034	35.5	100.0	25.7	13.8	43.9	26.3	2.3

Source: Appendix A.

283

per cent only for textile and leather machinery, aside from the miscellaneous category.

Both the United States and the United Kingdom lost ground as exporters of nonelectrical machinery, the former mainly between 1957 and 1961 and the latter in several smaller steps spread throughout the period (Table 12.2). Germany and other EEC countries both increased their shares rapidly during the years before 1961. The Japanese share doubled over the whole period but remained low, at only 3 per cent in 1964.

The outstanding features of the price data for nonelectrical machinery as a group, reported in Table 12.3, are the large price increases, concentrated in the early periods, and the striking similarity of price changes in the different countries. In Table 12.3, for the division as a whole, not a single price declined. There were, however, a few declines in the group and subgroup indexes.

The range of movement in price competitiveness among all the countries in all the years was only eight percentage points, and only three percentage points outside of 1957. The prices for the different countries thus appeared to have kept in step to an extraordinary degree, especially

Table 12.2

OECD Exports of Nonelectrical Machinery, 1953, 1957, 1961—64

(dollars in millions)

	Value of OECD Exports	Share in OECD Exports (per cent)					
		OECD	U.S.	U.K.	EEC		Japan
					Total	Germany	
INCLUDING SWITZERLAND AND SPAIN							
1964	$15,736	100.0	29.6	15.3	38.6	22.8	3.1
1963	14,164	100.0	28.6	17.0	38.8	23.3	2.5
1962	13.410	100.0	29.3	16.8	38.2	22.9	2.6
1961	12,088	100.0	28.8	18.0	37.8	23.4	2.6
EXCLUDING SWITZERLAND AND SPAIN							
1961	11,596	100.0	30.1	18.7	39.4	24.4	2.8
1957	8,264	100.0	39.3	19.0	31.9	21.2	1.5
1953	5,258	100.0	40.5	21.1	29.2	18.4	1.5

Source: Appendix B.

Table 12.3

International Prices, Price Competitiveness, and Price Levels of

Nonelectrical Machinery, 1953, 1957, 1961–64

	1953	1957	1961	1962	1963	1964
INTERNATIONAL PRICE INDEXES (1962 = 100)						
U.S.	81	92	99	100	101	102
U.K.	81	92	98	100	100	102
EEC	81	88	97	100	100	102
Germany	80	87	97	100	101	102
INDEXES OF U.S. PRICE COMPETITIVENESS (1962 = 100)						
Relative to						
U.K.	99	99	99	100	100	101
EEC	99	95	98	100	100	100
Germany	99	94	98	100	100	100
INTERNATIONAL PRICE LEVELS (U.S. FOR EACH YEAR = 100)						
U.S.	100	100	100	100	100	100
U.K.	89	90	90	90	90	91
EEC	92	89	91	93	93	92
Germany	92	88	91	93	93	93

Source: International price indexes from Appendix C; price competitiveness indexes, Appendix D; price levels, Appendix E.

in view of the substantial relative price changes in the individual groups that make up the nonelectrical machinery division.

Aircraft Engines and Parts [1]

Trade

Trade in aircraft engines and parts is dominated by the United States and the United Kingdom, which accounted for almost three-quarters of 1963 OECD exports in this group, as can be seen in Table 12.4. Subsidiaries of British and American companies probably accounted for all the trade of the third-ranking exporter, Canada. Most

[1] SITC 711.4. *Value of OECD exports in 1963:* $647.4 million; 1.5 per cent of study total. *Coverage:* Engines exported as spares or for installation in aircraft produced in the importing country. Over $125 million of aircraft engines exported as part of aircraft are not included (see note to Table A.11).

Table 12.4

OECD Exports of Aircraft Engines and Parts (SITC 711.4),
by Origin and Destination, 1963
(dollars in millions)

Destination	Value of Exports	Per Cent of OECD Exports in 711.4	Share in OECD Exports (per cent)				EEC		Japan
			OECD	U.S.	U.K.	Total	Germany	
Total, all destinations	$647.4	100.0	100.0	44.2[a]	27.2[a]	19.5	4.5	1.1
Destination								
U.S.	59.7	9.2	100.0		23.5	8.4	1.7	6.7
OECD Europe	297.9	46.0	100.0	32.2	29.9	33.9	7.7	0.3
U.K.	41.5	6.4	100.0	48.2		43.4	9.6	2.4
EEC total	212.5	32.8	100.0	27.3	36.2	34.8	8.0	[b]
Germany	57.1	8.8	100.0	12.3	45.5	40.3		
Canada	45.6	7.0	100.0	59.2	39.5			
Japan	26.5	4.1	100.0	86.8	11.3	0.7		
Latin America	23.6	3.6	100.0	63.6	29.7	4.2		
Other	75.8	11.7	100.0	9.2	59.4	23.7	6.6	2.6
Unaccounted for by destination	118.4	18.3	100.0	100.0				

Source: Data underlying Table A.11 and Note to Table A.5.
[a]See Note to Table A.11.
[b]Less than 0.05 per cent.

of the remaining 20 per cent was intra-EEC trade, and only a small part went outside Europe, mainly French exports to Israel and South Africa.

The ultimate destinations of the engines, as parts of aircraft, are more varied than Table 12.4 indicates. The concentration of destinations is partly due to the concentration of the aircraft manufacturing industry in a small number of countries.

The pattern of trade shown in Table 12.4 must be considered a very rough approximation. Since sales of engines for military aircraft are included, some of the data, particularly for the United States, are available only on exports to the world as a whole, and not by destination.

The United States accounted for about half or more of exports to most markets, except for the EEC and the "all other" market consisting mainly of Africa and Asia. The United Kingdom was the main exporter to the EEC, Africa, and Asia, as far as can be seen from this tabulation. However, the $118 million in the U.S. exports not accounted for by destination might, if properly distributed in the table, raise the U.S. share substantially in any of these markets. In addition, the data are beset by an unusual number of errors and inconsistencies, which we attempted to correct in Table 12.4.

Published data do not distinguish military from nonmilitary exports, but the classification of almost all the U.S. exports as special category suggests that military shipments are an important component of the total. The military element in the figures may account for some of the large discrepancy between exports reported by the United States ($286 million) and imports from the United States reported by importers (about $164 million, as shown in the note to Table A.5), although gaps in the country coverage of imports are also significant.

A high proportion of aircraft engine exports seems to be in the form of parts. However, the 3-to-1 ratio of parts to complete engines given in the U.S. data seems surprisingly large. The U.K. figures show parts as one-half of the total, and U.S. production data suggest a similar ratio.[2]

[2] The U.S. export parts total is from *United States Exports of Domestic and Foreign Merchandise; Commodity by Country of Destination,* 1963 Annual, U.S. Dept. of Commerce, Report FT 410, 1964, p. 440, Schedule B No. 79476 (misclassified under SITC 734). The complete engines and parts total is from unpublished revised data of the U.S. Department of Commerce. U.K. exports are from *Accounts Relating to Trade and Navigation of the United Kingdom,* U.K. Board of Trade, December 1964, p. 286. U.S. production data are from *Current Industrial Reports, Complete Aircraft and Aircraft Engines, Summary for 1964,* Series M37G (64–13), U.S. Bureau of the Census, April 1965.

A higher ratio is more in line with a statement that an aircraft engine consumes roughly one-third of its original purchase price in spare parts each year.[3] Assuming an average life of an engine of about nine years, and all parts purchased from the manufacturer, a ratio of parts to new engines of three to one would be plausible if the level of sales of new engines had remained constant. Any growth in sales, however, implies a lower ratio. We have, therefore, accepted the evidence of the U.K. exports and U.S. production data and weighted parts and complete engines equally in our indexes.

The pattern of trade in engines is probably determined mainly by the trade in aircraft, rather than by engine prices, since aircraft are usually supplied with engines of the same nationality. For example, U.S. imports of British engines have mostly been associated with purchases of British Viscounts and the BAC-111. However, aircraft intended for foreign markets can be fitted with foreign engines when that is commercially desirable. The French Caravelle used Rolls-Royce and American Pratt and Whitney engines and Boeing and Douglas offer versions of their large jets equipped with British, instead of the usual American, engines. An American sales agent for a French-built executive plane was reported to have insisted on the use of U.S.-built engines, and this aircraft was advertised with emphasis on the U.S.-built engine and without reference to the French origin of the airframe.[4]

Piston engines, which were the only ones traded in the early years of the period, were a small fraction of the total compared with jet engines at the end of our period. They were about one-quarter of U.S. exports, but data on OECD imports from all countries indicate that they were only about 15 per cent of total aircraft engine exports.[5]

Price Changes

According to the time-to-time price data summarized in Table 12.5, U.S. prices of aircraft engines and parts rose by almost 30 per cent between 1953 and 1964. Data are not sufficient for the calculation of U.K. prices in 1953, but during 1957–64, when indexes are available for

[3] "Aero-Engines: Rolls-Royce's Exports," *Economist*, March 31, 1962.

[4] "GE Said to be Getting $100 Million Contract for French-Built Jet," *Wall Street Journal*, August 13, 1963; *ibid.*, June 18, 1965.

[5] U.S. exports of piston and jet engines are from unpublished revised tabulation of the U.S. Department of Commerce. From the figure for 711.41 we deducted exports of aircraft engine parts (Schedule B No. 79476). OECD imports are from the *1963 World Trade Annual*, Walker & Company for the United Nations, Vol. IV.

Table 12.5
International Prices, Aircraft Engines and Parts, 1953, 1957, 1961–64
(1962 = 100)

	1953	1957	1961	1962	1963	1964
U.S.	85[a]	92[a]	95[a]	100	105	110
U.K.	NA	91	100	100	100	104

Source: Appendix C.
[a]Excluding parts before 1962, as in the U.K. index, 87 in 1953, 94 in 1957, and 99 in 1961.

both countries, U.S. prices rose by 20 per cent and U.K. ones by only 14 per cent.

Prices of parts tended to rise more rapidly than those of complete engines, particularly in the United States. All of the difference between U.S. and U.K. price change over the whole period is due to the rise in parts prices and to the inclusion of parts in the U.S. index for 1962/ 1961 when the U.K. index excludes them. Taking complete engines alone, we find prices in both countries to have risen only 12 per cent between 1957 and 1964.

The price changes incorporated in these indexes are those on individual engine models from the time they are introduced to the end of their production. Thus no price changes which involved the introduction of new engines enter the indexes at all. If new engines are introduced at a kind of promotional price to the first buyers and then sold to later buyers at prices fully reflecting their quality and production costs, this type of linked index might show rising prices even if there were no changes in the final prices from one engine to another. The past price patterns have, in fact, mostly shown price increases after the initial sales of each engine, but it is possible that these reflected trends in engine price levels rather than adjustments in specific prices.

A U.S. time-to-time index adjusted for quality change can be derived from the 1962 cross-sectional relationship between thrust and price which was calculated for the place-to-place comparisons (appendix to this chapter).[6] If we compare the actual prices paid in 1957 and 1962

---

[6] It would have been still better to use the superior equation containing both thrust and weight, but information on weight was not available for all the engines in the years other than 1962. The equation used here, not shown in the appendix to this chapter because the weight variable is omitted, is:

Y (price in dollars) $= 1,043 \, X_1$ (thrust in hundred pounds) $+ 47,326$.

with the 1962 equation (derived from order prices for a much larger range of engines), we find that the 1962 actual prices are more than 11 per cent above those calculated from the equation while 1957 prices were only 6 per cent higher. This difference indicates a price rise of 5.2 per cent, slightly below that indicated by the linked index we used. If we exclude from the 1957 data a small engine, far outside the range of sizes included in 1962, and we use a 1962 equation which covers only engines of 10,000 pounds' thrust and over, the measured price increase becomes 5.9 per cent, very close to the result of the linked index. Thus the correlation-based index supports the evidence of the linked index, and the support is the more impressive for the absence from the 1962 index of the engines appearing in the 1957 index.

Price Competitiveness

U.S. price competitiveness in aircraft engines relative to the United Kingdom apparently first rose and then, after 1961, declined (Table 12.6), mainly because U.S. prices rose substantially from 1962 to 1963 while U.K. prices remained stable.

We lack data for the computation of British indexes before 1957 but some information on cost per horsepower of British engines suggests a more rapid rise than in the United States, and therefore an improvement in U.S. competitiveness, between 1953 and 1957. However, the same data show a much greater rise between 1957 and 1960 than our U.K. index and must therefore be viewed skeptically as extrapolators.

It is not clear what effect price measures corrected for quality change, such as were discussed above in connection with the time-to-time

Table 12.6
U.S. Price Competitiveness Relative to the United Kingdom,
Aircraft Engines and Parts, 1957, 1961–64
(1962 = 100)

Year	Index		Year	Index
1957	97		1963	95
1961	101		1964	94
1962	100			

Source: Appendix D.

indexes, would have on the index of price competitiveness. The closeness of the U.S. regression-based price index to the linked index and the likelihood that adjustments for power would have been similar for the two countries suggest that the index of price competitiveness would not be strongly affected.

The main basis of the place-to-place index for complete aircraft engines in 1962 was an analysis, described in detail in the appendix to this chapter, of the cross-sectional relation between engine characteristics and price for twenty American and British aircraft engines. A regression equation was derived for price as a function of power (thrust) and weight, and British and U.S. engine prices were compared with the prices calculated from the equation. The U.K.-U.S. place-to-place index for complete engines, calculated by dividing the average U.K. ratio of actual to theoretical prices by the average U.S. ratio, equaled 100. Experimentation with several different forms of the equation did not affect the index significantly, giving results varying only from 99 to 101.

Since the lowest levels of engine power were represented only by U.S. engines and the next level by British ones, it seemed possible that these engines might distort the regression line; the four lowest-powered engines were therefore eliminated from the calculation to produce a regression line confined to the range within which we have both U.S. and British data. Inclusion of all twenty-four engines would have produced a somewhat higher U.K.-U.S. place-to-place index, around 102 or 103.

One rough check on the regression comparison is to match specific British engines with U.S. engines of similar, but not identical, thrust and weight. The method is crude because the results depend on the choice of pairs, which is difficult to standardize. The three pairs most similar in specifications gave U.K.-U.S. ratios ranging from 89 to 103 per cent, with an average of 95 per cent, as compared to the figure of 100 per cent used for the complete engines component of the index in Table 12.7.

The extrapolation of the 1962 place-to-place index for complete engines by time-to-time data gives U.K. price levels for other years ranging from 6 per cent below to 1 per cent above those of the United States.

Prices of engine parts in the United Kingdom were apparently considerably lower than in the United States in 1964—by more than 10 per cent. Our extrapolation by time-to-time indexes indicates a gap in

Table 12.7
U.K. Price Level Relative to the United States, Aircraft Engines
and Parts, 1957, 1961–64
(U.S. = 100)

Year	Index		Year	Index
1957	94		1963	92
1961	98		1964	91
1962	97			

Source: Appendix E.

1962 of only about 5 per cent, even then somewhat larger than that for complete engines. The sample is small, however, and is probably biased in favor of the United Kingdom since it consists of those parts which U.S. manufacturers choose to produce in the United Kingdom, possibly a minor and unrepresentative part of their total production.

Taking engines and parts together we find that U.K. prices were below U.S. prices in every year covered, and declined relatively after 1961 to a point almost 10 per cent lower by 1964. It seems likely, however, that the flow of trade in engine parts is determined more by the prices of engines than by those of individual parts, because many parts may be produced only in the factory making the complete engine. In that case, the engine prices should be taken as the appropriate place-to-place index for the group as a whole when the determinants of trade flows are being studied.

Internal Combustion Engines Other Than for Aircraft [7]

Trade

The United States and the United Kingdom were the leading exporters of internal combustion engines, each accounting for a quarter of OECD exports, with Germany following at about a fifth (Table 12.8). In OECD exports as a whole, diesel engines were more important by a considerable margin than all other types combined. In U.S. exports, how-

---

[7] SITC 711.5. *Value of OECD exports in 1963:* $900 million; 2 per cent of study total. *Coverage:* Gasoline, diesel, and other engines and parts, for automotive, marine, and other purposes, excluding engines exported as parts of vehicles.

Table 12.8

OECD Exports of Internal Combustion Engines Other Than for Aircraft (SITC 711.5), by Origin, Destination, and Type of Engine, 1963

(dollars in millions)

| | Value of Exports | Per Cent of OECD Exports in 711.5 | Share in OECD Exports (per cent) | | | EEC | | |
			OECD	U.S.	U.K.	Total	Germany	Japan
Total, all destinations and types of engine	$900	100.0	100.0	25.0	25.0	35.4	20.1	2.4
Destination								
U.S.	48	5.3	100.0		35.4	25.0	16.7	2.1
OECD Europe	351	39.0	100.0	14.0	20.8	49.9	31.3	0.6
U.K.	21	2.3	100.0	28.6		33.3	14.3	a
EEC total	192	21.3	100.0	14.6	21.4	54.2	32.3	0.5
Germany	29	3.2	100.0	10.3	34.5	37.9		a
Canada	82	9.1	100.0	79.3	13.4	3.6	2.4	
Japan	5	0.6	100.0	80.0	NA	20.0	NA	
Latin America	106	11.8	100.0	47.2	13.2	28.3	12.2	1.0
Other	308	34.2	100.0	18.5	35.7	31.8	15.6	5.8

(continued)

Table 12.8 (concluded)

| Type of engine[b] | Value of Exports | Per Cent of OECD Exports in 711.5 | Share in OECD Exports (per cent) | | | EEC | | |
			OECD	U.S.	U.K.	Total	Germany	Japan
Type of engine[b]	$449	100.0						
Complete engines	252	56.1	100.0	50.0	50.0	NA	NA	NA
Diesel	178	39.6	100.0	35.4	64.6	NA	NA	NA
Automotive	64	14.2	100.0	17.2	82.8	NA	NA	NA
Marine	40	8.9	100.0	50.0	50.0	NA	NA	NA
Other	75	16.7	100.0	44.0	56.0	NA	NA	NA
Other than diesel	70	15.6	100.0	88.6	11.4	NA	NA	NA
Automotive	19	4.2	100.0	84.2	15.8	NA	NA	NA
Marine	19	4.2	100.0	84.2	15.8	NA	NA	NA
Other	33	7.3	100.0	90.9	9.1	NA	NA	NA
Type not specified	4	0.9	100.0		100.0	NA	NA	NA
Engine parts	197	43.9	100.0	49.7	50.3	NA	NA	NA

Source: Appendix A and sources listed there.
[a]Less than 0.05 per cent.
[b]United States and United Kingdom only.

ever, other engines, particularly outboard motors and gasoline engines other than for marine use, were as important as diesel engines, and the United States was by far the major source of these engines. For diesel engines, on the other hand, the United Kingdom was almost twice as large an exporter as the United States, and Germany may also have been more important than the United States.

Among diesel engines, if we can judge by U.S. and U.K. export data, automotive diesels accounted for a little more than one-third and marine diesels for over a fifth. The United Kingdom and United States showed very different specialization, however. The United Kingdom was almost five times as important as the United States in exports of automotive diesels while the two countries were about equally important in marine diesels. In other diesel engines, for which the United Kingdom led the United States, its predominance was large in small diesel engines (under 100 horsepower) but not in very large ones (over 1,000 horsepower) where the United States may even have been more important, although the classification systems of the two countries do not permit an exact comparison.

In the exports of the United States and the United Kingdom, engine parts were almost as important as complete engines. A large share of parts, it will be recalled, also characterized the aircraft engine subgroup.

One feature of the data which may distort the comparisons among the engine industries in the various countries is the omission of engines exported as parts of vehicles. This factor may tend to exaggerate the relative strength of the automobile engine producers in the United States. Since exports are much more important to European than to U.S. automobile producers, engines exported as part of complete vehicles probably account for a much larger share of European than of U.S. engine output.

The major change in the relative importance of the exporting countries was a decline in the U.S. share between 1953 and 1961 (from 35 to 24 per cent), a small part of which was subsequently regained (Table 12.9). The U.K. share rose to 1961 and then declined to slightly under the initial level, and the German share declined by one or two percentage points. The most significant gains were made by two small exporters, France and Italy, which raised their combined share from less than 4 per cent in 1953 to more than 10 per cent in 1961–64.

Table 12.9
OECD Exports of Internal Combustion Engines Other than for Aircraft,
1953, 1957, 1961–64
(dollars in millions)

	Value of OECD Exports	Share in OECD Exports (per cent)			EEC		Japan
		OECD	U.S.	U.K.	Total	Germany	
		INCLUDING JAPAN					
1964	$1,027	100.0	27.0	23.8	34.0	19.9	2.7
1963	900	100.0	25.0	25.0	35.4	20.1	2.4
1962	847	100.0	26.0	24.6	34.9	20.7	2.5
		EXCLUDING JAPAN					
1962	826	100.0	26.6	25.2	35.8	21.1	
1961	783	100.0	24.0	27.7	35.6	21.3	
1957	626	100.0	28.3	24.8	32.3	21.4	
1953	353	100.0	34.6	24.6	29.7	22.1	

Source: Appendix B.

Price Trends and Price Competitiveness

The international price indexes in Table 12.10 indicate that the prices of U.S. and German internal combustion engines fluctuated within a narrow range during the last four years. Our data are not adequate for the publication of price indexes for the United Kingdom or the EEC as a whole, but they do suggest that British price history was roughly similar to that of the United States; the main exceptions are that more of the 1953–61 price rise came before 1957 and that prices rose relatively more in 1964. The U.S. position vis-à-vis Germany improved between 1961 and 1963, but the gains disappeared in 1964. The more limited data available for the United Kingdom suggest little change in U.K.-U.S. price relationships but a sharper rise in U.K. prices in 1964. In the earlier period the data show a sharp fall in U.S. price competitiveness relative to Germany between 1953 and 1957, and then little change to 1961. As can be seen in Table 12.9, the decline in U.S. price competitiveness was accompanied by a sharp decline in the U.S. share of internal combustion engine exports. The improvement in U.S. price competitiveness in 1962 was also matched by a gain in exports, but U.S. exports also gained in 1964, when the price movement appeared

Table 12.10

International Prices and U.S. Price Competitiveness, Internal Combustion
Engines Other than for Aircraft, 1953, 1957, 1961–64
(1962 = 100)

	1953	1957	1961	1962	1963	1964
INTERNATIONAL PRICE INDEXES						
U.S.	80	94	100	100	103	104
Germany	85	89	97	100	102	98
INDEX OF U.S. PRICE COMPETITIVENESS						
Relative to Germany	106	95	97	100	99	94

Source: International price indexes from Appendix C; price competitiveness indexes,
Appendix D.

quite unfavorable. Before 1964, at least, these data seem to confirm
the high estimates of elasticity of substitution between the United States
and Germany found in Chapter 6 for machinery and vehicles at the two-
digit level. However, we did not estimate elasticity for the subgroup,
since we had so few observations.

Price Levels

Estimates of international price levels for internal combustion engines have several deficiencies. One is that, although we have a large
number of observations, they are very unevenly distributed among the
various kinds of engines. In particular, there are very few for marine
diesels. A major shortcoming is our uncertainty about how best to
weight the types and sizes of engines within the group. Weighting is important because there is apparently a greater degree of national specialization within this category than in many others.[8] The United States,
for example, has a relative advantage in automotive gasoline engines mass produced in Detroit and elsewhere, particularly those in
the 150–400 horsepower range, built for heavy use over long distances.
In Europe and in many other markets the nature of the roads and truck
loads creates a demand for engines with 50 to 75 horsepower less than

[8] National specialization implies differences in the country-to-country price relatives
from one category of product to another. Differences in time-to-time relatives for various
categories within each country are likely to be smaller, and the data requirements for
such indexes are therefore not as stringent as for price level comparisons.

Table 12.11

Price Levels, Internal Combustion Engines Other than for Aircraft, 1962

(U.S. = 100)

| | | | EEC | |
	U.S.	U.K.	Total	Germany
Internal combustion engines and parts	100	90	96	94
Automotive diesel engines	100	70	NA	85
Outboard motors	100	94	100	NA
Parts of internal combustion engines	100	87	95	90

Source: Appendix E.

in the United States. The U.K. industry, which is much more export-oriented than that of the United States, tends to be better at lightweight, compact engines and at marine engines. The Germans tend to do well in industrial engines, particularly where each engine must be custom built. European countries also tend to be cheaper parts suppliers; and parts, as already noted, probably form a substantial fraction of the total trade.

In making our estimates of comparative price levels of internal combustion engines, we incorporated the results of regression analyses of prices of automotive diesel engines and outboard motors, for each of which we had prices of a wide range of models for a number of countries with the prices and specifications of each.[9]

When we combined the direct price comparisons for automotive and other diesel and gasoline engines and for parts with the regression-based indexes we found that for internal combustion engines as a whole U.K. prices in 1962 were 10 per cent and German prices 6 per cent lower than U.S. prices (Table 12.11). Prices in the EEC countries other than Germany were slightly higher than German prices.[10]

The very advantageous U.K. position shown in the price level comparisons is reflected in the trade data for automotive diesel engines

[9] The outboard motor analysis is in the appendix to this chapter; the diesel engine data are from Chapter 5.

[10] Some direct comparisons of automotive diesel engine prices, that is, comparisons between engines of closely matching specifications, show no difference between U.S. and U.K. prices. However, these are on engines outside the range of most U.K. exports and outside the range to which the U.K. regression line was fitted, although they were fairly typical of U.S. engines. If the specifications for these engines are inserted into the U.K. regression equations, the estimated U.K. prices and the U.K.-U.S. price ratios are far below the actual ones. This result indicates that the U.K. regression equation, while it fits the range of observations that produced it, cannot be extrapolated to the U.S. range of engine sizes. Fortunately, the U.K. size range is the one most important in world trade.

given in Table 12.8. U.K. exports were almost five times those of the United States in this subgroup. In outboard motors, on the other hand, for which U.K. prices were much closer to the U.S. level, the United States was by far the leader in exports.

Agricultural Machinery and Implements [11]

Trade

The United States, the United Kingdom, and Germany were the major exporters of agricultural machinery, with the first accounting for over one-third of OECD exports and the last for about one-eighth (Table 12.12). Canada was a smaller but notable exporter. Almost a quarter of total OECD exports represented trade between the United States and Canada. This exchange is facilitated by proximity, similarity of agricultural conditions and techniques, and the absence of U.S. or Canadian tariffs on most of the products in the group. In fact, the North American industry regards Canada and the United States as a single market, and this is often reflected in the organizational structure of the individual firms. Thus a single marketing subdivision may deal with the U.S. and Canadian market, and the location of plants on either side of the border tends to be governed to a large degree by the same kinds of considerations that might determine the choice, say, between Iowa and Illinois.

In 1963 tractors accounted for over half the agricultural machinery and implement exports of the OECD countries as a whole, for over 60 per cent of U.S. exports, and over 80 per cent of U.K. exports. U.S. tractor exports consisted largely of earth-moving tractors, particularly crawler-type, used more in construction than in agriculture, but nevertheless classified here by the SITC.[12] While the United States dominated

---

[11] SITC 712. *Value of OECD exports in 1963:* $1,398 million; 3.1 per cent of study total. *Coverage:* Tractors, farm and other, except those for tractor-trailers; harvesting, threshing, and sorting machines; cultivating machinery, etc.

[12] The trade patterns reported in the text must be considered in the light of the treatment of tractors in the SITC. SITC 712.5 is the basic classification for tractors designed to haul or push other vehicles, appliances, or loads, but certain types of tractors are classified elsewhere. Road tractors for tractor-trailer combinations are in SITC 732.5; tractors for the short-distance transport or handling of goods or materials (e.g., those with front-end loaders permanently attached) are in SITC 719.3 (mechanical handling equipment); and tractors with permanently attached earth excavating or moving appliances (e.g., bulldozers) are in SITC 718.4 (construction and mining machinery). As can be seen in the notes to Appendix A, there is some disagreement among national statistical offices as to the proper classification of some of these items. In addition, parts for tractors falling within 712.5 are classified in 732.8 (parts for motor vehicles).

Table 12.12
OECD Exports of Agricultural Machinery and Implements (SITC 712),
by Origin, Destination, and Commodity Subgroup, 1963
(dollars in millions)

| | Value of Exports | Per Cent of OECD Exports in 712 | Share in OECD Exports (per cent) | | | | | |
			OECD	U.S.	U.K.	EEC Total	EEC Germany	Japan
Total, all destinations and subgroups	$1,398	100.0	100.0	34.5	28.0	23.5	12.7	0.5
Destination								
U.S.	128	9.2	100.0		17.2	2.3	0.8	
OECD Europe	574	41.0	100.0	12.2	31.7	45.8	27.0	
U.K.	33	2.4	100.0	27.3		54.5	27.3	
EEC total	308	22.0	100.0	13.3	28.2	50.6	28.2	
Germany	61	4.4	100.0	16.4	36.1	32.8		
Canada	240	17.2	100.0	90.0	7.1	2.5	0.8	
Japan	10	0.7	100.0	30.0	50.0	20.0	20.0	
Latin America	111	7.9	100.0	59.4	26.1	8.1	1.8	
Other	335	24.0	100.0	38.2	41.2	13.7	4.2	1.8

(continued)

Table 12.12 (concluded)

SITC commodity subgroup	Value of Exports	Per Cent of OECD Exports in 712	Share in OECD Exports (per cent)			EEC		Japan
			OECD	U.S.	U.K.	Total	Germany	
Soil preparation or cultivating machinery (712.1)	$125	8.9	100.0	20.8	16.8	27.2	16.0	3.2
Threshing, harvesting, sorting machinery (712.2)	360	25.8	100.0	18.6	9.4	43.0	25.3	0.3
Dairy machinery (712.3)	41	2.9	100.0	26.8	22.0	24.4	14.6	
Tractors (712.5)	769	55.0	100.0	38.9	41.9	15.3	7.4	0.3
Agricultural machinery and appliances, n.e.s. (712.9)	103	7.4	100.0	77.7	5.8	11.6	2.9	1.9

Source: Appendix A and sources cited there.

the market for large earth movers, the United Kingdom was easily the leader in exporting the lighter, less powerful, usually wheel-type machines which are widely used in agriculture and which are more important in international trade. The strength of the U.K. position may be ascribed to the economies of large-scale production; British production is more concentrated in a few firms than is the case in other major countries, and the British firms concentrate only on two or three models.[13]

Harvesting, threshing, and sorting machines are the second most important subgroup, making up one-fourth of total exports. Germany and Canada are the leaders in the export of combines, which loom large in the subgroup. Combines play an important role in Canadian exports to the United States, reflecting the position in the North American market for the machines produced by a large Canadian-based agricultural equipment manufacturer.

Only in the miscellaneous subgroup (SITC 712.9), which includes poultry equipment and machines for extracting fruit juices, does the United States enjoy a dominant trade position.

Differences in local conditions and techniques create demands for somewhat different designs in different parts of the world. As a result, there tends to be a great deal of local specialization, through small-scale production, to meet local preferences, particularly for smaller products such as plows and harrows. Larger machinery is also affected, as, for example, the need for a combine in North America that will permit wheat farmers to plow straw back under, and for one in Europe that will permit them to harvest it. Again, cheap fuel costs in the United States have made it more economical for U.S. farmers to use tractors powered by gasoline engines, while high fuel prices in other areas have made the initially more expensive diesel engines more advantageous in the long run.

An important element in competition for the larger and more complicated machines such as tractors and combines is the availability of parts; fast parts replacement, especially during critical periods of use,

---

[13] Cf. *EFTA Bulletin,* European Free Trade Association, July 1962, p. 4. However, the exclusion of parts from SITC 712.5 and the assignment of certain types of tractors to other categories (see previous footnote) tend to enhance the U.K. share of exports in SITC 712.5 and to diminish that of the United States. Parts are more important in U.S. than in U.K. exports; when the 1963 exports of tractors and identifiable tractor parts (parts are not separately distinguished for some tractor categories in the trade statistics) are compared for the two countries, the U.S. total is $462 million and the U.K. total is $388; for 1964 the corresponding figures are $600 million and $377 million. One reason that parts are so important in U.S. exports is that the major U.S. firms are all extensively involved in production overseas.

is essential to the economical operation of such equipment. Thus dealer organization as well as price affects the competitiveness of different makes.

Changes in export shares were comparatively small during the four years for which we have data (Table 12.13). The United States lost somewhat in 1962 but more than regained its initial position by 1964, while the United Kingdom first gained but then lost more in 1964. Germany suffered some loss in its share in both 1962 and 1963 while other EEC countries gained to an extent that more than offset the German losses.

Price Trends and Levels

The two major problems in measuring price differences between times and between places were the lack of comparable models and existence of differential pricing between various markets. (The latter practice in the export trade seems to be a common feature of the agricultural equipment industry abroad and is not unknown in North America.) Our stress upon obtaining from each respondent comparative prices for two or more times or places helped meet both of these problems. In addition, to surmount the difficulty caused by the diversity of models, we used a regression analysis which enabled us to compare tractors of different weight and horsepower specifications over time for the United States and, to a more limited degree, between other countries and the United States. Nevertheless, it would have been desirable, because of the prevalence of differential pricing, to have had a larger sample of prices than we were

Table 12.13

OECD Exports of Agricultural Machinery and Implements, 1961–64

(dollars in millions)

	Value of OECD Exports	Share in OECD Exports (per cent)					
		OECD	U.S.	U.K.	EEC		Japan
					Total	Germany	
1964	$1,624	100.0	38.2	23.3	23.6	12.9	0.6
1963	1,398	100.0	34.5	28.0	23.6	12.7	0.5
1962	1,185	100.0	33.8	28.4	23.9	13.4	0.5
1961	1,067	100.0	36.6	26.2	22.3	15.7	0.6

Source: Appendix B.

Table 12.14
International Prices, Agricultural Machinery and Implements,
1953, 1957, 1961—64
(1962 = 100)

	1953	1957	1961	1962	1963	1964
AGRICULTURAL MACHINERY AND IMPLEMENTS (SITC 712)						
U.S.	83	89	98	100	102	103
U.K.	84	92	98	100	102	102
EEC	84	90	98	100	102	102
Germany	84	91	99	100	101	101
TRACTORS (SITC 712.5)						
U.S.	84	91	98	100	102	102
U.K.	86	95	99	100	101	102
EEC	86	92	98	100	103	104
Germany	88	94	100	100	102	103

Source: Appendix C.

able to gather. We believe, however, that the time-to-time indexes that we were able to put together for the United States and Germany are reliable; the United Kingdom and EEC temporal indexes are more tenuous.

In view of these problems it is somewhat reassuring to find that the indexes for the different countries, each built up from completely independent data,[14] behave in such similar ways. From 1953 to 1964, price increases on agricultural equipment ranged from 17 to 20 per cent, with the largest rise in the United States and the smallest in Germany (Table 12.14). Separate indexes for the important tractor subgroup indicate a slightly smaller increase but an otherwise generally similar timing and pattern of price change.

The same relationships are viewed from a somewhat different standpoint in the indexes of U.S. price competitiveness (Table 12.15). U.S. price competitiveness tended to decline, but only slightly in most cases. The data for tractors hint at some reversal of the U.S. decline in 1964.

The international price indexes and the derived indexes of price competitiveness may be compared with a similar set of indexes based on wholesale prices (Table 12.16). The coverage of these indexes differs

[14] Except, of course, for the overlap between the EEC and Germany.

Table 12.15

U.S. Price Competitiveness, Agricultural Machinery and Implements,
1953, 1957, 1961–64

(1962 = 100)

	1953	1957	1961	1962	1963	1964
AGRICULTURAL MACHINERY AND IMPLEMENTS (SITC 712)						
Relative to						
U.K.	102	105	101	100	99	100
EEC	101	102	100	100	100	100
Germany	102	102	101	100	99	99
TRACTORS (SITC 712.5)						
Relative to						
U.K.	102	105	101	100	99	100
EEC	103	102	100	100	101	102
Germany	105	104	102	100	100	101

Source: Appendix D.

Table 12.16

International Price and Price Competitiveness Indexes Based on Wholesale
Price Data, Agricultural Machinery and Implements, 1953, 1957, 1961–64

(1962 = 100)

	1953	1957	1961	1962	1963	1964
INTERNATIONAL PRICE INDEXES						
U.S.	81	88	99	100	101	103
EEC	86	91	96	100	101	102
Germany	79	85	96	100	100	101
Japan	86	102	101	100	101	99
INDEXES OF U.S. INTERNATIONAL PRICE COMPETITIVENESS						
Relative to						
EEC	105	102	97	100	100	99
Germany	98	96	98	100	99	98
Japan	104	114	103	100	99	96

Source: Appendix F. The EEC index is an average of Germany, weighted three
times, and France, weighted once.

widely from one country to another, and they refer, of course, to domestic rather than export transactions. They do not differ radically from the international price indexes, and the U.S. results are virtually identical, but the differences are sometimes large enough to lead to opposite conclusions. The indexes from wholesale prices, for example, show a larger rise in German prices up to 1962 than the international price indexes. As a result, they indicate a small increase in U.S. price competitiveness between 1953 and 1962, while the international prices point to stability or a deterioration in the U.S. price position. They also show a substantial decline in U.S. price competitiveness relative to the EEC while the indexes based on international prices show stability.

Qualifications similar to those mentioned in introducing the time-to-time indexes apply to our estimates of the levels of tractor prices in the different countries. We think it very unlikely, however, that the 1964 relationships below (from Appendix E) are far from the mark:

	SITC 712: Agricultural Machinery & Implements	SITC 712.5: Tractors
U.S.	100	100
U.K.	86	78
EEC	90	86

Considering the stability shown by these intercountry price relationships, we may say that over the period of our study the U.K. price level for the group as a whole has been about 15 per cent below that of the United States, and that EEC prices have been about 10 per cent lower than those of the United States. German prices on the average have been a shade below those of other common market countries.

The underlying data indicate substantial variations around these averages for different types of agricultural machinery and equipment. The United Kingdom, for example, is the low-priced source of tractors, but the United States is the low-priced source of preparation and cultivation machinery and of poultry and miscellaneous types of agricultural equipment. Even within the three-digit categories there are differences in the patterns of international specialization. For example, the United Kingdom undersells the United States on agricultural tractors by about 25 per cent but by a much smaller margin on heavy construction-type machines (the latter representing a branch of the industry in which U.S. subsidiaries are active both in the United Kingdom and on the Continent).

Office Machines [15]

Trade

The United States was the largest exporter of office machines in 1963, accounting for more than one-third of OECD exports, while the EEC countries combined accounted for about 40 per cent. More than three-quarters of OECD exports were shipped to other OECD countries, with the United States a large net exporter, Japan almost entirely an importer, and Europe as a whole roughly balancing its trade (Table 12.17).

The United States had a very small share in typewriter exports, but was a major importer and showed a substantial import surplus. Electric typewriters, which were much less important in world trade than portables, accounted for 60 per cent or more of U.S. typewriter exports.

The United States played a large role in exports of calculating and accounting machines (SITC 714.2) and other office machines and parts (SITC 714.9) mainly because of U.S. exports of electronic computers and parts. The former subgroup is composed of two very different components: electronic computers, mainly exported by the United States, and other calculating and accounting machines, in which the United States is much less important. The United States is a small exporter of punched-card and related equipment (SITC 714.3), but a very large factor in exports of the associated parts, which are included in subgroup 714.9.[16]

The role of United States firms in world trade in office machines is understated by the trade figures, since a substantial part of foreign exports is by overseas subsidiaries of U.S. firms. This is particularly the case for subgroups 714.2 and 714.3 (and the associated items in sub-

[15] SITC 714. *Value of OECD exports in 1963:* $1,024 million; 2.3 per cent of study total. *Coverage:* Typewriters; electronic computers and other calculating and accounting machines; punched card and related equipment; other office machines and parts.

[16] The indexes for office machinery as a whole are dominated by electronic computers and punched-card equipment, which are more than 50 per cent of the group total. In addition to the punched-card and related equipment (SITC 714.3) we have estimated that electronic computers account for half of subgroup 714.2 and that parts of electronic computers and punched-card equipment are more than half of subgroup 714.9.

Table 12.17
OECD Exports of Office Machines (SITC 714),
by Origin, Destination, and Commodity Subgroup, 1963
(dollars in millions)

	Value of Exports	Per Cent of OECD Exports in 714	Share in OECD Exports (per cent)			EEC			
			OECD	U.S.	U.K.	Total	Germany	Italy	Japan
Total, all destinations	$1,024	100.0	100.0	35.4	10.8	40.0	16.0	11.7	0.8
Destination									
U.S.	96	9.4	100.0		11.4	60.4	20.8	20.8	3.1
OECD Europe	567	55.4	100.0	31.7	9.2	45.8	19.0	11.1	0.2
U.K.	80	7.8	100.0	50.0		37.5	21.2	5.0	2.5
EEC total	350	34.2	100.0	31.7	9.7	44.8	14.8	12.0	0.3
Germany	131	12.8	100.0	32.1	9.2	41.2		11.4	0.3
France	114	11.1	100.0	37.7	9.6	40.4	20.2	17.5	0.3
Italy	40	3.9	100.0	27.5	10.0	47.5	27.5		
Canada	69	6.7	100.0	85.5	4.3	7.2	2.9	4.3	0.4
Japan	93	9.1	100.0	71.0	5.4	14.0	6.4	3.2	
Latin America	71	6.9	100.0	35.7	7.5	41.6	11.8	24.4	1.6
Other	127	12.4	100.0	25.2	26.8	34.6	15.7	11.0	2.4
SITC commodity subgroup									
Typewriters, etc. (714.1)	141	13.8	100.0	12.0	7.8	66.0	31.2	17.7	2.8
Calculating machines (714.2)	460	44.9	100.0	46.1	8.7	32.4	11.7	16.5	0.4
Statistical machines (714.3)	162	15.8	100.0	8.6	17.3	52.5	20.4	6.2	0.6
Office machines, n.e.s. (714.9)	260	25.4	100.0	45.8	12.3	31.9	12.7	3.5	0.4

Source: Appendix A and sources cited there.

308

group 714.9): It has been estimated that the leading U.S. producer of electronic computers and punched-card equipment sells more in the main European markets (outside of the United Kingdom) than all its U.S. and foreign competitors combined, and that the great majority of these sales consist of European-produced machines.[17] A substantial share of the rest of the European market is supplied by subsidiaries of other American firms.

The importance of U.S. firms in foreign production is less over-whelming in the other office machinery items. However, United States-owned firms produce, in European countries, items in all the other subgroups of office machines. In some cases they have transferred to their European plants their entire production of certain items, particularly portable typewriters and adding machines, including products for the U.S. market. A large part of U.S. typewriter imports, including virtually all from the Netherlands, is produced in United States-owned foreign plants.[18]

The U.S. share of OECD office machinery exports fell sharply between 1953 and 1957 and then changed little, increasing slightly after 1962 (Table 12.18). The U.K. share declined by about 60 per cent between 1953 and 1961, and then remained fairly stable. The EEC gained until 1962, mainly at the expense of the United States and the United Kingdom, but the gains of the United States and Japan after 1962 were matched by EEC losses.

International Price Indexes

From the measures of international price movements in Table 12.19 it is clear that office machine prices have behaved very differently from most prices since 1953. In the United States and the United Kingdom they were at almost the same level in 1964 as in 1953, and in Germany and the EEC countries they were considerably lower.

Our indexes since 1962 show a general decline in prices for all countries, partly attributable to the incorporation of cost data. Prices paid

[17] "Automation Abroad," *Wall Street Journal,* November 26, 1963; "Problems of Financing, Costs, and Competition Plaguing Europe's Computer Industry," *New York Times,* April 12, 1964; "European Computer Demand Widening US Firms' Horizons," *Journal of Commerce,* July 6, 1964; *Export Market Guide to Italy: Electronic Computers and Peripheral Equipment,* Bureau of International Commerce, U.S. Dept. of Commerce, 1965.

[18] "Burroughs Corp. to Close Plant in Mid-Detroit," *Wall Street Journal,* December 27, 1963; "Typewriters: The Status Symbol," *Economist,* October 8, 1960; *Typewriters, Report on Escape-Clause Investigation No. 7-84,* U.S. Tariff Commission, May 1960.

Table 12.18

OECD Exports of Office Machines, 1953, 1957, 1961–64

(dollars in millions)

	Value of OECD Exports	Share in OECD Exports (per cent)						
		OECD	U.S.	U.K.	Total	Germany	Italy	Japan
					EEC			
1964	$1,153	100.0	37.6	9.8	38.6	17.1	9.9	1.3
1963	1,024	100.0	35.4	10.8	40.0[a]	16.0	11.7	0.8
1962	971	100.0	33.3	9.6	42.7	17.0	12.0	0.5
1961	896	100.0	34.6	9.2	40.1	16.2	11.5	2.8
1957[b]	391	100.0	35.3	13.6	39.1	17.4	10.5	0.3
1953[b]	205	100.0	44.9	15.1	28.8	12.7	7.3	0.5

Source: Appendix B.

[a]Of which France, 7.6 per cent.

[b]Excluding Spain ($2 million in 1961) and Switzerland ($23 million in 1961).

by ultimate purchasers for these products tended to remain constant during 1962–1964. The use of these prices instead of cost data would therefore have tended to reduce or possibly eliminate the decline in U.S. and European prices shown in the last two years, but it would not have affected the movement of the indexes of price competitiveness presented below.

Our price indexes in this group take little or no account of the enormous improvements in quality that have taken place with the introduction of new computers. The price declines we show reflect mainly gains in the efficiency with which old machines were produced. Therefore, these

Table 12.19

International Prices, Office Machines, 1953, 1957, 1961–64

(1962 = 100)

	1953	1957	1961	1962	1963	1964
U.S.	92	100	103	100	96	92
U.K.	90	96	100	100	93	89
EEC	107	98	100	100	94	89
Germany	106	97	100	100	94	89

Source: Appendix C.

Table 12.20

U.S. International Prices, Office Machines: NBER Index vs. Indexes from
Wholesale Price and from Unit Value Data, 1953, 1957, 1961–64

	$\dfrac{1957}{1953}$	$\dfrac{1961}{1957}$	$\dfrac{1962}{1961}$	$\dfrac{1963}{1962}$	$\dfrac{1964}{1963}$
NBER international price index	109	103	97	96	96
Index derived from wholesale prices	112	102	99	101	100
Index derived from export unit values	106	124	106	91	108

Source: International price indexes: unlinked indexes underlying Table 12.19. Index derived from wholesale prices: Appendix F. Index derived from export unit values: Appendix G.

price indexes must be biased upward by a large margin. We did not have the data necessary for the type of regression analysis performed elsewhere in this study, but the dimensions of the upward bias are suggested by a comparison with regression-based indexes for U.S. domestic sales of computers, which show a decline of over 50 per cent in computer prices between 1961 and 1964 when our indexes report a decline of a little less than 15 per cent.[19]

In Table 12.20 our U.S. international price indexes for office machines are compared with indexes derived from BLS wholesale price series and from those U.S. export unit values of office machines that are used by the Department of Commerce in its export unit value index. These latter indexes, as year-to-year price changes, appear in the second and third lines of Table 12.20. There were not enough wholesale price series for the other countries to permit the construction of similar price indexes.

There are several large differences between the NBER indexes and the export unit value indexes. The NBER data show no upward price trend while the export unit values indicate a price rise of over 30 per cent and, in addition, fluctuate much more sharply. The unit value data cover a narrower list of products but nevertheless include a much wider range of price changes in some years than the NBER indexes. In 1961/1957,

[19] Gregory C. Chow, "Technological Change and the Demand for Computers," *American Economic Review*, December 1967.

for example, the export unit value changes in the three series covered ranged from −32 per cent to +36 per cent. Since the export unit values are averages for many transactions one would expect them to have, if the groups were homogeneous, a narrower range of price changes in any one year and greater stability over time than the individual transaction prices used in the NBER indexes.

The indexes derived from wholesale price data are in every year as close as or closer than the unit value indexes to the NBER indexes, particularly in 1961/1957 and 1962/1961, when there were large differences between the two trade indexes. One reason for the superiority of the wholesale price data is their wider coverage.

The wholesale price indexes do show some upward trend over the eleven years as a whole, but much less than the unit value indexes. One explanation for the differences in trends is that neither the unit value nor the wholesale price indexes include subgroup 714.3, electronic computers in subgroup 714.2, or the corresponding parts in subgroup 714.9, whereas the NBER indexes do. These items, particularly electronic computers, were responsible for the downward movement in the NBER price indexes in the later years. The NBER indexes for subgroups 714.1 and 714.2 other than electronic computers were all within two percentage points of the corresponding BLS indexes, except in the 1957/1953 segment when their rise was substantially less than that shown by the BLS.

Price Competitiveness

Relative to the United Kingdom, American price competitiveness barely changed during these years (Table 12.21). The relationship between the U.S. and British international price levels in 1964 was almost the same as in 1953. Germany and the EEC countries as a group gained substantially on the United States, the bulk of the improvement taking place between 1953 and 1957, with little or no change in price competitiveness after that.[20]

The data underlying both the time-to-time and place-to-place comparisons used in the indexes of price competitiveness for office machines

---

[20] It should be noted that the indexes prior to 1962 are seriously weak because they do not cover electronic computers, punched-card equipment, and the corresponding parts of machines in SITC 714.9. However, the evidence for later years does not suggest that changes in price competitiveness in these groups of commodities were very different from those in other subgroups of office machines, given the price measurement methods we are using. See, however, the discussion of international price measures, above.

Table 12.21
U.S. Price Competitiveness, Office Machines, 1953, 1957, 1961–64
(1962 = 100)

	1953	1957	1961	1962	1963	1964
Relative to						
U.K.	98	97	97	100	98	97
EEC	118	98	97	100	98	97
Germany	116	98	97	100	98	97

Note: Changes in price competitiveness can also be inferred from place-to-place data. The results of this calculation, although based on fewer and less reliable observations than the time-to-time calculations, are similar, as can be seen below:

	1953	1957	1961	1962	1963	1964
Relative to						
U.K.	102	100	99	100	98	98
EEC	NA	100	98	100	98	96
Germany	NA	100	98	100	98	96

Source: Appendix D.

differ from those in most of the other commodity groups in one major respect: the use of cost data in place of prices. Cost data were employed particularly in subgroups 714.2 and 714.3, but to some degree also in subgroups 714.1 and 714.9. Costs were used instead of prices in several cases in which sales were made through international companies which filled orders from production by subsidiaries in various countries but did not give the purchaser the option of selecting the source. It was felt that in such cases the international company could be regarded, for the purpose of measuring international price competitiveness, as the purchaser of the products rather than the seller, since it had no nationality as a manufacturer but determined, by its own "purchase" decisions, where the product was to be produced. These purchase decisions were undoubtedly influenced by many nonprice factors, notably the relative lengths of order books, but the cost of production in each country of manufacture may be taken as the closest measure of the price element in the international company's decisions.

Price Levels

As can be seen from the first section of Table 12.22 European prices were slightly lower than U.S. prices from 1957 on, except in 1962,

Table 12.22
Price Levels, Office Machines, 1953, 1957, 1961–64
(U.S. for each year = 100)

	1953	1957	1961	1962	1963	1964
U.S.	100	100	100	100	100	100
U.K.	98	97	97	100	97	97
EEC	117	98	97	99	98	96
Germany	115	96	96	99	97	96

Note: Independent, and probably less reliable, measures of international price levels are provided by the actual place-to-place comparisons for all years, rather than by extrapolation from the best year using the price competitiveness index, as described in Appendix E. The place-to-place data, based in some cases on a smaller number of observations, ranging from 7 to 36, are as follows:

	1953	1957	1961	1962	1963	1964
U.K.	102	100	99	100	97	98
EEC	NA	100	98	100	98	96
Germany	NA	100	98	100	98	95

Source: Appendix E.

when they were at almost the same level. At the beginning of our period, however, EEC prices, including German prices, were substantially higher than American ones.

The closeness of price levels shown in Table 12.22 conceals much larger differences among subgroup price levels. The United States was at a considerable competitive disadvantage in typewriters (SITC 714.1) and in calculating and accounting machines. Less technological change has taken place in these groups than in electronic computers (included in SITC 714.2) or in punched-card machines (included in SITC 714.3). The growth of world trade in typewriters and calculating and accounting machines has also been smaller, to judge by the more than tenfold growth of U.S. electronic computer exports between 1958 and 1964.

Our indexes for electronic computers show a competitive advantage for the United States, and those for punched-card machines suggest about equal prices in the United States and Europe. Even where the indexes are based mainly on cost data, new and old models of machines must be distinguished. After production of a model had continued for several years in both Europe and the United States, European costs were slightly lower than U.S. costs for components of electronic computer systems and 10 to 20 per cent lower for punched-card equipment. The advantage calculated for the United States was derived from the high cost in the early stages of European production for each model and the assumption of the same high initial level of European costs during the period before European production began, when the United States was the only source for a model. The level of the price differential in this calculation depended to a large degree on the lag between initial U.S. and initial European production for each model of a machine, and on the length of the period during which the model was produced. A long lag and a high rate of obsolescence (a short commercial life for each model) tend to raise the calculated ratio of foreign to U.S. costs.

Even within typewriters there were considerable differences among types of machines. The indexes are dominated by portables, which are estimated to have accounted for about two-thirds of world trade in typewriters in 1963. The unfavorable U.S. competitive position in these machines is confirmed by the fact that several typewriter producers that operate in both the United States and Europe have concentrated their production of portables in Europe. However, the United States remained an important exporter of electric typewriters, in which the competitive position was more advantageous. Costs and prices of electric typewriters were generally about as high in Europe as in the United States or higher, while EEC costs and prices for nonelectric standard and portable typewriters were 10 to 20 per cent below the U.S. level. Even this differential may be underestimated because we lack cost data from manufacturers who completely switched their production away from the United States.

Prices and the Pattern of Trade

Since price levels and price changes are not the only forces determining the direction of trade and changes in it, one could not hope to find very high simple correlations between prices and trade movements, but good correlations would be an indication that we have had some success in our price measurement.

For each pair of countries, we ranked five subgroups of office machines in the order of the price ratios, from highest to lowest, and compared this ranking with that of the export value and export-import ratios. For example, in the first section of Table 12.23, where we compare the

Table 12.23

Relation of Price Ratios to Export Shares and Export-Import Ratios, 1963

| | | | Export-Import Ratio | |
| | | | Based on | |
SITC Number[b]	Price Ratio	Export Value Ratio	Export Data[c]	Import Data[d]
U.K./U.S.				
714.2B	1	5	5	5
714.3	2	1	2	3
714.9	3	4	4	4
714.1	4	2	1	1
714.2A	5	3	3	2
EEC/U.S.				
714.2B	1	5	5	5
714.9	2	4	4	4
714.3	3	2	3	3
714.2A	4	3	2	2
714.1	5	1	1	1

The table is headed "Rank[a] of" spanning the four data columns.

Note: Price ratios are from subgroup indexes underlying Table 12.22. Export values, except for separation of 714.2 into 714.2A and 714.2B, are from Appendix A and the sources underlying it. U.S. exports for 714.2B are from *U.S. Export Statistics*, 1963 Annual, U.S. Bureau of the Census, Report FT 410, June 1964. Estimates of U.K. exports are from *Accounts Relating to the Trade and Navigation of the United Kingdom*, HMSO, December 1964. Those for other European countries are derived very roughly from *Market Information on Electronic Products in West Germany*, U.S. Dept. of Commerce, Overseas Business Reports, OBR 64-120, October 1964, and *Export Market Guide to Italy, Electronic Computers and Peripheral Equipment*, U.S. Dept. of Commerce, Bureau of International Commerce, 1965.

Import values from export data are OECD exports to the United States, the United Kingdom, and the EEC, from the same sources as the export values, except for 714.2B, which is roughly estimated from the sources mentioned above.

Import values from import data are total imports of the United States, the United Kingdom, and the EEC countries, from *Trade by Commodities*, OECD Statistical Bulletin, Series C, 1963, Vol. II, *Imports*, and for electronic computers, rough estimates based on the sources previously mentioned.

[a]High to low.

[b]The subgroups are 714.1, typewriters and check-writing machines; 714.2A, calculating, accounting machines other than electronic computers; 714.2B, electronic computers, 714.3, statistical machines; 714.9, office machines, n.e.s.

[c]For each country, exports as reported by that country and imports as the sum of other countries' reported exports to that country.

[d]For each country, exports and imports as reported by that country.

United Kingdom and the United States, we show in the first column that U.K. prices are highest relative to U.S. prices in electronic computers, and lowest in calculating and accounting machines other than electronic computers. In the second column we show the ranks of the export value ratios: the ratios of U.K. exports to U.S. exports for the five subgroups. As we might expect, the value ratio is lowest in subgroup 714.2B, for which the price ratio is highest. Similar sets of comparisons are made for the EEC vs. the United States.

All these comparisons of prices and trade values are subject to two serious drawbacks. One is the heterogeneity of the SITC trade groups, even on a four-digit level. In these comparisons, for example, it was necessary to break subgroup 714.2 down between electronic computers (714.2B) and other calculating and accounting machines (714.2A) because the price movements of the two items differed greatly. However, the division of the export and import values could be done only very crudely for lack of comparable data.

Even where the export classes do not combine such different commodities they suffer from inconsistencies among the trade classifications of the various countries, which produce spurious relationships among the export values. For example, the high ratio of U.K. to U.S. exports in subgroup 714.3 is at least partly due to the fact that the U.S. combines all electronic computers into one class, which is placed in subgroup 714.2, while the U.K. distinguishes those operating with punched-cards and puts them into subgroup 714.3 (see notes to Appendix A). There are probably similar difficulties with the EEC data.

There seems to be little relationship between price and export value ratios for the United Kingdom relative to the United States. In the comparison between the United States and the EEC countries, however, the relationship is inverse, as we would expect if the "product" substitution elasticities are greater than 1, as indicated in Chapter 6. The U.S. price advantage in electronic computers and related parts appears to be reflected in high shares of exports in subgroups 714.2B and 714.9, and the lower degree of U.S. price competitiveness in typewriters is reflected in comparatively low export ratios. In both the U.K. and the EEC comparisons, particularly the former, the U.S. export share for subgroup 714.3 is surprisingly low. To some extent, as has been mentioned, this apparently low U.S. share may be the result of differences in classification systems.

In a sense, export values or shares provide only a partial test of the price relationships, because the influence of prices should appear on the import as well as the export side of the trade account. It is partly to catch the influence on imports that we have included in the indexes domestic prices for commodities that a country does not export. For the second set of comparisons in Table 12.23 we therefore ranked ratios of exports to imports, by subgroup, for each country.

The comparison of EEC-U.S. export-import ratios with price ratios shows a perfect negative relationship. The U.K.-U.S. comparison, like that for the export ratios, shows little relationship. In particular, the U.K. trade ratio for SITC 714.3 is surprisingly high, given the price relationship. It may be that classification inconsistencies are again involved, since the import data are derived from other countries' exports while the export data follow the U.K. classification system.

To escape this classification problem a second set of export-import ratios was computed in which the import values were taken from each country's reported imports rather than from partners' exports. The advantage in this method was that the numerator and denominator for each country's ratios come from the same statistical system. However, even this method does not insure the comparability of export and import data, since some countries' export classifications differ substantially from their own import classifications.

This modification of the import data produces slightly better results in the U.K.-U.S. comparison. There is at least a tendency toward a negative relationship between price ratios and export-import ratios, although it is not a perfect one. The EEC-U.S. comparison remains perfectly negative, as it was using the earlier set of import data.

To summarize, we have some evidence for the idea that higher price levels for office machines do tend to be associated with lower levels of exports or, particularly, with lower ratios of exports to imports. The trade data thus do confirm, although somewhat weakly, the results of our price measurements.

It would be of great interest to relate changes in the movement of trade over ten years or more to changes in the price competitiveness of individual countries, but the possibilities for such comparisons are very limited in the office machines group. One difficulty is that changes in price competitiveness, as shown in these indexes, have been very small:

Only in two indexes for group 714 as a whole, both for 1953–57, were there changes of more than three percentage points. More price changes are to be found in the subgroup indexes, but there are no corresponding trade data available to compare them with, except for 1962 and 1963.

Most of the changes in price competitiveness shown in Table 12.21 are too small, especially in view of the probable margins of error surrounding the figures, to warrant any expectation of matching changes in trade flows. However, the one major change in price competitiveness, the substantial improvement for Germany and the EEC as a whole relative to the United Kingdom and the United States between 1953 and 1957, was accompanied by substantial changes in export shares. The German share of OECD exports rose from 13 to 17 per cent and the EEC share from 29 to 39 per cent, while the U.S. share declined from 45 to 35 per cent.

Summary

America tends to be a high-cost producer of business machines compared to Europe once the production of a particular machine is established in Europe and volume output achieved. The U.S. advantage lies in the continual introduction of new machines with superior capabilities and in the economies of mass production, which owing to the size of the American market, enable a firm to obtain large volume on a new machine quickly. Once a machine is developed and the U.S. market for it established, a market is fostered in Europe and other foreign areas through exports, licensing, and finally production abroad. In the initial stages foreign production may be 10 or 20 per cent more costly than U.S. production, but once the learning period is over and an optimum volume can be achieved European costs may be lower than those of the United States by 10 or 20 per cent. If a subsidiary of a U.S. firm is involved, the transition from high- to low-cost production may take place in as short a period as two or three years.

Taking old and new types of machines in the proportions in which they entered international trade, we found that U.S. international prices for office machines were usually slightly above U.K. and EEC prices. U.S. price competitiveness did not change significantly relative to the United Kingdom after 1953, or relative to the EEC countries after 1957, but the EEC countries gained substantially between 1953 and 1957. The

U.S. price position was most favorable in the technologically advanced lines—particularly electronic computers—and in electric typewriters, and weakest in portable and standard typewriters and in calculating and accounting machines. Data on the direction of trade show a pattern of competitive strength and weakness that tends to confirm the price indexes. Changes in trade flows support the finding of substantial gains in competitiveness by the EEC countries before 1957 but do not seem to have been closely related to the much smaller fluctuations in price competitiveness since then.

Both wholesale prices and unit values appear to give unsatisfactory measures of international price changes for office machines, mainly because the coverage of both sets of underlying data is inadequate and because individual unit value series display erratic movements. These probably do not correspond to any actual price changes but may represent shifts in composition within the export classes.

Metalworking Machine Tools [21]

Trade

More than half of OECD exports of metalworking machine tools were by the countries of the EEC, with Germany by far the leader in EEC and in the world as a whole (Table 12.24). The United States followed Germany in importance, but far behind, and the United Kingdom was the third ranking exporter, at about a third of the German level. In fact, the United States and the United Kingdom together exported less than Germany. As will be seen later, however, 1963 was a particularly poor year for U.S. machine tool exports and a particularly good one for German exports. The German lead was not usually as large as that shown here.

Total trade in machine tools can be broken down by type of machine, a separation which is desirable because the group contains a wide variety of products of different uses and degrees of technical sophistication. The leading position of Germany runs through the whole list, at least in the detail we have available. The German lead over the United States

[21] SITC 715.1. *Value of OECD exports in 1963:* $1,016 million; 2.3 per cent of study total. *Coverage:* Metal-cutting machine tools; presses and other metal-forming machine tools.

varied from a very wide one in lathes and milling machines (exports about three times as great as those of the United States) to less than 50 per cent for metal-forming machines. The United States, in turn, was consistently ahead of the United Kingdom, except in lathes and milling machines.

Much of international specialization seems to take place along different lines, dividing each group of machines according to the complexity or precision of the machine or the degree to which it is automatically controlled.

It is this specialization that explains the degree of cross-exporting (that is, trade in a product in both directions between a pair of countries) even within machine tool categories. Switzerland is reported to specialize in complex high-performance machine tools and to import its standard tools from Germany, while the United Kingdom concentrates on standard machine tools, exported mainly to the Commonwealth and to less industrialized countries. Germany sells both standard and specialized tools, and the United States concentrates mainly on numerically controlled tools and other sophisticated products such as those used for automobile production. The United States lead in numerical control has been attributed to military research, particularly in aircraft, largely financed from U.S. Air Force funds. Even when these machines are produced abroad they frequently use control systems built by U.S. electrical and electronic equipment firms and their foreign subsidiaries.[22]

Another basis for trade among the developed countries is differences in delivery time. Reports during the last few years about the rise of imports into the United States have stressed the effect of lengthening U.S. delivery delays relative to both Japan and European countries, particularly when full order books in one country coincide with recession in another.[23]

A recent study of 1956–62 U.K. export orders for machine tools found that waiting time for delivery of U.K. and German machine tools

[22] "Whose Revolution in Machine Tools?" *Economist,* November 26, 1960; "Machine Tools," *EFTA Bulletin,* March 1962; "The Numbers Game," *Economist,* July 2, 1966; "Consumersville USSR," *ibid.,* February 4, 1967; *Outlook for Numerical Control of Machine Tools,* BLS Bull. 1437, 1965, pp. 9–10.

[23] "More Machine Tools from Overseas Flow into U.S. Markets," *Wall Street Journal,* May 25, 1965; "Japan Pushes Tool Sales Drive," *Journal of Commerce,* January 13, 1966; "Tool Imports Rising as Delivery Slows," *ibid.,* February 23, 1966; "Big Hike in Machine Tool Exports for '66 Forecast," *ibid.,* March 28, 1966; "Tool Imports from Japan Up," *New York Times,* April 3, 1966; "U.S. Tool Order Backlog Opens Door to Imports," *Journal of Commerce,* April 29, 1966; "Foreign Machine-Tool Makers Profit from Domestic Shortage," *New York Times,* June 5, 1966.

Table 12.24

OECD Exports of Metalworking Machine Tools (SITC 715.1),
by Origin, Destination, and Type of Tool, 1963
(dollars in millions)

| | Value of Exports | Per Cent of OECD Exports in 715.1 | Share in OECD Exports (per cent) | | | EEC | | |
			OECD	U.S.	U.K.	Total	Germany	Japan
Total, all destinations	$1,016.1	100.0	100.0	21.0	12.4	51.2	36.2	1.7
Destination								
U.S.	34.6	3.4	100.0		17.3	39.3	28.9	2.9
OECD Europe	560.2	55.1	100.0	17.5	8.2	59.6	44.0	3.9
U.K.	67.9	6.7	100.0	30.0		51.2	39.8	0.9
EEC total	329.6	32.4	100.0	18.6	9.1	56.6	41.1	0.4
Germany	53.2	5.2	100.0	26.7	9.0	26.1		0.2
Canada	40.1	3.9	100.0	71.3	13.5	10.5	7.5	1.2
Japan	64.0	6.3	100.0	40.3	2.8	41.9	36.1	
Latin America	71.5	7.0	100.0	34.7	5.9	49.0	29.0	1.5
Other	245.6	24.2	100.0	14.5	25.6	43.4	26.5	4.9

(continued)

Table 12.24 (concluded)

	Value of Exports	Per Cent of OECD Exports in 715.1	Share in OECD Exports (per cent)			EEC		Japan
			OECD	U.S.	U.K.	Total	Germany	
All types of machine[a]	1,015.8	100.0						
Metal cutting	716.5	70.5	100.0	18.5	12.2	54.3	38.2	1.7
Boring machines	70.2	6.9	100.0	16.2	15.7	49.8	31.6	3.7
Drilling machines	38.4	3.8	100.0	16.4	13.0	54.9	29.2	2.6
Gear-cutting machines	49.6	4.9	100.0	28.8	7.0	49.2	46.0	0.8
Grinding machines	155.6	15.3	100.0	21.4	11.0	49.9	35.0	1.0
Lathes	194.1	19.1	100.0	13.4	16.1	55.8	39.0	1.8
Milling machines	90.0	8.9	100.0	12.7	12.7	60.2	38.2	1.7
Planers, broaching & miscellaneous cutting	118.7	11.7	100.0	25.1	6.7	57.6	44.6	1.2
Metal forming	299.3	29.5	100.0	25.3	11.8	55.1	43.1	1.1
Hydraulic pneumatic presses	43.0	4.2	100.0	20.0	19.5	56.0	41.6	1.4
Mechanical presses	73.8	7.3	100.0	28.6	9.5	56.9	41.6	0.8
Forming, except presses	182.5	18.0	100.0	25.2	10.8	55.1	44.0	1.0

Source: Appendix A and sources cited there.
[a]For explanation of differences between totals by destination and type of machine, see General Note to Appendix A.

Table 12.25
OECD Exports of Metalworking Machine Tools, 1953, 1957, 1961—64
(dollars in millions)

| | Value of OECD Exports[a] | Share in OECD Exports (per cent) | | | | | | |
| | | OECD | U.S. | U.K. | EEC | | | |
					Total	Germany	Switzerland	Japan
1964	$1,093.0	100.0	26.6	11.8	45.9	31.7	8.6	2.2
1963	1,016.1	100.0	21.0	12.4	51.2	36.2	8.6	1.7
1962	1,060.3	100.0	28.7	10.0	47.4	33.0	8.1	1.1
1962	1,059.8[b]	100.0	28.7	10.0	47.4	33.0	8.2	1.0[b]
1961	942.1[b]	100.0	28.2	9.4	47.3	33.6	8.4	1.7[b]
1961	920.9[c]	100.0	28.9	9.7	48.4	34.4	8.6[c]	1.7[c]
1957	518.4[c]	100.0	28.7	15.2	39.9	30.2	11.2[c]	0.8[c]
1953	404.6[d]	100.0	39.3	16.1	40.2	26.1	NA	NA

Source: Appendix B and sources cited there.
[a]Excluding Ireland.
[b]Data for Japan from Business and Defense Services Administration, U.S. Department of Commerce.
[c]Data for Japan and Switzerland from BDSA.
[d]Excluding Japan and Switzerland.

had a significant effect on the amount of foreign ordering of U.K. machine tools. U.S. waiting times, which were always lower than those in either the United Kingdom or Germany, were not significantly related, perhaps because the United States and the United Kingdom were offering different types of tools, or possibly because the differences between the United States and the other countries remained large even when U.S. waiting times rose.[24]

The main changes in shares of export trade (Table 12.25) were the large losses by the United States and the United Kingdom between 1953 and 1961—from 39 to 29 per cent for the former and from 16 to 10 per cent for the latter—and the rise in the German share from 26 to 34 per cent. Since 1961 however, there have been no clear trends. In 1963 every major exporter gained at the expense of the United States, but almost all the loss was recovered the next year.

[24] M. D. Steuer, R. J. Ball, and J. R. Eaton, "The Effect of Waiting Times on Foreign Orders for Machine Tools," *Economica*, November 1966.

Table 12.26
International Prices, Metalworking Machine Tools, 1953, 1957; 1961–64
(1962 = 100)

	1953	1957	1961	1962	1963	1964
METALWORKING MACHINE TOOLS, TOTAL						
U.S.	81	90	98	100	101	105
U.K.	75	85	95	100	101	107
EEC	71	82	98	100	100	103
Germany	75	85	98	100	103	107
METAL-CUTTING MACHINE TOOLS						
U.S.	81	89	97	100	101	105
U.K.	74	84	94	100	101	106
EEC	72	81	98	100	97	102
Germany	77	86	98	100	102	106
METAL-FORMING MACHINE TOOLS						
U.S.	NA	NA	101	100	100	105
EEC	NA	NA	97	100	106	102
Germany	NA	NA	98	100	106	108

Source: Appendix C.

Price Trends

Prices of metalworking machine tools rose throughout the period in all the countries covered by our international price indexes (Table 12.26).[25]

[25] The very rapid rise in the official German export price series before 1961 (see notes to Table C.4) seemed suspect to us. Our index, derived from data other than the official export price series, rises much more slowly until 1962 and is much closer to the U.S. international price index, as can be seen in the Note to Table C.4, where separate indexes are calculated from reports by buyers and reports by sellers. Buyers reported smaller price increases than sellers in four out of five periods in the United States, Germany, and the EEC countries as a whole, and in three out of five periods in the United Kingdom. The earlier data were less reliable and compiled from fewer observations; the large discrepancies may, therefore, arise from errors or sampling variation. The U.K. indexes do not show large differences over the period as a whole, but the United States and German data diverge substantially, by 15 and 25 per cent, respectively, over the decade.

The apparent long-term upward bias of sellers' reports relative to those of buyers agrees with the findings of Stigler and Kindahl for standard commodities (George J. Stigler and James K. Kindahl, *The Behavior of Industrial Prices,* New York, NBER, 1970).

The evidence is not conclusive, but it suggests that sellers may tend to report list prices and buyers to report transaction prices. We make this judgment because it is

For some countries and groups it is possible to compare our international price indexes with the corresponding domestic, mainly wholesale, price indexes. The main differences are at the two ends of the period. The international price indexes rose more rapidly in 1964 in both the United States and Germany. In the first period, 1953–57, the international indexes rose less than wholesale prices in the United States and more than wholesale prices in Germany. The result of these two differences was that the international price movements for the two countries were much more alike in these years than the wholesale ones. This greater similarity among international price indexes is a fairly general phenomenon, as is pointed out in Chapter 8.

All the price indexes shown here, and those for the United States in particular, probably tend to overstate the extent of price increases because they do not take account of productivity changes involved in important technological developments, especially the introduction of numerically controlled machine tools. There are no comprehensive data on the productivity of these machines, but some reports suggest that, for companies whose work permits their use, the substitution of these tools for the older ones produces large savings in total cost. The rapid rate of increase in the number of numerically controlled tools also suggests that they are relatively cheaper than types previously available. Of all those shipped between 1954 and 1963 almost two-thirds were shipped in the last two years of the period.[26]

Price Competitiveness

In metalworking machine tools the price competitiveness of the United States relative to the United Kingdom and the EEC countries increased substantially from 1953 to 1962 or 1963 (Table 12.27). The U.S. gains were larger in metal-forming than in metal-cutting machine tools. In both groups the gains were greater relative to the EEC countries than to the United Kingdom in the earlier years, but at the end of the period the EEC countries improved their price competitiveness relative to both the United Kingdom and the United States. The reversal in the movement of U.S. price competitiveness relative to the EEC appeared earlier in metal-cutting tools than in the metal-forming group.

buyers' prices that move more in conformity with the nonquantitative reports on the state of the trade, a pattern that would fit the hypothesis that buyers are more willing than sellers to reveal unannounced discounts or premiums.

[26] *Outlook for Numerical Control of Machine Tools,* BLS Bull. 1437, 1965, pp. 15, 29–31.

Table 12.27
U.S. Price Competitiveness, Metalworking Machine Tools,
1953, 1957, 1961–64
(1962 = 100)

	1953	1957	1961	1962	1963	1964
METALWORKING MACHINE TOOLS, TOTAL						
Relative to						
U.K.	90	94	96	100	101	102
EEC	87	90	100	100	99	98
Germany	92	94	100	100	103	101
METAL-CUTTING MACHINE TOOLS						
Relative to						
U.K.	92	95	96	100	100	102
EEC	89	90	102	100	96	97
Germany	95	96	102	100	101	101
METAL-FORMING MACHINE TOOLS						
Relative to						
U.K.	87	91	93	100	105	104
EEC	83	91	96	100	106	97
Germany	87	89	97	100	106	103

Source: Appendix D.

The movement of U.S. price competitiveness in these products stands in strong contrast to that in most other groups in this study. The typical pattern has been a decline in U.S. price competitiveness until some date in the early 1960s and then an improvement in 1964. Metalworking machine tools show the reverse movement, at least relative to the EEC countries: a large improvement followed by a small decline in the last year or two.[27]

The movements of the indexes of U.S. price competitiveness fail to explain the shifts in export shares shown in Table 12.25, particularly the

[27] Our index computations in this subgroup took account of the possibility that the differences between buyers' and sellers' price reports might represent bias in one or both types of data and that it was therefore logical to compute indexes of price competitiveness separately from the two sources. If that had not been done, the index relative to Germany would have shown a large rise in the indexes of U.S. price competitiveness, reflecting the heavier weight given to the fast-rising sellers' prices in the German index compared to the American.

large gain by Germany from 1953 to 1957. In fact, the changes in U.S. and German exports are the opposite of those one would expect from the price movements in almost every year. The comparisons with the United Kingdom do not show any consistent relationship in either direction between our measures of price competitiveness and exports.

One caution should be kept in mind in any comparisons of trade with price movements. There may be a considerable time lag between orders of machine tools, to which the prices apply, and the corresponding deliveries, which are reflected in the trade statistics. These lags may vary over time and among countries. The waiting times estimated in the previously cited study of machine tool orders ranged from eight to twelve months for the United Kingdom, two to nine months for the United States, and nine to 11 months for West Germany.[28] However, some data on actual waiting times, gathered in connection with the place-to-place comparisons discussed below, showed average waiting time of only about four months for the United States, the European countries, and Japan in the early 1960s.

Price Levels

The estimated price levels shown in Table 12.28 must be considered rough approximations even though the number of observations is not unusually small. In 1962, the year on which the price level comparisons are based, there were approximately fifty individual comparisons between the United States and the United Kingdom and more between the United States and EEC countries, but fewer for Germany. However, that number of observations is not sufficient because there is, as we point out below, a great deal of heterogeneity among the various types of machine tools and even within the usual categories.

The United Kingdom and the EEC countries appeared to have offered lower prices on machine tools than the United States throughout the whole period covered by the study, and the U.K. and EEC price levels were generally similar.

In 1964, the price differential was about 20 per cent in favor of European countries on metal-cutting tools, and there was little or no differential on metal-forming tools. For metalworking tools as a whole the United Kingdom and the EEC countries offered prices 10 to 15 per cent below those of the United States from 1962 through 1964.

[28] Steuer, Ball, and Eaton, *op. cit.*

Table 12.28
Price Levels, Metalworking Machine Tools, 1953, 1957, 1961–64
(U.S. for each year = 100)

	1953	1957	1961	1962	1963	1964
METALWORKING MACHINE TOOLS, TOTAL						
U.S.	100	100	100	100	100	100
U.K.	77	80	81	85	86	87
EEC	75	78	86	86	85	84
Germany	80	82	87	87	89	88
METAL-CUTTING MACHINE TOOLS						
U.S.	100	100	100	100	100	100
U.K.	73	76	77	80	80	81
EEC	72	73	82	80	78	78
Germany	76	78	82	81	82	81
METAL-FORMING MACHINE TOOLS						
U.S.	100	100	100	100	100	100
U.K.	84	88	90	97	101	100
EEC	82	90	96	99	105	97
Germany	88	90	99	101	108	104

Source: Appendix E.

Since Germany is the world's leading machine tool exporter (Table 12.24), it is not surprising that its price level is below that of the United States. However, the U.K. export performance does not square with its apparently low price level. Furthermore, the low U.K. price level is not a product of one or two exceptional groups but is evident in comparisons for almost all the individual machine tool types.

One explanation for the low export share of the United Kingdom, despite its low price level, may be that its delivery delays were longer than those of the United States and Germany. Steuer, Ball, and Eaton estimated that U.K. delivery periods were twice as long as those of the United States and 20 per cent longer than the German ones.

Another possible explanation is that these price ratios are from a biased sample of machine tools. As was mentioned earlier, the United Kingdom tends to specialize in standard types of machine tools, the

United States in special tools, and Germany exports both types. Our ratios of foreign subsidiary prices to U.S. parent company prices for equivalent products are likely to be for standard tools because the most advanced types may be produced only in the United States. A large proportion of the other price comparisons are from less developed countries lacking the industries that would use advanced types of tools. Therefore, these data also would tend to relate to standard types of machine tools. The only way to cover the full range of products in such an index would be through regression analyses or other methods which permit comparison between two very different products that serve the same function. Being unable to collect the extensive data on specifications and performance needed for such a measure, we are obliged to use an index which is restricted to standard machine tools.

A completely independent estimate of price differentials can be derived from a survey of distributors of U.S. machine tools in thirty-six foreign countries by the National Machine Tool Builders' Association.[29] This involved asking distributors of U.S. machine tools in foreign countries to estimate the price differentials and the quality differentials between U.S. and foreign tools sold in their countries. We used the two estimated differentials to calculate price levels unadjusted and adjusted for quality differences. These quality-adjusted ratios on the whole confirmed the NBER price level indexes, coming to 87 for the United Kingdom, 85 for the EEC countries, and 84 for Germany, as compared

[29] *Survey of Foreign Machine Tool Markets,* National Machine Tool Builders' Association, Washington (no date, but probably 1963). These foreign distributors were asked to estimate both the price differential and the quality differential between U.S. and foreign machine tools in their countries. For each importing country we computed a quality-adjusted place-to-place comparison among the exporters' prices from these two estimates by dividing the price ratio by the quality ratio, and further adjusted it for differences in tariffs levied on tools from different sources of supply. We then averaged these across the list of purchasing countries, weighting each purchasing country's observations equally. The results were as follows, for the indexes unadjusted and adjusted for quality differences:

Country of Origin of Tools	Unadjusted	Adjusted
U.S.	100	100
U.K.	72	87
EEC, total	68	85
Germany	70	84
France	71	90
Italy	62	90
Switzerland	82	86
Japan	57	94

(Both sets of indexes were adjusted to take account of tariff differences, to place the sellers' prices on an f.a.s. basis.)

to 86 for all three in Table 12.28. The Swiss index calculated from this survey was close to the German one while the French and Italian indexes were higher and the Japanese still higher, although still below the U.S. level.[30]

Textile and Leather Machinery [31]

Trade

Germany was the leading exporter of textile and leather machinery, responsible for over one-fourth of OECD exports, followed by the United Kingdom, the United States, and Switzerland with shares of 17 per cent, 14 per cent, and 12 per cent, respectively (see Table 12.29). Europe was the major destination of Swiss and German exports, while for the United States, the American republics, Asia, and Canada were the main markets; and for the United Kingdom, Asia was a more important destination than Europe. Trade sources reported that a significant amount of U.S. exports consisted of used machinery which was exported to Latin America and Canada. The relative importance of used machinery in exports may well be higher for the United States than for the other major exporters because of the higher U.S. rate of obsolescence of equipment due to more rapid technological change and also, in some branches of the textile industry, notably knitted outerwear, to frequent style changes.

Textile machinery accounted for over three-quarters of total OECD exports in this group, and sewing machines constituted the bulk of the remainder; the other subgroup, machinery for leather, made up less than 5 per cent of exports.

Textile Machinery

Textile machinery tends to be highly specialized because of the variety of fibers and processes, and the lines of specialization seem to be drawn more sharply between firms than between countries. The possession of a particular type of machine provides a given firm with

---

[30] The price estimates uncorrected for quality differences suggested much wider gaps in levels, and the ranking of the countries was quite different. The disregard for quality differences in this type of comparison may account for some of the wide price discrepancies reported in the press.

[31] SITC 717. *Value of OECD exports in 1963:* $1,294 million; 2.9 per cent of study total. *Coverage:* Textile machinery; leather machinery; sewing machines.

Table 12.29

OECD Exports of Textile and Leather Machinery (SITC 717),
by Origin, Destination, and Commodity Subgroup, 1963
(dollars in millions)

| | Value of Exports | Per Cent of OECD Exports in 717 | Share in OECD Exports (per cent) | | | | | | |
			OECD	U.S.	U.K.	EEC Total	Germany	Switzerland	Japan
Total, all destinations	$1,296	100.0	100.0	14.7	17.5	42.9	27.5	12.2	9.2
Destination									
U.S.	98	7.6	100.0		20.4	31.6	23.5	9.2	30.6
OECD Europe	618	47.7	100.0	11.2	11.3	53.2	35.0	17.8	2.3
U.K.	63	4.9	100.0	23.8		44.4	28.6	23.8	1.6
EEC total	364	28.1	100.0	10.7	11.8	51.9	32.4	20.3	1.4
Germany	84	6.5	100.0	13.1	13.1	28.6		33.3	1.2
Italy	86	6.6	100.0	7.0	12.8	59.3	45.3	19.8	0.2
Switzerland	25	1.9	100.0	8.0	8.0	80.0	64.0		
Canada	49	3.8	100.0	73.5	12.2	8.2	6.1	4.1	4.1
Japan	51	3.9	100.0	27.4	13.7	52.9	29.4	5.9	
Latin America	120	9.3	100.0	35.0	10.0	40.0	25.8	6.6	5.8
Other	360	27.8	100.0	8.1	31.1	32.8	19.2	7.8	18.0
SITC commodity subgroup									
Textile machinery (717.1)	1,006	77.6	100.0	14.7	18.5	44.2	27.6	14.4	5.6
Leather machinery (717.2)	46	3.5	100.0	13.0	19.6	56.5	41.3	0.2	0.3
Sewing machines (717.3)	244	18.8	100.0	14.8	12.7	34.8	24.2	5.3	25.8

Source: Appendix A and sources cited there.

an advantage both in its domestic and in the world market. The industry has been characterized by very rapid technological advance in the last ten or fifteen years. The timing of these changes has varied somewhat from one segment of the industry to another. In most fields the United States has been the technological leader, but many think the gap has been closing. The U.S. textile industry tends somewhat to produce more complex machines than the European and Japanese industries. U.S. industry is geared largely to the home market, only about 20 per cent of its production being exported, while exports absorbed around 70 per cent of German and 90 per cent of Swiss output.[32] The underdeveloped countries, which are significant purchasers of textile machinery in world markets, tend to favor the simpler designs. It is interesting to note that in sectors in which the U.S. textile industry is geared to rapid style changes, the U.S. equipment industry appears to have adapted to its market by producing more versatile, less speedy, and sometimes less durable machines. It is the Europeans, for example, who have been turning out machines that will make standard sweaters at high speed. In general, however, U.S. equipment tends to be more durable than foreign although not always so well finished (e.g., castings may be polished on a foreign but not on a U.S. machine).

The distribution of textile and leather machinery exports did not change greatly over the period for which we have data. The EEC countries as a group showed consistent gains in their share; and the United Kingdom, fairly consistent losses (Table 12.30). Since total OECD exports of textile machinery were growing slowly, the decline in the U.K. share and the slight fall in the U.S. share left both countries' exports virtually static over the four-year period.

Textile machinery export prices in general have followed similar movements in the United States and the Common Market. As may be seen in Table 12.31 (top panel), prices rose by about 25 per cent between 1953 and 1964. We do not have sufficient data for the United Kingdom and Switzerland to warrant the publication of separate series for these countries, but the information we do have indicates a somewhat larger rise in the United Kingdom and a still greater one in Switzerland.

[32] These figures, which refer to 1962, were reported in a statement to the U.S. Tariff Commission by Mr. Robert S. Pennock on behalf of the American Textile Machinery Association, March 2, 1964. The statement quoted the German and Swiss figures from trade association sources in those countries.

Table 12.30
OECD Exports of Textile and Leatherworking Machinery, 1961–64
(dollars in millions)

	Value of OECD Exports	Share in OECD Exports (per cent)						
					EEC			
		OECD	U.S.	U.K.	Total	Ger- many	Switzer- land	Japan
		INCLUDING JAPAN						
1964	$1,504	100.0	15.2	15.3	43.6	27.4	11.4	10.8
1963	1,296	100.0	14.7	17.5	42.9	27.5	12.2	9.2
1962	1,278	100.0	15.6	17.6	41.5	26.1	11.3	10.4
		EXCLUDING JAPAN						
1962	1,145	100.0	17.4	19.7	46.4	29.1	12.6	
1961	1,124	100.0	18.7	20.6	45.5	28.0	11.6	

Source: Appendix B.

Table 12.31
International Prices, Price Competitiveness, and Price Levels, Textile
Machinery, 1953, 1957, 1961–64

	1953	1957	1961	1962	1963	1964
	INTERNATIONAL PRICE INDEXES (1962 = 100)					
U.S.	80	91	98	100	100	101
EEC	81	88	97	100	100	102
Germany	81	88	97	100	101	103
	INDEXES OF U.S. PRICE COMPETITIVENESS (1962 = 100)					
Relative to						
EEC	102	97	99	100	100	101
Germany	102	97	99	100	101	102
	INTERNATIONAL PRICE LEVELS (U.S. FOR EACH YEAR = 100)					
U.S.	100	100	100	100	100	100
EEC	88	84	85	86	86	87
Germany	88	84	86	86	87	88

Source: International price indexes from Appendix C; price competitiveness indexes,
Appendix D; price levels, Appendix E.

The export prices of Germany and of the EEC as a whole have been lower than U.S. prices for comparable goods by 12 to 16 per cent. The data in Table 12.31 (bottom panel) indicate that the European prices were at their lowest relative to the United States in 1957 and at their highest in 1964, but the differences between the years are small and probably fall within the margins of error that must be assigned to the estimates.

The data for the United Kingdom and Switzerland are adequate to provide estimates of their export price levels for one or two individual years. We estimate that U.K. prices were at about the same level in 1963 as EEC prices, whereas Swiss prices were several percentage points above EEC prices. These facts in conjunction with what has already been said about time trends suggest that the United Kingdom and to a smaller degree, Switzerland, started out the 1953–64 period with price levels that were lower than those of Germany and the Common Market. The scattered data we have for Japanese textile machinery prices in 1964 seem to indicate they were about the same as those of western Europe.

Although there are no sharply drawn lines of international specialization, a few tentative generalizations may be offered. The United Kingdom seems able to offer cotton spinning machinery at lower prices than other countries, while Italy tends to be cheaper on standard looms. Germany has an advantage in finishing equipment; and the United States, in handling machinery (e.g., cloth spreaders). As already noted, each country has firms which offer unique goods in different branches of the textile machinery industry, with U.S. exports probably most heavily dependent upon uniqueness.

While purchases of textile machines are often made on the basis of design, price is undoubtedly a key variable, especially for the less complex machines that probably loom large in world trade. It also seems likely that textile machinery buyers are very sensitive to the trade-off between design and price, so that price is a significant factor even for the more sophisticated type of product.

Machinery for Hides, Skins, and Leather

Germany was the most important exporter of leather machinery in 1963, accounting for over 40 per cent of the OECD total (see Table 12.29). The data indicate that the margins by which European prices are lower than those of the United States are larger than in the case of textile machinery. Also, unlike the textile machinery case, European vis-à-vis U.S. prices declined between 1963 and 1964.

This, too, appears to have been a field of rapid technological change, especially in the important shoe machinery component, and machine design has been an important factor in a country's ability to export.

Sewing Machines

Japan is the world's leading exporter of sewing machines, having nosed out Germany in the mid-1950s; the two countries accounted for about one-half of OECD exports in 1963 (see Table 12.29). Japan's exports are primarily of the household type while German exports are evenly divided between household and industrial machines. The United States, which absorbs about half of Japan's exports, is the third largest exporter, with virtually all of its exports consisting of industrial machines. Indeed, the bulk of U.S. output consists of industrial machines; by the end of our period only one U.S. firm was continuing to produce household machines in the United States.

The factors affecting the ability of each country to sell in world markets are similar to those that have been described in the case of textile machinery. The U.S. export position rests upon its capacity to provide machines embodying the latest technology and highest productivity. This type of machine can be marketed most readily in countries where labor is relatively scarce, and indeed it is to such destinations that most U.S. exports go. The different character of various foreign markets is clearly suggested by Table 12.32 in which the unit values of U.S. exports of industrial sewing machines are arrayed in ascending order. The first five destinations are clearly low-wage countries which are buying either used or less sophisticated machines. U.S. trade sources state that the market for industrial sewing machines in underdeveloped countries tends to consist largely of the types that are commercially obsolete in the advanced countries. The prices of such machines tend to be lower in Europe and Japan than in the United States, and prices have not been rising as much as they have for the more sophisticated machines. Some of the major U.S. companies produce their more standard models abroad in order to lower their costs.

As in the case of textile machinery, the time-to-time movements of export prices of sewing machines in the three countries are remarkably similar (Table 12.33). The place-to-place data were not sufficient to

Table 12.32
U.S. Exports and Unit Values of Industrial Sewing Machines, 1964

	Exports (millions)	Unit Value
Hong Kong	$0.8	$107
Mexico	1.1	236
Japan	1.3	246
Venezuela	0.8	283
Brazil	0.5	305
Belgium	2.4	322
Germany	1.7	333
United Kingdom	2.9	388
Australia	1.0	437
Italy	0.9	446
France	1.4	492
Canada	3.2	497
Republic of S. Africa	1.0	616
All U.S. exports	24.9	340

Source: *United States Exports of Domestic and Foreign Merchandise; Commodity by Country of Destination,* 1964 Annual, U.S. Dept. of Commerce, Report FT 410, June 1965, pp. 329–330. All countries which received at least $500,000 worth of exports are included in the table. These exports are recorded as complete head assemblies (Schedule B, item 75525).

Table 12.33
International Prices and Price Competitiveness, Sewing Machines,
1953, 1957, 1961–64
(1962 = 100)

	1953	1957	1961	1962	1963	1964
INTERNATIONAL PRICE INDEXES						
U.S.	88	100	99	100	99	103
Germany	88	99	97	100	98	102
Japan	NA	NA	99	100	101	105
INDEXES OF U.S. PRICE COMPETITIVENESS						
Relative to						
Germany	99	99	98	100	99	99
Japan	NA	NA	100	100	102	102

Source: International price indexes from Appendix C; price competitiveness indexes, Appendix D.

enable us to include them in the table. The U.K. export prices in 1964 were several percentage points higher, and the German prices several percentage points lower than those of the United States. More scattered data suggest that other EEC prices were in the same range as German prices, while Japanese prices were definitely lower.

Textile and Leather Machinery as a Whole

When the subgroups are combined (Table 12.34), the results more closely resemble those for textile machinery than for sewing machines, as is to be expected from the better than four-to-one ratio of the weights of the two subgroups. The slower rise of sewing machine prices and the more competitive price position of U.S. manufacturers of sewing machines are, however, revealed in the figures. All in all, European

Table 12.34

International Prices, Price Competitiveness, and Price Levels, Textile and Leather Machinery, 1953, 1957, 1961–64

	1953	1957	1961	1962	1963	1964
INTERNATIONAL PRICE INDEXES (1962 = 100)						
U.S.	81	92	98	100	100	101
U.K.	80	90	98	100	102	104
EEC	82	90	97	100	100	102
Germany	82	90	97	100	100	103
Japan	NA	NA	100	100	101	102
INDEXES OF U.S. PRICE COMPETITIVENESS (1962 = 100)						
Relative to						
U.K.	98	97	99	100	102	102
EEC	101	98	99	100	100	101
Germany	101	98	99	100	101	101
Japan	NA	NA	102	100	101	100
INTERNATIONAL PRICE LEVELS (U.S. FOR EACH YEAR = 100)						
U.S.	100	100	100	100	100	100
U.K.	83	83	84	85	86	87
EEC	89	86	87	88	88	88
Germany	89	86	87	88	88	89

Source: Same as Table 12.31.

prices have been a little more than 10 per cent below U.S. prices for SITC 717 as a whole with very little change in price relationships over the last four years, during which prices rose by 4 or 5 per cent both in the United States and in Europe. According to the index we produced (based on ten series from the export price index of the Bank of Japan and a smaller number of series obtained from the United States and other sources), the price increase in Japan has been somewhat smaller.

Mechanical Handling Equipment [33]

Trade

The United States was the leading supplier of mechanical handling equipment, followed by Germany, the United Kingdom (a poor third), and then France (Table 12.35). The poor showing of the United Kingdom is partly a product of differences in classification methods, as is pointed out in the notes to Appendix A, but its rank would not be altered by a reclassification of the U.K. figures to match those of the United States.

Within Europe itself, Germany was the largest supplier, although the United States was also important. Outside of Europe, however, the United States dominated the market by a large margin, and the United Kingdom, rather than Germany, was often the second most important source of equipment. Lifting and loading machinery account for 85 per cent of the group total; and forklift and other industrial trucks, for about 15 per cent. The lifting and loading machinery item is itself a composite of several very different types of machinery. The largest single item is self-propelled loading shovels for the construction industry, but such varied items as cranes and conveyors for construction, mining, and factory use, and oil field derricks are also important.

Some of the elements of U.S. competitiveness are concealed by the broadness of the published trade classes. U.S. companies led in producing self-propelled loaders for construction; and it was not unusual, even when worldwide bidding was solicited, to find only American companies, and sometimes their foreign subsidiaries, offering such machines. It has also been reported that U.S. companies have led in

[33] SITC 719.3. *Value of OECD exports in 1963:* $810 million; 1.8 per cent of study total. *Coverage:* Lifting and loading machinery; forklift and other industrial trucks.

Table 12.35

OECD Exports of Mechanical Handling Equipment (SITC 719.3),
by Origin, Destination, and Commodity Item, 1963

(dollars in millions)

| | Value of Exports | Per Cent of OECD Exports in 719.3 | Share in OECD Exports (per cent) | | | | EEC | | |
			OECD	U.S.	U.K.	Total	Germany	Japan
Total, all destinations and items	$810	100.0	100.0	34.7	12.0	40.5	24.7	1.6
Destination								
U.S.	18	2.2	100.0		5.6	33.3	22.2	5.6
OECD Europe	424	52.4	100.0	25.5	7.5	55.0	36.6	0.0
U.K.	29	3.6	100.0	34.5		48.3	24.1	
EEC total	238	29.4	100.0	26.5	6.7	56.3	36.1	
Germany	48	5.9	100.0	39.6	8.3	35.4		0.0
Canada	63	7.8	100.0	85.7	7.9	3.2	1.6	0.0
Japan	5	0.6	100.0	25.5	21.3	40.4	31.9	
Latin America	74	9.0	100.0	62.2	5.4	23.0	9.5	1.4
Other	226	27.9	100.0	32.3	23.9	30.1	14.2	4.9
SITC commodity item								
Lifting and loading mach. (719.31)	689	85.0	100.0	34.5	11.3	40.9	25.5	1.7
Fork lift and other industrial trucks (719.32)	121	15.0	100.0	36.4	15.7	37.2	19.8	0.8

Source: Appendix A.

Table 12.36

OECD Exports of Mechanical Handling Equipment, 1961–64

(dollars in millions)

| | Value of OECD Exports | Share in OECD Exports (per cent) | | | | | |
		OECD	U.S.	U.K.	EEC Total	Germany	Japan
			INCLUDING JAPAN				
1964	$917	100.0	35.2	11.5	38.7	22.4	2.6
1963	810	100.0	34.8	12.0	40.5	24.8	1.6
1962	694[a]	100.0	33.6	11.2	42.6	26.5	1.5
			EXCLUDING JAPAN				
1962	684[b]	100.0	34.1	11.4	43.3	26.9	
1961	613[b]	100.0	37.0	12.0	41.0	25.7	

[a]Excluding Iceland and Ireland.

[b]Excluding Iceland, Ireland, and Japan.

the design and production of large cranes for container handling at docks, partly because the United States led in the use of containers for shipping.[34]

Most of the major American firms manufacture abroad as well as in the United States, but the contribution of overseas subsidiaries to foreign exports is not clear. Some indication of the importance of exports for foreign subsidiaries is given in a recent report on one of the important manufacturers of loading equipment. One foreign subsidiary was expected to export 95 per cent of its production, and two others, in larger countries, exported 60 and 70 per cent of their production.[35] Overseas facilities are particularly important in the supply of elaborate conveying systems and elevators, because they must be fitted to the particular job and cannot be standardized. A fairly large part of the sales in this group are supplied mainly through bids for specific jobs, because of their nonstandardized nature.

Data on changes in the share of the various countries, available only back to 1961, show fairly small shifts (Table 12.36). Both the EEC

[34] "Gantry Cranes: Why Buy British?," *Economist*, October 22, 1966, p. 409.

[35] "The Multinational Diet That Helps 'Cat' Thrive," *Business Week*, August 13, 1966. The description applies to the whole range of the company's products, most of which fall into SITC subgroups 711.5, 712.5, and 718.4.

Table 12.37

International Prices, Mechanical Handling Equipment, 1953, 1957, 1961–64
(1962 = 100)

	1953	1957	1961	1962	1963	1964
U.S.	NA	91	100	100	101	103
U.K.	NA	101	99	100	100	103
EEC	76	86	95	100	100	102
Germany	75	85	95	100	100	102

Source: Appendix C.

and the German shares were lower in 1964 than in 1961, falling particularly in 1963 and 1964. The U.S. share, after falling in 1962, rose slightly between 1962 and 1964 but remained below the initial level. Gains were made by Japan and several smaller countries.

Price Trends

International price trends for materials handling equipment are described by the indexes of Table 12.37. For the group as a whole, they indicate a gradual rise in price after 1962 in both the United States and the European countries. Before that date there were widely contrasting price movements: stability from 1957 to 1962 in the United Kingdom (judged on the basis of rather poor data), large increases in both 1957–61 and 1961–62 in Germany and the EEC as a whole, and a slightly smaller price increase in the United States. Since lifting and loading machinery account for 85 per cent of the weight of the whole group, its indexes tell essentially the same story and need not be described separately.[36]

In the small subgroup SITC 719.32, forklift and other industrial trucks, the indexes for the United States and the EEC countries moved almost identically between 1957 and 1963, but diverged in 1964 as

[36] On the whole, indexes derived from U.S. wholesale price data for both SITC 719.31 and SITC 719.3 move closely with the international price indexes, never deviating by more than two percentage points. If the difference is at all significant, it is in the direction of showing a slightly slower price increase in domestic prices than in international prices over the period as a whole.

Foreign wholesale price series are available only for Japan, and they fell substantially between 1961 and 1964 for subgroup 719.31. This contrasts with a rising trend in the U.S. wholesale price series and in the U.S. and European international price series.

Table 12.38

Price Levels, Mechanical Handling Equipment, 1953, 1957, 1961—64

(U.S. for each year = 100)

	1953	1957	1961	1962	1963	1964
U.S.	100	100	100	100	100	100
U.K.	NA	86	84	83	89	91
EEC	72	80	81	86	85	85
Germany	NA	73	74	78	78	77

Source: Appendix E.

U.S. prices took a major jump (which is partly responsible for the larger increase, in SITC 719.3 as a whole, in the United States compared with other countries). The validity of the observed international price change is, however, suspect: The international price data can be divided between sellers' reports and buyers', and while the former showed a substantial rise in 1963–64, the latter showed a very small one. Furthermore, the index from buyers' prices resembles that for SITC 719.31 more closely than the sellers' price index does.[37] None of this is conclusive evidence, of course, but it suggests some doubt about the 1964 increase in SITC 719.32.[38]

Price Levels

Working from a set of data largely independent of those used in the international price indexes we can calculate relative international price levels for mechanical handling equipment. These, summarized in Table 12.38, show that German price levels for the group as a whole have

[37] The wholesale price index, which followed the international price index closely between 1957 and 1962, showed no increase after that date.

[38] Still another set of observations relating to U.S. exports is provided by export unit values for two items in this group which are used for the official Department of Commerce export unit value index. The unit value for loaders resembles our U.S. international price index in showing a large rise between 1958 and 1961 and a 1964 value a little above 1961 and 1962. However, the rise in the unit value between 1958 and 1961 is much larger than that in either the international price index or the wholesale price index between 1957 and 1961, and may well include the effects of increases in the size and power of these machines.

For SITC 719.32 the export unit value fell between 1961 and 1962, when wholesale and international prices rose, and increased sharply in 1963 when the other two moved very little. In 1964, when the international price index and the wholesale price both rose, the unit value declined.

We conclude that the unit value series is not a reliable guide to international price changes in either of these subgroups.

consistently been the lowest among the countries listed. The EEC countries taken together show price levels somewhat higher than the German ones but lower than those of the United Kingdom; and the United Kingdom, in turn, has been below the U.S. level in every year shown.

When the materials handling equipment group is divided up into its components, major differences appear. In the category of forklift and other industrial trucks, which are used for materials handling within factories and warehouses, prices in the United Kingdom and, on the average, in the EEC countries have been above U.S. prices. German prices have been at about the U.S. level, except in 1964, when they dipped slightly.

In the much larger category of lifting and loading machinery, only France apparently had higher prices than the United States, while all the other countries in the group reported substantially lower prices—ranging from 10 to 20 per cent lower in the United Kingdom and 25 to almost 40 per cent lower in Germany, with Japan at about or slightly above the German level. Even within this subgroup, however, there was a great deal of variation. For front-end loaders, used in construction, countries other than the United States and the United Kingdom rarely even submitted offers, and U.S. offers were generally equal or superior to those of other countries, including the United Kingdom.[39] The United States was sometimes at an advantage, also, in complex conveying systems, such as for ores. In the larger group of cranes, hoists, and parts of materials handling equipment, the price relatives ranged from half to twice the U.S. offers, but low ratios predominated, particularly on smaller items, bringing down the averages to considerably below U.S. levels. A fair number of bids on these products were at prices more than 40 per cent and sometimes more than 50 per cent below U.S. prices, without, according to the purchasers, any clear U.S. quality margin.

In loaders and forklift trucks, in which the competitive position of the United States is strongest, prices offered by U.S. companies can be compared with those offered for the same models by the companies' foreign subsidiaries. The number of cases is too small to be conclusive, but they suggest that the foreign subsidiaries of U.S. firms compete on more favorable terms with their U.S. parents than the general run of

[39] The inclusion of front-end loaders in SITC 719.3 has been questioned. They are more akin to the construction machinery of SITC 718.42, and are so placed in the U.K. export statistics (see note to Appendix A).

firms in those countries. The differences average about 5 or 6 per cent, for both the United Kingdom and the Common Market countries, on items for which the place-to-place indexes run between 100 and 110 per cent.

If we compare the price levels for SITC 719.32 with the export data of Table 12.35 we find that the United States and Germany, with the lowest prices, were the leading exporters, although there is nothing in the price data to explain the large U.S. lead over Germany. The United Kingdom, next in price level by a very narrow and probably not significant margin, followed in importance as an exporter, while France, Italy, and Belgium, all higher-priced sellers, exported comparatively minor amounts.

Comparisons for SITC 719.31 are made difficult by inconsistencies among the trade statistics of the various countries. The dominance of the United States is somewhat surprising, since price levels in the other countries are much lower. However, a large part of U.S. exports, about $110 million, were front-end loaders, in which the United States was clearly the major world exporter by a considerable margin. These machines, in which the United States has a favorable price position, are omitted from the U.K. export total and may not be included in the figures for other countries. Furthermore, the German price level for SITC 719.31 may be understated because there were no German price data for loaders, an item for which U.S. prices tended to be much more competitive than for the cranes and hoists which make up the rest of the subgroup. The U.K. index for 1963, for example, would have been almost five percentage points lower if loaders had been excluded.

Another large element of U.S. exports was petroleum and natural gas field production equipment and parts, for which we have no price data. The U.S. competitive position was probably stronger in this item than in the rest of SITC 719.31.

If the loaders are excluded from U.S. exports, Germany becomes the largest exporter by a substantial margin. However, the United States remains a considerably larger exporter than the United Kingdom despite the apparently lower U.K. prices.

Price Competitiveness

Combining the place-to-place and time-to-time price data, we derived the indexes of U.S. price competitiveness set out in Table 12.39. For

Table 12.39
U.S. Price Competitiveness, Mechanical Handling Equipment,
1953, 1957, 1961–64
(1962 = 100)

	1953	1957	1961	1962	1963	1964
Relative to						
U.K.	NA	104	101	100	107	110
EEC	84	94	95	100	99	99
Germany	NA	94	95	100	99	98

Source: Appendix D.

the group as a whole, and for the main component, SITC 719.31, they show U.S. price competitiveness to have improved relative to both the United Kingdom and the EEC, if the final year's indexes are compared with the earliest ones. The improvement in the U.S. position between 1953 and 1962 relative to the EEC and Germany was followed by a slight decline. The United States lost ground relative to the United Kingdom until 1962 and then gained. The indexes for SITC 719.32 suggest smaller changes in price competitiveness, with the United States gaining slightly over the United Kingdom and declining relative to Germany and the EEC as a group.[40]

Appendix: Price Estimates Based on Regression Analysis

Aircraft Engines

Place-to-place indexes of aircraft engine prices, shown earlier in this chapter, were based mainly on a regression analysis of prices of British and American aircraft engines as related to power and weight. As is the case for many machinery products, we are unable to make

---

[40] Two of the larger changes in price competitiveness shown by the indexes are questionable because data not included in the indexes, and too weak to be conclusive, do show different relative price movements. U.K. time-to-time data for SITC 719.31 fail to confirm the large jump in U.S. price competitiveness in 1963. They suggest approximate stability since 1961 and, therefore, that the U.S. position has deteriorated somewhat since 1957, rather than improved. Similarly, place-to-place data on SITC 719.32 for Germany indicate very little change in 1962–64, rather than a decline in U.S. price competitiveness, and therefore imply that the U.S. position in this subgroup remained virtually unchanged throughout the whole period. It must be stressed, however, that both of these are suggestions from very fragmentary data, and that the indexes shown in the table are supported by greater numbers of observations.

direct comparisons of U.S. and foreign prices because the engines produced in one country do not have exact counterparts in the other, even though the range of weight and power is similar. Therefore, the comparison between the two countries has been made by fitting an equation to price, take-off thrust, and weight of engines produced in both countries. Each country's price level was estimated by inserting the country as a variable in the equation or by taking the ratio of each actual engine price to that derived from the equation for an engine of identical characteristics, and averaging these ratios separately for the United Kingdom and the United States.

Unfortunately the number of engines available for this analysis was small. One set of equations includes 24 engines and another set, limited to the range of thrust in which most U.S. and U.K. engines fall, is based on only 20 engines. However, these engines do include a very high proportion of the value of commercial jet engines produced in the two countries in 1962, and the five major producers are all represented in the sample. The sample is weakest at the low end of the scale, and omits all military engines and the piston engines that were used for executive, private, and other small aircraft.

Some problems were encountered in determining which engines were available for sale in 1962. Four U.S. engines were eliminated from the initial list because Civil Aeronautics Board data on purchases by U.S. airlines showed that none of them was delivered after 1961. Since these data were intended to represent prices of engines for order in 1962 we felt that these four were probably obsolete by the standards of 1962 and that the prices were therefore nominal. However, it was not possible to make the same analysis of the U.K. engines, and some out-of-date engines may therefore be included in that list.

The whole list of twenty-four engines covered a range of take-off thrust from about 3,000 pounds to 22,000 pounds. The lowest pair were U.S. engines in the 3,000–4,000 pounds thrust range, and the next two were U.K. engines in the 7,000–8,000 pounds range. Only at about 10,000 pounds and over was there a fair representation from both countries all along the scale. For this reason, all equations were computed not only for the entire range of engines but also excluding the four low-power engines, the smaller group representing those engines sold by both countries.

Seventeen equation forms were used for both sets of data, yielding thirty-four equations. The coefficients for thrust were all statistically significant at the 1 per cent level. A majority of those for weight were significant at the 5 per cent level, and only one of those for country was even equal to the associated standard error. In eight cases we could compare equations including thrust, country, and weight as variables with corresponding equations excluding weight. The coefficient for the dummy variable representing the United Kingdom was negative (U.K. prices lower than U.S.) in seven of the eight equations without weight as a variable, but when weight was included, it shifted to positive in six of the seven cases and increased in the other two also. Thus the U.K. engines were cheaper, but heavier, than U.S. engines of corresponding thrust, and they were no longer cheaper when the negative value of extra weight was taken into account. Since the country coefficients were not significant and the weight coefficients were, we discarded all the eight equations excluding weight, along with six others which excluded both weight and country.

Thrust and weight, taken separately, are both highly correlated with engine price. However, the two are also highly correlated with each other, and it seems likely that the thrust-weight relationship accounts for the high positive gross correlation of weight and price.

We have, in several equations, substituted residuals from the relationship between thrust and weight for the weight variable. Thus, instead of

$$Y \text{ (Price)} = aX_1 \text{ (Thrust)} + bX_2 \text{ (Weight)} + cX_3 \text{ (Country)} + d$$

we calculated the regression of weight on thrust

$$X_2 = eX_1 + g$$

and substituted the residuals from this relationship for the weight variable above, to give

$$Y = hX_1 + k(X_2 - eX_1 - g) + mX_3 + n$$

The effect of this transformation of the weight variable is to change the thrust coefficient and the constant term, leaving the weight coefficient, the country coefficient, and the level of $\bar{R}^2$ unchanged. The effect on the coefficients can be seen in the following rearrangement of terms:

$$Y = (h - ke)X_1 + kX_2 + mX_3 + (n - kg)$$

The relationships with the original equation are thus that:

$$h - ke = a$$

$$k = b$$

$$m = c$$

$$n - kg = d$$

The country variable was also measured in two different ways. One was to insert it in the equations. The other was to omit it from the equations and compare the relative deviations from the regression line for U.S. engines with those for U.K. ones. The latter procedure was, in effect, a decision to put under thrust and weight any effects on price which, because of interrelations between country and the other variables, might have been attributed to the country variable if all three variables had been combined in one equation.

The twenty equations remaining after those omitting the weight variable were dropped, are summarized in Table 12.40. The $\bar{R}^2$ range from .85 to .95, and the standard errors are all between 5 and 7 per cent of the mean price. Despite changes in the coefficients as the form of the equations is altered, the ratio of U.K. to U.S. prices, which was the main object of the regression analysis, is extremely stable, varying only from 102 to 103 among the equations for all twenty-four engines; and from 99 to 101 among the equations which excluded the small engines. The stability of the index estimates is important for this study because it suggests that the country-to-country price relationships may be satisfactorily estimated by regressions that are not reliable for the estimation of other influences on price, and that it may therefore be possible to ignore some of the problems that frequently arise in the estimation of other variables. However, there are dangers in the omission of variables correlated with country of origin, since these could seriously affect the country coefficients.

For the place-to-place indexes of Table 12.7 a single choice among the country indexes of Table 12.40 was required. For several reasons we decided not to use the 24-engine equations, although they covered a wider range of engine types. The number of engines of low take-off thrust was small, and the U.S. and U.K. engines occupied different parts of the power range. We were therefore unable to separate the

Table 12.40

Regression Analysis of Aircraft Engine Prices

(figures in parentheses are ratios of coefficients to standard errors)

	Coefficients of Independent Variables									
	Take-off Thrust (100 pounds)		Weight (100 pounds)						S.E. (as % of Mean)[c]	Index: U.K./U.S.
Equation Number	Actual	Log	Actual	Weight-Thrust Residual[a]	Log Weight	U.K.[b]	Constant Term	$\bar{R}^2$		
A. ALL ENGINES										
1A	1,444 (6.83)		-1,693 (1.96)				46,836 (6.01)	.9449	6.8	103.4
2A	1,485 (6.54)		-1,861 (2.00)			3,281 (.55)	45,443 (5.46)	.9431	6.9	101.7
3A	1,043 (19.82)			-169 (1.96)			47,327 (6.07)	.9449	6.8	103.4
4A	1,044 (19.50)			-186 (2.00)		3,280 (.55)	45,983 (5.55)	.9431	6.9	101.7
5A		226,882 (8.67)			-100,159 (4.70)		-569,284 (9.70)	.9452	6.8	102.2
6A		235,234 (8.34)			-107,179 (4.65)	4,949 (.83)	-587,973 (9.29)	.9444	6.8	102.6
7A	.0063 (2.93)		.0006 (.07)				2.0051 (25.23)	.8617	5.9	102.6
8A	.0067 (2.88)		-.0008 (.09)			.0285 (.47)	1.9930 (23.45)	.8564	6.0	102.8
9A		.9598 (5.95)			-.2121 (1.62)		-1.0289 (2.84)	.9498	5.6	101.8
10A		.9941 (5.66)			-.2410 (1.68)	.0203 (.55)	-1.1056 (2.81)	.9480	5.6	102.0

(continued)

Table 12.40 (concluded)

	Coefficients of Independent Variables									
	Take-off Thrust (100 pounds)		Weight (100 pounds)						S.E. (as % of Mean)[c]	Index: U.K./U.S.
Equation Number	Actual	Log	Actual	Weight-Thrust Residual[a]	Log Weight	U.K.[b]	Constant Term	$\bar{R}^2$		
B. ENGINES OTHER THAN FOUR OF LOWEST THRUST										
1B	1,495 (8.08)		-2,461 (3.01)				68,295 (5.97)	.9176	5.2	99.5
2B	1,494 (7.43)		-2,456 (2.75)			-90 (.02)	68,308 (5.78)	.9125	5.4	100.0
3B	976 (14.30)			-246 (3.01)			58,159 (5.32)	.9176	5.2	99.5
4B	976 (13.87)			-246 (2.75)		-90 (.02)	58,192 (5.09)	.9125	5.4	100.0
5B		245,841 (7.94)			-106,551 (3.42)		-642,465 (9.64)	.9009	5.7	100.6
6B		248,805 (7.57)			-109,610 (3.31)	2,108 (.35)	-647,121 (9.28)	.8955	5.9	101.0
7B	0.0072 (7.20)		-.0124 (2.80)				2.3662 (38.32)	.8944	5.0	99.0
8B	0.0071 (6.54)		-.0118 (2.46)			-.0108 (.36)	2.3677 (37.27)	.8887	5.0	98.9
9B		1.1955 (7.76)			-0.5406 (3.49)		-1.0366 (3.12)	.8918	5.0	100.0
10B		1.1959 (7.27)			-0.5411 (3.27)	.0003 (.01)	-1.0359 (2.97)	.8850	5.1	100.0

351

Notes to Table 12.40

Note: In equations 1A–6A and 1B–6B, the dependent variable is priced in dollar amounts. In the other equations, the dependent variable is the natural logarithm of price in tens of thousands of dollars.

Data are order prices for 24 U.S. and U.K. jet aircraft engines available early in 1962. They were supplied by both buyers and sellers of engines and were checked also against Civil Aeronautics Board data on engines purchased by U.S. airlines. Four U.S. engines nominally available for sale at this date were excluded because they appeared to belong to an earlier generation of engines, and no deliveries were reported after 1960 or 1961. It is possible that further exclusions should have been made on the same grounds.

Of 34 equations originally fitted, 14 were dropped immediately for the reasons cited in the text. The equations dropped were identical to numbers 1, 2, 5, 6, 7, 8, and 10, both A and B, except that they omitted the weight variable.

The indexes were calculated in several different ways. Where there was a U.K. term in an equation for the log of price the coefficient (actually 100 [coefficient plus one]) was taken as the price index. Where there was a U.K. term in an equation for the actual price, the average specifications for 20 or 24 engines were inserted, U.K. and U.S. prices computed for that point, and the ratio taken as the index. Where there was no U.K. term in the equation the index was measured, in the actual price equations, from the averages of ratios of actual to expected price for U.K. and U.S. engines. In the log equations, the index was the antilog of the difference between average U.K. and average U.S. residuals. The last two procedures imply two different types of average: an arithmetic mean of ratios in the former case and a geometric mean in the latter.

[a]Residual from equation relating weight to thrust.

[b]Dummy variable taking value of 1 for U.K. engines and zero for U.S. engines.

[c]For the logarithmic equations these are ratios of the antilog of the logarithmic standard error to the mean of actual prices.

influence of country of origin from the influence of the other variables in this range.

Among the 20-engine regressions, the highest correlations were for 1B and 3B, which produced U.K.-U.S. indexes of 99.5. The logarithmic equations had slightly lower standard errors, but the average of their U.K.-U.S. price indexes was also 99.5. We used this value as the 1962 place-to-place index for the complete aircraft engine component of the index for aircraft engines and parts in the computations for Table 12.7.

Outboard Motors

Retail prices of outboard motors ranging from 3 to 100 horsepower were made available from a market survey by a large producer. The survey included motors of four U.S. producers and six producers in

Belgium, Canada, Italy, Sweden, and the United Kingdom (see Table 12.41).

For our study we would have preferred to have f.a.s. export prices for each country's producers. Instead, we had each producer's retail prices in a number of different places, usually including his home market and one or more foreign markets. We tried to come a little closer to the approximation of relative export prices by excluding the observations relating to a producer's price in his home market.

There were 127 usable observations for 1962 and 97 for 1963, of which, it may be seen from Table 12.41, 79 and 54, respectively, were U.S. models. The prices were those prevailing on the French, German, Italian, or British markets. Where a producer sold the same model in two or more different markets the prices usually differed, and

Table 12.41
Number of Observations and Average Horsepower of
Outboard Motors, 1962 and 1963

| Country of Producer | No. of Producers | No. of Observations in Market of | | | | | Average Horsepower |
		France	Germany	Italy	U.K.	Total	
1962							
U.S.	4	26		22	31	79	34
U.K.	1		8			8	23
Belgium	2	7		8		15	27
Italy	1				8	8	19
Sweden	2				7	7	16
Canada	1				10	10	26
Total	11	33		38	56	127	30
1963							
U.S.	4	21	8		25	54	35
U.K.	1	4	5			9	22
Belgium	1	7				7	26
Italy	1	5			7	12	16
Sweden	1	4			3	7	8
Canada	1				8	8	29
Total	9	41	13		43	97	28

the model was treated as a separate observation in each market. The number of different U.S. models was in each year about half the number of U.S. observations. Non-U.S. firms tended more to restrict their operations to one foreign market, so there were only about a dozen foreign models that had to be treated as more than one observation.

The 1962 data also contained information on motors equipped with electric starters, generators, and stern drive. The few that had the last two features were eliminated, but those with electric starters, accounting for about a fourth of both the U.S. and foreign observations, were retained. Two small, inexpensive motors made by a Japanese producer were excluded because they used kerosene as fuel rather than gasoline.

In deriving price comparisons from these data, we experimented with several approaches to regression analysis. Partly because we had information about the electric starter in one year but not in the other, it was more convenient to do separate regressions for the two years. In each case, there was one continuous independent variable, horsepower. The other variables—country of producer, market, and (in 1962 only) an electric starter—were used as dummies.[41]

Arithmetic and logarithmic regressions for the two years yielded $\bar{R}^2$'s of 0.95 or 0.96; the coefficients are presented in Table 12.42.[42] The producer coefficients tell us the amount by which the price or log price of each country differed from that of the United States. For example, the 1962 arithmetic regression indicates the U.K. retail prices in foreign markets were $28.34 less than U.S. retail prices in foreign markets. The difference, like all the other differences for producing countries, is not statistically significant. Indeed, all the Canadian coefficients are less than half their standard errors and the same is true for Italy, Belgium, and Sweden in at least one of the four regressions. We nevertheless converted the coefficients to price index numbers with the United States as the base in Table 12.43, since they represent our best, if somewhat uncertain, estimates of the price relationship. We took the arithmetic price differences as percentages based first on a 30-horse-

---

[41] The omitted variable for the producer dummies was for U.S. firms; thus each of the regression coefficients for the included variables could be regarded as giving the difference in price between the United States and the country to which the particular dummy variable referred. For the market variables, the United Kingdom was omitted.

[42] Correlations involving the log of price and arithmetic horsepower or arithmetic price and the log of horsepower yielded $\bar{R}^2$'s around 0.82.

Table 12.42
Regressions for Outboard Motors, 1962 and 1963

| | Pooled Regressions | | | |
| | Arithmetic | | Logarithmic[a] | |
	1962	1963	1962	1963
Horsepower	14.52	15.30	.5593	.5857
	(0.30)	(0.35)	(.0119)	(.0151)
Producers				
United Kingdom	-28.34	-25.92	-.0636	-.0547
	(29.94)	(32.14)	(.0468)	(.0557)
Italy	20.37	-45.34	-.0012	-.0905
	(29.07)	(26.87)	(.0457)	(.0470)
Belgium	-16.75	33.51	-.0129	.0523
	(21.18)	(34.41)	(.0343)	(.0602)
Sweden	7.08	-20.64	-.0290	.1107
	(30.77)	(33.95)	(.0487)	(.0615)
Canada	-7.40	-10.59	-.0159	-.0026
	(26.61)	(32.49)	(.0418)	(.0569)
Markets				
France	149.88	104.29	.2250	.1862
	(19.25)	(19.88)	(.0302)	(.0348)
Germany		90.71		.1785
		(29.46)		(.0513)
Italy	112.71		.1924	
	(19.74)		(.0309)	
Electric starter	101.29		.1320	
	(15.99)		(.0258)	
Constant	168.21	172.83	4.5630	4.5147
	(16.02)	(19.27)	(0.0296)	(0.0374)
$\bar{R}^2$	0.9639	0.9601	0.9633	0.9501
Standard error				
(per cent of mean)	10.4	12.5	1.9	2.2

[a]In terms of natural logarithms.

power motor, which is close to the overall average of the whole sample, and then on a 15-horsepower motor, which is closer to the average size of the Italian and Swedish exports. The logarithmic form yields a constant percentage difference for every size motor.

Table 12.43
Comparative Prices of Outboard Motors, Based on Pooled
Regressions, 1962 and 1963

| | Arithmetic | | | | Logarithmic | |
| | 1962 | | 1963 | | | |
	30 H.P.	15 H.P.	30 H.P.	15 H.P.	1962	1963
Prices of producing countries						
U.S.	100	100	100	100	100	100
U.K.	95	93	96	94	94	95
Italy	103	105	93	89	100	91
Belgium	97	96	105	108	99	105
Sweden	101	102	97	95	97	112
Canada	99	98	98	97	98	100
Prices in various markets						
U.K.	100	100	100	100	100	100
France	125	139	117	126	125	120
Germany			114	123		119
Italy	119	129			121	

Confining ourselves to the cases in which the arithmetic and logarithmic forms yield substantially similar price comparisons [43] and in which standard errors are not much larger than the coefficients, we hazard the following conclusions about European vs. U.S. producers' prices: (1) U.K. prices were about 5 per cent lower than U.S. prices in 1963, and perhaps a shade lower still in 1962. (2) Italian prices in 1963 were around 9 per cent below those of the United States. (3) Belgian prices were probably around 3 per cent lower than U.S. prices in 1962 and about 5 per cent higher in 1963. Reliable comparisons between the United States and Italy in 1962 and between the United States and Sweden or Canada in either year could not be made from the available data.

Retail prices on the Continent were higher than those in the United Kingdom. Foreign producers charged about 20 per cent more in the

[43] The arithmetic form produces $\bar{R}^2$'s which are marginally higher than those of the log form, but the differences are too small to warrant ignoring the results given by the latter.

French and Italian markets in 1962 and the French and German markets in 1963 than in the U.K. market in the same years.

We could not readily derive time-to-time indexes from the data because we did not know whether or not motors with electric starters were included in the 1963 observations. If we assume that they were not, the estimated U.S. price increase, for example, would be about 3 per cent between 1962 and 1963.[44] It seems more likely, however, that electric starters were included, and that their inclusion rather than a genuine rise in prices, accounts for the 3 per cent increase.

Regressions for the individual producing countries yielded similar coefficients. In the arithmetic form, for example, horsepower coefficients were almost invariably in the $15 to $17 range. The U.S. coefficients tended to be near the bottom of the range.

U.S. Tractors

Data obtained from six U.S. manufacturers included 61 diesel engine tractors for which export prices (to distributors), weight, and net or belt horsepower were available. The distribution of these observations by type of tractor and reference years is shown below:

	Crawler	*Wheel*	*Total*
1953	4	–	4
1957	5	1	6
1961	9	1	10
1962	10	4	14
1963	9	5	14
1964	9	4	13
Total	46	15	61

Our sample is heavily weighted in favor of crawler tractors, correctly reflecting their importance in U.S. exports but not in world trade. Ten of the wheel-type tractors were intended for farm use and five were construction-type (i.e., large earth movers, graders, or scrapers); some of the smaller crawler tractors were also used in agriculture.

The basic procedure was to correlate tractor prices with horsepower

[44] This result is produced consistently by log equations including those given in Table 12.42, others relating to the United States only, and still others in which data for all years and countries are pooled. The results given by arithmetic equations vary from 2 to 5 per cent.

or weight or both, in a regression in which data for all years were pooled. A dummy variable was used to distinguish the prices of wheel tractors from crawlers, and dummy variables were employed also to distinguish the 1962 level of prices from the level in each of the other years.

Horsepower obviously should be included as an explanatory variable; it is probably the key element in the product mix that makes up a tractor. There are, however, many other significant specifications which affect price and which have been changing over the years.[45] Lacking these variables, we used weight as a proxy for the many other features of a tractor which add to its utility. Weight, however, is itself highly correlated with horsepower, and when both are included, their sampling errors are much larger than when only one is used.

A regression in which the log of price rather than price in arithmetic terms is the dependent variable is preferable if, as seems likely, price changes for all sizes of tractors (from 2,900 to 70,000 pounds and from 30 to 425 horsepower) can be expected to conform more nearly to a uniform percentage change than to a uniform dollar price change. Partly on this basis, the regression that has been chosen as most appropriate for measuring price changes is one in which price and the two independent continuous variables are all expressed as logs. The regression contains dummy variables for wheel tractors and for years other than 1962. The coefficients of the regression, which yielded an $\bar{R}^2$ of .990, are shown in Table 12.44, and the price indexes derived from it in Table 12.45.

A number of other regressions were computed, and we comment briefly on them. From a purely statistical standpoint, a log regression in which horsepower was omitted was marginally better since its $\bar{R}^2$ was the same and its standard error was slightly smaller. However, horsepower rather than weight is the important economic variable, and this fact more than offsets the slight statistical ground for excluding it. In any case the two log equations yield price indexes that differ by no more than one percentage point at any date. Correlations in which the log of price was made dependent upon the arithmetic values of the

[45] Cf. Lyle P. Fettig, "Price Indexes for New Farm Tractors in the Postwar Period," unpublished Ph.D. dissertation, University of Chicago, 1963; and Fettig, "Adjusting Farm Tractor Prices for Quality Changes, 1950–1962," *Journal of Political Economy*, August 1963. See also Deere & Co., *Facts about John Deere Tractor Wholesale Prices in the U.S., 1935–61*, May 1961.

Table 12.44
Coefficients of Tractor Regressions, 1953, 1957, 1961–64

	All Tractors		Construction Type	
	Arithmetic	Log	Arithmetic	Log
Weight	.2407	.8918	.2293	.2611
	(.0550)	(.0915)	(.0351)	(.0540)
Horsepower	67.88	.0996	66.21	.6554
	(9.00)	(.1000)	(5.82)	(.0525)
Wheel	-1,624	.0748		
	(677)	(.0601)		
Constant	1,067	.1640	1,836	3.8578
	(598)	(.0478)	(497)	(0.6688)
1953	-4,422	-.4304	-4,763	-.3967
	(787)	(.0542)	(671)	(.0289)
1957	-2,378	-.1265	-2,750	-.1566
	(671)	(.0437)	(579)	(.0241)
1961	-24.98	-.0112	-234.1	-.0155
	(562.81)	(.0374)	(489.8)	(.0206)
1963	397.0	.0256	573.1	.0355
	(509.5)	(.0337)	(489.7)	(.0206)
1964	1,092	.0399	1,345	.0664
	(518)	(.0343)	(490)	(.0206)
$\bar{R}^2$	.988	.990	.990	.993
Standard error (per cent of mean)	7.2	1.8	5.2	0.9

Table 12.45
Tractor Price Indexes Derived from Regressions, 1953, 1957, 1961–64
(1962 = 100)

	All Tractors		Construction Type	
	Arithmetic	Log	Arithmetic	Log
1953	76	65	78	67
1957	87	88	88	86
1961	99	99	99	98
1962	100	100	100	100
1963	102	103	103	104
1964	106	104	106	107

continuous variables did not produce any $\bar{R}^2$ in excess of 0.859. However, the explanatory power of an equation in which all variables were taken in arithmetic terms was almost as good as that of the preferred log equation, and its coefficients and the price indexes derived from it are shown in Tables 12.44 and 12.45. On the other hand, the arithmetic equation, which indicated somewhat different price changes for some of the time links, did not provide a good fit for the ten lower-priced farm-type tractors (wheel tractors under 6,000 pounds and under 70 horsepower) in the sample.[46]

It is questionable whether we are justified in including the ten farm tractors in the same regression with the construction-type tractors. Even in terms of the simplified models of price explanation used here, the two types of tractors are strikingly different. Farm tractors are built to give more power for their weight than earth-movers; in our sample, for example, the ten farm tractors averaged about 1 horsepower per 100 pounds, while the others were closer to 0.5 horsepower per 100 pounds. Farm tractors tend to be cheap in terms of horsepower; and construction-type tractors, cheap in terms of weight.[47]

In addition, the two types of tractors are not only sold largely to different industries but they are produced, to a considerable degree, by different firms, both in the United States and in Europe. Thus, the prices of construction and farm tractors may behave differently. This, indeed, seems to have happened between 1963 and 1964 when farm tractors did not rise in price while the others did. In the regressions the price rise of the construction-type tractors dominates the results, and the price indexes do not adequately reflect the importance of the price movements of farm tractors in international trade.

We could try to meet this problem by introducing weights into the regression, but our sample of ten tractor prices is much too limited to rely upon for the measurement of price changes for the four time links.

[46] The residuals obtained by subtracting the estimated from the actual values for the small tractors were all negative, indicating consistent price overestimation. This was not the case in the log equation.

[47] Thus, when weight is excluded and horsepower used as the only continuous independent variable, wheel tractors will be cheaper in both the arithmetic and logarithmic forms, and when only weight is used they will be more expensive in both forms. When weight and horsepower are included together, a different balance in each equation is struck between these opposite tendencies. Hence, the arithmetic equation in Table 12.44 shows that wheel tractors (mainly farm-type) were $1,624 cheaper than crawlers (mainly construction-type) in 1962, holding weight and horsepower constant, while the log equation indicates that wheel tractors were 7 per cent more expensive.

This would be particularly inadvisable since we have a number of other price comparisons between the periods made by respondents who did not supply weight or horsepower data, and thus have the opportunity to make conventional indexes based on a larger sample of time-to-time price relatives.

In these circumstances, we prepared regressions in which only the construction-type tractors were included. The coefficients of these regressions and the indexes based upon them are shown in Tables 12.44 and 12.45.[48]

We used the log regression for construction-type tractors as a component of the U.S. international price index given in the main body of this report. It was weighted in with indexes for farm tractors and tractor parts produced by conventional methods.

[48] It will be noted that we omitted the dummy variable for wheel tractors from the regressions although 5 of the 51 prices represent construction-type wheel tractors. The coefficient for this variable was not statistically significant, and we have no basis for believing that wheel tractors should be more or less expensive than crawlers when weight and horsepower are the same. Fortunately, the price indexes resulting when the wheel variable is included are virtually identical with those given in Table 12.45.

13

ELECTRICAL MACHINERY, APPARATUS, AND APPLIANCES

THE UNITED STATES was the leading exporter of electrical machinery and apparatus, followed by Germany, the United Kingdom, and Japan (Table 13.1). The EEC countries accounted for two-thirds of the EEC market, while the United States dominated the Canadian, Japanese, and Latin American trade. The United Kingdom led all the other sellers by a wide margin in sales to other countries, and Japan was the major outside source for the U.S. market. All these statements are subject to an important reservation: More than $340 million in exports, mainly from the United States, were not identified by destination. These were over 20 per cent of U.S. exports and more than 5 per cent of OECD exports in this division.

The major shifts in export shares in this division took place between 1953 and 1961 (Table 13.2). The U.S. share was cut by fifteen percentage points (more than a third) and the smaller U.K. share by six percentage points (over a quarter). The main beneficiary was Japan, whose share was less than 1 per cent in 1953 and rose to more than 7 per cent in 1961. Germany's share gained by nine percentage points, an increase of 70 per cent over its initial share of exports. France and the other EEC countries also improved their position substantially.

After 1961 the U.S. share changed little but the U.K. position continued to deteriorate. Germany's share, which had risen so rapidly before 1961, declined in the next few years. The shares of Japan and of

Note: SITC 72. *Value of OECD exports in 1963:* $6,005 million; 13.5 per cent of study total. *Coverage:* Equipment for producing and transmitting electricity, telecommunications apparatus, domestic electrical equipment, and all other electrical machinery and appliances.

Table 13.1

OECD Exports of Electrical Machinery, Apparatus, and Appliances (SITC 72),
by Origin, Destination, and Commodity Group, 1963
(dollars in millions)

| | Value of Exports | Per Cent of OECD Exports in 72 | Share in OECD Exports (per cent) | | | EEC | | |
			OECD	U.S.	U.K.	Total	Germany	Japan
Total, all destinations and groups	$6,005	100.0	100.0	24.8	14.8	41.2	19.5	8.6
Destination								
U.S.	397	6.6	100.0		10.6	22.2	11.6	47.1
OECD Europe	2,660	44.3	100.0	13.8	10.2	61.8	30.5	2.1
U.K.	173	2.9	100.0	33.5		45.7	17.3	2.9
EEC total	1,535	25.6	100.0	13.9	8.9	65.2	27.8	1.6
Germany	344	5.7	100.0	15.1	9.6	53.8		3.5
Canada	338	5.6	100.0	78.1	13.0	4.4	2.4	3.0
Japan	67	1.1	100.0	70.1	7.5	16.4	9.0	
Latin America	490	8.2	100.0	40.8	7.8	30.2	12.2	10.6
Other	1,708	28.5	100.0	15.9	28.8	33.4	14.1	12.5
Unaccounted for by destination	344	5.7	100.0	100.0				

(continued)

363

Table 13.1 (concluded)

| SITC commodity group | Value of Exports | Per Cent of OECD Exports in 72 | Share in OECD Exports (per cent) | | | | EEC | | |
			OECD	U.S.	U.K.	Total	Germany	Japan
Electric power machinery and switchgear (722)	$1,403	23.4	100.0	23.2	15.4	43.2	22.5	4.1
Electricity distribution equipment (723)	343	5.7	100.0	10.5	28.6	39.1	17.5	11.4
Telecommunications equipment (724)	1,715	28.6	100.0	22.8	12.8	37.9	16.3	16.5
Domestic electrical equipment (725)	554	9.2	100.0	17.7	18.0	49.4	24.0	3.5
Miscellaneous electrical machinery and apparatus (726, 729)	1,989	33.1	100.0	32.3	13.0	40.8	19.3	6.1

Source: Appendix A and sources cited there.

Table 13.2
OECD Exports of Electrical Machinery, Apparatus, and Appliances,
1953, 1957, 1961–64
(dollars in millions)

| | Value of OECD Exports | Share in OECD Exports (per cent) | | | | | |
		OECD	U.S.	U.K.	EEC Total	EEC Germany	Japan
		INCLUDING SWITZERLAND AND SPAIN					
1964	$6,836	100.0	24.4	12.9	42.6	19.2	9.3
1963	6,005	100.0	24.9	14.8	41.2	19.5	8.6
1962	5,312	100.0	25.6	15.1	40.7	20.4	8.1
1961	4,748	100.0	24.9	16.0	41.8	21.5	7.1
		EXCLUDING SWITZERLAND AND SPAIN					
1961	4,599	100.0	25.7	16.5	43.2	22.2	7.4
1957	3,063	100.0	32.8	20.8	37.5	21.0	2.5
1953	2,112	100.0	40.4	22.8	29.5	13.1	0.7

Source: Appendix B.

EEC countries outside of Germany and France also increased between 1961 and 1964.

The rapid growth in Japan's exports before 1961 was associated with a great increase in Japanese price competitiveness, at least during 1957–61, and the continued gains after that matched a favorable relative price movement until 1963 (Table 13.3). During 1953–57, export shares of the United States and the United Kingdom and their price competitiveness declined. After that, U.S. price performance improved steadily but its export share continued to fall until 1961.

Price increases in this division were smaller than in most others covered by the study. Japanese prices in 1964 were far lower than in the first year shown, and U.S. prices ended somewhat below the initial level. Only the United Kingdom had a price increase of over 5 per cent.

The U.S. price position in SITC 72 was relatively favorable at the end of the period, as compared with that in other products. Even the Japanese price level was only 10 per cent lower. German prices were slightly below those of the United States, and British prices were higher.

Table 13.3

International Prices, Price Competitiveness, and Price Levels, Electrical
Machinery, Apparatus, and Appliances, 1953, 1957, 1961–64

	1953	1957	1961	1962	1963	1964
INTERNATIONAL PRICE INDEXES (1962 = 100)						
U.S.	102	108	104	100	97	97
U.K.	96	98	103	100	101	101
EEC	98	100	102	100	100	99
Germany	96	98	101	100	99	98
Japan	NA	124	106	100	97	99
INDEXES OF U.S. PRICE COMPETITIVENESS (1962 = 100)						
Relative to						
U.K.	94	91	99	100	105	103
EEC	96	92	97	100	103	101
Germany	94	91	97	100	102	101
Japan	NA	115	102	100	100	102
INTERNATIONAL PRICE LEVELS (U.S. FOR EACH YEAR = 100)						
U.S.	100	100	100	100	100	100
U.K.	97	94	102	103	108	106
EEC	90	86	91	94	97	95
Germany	90	87	93	96	98	97
Japan	NA	103	91	89	90	91

Source: International price indexes from Appendix C; price competitiveness indexes, Appendix D; price levels, Appendix E.

In the following sections four specific groups in the electrical machinery division—electric power machinery and switchgear, electricity distribution equipment, telecommunications equipment, and domestic electrical equipment—are discussed in detail. These groups account for over $4 billion in OECD exports, more than two-thirds of the total for the division. The most important group not covered is miscellaneous electrical machinery and apparatus (SITC 729), which is a collection of heterogeneous subgroups not appropriately treated as one group.

Electric Power Machinery and Switchgear [1]

Trade

In 1963, the United States was the leading exporter of electric power machinery and switchgear (SITC 722) by a narrow margin over Germany, and the United Kingdom ranked third, a considerable distance behind (Table 13.4). Germany was the dominant exporter to Europe, but the United States exported almost twice as much or more to the other areas shown in the table. Among the countries not listed separately, France was a major exporter, along with Sweden and Switzerland.

The two large subgroups which make up this group are electric power machinery (57 per cent), in which the United States was the largest exporter, and switchgear (43 per cent), in which Germany was more important. For the United States and the United Kingdom it is possible to break the electric power machinery down into its main components. Generators were the largest item, and the one in which the U.S. lead was greatest. Electric motors were the next most important in both the United States and the United Kingdom, followed by transformers, in which the United Kingdom had a slight lead as an exporter.

The U.S. share of OECD exports of electric power machinery and switchgear fell sharply between 1957 and 1961 but then remained stable and even increased slightly (Table 13.5). The share of the United Kingdom, on the other hand, fell steadily—from 30 per cent in 1953, which was close to the U.S. share, to less than 15 per cent at the end of the period. The EEC countries as a whole, and Germany in particular, made rapid gains between 1953 and 1961, but after that the German share fell back and France's remained approximately constant. Other large increases, amounting almost to a tripling of their share between 1953 and 1962, were made by other OECD countries, particularly Sweden.

Within the electric power machinery subgroup, the United States has been a leader in the movement toward larger units and has tended to be an exporter at the upper end of the size scale for generators and transformers. It has also led in the development of atomic power generating

[1] SITC 722. *Value of OECD exports in 1963:* $1.4 billion; 3.1 per cent of study total. *Coverage:* Generators, transformers, electric motors, circuit breakers and other apparatus for making, breaking, or protecting electrical circuits.

Table 13.4

OECD Exports of Electric Power Machinery and Switchgear (SITC 722),
by Origin, Destination, and Commodity Subgroup, 1963

(dollars in millions)

	Value of Exports	Per Cent of OECD Exports in 722	Share in OECD Exports (per cent)					
						EEC		
			OECD	U.S.	U.K.	Total	Germany	Japan
Total, all destinations and subgroups	$1,403	100.0	100.0	23.2	15.4	43.2	22.5	4.1
Destination								
U.S.	31	2.2	100.0		19.4	19.4	12.9	22.6
OECD Europe	584	40.8	100.0	13.2	6.0	63.0	37.8	0.3
U.K.	28	2.0	100.0	25.0		50.0	25.0	a
EEC total	329	23.4	100.0	12.8	4.2	67.2	35.6	0.3
Germany	62	4.4	100.0	11.3	3.2	51.6		a
Canada	65	4.6	100.0	81.5	12.3	3.1	1.5	a
Japan	19	1.4	100.0	73.7	5.3	10.5	10.5	
Latin America	171	12.2	100.0	39.8	8.8	32.2	9.9	8.2
Other	531	38.7	100.0	21.5	28.2	32.2	13.6	6.3
Unaccounted for by destination	2	0.1	100.0					100.0
SITC commodity subgroup								
Electric power machinery (SITC 722.1)	803	57.2	100.0	24.9	16.1	40.2	20.7	4.7
Switchgear (SITC 722.2)	600	42.8	100.0	21.0	14.5	47.0	25.0	3.2

Source: Appendix A and sources cited there

aLess than 0.05 per cent.

Table 13.5
OECD Exports of Electric Power Machinery and Switchgear,
1953, 1957, 1961–64
(dollars in millions)

| | Value of OECD Exports | Share in OECD Exports (per cent) | | | EEC | | |
		OECD	U.S.	U.K.	Total	Ger-many	Japan
ELECTRIC POWER MACHINERY AND SWITCHGEAR (SITC 722)							
Including Japan							
1964	$1,547	100.0	23.0	13.3	43.9	22.8	3.8
1963	1,403	100.0	23.2	15.4	43.2	22.5	4.0
1962	1,228	100.0	21.5	15.6	44.7	24.8	3.7
Excluding Japan							
1962	1,182	100.0	22.3	16.2	46.4	25.7	NA
1961	1,096	100.0	22.3	17.4	45.6	26.3	NA
Excluding Japan, Switzerland, and Spain							
1961	1,067	100.0	23.0	17.9	46.9	27.0	NA
1957	755	100.0	34.7	24.5	35.7	23.5	NA
1953	555	100.0	34.1	29.9	30.8	17.1	NA
ELECTRIC POWER MACHINERY (SITC 722.1)							
Including Japan							
1964	875	100.0	26.3	13.5	39.5	20.1	4.1
1963	803	100.0	24.9	16.1	40.3	20.6	4.7
1962	702	100.0	22.1	17.4	41.4	23.0	4.8
Excluding Japan							
1962	669	100.0	23.2	18.2	43.3	24.2	NA
1961	635	100.0	23.5	18.4	43.9	24.7	NA
SWITCHGEAR (SITC 722.2)							
Including Japan							
1964	672	100.0	18.8	13.1	49.7	26.3	3.3
1963	600	100.0	21.0	14.4	47.1	25.1	3.1
1962	526	100.0	20.7	13.2	49.2	27.2	2.5
Excluding Japan							
1962	513	100.0	21.2	13.5	50.5	27.9	NA
1961	461	100.0	20.8	16.1	48.1	28.4	NA

Source: Appendix B.

systems. Bids on these are not included in our indexes, however, partly
because most of the development came after the period covered by the
study. Although the United Kingdom was a leader in the earlier development of atomic power, it later fell behind, particularly when U.S. companies, anticipating the gains from the larger scale of production of components, cut prices in 1963 and after. In early 1967 it was reported
that the United Kingdom had received no export orders for nuclear
plants for several years; France received its first export order in 1966.
The American companies had, in the meantime, won a substantial number of contracts for atomic power generating stations in several different
foreign countries. The success of U.S. companies in bidding does not
necessarily imply that the full amount of the bid was purchased in the
United States, because some foreign purchasers insisted on producing as
many of the components as they could, even at the expense of raising
the cost considerably by foregoing the economies of scale available in
U.S. component production.[2]

Sweden's technological leadership in high-voltage direct current transmission systems was responsible for some of its successes in the American
and Canadian markets after 1964, and probably accounted for some of
the increases in its share of exports in this group before that date.[3]

Nonprice Influences on Trade

Trade in heavy electrical equipment of the type bought mainly by
utilities, such as large generators, transformers, and circuit breakers, is
both restricted and promoted by governmental actions, and has been
influenced also by various private arrangements among companies within

---

[2] "The Atomic Flood-Tide," *Economist*, September 24, 1966; "GE to Publish Prices of
Atomic Power Plants up to Million Kilowatts," *Wall Street Journal*, February 28, 1964;
"Atomic Power: Wide of Target," *Economist*, May 6, 1967; "Atomic Power: Bargain
and Barter," *ibid.*, October 22, 1966; "GE Plant in Japan," *Wall Street Journal*, Decem-
ber 12, 1963; "Westinghouse to Build Swiss Atomic Plant," *ibid.*, July 19, 1965; "U.S.
Firms Seek to Win Atomic Power Order," *Journal of Commerce*, April 11, 1966;
"Spain Will Get Its Second Nuclear Power Plant; GE Shares in $61-million Contract,"
Business Week, May 14, 1966; "GE Wins Contract: Swiss Opt for Nuclear Power,"
Journal of Commerce, September 9, 1966; "Atomic Push Abroad: Growing World
Market in Nuclear Power Field Attracts U.S. Firms," *Wall Street Journal*, September
13, 1966; "Atomic Energy: Bidding," *Economist*, September 10, 1966.

[3] "Swedish Electrical Producer Spreads Its Production and World Facilities," *Journal
of Commerce*, February 19, 1964; "Swedish Firm Has High Hopes for System of Long-
Distance Transmission of Power," *Wall Street Journal*, June 11, 1964; "Swedish Producer Receives Electric Transmission Order," *New York Times*, January 31, 1965; "GE
Wins Order in Power Project," *ibid.*, May 1, 1965; "GE, Swedish Firm Get $52 Mil-
lion in Pacts for Two Terminals on Pacific Power Intertie," *Wall Street Journal*, May 3,
1965; "Swedish Electrical Firm Seeks U.S. Sales," *Journal of Commerce*, May 24, 1965;
"Power Lines Get Higher Voltage," *New York Times*, July 4, 1965.

and among different countries. In many countries the production and distribution of electricity are governmental functions, and the electricity authorities consider themselves obliged to purchase their equipment from domestic producers without inviting offers from foreign firms.[4] The relation of government enterprises to foreign suppliers was the opposite in the United States. Privately owned utilities, far more important than government-owned ones, were reluctant to purchase abroad, and the ratio of imports to domestic output was very low.[5] However, government-owned authorities, both federal and local, took the lead in encouraging foreign producers to enter bids and at times purchased substantial fractions—as much as a quarter or a third—of some types of equipment from overseas despite "buy-American" differentials of 6 per cent or more (up to 50 per cent for the Defense Department).[6]

Governmental actions affecting trade in electric power and related machinery are not confined to imports but include also the encouragement of exports through tied loans. Some international aid is not tied, particularly loans by the IBRD and IDA, which lent almost $3 billion for electric power projects during 1953–64.[7] Total exports of electric power machinery and switchgear by OECD countries during these years came to over $10 billion.

Most U.S. government loans under the Agency for International Development (AID) have been tied in recent years and Export-Import Bank loans have always been tied to procurement in the United States.

[4] Imports of electric power and related equipment were about 2 per cent of home consumption in the United Kingdom in 1951 (*Report on the Supply and Exports of Electrical and Allied Machinery and Plant,* Monopolies and Restrictive Practices Commission, London, 1957, p. 337). The Central Electricity Authority considered any attempt ". . . to stimulate competition and obtain a check on price levels . . . by importing . . . impracticable for political reasons" (*ibid.,* pp. 222–223). In 1961, however, the Central Electricity Generating Board, which had previously purchased only those foreign products not available at home, did buy transformers from Canada ("Electricity: Buying Abroad," *Economist,* November 18, 1961).

[5] U.S. imports of motors, generators, and transformers in the early 1960s were about 1 per cent of the new supply, that is, output plus imports (*U.S. Commodity Exports and Imports as Related to Output, 1964 and 1963,* U.S. Bureau of the Census, Series ES 2, No. 7, 1966). After 1964 the attitudes of private utilities showed signs of change. The most notable of these was a purchase of turbine generators, in 1967, but that was only one of a number of recent private orders ("American Electric Buys 2 Turbines from Swiss Firm," *Wall Street Journal,* Dec. 12, 1967; "Switzerland's New Peak," *Economist,* Dec. 16, 1967; "Edison Buys Huge Turbine Generator," *Journal of Commerce,* Aug. 31, 1967; "AEI Awarded Contract for Generators," *ibid.,* Jan. 18, 1968; "Utilities Looking Abroad for Quality," *New York Times,* March 2, 1969).

[6] "Electrifying Surrender," *Economist,* December 10, 1960; "English Electric Pushes Export Drive," *Journal of Commerce,* August 4, 1965.

[7] *Annual Report,* International Bank for Reconstruction and Development and International Development Association, 1952–53 and 1964–65.

These two agencies lent over $1.25 billion on projects related to electric power during the decade of this study, of which only about $200 million was in AID loans before the period when they were tied to purchases in the United States.[8] Other countries have frequently insisted on tying their aid loans and grants, and these measures have influenced the direction of trade in this commodity group.

In addition to governmental restriction and encouragement of exporting there have been, at times at least, private agreements which allocated markets, often as part of licensing arrangements. The British report, cited earlier, mentions two agreements on generators, one ". . . a technical aid agreement with an associated foreign company. . . . Each party also agrees not to supply in the other's specified exclusive territory without the other's consent"; and the second ". . . an agreement between a United Kingdom manufacturer and a foreign manufacturer under which the British company receives the right to the use of certain designs, test and manufacturing data . . . and undertakes . . . not to export machinery of the types concerned without the foreign manufacturer's consent. . . ."[9]

The antitrust cases against the U.S. electrical equipment manufacturers did not involve prices charged to foreign buyers; and we do not know, therefore, whether the collusion among the U.S. companies extended to foreign sales (see the appendix to this chapter). The steep drop in export prices after 1957, parallel to that in domestic sales, suggests that similar agreements might have been keeping export prices artificially high. The high prices and the decline are particularly notable because our indexes exclude prices under tied aid, which we might have expected to be most strongly affected by collusion among domestic companies.

Price Competitiveness

The price competitiveness of the United States in electric power machinery and switchgear rose through most of the period from 1957

---

[8] Over $830 million in Eximbank credits were extended for electric power projects (not all for equipment in this group) during fiscal 1957–64 (*Report to the Congress,* Export-Import Bank of Washington, various years), and over $530 million in AID procurement expenditures for electrical apparatus in fiscal 1956–65, of which about $360 million were disbursed during fiscal 1962–65 (*Operations Report,* ICA and AID, various issues). The proportion procured in the United States doubled after 1962, from 36 per cent in fiscal 1956–61 to 76 per cent in 1962–65.

[9] *Report on the Supply and Exports of Electrical and Allied Machinery and Plant,* p. 104.

Table 13.6
U.S. Price Competitiveness, Electric Power Machinery and Switchgear,
1957, 1961–64
(1962 = 100)

	1957	1961	1962	1963	1964
ELECTRIC POWER MACHINERY AND SWITCHGEAR (SITC 722)					
Relative to					
U.K.	84	102	100	110	107
EEC	86	96	100	105	105
Germany	82	94	100	104	106
Japan	NA	97	100	102	113
ELECTRIC POWER MACHINERY (SITC 722.1)					
Relative to					
U.K.	75	91	100	109	101
EEC	81	92	100	108	109
Germany	76	90	100	105	111
Japan	NA	100	100	106	128
Sweden	NA	82	100	102	87
Switzerland	72	91	100	112	104
SWITCHGEAR (SITC 722.2)					
Relative to					
EEC	NA	101	100	101	100
Germany	NA	101	100	101	100

Source: Appendix D.

through 1964 (Table 13.6). Foreign prices, in other words, increased relative to U.S. prices, and the highest levels of U.S. price competitiveness were reached in 1963 or 1964.

The improvement in U.S. price competitiveness through 1963 is even stronger in the major subgroup, electric power machinery. The data here are more reliable, and some additional countries could be included in the comparison. The number of reversals in direction in 1964 is also greater, and the declines in U.S. price competitiveness were sharper than in the group as a whole. Sweden showed the outstanding gain that year, almost back to the 1961 level relative to the United States. With this one exception, however, the peak in the U.S. position relative to each country was in 1963 or 1964, as it was for the whole group.

Only fragmentary data, insufficient for the calculation of indexes, are available before 1957. The best series, that for the U.K., shows a very large decline in U.S. price competitiveness between 1953 and 1957.

The indexes of price competitiveness for electric power machinery and switchgear, unlike most of the others in this study, have been calculated mainly from place-to-place price comparisons for contract bids on large installations. Price competitiveness measured from place-to-place data tends to be more volatile than that from the time series data used in most other commodity groups; consequently, the year-to-year fluctuations may not be very significant. The trends, however, seem unmistakable despite the wide fluctuations.

The gains in U.S. price competitiveness after 1957 are partly due to the high U.S. price level in that year, as we point out below, in the discussion of international price indexes. The sharp declines in U.S. domestic prices are frequently attributed to governmental attacks on collusive bidding practices within the United States, culminating in the Philadelphia indictments against twenty-nine electrical equipment manufacturers in July 1960 and their pleas of guilty or no contest in December of that year.[10] Reductions in prices offered to foreign countries apparently reflect the collapse of those domestic price arrangements. The large gains in U.S. price competitiveness after 1957 were exceptional among the commodity groups covered in the study.

It is difficult to compare movements in price competitiveness with changes in export shares for this group because the lag between order and delivery is so long for at least the major equipment. The U.S. export share did not decline between 1953 and 1957, when, we believe, U.S. price competitiveness greatly deteriorated. However, the U.S. share fell sharply from 1957 to 1961, perhaps in consequence of the earlier high prices exemplified by those of 1957, the effects of which may well have been felt in most of the 1961 deliveries. After 1962 U.S. and Swedish shares rose a little and U.K. and EEC shares declined, movements which appear consistent with changes in prices.

The price movements, as we have mentioned, were both sharper and more reliably measured for electric power machinery alone, but the export data are unfortunately available only back to 1961. In this period, how-

_____
[10] See discussion in chapter appendix, below.

ever, the gains in U.S. and Swedish exports were much more marked than for the group as a whole, and U.K. and German shares clearly declined, as one would expect from the changes in price competitiveness. EEC countries other than Germany, with a more favorable price record, also increased their export shares, and the Japanese decline in price competitiveness was matched by a decline in exports relative to other countries. Thus, in the electric power machinery subgroup at least, the degree of consistency between price movements and export shares was substantial.

Since changes in international price competitiveness are often inferred from comparisons of wholesale price series, in the absence of international price data, we compared the indexes so derived, as given in Appendix F, with our indexes. Some of the differences between the two measures are quite large, particularly in electric power machinery (SITC 722.1). Both indexes for Germany in that subgroup show an improvement in U.S. price competitiveness from 1961 to 1962, but the index from wholesale prices shows little gain after that, while the NBER indexes show an improvement of more than 10 per cent. Relative to Japan, the wholesale price data suggest only a small gain in U.S. price competitiveness in 1964; the NBER indexes, a very large one. On the whole, if the NBER data are correct, the wholesale price series seriously understate the gains in U.S. price competitiveness in this group in the later years.

Price Levels

Most countries' prices of electric power machinery and switchgear were close to the U.S. price level in 1964, after a long period of improvement in U.S. price competitiveness (Table 13.7). The U.S. price level was lowest in switchgear, but in the more important electric power machinery subgroup, its level was higher than that of all but the United Kingdom.

From the point of view of U.S. competitiveness, the earliest price relationships, for 1957, were the most unfavorable. For the total group, European prices were more than 20 per cent lower than U.S. prices, and for electric power machinery the foreign price levels ranged between 25 and 40 per cent lower.

We have not shown separate price level indexes by type of machinery within electric power machinery, but the data indicate that for the United

Table 13.7

Price Levels, Electric Power Machinery and Switchgear, 1957, 1961–64
(U.S. for each year = 100)

	1957	1961	1962	1963	1964
ELECTRIC POWER MACHINERY AND SWITCHGEAR (SITC 722)					
U.S.	100	100	100	100	100
U.K.	79	96	94	103	101
EEC	77	86	90	94	94
Germany	79	90	95	99	101
Japan	NA	85	88	90	99
ELECTRIC POWER MACHINERY (SITC 722.1)					
U.S.	100	100	100	100	100
U.K.	74	90	99	108	100
EEC	64	73	79	85	86
Germany	60	71	79	83	87
Japan	NA	73	73	77	93
Sweden	NA	67	82	83	71
Switzerland	59	76	83	93	87
SWITCHGEAR (SITC 722.2)					
U.S.	NA	100	100	100	100
U.K.	NA	NA	NA	NA	102
EEC	NA	106	105	106	105
Germany	NA	118	117	119	117
Japan	NA	NA	NA	NA	101

Source: Appendix E and the appendix to this chapter.

Kingdom, prices of electric motors were lower relative to the U.S. level than prices of generators and transformers. Among the latter two groups U.K. offers were quite commonly above those from U.S. companies in 1962 and 1963, on jobs both inside and outside the United States.

The German relationship was in the opposite direction. Generators and transformers were priced considerably lower, relative to the United States, than electric motors. For other EEC countries, and for Sweden and Switzerland, the data are insufficient to permit this comparison.

Among the transformers and generators the U.S. price level was particularly high relative to Germany, Sweden, and Switzerland on instrument transformers. Foreign offers that were a third below or even half of U.S. bids were not uncommon. Between generators and power transformers the relationship was not so regular, but the U.S. position in the last year was at least slightly more favorable for generators. Most of the foreign countries were offering bids on generators in 1964 that were above the corresponding U.S. bids.

These price level indexes are based mainly on comparisons of bids. For some of the bids, data were available on quality differences among the individual offers, usually in the form of adjustments, calculated by the purchaser, to take account of differences in efficiency. The basis for the purchase decision was the offer price adjusted for quality differences. In cases where the number of adjusted bid prices was adequate, only these were used to calculate the price level indexes. The quality-adjusted data were used for most generator and transformer price level indexes other than those for the United Kingdom.

It has been said that U.S. electrical equipment is superior to foreign makes and that published comparisons for equipment of specific sizes or capacity are often biased against the United States on this account. To test whether such biases might have affected place-to-place comparisons from non-quality-adjusted bids we compared place-to-place indexes from adjusted and unadjusted data. The results did not suggest very large or consistent relationships between the two sets of indexes, but on the whole the adjusted indexes were more favorable to the United States than the unadjusted ones through 1962 and less favorable after that. A defect of these comparisons is that the unadjusted data included many bids not covered by the adjusted data and the price relationships may thus have been affected by the characteristics of the items not in both samples. For part of the collection comparisons were made between adjusted and unadjusted prices on identical bids from 1961 through 1964. The price level indexes for adjusted data in 11 of 12 cases fell within 10 per cent of those from unadjusted data, the one exception being a price level estimate for Japan which was more than 20 per cent higher relative to the United States in the adjusted data. However, eight of the twelve adjusted indexes were less favorable to the United States than the corresponding unadjusted ones. From these tests we infer that quality differences are not uniformly in favor of the United States. This inference is supported by some recent discussions provoked by American utilities' purchases of foreign equipment.[11]

A somewhat surprising result of the regression analysis in the appendix to this chapter, on which our price level estimates are based, is the significant positive coefficient for foreign projects. It might have been expected, since foreign power transformer prices were lower than U.S. prices, that U.S. companies would tend to offer lower prices to purchasers abroad than to U.S. purchasers. The data appear to show the opposite. U.S. companies' offers to foreign purchasers, most of whom were in less developed countries, were higher than their bids on the domestic projects in our sample; the differences were large (about 50 per cent) and were statistically significant, whether or not large transformers were included in the comparison. The finding is particularly unexpected because U.S. firms have the benefit of the buy-American differential on domestic projects and were competing on equal terms with others for the foreign projects.

One possible explanation for this difference in price levels is that our sample of domestic offers is biased because it is confined to that small proportion of domestic bids on which there is foreign competition. These are all bids to government agencies, since privately owned U.S. utilities had not, during the period covered by our data, sought foreign equipment bids. The American suppliers may have felt that foreign bidders would be offering particularly low prices to the U.S. government or particularly low prices on these projects in order to break into the U.S. market or to gain the prestige involved in beating the U.S. companies in their own market.

Another possibility is that foreign firms did not offer particularly low bids on U.S. government projects but American firms did, either because costs of supplying machinery to this country were lower than for supplying it to other countries or because American firms felt that it was a blow to their prestige when foreign companies won U.S. government contracts.

One way of investigating this question is to examine the average foreign-U.S. price ratios for particular suppliers and years on projects in the United States and abroad. If foreign companies charged the same prices in both markets, while U.S. companies charged 50 per

11 "Utilities Looking Abroad for Quality," *New York Times*, March 2, 1969.

cent more abroad, the foreign-U.S. price ratios on U.S. government projects would be 50 per cent higher than on foreign contracts. If foreign companies maintained the same price differentials as U.S. companies, foreign and U.S. projects would show the same ratios.

Our data are too thin to give an authoritative answer to this question. What evidence there is suggests it is unusual for foreign-U.S. price ratios to be as much as 50 per cent higher on foreign than on U.S. projects and, therefore, that both foreign and U.S. companies charged more outside the United States. U.K. companies seemed to be selling abroad at levels more than 50 per cent higher than those charged to the United States, while suppliers in other countries offered prices abroad that were higher than their prices to the United States but not by the 50 per cent margin.

Price Trends

In most of the other commodity groups included in this study, international price indexes from time-to-time price comparisons are the most reliable source of information on relative price changes. In this group, because most of the products, with electric motors the chief exception, are made to order for specific contracts, it is almost impossible to collect transactions prices for an identical product at two different times.

The international price indexes shown in Table 13.8 are, for this reason, less reliable relative to the other types of indexes than those for most other commodity groups in the study. The U.S. indexes are based on the regression analysis described in the appendix to this chapter for electric power machinery other than motors, and on the usual type of time-to-time price data for electric motors and switchgear. The German indexes for switchgear are calculated from price competitiveness indexes based on time series data, but the German indexes for electric power machinery and all those for the other countries listed are estimated from indexes of price competitiveness based on place-to-place data. This procedure entails the drawback of multiplying the errors of the two types of indexes, a drawback that is the more serious because both are derived from the rather volatile prices offered in bidding on large projects.

For electric power machinery other than motors our U.S. index is based on a regression, for power transformers, of price on capacity

Table 13.8
International Prices, Electric Power Machinery and Switchgear,
1953, 1957, 1961–64
(1962 = 100)

	1953	1957	1961	1962	1963	1964
ELECTRIC POWER MACHINERY AND SWITCHGEAR (SITC 722)						
U.S.	NA	124	110	100	94	94
EEC	NA	107	105	100	99	99
Germany	NA	102	104	100	97	100
Japan	NA	NA	106	100	96	106
ELECTRIC POWER MACHINERY (SITC 722.1)						
U.S.	132	154	120	100	91	91
U.K.	NA	116	110	100	100	92
EEC	NA	125	111	100	98	99
Germany	NA	117	108	100	96	100
SWITCHGEAR (SITC 722.2)						
U.S.	NA	NA	99	100	98	99
Germany	88	90	100	100	99	99

Source: Appendix C.

(kilovolt-amperes, KVA, or millivolt-amperes, MVA), year, and market to which sold (United States vs. rest of the world). As is explained in the appendix to this chapter, it would have been desirable to include several more specifications, but the data did not contain enough information. This international price index was compared with domestic price indexes which, also, were constructed so as to take account of the widespread discounts from list price that prevailed in some years; and the results confirmed the correctness of at least the major price trends revealed by the regression analysis.

The U.S. international price index for the group as a whole shows a steep decline from 1957 through 1963, clearly accounted for by the electric power machinery subgroup, in which the fall was approximately 40 per cent, one of the largest declines among machinery items. Only for the United States do we have an estimate of the price change before 1957, and that suggests a substantial rise during that period but not an unusually large one for machinery.

As we pointed out earlier, the fall in U.S. prices after 1957 was from a high level relative to other countries. The decline was precipitated by a number of events, including outbreaks of competition on some products, the indictments of the electrical equipment manufacturers in 1960, and technological developments in the production of electric power equipment, and was influenced also by the increase in the size of individual units of equipment.

Prices of electric power machinery in other countries also declined between 1957 and 1963, although none as far as in the United States. But in these countries, as in the United States, the fall in price was particularly rapid between 1961 and 1962, which was not, in general, a period of declining price levels.

In 1964 U.S. prices remained unchanged and prices in several other countries increased for the first time since 1957. In the United Kingdom, however, and particularly in Sweden, the price decline continued; the indicated fall in Swedish prices for 1961 through 1964, not shown in the table, was at least as large as that in any other country. These international price indexes differ widely from other price measures. An index taken from official Japanese export price data, for example, shows almost no change in electric power machinery prices from 1961 through 1964, while our indexes for Japan and for all other countries showed substantial declines.

Two comparisons with U.S. wholesale price indexes gave contrasting results. For switchgear, both the international and the wholesale price index were quite stable from 1961 through 1964, but in electric power machinery the wholesale index, although it declined from 1957 through 1964, as few machinery prices did, fell much less than our international index. The difference in movement was apparently due to the failure of the wholesale price index to take account of extensive discounting from list prices in both domestic and foreign markets rather than from any major differences between domestic and export price movements (see the appendix to this chapter).

Electric power equipment is represented in the official export unit value index of the U.S. Department of Commerce by only three series on electric motors and generating sets. The export price movement implied by these series is in direct contradiction to that shown by the NBER index. The unit value series show price increases in every period except for 1964, cumulating to a total increase of about 40 per cent. The NBER index, on the other hand, shows a 30 per cent fall in U.S.

international prices over the same period. Given our knowledge about even list prices in the United States and the extent of discounting from list prices in the 1960s it seems fair to say that the unit value data in this subgroup seriously misrepresent the price trends.

Electricity Distribution Equipment [12]

Trade

In 1963, the United Kingdom was by far the leading exporter in the group as a whole and in the major subgroup (Table 13.9). Germany followed, and then Japan and the United States. More than two-thirds of the exports went to countries outside the OECD; and the proportion shipped to these, mainly less developed, countries by the United Kingdom and Japan was particularly high. Only Germany exported mainly to other developed countries. Japan was the leading exporter of insulating equipment (SITC 723.2), with a wide lead over the United States, the United Kingdom, and Germany, which were all at about the same export level.

The products involved in this group are very different from most of those in the electric power machinery group (SITC 722). Both cable and insulators are relatively standardized items made to a single specification in large quantities, while much of the power equipment is produced to order, with each piece of equipment somewhat different from the previous order. Also, a greater degree of technological change took place in power equipment than in cable and insulators. The lower rate of technological change may partly explain the unusually small importance of the United States as an exporter.

The shares of the United States and the United Kingdom in OECD exports did not change very greatly in the four years for which we have data (Table 13.10). The major shifts were the growth in Japanese exports, almost doubling between 1962 and 1964, and declines in the EEC share, applying to both Germany and other EEC countries, particularly the latter. The shift in export shares from the EEC countries to Japan was even stronger in the main subgroup, insulated wire and cable, than in the group as a whole.

[12] SITC 723. *Value of OECD exports in 1963:* $343 million; three-fourths of 1 per cent of study total. *Coverage:* Insulated wire and cable (80 per cent); electrical insulating equipment.

Table 13.9

OECD Exports of Electricity Distribution Equipment (SITC 723),
by Origin, Destination, and Commodity Subgroup, 1963

(dollars in millions)

| | Value of Exports | Per Cent of OECD Exports in 723 | Share in OECD Exports (per cent) | | | EEC | | |
			OECD	U.S.	U.K.	Total	Germany	Japan
Total, all destinations and subgroups	$343	100.0	100.0	10.5	28.6	39.1	17.5	11.4
Destination								
U.S.	17	5.0	100.0		41.2	17.6	17.6	17.6
OECD Europe	97	28.3	100.0	9.3	11.3	64.9	37.1	2.1
U.K.	5	1.4	100.0	60.0		20.0	20.0	
EEC total	50	14.6	100.0	4.0	8.0	74.0	38.0	2.0
Germany	13	3.8	100.0	7.7	15.4	53.8	a	2.2
Canada	16	4.7	100.0	37.5	56.2	0.6	a	6.2
Japan	1	0.3	100.0	60.0	40.0	a	a	
Latin America	21	6.1	100.0	28.6	9.5	38.1	14.3	14.3
Other	185	53.9	100.0	7.6	36.7	31.4	9.2	16.2
Unaccounted for by destination	5	1.4	100.0	a	15.4	44.2	9.6	19.2
SITC commodity subgroup								
Insulated wire and cable (723.1)	282	82.2	100.0	9.2	31.6	40.1	18.1	8.5
Electrical insulating equipment (723.2)	61	17.8	100.0	14.8	16.4	32.8	14.8	24.6

Source: Appendix A and sources cited there.
aLess than 0.05 per cent.

Table 13.10
OECD Exports of Electricity Distribution Equipment, 1961–64
(dollars in millions)

	Value of OECD Exports	Share in OECD Exports (per cent)					
					EEC		
		OECD	U.S.	U.K.	Total	Germany	Japan
				INCLUDING JAPAN			
1964	$377	100.0	9.0	26.2	39.5	17.5	14.1
1963	343	100.0	10.4	28.7	39.0	17.4	11.4
1962	320	100.0	9.4	25.0	45.3	19.4	7.8
				EXCLUDING JAPAN			
1962	295	100.0	10.2	27.1	49.2	21.0	
1961	268	100.0	10.8	28.3	48.1	20.5	

Source: Appendix B.

Price Trends

International prices for electricity distribution equipment rose throughout most of the period of the study in both the United Kingdom and Germany, while U.S. prices, after rising sharply between 1953 and 1957, declined until 1963 (Table 13.11). The fall in U.S. prices in 1962 is surprisingly large for a year in which other countries' prices were stable. One possible explanation is that the American data were much more heavily weighted with prices supplied by purchasers than at least the German information. However, the data for the United Kingdom from

Table 13.11
International Prices, Electricity Distribution Equipment, 1953, 1957,
1961–64
(1962 = 100)

	1953	1957	1961	1962	1963	1964
U.S.	100	114	111	100	97	99
U.K.	85	95	106	100	101	98
EEC	90	94	100	100	94	94
Germany	90	94	100	100	94	102

Source: Appendix C.

purchasers did not show any similar decline, and the U.S. prices from sellers, while they did not decline quite as fast as those reported by buyers, did show a fall in 1962. Thus, differences in type of respondent do not completely explain the differences in price behavior.

The decline in the U.S. international price index from 1961 to 1963 had a parallel in the even sharper decline in wholesale prices reported by Japan, followed, as in every country, by a rise in 1964. The U.S. domestic wholesale price index itself showed a strong downward trend, but it began earlier than that in the international index, and the wholesale price series did not rise from 1953 to 1957.

The evidence is fairly strong, therefore, that U.S. prices for electricity distribution equipment did decline, starting near the beginning of the period and ending in 1963, and then rose in 1964.

Price Levels

American price levels for electricity distribution equipment were higher than those of the other countries in our study in all the years for which we have data (Table 13.12). The margin by which U.K. prices

Table 13.12

Price Levels, Electricity Distribution Equipment, 1957, 1961–64

(U.S. for each year = 100)

	1957	1961	1962	1963	1964
ELECTRICITY DISTRIBUTION EQUIPMENT (SITC 723)					
U.S.	100	100	100	100	100
U.K.	73	83	87	90	86
EEC	62	68	76	73	72
Japan	NA	79	69	77	77
INSULATED WIRE AND CABLE (SITC 723.1)					
U.S.	100	100	100	100	100
U.K.	70	80	84	87	87
Japan	NA	79	69	78	78
ELECTRICAL INSULATING EQUIPMENT (SITC 723.2)					
U.S.	NA	100	100	100	100
Japan	NA	77	72	70	69

Source: Appendix E.

were lower ranged between 10 and almost 20 per cent, and the EEC countries and Japan undercut the United States by margins of 20 to 30 or even 40 per cent.

Few clear trends are evident in the levels in general. In insulated wire and cable, the subgroup for which we had somewhat better data, U.K. prices seemed to be closer to U.S. levels at the end of the period than initially. EEC prices appear to have been lower in 1964 than earlier. The Japanese relative price level, except for a dip in 1962, did not show any trend.

The price level data for Germany are too weak to be shown separately, but as far as they go, they suggest that German prices were higher than those of other EEC countries in the last two years after having been lower in the first two.

The poor export showing of the United States, described in Table 13.9, seems reasonable in the light of the price levels shown here, as do the unusually strong export positions of Japan and the EEC countries other than Germany. But the price data show the United Kingdom as being a higher-priced exporter than the EEC countries and Japan, a finding which seems anomalous in view of the United Kingdom's dominance of export trade in this group. However, the main strength of the United Kingdom is in insulated cable sold in Africa and the Far East, and it may be that, in the face of high prices, British sales were aided by the experience with British equipment and the adoption of British standards in Commonwealth countries.

The many place-to-place comparisons we have for this group are a potential source of information on differences in price levels by market of sale. Unfortunately, in only three years do we have samples of as many as five observations for a particular competitor in both U.S. and foreign markets. For electrical generating equipment (SITC 722.1) we found that the ratio of foreign to American prices was substantially lower on bids in the United States than abroad. In each case in electricity distribution equipment, the average ratio of foreign to U.S. prices was lower outside the United States than on U.S. projects, the opposite result to that in generating equipment.

This result may point to a possible bias in the comparison of price levels among foreign countries in this group. Only a small proportion of the EEC bids were on U.S. projects, for which we found that the ratios of foreign to U.S. prices were relatively high. However, a considerable number of British bids and a majority of the Japanese bids used for our indexes were on U.S. contracts. If U.S. market price ratios were unfavorable to foreign firms, as the data suggest, we may have overestimated British and particularly Japanese price levels by overweighting that market, or underestimated EEC price levels by underweighting the U.S. market.

Price Competitiveness

The United States improved its price competitiveness relative to its European competitors, during 1953–64, particularly before 1962 (Table 13.13). Relative to Japan, the U.S. position declined greatly and then recovered almost to the 1961 level.

Data for insulated cable, the main subgroup, show a constant increase in American price competitiveness relative to the United Kingdom, but a sharp fall followed by a gain relative to Japan. In electrical insulating equipment, however, where only the Japanese data are adequate for

Table 13.13
U.S. Price Competitiveness, Electricity Distribution Equipment,
1953, 1957, 1961–64
(1962 = 100)

	1953	1957	1961	1962	1963	1964
ELECTRICITY DISTRIBUTION EQUIPMENT (SITC 723)						
Relative to						
U.K.	85	84	96	100	103	99
EEC	90	82	90	100	96	95
Germany	90	82	90	100	97	103
Japan	NA	NA	113	100	110	111
INSULATED WIRE AND CABLE (SITC 723.1)						
Relative to						
U.K.	NA	83	95	100	103	103
Japan	NA	NA	115	100	113	114
ELECTRICAL INSULATING EQUIPMENT (SITC 723.2)						
Relative to Japan	NA	NA	108	100	98	96

Source: Appendix D.

the publication of an index, the U.S. position declined throughout the four years for which we have data.

The export data of Table 13.10 show a substantial shift from the EEC countries to Japan during a four-year period, 1961–64, when EEC prices rose relative to Japanese prices. U.S. and U.K. price movements were between those of the other two countries, as were their export changes. However, the matching of price and export changes was poor for 1962–64, when price changes seemed to favor the EEC countries. That finding suggests that the sharp decline and rise in Japanese prices from 1961 to 1963 may reflect the erratic nature of the bidding data rather than actual price changes.

Telecommunications Equipment [13]

Trade

The United States was the leading exporter of telecommunications equipment in 1963. Japan, a comparatively minor factor in most machinery groups, was in second place, followed by Germany and the United Kingdom (Table 13.14). The ranking of the exporters varied greatly among the subgroups. In television receivers, Germany ranked first, followed closely by Japan. The United States and the United Kingdom were far behind. Japan completely dominated the trade in radio receivers, accounting for almost half the exports, largely with its portable transistor radios. U.S. and U.K. exports were negligible by comparison. In other telecommunications equipment the United States had a long lead over the United Kingdom, its nearest competitor, mainly in special-category exports classified under "electronic detection and navigational apparatus." These accounted for the great bulk of U.S. exports in the subgroup and even for three-quarters of U.S. exports of telecommunications equipment as a whole. We infer that exports by the Netherlands also were mainly of military products because no data on destination were reported in this category.

Exports of telecommunications equipment grew rapidly during the four years for which we have data. Exports by countries other than

[13] SITC 724. *Value of OECD exports in 1963:* $1.7 billion; 3.9 per cent of study total. *Coverage:* Television and radio receivers, telephone equipment, other telecommunications equipment, including telegraph equipment, microphones, loudspeakers, radar and other communications devices, and other components.

Table 13.14

OECD Exports of Telecommunications Equipment (SITC 724), by Origin, Destination, and Commodity Subgroup, 1963

(dollars in millions)

	Value of Exports	Per Cent of OECD Exports in 724	Share in OECD Exports (per cent)			EEC		
			OECD	U.S.	U.K.	Total	Germany	Japan
Total, all destinations and subgroups	$1,715	100.0	100.0	22.7	12.8	37.9	16.3	16.5
Destination								
U.S.	210	12.3	100.0		4.3	12.4	9.3	63.8
OECD Europe	672	39.2	100.0	14.7	9.9	59.7	27.1	5.2
U.K.	44	2.6	100.0	50.0		34.1	15.9	6.8
EEC total	383	22.3	100.0	15.4	7.3	65.3	25.6	3.9
Germany	81	4.7	100.0	8.6	8.6	64.2		9.9
Canada	89	5.2	100.0	66.3	19.1	6.7	4.5	6.7
Japan	14	0.8	100.0	85.7	7.1	7.1	1.4	
Latin America	99	5.8	100.0	24.2	7.1	26.3	17.9	21.2
Other	392	22.9	100.0	8.2	30.1	29.8	14.7	21.7
Unaccounted for by destination	236	13.8	100.0	69.5	0.0	30.5		0.1

(continued)

389

Table 13.14 (concluded)

SITC commodity subgroup	Value of Exports	Per Cent of OECD Exports in 724	Share in OECD Exports (per cent)					
			OECD	U.S.	U.K.	EEC Total	Germany	Japan
Television receivers (724.1)	$149	8.7	100.0	14.8	7.4	43.0	28.8	27.5
Radio receivers (724.2)	386	22.5	100.0	1.8	4.4	40.7	17.9	49.0
Telecommunications equipment, n.e.s. (724.9)	1,180	68.8	100.0	30.6	16.2	36.4	14.2	4.4
Electric line telephone and telegraph equipment (724.91)	358	20.9	100.0	9.4	22.4	38.9	22.6	2.6
Microphones, loudspeakers, amplifiers (724.92)	67	3.9	100.0	32.0	7.4	36.8	13.7	19.2
Other telecommunications equipment (724.99)	754	44.0	100.0	40.6	14.1	35.1	10.3	4.0

Source: Appendix A and sources cited there.

Japan increased by more than 40 per cent from 1961 to 1964, and Japanese exports grew by that amount between 1962 and 1964 (Appendix B). The U.S. share of OECD exports rose sharply in 1962, mainly at the expense of Germany. It then fell back to about the initial proportion of exports other than Japanese (Table 13.15). The U.K. share fell in every year, while the main gains were scored by Japan and Italy.

The shifts in export shares showed up more strongly in the subgroup data. In television receivers the United Kingdom made a large gain in 1962 at the expense mainly of Germany. After that all the main exporters except Japan lost heavily (in relative terms), as Japan doubled its share from 15 to 30 per cent in two years. The rise in the Japanese share was the result of the rapid growth in exports of small television sets, principally to the U.S. market, in which the Japanese succeeded in capturing something like 10 per cent of sales of black and white sets at the end of our period and probably a greater share later, mostly under the brand names of U.S. television set producers and retail chains. The U.S. producers specialized in larger sets, for which the market was greatest in the United States, while the Japanese were innovators and specialists in small-screen sets which accounted for the bulk of the Japanese home market. The same specialization seemed to be taking

Table 13.15

OECD Exports of Telecommunications Equipment, 1961–64

(dollars in millions)

| | Value of OECD Exports | Share in OECD Exports (per cent) | | | | | | |
| | | OECD | U.S. | U.K. | EEC | | | Japan |
					Total	Ger-many	Nether-lands	
				INCLUDING JAPAN				
1964	$1,961	100.0	20.6	11.5	40.5	16.1	10.2	17.8
1963	1,715	100.0	22.7	12.8	37.9	16.3	7.9	16.5
1962	1,538	100.0	24.0	13.4	37.0	15.9	7.5	15.8
				EXCLUDING JAPAN				
1962	1,296	100.0	28.5	15.9	43.6	18.9	11.5	
1961	1,106	100.0	24.8	16.8	47.4	22.2	6.4	

Source: Appendix B.

place in color television after the end of the period covered by this study.[14]

Japan's dominance in radio receivers antedated the period covered in our table, and the Japanese share continued to increase while that of the EEC countries declined. By the end of the period, Japan was meeting increasing competition from producers in Hong Kong, Taiwan, and South Korea, none of which is included in the export data of Tables 13.14 and 13.15.[15]

In the largest subgroup, other telecommunications equipment (SITC 724.9), both the United States and the United Kingdom lost ground to the EEC countries as a group. The Netherlands and Italy made the largest gains, but the other EEC countries also improved their position.

Trade in telecommunications equipment, particularly in the 724.9 subgroup, is affected to an important degree by nonprice factors. Most telephone systems outside the United States are government owned, and favor domestic over foreign suppliers in their purchasing. The Australian government, for example, favors home producers of telephone equipment by imposing hypothetical tariffs on foreign products in comparing offers, and has thereby encouraged the replacement of imports through the establishment of foreign subsidiaries and joint ventures with local firms. The British and German telephone systems also apparently confine their purchases to domestic producers. Several countries aid exports by supplying or guaranteeing finance, and it was said to be a principal handicap to exports by Sweden, a major producer of telephone equipment, that little government financing was available.[16]

Another factor in the telephone equipment industry is that the telephone systems of different producers are incompatible. It is, therefore, the bidding on the first major installation that determines the course of trade for additional equipment in succeeding years, because the customer

[14] "TV Exports Counter Sluggish Home Market," *Journal of Commerce,* September 29, 1965; "TV Importers Seeks Sales Mark," *ibid.,* May 25, 1965; "GE Slates Output of Small TV Sets to Counter Imports," *New York Times,* September 3, 1965; "Japan to Sell Color TV's in the U.S.," *Journal of Commerce,* December 15, 1965; "Japanese Color TV Drive Set," *ibid.,* August 22, 1966; "Japan's Hold on Small Color-TV Set Sales in U.S. Grows, Hidden by American Labels," *Wall Street Journal,* August 25, 1967.

[15] "Standard Kollsman to Offer Low-Priced, Small TV Tuner," *Wall Street Journal,* August 31, 1965; "U.S. Boom: Japanese Export Boon," *Journal of Commerce,* June 15, 1966.

[16] *Market Information on Electronic Products in Australia,* U.S. Dept. of Commerce, August 1967; "Telecommunications: A Very Close Look," *Economist,* January 14, 1967; "Sweden's Ericsson Phone Firm Wins Big Slice of Growing World Market," *Wall Street Journal,* August 29, 1963; "The Secrets of the Ring," *Economist,* July 23, 1960; "L. M. Ericsson Pushes U.S. Sales," *Journal of Commerce,* June 7, 1965.

is fairly well committed to the firm performing the initial installation. This fact, of course, affects pricing policy and at the same time tends to weaken the relationship between the flow of trade and contemporaneous price relationships.

Price Trends

International price data for telecommunications equipment are sparse throughout the period, particularly in the early years, but the evidence for a decline in prices after 1961 seems fairly strong (Table 13.16). This decline is evident in some of the unpublished indexes, such as the separate series for television receivers and radio receivers, as well as in those shown in the table. The few observations for portable transistor radios show some of the sharpest price declines found in the study, including price cuts of two-thirds or more between 1957 and 1961, as well as substantial declines in other periods.

Table 13.16
International Prices, Telecommunications Equipment, 1953, 1957, 1961–64
(1962 = 100)

	1953	1957	1961	1962	1963	1964
TELECOMMUNICATIONS EQUIPMENT (SITC 724)						
U.S.	NA	NA	101	100	95	96
U.K.	NA	NA	101	100	101	99
EEC	NA	NA	101	100	100	97
Germany	NA	NA	101	100	100	96
Japan	NA	NA	107	100	100	98
TELEVISION AND RADIO RECEIVERS (SITC 724.1 and 724.2)						
U.S.	NA	NA	102	100	90	85
EEC	125	113	103	100	96	94
Germany	119	108	103	100	97	94
OTHER TELECOMMUNICATIONS EQUIPMENT (SITC 724.9)						
U.S.	NA	NA	101	100	98	102
U.K.	NA	90	100	100	106	107
EEC	88	88	100	100	102	98
Germany	86	86	100	100	101	95

Source: Appendix C.

There were no U.K. data for radios other than portable transistor sets, and no U.S. data before 1961. The data for television sets and portable transistor radios indicate clearly that prices on both of these items fell, and that if we had been able to calculate an index for the combination of television and radio receivers it would have shown falling prices, as the indexes for Germany and the EEC countries do.

The main component of telecommunications equipment is SITC 724.9, which is dominated by telephone equipment. Prices in this subgroup rose in the EEC countries until 1963 and in the United Kingdom throughout the period. American prices were comparatively stable after 1961, declining at first and then recovering, but had risen sharply before then, according to fragmentary data.

In general, the main directions of movements in international prices are reflected in wholesale prices, too, with declines in television and radio receivers and comparative stability in other telecommunications equipment. The differences appear to involve mainly a widespread tendency toward smaller price declines in domestic wholesale prices than in international prices. Coverage, however, is very inconsistent. The U.S. wholesale price index excludes portable transistor radios, since they are unimportant in U.S. production, although they make up a large part of international trade in radio receivers. The Japanese wholesale price index for radio receivers, on the other hand, contains only transistor radios.

The U.S. Department of Commerce export unit value series for television and radio receivers, which are components of the official export unit value indexes, do not resemble any of the other price data in their trends or fluctuations. The export unit value for television sets declined sharply from 1961 through 1963 and then greatly increased. Both international and wholesale price series showed gradual declines with no reversals during those years. The export unit value for radios increased substantially from 1957 to 1963 and then fell precipitously, to considerably below the initial level. Wholesale and international prices of radios were declining throughout this whole period. In view of the intense competition from Japanese transistor radios, it seems very unlikely that any appropriate measure of U.S. prices could have shown an increase such as that of the unit value series. In this group, it seems safe to say, the official export unit value data are useless as measures of the behavior of U.S. export prices.

Price Competitiveness

American price competitiveness in telecommunications equipment as a whole moved within a fairly narrow range between 1953 and 1964, except for Japan (Table 13.17). It ranged from 98 to 106 per cent of the 1962 level relative to each of the other major competitors. Concealed in this apparent stability, however, were contrasting movements in competitiveness in television and radio receivers on the one hand and in other telecommunications equipment on the other. In television and radio receivers U.S. price competitiveness declined relative to Japan between 1957 and 1962, and relative to the EEC countries especially from 1953 to 1962 (see note to Table 13.17). The recovery fell far short of regaining the early levels. In other telecommunications equipment the U.S. gained relative to the EEC countries until 1963 and then lost the gains in 1964.

The comparison with the United Kingdom showed some gains in U.S. price competitiveness, mainly in the later years and for other telecommunications equipment. The index remained comparatively stable for television and radio receivers.

The widest movements in U.S. price competitiveness were relative to Japan, a very large fall for both television and radio receivers and for other telecommunications equipment after 1957. The supplementary data on wholesale prices suggest that even the large movements shown are smaller than the earlier losses, from 1953 to 1957, and that the U.S. recovery after 1962 was minor in comparison to the original decline.

Some of the differences among price competitiveness indexes in Table 13.16 are due to differences in coverage rather than relative price movements for specific commodities. The main one involves radio receivers (SITC 724.2) for which some countries' data include only portable transistor radios. The indexes in the note to Table 13.17, less complete in coverage than those in the table but more comparable among countries because only portable transistor radios were used in the subgroup index for SITC 724.2, suggest that U.S. price competitiveness relative to the EEC countries did not improve much more than that relative to the United Kingdom after 1962. There was, however, a large decline in the former before 1962, comparable to the decline relative to Japan.

U.S. price competitiveness indexes relative to Japan for television and radio receivers computed from wholesale price data declined moder-

Table 13.17
U.S. Price Competitiveness, Telecommunications Equipment,
1953, 1957, 1961—64
(1962 = 100)

	1953	1957	1961	1962	1963	1964
TELECOMMUNICATIONS EQUIPMENT (SITC 724)						
Relative to						
U.K.	98	98	100	100	106	103
EEC	NA	NA	100	100	105	101
Germany	NA	NA	100	100	105	99
Japan	NA	121	106	100	105	102
TELEVISION AND RADIO RECEIVERS (SITC 724.1 AND 724.2)						
Relative to						
U.K.	100	94	102	100	99	98
EEC	NA	NA	101	100	107	111
Germany	NA	NA	101	100	108	111
Japan	NA	151	124	100	110	110
OTHER TELECOMMUNICATIONS EQUIPMENT (SITC 724.9)						
Relative to						
U.K.	97	100	99	100	109	105
EEC	96	97	99	100	104	96
Germany	94	95	99	100	104	94
Japan	NA	110	99	100	102	98

Note: *Alternative calculation:* The indexes for Germany and the EEC above are not strictly comparable to those for the United Kingdom and Japan because they include both portable transistor and other radios in SITC 724.2. A more comparable, but less complete, set of calculations using only transistor radios in SITC 724.2 and giving SITC 724.2 only the weight of the transistor ratio portion results in the following indexes of U.S. price competitiveness (1962 = 100):

	1953	1957	1961	1962	1963	1964
TELECOMMUNICATIONS EQUIPMENT (SITC 724)						
Relative to						
U.K.	98	99	100	100	107	104
EEC	97	102	100	100	102	98
Germany	96	100	100	100	102	97
Japan	NA	115	103	100	103	100

(continued)

Notes to Table 13.17 (concluded)

TELEVISION AND RADIO RECEIVERS (SITC 724.1 AND 724.2)
Relative to

U.K.	98	96	101	100	100	100
EEC	119	110	102	100	96	102
Germany	122	122	102	100	96	102
Japan	NA	137	117	100	106	107

All these indexes are based on small numbers of observations, considerably smaller, in the case of the EEC countries, than those used in table 13.17. Some indexes for 1953 and 1957, omitted there, are shown here because, although the number of observations is smaller, we have more assurance of comparability between countries.

ately after 1961 instead of declining and recovering like the indexes from international price data. For the earliest period, on which no international price data are available, the wholesale price data indicate a considerable deterioration in the U.S. position.

Wherever possible, the price competitiveness indexes were computed separately for portable transistor radios and for all other radios. But it may very possibly be that the two items are such close substitutes that we should have derived the index by comparing Japanese prices for the transistor radios with other countries' prices for radios of other types. The result would have been an even larger estimate of the gain in price competitiveness of Japan in radio receivers, since prices of portable transistor radios fell relative to other radio prices. The wholesale price comparison is of this nature, and that fact accounts for the steady or declining trend after 1961 in this measure of U.S. price competitiveness during a time when the comparisons among like types of radios showed an improvement in the U.S. position. The great increase in Japanese exports (see Appendix B) was mainly a matter of increases in portable transistor exports and later in exports of small-screen television sets rather than of improvements in their share within each of these items. Our method of measuring price competitiveness, involving comparisons within homogeneous groups, tends to conceal the basis for rising export shares in a case like this (see discussion in Chapter 3).

Price Levels

British prices of telecommunications equipment were apparently above U.S. ones throughout the whole period of the study, while EEC prices were consistently lower. Japanese prices were at first above the U.S. level and then fell to the EEC levels or below (Table 13.18). At the

Table 13.18

Price Levels, Telecommunications Equipment, 1953, 1957, 1961–64

(U.S. for each year = 100)

	1953	1957	1961	1962	1963	1964
TELECOMMUNICATIONS EQUIPMENT (SITC 724)						
U.S.	100	100	100	100	100	100
U.K.	113	112	115	115	122	118
EEC	NA	NA	89	89	93	89
Germany	NA	NA	88	88	93	87
Japan	NA	104	91	86	90	88
TELEVISION AND RADIO RECEIVERS (SITC 724.1 and 724.2)						
U.S.	100	100	100	100	100	100
U.K.	111	104	113	111	109	108
EEC	NA	NA	83	82	88	91
Germany	NA	NA	85	84	90	92
Japan	NA	135	111	89	98	98
OTHER TELECOMMUNICATIONS EQUIPMENT (SITC 724.9)						
U.S.	100	100	100	100	100	100
U.K.	114	116	116	117	127	123
EEC	88	89	91	92	96	88
Germany	85	86	90	90	94	85
Japan	NA	93	84	84	87	83

Note: An alternative set of indexes for 724, 724.1 and 724.2, more comparable among countries but less complete in coverage, can be derived by using only data on transistor radios in the level for 724.2 and extrapolating by corresponding indexes of price competitiveness, as described in the notes to Table 13.16. These indexes are as follows (U.S. for each year = 100):

	1953	1957	1961	1962	1963	1964
TELECOMMUNICATIONS EQUIPMENT (SITC 724)						
U.S.	100	100	100	100	100	100
U.K.	119	121	121	122	130	127
EEC	86	90	88	88	90	87
Germany	85	89	88	88	90	85
Japan	NA	94	84	82	84	82
TELEVISION AND RADIO RECEIVERS (SITC 724.1 and 724.2)						
U.S.	100	100	100	100	100	100
U.K.	103	101	107	105	105	105
EEC	97	97	83	81	78	83
Germany	99	99	83	81	78	83
Japan	NA	98	84	72	76	76

(continued)

Notes to Table 13.18 (concluded)
The differences between the two sets of indexes are greater in the case of radio and television receivers alone. The Japanese are shown to have offered the lowest prices among the leading exporters since 1962 instead of being above the EEC price level, and are described as having a price level consistently below that of the United States instead of being at first far above American prices. In addition, a much larger gap is indicated between Japanese and American prices and between EEC and U.S. prices at the end of the period. British prices, on the other hand, appear in these calculations to have been closer to U.S. prices than is suggested by the estimates in the table.

Source: Appendix E.

end, the price level differences were wider for other telecommunications equipment than for television and radio receivers, in which the range was surprisingly narrow. The range of price levels within that subgroup was much larger than for the aggregate, however, with EEC and Japanese prices for portable transistor radios far lower than American prices. Fragmentary data suggest that the United States, in turn, was in a superior position in the more important group of other radio receivers.

The data on radios other than portable transistor radios are particularly weak and do not cover the same items or all the years in each country. There may be some advantage, therefore, in comparing price levels estimated by using only the portable transistor portion of SITC 724.2 in combination with the other subgroups. The results, given in the note to Table 13.18 show EEC, particularly German, prices to have been the lowest of all in 1957, and to have been below U.S. and U.K. prices since 1953. The Japanese price level reached its position as the lowest among all the countries at an earlier date in these calculations than in our main indexes, and the margin relative to the United Kingdom and the United States was consistently greater.

It is difficult to choose between the indexes in the table, which are the more comprehensive in coverage, and those in the notes, which are the more reliable for the items covered. Those in the table represent our best estimates for the relationship of each country to the United States, but those in the notes are probably superior for comparisons among the foreign countries.

A juxtaposition of the price level estimates with the 1963 trade pattern, as given in Table 13.14, supports the indexes in the notes, at least as regards the radio receivers subgroup itself. The position of the Japanese as exporters of radio receivers fits in far better with the price level indexes for portable transistor radios alone than with that for all radios. The levels for portable transistor radios show Japan far below Germany and the EEC as a whole, and those, in turn, far below the United Kingdom and the United States. The only anomaly is the relation between the United Kingdom and the United States, with the former exporting substantially more despite an apparently higher price level.

The export pattern for other telecommunications equipment did not confirm the reported price levels at all, possibly because military exports, which did not enter the price estimates, were important in trade. The United States, by far the major exporter, showed prices substantially higher than the EEC countries and Japan, while the United Kingdom was a major exporter despite prices considerably higher than even those of the United States. Japan, on the other hand, reported to be the lowest-priced equipment source, was a minor factor.

Household Electrical Equipment [17]

Trade

Germany was the leading exporter of household electrical equipment, followed by the United Kingdom, the United States, and Italy, here making a rare appearance as a major machinery exporter (Table 13.19). Italy's importance was concentrated in refrigerators, in which it was a close second to the United States as an exporter and was also a major producer. It was surpassed only by the United States and Germany in 1963 and only by the United States in 1964. The Italian industry was heavily dependent on exports, sending a third or more of its production abroad, mainly to other Common Market countries and Great Britain.[18] By comparison with Great Britain, at least, Italy specialized in large refrigerators, although it was also a major producer at the small end of the line.[19]

The major successes in recent trade in household electrical equipment were the expansions in exports by Italy and Japan, the former more than doubling its exports in three years and the latter almost doubling in

[17] SITC 725. *Value of OECD exports in 1963:* $554 million; 1.2 per cent of study total. *Coverage:* "Domestic" (i.e., household) refrigerators, domestic washing machines, other electromechanical domestic appliances, electric shavers and hair clippers, and other domestic electrical equipment.

[18] *Free World Production and Trade in Selected Household Appliances,* Overseas Business Reports, U.S. Dept. of Commerce, December 1966.

[19] "Italian Invasion," *Economist,* March 6, 1965.

Table 13.19

OECD Exports of Household Electrical Equipment (SITC 725),
by Origin, Destination, and Commodity Subgroup, 1963

(dollars in millions)

| | Value of Exports | Per Cent of OECD Exports in 725 | Share in OECD Exports (per cent) | | | | | |
			OECD	U.S.	U.K.	EEC Total	EEC Germany	Japan
Total, all destinations and subgroups	$554.4	100.0	100.0	17.7	18.0	49.4[a]	24.0	3.5
Destination								
U.S.	26.8	4.8	100.0		25.0	40.7	9.0	11.2
OECD Europe	336.8	60.8	100.0	4.9	16.0	64.8	34.6	0.5
U.K.	23.6	4.2	100.0	9.3		38.1	10.6	0.0
EEC total	186.2	33.6	100.0	5.0	17.1	69.6	33.1	0.7
Germany	30.9	5.6	100.0	6.5	29.4	43.4		1.0
Canada	35.2	6.3	100.0	89.5	5.7	3.7	0.8	0.3
Japan	2.1	0.4	100.0	33.3	9.5	42.8	23.8	
Latin America	37.9	6.8	100.0	68.1	6.6	12.9	6.1	3.4
Other	115.7	20.9	100.0	17.3	29.6	32.6	9.8	11.7

(continued)

Table 13.19 (concluded)

SITC commodity subgroup	Value of Exports	Per Cent of OECD Exports in 725	Share in OECD Exports (per cent)				EEC		
			OECD	U.S.	U.K.	Total	Germany	Japan
Domestic refrigerators (725.01)	$168.1	30.3	100.0	25.2	8.6	53.3[b]	20.3	2.3
Domestic washing machines (725.02)	128.6	23.2	100.0	14.2	30.6	50.1	32.7	1.1
Electromechanical domestic appliances, n.e.s. (725.03)	110.5	19.9	100.0	14.8	21.4	39.4	17.4	9.7
Electric shavers and hair clippers (725.04)	43.4	7.8	100.0	11.3	12.7	70.5	17.0	0.2
Electric spaceheating equipment (725.05)	102.6	18.5	100.0	15.8	16.2	44.8	29.5	3.4

Source: Appendix A and sources cited there.
[a]Of which Italy, 10.8 per cent.
[b]Of which Italy, 24.9 per cent.

Table 13.20
OECD Exports of Household Electrical Equipment, 1961–64
(dollars in millions)

| | Value of OECD Exports | Share in OECD Exports (per cent) | | | | | | |
		OECD	U.S.	U.K.	EEC Total	Germany	Italy	Japan
				INCLUDING JAPAN				
1964	$640	100.0	17.5	15.3	50.9	23.2	13.7	4.3
1963	554	100.0	17.7	18.0	49.4	24.0	10.8	3.5
1962	478	100.0	20.9	16.6	50.1	24.7	10.5	3.3
				EXCLUDING JAPAN				
1962	462	100.0	21.6	17.2	51.8	25.5	10.9	
1961	452	100.0	23.5	16.7	50.8	25.1	8.9	

Source: Appendix B.

two (Appendix B). Italy increased its share from 9 to 14 per cent while the other major exporters, the United States, the United Kingdom, and Germany, all lost ground (Table 13.20). The growth in Italian exports of refrigerators was so great that, in combination with an increasing degree of market saturation it led to declines in domestic production in the other Common Market countries; by the end of the period, Italian exports of washing machines were also gaining in importance.[20]

Price Trends

International prices of household electrical equipment changed relatively little over the period of the study (Table 13.21). The price stability for the group as a whole reflects a sharply declining trend in household refrigerators and mostly rising or stable prices for the other items in the group. The only other clear downward trend, not shown in the table because the number of observations was very small, was for prices of household washing machines in the EEC countries.

Refrigerator prices in the United States and the United Kingdom, based on too few reports for publication, showed major declines, al-

[20] From sources in footnotes 18 and 19. See also "Appliance Sales Abroad Building Up Momentum," *Journal of Commerce,* June 14, 1965; "Italy Appliance Makers Boost Exports to Britain," *ibid.,* April 8, 1965; "Washing Machines: A New Growth Point?" *Economist,* September 9, 1967.

Table 13.21

International Prices, Household Electrical Equipment, 1953, 1957, 1961–64
(1962 = 100)

	1953	1957	1961	1962	1963	1964
HOUSEHOLD ELECTRICAL EQUIPMENT (SITC 725)						
U.S.	NA	102	98	100	102	102
U.K.	NA	NA	NA	100	98	102
EEC	NA	102	100	100	99	100
Germany	NA	101	100	100	99	99
HOUSEHOLD REFRIGERATORS (SITC 725.01)						
EEC	140	118	101	100	97	96
Germany	132	114	100	100	96	96
ELECTROMECHANICAL HOUSEHOLD APPLIANCES, N.E.S. **(SITC 725.03)**						
EEC	94	94	100	100	101	104
Germany	92	93	100	100	101	104
ELECTRIC SPACE-HEATING AND OTHER ELECTRIC HEATING **EQUIPMENT (SITC 725.05)**						
EEC	NA	91	99	100	100	101
Germany	NA	91	99	100	101	101

Source: Appendix C.

though not as large as those for EEC countries. In the United Kingdom the price decline continued through 1964, probably in response to the pressure of imports from EEC countries, whose prices were also falling.

Wholesale prices in several cases moved quite differently from the international price indexes. They showed a strong downward trend in the United States, while the international prices were fairly stable; and a large price rise in the United Kingdom in 1962–64, when international price series showed little change (see Appendix F). In Japan, for which international price data were unavailable, wholesale price data indicated that the price level was falling between 1961 and 1964.

A downward price trend was pervasive in the U.S. wholesale price data, not only in refrigerators, where it was considerably stronger than the trend in international prices, but also in the other items, for which international prices were rising or stable. The group is unusual in this respect; there are few groups in which most wholesale prices did not rise during this decade.

Both household refrigerators and washing machines were used in the construction of the official export unit value index. The decline in unit value for refrigerators was considerably smaller than the fall in international prices or in wholesale prices. In particular, the stability shown after 1962 seems doubtful in view of the declines in the other two series and in foreign prices. In the case of washing machines the large decline in the last year is not reflected in either of the other two sources and is also suspect on that account.

Price Competitiveness

Only very minor changes in price competitiveness between the major world exporters are seen in the indexes for household electrical equipment as a whole (Table 13.22). The U.S. position weakened somewhat relative to the EEC countries between 1961 and 1963, but that followed a slight rise in the previous period, and the net change over seven years was small.

Indexes for earlier years, not published because they cover too small a part of the total value of trade in the group, suggest a deterioration in the U.S. price position relative to the EEC countries at the beginning of the period, and a gain relative to the United Kingdom, followed by a rapid fall, all before 1962. These early indexes, however, mainly reflect the movement of refrigerator prices, in which first the EEC countries (particularly in 1953–57) and then the United Kingdom (in 1961–62 and 1962–63) improved their price competitiveness rela-

Table 13.22

U.S. Price Competitiveness, Household Electrical Equipment, 1957, 1961–64
(1962 = 100)

	1957	1961	1962	1963	1964
Relative to					
U.K.	NA	NA	100	97	100
EEC	100	102	100	98	98
Germany	99	102	100	97	97

Source: Appendix D.

tive to the United States by 15 per cent or more. In this item U.S. price competitiveness quite generally fell until 1963, but recovered sharply in 1964.

Indexes of price competitiveness from wholesale price data record a different story, mainly gains in U.S. price competitiveness throughout the period. The chief exceptions are several declines relative to Japan. The indexes from wholesale prices show a 9 per cent gain in U.S. price competitiveness relative to the United Kingdom between 1962 and 1964, while the indexes from international prices show no change. The indexes from wholesale prices show a gain relative to Germany of 5 per cent between 1961 and 1964; those from international prices, a 5 per cent decline.

Data on trade shares given in Table 13.20 fit better with the price competitiveness indexes from international price data than with those from wholesale price data. They show no gain in exports relative to the United Kingdom between 1962 and 1964, as might be expected from the wholesale price data. If anything they show some loss in the U.S. relative share. The U.S. export share also declined relative to Germany between 1961 and 1964, as might be expected from the international price data, instead of gaining, as one might expect from looking at the relative movements of wholesale prices.

Price Levels

Both U.K. and EEC household electrical equipment prices have been between 5 and 10 per cent below U.S. prices throughout the period of the study, with no strong trend visible in the data for the group as a whole (Table 13.23). The European level was lower for refrigerators

Table 13.23
Price Levels, Household Electrical Equipment, 1957, 1961–64
(U.S. for each year = 100)

	1957	1961	1962	1963	1964
U.S.	100	100	100	100	100
U.K.	NA	NA	92	90	93
EEC	93	95	93	90	90

Source: Appendix E.

than for the other items in 1964, particularly in the case of the EEC countries, and there is some evidence of a strong downward trend before that. There is a little evidence that EEC prices in the earlier years were substantially above U.S. ones.

A few scattered observations for Japan, not shown in the table, suggest that the Japanese price level was the lowest of all, but the data do not include any prices on the major household appliances; their inclusion might give a different impression.

In general, these place-to-place comparisons are considerably weaker than those in many other groups because of the large differences in the specifications of products produced and used in each country.

For example, as was mentioned earlier, the most popular household models of refrigerators in the United Kingdom were in the 3.5–4.5 cubic foot range even at the end of the period, and a British firm supplied the demand for larger models by importing those of about 4.5–8.5 cubic foot capacity from Italy, where the most popular range of sizes was 4.8–6.4 cubic feet.[21] In the United States, by way of contrast, the most popular size was 13.5–14.5 cubic feet, and only 45,000 units, about 1 per cent of the units produced, were under 8.5 cubic feet.[22] The value of comparing European and British refrigerator data with American data for the same products is questionable; it means comparing a small fringe of the U.S. industry with a high proportion of the Continental and British output, giving no weight to the bulk of U.S. output, which meets little or no competition. If we had received additional data we might have been able to apply regression analysis to the various countries' data to give a wider range of price comparisons. The small refrigerators are more important in world trade than the large ones, but U.S. exports were important, at about one-quarter of OECD exports, as can be seen in Table 13.19. The average U.S. export unit value of $166 in 1963 [23] suggests an average size of exported refrigerators in the 12.5–13.5 cubic foot range, which is not represented in our price comparisons. That size would, if included, almost certainly raise the ratio of foreign-U.S. prices in the refrigerator subgroup.

Other appliances also differ substantially from country to country, with foreign products being generally less automatic and of smaller

21 "Italian Invasion," *Economist,* March 6, 1965; *Free World Production and Trade.*
22 *Census of Manufactures: 1963, Industry Statistics: Household Appliances,* U.S. Bureau of the Census, 1966.
23 *United States Exports of Domestic and Foreign Merchandise; Commodity by Country of Destination, 1963 Annual,* U.S. Bureau of the Census, Report FT 410, 1964.

capacity, although some contained features not wanted or not needed in the United States, such as water heaters in washing machines or water softeners in dishwashers. Where comparability was obtained in some price comparisons for freezers and dishwashers the European prices were far above the U.S. levels.

Appendix: Regression Analysis of Power Transformer Prices

Little direct information on price trends for power transformers was collected in the course of this study, mainly because the data for these products are almost entirely from purchasers and no purchaser is likely to buy identical items year after year. Even when we pooled the data from many purchasers it was difficult to find observations in successive years for products identical with respect to the short list of specifications available, and those that did have corresponding specifications probably differed in other characteristics for which we did not have information.

In such a product, for which each individual sale involves some degree of custom tailoring, prices supplied by sellers for an identical product over time are likely to be somewhat artificial. The agency requesting the price cannot even request actual prices because there will be few, if any, sales of the exact product specified by the collecting agency. The reported price is even more likely than usual to represent a list price, i.e., without adjustments to meet competition. Since we do not have time-to-time sellers' data on identical products, and each buyers' report is of an item somewhat different from the previous one, our choice of methods for making price comparisons is narrowed. Place-to-place comparisons for power transformers, and for most of the other items in this subgroup, were made from bidding data, as described in the text. For comparisons over time, however, the only possible technique was to fit regressions to each year's bid prices and to measure the price changes from these.[24] This procedure was applied only to U.S. prices, because observations for the other countries were too few. Indexes for the other countries were inferred from the U.S. ones by using the place-to-place relatives from bid data.

The basic data for the regression analysis were approximately 150 offers by U.S. companies in bidding on power transformers in the United

[24] For a discussion of the use of regression methods, see Chapter 5.

States and abroad in 1957 and 1961 through 1964. Only the lowest U.S. offer was taken for each bidding, on the ground that it was the only one relevant for the buyers. It undoubtedly would have been desirable to include several characteristics of the transformers in the equation.[25] However, we did not collect detailed specifications, although they were available in any degree of completeness desired, because the data were intended for use in place-to-place comparisons, in which the requirement that buyers' specifications be met and the evaluation of offers by purchasers insured comparability among suppliers. For that reason, the only characteristic of the equipment that could be included in our equations was transformer capacity, and we were obliged to assume that either the other characteristics were not correlated with capacity or the year of purchase or that they did not affect the price.

It would have been possible to calculate place-to-place indexes through regression analysis also, but this procedure would not have been efficient. Bidding produces the effect sought from the regression analysis; i.e., the comparison of prices of comparably specified items, or at least having comparable minimum specifications. The advantage is that the number of specifications matched or otherwise taken into account is much greater than could be included in any regression possible from the existing data.

Given the limitations on the number of characteristics to be used in the equations the main remaining decisions concerned the form of the equations. The variables included were the capacity of the transformer, measured in millivolt-amperes, the year in which the bidding took place, and a dummy variable to distinguish bids on projects in the United States from those on foreign projects. The equations with the greatest number of variables included those listed plus interaction terms to permit the coefficient for capacity to vary from year to year. Four equation forms were fitted for each set of variables, arithmetic in both dependent and independent variables, logarithmic in both, the dependent variable arithmetic and the independent variables logarithmic, and vice versa.

The mixed equation forms could be dismissed immediately. Many fitted the data poorly, and the best of them were inferior to the corre-

[25] Dean and De Podwin included not only capacity (kilovolt-amperes) but also dummy variables for phase and load tap changing, and calculated separate equations for self-cooled and forced oil auto and conventional transformers. See Charles R. Dean and Horace J. De Podwin, "Product Variation and Price Indexes: A Case Study of Electrical Apparatus," *Proceedings of the American Statistical Association,* December 29, 1961.

sponding arithmetic or logarithmic equations. The arithmetic equations produced some high levels of $\bar{R}^2$ but the residuals gave clear evidence of curvilinearity in the relationship of price to capacity.

The arithmetic equations show substantial differences in slope from year to year as well as differences in level. In equation 1 of Table 13.24, for example, the coefficient for MVA ranges from .82 in 1962 ($820 per MVA) to 2.33 in 1957, and the other equations show similarly wide ranges. However, the slope measures are sensitive to the presence or absence of large transformers in the sample. They sometimes increased sharply when the largest ones were dropped, as in 1962 and 1964, and sometimes declined, as in 1957 and 1963. This effect can be seen by a comparison of Table 13.24, which includes all transformers, with Table 13.25, which excludes nine transformers of 300 MVA or over. The elimination of the large transformers narrows the range of year-to-year variation in slope, although it remains large in Table 13.25. The most drastic change in coefficients is in 1963, the year in which most of the large transformer bids took place. The coefficient was cut from 1.18 to 0.69, the lowest of all the years shown.

The results from dropping the large transformers illustrate their role in the high levels of $\bar{R}^2$ reached in the arithmetic regressions. The equations of Table 13.25, without the few largest transformers, produce much lower levels of $\bar{R}^2$, ranging from .73 to .78 instead of .85 to .86, most of them about one-tenth below the corresponding ones in Table 13.24.

The logarithmic equations, which are superior to the arithmetic, are shown in Table 13.26. Differences in slopes, by year, were not statistically significant except for 1964. We therefore settled on equation 12, with only a single slope for the other years and with year-to-year price changes represented by the coefficients of the year dummy variables. For 1964, since the dummy variable for the slope was significant, the measured price change was different at each size of transformer. Price relatives were calculated for several different sizes, and these were weighted by our estimate, from bidding data, of the relative importance of each size in terms of the value of the trade involved. All of the year dummy coefficients were statistically significant, and the preferred equation, 12, shows a sharp fall in price from 1957 to 1961, smaller declines to 1963, and the smallest of all in 1964.

The logarithmic equations present a number of contrasts with the arithmetic ones. Not only are the $\bar{R}^2$ higher, all between .93 and .94,

Table 13.24
Arithmetic Regression Equations for Prices of Power Transformers,
All Observations
(price in thousands of dollars; figures in parentheses are *t*-ratios)

	Equation Number				
	1	2	3	4	5
Constant term	36.272	40.359	23.545	23.594	17.144
	(3.6)	(4.3)	(3.6)	(4.7)	(2.2)
Dummy coefficient for					
1957	22.53	18.44			41.65
	(9.6)	(0.8)			(1.8)
1961	-10.90	-11.72			10.22
	(-0.8)	(-0.8)			(0.8)
1963	-34.47	-35.18			
	(-2.5)	(-2.6)			
1964	-38.71	-31.33			
	(-2.4)	(-2.2)			
Foreign project	12.10		0.12		4.75
	(1.1)		(0.01)		(0.5)
Slope (MVA)	0.8188	0.8066	0.8764	0.8762	0.9011
	(10.6)	(10.5)	(12.1)	(12.4)	(12.2)
Slope dummy coefficient					
1957	1.5094	1.5216	1.6189	1.6188	1.4271
	(8.1)	(8.2)	(10.4)	(10.5)	(7.6)
1961	0.6040	0.5965	0.5849	0.5846	0.5098
	(2.7)	(2.7)	(3.1)	(3.1)	(2.3)
1963	0.3662	0.3677	0.2293	0.2293	0.2278
	(3.7)	(3.7)	(2.6)	(2.7)	(2.6)
1964	0.7565	0.7353	0.6115	0.6116	0.6071
	(4.9)	(4.8)	(4.2)	(4.2)	(4.2)
Standard error	5.12	5.12	5.27	5.25	5.24
$\bar{R}^2$	.86	.86	.85	.85	.85

Table 13.25
Arithmetic Regression Equations for Prices of Power Transformers,
Excluding Large Transformers
(price in thousands of dollars; figures in parentheses are t-ratios)

	Equation Number				
	1	2	3	4	5
Constant term	36.835	40.562	31.313	29.296	24.781
	(5.7)	(6.8)	(6.9)	(8.3)	(4.6)
Dummy coefficient for					
1957	47.16	43.34			66.18
	(2.7)	(2.5)			(3.9)
1961	-10.84	-11.92			3.73
	(-1.3)	(-1.4)			(0.5)
1963	-19.20	-19.62			
	(-2.5)	(-2.5)			
1964	-38.82	-32.04			
	(-3.7)	(-3.4)			
Foreign projects	9.82		-4.50		0.50
	(1.4)		(-0.7)		(0.1)
Slope (MVA)	0.8797	0.8576	0.8497	0.8621	0.9644
	(10.4)	(10.3)	(10.6)	(11.1)	(11.3)
Slope dummy coefficient					
1957	1.0750	1.0974	1.6369	1.6443	0.9573
	(4.5)	(4.5)	(8.7)	(8.7)	(3.8)
1961	0.5394	0.5456	0.5295	0.5335	0.4395
	(3.7)	(3.7)	(4.0)	(4.1)	(2.9)
1963	-0.1890	-0.1870	-0.1799	-0.1784	-0.2736
	(-2.6)	(-2.6)	(-2.7)	(-2.6)	(-4.0)
1964	1.0125	0.8688	0.2011	0.1752	0.2441
	(2.23)	(2.0)	(0.5)	(0.4)	(0.6)
Standard error	3.02	3.04	3.32	3.32	3.17
$\bar{R}^2$	.78	.77	.73	.73	.75

Table 13.26
Logarithmic Regression Equations for Prices of Power Transformers, All Observations
(natural logarithm of price in thousands of dollars; figures in parentheses are t-ratios)

	Equation Number					
	7	8	9	10	11	12
Constant term	1.4781	1.7510	1.4631	1.7139	1.7395	1.4886
	(15.8)	(19.1)	(17.7)	(22.0)	(21.9)	(18.1)
Dummy coefficient for						
1957	0.838	0.714	0.820	0.735	0.740	0.830
	(6.2)	(4.8)	(7.3)	(6.0)	(6.0)	(7.5)
1961	0.289	0.240	0.262	0.227	0.224	0.260
	(3.6)	(2.7)	(3.8)	(3.0)	(2.9)	(3.8)
1963	-0.165	-0.197	-0.164	-0.180	-0.178	-0.159
	(-2.2)	(-2.3)	(-2.4)	(-2.4)	(-2.4)	(-2.4)
1964	-0.253	-0.068	-0.187	-0.016	-0.061	-0.258
	(-2.7)	(-0.7)	(-2.2)	(-0.2)	(-0.6)	(-2.8)
Foreign project	0.419		0.399			0.417
	(6.0)		(5.8)			(6.1)
Slope (ln MVA)	0.7555	0.7047	0.7620	0.7166	0.7084	0.7523
	(32.6)	(29.2)	(41.4)	(38.9)	(36.8)	(40.4)

(continued)

Table 13.26 (concluded)

	Equation Number					
	7	8	9	10	11	12
Slope dummy coefficient						
1957	-0.0013	0.0036				
	(-0.1)	(0.3)				
1961	-0.0094	-0.0059				
	(-0.7)	(-0.4)				
1963	0.0006	0.0023				
	(0.1)	(0.5)				
1964	0.0179	0.0134			0.0128	0.0183
	(2.2)	(1.4)			(1.4)	(2.3)
Standard error	.30	.33	.30	.33	.33	.30
$\overline{R}^2$	.94	.93	.94	.93	.93	.94

and the slopes virtually constant from year to year, but the equations calculated from the sample excluding the largest transformers (Table 13.27) are almost identical to those from the complete sample. The $\bar{R}^2$ are hardly reduced by the reduction in the sample, ranging from .91 to .94, and the coefficients are mostly very close as well, except those for 1964 and the constant term for 1957, which is unstable because of the small number of observations for that year.

Price indexes are derived below (Table 13.28) from equation 12 (previously mentioned as preferred), which includes a dummy variable for foreign projects and a slope dummy variable for 1964, and from two others. Of these, equation 11 is equation 12 minus the dummy variable for foreign projects, and equation 10 also excludes the 1964 slope dummy.

The movements of all three price indexes are fairly similar between 1961 and 1963 and those from equations 10 and 11 are similar throughout. However, the index from equation 12 declines in 1964 while the other two rise. It also declines more than the other two in 1957–61 and 1961–62, and rises more in 1962–63. The only really large difference is in the last year, when almost all the observations were from foreign projects; equation 12 implies that the apparent rise in U.S. prices between 1963 and 1964 is due entirely to this fact, and that the comparison with foreign projects alone shows a continuation of the price declines.

This international price index can be compared with a number of measures of domestic prices of power transformers and other electrical equipment, although the methods and time period covered differ from our own and the differences among the indexes cannot, therefore, be assumed to represent differences between domestic and international price behavior. These indexes and the international price index are shown on Chart 13.1 and Table 13.29.

The BLS series relies essentially on list or catalog prices and does not reflect what were apparently sharp short-term fluctuations in actual transaction prices. The indexes published by Dean and De Podwin and by Kuhlman [26] use transaction prices calculated by the electrical equipment manufacturers and fluctuate more sharply than the BLS series. The Dean and De Podwin index is, in addition, based on a regression

---

[26] Dean and De Podwin, *op. cit.;* John M. Kuhlman, "Theoretical Issues in the Estimation of Damages in a Private Antitrust Action," *Southern Economic Journal,* April 1967.

Table 13.27

Logarithmic Regression Equations for Prices of Power Transformers, Excluding Large Transformers
(natural logarithm of price in thousands of dollars; figures in parentheses are t-ratios)

	Equation Number					
	7	8	9	10	11	12
Constant term	1.4978	1.7557	1.5447	1.7992	1.8167	1.5680
	(17.0)	(19.5)	(18.8)	(22.5)	(21.9)	(19.0)
Dummy coefficient for						
1957	0.981	0.851	0.816	0.721	0.722	0.822
	(6.6)	(5.0)	(7.2)	(5.7)	(5.7)	(7.4)
1961	0.276	0.233	0.248	0.213	0.212	0.247
	(3.7)	(2.7)	(3.7)	(2.8)	(2.8)	(3.7)
1963	-0.153	-0.173	-0.215	-0.235	-0.237	-0.218
	(-2.2)	(-2.1)	(-3.2)	(-3.1)	(-3.1)	(-3.3)
1964	-0.302	-0.078	-0.264	-0.085	-0.132	-0.360
	(-3.0)	(-0.7)	(-3.1)	(-0.9)	(-1.2)	(-3.6)
Foreign project	0.422		0.403			0.419
	(6.5)		(6.1)			(6.3)
Slope (ln MVA)	0.7519	0.7058	0.7376	0.6908	0.6849	0.7281
	(32.7)	(28.2)	(37.2)	(33.5)	(31.4)	(35.8)

(continued)

Table 13.27 (concluded)

	Equation Number					
	7	8	9	10	11	12
Slope dummy coefficient						
1957	-0.0187	-0.0119				
	(-0.9)	(-0.5)				
1961	-0.0087	-0.0061				
	(-0.7)	(-0.4)				
1963	-0.0140	-0.0139				
	(-2.5)	(2.1)				
1964	0.0626	0.0270			0.0412	0.0784
	(1.4)	(0.5)			(0.8)	(1.8)
Standard error	.28	.32	.29	.32	.32	.28
$\bar{R}^2$	.94	.92	.93	.92	.91	.93

Table 13.28

Price Indexes for U.S. Power Transformers from Regression Equations,
1957, 1961–64
(1962 = 100)

Equation Number	1957	1961	1962	1963	1964
10	204.8	123.3	100.0	82.0	96.6
11	209.7	125.2	100.0	83.7	99.6
12	229.2	129.7	100.0	85.4	84.1

Source: Table 13.26.

Chart 13.1

Indexes of U.S. Power Transformer Prices, 1953–64

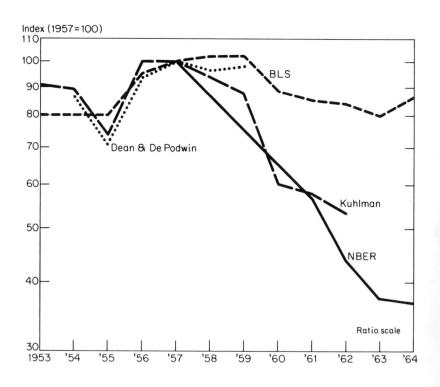

Table 13.29
Comparison of Several Indexes of U.S. Power Transformer
Prices, 1953, 1957, 1961—64

	1953	1957	1961	1962	1963	1964
1962 = 100						
NBER	NA	229.2	129.7	100.0	85.4	84.1
Kuhlman	170.2	187.4	108.7	100.0		
BLS	95.1	118.8	101.4	100.0	95.1	102.6

	$\dfrac{1957}{1953}$	$\dfrac{1961}{1957}$	$\dfrac{1962}{1961}$	$\dfrac{1963}{1962}$	$\dfrac{1964}{1963}$
Each year on earlier year as 100					
NBER		56.1	77.1	85.4	98.5
Kuhlman	110.1	58.0	92.0		
Dean and De Podwin	115.8				
BLS	125.0	85.4	98.6	95.1	108.0

Note: NBER index: Table 13.28 index, from equation 12. Kuhlman index: John M. Kuhlman, "Theoretical Issues in the Estimation of Damages in a Private Antitrust Action," *Southern Economic Journal,* April 1967. Dean-De Podwin index: Charles R. Dean and Horace J. De Podwin, "Product Variation and Price Indexes: A Case Study of Electrical Apparatus," *Proceedings of the American Statistical Association,* December 1961; the first year is 1954 rather than 1953. BLS index: Price relative for 5,000 KVA power transformer (see notes to Appendix F).

analysis of prices similar to that used in calculating the NBER international price indexes, but it is more elaborate because their data permitted the use of additional variables. The Kuhlman index seems to have been based on a comparison of each transaction price with a 1954 book price—the price that would have been charged for that set of specifications if the 1954 price list had been used. The difference between that procedure and the regression method is that in the regression analysis the prices of particular characteristics, such as capacity, are inferred from market prices while in Kuhlman's index the characteristic prices are taken from the price list. If the difference between actual and book prices were greater for transformers of higher capacity and if this relationship had remained constant over time but there had been a shift toward larger transformers, Kuhlman's index would have declined relative to a regression-based index.

In fact, Kuhlman's index resembles Dean and De Podwin's closely except in 1959, when it declined sharply while the Dean-De Podwin index rose. Even this divergence may have been only in timing, since the Dean-De Podwin index turned sharply downward in the first quarter of 1960, the last period for which it is available. The NBER and Kuhlman indexes show similar large declines from 1957 to 1961, but we do not have data on intermediate years with which to compare year-to-year fluctuations. In 1962 the NBER index continued its rapid fall, while the Kuhlman series dropped by only 8 per cent.

The resemblances among the three series are particularly striking in view of the large differences in methods of construction, source of data, and even in the transactions covered, since the NBER data referred to foreign and U.S. government sales and the other two mainly or entirely to sales to private utility companies. The similarity among these indexes reinforces the impression that the BLS index greatly exaggerates the stability of power transformer prices and may well give an incorrect impression of the trend as well.

Some independent confirmation of the price changes shown by the indexes other than the BLS can be found in newspaper and magazine reports on the antitrust case against the electrical equipment manufacturers. For example, the "white sale" of 1954–55, which began at about the end of 1954, and the reported resumption of price-fixing arrangements in 1956 are clearly marked in both the Kuhlman and Dean-De Podwin indexes, particularly in the quarterly data, not reproduced here, but the BLS index shows no trace of them.[27] The defense in the trial was quoted as reporting that power transformer prices ". . . sagged badly in 1958, well before the end of the conspiracy." [28] The BLS series showed a rise in price in 1958 while both Kuhlman and Dean-De Podwin confirm the reported decline. The reported decline after the ending of the conspiracy—". . . 30 per cent or more below the price levels of a year ago" [29]—matches closely the Kuhlman figure of 29 per cent from the fourth quarter of 1959 to the fourth quarter of 1960. The BLS reported a fall of less than 15 per cent in the same period.

[27] Richard Austin Smith, "The Incredible Electrical Conspiracy, Part I," *Fortune*, April 1961.
[28] "Electrical-Gear Makers Go on Trial Today in First Civil Suit on Price-Fixing Charges," *Wall Street Journal*, March 16, 1964.
[29] "Electrifying Surrender," *Economist*, December 10, 1960.

On the other hand, the continuation of declining prices after 1962 or 1963 shown by the NBER indexes is contradicted by some newspaper reports in late 1963. These suggested that prices may have reached a low point in late 1963 and then rebounded, a pattern more like that of the BLS index or of indexes from the NBER equations that did not include a foreign project variable. The reports of price increases were frequent from September 1963 through the end of the year.[30] However, beginning in March 1964, reports of increases and decreases in transformer prices alternated frequently, suggesting that attempts to raise prices were being defeated by undercutting of the new levels,[31] and that the rise in prices shown by the BLS that year may have been very temporary or may have reflected only list prices, not transactions prices. It must also be remembered that the NBER data for 1964 relate almost entirely to foreign sales, for which the price movement could have been different from that in domestic sales.

In general, from the combination of evidence from several sources, we conclude that the large decline in transformer prices shown by the NBER international price index is probably a valid description of the course of prices in these years despite the divergence from price trends given by BLS data. In addition, since the Kuhlman index follows at least the major movement of the NBER series after 1961, we used it to extrapolate the international price index back to 1953.

[30] "Prices of Heavy Electrical Goods Are Seen Firming," *Wall Street Journal,* September 18, 1963; "GE Increases Network Transformer Prices," *ibid.,* September 30, 1963; "Westinghouse Raises Prices 5% on Network Transformers," *ibid.,* October 4, 1963; "GE Increases Price 6% on Power Transformers," *ibid.,* October 14, 1963; "Electrical Comeback: Power Equipment Field Lifts Prices, Indicating Long Slump Is Ending," *ibid.,* December 11, 1963.

[31] "Westinghouse Reduces Prices on Large-Rated Power Transformers," *Wall Street Journal,* March 19, 1964; "McGraw-Edison Unit Lifts Prices of Some Transformers by 6%," *ibid.,* April 1, 1964; "McGraw-Edison Unit Lifts Prices of Larger Power Transformers," *ibid.,* May 15, 1964; "Westinghouse Raises Prices for Large Transformers," *New York Times,* May 22, 1964; "G.E. Cuts Its Price for Transformers," *ibid.,* August 8, 1964; "Electrical Equipment Price Increased by Westinghouse," *ibid.,* October 15, 1964; "Westinghouse Raises Prices on Some Power, Network Transformers," *Wall Street Journal,* October 15, 1964; "Big-Transformer Prices Cut by Westinghouse," *ibid.,* November 4, 1964.

14

TRANSPORT EQUIPMENT

TRANSPORT EQUIPMENT accounted for nearly a quarter of OECD exports of manufactured metals and machinery in 1963. Over half of these exports represented trade among the OECD countries themselves; an even higher proportion of aircraft exports (probably near 75 per cent) had OECD destinations while railway equipment was exported mainly (nearly 80 per cent) to non-OECD countries (Appendix A and sources cited). The United States accounted for about one-fourth of OECD transport equipment exports; and Germany, for almost as much. The addition of the United Kingdom raises the three-country share to nearly two-thirds of the OECD total (Table 14.1). At over 50 per cent, the U.S. share was highest in aircraft, one of the highest single-country proportions for any major manufactured product. The German share was highest in road motor vehicles. In ships, Japan was already by 1963 the most important single exporter. Import sources among markets differed greatly, with the United States dominant in the Western hemisphere and Japan; and the EEC countries, in Europe.

The U.S. share of OECD exports declined from almost half in 1953 to a quarter in 1964, with the main change taking place before 1961 (Table 14.2). The U.K. share also fell, although not quite as sharply. Large gains were made by Germany, the other EEC countries, and Japan. Between 1961 and 1964 the U.S. and U.K. shares in transport equipment exports declined, while the EEC and Japan gained.

International prices of transport equipment rose by 10 to more than 20 per cent between 1953 and 1964 (Table 14.3). Most of the increases occurred in the earlier years, prices having been rather stable in 1961–64 except for a U.K. rise. During these recent years the decline in the

Note: SITC 73. *Value of OECD Exports in 1963:* $10.5 billion; 23.6 per cent of study total. *Coverage:* Railway and road vehicles, aircraft, ships, and boats.

Table 14.1

OECD Exports of Transport Equipment (SITC 73),
by Origin, Destination, and Commodity Group, 1963
(dollars in millions)

	Value of Exports	Per cent of OECD Exports in 73	Share in OECD Exports (per cent)			EEC		Japan
			OECD	U.S.	U.K.	Total	Germany	
Total, all destinations and groups	$10,496	100.0	100.0	25.8	16.8	42.6	22.3	6.0
Destination								
U.S.	866	8.3	100.0		20.0	58.1	45.7	5.1
OECD Europe	4,233	40.3	100.0	7.1	14.6	65.7	32.6	1.9
U.K.	262	2.5	100.0	11.5		56.1	17.9	10.7
EEC total	2,186	20.8	100.0	7.2	12.7	76.3	30.4	0.2
Germany	529	5.0	100.0	7.6	7.0	79.0		0.4
Canada	690	6.6	100.0	86.7	5.9	5.9	4.9	0.1
Japan	73	0.7	100.0	64.4	11.0	21.9	12.3	
Latin America	946	9.0	100.0	55.6	7.7	22.3	9.7	6.8
Other	2,969	28.3	100.0	17.3	28.7	31.0	14.6	14.7
Unaccounted for by destination	719	6.9	100.0	100.0				a
SITC commodity group								
Railway vehicles (731)	459	4.4	100.0	30.5	12.6	35.5	16.1	10.9
Road motor vehicles (732)	6,802	64.8	100.0	24.7	20.4	47.2	28.1	3.1
Other road vehicles (733)	221	2.1	100.0	11.4	30.3	43.0	20.4	7.2
Aircraft (734)	1,543	14.7	100.0	53.0	8.4	32.1		0.4
Ships and boats (735)	1,467	14.0	100.0	2.7	8.1	34.4	17.4	23.1

Source: Appendix A.
[a]Less than 0.05 per cent.

Table 14.2
OECD Exports of Transport Equipment, 1953, 1957, 1961–64
(dollars in millions)

| | Value of OECD Exports | Share in OECD Exports (per cent) | | | | | |
		OECD	U.S.	U.K.	EEC Total	Germany	Japan
		INCLUDING SWITZERLAND AND SPAIN					
1964	$11,924	100.0	25.1	15.3	42.6	22.1	7.0
1963	10,496	100.0	25.8	16.8	42.6	22.3	6.0
1962	9,437	100.0	29.0	16.8	40.9	20.8	5.0
1961	8,882	100.0	28.0	18.3	41.0	21.4	5.4
		EXCLUDING SWITZERLAND AND SPAIN					
1961	8,865	100.0	28.0	18.3	41.0	21.4	5.4
1957	7,226	100.0	36.3	20.3	30.1	16.2	5.9
1953	4,720	100.0	46.9	22.0	21.5	9.1	2.5

Source: Appendix B.

U.K. share is thus in the direction that would be expected from changes in relative prices. The same cannot, on the other hand, be said of the decline in the U.S. share; U.S. price competitiveness improved after 1961, markedly with respect to the United Kingdom and marginally vis-à-vis the EEC countries. However, the largest share gainers during this period were Japan and other OECD countries, for which we do not have price indexes except for some individual groups for Japan. U.S. price levels in 1964 were notably above those of Germany and the United Kingdom and slightly above those of the EEC as a whole.

These overall average price relationships conceal widely differing situations for the major types of transport equipment. In railway vehicles and aircraft, price trends were favorable to the United States, and its prices were lower, particularly at the end of the period, than those of its chief OECD competitors. For ships and boats the opposite was true: EEC and Japanese prices declined from around two-thirds of U.S. prices in 1953 to roughly half in 1964. The picture was more mixed in the important road motor vehicle group.

Table 14.3
International Prices, Price Competitiveness, and Price Levels, Transport
Equipment, 1953, 1957, 1961–64

	1953	1957	1961	1962	1963	1964
INTERNATIONAL PRICE INDEXES (1962 = 100)						
U.S.	89	94	96	100	99	100
U.K.	87	94	100	100	102	107
EEC	94	98	97	100	101	102
Germany	90	95	96	100	101	101
INDEXES OF U.S. PRICE COMPETITIVENESS (1962 = 100)						
Relative to						
U.K.	98	100	104	100	103	107
EEC	107	105	101	100	101	102
Germany	102	101	100	100	102	101
INTERNATIONAL PRICE LEVELS (U.S. FOR EACH YEAR = 100)						
U.S.	100	100	100	100	100	100
U.K.	85	87	90	87	89	93
EEC	102	100	96	96	97	98
Germany	94	94	92	93	94	93

Source: International price indexes from Appendix C; price competitiveness indexes,
Appendix D; price levels, Appendix E.

Railway Vehicles [1]

Trade

Most OECD exports of railway vehicles were to the less developed
countries. The OECD countries were the destination of only about $110
million of railway vehicle exports in 1963 (Appendix A), and only
Germany sold most of its exports within Europe. The United States,
the United Kingdom, and Japan had practically no sales to European
countries; the great bulk of their sales went to less developed countries.
Exports to all the main railway vehicle exporting countries—the United

[1] SITC 731. *Value of OECD exports in 1963:* $0.5 billion; 1.0 per cent of study total.
Coverage: Railway locomotives, freight and passenger cars, and parts.

States, the United Kingdom, Germany, and Japan—came to less than $15 million.

To some extent, the country pattern of trade reflects its commodity composition. The United States specialized in diesel locomotives (SITC 731.3), in which it was the dominant exporter (Table 14.4), and these were mainly imported by less developed countries. Germany, on the other hand, specialized in freight and passenger cars, of which a much higher proportion was bought by European countries. Freight cars in particular are bulky to ship and comparatively easy to manufacture or assemble, and therefore have been more subject to competition from local manufacture in less developed countries than locomotives. Electric locomotives, a minor item in which the EEC countries were the chief exporters, were sent almost entirely to less developed countries.

A specialization not revealed by the published trade data is that within diesel locomotives, U.S. firms produced mainly diesel electric locomotives,[2] while European firms led in production of diesel hydraulic locomotives. This specialization produced the rare phenomenon of locomotive imports into the United States: Twenty-one high-horsepower diesel hydraulic locomotives were ordered from Germany by two western railroads, operating along mountainous routes.[3] In these very high horsepower ranges, European, rather than U.S., producers, have been the technological leaders.

Railway vehicle exports by OECD countries have been relatively stagnant during the years covered by the study, ranging only between $400 and $500 million except in 1961 (Table 14.5). Export origins changed, however. The chief trends were a drastic decline in the U.K. share—from 28 per cent in 1953 to only 12 per cent in 1964—which involved a fall in the absolute value of exports as well, and a gain in the share of Canada and Japan from 4 to 12 per cent. The fall in the U.K. export share took place mainly between 1953 and 1961, and was accompanied by a substantial rise in the shares of both the United States and Japan, but the U.S. share fell back sharply by 1964.

Within the EEC, Germany gained at the expense of its partners, whose exports in 1964 were lower in absolute value than in 1953.

U.S. dominance in locomotive exports goes back at least to 1957,

---

[2] As can be seen in the locomotive orders data for the earlier years of the study published in various issues of *Railway Age* (January 14, 1957, for example).

[3] *Railway Age*, November 23, 1959, January 18, 1960, and January 7–14, 1963.

Table 14.4

OECD Exports of Railway Vehicles (SITC 731),
by Origin, Destination, and Commodity Subgroup, 1963

(dollars in millions)

| | Value of Exports | Per Cent of OECD Exports in 731 | Share in OECD Exports (per cent) | | | EEC | | |
			OECD	U.S.	U.K.	Total	Germany	Japan
Total, all destinations and subgroups	$459	100.0	100.0	30.5	12.6	35.5	16.1	10.9
Destination								
U.S.	4	0.9	100.0		17.1	12.2	2.4	
OECD Europe	90	19.6	100.0	4.4	5.6	81.1	51.1	
U.K.	2	0.4	100.0	5.6		55.6	5.6	
EEC total	38	8.3	100.0	5.4	4.7	80.5	43.6	
Germany	6	1.3	100.0	6.2	14.1	62.5		
Canada	16	3.5	100.0	93.8	6.2	a	a	
Japan	a	a	100.0	a	a	a	a	
Latin America	115	25.1	100.0	39.8	1.7	28.7	1.7	8.7
Other	234	51.0	100.0	32.5	20.9	23.9	11.1	17.1

(continued)

Table 14.4 (concluded)

SITC commodity subgroup	Value of Exports	Per Cent of OECD Exports in 731	Share in OECD Exports (per cent)						
			OECD	U.S.	U.K.	EEC Total	Germany	Japan
Steam locomotives (731.1)	$ 1	0.3	100.0		6.8	16.6	16.6	76.6
Electric locomotives (731.2)	28	6.1	100.0	20.3	1.1	65.9	11.6	10.1
Other locomotives (731.3)	173	37.7	100.0	56.9	7.1	15.6	3.5	1.4
Mechanically propelled cars (731.4)	23	5.0	100.0	8.4	4.0	47.1	23.3	38.3
Passenger cars, not mech. prop. (731.5)	36	7.8	100.0	6.1	1.1	52.1	34.3	32.3
Freight and maintenance cars, not mech. (731.6)	61	13.3	100.0	10.9	18.6	56.1	28.7	11.2
Parts of locomotives and rolling stock (731.7)	139	30.3	100.0	18.7	23.8	39.4	21.3	12.4

Source: Appendix A.
aLess than 0.05 per cent.

Table 14.5
OECD Exports of Railway Vehicles, 1953, 1957, 1961–64
(dollars in millions)

	Value of OECD Exports	Share in OECD Exports (per cent)					
		OECD	U.S.	U.K.	EEC Total	Ger-many	Japan
		INCLUDING SWITZERLAND AND SPAIN					
1964	$446	100.0	25.2	11.6	43.1	23.7	5.7
1963	459	100.0	30.5	12.6	35.5	16.1	10.9
1962	442	100.0	35.0	12.7	33.5	15.2	14.4
1961	404	100.0	38.6	9.7	36.4	19.2	8.4
		EXCLUDING SWITZERLAND AND SPAIN					
1961	399	100.0	39.1	9.8	36.8	19.5	8.5
1957	478	100.0	30.9	24.5	30.2	13.0	7.0
1953	426	100.0	25.4	27.9	40.5	14.2	2.2

Source: Appendix B.

but it has declined since then, and the U.S. share in other rolling stock has fallen substantially. The United Kingdom has lost ground as an exporter in both major types of rolling stock, while Germany has gained substantially in exports of railway vehicles other than locomotives.

Over time, the horsepower range of locomotives exported from the United States shifted considerably (see Table 14.6). More than 40 per cent, by number, of the locomotives exported in 1953 were of less than 600 horsepower, while in later years the proportion was rarely as high as the 16 per cent of 1964. On the other hand, locomotives of more than 2,400 horsepower, which did not appear in the export records at all before 1962, accounted for almost a quarter of exports in the last two years shown. In value of exports, of course, the more powerful locomotives are of still greater importance, since their prices are as much as twice as high as those of the smaller locomotives.

Nonprice Factors in Trade

One feature of the trade pattern for railway vehicles that suggests the unlikelihood of finding a close relationship between our measures

Table 14.6
U.S. Exports of Diesel Locomotives, by Horsepower,
1953, 1957, 1961–64

H.P. Range	1953	1957	1961	1962	1963	1964
NUMBER OF LOCOMOTIVES						
Under 600	52	4	29	40	18	39
600–1,200	55	101	276	78	164	58
1,300–2,400	13	206	267	313	209	104
Over 2,400			6	40	133	60
Total	120	311	578	471	524	261
PER CENT DISTRIBUTION						
Under 600	43	1	5	8	3	16
600–1,200	46	32	48	17	31	22
1,300–2,400	11	66	46	66	40	40
Over 2,400				8	25	23
Total	100	100	100	100	100	100

Note: Data are from *Railway Age,* January 20, 1964, and from corresponding
Review and Outlook issues for earlier and later years.

of prices and the flow of trade is the concentration among sources of
supply for particular importing countries; that is, many importing countries tend to purchase all, or almost all, of their locomotives or freight
cars from a single exporter in any one year and even over considerable
periods of time.

A possible explanation for this concentration is that the flow of
trade might be determined almost without regard to current prices, by
long-standing supplier relationships, by the need for compatibility between existing and new equipment, by the economy of taking advantage of existing stocks of spare parts and of employees' familiarity with
previously purchased equipment, by special financing arrangements, and
by other factors not reflected in price as we measure it. The operation
of such factors is suggested by some aspects of the trade pattern.

The operation of nonprice factors is suggested by the tendency of
many importers to buy from countries with which there is, or was, a

political relationship. The formerly French territories of Mauritania, Senegal, the Malagasy Republic, Niger, and Algeria, for example, purchased more than 96 per cent of their imports of railway vehicles and parts from France during the period 1958–64, while Kenya, Rhodesia, and Tanganyika imported almost entirely from the United Kingdom. The concentration is even greater for diesel locomotives in the four years for which data are available, 1961–64. The former French territories mentioned above imported all their locomotives from France.

Some flows of trade may have been associated with military or foreign aid relationships (South Korea and South Vietnam purchasing locomotives from the United States), and some may be examples of the influence of price, or of the other factors mentioned above. Peru, Israel, and Tunisia bought their diesel locomotives in the United States; New Zealand, in Canada; and Nigeria, in Germany. Data on freight cars are available only for 1961–63, but the same pattern emerges, with many countries buying all or almost all of their imports from a single source.

Because railroad investment for any particular line, and often for a whole country, is made in large lumps, the tendency to stay with one supplier is reinforced. A frequent pattern is of large-scale re-equipping for a few years followed by several years of small purchases, for which a change in supplier would be even more uneconomical than for a large investment. For example, Algeria made large purchases in 1958–59, and then much smaller ones in the following years. Nigeria's purchases were concentrated in 1958–60; Greece's in 1958–59 and 1962–63; Chile's in 1962–63; and those of the Union of South Africa, 1958–60. This concentration in time implies active bidding in one or two years, followed by several years in which at least part of the trade flow is determined by the results of the first year's competition.[4]

If the entire country is taken as a unit in examining trade data, the degree to which one year's purchase source determines the next year's tends to be underestimated. The larger countries have more than one railway line, and for any particular railroad the tendency to remain with the same supplier, ignoring current prices, would be stronger than for the country as a whole. Whatever the reason, the origin of a country's imports in any one year is clearly not independent of the origin

[4] *Trade by Commodities*, OECD Statistical Bulletin, Series C, 1964, and earlier volumes.

of the previous year's imports, and this correlation goes far beyond what could be explained on grounds of geographical proximity.

The pattern of trade in railway vehicles may be determined more by sources and types of financing than by what are usually regarded as price considerations. A large fraction of railway equipment imports were financed outside the importing countries, particularly in the case of imports by less developed countries. Total exports of railway vehicles by OECD countries to non-OECD countries amounted to almost $4 billion for 1953–63. As of the end of 1963, the International Bank had disbursed approximately three-fourths of a billion dollars in railroad loans signed in the years beginning with fiscal year 1953, the Export-Import Bank disbursed almost one-half a billion dollars for the same purpose in that period, and the Agency for International Development and its predecessor agencies lent more than $200 million for railroad equipment.[5]

World Bank loans have always involved international competitive bidding, but Eximbank and, in the later years of the study, AID financing were tied to the purchase of equipment in the United States. It is likely that a substantial proportion of other countries' aid has also been tied to the purchase of equipment from the lending country.

For the United States alone, total exports of railway vehicles were about $1.2 billion between 1953 and 1963, and U.S. aid financing was large enough to have accounted for a substantial part of that sum. However, it is difficult to make direct comparisons because the proceeds of a railroad development loan can be spent on products outside of SITC 731, such as rail or ties, construction or repair of vehicles, track, or other facilities, machine tools for repair shops, or various iron or steel products. On the other hand, some purchases of locomotives or other railway vehicles may be financed under loans for port or mining development or under mixed-purpose loans.

Price Trends

Information on price trends for all railway vehicles since 1953 is available only for the EEC, Germany, and the United States. All show price increases over the period as a whole, somewhat greater in the

---

[5] See *Statement of Loans*, IBRD, December 31, 1963; *Report to the Congress*, Export-Import Bank of Washington, annual issues, 1952–63, Part II; and various issues of the *Operations Report* of the Agency for International Development and the International Cooperation Administration, and *Paid Shipments* reports of the Mutual Security Agency.

Table 14.7
International Prices, Railway Vehicles, 1953, 1957, 1961–64
(1962 = 100)

	1953	1957	1961	1962	1963	1964
ALL RAILWAY VEHICLES (SITC 731)						
U.S.	83	96	102	100	101	102
U.K.	NA	NA	103	100	104	NA
EEC	74	84	95	100	101	103
Germany	74	84	95	100	101	103
LOCOMOTIVES (SITC 731.1–731.3)						
U.S.	100	108	103	100	99	98
U.K.	NA	NA	106	100	98	NA
Germany	74	83	94	100	101	103

Source: Appendix C.

EEC and Germany than in the United States, where the 1964 level was only six percentage points above that of 1957 as compared with nineteen percentage points in the other cases (Table 14.7).

Locomotive export price behavior for the two areas contrasted particularly strongly: U.S. prices apparently fell after a rise in 1957, while German prices, the only EEC prices available, increased by more than 25 per cent. Both countries' prices rose substantially between 1953 and 1957, but after that date U.S. locomotive prices fell in every year shown, while German prices increased in every year. The German price indexes are supposed to be free of the influence of quality changes, but it is possible that, with the aid of a larger amount of information on the relationship of horsepower to price of locomotives, we were more successful in producing a quality-adjusted index for the United States than for Germany, for which we relied heavily on the official export price data. However, there is evidence that almost any kind of index for the United States would show a smaller increase in price than the German series.[6]

[6] The index in Table 14.7 indicates a fall of 2 per cent in U.S. prices between 1953 and 1964, and the alternative indexes listed in the appendix to this chapter offer a range from a 10 per cent decline in U.S. prices to a 10 per cent rise. The 10 per cent decline is given by a price index constructed by valuing all locomotives purchased in 1963 at the prices that would have been charged in each of the other years, as estimated from regressions of price on horsepower for each year; and the 10 per cent rise, by

The German index can be compared with additional U.S. indexes for 1961–64. All the U.S. indexes, some derived from completely independent basic data, show stability in U.S. locomotive prices and even some decline in the last two years, while the German index continued to rise.[7]

Like the U.S. index, the U.K. locomotive index, in the few years for which it is available, declined substantially.

In railway vehicles as a whole in the first few years, U.S. prices rose more rapidly than Common Market prices. After 1961, American prices were stabilized, while EEC prices continued to increase. U.S. prices of freight cars rose much more than European ones, and much more than U.S. parts prices.

Possibilities for comparing the NBER indexes for the United States with other time-to-time measures, such as unit values and wholesale prices, are very few. No railroad equipment is included in the export unit value index of the U.S. Department of Commerce, and the Bureau of Labor Statistics wholesale price index covers railway rolling stock only since 1961.

The BLS index was very stable, showing only a rise of half a percentage point in 1962 and a decline, later reversed, of about the same amount after mid-1963. The NBER international price index declined slightly in 1962 and then rose, but ended in 1964 at virtually the 1961 level. Thus, the two indexes were almost identical in this period. Unfortunately, the components of the BLS index have not been published, and we do not know, therefore, whether the stability in the BLS index results, as in the NBER index, from a rise in freight car and parts prices offset by a decline in locomotive prices.

The Department of Commerce does not use locomotives in its export unit value index; but the unit value for diesel electric locomotives, except switching, was quite stable. For 1961–64 the unit value (dollars per locomotive) rose by about 2 per cent, while the NBER index fell by 4 per cent. The direction of the difference is as expected: Because

an ICC price index, the method of construction of which is not revealed by the source. The index actually used lies between the other two for 1953–61 and 1953–64. The first segment is constructed by linking indexes for locomotives of identical horsepower from year to year. The second segment, based on company reports of export prices, includes some adjustments, based on the regression, for changes in horsepower of specific locomotive models.

[7] See, however, the section on price competitiveness, below, and the appendix to this chapter for alternative measures of German price movements.

the average horsepower of locomotives has been increasing, the unit value should be biased upward as a measure of price.

International Price Levels

The United States appears to have been the lowest-priced exporter of diesel locomotives, except at the beginning of the period, and the lowest-priced exporter of railway vehicles as a whole, but by a smaller margin (Table 14.8). Indexes for railway vehicles other than locomotives, not shown in the table except as part of the total, indicate that the United Kingdom offered lower prices than the United States for parts of railway vehicles and that EEC prices were higher than those of the United States by more than 25 per cent in 1953 and by between 5 and 15 per cent in later years. Japanese prices for locomotives also

Table 14.8
Price Levels, Railway Vehicles, 1953, 1957, 1961–64
(U.S. for each year = 100)

	1953	1957	1961	1962	1963	1964
ALL RAILWAY VEHICLES (SITC 731)						
U.S.	100	100	100	100	100	100
U.K.	NA	NA	103	102	105	NA
EEC	109	105	115	122	123	125
DIESEL LOCOMOTIVES (SITC 731.3)						
U.S.	100	100	100	100	100	100
U.K.	NA	NA	112	110	115	NA
EEC	NA	NA	114	NA	NA	NA
Japan	NA	NA	104	NA	NA	NA

Note: Some of these indexes can be compared with indexes derived entirely from place-to-place data. Taking the United States as 100 in each case, the alternative indexes are as follows:

	1953	1957	1961	1962	1963
ALL RAILWAY VEHICLES					
EEC	101	113	115	133	111
DIESEL LOCOMOTIVES					
U.K.		118	112	128	111
EEC	94	112	114	140	110

Source: Appendix E.

were substantially higher than U.S. prices for the few years in which data are available.[8]

In most of the place-to-place comparisons, of which the indexes of Table 14.8 are composed, the equivalence, but not exact identity, of the locomotives offered by the various countries was insured by the requirement that each one meet the purchasers' specifications. In a number of instances, U.S. companies bid against their European licensees on the same locomotive models, and these give something of a check on the other bidding data, since the locomotives offered are alike in more respects than specified. Unfortunately, these cases are confined to 1959 and 1960, years for which we did not compute most of our measures. The ratios of European to U.S. prices for the same locomotive models ranged from 99 to 116 per cent, with an average of not quite 110 per cent. These comparisons confirm the finding of a U.S. price advantage in diesel locomotives but suggest a somewhat smaller difference than that shown in the more comprehensive listing.

The bid data on which the place-to-place indexes are based fall far short of covering all trade in railway vehicles. Particularly in locomotives, however, some very crude estimates suggest that they cover a significant part of the trade. The total value of contracts for which bidding data were examined was over $80 million, and almost all of them yielded some useful price comparisons, roughly $60 million in locomotive bids and $15 million in freight car bids. The coverage of the bids is uncertain, but it is clear that intra-OECD trade and exports under tied loans or grants are not covered at all. Exports of diesel locomotives by OECD countries to countries outside the OECD amounted to about $430 million from 1961 through 1963. Over $200 million in loans for railroad equipment were made by U.S. government agencies, mostly under arrangements which tied purchasers to U.S. suppliers. These figures suggest that purchases of locomotives not so

---

[8] Some price level comparisons can be made from place-to-place data alone, but they are more erratic and may be less reliable than those in Table 14.8 because they are based on a smaller number of observations. As summarized in the note to the table they confirm that diesel locomotive prices in both the United Kingdom and the EEC tended to be higher than U.S. prices, and that EEC prices for railway vehicles as a whole were also generally high. They confirm the upward trend in relative EEC prices from 1953 to 1961, but the picture for later years is not clear because of the very large rise in 1962 and fall in 1963. The low 1963 EEC-U.S. ratio casts some doubt on the steadily rising trend of German locomotive prices after 1961, a trend which is in any case doubtful because of the reportedly fierce competition in this area. However, the Germans had not, until 1964, been notably successful in this competition.

Table 14.9
U.S. Price Competitiveness, Railway Vehicles, 1953, 1957, 1961–64
(1962 = 100)

	1953	1957	1961	1962	1963	1964
ALL RAILWAY VEHICLES (SITC 731)						
Relative to						
U.K.	NA	NA	102	100	103	NA
EEC	89	86	94	100	100	102
Germany	88	85	94	100	100	101
LOCOMOTIVES AND SELF-PROPELLED CARS (SITC 731.1–731.4)						
Relative to						
U.K.	NA	NA	102	100	102	NA
Germany	74	77	91	100	102	105

Source: Appendix D.

tied were somewhat above $200 million in these three years, and some of these may have been tied to other countries' exporters. During that period our bid data on locomotives covered roughly $40 million in contract values.

Price Competitiveness

For railway vehicles as a whole, and notably for locomotives, U.S. price competitiveness relative to the EEC improved substantially over 1953–64, particularly in the five years 1957–62 (Table 14.9). The index for all railway vehicles declined from 1953 to 1957 and was almost stable after 1962, while that for locomotives shows constant improvement.[9] The data for U.S. price competitiveness relative to the United Kingdom run for too short a period to indicate a trend, but suggest little change from 1961 through 1963.

Since there were such large changes in price competitiveness of locomotives, it might be expected that they would be reflected in shifts in trade. We compare U.S. price competitiveness relative to Germany with ratios of German to U.S. exports in Chart 14.1. The shifts in trade do

[9] The alternative indexes, derived from the bid data, which are more erratic and are composed of a smaller number of observations, confirm the great improvement in U.S. price competitiveness between 1953 and 1962 and between 1957 and 1962, but suggest a reversal in 1963.

Chart 14.1

Price Competitiveness and Export Shares in Locomotives, United States
and Germany, 1957, 1961–64

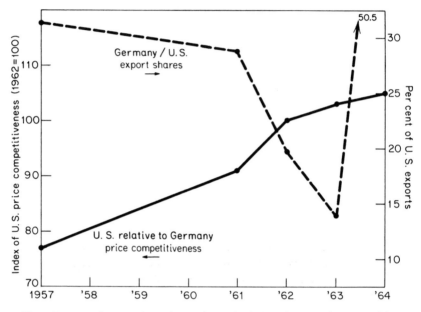

Note: Export values are from Appendix B; the index of U.S. price competitiveness
is from Table 14.9.

seem consistent with the changes in price competitiveness, except in
1964. In the other three cases the directions of movement are opposite,
as we would expect, and the rates of change appear to be in the appropriate order.

The high 1964 ratio of German to U.S. exports might be an accident,
not related to price movements, but it might also reflect on the validity
of the German export price indexes we use. As is mentioned in the
appendix to this chapter, bidding data suggest a considerable decline
in German prices in 1963 and 1964, but there were so few observations
that we did not calculate an index past 1963. The same data also suggest that the price ratio may have moved sharply against the United
States to the extent that the German place-to-place index relative to
the United States may have gone below 100. However, because of the
lack of adequate data, this must be considered only a suspicion, somewhat reinforced by the change in trade flows.

Just as changes in trade appear to be consistent with changes in price competitiveness, the structure of trade seems to fit the estimated price level relationships reasonably well. U.K. price competitiveness relative to the United States appears high in railway vehicle parts but low in locomotives, and U.K. exports of locomotives are much smaller than those of the United States, while U.K. exports of railway parts are higher. The EEC price position relative to the United States is more favorable in freight cars than in locomotives, and EEC exports of freight cars are far larger than those of the United States, while locomotive exports are lower.

In summary, we can say that the United States had a dominant competitive position in locomotives, as measured by both price relations and trade flows, but a lower and declining position in other railway vehicles, and that these indicators of price competitiveness were apparently reflected in the trade flows despite the many interferences with price competition mentioned earlier.

Road Motor Vehicles [10]

Trade

Motor vehicles, which constitute over 15 per cent of the total OECD exports covered by our study, have been one of the most dynamic commodity groups in the world economy. During the period of the study (1953–64) motor vehicle production grew more rapidly than industrial production as a whole, and world trade in motor vehicles expanded more rapidly than world vehicle production, total world commodity exports, or world exports of manufactured goods.[11]

---

[10] SITC 732. *Value of OECD exports in 1963:* $6.8 billion; 15.3 per cent of study total. *Coverage:* Passenger cars, buses, trucks, road tractors, and motorcycles.

[11] These statements are based on the following data:

	1953	1964	Ratio: 1964/1953
1. Motor vehicle production, excl. motorcycles (millions of units)	10.5	22.0	210
2. World industrial production (1958 = 100)	78.0	155.0	199
3. Motor vehicle exports (billions of dollars)	2.4	7.8	338
4. Manufactured exports (billions of dollars)	35.6	96.7	272
5. Total exports (billions of dollars)	78.3	169.8	217

The data above and in the two following paragraphs of text are from: Line 1: *Statistical Yearbook, United Nations,* 1962 and 1966; line 2: *Monthly Bulletin of Statistics,* United Nations, September 1964, September 1967; line 3: OECD exports (see Table 14.11); lines 4–5: *International Trade, 1965,* GATT, p. 1.

World production of both passenger and commercial vehicles doubled in terms of units, between 1953 and 1964. U.S. output expanded only by about a quarter, while in western Europe, where there was a smaller starting degree of market saturation, the rate of expansion was much more rapid. The output of commercial vehicles doubled in the four leading European producing countries, and the production of passenger cars increased more than threefold in the United Kingdom and France and more than sevenfold in Italy and Germany. Japan, starting from very low levels, developed an important motor vehicle industry with a commercial vehicle capacity second only to that of the United States.[12]

Despite a decline in its share of world production—from 71 per cent in 1953 to 42 per cent in 1964, the U.S. industry still produced more than three times as many units as Germany, the next biggest producer; and in value terms the gap was greater. Production became less concentrated not only as a result of the rise in the shares of the main European countries and Japan vis-à-vis the U.S. share, but also because of rapid growth in other countries including the U.S.S.R., Australia, Sweden, Brazil, Argentina, Spain, and East Germany.[13]

The growth in the output of the major European producers was stimulated by their ability to sell motor vehicles, particularly passenger cars, in foreign as well as home markets.[14] In 1964, for example, about half of German vehicle output was exported. For the United Kingdom and France exports were about a third of production; and for Italy, about a quarter. The great growth in Japanese output, on the other hand, was, at least through 1964, largely directed toward the home market; only about 10 per cent of output was exported. The United States, with its major producers owning many foreign manufacturing subsidiaries, exported only around 3 per cent of its output.

By 1964 Germany was the leading exporter of motor vehicles, having increased its share of OECD exports from 11 per cent in 1953 to 28 per cent (see Table 14.11). France and Italy also expanded their shares. The United States and the United Kingdom, on the other hand, dimin-

---

[12] The relative changes described in the text are generally valid descriptions of what took place, but the actual ratios would vary if other terminal years were compared. Between 1952 and 1965, for example, U.S. passenger vehicle output more than doubled, while that of France and the United Kingdom nearly quadrupled and that of Germany and Italy increased more than ninefold.

[13] All these countries produced at least 100,000 vehicles in 1964, with the U.S.S.R.'s 835,000 by far the largest output.

[14] See Chapter 15.

Table 14.10

OECD Exports of Road Motor Vehicles (SITC 732), by Origin, Destination, and Commodity Subgroup, 1963
(dollars in millions)

Destination	Value of Exports	Per Cent of OECD Exports in 732	Share in OECD Exports (per cent)					EEC			Japan
			OECD	U.S.	U.K.	Total	Germany	France	Italy		
Total, all subgroups	$6,802	100.0	100.0	24.7	20.4	47.2	28.1	9.9	5.7		3.1
U.S.	697	10.2	100.0		20.9	64.7	53.4	6.0	3.7		5.2
OECD Europe	2,816	41.4	100.0	6.8	18.2	69.8	39.3	14.5	8.6		0.5
U.K.	94	1.4	100.0	14.9		68.1	23.4	14.9	13.8		8.5
EEC total	1,596	23.5	100.0	6.3	14.9	76.1	35.3	18.8	10.6		0.2
Germany	266	3.9	100.0	10.9	8.6	75.2		36.1	28.2		0.4
France	284	4.2	100.0	6.0	19.7	73.2	44.7		19.0		0.1
Italy	326	4.8	100.0	1.5	20.2	77.6	48.2	28.5			0.3
Canada	605	8.9	100.0	87.4	5.3	6.4	5.6	0.8	0.2		0.2
Japan	26	0.4	100.0	46.2	15.4	38.5	34.6	1.7	1.4		
Latin America	643	9.5	100.0	65.8	7.9	20.7	12.3	3.9	4.0		2.5
Other	1,879	27.6	100.0	20.9	34.4	32.7	16.5	10.4	5.1		7.7
Unaccounted for	137	2.0	100.0	97.4					0.2		2.6

(continued)

Table 14.10 (concluded)

SITC commodity subgroup	Value of Exports	Per Cent of OECD Exports in 732	Share in OECD Exports (per cent)							
						EEC				
			OECD	U.S.	U.K.	Total	Germany	France	Italy	Japan
Passenger cars and chassis (732.1, 732.6)	$3,360	49.4	100.0	8.8	19.8	66.5	39.4	14.8	7.5	1.2
Buses (732.2)	90	1.3	100.0	28.3	21.0	44.8	21.1	2.7	5.4	4.3
Trucks (732.3)	1,032	15.2	100.0	30.6	23.6	31.7	20.5	6.2	3.1	7.3
Special purpose trucks (732.4)	155	2.3	100.0	72.8	8.3	13.8	6.1	4.3	0.8	2.3
Road tractors (732.5)	18	0.3	100.0	a	15.6	71.5	31.8	14.5	14.0	3.4
Chassis (excl. passenger cars) (732.7)	138	2.0	100.0	a	57.0	25.3	19.4	0.7	1.2	9.8
Bodies and parts (732.8)	1,842	27.1	100.0	50.5	19.1	25.1	15.8	4.9	3.2	1.0
Motorcycles and parts (732.9)	166	2.4	100.0	0.8	10.6	47.2	13.1	8.3	23.3	35.3

Source: Appendix A.
aNot reported separately by United States.

Table 14.11
OECD Exports of Road Motor Vehicles, 1953, 1957, 1961–64
(dollars in millions)

| | Value of OECD Exports | Share in OECD Exports (per cent) | | | | | | | |
| | | | | | EEC | | | | |
		OECD	U.S.	U.K.	Total	Ger-many	France	Italy	Japan
		INCLUDING SWITZERLAND AND SPAIN							
1964	$7,792	100.0	24.6	19.3	46.9	28.2	8.3	5.9	3.8
1963	6,802	100.0	24.7	20.4	47.2	28.1	9.9	5.7	3.1
1962	6,040	100.0	25.2	20.8	47.0	27.1	9.7	6.5	2.7
1961	5,336	100.0	24.8	20.8	47.6	28.0	9.9	6.4	2.6
		EXCLUDING SWITZERLAND AND SPAIN							
1961	5,324	100.0	24.8	20.8	47.7	28.1	10.0	6.4	2.6
1957	3,929	100.0	37.9	22.0	35.6	20.7	8.4	4.5	0.7
1953	2,367	100.0	46.0	26.1	22.9	11.1	7.4	2.6	0.2

Source: Appendix B.

ished in relative importance, the former dropping from 46 to 25 per cent and the latter from 26 to 19 per cent. Even their smaller shares in the rapidly expanding market, however, gave the United States and the United Kingdom substantially larger motor vehicle export proceeds in 1964 than they had in 1953.

Exports of the major countries differed substantially in their geographical destination and commodity composition. U.S. exports went largely to Canada (31 per cent) and to the less developed countries of Latin America and Asia (48 per cent); only a small fraction (11 per cent) went to European OECD countries (Table 14.10). The dominant markets for the United Kingdom and Japan were in Asia and Oceania, with OECD Europe a close second destination for the United Kingdom. Well over half of Germany's exports went to OECD Europe, but another third went to the United States and Asia.

The United States and Japan, unlike the European countries, exported more commercial vehicles (SITC 732 subgroups 2, 3, 4, 5, and 7) than passenger cars. Commercial vehicles comprise a wide range of products that vary in size and purpose. Their single most important use is to haul goods from one place to another. Within this category light vans and trucks with gross vehicle weights (GVW) of three tons or less are the most numerous.[15] The vehicles at this smaller end of the range are mass produced like automobiles, often under the same brand names and largely from the same parts. Numbers diminish and the large automobile producers' shares of the market decline with increasing size of vehicle, since the comparative advantage shifts to smaller and more specialized truck manufacturers. Styling becomes less important, and the difficulties of standardization increase with size, especially as purchasers with large freight volume have greater incentives to seek cost savings through trucks closely adapted to their specific needs. Thus, in the United States, for example, the big-three auto manufacturers accounted for nearly 90 per cent of new-truck registrations in 1965 for vehicles with a GVW of 6,000 pounds or less but for only around 30 per cent of those with a larger GVW.[16] The lighter vehicles almost all use gasoline engines even in Europe, while the heavier ones are more likely to be diesel, even in the United States. However, the proportion of diesel vehicles is higher in Europe; it has recently been estimated at 35 per cent, while diesels have been accounting for only 5 to 6 per cent of U.S. factory sales of trucks.[17]

Aside from goods delivery, commercial vehicles are designed for passenger transport (buses) and a variety of special purposes including fire fighting, street cleaning, concrete mixing, and mobile lighting, generating, and testing equipment.

Both in production and in international trade, however, trucks per se are of overwhelming importance, and we therefore do not regard it as a serious disadvantage that we rely on truck prices for our time-to-time index of commercial vehicle prices. In 1963, trucks (SITC 732.3) accounted for over 70 per cent of OECD commercial vehicle exports. Most of the balance was made up of special-purpose trucks (SITC 732.4) and chassis for trucks (included with bus chassis in SITC 732.7).

Japan and Italy were the main exporters of motorcycles. Japan's exports of motorcycles, which exceeded its passenger car exports in

---

[15] Gross vehicle weight is the weight of the vehicle plus its payload. The proportion of the payload rises from around 25 per cent for small vans to more than 75 per cent for very large trucks. On this and other points see the informative report in the *Economist*, July 8, 1967, pp. vii ff.

[16] *Automotive Industries*, March 15, 1967, p. 103.

[17] *Economist*, July 8, 1967, p. xxv; and *Automotive Industries*, March 15, 1967, p. 97.

value in 1963, more than tripled between 1962 and 1964, and Japan replaced Italy as the largest motorcycle exporter.

Over half of U.S. exports in this division consisted of parts. For the European exporters complete vehicles, particularly passenger cars, dominated exports (see Appendix A). The reason for the difference is probably that, to a much greater extent than the other countries, the United States had direct investments in automobile plants in Canada, Latin America, and other areas to which parts that could not be produced locally on an economical basis were shipped. In many of these markets, government policies were directed toward the local production of an increasing proportion of the completed vehicle; however, the expansion of production in those areas was great enough to keep U.S. parts exports rising. It is interesting to note that in Latin America where Germany was also involved with direct investment, the share of parts in German exports approached that of the United States. The United States also had a relatively favorable price position for parts (see below), but the low share of parts in U.S. exports to Europe does not support the hypothesis that price was the main factor accounting for large U.S. parts exports.[18]

Price Trends

For passenger cars, which accounted for about half of 1963 trade in motor vehicles, regression methods were used to estimate price changes. The nature of the data, the problems encountered in their use for our purposes, and the results, which are merely summarized in part of Table 14.12, are considered more fully in the next chapter. Regression methods were applied also to trucks for U.S. and U.K. indexes.[19]

---

[18] It is possible also that the U.S. reporting system tended to classify incomplete vehicles with parts to a greater extent than that of other countries. The Europeans followed the Brussels nomenclature while the United States did not. The Brussels classification, which underlies the SITC, calls for the assignment of incomplete vehicles to the same category as complete ones as long as they have "the essential character" of the completed vehicle (e.g., a vehicle without its engine or interior fittings). Cf. *Explanatory Notes to the Brussels Nomenclature*, Customs Co-operation Council, 1955, Vol. III, p. 990. The U.S. classification, at least before 1965, contained a category of "parts and accessories, n.e.c.—for assembly" which seemed to include all except "complete knockdown vehicles," and these incomplete vehicles were classified as parts in U.S. export data. Cf. *Schedule B—Statistical Classification of Domestic and Foreign Commodities Exported from the United States*, January 1, 1958 Edition. Changes effective through July 1, 1964, U.S. Bureau of the Census.

[19] The indexes were derived from double log equations using as independent variables GVW, wheelbase, displacement, and dummy variables for trucks equipped with a cowl, for those with a diesel engine (for the United States after 1962 and for the United Kingdom), and for forward control (United Kingdom only). The method of flexible

Table 14.12

International Prices, Road Motor Vehicles, 1953, 1957, 1961—64

(1962 = 100)

	1953	1957	1961	1962	1963	1964
United States						
Passenger cars	90	89	94	100	100	100
Commercial vehicles	86	92	93	100	97	93
All motor vehicles	89	91	94	100	99	98
United Kingdom						
Passenger cars	98	93	99	100	101	106
Commercial vehicles	81	95	98	100	100	102
All motor vehicles	92	95	100	100	101	106
EEC						
Passenger cars	102	100	95	100	102	102
Commercial vehicles	81	84	94	100	101	102
All motor vehicles	95	95	96	100	102	103
Germany						
Passenger cars	95	95	94	100	102	100
Commercial vehicles	81	84	94	100	100	100
All motor vehicles	90	92	95	100	102	101

Source: Appendix C.

The independent variables in the equation relate only to certain standard features of trucks. Truck sales, especially in the larger sizes, usually involve custom combinations of features that fit the special needs of buyers more sophisticated and more expert than passenger car purchasers. Not only are there many body styles [20] that can be combined with a given model having a certain gross vehicle weight and displacement, but many of the manufacturers offer a wide choice of options

pooling (see Chapter 5 on regression methods) was applied to successive pairs of years for each country. The resulting estimates of price changes for U.S. and U.K. commercial vehicles, shown in Table 14.12, would not have been radically different if alternative equations with almost equal economic and statistical claims to selection had been used. The price changes between successive years were usually within one or two percentage points of those in Table 14.12 and rarely different by more than three or four points. The differences for successive periods tended to be offsetting, so that the consistent use of an alternative equation would have in most cases produced a similar estimate of price change between 1953 and 1964.

[20] However, truck manufacturers generally build only the smaller truck bodies.

with respect to engines, rear axles, and transmissions, and other features. However, the high proportion of price variation that our variables were able to explain is encouraging.

For motor vehicle parts, which account for over one-fourth of the total trade for the group, we based our indexes partly on the car and truck price indexes and partly on direct price observations for parts. Car and truck prices are relevant because a large portion of the so-called parts trade probably consists of partially completed cars and trucks.

Over the period 1953–64 the international price indexes for motor vehicles as a whole rose about 10 per cent in the United States and Germany (with generally similar timing) and by somewhat more in the United Kingdom (see Table 14.12). However, there is an important difference in the pattern of the price changes: In the United States, passenger car prices rose more and truck prices substantially less than in Europe.

Our data are presented in Table 14.13 in the form of price relatives for successive pairs of years so that they may be more readily compared with official wholesale and export price series reweighted by our international trade weights. For the United States and Germany, the major differences between the NBER international price indexes and the wholesale indexes are in the 1957-to-1953 comparisons, when the former show only slight price increases whereas the latter show a notable rise in U.S. prices and a fall in German ones. These differences dominate the results for the period as a whole, and lead to opposite conclusions about the change in the relative price position of the United States vis-à-vis Germany. Our indexes show a relative decline in U.S. prices of commercial vehicles but little overall change, while the wholesale price indexes show a fairly large rise in U.S. prices. In France, the wholesale prices seem to be biased downward, relative to the NBER indexes for passenger cars, while in Japan they appear to have an upward bias. Since our prices for the motor vehicle group for the most part refer to domestic list prices rather than to export prices (which have been gathered for virtually all other parts of our study), we attribute the differences to method and, possibly, to sampling variation. As we stated in Chapter 5, we believe that our regression methods take account of a wider segment of the market and are more consistent and more systematic than those that underlie the official indexes.

Table 14.13

Official Wholesale and Export and NBER International Price Indexes for
Total, Passenger, and Commercial Motor Vehicles, 1953, 1957, 1961–64

	$\dfrac{1957}{1953}$	$\dfrac{1961}{1957}$	$\dfrac{1962}{1961}$	$\dfrac{1963}{1962}$	$\dfrac{1964}{1963}$
UNITED STATES					
NBER					
Passenger cars	99	105	107	100	100
Commercial vehicles	107	101	108	97	96
Total	102	104	106	99	99
Wholesale price index					
Passenger cars	112	104	99	99	100
Commercial vehicles	113	106	100	99	100
Total	113	105	100	100	99
GERMANY					
NBER					
Passenger cars	100	99	106	102	98
Commercial vehicles	103	113	106	100	100
Total	101	104	106	101	99
Wholesale price index					
Passenger cars	88	105	103	101	100
Commercial vehicles	97	110	102	101	100
Total	93	107	102	101	100
Export price index					
Passenger cars	99[a]	103	100	99	100
Commercial vehicles	NA	104[b]	101	100	100
Total	100	105	100	100	101
FRANCE					
NBER					
Passenger cars	101	86	105	103	105
Wholesale price index					
Passenger cars	103	77	102	102	101
Commercial vehicles	110	86	103	103	104
Total	105	80	102	102	102

(continued)

Table 14.13 (concluded)

	$\dfrac{1957}{1953}$	$\dfrac{1961}{1957}$	$\dfrac{1962}{1961}$	$\dfrac{1963}{1962}$	$\dfrac{1964}{1963}$
		JAPAN			
NBER					
Passenger cars	NA	71	95	95	97
Wholesale price index					
Passenger cars	73	82	99	99	97
Commercial vehicles	105	92	99	99	100
Total	90	88	99	99	98
Export price index					
Passenger cars	NA	NA	98	98	100
Commercial vehicles	NA	NA	100	99	100
Total	NA	NA	99	99	100

Source: International prices from Appendix C; wholesale prices from Appendix F. Export prices for Germany are from *Preise-Löhne-Wirtschaftsrechnungen,* Reihe 1, Preise und Preisindices für Aussenhandelsgüter, Statistisches Bundesamt, Wiesbaden, various issues; for Japan, *Export and Import Price Index Annual,* Bank of Japan, various issues.

[a]For 1957/1954.

[b]For 1961/1958.

Another way of looking at these changes is through the indexes of price competitiveness in Table 14.14. In passenger cars, U.S. price competitiveness declined relative to Germany and the EEC; it declined relative to the United Kingdom also, but recovered in the final year as U.K. prices rose relative to all the others. Larger changes in price competitiveness, rather consistently favorable to the United States, were found for trucks. This finding seems consistent with the relatively better export performance of the United States in commercial vehicles as compared to passenger cars.

Price Levels

We are able to provide only very rough estimates of differences in levels of export prices for motor vehicles.

Even in the case of passenger cars, where we had relatively extensive data (see Chapter 15), product differentiation and differential pricing between markets made it difficult to summarize price relationships between each pair of countries in a single average figure. We obtained

Table 14.14
U.S. Price Competitiveness, Road Motor Vehicles, 1953, 1957, 1961–64
(1962 = 100)

	1953	1957	1961	1962	1963	1964
BASED ON NBER INTERNATIONAL PRICE INDEXES						
Relative to U.K.						
Passenger cars	109	105	106	100	101	106
Commercial vehicles	94	104	106	100	103	110
All motor vehicles	104	105	106	100	102	107
Relative to EEC						
Passenger cars	114	113	102	100	102	102
Commercial vehicles	95	91	102	100	104	110
All motor vehicles	107	105	102	100	103	104
Relative to Germany						
Passenger cars	106	107	101	100	102	100
Commercial vehicles	95	91	102	100	103	107
All motor vehicles	102	102	101	100	102	102
BASED ON WHOLESALE PRICE INDEXES						
Relative to Germany						
Passenger cars	121	95	96	100	102	102
Commercial vehicles	111	95	98	100	102	102
All motor vehicles	118	95	97	100	100	102
Relative to France						
Passenger cars	143	132	97	100	103	104
Commercial vehicles	124	120	98	100	104	108
All motor vehicles	137	128	98	100	103	105
Relative to Japan						
Passenger cars	196	128	101	100	100	96
Commercial vehicles	126	117	101	100	100	100
All motor vehicles	169	124	101	100	99	98

Note: Figures show ratios of foreign to U.S. international price indexes. The international price indexes used in each foreign-U.S. comparison for the table are comparable in coverage and method, while those in Table 14.12 represent the best estimates that could be made for each country, regardless of comparability. The differences, however are slight.

Source: Appendixes D and F.

different results in each of the four comparisons we made—of home prices, of prices in the U.S. market, of prices in the U.K. market, and of prices in the French market. We regard the comparisons made for the domestic markets and for the French market as the most reliable, but knowing that some motor car manufacturers pursue pricing policies that discriminate between various markets, we do not feel warranted in discarding the other two sets of results.

Even if all four sets of results were perfectly reliable, their valid combination into overall averages for each pair of countries would require knowledge that we do not possess. That is, we would have to know to what extent the price relationships observed in these comparisons represent other export markets for which we have no data. In the absence of this information, we used the U.S. market price relationships to represent the 18 per cent of world exports that went to the United States and Canada, the U.K. market data to carry the 21 per cent weight of exports to OECD Europe other than the EEC, the French market data to stand for the 33 per cent of exports to the Common Market, and the home market comparisons to represent the 28 per cent of world exports that went to other destinations.[21] The results for 1964 are: United States, 100; United Kingdom, 84; Germany, 89; France, 114; and Italy, 102.

Thus, this method of averaging indicates that U.S. and Italian passenger car export prices were about the same, that U.K. and German passenger car export prices were lower (and not very different from one another), and that French prices were higher.

Regression methods like those used to derive the automobile results could be employed in the case of trucks only for the U.K.-U.S. comparison.[22] Our data indicated widely differing U.K.-U.S. price relationships for diesel- and gasoline-powered trucks, and since U.S. diesel

[21] The weights refer to 1963, the year used for weighting purposes in the study as a whole.

[22] The numbers of trucks included in the sample by size and type of engine, were as follows:

GVW (lbs.)	United States			United Kingdom		
	Diesel	Gas	Total	Diesel	Gas	Total
Under 6,000	0	3	3	2	4	6
6,000–9,999	0	2	2	2	2	4
10,000–14,999	0	3	3	4	4	8
15,000–19,999	0	3	3	12	14	26
20,000–24,999	5	21	26	14	20	34
25,000–29,999	2	8	10	11	3	14
Total	7	40	47	45	47	92

observations were available only for large trucks, it seemed best to treat the two kinds of trucks separately. A pooled U.K.-U.S. double log regression for gasoline trucks indicated that U.K. list export prices were 9 per cent higher than those of the United States.[23] When, on the other hand, the United Kingdom prices of the seven U.S. diesel trucks were estimated from a U.K. equation for diesels only,[24] the U.K.-U.S. price relatives ranged from 41 to 53 and averaged 49. Our overall estimate for trucks thus turns critically on the relative importance of diesel and gasoline trucks in OECD exports. On the basis of very incomplete information,[25] we place the share of diesels at one-third. On this basis, the U.K.-U.S. relative for trucks comes to 88. We also had more than a score of direct export price comparisons for 1961–64 from foreign purchasers, including a number of comparisons based on bidding procedures. Many of these were for heavy trucks designed for construction projects, such as dump trucks and cement mixers, and the United States tended to show up more favorably; U.K. prices were 8 per cent higher on the average. Ideally, we should have had trade data on the importance of these kinds of trucks relative to urban or interurban delivery trucks, but we simply averaged the results of the direct comparisons and the regressions. When we added bid data for special-purpose vehicles (e.g., trucks equipped with cranes) and road tractors, allowing these to represent 15 per cent of total commercial vehicle exports and trucks, the other 85 per cent, our final estimate of the U.K.-U.S. price relative for commercial vehicles came to 100.

The evidence on the price position of German trucks relative to that of the United States and the United Kingdom pointed fairly consistently to higher German prices. The list export prices of the four rather small trucks used for the measurement of time-to-time price changes were about 5 per cent higher than U.K. prices estimated from a U.K. equa-

[23] $\bar{R}2 = .9840$. Independent variables: GVW, wheelbase, displacement, and dummies for cowl and forward control. Coefficients more than two times their standard errors except forward control (1.9). Retained slope dummies: cowl and displacement.

[24] $\bar{R}^2 = .91$. Independent variables: GVW, wheelbase, displacement, and dummies for cowl and forward control. The forward control coefficient was 1.5 times its standard error; all others were more than two times their standard errors.

[25] Diesels were 18 per cent of the total dollar value of 1964 truck exports for the United States and probably between 40 and 45 per cent of the value of U.K. exports. If it is assumed that the other OECD countries had diesel ratios of around 40 per cent the trade shares of Table 14.6 indicate that diesels accounted for about one-third of truck exports (*United States Exports of Domestic and Foreign Merchandise; Commodity by Country of Destination*, 1964 Annual, U.S. Dept. of Commerce, Report FT 410, June 1965; *Accounts Relating to the Trade and Navigation of the United Kingdom*, U.K. Board of Trade, December 1964).

tion for gasoline trucks.[26] However, two private purchasers, one in the United States and one abroad, reported German prices for smaller vehicles at about the same level as or lower than the U.S. prices. In international bidding, on the other hand, German prices turned out to be substantially higher (not as much higher for special-purpose vehicles as for ordinary trucks). Putting together these various sources of information as in the U.K.-U.S. comparison, we arrived at a German-U.S. price relative for commercial vehicles of 105. Scattered bid data and price comparisons by purchasers indicate that French and Italian commercial vehicle export prices were in general slightly higher than German ones.

The estimates for bodies and parts (SITC 732.8), the remaining major component of SITC 732, were based on direct U.K.-U.S. comparisons of about sixty parts and on direct German-U.S. comparisons of about forty parts. Most of the data came from a survey made by a major manufacturer to select its own sources of supply; the rest of the information came from two equipment manufacturers and several purchasers. Although there was a wide dispersion of price relatives, U.K. prices tended to be higher than those of the United States, and German and EEC prices higher still.

Our final 1964 indexes for motor vehicle price levels are: United States, 100; United Kingdom, 93; EEC, 106; Germany, 100.

Aircraft [27]

Trade

The United States was by far the chief exporter of aircraft and parts, accounting for more than half of all exports in 1963 (Table 14.15). Next in importance, but far behind, came the Netherlands, the United Kingdom, France, Belgium-Luxembourg, Canada, Italy, and Germany. The EEC countries as a group were responsible for almost one-third of OECD exports.

---

[26] The equation ($\bar{R}^2 = .98$) is analogous to that used in the pooled U.K.-U.S. regression and gives the same result for the U.K.-U.S. price relative (108) when used in conjunction with a corresponding U.S. equation. We did not estimate U.S. prices for the German specifications because the displacement of the German trucks was smaller than that of any trucks in the U.S. sample.

[27] SITC 734. *Value of OECD exports in 1963:* $1.5 billion; 3.5 per cent of study total. *Coverage:* Almost entirely heavier-than-air aircraft and parts.

Table 14.15

OECD Exports of Aircraft and Parts, by Subgroup, 1963, and by Year, 1953, 1957, 1961–64
(dollars in millions)

| | Value of OECD Exports | Share in OECD Export (per cent) | | | EEC | | Japan |
		OECD	U.S.	U.K.	Total	Ger-many	
SITC commodity subgroups; 1963	$1,543	100.0	53.0	8.4	32.1	3.9	0.4
Heavier than air (734.1)	847	100.0	56.0	6.7[a]	32.6	0.5	0.4
Parts and airships (734.9)	697	100.0	49.3	10.5	31.4	8.1	0.3
Group as a whole							
1964	1,764	100.0	48.4	6.9	31.7	2.3	0.3
1963	1,543	100.0	53.0	8.4	32.1	3.9	0.4
1962	1,507	100.0	65.0	7.6	18.6	0.7	0.3
1961	1,436	100.0	63.9	11.5	17.2	0.5	0.4
1957	1,125	100.0	71.8	17.3	6.2	b	b
1953	975	100.0	80.2	12.1	2.7	b	b

Source: Appendix A and B.
[a]Includes airships
[b]Less than 0.05 per cent

The statistics on aircraft exports, particularly those on destination, have a number of deficiencies. Almost 40 per cent of OECD exports are U.S. special-category items for which no destinations are shown. Furthermore, the figures for the United States published by the United Nations and the OECD contain numerous errors resulting from misclassification in the translation of U.S. export data into SITC categories. (These errors, and the corrections made in the U.S. figures, are described in the notes to Appendix A.) Another indication of unreliability in the published information are the very large differences between import and export records for the same pairs of countries. Germany, for example, is reported as the destination for $133 million in exports of complete aircraft (SITC 734.1) from EEC countries, but reports only $6 million in imports from these countries. Belgium reports exports of $18 million in complete aircraft to the United Kingdom, but the United Kingdom reports less than $9 million in imports of all aircraft and parts (probably mostly parts) from all countries except the United States, France, Canada, and the Commonwealth. The most likely explanation for at least some of these discrepancies is that military aircraft were involved, and therefore importing countries did not report them for security reasons or because they were for the use of international forces.

The destinations of U.S. aircraft and parts exports, as far as they could be surmised from the data, were less concentrated in Europe than those of the EEC countries (see sources listed in Appendix A). Almost two-thirds of EEC exports were to other EEC countries; and more than three-quarters, to OECD Europe. The U.S. ratios, estimated from import data, were one-third to the EEC and one-half to OECD Europe. The U.K. export ratios to Europe were even lower. The true U.S. ratios were undoubtedly lower than the reported ones because unreported exports must have been mainly to countries outside Europe.

Exports by countries other than the United States and the United Kingdom are, in a sense, inflated by the process of subcontracting large portions of the total cost of an aircraft to other countries. The individual part is thus frequently reported twice in the export data, once as a part and once as part of a complete aircraft. The Fokker Friendship, one of the main factors in Netherlands aircraft exports, includes elements manufactured in the United Kingdom, Germany, and France.[28] The

[28] "That Company, Fokker," *Economist,* August 28, 1965.

building of F104 and F104G fighter aircraft, some of which were exported by four European countries, Canada, and Japan, at a cost of $2.8 billion, resulted in $1.2 billion of expenditures in the United States, more than 40 per cent of the total.[29] The largest element of "duplication" in aircraft exports probably consists of engines (SITC 711.4 when reported separately), but electronic equipment and other items are also important.

Parts of aircraft, with other minor items, make up about 45 per cent of exports. The United Kingdom showed a considerably higher ratio of parts to complete aircraft than the United States or the Continental countries; and Japan, a lower ratio. One reason for the high U.K. ratio may be its decline as an aircraft supplier, which means that the ratio of old aircraft in use to new aircraft exported is higher for planes of U.K. manufacture than for aircraft produced by other countries.

The main change in the direction of trade in aircraft and parts was the rise of the EEC countries from a negligible level in 1953 to almost 30 per cent of OECD exports in 1963 and 1964 (Table 14.15). The U.S. proportion, around 80 per cent in 1953, had shrunk to less than 50 per cent by the end of the period.

Nonprice Factors in Trade

Clearly, many factors governing the flow of trade in aircraft and parts are not reflected in prices as we are able to measure them. Among these are the early availability of new types of aircraft, delivery time, reliability of service, subsidies, free services included as part of sales contracts, compatability with existing equipment, trade-in deals, and the cost of credit. These could, theoretically, be priced if we had adequate information, and the purchasing agencies presumably do put prices on them. That is, each purchaser evaluates the utility of these factors to his own company.

Some nonprice factors cannot be evaluated by the purchasers. These involve governmental decisions based on interests outside those of the purchasing agency; for example, consideration of employment levels in the domestic aircraft industry or prospects of promoting exports by that or other domestic industries.

An example of the influence of nonprice factors was the purchase of

[29] "U.S. Balance Fattened by Plane Purchases," *New York Herald Tribune*, July 1965.

the Super VC-10 by BOAC in the early 1960s. The decision to buy this aircraft was widely reported to be contrary to the wishes of the management of the airline, and was clearly a measure of support for the British aircraft industry.[30]

Other cases of the influence of factors external to the purchaser involved the purchase of aircraft as a *quid pro quo* for the purchase of parts or other items by the aircraft supplier. A possible arrangement for building British jet plane parts in Germany was expected to involve the requirement that a German airline would be committed to buying British aircraft. A British purchase of U.S. military aircraft included, as part of the trade, a waiver of buy-American rules to enable British firms to compete on equal terms with U.S. firms for American defense contracts. The arrangement included a suspension of buy-American provisions for some amount of British military sales to the United States and an agreement by the Americans not to compete with the British for military sales in the Middle East market, so that Great Britain's military orders there could balance the cost of its U.S. purchases.[31] Military aircraft and parts, again, are purchased under a number of different types of arrangement, including substantial subsidies not reflected in quoted prices. In the case of the $2,753 million program for equipping European countries with F104 fighter aircraft, the United States contributed $215 million of the $1,159 million which was spent in the United States. It was reported that U.S. and British bidders for an Argentine civil aircraft order offered military aircraft at low prices as part of a tie-in sale. Quite commonly an aircraft supplier will take an existing fleet in trade-in as part of a sale of new aircraft.[32]

Among the larger civil airlines the most important factors are probably service and the economy of standardization. The size of American aircraft companies, a result of the large scale of U.S. military procure-

---

[30] "Over the Atlantic," *Economist*, March 13, 1965; "The New Battle of Britain: Can Air Industry Survive," *New York Herald Tribune*, March 12, 1965; "BOAC Buys British, Boeing 707's Stymied," *ibid.*, July 20, 1964; "Britain Expected to Ask BOAC to Make Good Order for VC-10 Planes," *Wall Street Journal*, July 14, 1964; "Second Best?" *Economist*, June 16, 1962.

[31] "America Expects Every Briton . . . ," *Economist*, January 13, 1968; "Arms Exports, On the Warpath," *ibid.*, February 4, 1967; "Arms Sales: Markets Are Where You Find Them," *ibid.*, May 7, 1966; "Defence: The Next Orders," *ibid.*, February 26, 1966.

[32] "West German Company Is Discussing Making British Jet-Plane Parts," *Wall Street Journal*, June 22, 1964; "The Next Orders," *Economist*, February 26, 1966; "U.S. Balance Fattened by Plane Purchases," *New York Herald Tribune*, July 1965; "Argentina Given War Plans Offers," *New York Times*, March 3, 1965; "3 Companies Woo Mideast Airlines," *ibid.*, March 22, 1965.

ment and civilian aircraft purchases, is probably of great benefit in international competition, partly because a purchaser, faced with two similar aircraft, will buy from the larger firm in the expectation that service will be superior.[33] The large company has another, related, advantage, in that it can offer a wider variety of aircraft, all sharing certain spare parts. An airline can standardize on one supplier for several types of aircraft, thus economizing on stocks of parts and probably on the learning time of its mechanics as well. This economy, among other factors, may explain the speed with which American companies came to dominate the short-range jet market despite a very late start compared with the British.[34]

Changes over time in the type of aircraft purchased also affect market shares of the main exporters. The market for commercial jet aircraft has gone through several phases, each of which favored one or the other major exporter. During 1955–57, for example, purchases of long-range aircraft were particularly important, and the United States met virtually no competition in that class. At the end of the period demand surged for small jets to replace piston aircraft on shorter flights. This demand was beneficial to British manufacturers, who began production of such aircraft two years before the first American company to enter the field. The advantage may have been temporary, but it did affect the flow of orders for several years.[35]

Price Trends

Prices for aircraft and parts sold by the United States, the United Kingdom, and France rose steadily during this period (Table 14.16). U.S. prices for complete aircraft rose less than those of the other two countries, but parts prices seem to have risen at least as quickly in the United States as in the European countries.

The French index is very weak. For one thing the data cover essentially one aircraft, the middle-range Caravelle, in various versions, while the U.K. and U.S. prices cover a range from the comparatively small jets, such as the Douglas DC-9, and the BAC-111, through the large

[33] "That Company, Fokker," *Economist*, August 28, 1965.

[34] "War of Small Jets," *Economist*, February 27, 1965; "British Pin Hopes on Selling Shorter-Range Craft in the U.S.," *New York Times*, April 11, 1965; "Boeing is Making Short-Range Jets," *ibid.*, February 20, 1965.

[35] "Industry Awaits UAL Jet Choice," *New York Herald Tribune*, March 22, 1965; "United to Buy 75 Jetliners for Record $375 Million," *New York Times*, April 6 1965; also see sources in previous footnote.

Table 14.16
International Prices, Aircraft and Parts, 1953, 1957, 1961–64
(1962 = 100)

	1953	1957	1961	1962	1963	1964
AIRCRAFT AND PARTS (SITC 734)						
U.S.	83	89	99	100	102	108
U.K.	NA	NA	NA	100	108	112
France	NA	76	93	100	102	104
COMPLETE AIRCRAFT (SITC 734.1)						
U.S.	80	86	95	100	103	104
U.K.	NA	74	97	100	106	107
France	NA	69	93	100	103	107

Source: Appendix C.

transatlantic aircraft. Also, improvements in the Caravelle have probably not been adequately accounted for, and the price increase therefore
includes more unidentified quality change than the U.S. index, for which
we had a finer breakdown of aircraft by type.

All these time-to-time indexes are based on price series for individual
aircraft types, in which an attempt was made to compare the price of an
identical aircraft in several years. However, this method does not measure
the decline in the efficiency price of air transportation equipment, mostly
decreases in costs resulting from the shift to larger and faster planes,
and particularly the shift from piston to jet aircraft. The older aircraft
were forced from the market altogether, or pushed into different types of
route, where they did not have to compete with the new models. We
can rarely observe the decline in price of older models which would
permit us to measure the degree of quality improvement contained in
the new models, although a study of the active market for secondhand
aircraft might permit some judgments on this score.[36]

Some indication of the degree of quality improvement involved in the
change from piston to jet aircraft is given by data on operating costs
of various types of aircraft.[37] We can compare the 1963 direct operating

[36] A method for using secondhand prices is described in Phillip Cagan, "Measuring
Quality Changes and the Purchasing Power of Money: An Exploratory Study of Automobiles," *National Banking Review,* December 1965.
[37] "A basic reason for the sizable and continuing acquisition of jet aircraft by the
trunk airlines is evident from . . . unit cost data. . . . In 1963, as in previous years,

costs per seat-mile for the types of aircraft delivered to U.S. airlines in 1963 (mainly four-engine jets) with the 1963 costs for the types of aircraft delivered in 1953 (mainly two- and four-engine piston aircraft).[38] Costs for the older plane types were 2.49 cents per seat-mile; and for the newer types, only 1.65 cents per seat-mile, mainly because the new planes were larger and faster than the old ones but partly also because jet engines are cheaper to maintain.

For many reasons this comparison cannot be used as a direct measure of the decline in price of air transport equipment. The piston aircraft in use in 1963 may have cost more to operate than the jets not only because of their size and engine characteristics but also because they were older than the jet aircraft and because they were used on shorter routes for which jets might have been uneconomical. However, it does not seem likely that these factors account for most of the difference in cost, in view of the difference in seating capacity (around 50 for the older planes as compared with more than 100 for the later types), and in speed (200 miles an hour as compared with more than 450).

It seems reasonable to conclude, therefore, that a quality- or productivity-adjusted index of U.S. aircraft prices would show a decline between 1953 and 1963 instead of the price increase of almost 30 per cent given in Table 14.16.

Price Levels

Very little information on comparative aircraft price levels was collected in the course of this study. Ideally we would have wished to gather data on comparative capital costs and operating costs for various aircraft from the airlines that were contemplating purchases. Lacking these, we can only suggest a rough approximation derived from press discussion and other published information.

We estimated that U.K. prices in 1964 were more than 10 per cent above U.S. prices for roughly comparable aircraft (Table 14.17). Price ratios for the other years suggest that U.K. prices were higher

unit costs of the 4-engine jets were substantially lower than those of either piston-engine or turboprop aircraft. Direct operating costs of the jets . . . averaged . . . 1.50 cents per seat-mile . . . 4-engine piston aircraft averaged . . . 2.61 cents per seat-mile while . . . 4-engine turboprops averaged . . . 2.36 cents per seat-mile" (*Direct Operating Costs and Other Performance Characteristics of Transport Aircraft in Airline Service, Calendar Year 1963*, Federal Aviation Agency, July 1964, p. 5).

[38] These are not, of course, necessarily the same aircraft as were delivered in 1953. A single model is sold for several years, and those of 1953 type in operation in 1963 may have been purchased in 1954 or later.

Table 14.17
U.K. International Price Levels, Aircraft, 1957, 1961–64
(U.S. = 100)

Year	Index	Year	Index
1957	93	1963	111
1961	110	1964	111
1962	107		

Source: Appendix E.

than U.S. prices by close to 10 per cent in each year except 1957, when they were lower. These ratios apply to complete aircraft, but we did not combine them with our parts price ratios. The latter varied widely and therefore produced an unreliable index; furthermore, the data covered parts of American aircraft, the price ratios for which might not have been typical of aircraft in general. For these parts the data we collected showed U.K. prices more than twice as high as U.S. prices.

Among the various types of aircraft, the U.S. price position appeared to be strongest in the long-range aircraft and weakest in those of shortest range. During 1961–63 the ratio of U.K. to U.S. aircraft orders was, correspondingly, lowest for the very long-range planes and highest for the short-range ones. The relationship, which was calculated on the basis of gross orders, would have been even stronger if it had taken account of the large number of cancellations of orders for British aircraft during these years, for planes ordered earlier, and in later years, for planes ordered in 1961–63. The data on aircraft sales thus tend to confirm the order of the price ratios.

A different measure of place-to-place price differences can be derived from the operating cost data discussed earlier. Only a few foreign aircraft were in service in the United States in 1963, but these permit some very rough price comparisons. Neither the British nor the French aircraft had exact U.S.-made counterparts, but both were in the high ranges of direct operating costs per seat-mile: 2.88 cents for the Caravelle and 2.19 and 2.87 cents for the two Vickers planes. These levels were similar to the costs of U.S. piston aircraft (2.61 cents) and U.S. turbo-props (2.29 and 2.55 cents—the latter for a local-service aircraft), but were considerably more expensive than the American jet aircraft which were replacing them. The large American jets in operation in 1963 had average costs of 1.50 cents per seat-mile, and the smaller Boeing, the 727, appearing in the records for the first time in 1964, had costs of slightly over 1.50 cents.

Price Competitiveness

U.S. price competitiveness in aircraft and parts apparently increased from 1957 to 1963 but declined somewhat in 1964 (Table 14.18). However, since the parts indexes are a very narrow selection of the total trade in parts, the indexes for complete aircraft, which do not show the 1964 decline, might represent price competitiveness in aircraft and parts better than the indexes that include parts prices.

The indexes of U.S. price competitiveness relative to the United Kingdom do not seem unreasonable in relation to the trade data of Table 14.15. The least favorable price relationship for the United States was in 1957, and that was the year in which U.K. exports were relatively (and absolutely) highest. The U.S. price position improved greatly by 1961, declined slightly, and then improved somewhat, while U.S. exports reached their peak relative to those of the United Kingdom in 1962 and then fell back somewhat. Thus the trade flows for the United States and United Kingdom do not seem inconsistent with the price competitiveness indexes we have compiled, particularly in view of the coverage differences.

Table 14.18
U.S. Price Competitiveness, Aircraft and Parts, 1957, 1961—64
(1962 = 100)

	1957	1961	1962	1963	1964
AIRCRAFT AND PARTS					
Relative to					
U.K.	NA	NA	100	106	103
France	85	94	100	100	96
COMPLETE AIRCRAFT					
Relative to					
U.K.	86	102	100	103	103
France	80	98	100	101	103

Source: Appendix D.

On the other hand, the movement of United States prices relative to France does not explain the great increase in the EEC share of world trade in aircraft and parts, from 3 to 32 per cent of OECD exports. The bulk of the growth in EEC exports after 1961 took place in Belgium and the Netherlands, for which we have no price data. We suspect that much of the growth must have taken place in military aircraft, Belgium was not an important competitor for civil aircraft orders and the Netherlands' main civilian aircraft, the highly successful F-27 Friendship (perhaps involving roughly $300 million in sales over a ten-year period, including spare parts) [39] could not account for sales reaching beyond $130 million in 1963 and over $200 million in 1964.

Ships and Boats [40]

Trade

Japan was the leading exporter of ships and boats in 1963, accounting for nearly one-fourth of OECD exports, with Germany, Sweden, Great Britain, and France as the other major shipbuilders for the world market (Table 14.19).

The figures on exports to the United States understate its role as a source of the orders that give rise to other OECD countries' exports. [41] The reason is that purchases of foreign-built ships by U.S. companies were often made through affiliates and subsidiaries which then operated the vessels under Liberian, Panamanian, or other foreign flags. [42] Such arrangements seemed to be most common in connection with bulk carriers, which are specially designed for the low-cost loading, transport, and unloading of some particular material—most often oil and, less frequently, iron ore, bauxite, or coal. The owners of these vessels were

[39] "Fokker Planes Keep Role in Europe," *New York Times,* December 4, 1965; "That Company, Fokker," *Economist,* August 28, 1965.

[40] SITC 735. *Value of OECD exports in 1963:* $1.5 billion; 3.5 per cent of study total.

[41] Recreational craft, which are of minor importance in world trade, loom large in U.S. trade. It should also be mentioned that the export figures for the United States, and probably for other countries, include used ships even where the transfers of registry change only the legal form and not the ultimate beneficiary of ownership.

[42] More than one-fourth of the tonnage launched "for registration in other countries" in the six reference years of our study (1953, 1957, and 1961–64) was for Liberian registry, and U.S. firms were probably responsible for a large percentage of these orders (*Lloyds Register of Shipping, Annual Summary of Merchant Ships Launched During 1964,* London, 1965, and earlier issues). Aside from the United States, Greek shipowners are the largest users of "flags of convenience," as the Liberian, etc., registries are often referred to.

Table 14.19

OECD Exports of Ships and Boats (SITC 735), by Origin and Destination, 1963

(dollars in millions)

Destination	Value of Exports	Per Cent of OECD Exports in 735	Share in OECD Exports (per cent)							
			OECD	U.S.	U.K.	EEC Total	Germany	France	Sweden	Japan
Total, all destinations	$1,467	100.0	100.0	2.7	8.1	34.4	17.4	7.1	17.2	23.1
Destination										
U.S.	38	2.6	100.0		1.6	54.7	45.9			8.5
OECD Europe	714	48.7	100.0	1.3	8.0	42.2	19.5	9.0	26.7	9.2
U.K.	120	8.2	100.0	0.2		47.5	18.3	11.7	25.0	16.7
Sweden	57	3.9	100.0			66.7	21.0	22.8		
EEC total	90	6.1	100.0	3.3	10.0	67.8	17.8	4.4	5.6	1.1
Germany	19	1.3	100.0	3.7	15.3	38.4		7.4	15.8	2.1
France	22	1.5	100.0	6.0	14.7	63.6	7.4			
Canada	4	0.3	100.0	53.8	20.5	17.9	a	a	a	5.1
Japan	1	0.1	100.0	15.4	7.7	15.4				
Latin America	98	6.7	100.0	8.2		26.5	10.2	4.1	7.1	37.8
Other	596	40.6	100.0	0.9	10.0	26.1	15.0	5.8	9.2	39.1
Unaccounted for	16	1.1	100.0	96.1						1.9

Source: Appendix A.
aLess than 0.05 per cent.

464

freer to buy ships in the cheapest shipbuilding country than the operators of general cargo or passenger vessels. As a result, bulk cargo vessels
tended to be more important in exports than in world production.[43]

Japan, which accounted for only about 11 per cent of world launchings and 12 per cent of exports (on a gross tonnage basis)[44] in 1953,
emerged during the period as the world's greatest shipbuilding country;
in 1964, its total launchings were 40 per cent and its export launchings
50 per cent of the world totals. The United States virtually disappeared
from the world market; and the United Kingdom, which was the leader
at the beginning of the period, had its share reduced from over 20 per
cent in 1953 to 3 per cent in 1964 (Table 14.20).[45] The German share
also declined, while Sweden was able to maintain its position in the
rapid expansion of the 1961–64 period largely by continuing its domi-
nation of the important Norwegian market. The Japanese ascendancy
cannot be ascribed to efficient imitation of Western methods with low-
wage labor; it is attributable, in part at least, to leadership in designing
and building larger and more automated ships, particularly tankers,
that have enabled their owners to achieve substantial economies.[46]
Another factor favorable to Japan, according to U.S. and U.K. shipbuilders, was the high rate of utilization of its shipyards, made possible
in part by the rapid expansion of its own maritime fleet.[47]

[43] Tankers, for example, accounted for about 45 per cent of all tonnage launched
in the six reference years of our study, but for about 55 per cent of tonnage launched
for registration in countries other than the country of construction (*ibid.*).

[44] Gross tonnage is a measure of space available for cargo, crew, and passengers.
The other common measure of ship size, deadweight tonnage, is a measure of capacity
to carry weight; it is defined as the difference between the ship's displacement at load
and light drafts. Deadweight tonnage (DWT) runs higher than the gross tonnage; see,
for example, the figures on Japanese export ships in Table 14.26, below.

[45] The relative importance of the EEC and Japan in 1963 as measured by the value
figures (Table 14.19) differs from that measured in tonnage (Table 14.20) because of
differences in coverage and in units of measurement. The OECD data used for exports
are expressed in dollar values and include all kinds of vessels, such as ferries, tugs,
and small fishing craft, while Lloyd's launchings are expressed in tons and are confined
to merchant ships of 100 gross tons or more.

[46] See, for example, *Wall Street Journal*, August 22, 1963, and *Journal of Commerce*,
February 28, 1964, March 2, 1964, March 29, 1965, and September 30, 1965, for
accounts of developments in the Japanese industry. On the economy of large tankers,
an oil company estimated that fuel and crew economies enabled a 90,000 ton tanker
to carry oil at one-third to one-half the cost of the standard 16,600 ton tankers used
during World War II (*New York Times*, September 1, 1963). See also S. G. Sturmey,
British Shipping and World Competition, London, 1962, p. 265.

[47] About 13 per cent of all tonnage launched in 1961–64 was Japanese built for
Japanese registry; Japan's launchings for foreign and domestic owners accounted for
about 30 per cent of the world total in the same period (*Lloyds Register*). The statement in the text about the advantage of high utilization implies either that it encour-
ages the rapid adoption of new techniques or, what is more questionable, that average
cost rather than marginal cost pricing is followed in the shipbuilding industry.

Table 14.20
Tonnage and Distribution of Ships Launched for Registration in
Other Countries, 1953, 1957, 1961—64

Country of Origin	1953	1957	1961	1962	1963	1964
		1,000 GROSS TONS				
U.S.	106	64	2			2
U.K	365	261	281	165	284	149
Germany	364	778	542	684	644	588
France	93	181	172	309	282	239
Netherlands	185	157	317	244	143	175
Italy	18	159	12	27	148	130
Sweden	242	437	479	596	698	830
Japan	201	1,513	748	877	1,497	2,721
World	1,728	3,886	3,178	3,450	4,335	5,421
		PER CENT				
U.S.	6.1	1.6	0.1			a
U.K.	21.1	6.7	8.8	4.8	6.6	2.7
Germany	21.0	20.0	17.1	19.8	14.9	10.8
France	5.4	4.7	5.4	9.0	6.5	4.4
Netherlands	10.7	4.0	10.0	7.1	3.3	3.2
Italy	1.0	4.1	0.4	0.8	3.4	2.4
Sweden	14.0	11.2	15.1	17.3	16.1	15.3
Japan	11.6	38.9	23.5	25.4	34.5	50.2
World	100.0	100.0	100.0	100.0	100.0	100.0

Source: *Lloyd's Register of Shipping, Annual Summary of Merchant Ships Launched During 1964*, London, 1965, and earlier issues. Excludes ships under 100 gross tons, sailing vessels, and nonpropelled craft and ships built of wood.
[a]Less than 0.05 per cent.

Nonprice Factors in Trade

Operators of general cargo or passenger vessels of the major industrial countries were under a variety of pressures to have their ships built in domestic yards. Each country wished to maintain its own merchant marine and shipbuilding capacity, the usual justification being the need for such facilities for defense purposes. The measures adopted to carry out this policy were varied; they included the restriction of coastwise and government cargoes to domestic flag vessels, direct subsidies for construction and operation, and tax relief, accelerated depreciation, and special credit provisions.[48] The United States, for example, reserved its coastwise trade exclusively to U.S. flagships and required that at least 50 per cent of government-sponsored cargoes be transported in American bottoms. Operating subsidies and cargo preferences were restricted to ships constructed in U.S. yards, and construction subsidies were paid to offset the higher cost to the operator as a result of building in U.S. rather than foreign yards.[49] Both operating and shipbuilding subsidies were confined to vessels used in foreign commerce. Shipbuilding subsidies were used by other countries, notably France and Italy, not only to build ships for the domestic flag lines but also for foreign owners. U.K. shipowners got more favorable tax treatment on new investment than firms in other industries, and for a time the government provided favorable credit terms for ships built in British yards. In Germany, shipbuilders received a turnover tax reimbursement equal to 7 per cent of the final price to foreign buyers when a ship was constructed for foreigners, and in Japan, shipbuilders' exports were supported by the provision of government credit on favorable terms.[50]

These governmental measures not only caused ships flying the flags of the main industrial countries such as the United States, Germany, France, and Japan to be constructed domestically regardless of cost,[51] and thus to reduce the volume of trade in ships, but also to maintain larger world shipyard capacity than there otherwise would have been. Given the large overhead costs of shipyards and the sensitivity of unit costs to the rate of capacity utilization, the intense competition for busi-

[48] *Economic Policies and Practices: Subsidies to Shipbuilding by Eleven Countries,* Joint Economic Committee, 88th Cong., 2nd sess., 1964. See also Sturmey, *op. cit.*

[49] For a review of the construction subsidy program see Statement of G. F. Nuse, *Construction Differential Subsidies,* House Subcommittee on Merchant Marine, Committee on Merchant Marine and Fisheries, 89th Cong., 1st sess., March 3, 1965, pp. 40 f.

[50] Japanese shipyards were also able to buy steel at especially low prices. The European Economic Commission, the executive body of the Common Market, concluded that Japanese aids to shipbuilders, including low interest rates, long-term credits, and subsidies for steel plate, were equivalent to a 10 per cent subsidy (*European Community,* Washington, D.C., EEC Information Service, May 1966, p. 14). It was reported at the same time that French and Italian shipyards were receiving subsidies of about 15 per cent (*New York Times,* April 18, 1965). See also *Economist,* September 15, 1962, pp. 1035–36 and March 20, 1965, p. 1293; the 1962 *Economist* article reported subsidy rates in France and Italy higher than 15 per cent.

[51] *Hearings, Construction Differential Subsidies,* 88th Cong., 2nd sess., April 7, 8, and 9, 1964, pp. 9–10. The United Kingdom and the Netherlands were exceptions; at the end of 1962, for example, 29 per cent of ships under construction for U.K. registry and 21 per cent of those for Netherlands registry were being built abroad.

Table 14.21
International Price Indexes, Ships and Boats, 1953, 1957, 1961–64
(1962 = 100)

	1953	1957	1961	1962	1963	1964
U.S.	98	116	101	100	96	97
EEC	111	130	99	100	91	90
Germany	108	124	95	100	93	92
Japan	112	140	99	100	86	87

Source: Appendix C.

ness is not surprising. From time to time determined efforts of secondary builders such as Yugoslavia and Spain to obtain orders added to the price pressures.[52]

Whatever the competitive, technological, or other forces responsible, world ship prices were substantially lower in 1964 than in 1953 despite increases in wages and in the prices of materials used in shipbuilding.[53]

Prices

Prices in Europe and Japan rose more sharply than in the United States under the impetus to demand given in 1957 by the Suez crisis, but foreign prices also fell more drastically after that date, especially the Japanese (Table 14.21). Japanese prices were more than 25 per cent and Common Market prices about 15 per cent lower in 1964 than in 1953, while U.S. prices were at about the same level at the two terminal dates.[54]

We do not have enough direct information to produce a time-to-time index for the United Kingdom. However, a widely recognized source prepared estimates of the costs of ship construction for two or three

[52] For further details about the statements made in this paragraph see *ibid.*, pp. 76 and passim.; Committee of American Steamship Lines, *Shipbuilding Survey*, July 1961, July 1962, and July 1963. In addition, an estimate made in 1960 placed Polish and Yugoslav prices at 35 to 40 per cent of the United States at a time when German and Japanese prices were estimated at 46 per cent of the United States (J. J. Henry, "Shipbuilding Costs," *Marine News*, April 1960).

[53] Average hourly earnings in U.S. manufacturing rose by 45 per cent (*Economic Report of the President*, January 1966, p. 24) and more in the other industrial countries. One key material for shipbuilding, steel, increased in price by around 15 per cent (Chapter 9). The steel price increase taken by itself might have been expected to increase ship prices approximately 3 per cent (*Metal Bulletin*, May 8, 1964, p. 12), and there were, of course, other materials that increased in price.

[54] See the appendix to this chapter for a regression analysis of Japanese ship prices.

vessels of standard design and, also, of the prices of used vessels of the same specifications. In order to convey a general impression of the order of magnitude of export price changes in the United Kingdom, we have tried to adapt these data to our purposes.[55] The resulting index is as follows:

1953—93	1962—100
1957—113	1963—101
1961—101	1964—107

In Table 14.22 the price competitiveness of the U.S. vis-à-vis each foreign area is calculated by dividing each foreign index by the U.S. international price index for ships. It is clear that except for a small improvement relative to Europe between 1961 and 1962, the price competitiveness of the United States declined, particularly between 1957 and 1961.

[55] The indexes in the text are based on the estimates of ship prices for June of each year made by the *Fairplay Shipping Journal*. The estimates refer to two or three vessels of standard design, and larger and more modern vessels are substituted from time to time for vessels formerly priced. The "building cost price" includes cost plus "full overheads and a fair profit margin" . . . "not in competition with other firms . . ." (*ibid.*, January 11, 1962, pp. 77 and 79). The "ready ship price" is the market price of such a ship already in service. The relationship between these prices fluctuates with changes in the cost of ship construction and changes in the demand for shipping (freight rates). For our dates of reference, the prices (£1,000) follow:

	Cargo Vessels					
	9,500 DWT		11,000–13,000 DWT		Bulk Carrier, 24,000 DWT	
June	Bldg. Cost	Ready Price	Bldg. Cost	Ready Price	Bldg. Cost	Ready Price
1953	620	600				
1957	775	900	1080	1250		
1961	730	650	1015	900		
1962			1020	875	1320	1200
1963			1025	850	1330	1250
1964			1035	975	1340	1400

The data are from *Fairplay Shipping Journal*, January 11, 1962, pp. 77 and 79; *ibid.*, January 13, 1966, pp. 89 and 91. Comments in the *Fairplay* articles presenting its estimates make it clear that at least during the 1960s and perhaps also in 1953, actual contracts were concluded at less than the building cost price. We based the index in the text on the averages of the building cost and ready prices for each vessel, except for 1957 for which we used the building cost price.

The time-to-time indexes were derived by linking up price changes between successive dates (and taking simple averages for the four out of the five links for which price changes were available for two different ships). Indexes, based on building costs and ready prices, are compared below with the index offered in the text (1962 = 100):

	1953	1957	1961	1962	1963	1964
Building cost	85	106	100	100	101	102
Ready price	95	143	103	100	101	114
Index in text	93	113	101	100	101	107

Table 14.22
U.S. Price Competitiveness, Ships and Boats, 1953, 1957, 1961—64
(1962 = 100)

	1953	1957	1961	1962	1963	1964
Relative to						
EEC	114	112	98	100	95	93
Germany	110	106	94	100	97	95
Japan	114	120	98	100	90	90

Note: The U.K. index given in the text produces the following index of U.S. price competitiveness relative to the United Kingdom: 1953, 97; 1957, 97; 1961, 100; 1962 100; 1963, 105; and 1964, 110.

Source: Appendix D.

This is shown also in Table 14.23 where the levels of ship prices are compared. For the last few years of the period prices in Japan were about half or even less and prices in Germany and the other EEC countries a little more than half those of the United States. We have less information about the U.K. levels. At the beginning of our period, U.K. prices seem to have been as low as any in the world, but by 1957 they appear to have been well above those of Germany.[56]

It seems clear that the exclusion of the United States from the world ship market is due to high prices and that the dominance of Japan is due to low and declining prices. The role of prices is apparent in the changes between 1953 and 1964 involving the other countries as well: [57]

	Rank with Respect to	
	Price Change	Increase in Export Tonnage
U.S.	4	5
U.K.	5	4
Germany	3	3
Other EEC	2	2
Japan	1	1

[56] An official report relating to 1959–61 summarized United Kingdom and Continental European bidding for 34 vessels by stating that over half of the Continental bids were 12 to 17 per cent below the U.K. bids. See *Shipbuilding Orders Placed Abroad by British Shipowners*, Report to Minister of Transport by Messrs. Peat, Marwick, Mitchell & Co., London, 1961, p. 5.

[57] Price change is based on the ratio of 1964 to 1953 prices, and the ranking is from low to high (from Table 14.21 and text). Export tonnage is ranked from high to low (from Table 14.20). "Other EEC" covers France, Italy, and the Netherlands.

Table 14.23

Price Levels, Ships and Boats, 1953, 1957, 1961—64

(U.S. for each year = 100)

	1953	1957	1961	1962	1963	1964
U.S.	100	100	100	100	100	100
EEC	68	66	58	59	56	55
Germany	62	60	53	56	54	53
Japan	59	62	50	51	46	46

Source: Appendix E.

The role of prices in this group cannot be ascertained simply by a juxtaposition of contemporaneous price and quantity changes as can be seen in the data below for German and Japanese prices and exports: [58]

	Movements of German Prices Relative to Japanese Prices	German as Percentage of Japanese Export Tonnage		
		Current	1-yr. Lag	2-yr. Lag
1953	96	180	366	69
1957	88	51	68	95
1961	97	73	78	43
1962	100	78	43	22
1963	108	43	22	23
1964	106	22	23	—

If the terminal years are compared, we find, as already noted, a rise in German relative prices and a substantial decline in relative exports. However, if successive pairs of years are examined, we find a contraction of the German export share between 1953 and 1957, when German price competitiveness improved, and a large expansion in German relative exports between 1957 and 1961, when German prices increased. The connection between the price changes and relative exports is not any better if a one-year lag is allowed for between the date of order, to which the prices refer, and the date of launching, to which the tonnage figures refer, but there is an improvement with a two-year lag. Even so,

[58] The German-Japanese price ratios are computed from data in Table 14.21. The German-Japanese tonnage ratios are from Table 14.20 and sources cited there.

the decline in relative German exports which came in the last two years seems quite large relative to the German prices. Among a number of possible explanations for such situations, two seem to apply to this case.

First, some of the expansion in Japanese sales in the last two years was to Dutch and other European shippers who had formerly bought ships from European yards. By 1962, the differential between European and Japanese prices had widened enough to make worthwhile the inconvenience and extra inspection costs of shifting purchases from Europe.[59] A second factor is that the German yards were able to stay in the price range in which they were bidding in the early 1960s only by setting prices below their costs.[60] The effort to maintain high utilization of capacity could not, however, be sustained, particularly in the face of further declines in Japanese prices. At least one large German yard was forced out of business in 1962, and German shipbuilding contracted. Total tonnage launched was 11 per cent less and export tonnage launched was 14 per cent less in 1964 than in 1962, while for the world as a whole the corresponding figures increased by 21 and 57 per cent.[61]

Delivery time is another element that has sometimes played a role in determining trade flows. The closing of the Suez Canal in the fall of 1956, for example, created a large demand for shipping. Freight rates soared, and there was a rush to place orders for large ships to move oil. Delivery periods in major yards rose to three years. With freight rates so high that the cost of a vessel might be paid off in a few trips, orders were placed in U.S. yards which could offer quick delivery, albeit at high prices.

In summary, in the period under study, competition in the world shipbuilding industry was intense. The period was marked by a shift to larger-size vessels, and by the emergence of Japan as the leading shipbuilding nation. There were notable changes in international price relationships. Japanese prices declined most sharply, but there were also price cuts in Germany and the other EEC countries. U.S. prices were about the same at the end of the period as at the beginning, and U.K. prices

[59] For example, Dutch shipping officials reportedly stated in connection with one order that went to Japan that if the 20 per cent differential had been reduced to 6 or 7 per cent it would have paid to place the order in Europe (*Journal of Commerce*, February 16, 1965). Our estimates for 1964 do not place the average difference between Japanese and EEC prices as high as 20 per cent (cf. Table 14.23).

[60] *Economist*, September 5, 1962, pp. 1035–36.

[61] Cf. *Lloyds Register*.

were higher. The changes in prices in the different countries, at least for the period as a whole, were well correlated with the changes in shares of the world market for ships.

Appendixes

Comparisons Among Various Measures of Diesel Locomotive Price Trends

Diesel locomotives (SITC 731.3) provide an unusual opportunity for comparing measures of price trends derived from different sets of data and by different methods. We are interested in this comparison not only because of the importance of locomotive exports, but also because it has implications for measures of price change and price competitiveness in other commodity areas.

Two types of data entered into the time-to-time indexes actually used in this paper: ICC reports on locomotive purchases by railroads in the United States, classified by type of locomotive; and export price data, collected by the National Bureau from American locomotive producers for this study. There is, in addition, a locomotive price index published by the ICC without any detailed description of its construction. This index does not appear to have been derived from the ICC purchase data which we used for our index.

A further source of data is the information on bidding that is used to calculate the place-to-place indexes described earlier. The chief defect in the bidding data is the incompleteness of our knowledge of the characteristics of the locomotives offered. This information on characteristics could have been much more complete, but more detailed specifications were not collected because they were not necessary for the primary purpose of the bid data collection: place-to-place comparisons. For these, it was only necessary to know which of the offers were comparable and met the specifications, whatever the specifications were. For this reason we could standardize for only some of the characteristics in making time-to-time comparisons, particularly horsepower, type of transmission, and wheel arrangement. At times, however, there were additional data giving type of body, more detailed information on transmissions, or even specific model numbers.

Table 14.24

Comparison of U.S. Time-to-time Indexes from Various Sources, Diesel
Electric Locomotives, 1953, 1957, 1959, 1961–64

	$\frac{1957}{1953}$	$\frac{1959}{1957}$	$\frac{1961}{1959}$	$\frac{1962}{1961}$	$\frac{1963}{1962}$	$\frac{1964}{1963}$
NBER indexes from ICC data						
1. Linked	108	104	92	104	95	97
2. Regression	107		88[a]	105	94	97
3. ICC index	110	100	100	100	100	100
4. NBER index from						
company export data	NA	100	97	98	99	99
NBER index from bidding data						
5. Selected data	NA	NA	103	97	98	100
6. All data	NA	NA	109	94	98	100

Note: For sources and general descriptions of series see text of this appendix. Figures
for 1964 in lines 4–6 include some early 1965 prices. The year 1959, in lines 5 and 6,
represents a combination of observations for dates ranging from fall 1959 through the
first half of 1960.

Lines 1 and 2 are based on virtually full coverage of domestic locomotive purchases,
from data published in various issues of *Transport Statistics of the United States*,
Interstate Commerce Commission. The company data of line 4 are from no more than
six observations for each link, but the major producers and items are represented. The
selected bidding data of line 5 contain a somewhat larger number of observations, also
with coverage of all major U.S. producers, and the index of line 6 is based on at least ten
observations for every link except the last.

[a] 1961/1957.

Several measures of time-to-time price movements, comparing pairs
of years, are given in Table 14.24. The indexes from ICC data on purchases by U.S. railroads are shown in lines 1 and 2. The first of these
is a conventional index constructed by comparing each year's prices
with those of the preceding year for locomotives of identical horsepower
and wheel arrangement, with numbers purchased in the earlier year as
the weights. The second is a regression-based index, calculated by fitting
a linear regression line to price and horsepower of B-B [62] locomotives
for each year, and pricing the locomotives actually bought in 1963 at

[62] Single-unit locomotives with two four-wheel trucks, all driving axles.

the prices (as described by the regression lines) of the other years. The regression lines and coefficients of determination were as follows ($Y =$ price, in dollars; $X =$ horsepower):

Year	Constant Term	Coefficient of X	$\bar{r}^2$	Number of H.P. Categories
1964	$74,246	$ 54.80	.89	6
1963	13,766	84.97	.94	13
1962	17,995	88.80	.98	8
1961	21,970	82.73	.97	8
1957	10,971	100.29	.94	14
1953	28,912	85.20	.89	17

The regression-based index was not used for a number of reasons. One was that differences in the coefficients from year to year were substantial, particularly in 1957 when the marginal cost per horsepower was $100 instead of the $83–$89 of the other years through 1963. The last year, 1964, is a special case because the data were from a different source [63] and were less complete. Another problem affecting the regression-based index was the shift toward higher-horsepower locomotives. This shift meant that the earlier regressions contained more observations at the lower horsepower levels while the later ones were concentrated at the 2,000 horsepower and over range. The 1957 data in particular were all for locomotives of 1,800 horsepower or less.

In any case, the trend in the price-horsepower regression line does appear to have been downward, at least within the horsepower ranges actually built.

The ICC indexes (line 3) are not fully annotated in any public source but they are briefly described in one publication [64] as having been "developed from analyses of major construction contracts and projects . . . studies of carriers' returns to Valuation Order No. 14, joint studies made with various railroad committees, well-known engineering and trade publications, and information furnished by suppliers, manufacturers, and individual carriers." However, the great degree of stability in the diesel electric locomotive index (no change from 1957 through 1963) suggests that it is not derived from data on prices actually paid.

[63] *Joint Equipment Committee Report, Costs of Railroad Equipment and Machinery,* Association of American Railroads, July 1, 1965.
[64] "Schedule of Annual Indices for Carriers by Railroad, 1914 through 1963," Bureau of Accounts, Interstate Commerce Commission, mimeo., n.d.

The NBER index from company export data is derived from information on the prices at which U.S. producers actually offered specific locomotive models. The number of observations is small, but all the major producers and most of the important models are represented. Some list prices are included, and the major consequence of their exclusion would be to lower the 1961/1957 index by a few points. There would be virtually no effect after 1962.

The bidding data on which the last set of NBER indexes is based are quite imperfect. However, their coverage of trade in locomotives is more comprehensive than the company data, and they are therefore of interest as a check on other measures. The time-to-time estimates do not necessarily refer to the lowest bid from a country but rather compare bids at two dates on comparable locomotives, identified by specifications on horsepower, body style, wheel arrangement, and, usually, model number. Line 5 is an index derived from a selection of the bidding data for which a high degree of comparability was insured by the completeness of specifications. It excludes incompletely identified locomotives; and, in particular, it omits a large amount of data from several major bids in 1961 which drew particularly low offers from most countries on smaller locomotives and very high bids on the larger ones. These bids are, however, included in line 6, for which the standard of selection was not as high. For this index we tried to make comparisons for every pair of bids, even where offers from two different companies had to be matched or where locomotives of somewhat different horsepower had to be compared, after a rough price adjustment for the differences in power.

Despite the wide diversity of sources and the considerable defects of the basic data, the various NBER indexes in Table 14.24 are alike in several ways. In all of them U.S. prices decline from 1962 to 1963, and decline or remain unchanged from 1963 to 1964. They all also show a 1964 price level lower than that for 1961. There are greater differences in 1961–62, and the bid data here support the company reports of price declines. The widest range occurs in 1959–61, but the reason for these large discrepancies is not clear.

The bid data, rough as they are, provide the only time-to-time comparisons available for the United Kingdom and Japan, and for the EEC countries as a group. These comparisons, for three subperiods between 1959 and 1963 and for the period as a whole, are shown in Table 14.25.

Table 14.25
Comparison of Time-to-time Indexes from Bidding Data, Diesel
Electric Locomotives, 1959, 1961–63

	$\frac{1961}{1959}$	$\frac{1962}{1961}$	$\frac{1963}{1962}$	$\frac{1963}{1959}$
All locomotives, all data				
U.S.	109	94	98	99
EEC	95	124	87	102
All locomotives, selected data, U.S.	103	97	98	98
Locomotives of 800–1,500 H.P., all data				
U.S.	91	108	96	95
U.K.	93	106	98	97
EEC	85	116	97	96
Japan	85	117	96	95
Locomotives of 800–1,500 H.P., selected data				
U.S.	102	96	96	95
U.K.	104	95	98	97

Note: U.S. data are described in notes to Table 14.24, lines 5 and 6. The U.K. and EEC indexes are each based on from 5 to 20 bids in each link, and the Japanese on only 1 to 7 observations. The comparison of the data from selected bids with the data from all bids for the United States was used for some decisions on the comparability of specifications from one bidding to another for foreign offers, since we had a greater amount of detail, including company data, to aid in interpreting the U.S. bids.

EEC indexes are a combination of indexes for France, weighted twice, and Germany, weighted once.

Data for 1959 include bids ranging from the fall of 1959 through June 1960 and those for 1961 cover offers from late 1960 through the fall of 1961. The timing of the comparisons is thus somewhat blurred, but it is comparable from one country to another.

All the indexes for countries outside the United States, except the EEC index for all locomotive sizes and all data, declined over the four years, 1959–63, taken as a whole, as did the U.S. indexes. There are very slight indications that U.S. prices fell more than those of the other countries, but the differences are too small to deserve confidence. However, their combined evidence reinforces the impression of falling prices derived from some of the other data presented earlier.

A rough comparison can be made between the German bidding data underlying the EEC indexes in Table 14.25 and the German export price information used in the text of this report, for Table 14.7. The bidding data are weak, and for that reason are not shown separately in Table 14.25. The export price data cover not only diesel locomotives but also electric locomotives and self-propelled railway cars, which together account for more of German exports than diesel locomotives. Even within diesel locomotives, the export price data cover not only diesel electric but also diesel hydraulic locomotives, for which we lack bidding data.

Given these limitations of the comparison, the differences between the two indexes shown below are not startling, although they cumulate over time. The indexes for the first two years are quite close, but the last period and the total for the four years show large discrepancies.

	1961/1959	1962/1961	1963/1962	1963/1959
Bidding data	110	104	95	110
Export price data	112	107	101	121

The bidding data for the link for 1963/1962 are particularly sparse and might be dismissed on that account were it not that the decline in prices is confirmed by bidding and other data from most of the countries other than Germany.

If the bidding data were continued for one more year the index would show an even larger decline, while the export price index would rise slightly. However, the number of observations in the bidding data is too small to provide a reliable estimate of the change in price.

Regression-based International Price Index for Japanese Ships [65]

Tabulations were obtained covering all contracts between Japanese shipyards and foreign firms signed during the Japanese fiscal years 1957, 1961, 1962, 1963, and 1964.[66] Of the total of 256 contracts, 229 related to cargo ships, tankers, and bulk carriers and the other 27 to a variety of ships such as trawlers and scientific vessels. The latter were deleted; so too were 24 contracts for which information was incomplete or so far out of line with the other data as to make it seem either erroneous or the consequence of special factors not known to us. As a result

[65] This summary is based on the work of Steven Hitchner, a Swarthmore College student who was an undergraduate research participant in a National Science Foundation program at the University of Pennsylvania during the summer of 1966.

[66] The Japanese fiscal year begins on April 1; thus our 1957 data, for example, refer to the period April 1, 1957, to March 31, 1958. For 1964, data were available only for the first nine months of the fiscal year.

Table 14.26
Japanese Export Ship Contracts, Summary of Data, 1957, 1961–64

	1957	1961	1962	1963	1964[a]	Total
No. of contracts	32	25	21	79	48	205
Average						
Price ($1,000)	7,019	3,968	5,710	5,253	4,476	5,287
Gross tons (1,000)		17.6	28.6	31.4	25.1	23.1
Deadweight tons (1,000)	36.0	27.2	44.8	49.5	39.7	42.1
Horsepower (1,000)	13.2	10.7	15.4	16.8	13.9	14.8
Speed (m.p.h.)	15.2	15.3				
Ships per contract	1.65	1.56	1.90	1.61	1.44	1.61
Proportion of contracts calling for turbine engine		24%	29%		8%	9%
Proportion of contracts for						
Tankers	56%	28%	57%	63%	36%	51%
Bulk carriers	9	40	19	28	54	32
Cargo vessels	35	32	24	9	10	17

[a]Data for first nine months of fiscal year (i.e., April–December 1964).

the analysis was based on 205 contracts. The characteristics of the data are summarized in Table 14.26. About one-third of the contracts called for the building of more than one vessel; the average contract involved 1.6 ships. We treated each contract rather than each ship as a unit of observation.

In addition to price and number of ships, information was available, for at least one of the years, for gross tons, deadweight tons, horsepower of the main engine, normal operating speed, type of engine (diesel or turbine), and kind of ship (tanker, bulk carrier, or other). However, only deadweight tons, horsepower, and number and type of ship were available for all five of the years.

The basic procedure was to regress price against the variables relating to the size, power, and other characteristics of the vessels. After substantial experimentation with various ways of calculating the relationship, a logarithmic equation, in which the data for all the years were pooled, was chosen as the best means for estimating changes in price

during the period. The equation, which was computed in natural logarithms, had an $\bar{R}^2$ of .94 and a standard error of estimate equivalent to
3.1 per cent of the (geometric) mean price:

$$\text{Log } P = 6.0874 + .3290 \log DWT + .4356 \log HP - .0513BC -$$
$$\quad\quad\quad (.3378)\ (.0377) \quad\quad\quad (.0450) \quad\quad\quad (.0228)$$

$$.0597C + .4810Y_{57} + .1369Y_{61} + .1488Y_{62} + .0174Y_{64}$$
$$(.0415)\quad (.0263)\quad\quad (.0294)\quad\quad (.0301)\quad\quad (.0230)$$

The first three terms on the right represent the constant and the "prices"
of deadweight tons (DWT) and horsepower (HP).[67] In the next two
terms, the prices of bulk carriers (BC) and cargo vessels (C) are compared to the prices of tankers; the coefficients indicate that on the average, bulk carriers were 5 per cent and cargo vessels 6 per cent cheaper
than tankers, holding everything else (i.e., deadweight tons, horsepower,
and year) constant. The last four terms (in Y) in the equation show
the differences in prices between 1963 and each other year. For example, the natural logarithm of price in 1957 was .4810 higher than in
1963, all other things being equal; this is equivalent to a 62 per cent
difference. Converting this and the other coefficients to index numbers
on a 1963 base yields the following series: [68] 1957, 162; 1961, 115;
1962, 116; 1963, 100; 1964, 102.

In the balance of this appendix we discuss alternative computations
we made and explain our reasons for rejecting them in favor of the
estimates just summarized.

The log form produces directly, in the form of regression coefficients,
the estimates of the percentage change in prices between the observed
years. The arithmetic equation, on the other hand, gives the absolute
amount of the difference between two years. This seems less reasonable,
since we would ordinarily expect, for example, that the price increase
for an expensive ship would be in the same proportion rather than in
the same absolute amount as the price increase for a smaller, less costly
vessel. In the arithmetic form we must estimate a price from the equation by inserting appropriate values for the various vessel specifications
included in the equation.

---

[67] Observations for prices, deadweight tons, and horsepower are in thousands. The
figures in parentheses are the standard errors of the coefficients.

[68] The 1964 index is taken as 101 in Table 14.21, since a 1 per cent rather than a
2 per cent increase was indicated by a regression in which observations for similar
nine-month periods in 1963 and 1964 were included.

Table 14.27

Ship Price Indexes Computed from Pooled Regressions, 1957, 1961–64

	1957	1961	1962	1963	1964
Logarithmic	162	115	116	100	102
Semilogarithmic	162	114	120	100	101
Arithmetic					
1961 specifications	211	133	134	100	107
1963 specifications	163	119	119	100	104
Average specifications	174	122	123	100	105

Note: Independent variables: deadweight tons, horsepower, type of ship, and year.

The measure of percentage price change varies according to the choice of specifications. In Table 14.27, for example, the indexes derived from the arithmetic form on the basis of 1961 and 1963 average specifications, which differed more than any other pair, are compared with the indexes derived from the logarithmic equation described above. If we were using the arithmetic form, we would select the 1963 trade weights in our study of international competition.

Aside from its other advantages, the log form gives a better fit to the data; its $\bar{R}^2$ is .94 compared to .87 for the arithmetic form.

The semilog form, in which the log of price is regressed against the variables in natural numbers, shares many of the advantages of the log form but for Japanese ships, its $\bar{R}^2$ was only .89 compared to .94 for the log form. Its correlation was lower than the arithmetic one for most of the combinations of independent variables we employed, except for the combination reported upon, where it was slightly higher. It can be seen from Table 14.27 that our indexes would not be much different if we had used the semilog equation.[69]

Another question concerns the choice of independent variables used in the equation to explain price. In addition to the variables we used in the log equation described above, we had data on number of ships per contract for all years, and on gross tons, operating speed, and type of engine for some years.

[69] A semilog regression of price in arithmetic numbers on the logarithms of the independent variables consistently gave a poorer fit to the data than any of the other forms; for the variables included in the above equation, for example, it yielded an $\bar{R}^2$ of .81.

The number-of-ships variable was excluded because its coefficient was usually positive. It was ordinarily not large enough to be statistically significant, but we would normally expect a multiple order to reduce the price per ship. If contract prices on multiple orders were indeed higher, the reason may have been that shipowners with enough financial strength to place multiple orders also were in a position to set special requirements concerning the equipment of a ship or its general quality which could not be measured through the variables about which we had information. In any case, the inclusion of the number-of-ships variable in the log equation did not change any of the price indexes.

The price indexes computed from the regressions do not, indeed, appear to be sensitive to the inclusion or exclusion of marginal variables once enough are included to achieve high $\bar{R}^2$'s. When gross tonnage, for example, was added to the variables in the logarithmic equation set out above, the indexes were changed by one or two points at the most. (The pooled data in this case omitted 1957, for which gross tonnage figures were not available.)

Of the variables that were included, deadweight tons and horsepower obviously are important indicators of the capacity and power of a vessel. They represent major cost factors to the shipbuilder and major elements of utility to the shipowner. It also seemed desirable to differentiate among tankers, cargo vessels, and bulk carriers.

Aside from questions of mathematical form and the appropriate independent variables to include in the regression, the remaining important issue is whether we should compare prices estimated from separate regressions for each year rather than use the pooled regression we have selected. The assumption underlying the pooled regression is that the relative prices (i.e., coefficients) of horsepower, deadweight tons, and type of ships were the same in all the years. Regressions computed for individual years in fact yield very different coefficients from one time to the next. The coefficients do not, however, appear to change in any systematic or other way which can be rationalized in economic terms. Furthermore, the individual-year regressions are necessarily based on a smaller number of observations and their coefficients are therefore more likely to be erratic. We prefer, therefore, to rely upon the pooled regression.[70]

[70] For further discussion of these choices see Chapter 5.

The indexes derived from the individual-year regressions are compared below with those based on our preferred pooled regression:

	1957	1961	1962	1963	1964
Pooled, logarithmic	162	115	116	100	102
Individual year					
Arithmetic					
1963 specifications	171	119	120	100	100
1961 specifications	156	111	127	100	98
Average specifications	168	117	122	100	99
Logarithmic					
1963 specifications	167	114	118	100	101
1961 specifications	144	109	115	100	100
Average specifications	159	113	117	100	101

It is necessary to present both arithmetic and log forms because the log form is not consistently superior to the arithmetic for the individual years.[71] There are not, however, substantial differences between the two sets of results. Furthermore, at the 1963 specifications, the ones of most interest to us, the logarithmic regressions produce indexes that are close to those of the pooled regression. The individual arithmetic regressions yield measures of price change that are a little further away from those derived from the pooled regression, but even between these sets of results the largest difference is less than 6 per cent.

[71] Each, however, is consistently superior to either of the semilog forms; the differences in $\bar{R}^2$'s are generally around .10.

15

PASSENGER MOTOR CARS

Background

During the period covered by this study, world production of passenger cars more than doubled (see Table 15.1). The largest gains in numbers of units produced were achieved by Germany, the United Kingdom, France, Italy, and Japan, in that order. Growth in output in the United States, where the automobile industry was already highly developed in 1953, was only 26 per cent. The U.S. share in world output declined from three-quarters of the world total to 43 per cent. (These figures refer to domestic production; U.S.-owned or -controlled production abroad, which is particularly important in the United Kingdom and Germany, is included in the data for those countries.)

World trade in passenger cars expanded even more rapidly than production. The extent to which the producing countries shared in the expansion of trade varied widely. Germany, which led in the growth of production, raised its export ratio from over a third of domestic production in 1953 to about a half in 1964. The United States exported about 2.5 per cent of its output both in 1953 and 1964, but its imports expanded from less than 0.5 per cent of domestic production to more than 7 per cent. The U.K. export ratio fell from half of domestic production to a third, partly because of a relaxation of government allocation policies that were still favoring export markets at the beginning of the period.

These figures understate the importance of U.S. exports, since they exclude exports of parts for assembly abroad, which played a larger role

Note: SITC 732.1 and 732.6. *Value of OECD exports in 1963:* $3.4 billion; 7.5 per cent of study total. *Coverage:* Passenger motor cars (other than buses or special vehicles) including chassis with engines mounted.

Table 15.1
Output and Exports of Passenger Cars, 1953 and 1964
(number of cars in thousands)

	1953			1964		
		Exports			Exports	
	Output (number)	Number	As Per Cent of Output	Output (number)	Number	As Per Cent of Output
U.S.	6,122	154	2.5	7,751	192	2.5
U.K.	595	302	50.8	1,868	673	36.0
Germany	369	135	36.6	2,650	1,437	54.2
France	368	81	22.0	1,321	444	33.6
Italy	143	31	21.7	1,029	282	27.4
Japan	7	NA	NA	580	79	13.6
Total	7,597	703	9.3	15,199	3,107	20.4
Total world	8,110			17,826		

Source: For 1953: Data for Japan and world production from *Statistical Yearbook,* United Nations, 1957, p. 282. All other data from *International Trade, 1955,* GATT, May 1956, p. 65. For 1964: Production from *World Motor Vehicle Production and Registration, 1965–66,* U.S. Dept. of Commerce, November 1966. Exports from *Statistisches Jahrbuch für die Bundesrepublik Deutschland, 1966,* Federal Republic of Germany, 1966, p. 101.

in the trade of the United States than in that of the other countries. Even allowance for this factor, however, could hardly raise the U.S. export percentage above 5 or 7 per cent.[1]

Despite the notable development during these years of automobile industries outside of North America and western Europe, the older centers of production still accounted for 90 per cent of all the cars produced in 1964. The largest new producers were Japan, with 580,000 cars, and Australia, with 341,000. Among the other countries, the Soviet Union, the Union of South Africa, Argentina, and Brazil passed the 100,000 mark.

[1] The exact figure is somewhat uncertain because exports of parts for assembly were not reported separately for passenger cars but only for passenger cars in combination with trucks and buses. In 1964, the aggregate of such exports was $520 million, compared with complete-vehicle exports of $295 million for passenger cars, $316 million for trucks, and $26 million for buses. If all the parts exports were for passenger cars, the percentages of U.S. passenger car production that was exported would still be under 7 per cent. The importance of parts exports for the United States is connected with direct U.S. investments in automobile production in Canada, Latin America, Oceania, and other regions. For further comment on this point and for the sources of the statistics cited in this note, see Chapter 14.

The OECD countries, including Japan, accounted for well over 90 per cent of world exports by value. The six largest OECD members— the United States, the United Kingdom, Germany, France, Italy, and Japan—accounted in turn for over 90 per cent of OECD exports by value (Table 15.2).

The United States was the major supplier to the Latin American market, but Germany dominated the much larger European market. The EEC itself absorbed about 30 per cent of German exports and 50 per cent of French exports.

The U.S. share in OECD exports declined precipitously from 32 per cent to less than 9 per cent, although in absolute terms the dollar volume expanded a little (Table 15.3). The United Kingdom also lost in terms of shares—31 per cent to 19 per cent—although the dollar value of its exports increased more than two and a half times. Germany made the largest gains: Its share increased from 15 per cent to 40 per cent, and its foreign exchange earnings went up more than elevenfold. Japan's gains, though small in comparison to Germany's, represented a phenomenal rate of growth. Her exports of passenger cars were negligible in 1953, but by the end of the period, she was the sixth largest exporter of passenger cars.

Time-to-time Changes in Domestic Automobile Prices

Data

Our price data include more than 1,000 observations for the United States and 700 for five foreign countries—the United Kingdom, Germany, France, Italy, and Japan. Six model years (1953, 1957, 1961, 1962, 1963, and 1964) and every important make in every country are represented. The distribution of the observations over time and among the countries is shown in Table 15.4. The six countries accounted for 85 per cent of world production of passenger cars in 1964 and for a substantially higher percentage of world exports.

A major disadvantage of the data for our purposes is that the prices are domestic list prices (excluding sales and purchase taxes) rather than the export prices which are most relevant to international price competitiveness. In a number of cases, particularly in regard to U.S. exports we were informed that the domestic and export prices were the same but no one claimed that this was true for all countries and periods. Also

Table 15.2

OECD Exports of Passenger Cars (SITC 732.1 and 732.6), by Origin and Destination, 1963

(dollars in millions)

| | Value of Exports | Per Cent of OECD Exports in 732.1+732.6 | Share in OECD Exports (per cent) | | | | EEC | | | | |
			OECD	U.S.	U.K.	Total	Germany	France	Italy	Japan	Canada
Total, all destinations	$3,360	100.0	100.0	8.8	19.8	66.5	39.4	14.8	7.5	1.2	0.8
Destination											
U.S.	531	15.8	100.0		20.1	72.9	62.2	6.8	2.9	0.7	0.3
OECD Europe	1,805	53.7	100.0	3.6	15.1	78.5	42.1	18.2	9.8	a	0.1
U.K.	53	1.6	100.0		1.7	85.0	26.9	19.5	12.1		2.8
EEC total	1,102	32.8	100.0	3.6	12.8	82.8	36.5	22.6	11.7	a	0.1
Germany	188	5.6	100.0	3.9	6.6	87.9		42.2	34.3		a
France	184	5.5	100.0	2.6	20.6	76.2	45.4		20.0		a
Italy	251	7.5	100.0	0.4	14.6	84.9	50.4	33.4			a
Canada	83	2.5	100.0	32.5	22.5	40.0	34.7	5.0	0.4	0.1	
Japan	20	0.6	100.0	42.6	16.7	40.2	36.8	2.0	1.5		
Latin America	195	5.8	100.0	54.5	6.0	34.3	20.0	9.4	4.4	2.1	1.6
Others	727	21.6	100.0	12.1	34.7	44.6	21.8	14.9	6.9	4.1	2.7

Source: Appendix A.

aLess than 0.05 per cent.

Table 15.3

OECD Exports of Passenger Cars, 1953, 1957, 1961–64

(dollars in millions)

| | Value of OECD Exports | | | | Share in OECD Exports (per cent) | | | | | |
| | | | | | | EEC | | | | |
		OECD	U.S.	U.K.	Total	Ger-many	France	Italy	Japan	Canada
1964	$3,795	100.0	8.6	19.0	65.8	39.9	11.6	7.4	2.0	1.7
1963	3,360	100.0	8.8	19.8	66.5	39.4	14.8	7.5	1.2	0.8
1962	2,936	100.0	9.3	20.5	65.7	36.8	14.6	9.1	1.0	0.7
1961	2,334	100.0	9.6	17.8	69.1	41.0	15.2	7.9	0.7	0.7
1957	1,643[a]	100.0	18.6	25.9	51.9	30.2	13.0	6.1	NA	1.4
1953	874[a]	100.0	32.3	30.9	32.3	15.4	10.6	4.2	NA	4.2

[a]Excluding Switzerland and Spain. Their exports were only about $1 million in 1961 and would not affect the percentages shown.

Table 15.4

Number of Models Included in Regressions Based on Domestic List Prices
of Domestic Cars, 1953, 1957, 1961–64

Model Year	U.S.	U.K.	Germany	France	Italy	Japan
1953	106	23	12	8	4	
1957	130	39	20	15	7	9
1961	210	36	30	13	14	19
1962	195	45	33	18	14	21
1963	216	54	29	21	16	34
1964	207	67	40	17	17	50
Total	1064	264	164	92	72	133

the size of the average discount from list price given to domestic purchasers may change from time to time, and thus make the list prices
unreliable guides to actual price movements even in home markets. This
possibility is reduced, but not eliminated, by our practice of taking prices
as of the beginning of the model year, when discounting is generally at
a minimum.

Changes in the extent of discounting from list prices in retail sales
could have come about through changes in the discount from list allowed to dealers by the manufacturers or through changes in dealer
profit margins. Information on profit margins supplied by the National
Automobile Dealers Association suggests that they did not change enough
to be a serious source of error in our indexes. The averages for the
years covered in our study were as follows: [2]

	Ratio (per cent)	
	Gross Profit to All Sales	Washout Profit to New and Used Unit Sales
1953	15.2	NA
1957	14.4	9.6
1961	15.3	10.1
1962	15.2	10.3
1963	14.8	10.1
1964	14.7	10.1

[2] It must be noted, however, that new passenger cars account for less than half of
the total sales of the dealers, since their sales include trucks, used vehicles, parts, and

The main factor tending toward change in the discount from list allowed to dealers was the introduction of compact cars, on which the discount was smaller than on full-sized cars. However, even if compact cars had risen from zero to a quarter of our sample between 1957 and 1961, the effect on our price index would not have been more than about 1 per cent.[3]

As far as possible, the sample is limited to standard sedans.[4] Station wagons, convertibles, hardtops, and sports cars were excluded in order to avoid the uncertainties that would be encountered in classifying cars into these sometimes overlapping categories, and, secondarily, to avoid adding more variables to a list already long. We had intended to include only four-door sedans, since the deletion of two-door cars would have resolved some uncertainties about the classification of a car as a sedan or sports car. However, two-door cars figured prominently in our German data, and their exclusion would have eliminated a number of German observations. Thus both two-door and four-door variants of a particular car were included whenever separate data on price and physical characteristics could be obtained for them.

Deluxe models were excluded unless they were larger or more powerful than the standard models for which we had data. Since we had no independent variables designed to measure the amount of chrome or the luxuriousness of the interior, including cars differentiated from standard models solely by such characteristics seemed pointless. Of course, heavier and more powerful cars may also have more chrome and more luxurious interiors, and to the extent this is the case, our regression coefficients for the included characteristics such as weight and displacement will be biased upward, since they will reflect in part higher prices really attributable to the missing variables.

The data on U.S. automobiles were taken in the first instance from *Ward's Statistical Report* or *Automotive Industries*. Data on weight,

service. The gross profit figures include parts, service, and finance, as well as new and used vehicles. The washout profit covers only new and used vehicles but is net of gains and losses from resale of traded-in vehicles.

[3] There is little information in the public domain concerning discounts at the retail level. A series of articles by A. F. Jung in the *Journal of Business*, 1959 and 1960, indicated that discounts in the Chicago area averaged around 15 per cent in 1959 and 1960. At about the same time, the *Economist* (July 23, 1960, p. 383) reported that current discounts in England on one major make were around 10 per cent.

[4] Two- and four-door sedans accounted for 44 per cent of U.S. passenger car factory sales in 1964. Hardtops, the next most important category, accounted for 38 per cent (*Automotive Industries*, March 15, 1966, p. 96).

length, horsepower, engine displacement, number of cylinders, and price were gathered. The prices were retail and excluded federal and local taxes, delivery, and handling charges. The material in these sources was usually so arranged that it was necessary to collate data from different tables in order to complete the information about each car. It was sometimes difficult to be certain that this could be done correctly from the published data. Information transcribed from these published sources was therefore sent to the automobile companies for their review and correction. Although the entire sample was not subject to this process of review and correction, we believe few errors remain.

The starting point for accumulating the data on European cars was a series of production surveys in the United Kingdom, Germany, France, and Italy made available to us by a large automobile manufacturer. For each of the more important models produced by makers whose annual output exceeded a certain minimum (15,000 cars in most years), the surveys gave the model name or number, list price, number of cylinders, number of doors, engine displacement, and estimated volume of production. For the United Kingdom, where the number of makes is larger than in any of the other three countries, a few of the most important producers with outputs less than the minimum were also listed. The listed makes thus accounted for at least 95 per cent of national output in every case, and for more than 99 per cent in the last few years.

The next step was to add information on weight, length, and brake horsepower for each model. Basic reliance was placed on tabulations of foreign car characteristics appearing in the mid-March issues of the U.S. publication *Automotive Industries*. The matching of cars between the two sources was based on model name or number and on engine displacement. Other sources were the *London Times* "Survey of the British Motor Industry" and the *Autocar* "Buyers Guide" and the French publication *Argus*. For 1953 models some data were drawn from a tabulation in the *Economist* of October 25, 1952.

In a number of instances, these sources gave conflicting information— particularly on price and weight—about what seemed, on the basis of model name or number and engine displacement, to be the same car. Where the numerical differences were substantial and there was no clear-cut basis for thinking one was right and the other wrong, the car was generally dropped. Small differences (generally within 1 or 2 per cent) in list prices for British cars between our private source and the published materials referred to above were resolved by taking the lower of the two prices. In the case of French cars, apparently unsystematic differences between prices given by our private source and those in *Argus,* sometimes reaching as high as 7 or 8 per cent, were settled by using *Argus* prices. Since there were some discrepancies between *Argus* and *Automotive Industries* about length, horsepower, and weight, *Argus* data were chosen for these characteristics also, in order to minimize errors in the matching of prices and physical characteristics. This had the disadvantage of using "running weight" for French cars, and "shipping weight" for all other cars; the former includes water, oil, and possibly some gasoline, while the latter is dry weight.

The surveys prepared by the private source reported retail list prices (excluding sales and purchase taxes) as of the beginning of the model year, which was taken as the October or November preceding a given calendar year. Thus the 1964 data we used are based on tables for November 1963 prepared by our private source, on French (*Argus*) and English (*Autocar* and the *London Times* "Survey") publications appearing in October 1963, and on a U.S. publication (*Automotive Industries*) appearing in March 1964. While the change-over from one year's model to the next in the fall of each year is less systematic in Europe than in the United States, all things considered there seemed to be no better way to maximize comparability than by placing the prices for all countries on a beginning-of-model-year basis.

All the Japanese data were obtained from a single Japanese source.

Foreign prices were converted to dollars at the exchange rates prevailing as of the month of the price list. The sample averages (unweighted) for the terminal year are shown in Table 15.5.

Independent Variables

The physical characteristics considered for use as independent variables—weight, length, horsepower, displacement, number of cylinders, and number of doors—represent only a few of the literally hundreds of specifications that are used to describe an automobile. Beyond a certain point, the gain from including a larger number is not worth the statistical complications. Our experience with regression methods (see Chapter 5) indicates that it is usually possible to account for a high proportion of the price variation (something like 90 per cent) with three to five variables; once a very high correlation coefficient is reached, further additions

Table 15.5
Average Price and Characteristics of 1964 Models Included in Regressions of Domestic Cars

	Price (dollars)	Weight (pounds)	Length (in.)	Horse-power (number)	Piston Displacement (cu. in.)	Mean Effective Pressure[a]
U.S.						
All cars	2,407	3,206	202.4	200.4	282.9	69.03
Excl. auto. trans.[b]	2,228	3,121	201.1	192.5	274.3	68.50
U.K.	2,004	2,233	164.9	79.6	106.4	74.54
Germany	1,974	2,053	169.9	71.3	91.8	76.94
France	1,656	1,894	167.0	51.5	68.4	76.15
Italy	2,494	2,264	163.7	81.9	94.7	85.28
Japan	2,160	2,249	162.5	66.5	89.9	74.87

[a](Horsepower x 100) divided by piston displacement.
[b]All cars, excluding twelve with automatic transmission as a standard feature.

of independent variables often have little impact on either the correlation coefficient or the price indexes derived from the regressions. The variables we included are strategic in that they are closely related to many of the omitted ones [5] and are also, among the alternatives available, those used most by consumers to differentiate one sedan from another. (There are international differences on this last point; horsepower is used more widely as an indicator of power in the United States, while displacement is relied upon more in Europe.)

The independent variables tend to be highly intercorrelated. The correlation coefficients below were found, for example, when 1963 and 1964 data for the United States were pooled:

	Weight	Length	Displacement	Horsepower
Length (L)	.91			
Displacement (D)	.81	.73		
Horsepower (H)	.74	.67	.95	
Mean effective pressure (M)	.48	.45	.67	.85

Mean effective pressure as used in our calculations is simply the ratio of horsepower to piston displacement. Actually, the correct formula is

$$M = \frac{Hk}{DR}$$

where k is a constant, and R is revolutions per minute.[6] R is not included in our data, but its range of variation is small and H/D is probably a good surrogate for M.[7]

The variables we have do not, of course, measure all of the qualities that are important to the automobile purchaser. Style, size and comfort, and power are probably the key considerations, although factors such as reliability and economy of operation may also be significant. We have variables that represent size and comfort and power, but none that can be regarded as a proxy for style. We tried to minimize the effect of this omission by basing our study on sedans and excluding

[5] The multicollinearity between the included and excluded is no advantage in obtaining unbiased estimates of the coefficients of the included variables, but helps to explain a large portion of the variance in prices.

[6] See A. R. Rogowski, *Elements of Internal-Combustion Engines*, New York, 1953, p. 53.

[7] For the 173 cars included in the French market data, referred to below, the coefficient of correlation between D and DR was 0.98.

sports cars and other models for which styling is a more important factor.

Size and at least the gross differences in comfort are probably reflected in length and weight.[8] Length and weight are usually highly correlated, as in the illustration of U.S. cars given above, but sometimes one and sometimes the other explains price variation better. We could, of course, include whichever was better in each situation, but we prefer if possible to establish a common set of independent variables to use for all price comparisons. The inclusion of both length and weight usually adds to the correlation coefficient; even where it does not, there is little impact on our price comparisons.

In measuring power we must limit ourselves to three of the four variables in the expression $H = MDR/k$; otherwise we should be including the same thing twice.[9] One possibility is to include horsepower alone. (It would be desirable to have an objective test measurement of horsepower, performed by the same impartial body on the engines of all countries, rather than the manufacturer's advertised horsepower, which is what we have.) There is, however, an advantage to including the elements that determine horsepower—that is, M, D, and R—rather than horsepower itself, for reasons given in Chapter 5.

The basic independent variables that we used, therefore, were W, L, D, and M. Since we have no independent data on M and no data on R, we derive what we shall call "M" by dividing D into H.

We considered and rejected as independent variables the number of doors and volume of production. The door variable frequently had insignificant coefficients and created computational difficulties in some cases where there were only one or a few observations of two-door models. Since four-door models are heavier than two-door ones, the effect of dropping this variable was to allow the weight variable to

---

[8] Weight has both a positive aspect in adding to the size and comfort of a car and a negative aspect in requiring a more powerful motor and greater fuel costs. Technical progress has aimed in part at weight reduction, and thus tended to make weight an unreliable guide to quality over time. However, in any one year, weight often adds significantly to the explanatory power of the regression, and the amount of weight-saving technical change has probably been small from one of our reference years to the next. Even one of the more important changes, the shift to aluminum block engines and subsequently to lightweight cast-iron engines, must be assessed in terms of the fact that the engine is only around 15 per cent of the weight of the total car.

[9] This is one of the points, referred to earlier, at which we could further split out variables. Displacement, for example, is the product of the displacement per piston and the number of pistons; the advantage of more pistons, given the total displacement, is that firing is more continuous and performance therefore smoother.

bear the burden of explaining price differences attributable to the number of doors.[10]

Although the scale of production is not per se an element of utility to consumers [11] (unless it is considered to bring about such benefits as more widespread and less costly repair services and higher resale values) differences in scale may produce direct price differences for cars of equivalent quality. In that event, a scale variable should be included in our equations; otherwise price differences attributable to scale might be incorrectly ascribed to the other independent variables (W, L, etc.), and the coefficients used to estimate the price differences might also be biased. We would, of course, regard scale as one of the reasons for real price differences confronting consumers, unlike differences in the quality variables (W, L, etc.) which produce differences in nominal prices for which corrections must be made.[12] Since the effects on price were uniformly small and not always in the same direction, it seemed preferable to delete this variable.[13]

[10] The coefficient for two-door cars was usually negative. However, positive coefficients are also credible; they signify that two-door models were expensive relative to four-door models, holding weight, length, displacement, and pressure constant.

[11] Small volume may, however, help provide prestige for the purchasers. It may, on the other hand, merely reflect the failure of the producer to gain acceptance for the car.

[12] We considered a number of alternative ways of associating a scale variable—i.e., volume of production—with each passenger car in our sample:

1. The output of the maker (e.g., Chevrolet in the United States or Austin in England).
2. The output of a whole group of commonly owned makes (e.g., G.M. rather than Chevrolet in the United States, and the British Motor Corporation rather than Austin in the United Kingdom).
3. The output of the particular model whose price and other characteristics were taken as an observation.
4. The output of the particular model plus some or all of the output of closely related models. (E.g., in the case of the two-door Falcon standard 6, all or part of the output of four-door Falcon standard 6 or of all other Falcons might be added to the number of two-door standard sizes.)

We experimented with maker's output (No. 1) and a variant of series output (No. 4) in which we took model volume as the output of the particular model plus half the output of closely related models. The estimation of series output for each car necessarily involved heavy reliance on similarity or dissimilarity of the names assigned to different models, and a number of arbitrary decisions had to be made. Without detailed knowledge of the manner in which different models share common parts and overhead items (such as design costs), it is impossible to get good measures of the true scale of production for each observation.

[13] Another variable falling outside of the category of performance characteristics that we considered was size classification into compacts, standards, etc. It seemed preferable to allow length to explain price differences on this score, particularly since lengths regarded as standard in some years were regarded as compact in others. (The standard four-door sedans of the three major U.S. producers in 1953 were all under 200 inches, the length regarded as the upper limit for compacts when they were first introduced. Later, some of the compacts of the more expensive brands crept over the 200-inch limit.)

About 10 per cent of the U.S. cars in our sample came equipped with automatic transmission as a standard item, and a dummy variable was added to take account of this influence on price. Some of the same cars also came with power brakes and/or power steering as standard equipment, but we did not add separate dummy variables for these items. Cars in which these features were standard items were higher priced, and the coefficient for automatic transmission probably reflects not only the addition to price for this feature (and sometimes power brakes and power steering) but also luxury features such as exterior and interior trim that are not picked up by W, L, D, or M.

Scope and Form of the Regressions

The basic approach was to pool data for successive pairs of years in the regression analysis for each country. For each pair of years price was correlated with W, L, D, M, and one or more dummy variables which were inserted to measure the difference in price between the two years.[14] We begin by estimating an equation in which there is a dummy variable for the second year and an interaction term for each combination of time and characteristic (W, L, D, M). The time dummy distinguishes the intercept of the second year from that of the base year; the interaction terms distinguish the slope of each characteristic in the second year from the slope of the same characteristic in the base year. By dropping the dummy and interaction terms that do not prove to be significant and retaining those that do, we use the whole size and range of the combined sample for the two years to estimate the coefficients which seem to be common to them while permitting the estimation of separate coefficients where these appear to be warranted. We thus avoid the imposition of equal coefficients for W, L, D, and M on equations for the two years.

In each pooled regression we tested each of the intercept and slope dummies to see whether it should be retained, according to the rules described in Chapter 5.[15]

---

[14] For further details and for other regression approaches, including pooling of all the situations and use of separate regressions for each situation, see Chapter 5.

[15] See section on "Pooling with International Differences in Element Prices." However, a minor difference in the rules was that in the automobile comparisons, the intercept dummy was retained when it was at least as large as its standard error even when the constant term was not significant. This treatment assumes that the constant term, which refers to the price of a car with zero weight, length, etc., does not have an economic interpretation but is merely a device for providing a better fit within the range of observation.

With respect to mathematical form, a number of experimental regressions were computed for each of the six countries using linear, semilog, inverse semilog, and double log equation forms. The inverse semilog form (in which logarithmic price is the dependent variable and the independent variables are in arithmetic form) was chosen chiefly because it almost always accounted for a higher proportion of the price variation than any other form, regardless of the country or the combination of independent variables used. This form (like the double log form) has the advantage for our purpose of minimizing the squares of percentage deviations rather than the squares of absolute deviations: A larger absolute error is acceptable in estimating the price of a $4,000 automobile than of a $2,000 one.

Time-to-time Movement of Domestic Automobile Prices

The year-to-year changes in domestic automobile prices estimated by these methods are shown for each of the six countries in Table 15.6 and as indexes on a 1962 base in Table 15.7. Since the automobile prices were always converted into dollars before being used, adjusted figures in parentheses are given for Germany and France (the two countries which changed their exchange rates within our period) to show how the indexes would appear to persons spending the domestic currencies of those countries rather than dollars.

Automobile prices declined by 17 per cent in Italy between 1953 and 1957 and by 29 per cent in Japan between 1957 and 1961. In both cases the volume of production greatly increased, and the price movements were probably associated with the attainment of greater economies of scale. The price decline was arrested in Italy after 1961 but continued in Japan, although at a diminishing rate. In France, automobile prices rather consistently increased in terms of domestic currency during the period, although for 1957–61, owing to a 29 per cent currency devaluation, dollar prices declined by 14 per cent. For the period as a whole, only Japanese and Italian prices declined significantly. French prices converted to dollars at official exchange rates were almost as high at the end as at the beginning. German prices did not change much in domestic terms but rose slightly in dollar terms after the appreciation of the mark in 1961. U.K. prices were about 8 per cent higher and U.S. prices about 11 per cent higher in 1964 as compared to 1953.

While these results are the best we were able to derive from our data

Table 15.6
Price Relatives, Domestic Cars, Preferred Regressions, 1953, 1957, 1961−64

	$\dfrac{1957}{1953}$	$\dfrac{1961}{1957}$	$\dfrac{1962}{1961}$	$\dfrac{1963}{1962}$	$\dfrac{1964}{1963}$
United States					
Price relative	99	105	107	100	100
$\bar{R}^2$	.91	.85	.85	.88	.90
Dummies	TLD	TWL	TLD	WDM	WM
United Kingdom					
Price relative	95	106	101	101	105
$\bar{R}^2$	.92	.93	.96	.96	.94
Dummies	TM	TLM	TM	T	TWLM
Germany					
Price relative	100	99	106	102	98
$\bar{R}^2$	.96	.96	.97	.97	.98
Dummies	WL	TWLM	TL	M	LM
France					
Price relative	101	86	106	103	104
$\bar{R}^2$	.90	.94	.91	.89	.90
Dummies	TWLM	DM	TL	M	M
Italy					
Price relative	83	92	100	101	100
$\bar{R}^2$	.99	.93	.93	.94	.96
Dummies	TW	WLD	WL	T	T
Japan					
Price relative	NA	71	95	95	97
$\bar{R}^2$	NA	.88	.89	.87	.89
Dummies	NA	WM	TLD	W	TLD

Note: All regressions involve log of price and arithmetic values of the independent variables, which were weight (W), length (L), piston displacement (D), and mean effective pressure (M). A separate regression was computed for each pair of years. Since the method of flexible pooling was used, the independent variables included not only W, L, D, and M but also dummy variables as indicated in the table. T stands for a time or intercept dummy. The basis for selecting the dummy variables is described in the text.

Table 15.7
Indexes of Domestic Car Prices, 1953, 1957, 1961–64
(1962 = 100)

	1953	1957	1961	1962	1963	1964
U.S.	89	89	93	100	100	100
U.K.	98	93	99	100	101	106
Germany	96	96	94	100	102	100
	(101)	(101)	(99)	(100)	(102)	(100)
France	109	110	95	100	103	108
	(84)	(85)	(95)	(100)	(103)	(108)
Italy	133	109	100	100	101	101
Japan	NA	147	105	100	95	92

Note: Based on data summarized in Table 15.6 (with slight rounding differences). Figures in parentheses reflect trend of prices in terms of domestic currency; other figures in terms of dollars.

in terms of the economic rationale and statistical methods we employed, we must point out that other choices of regression method would yield different answers. Results from some of the more likely alternatives are shown in Table 15.8, and in Table 15.9 our preferred results are compared with the automobile price changes measured by wholesale and consumer price indexes. For the United States, the largest differences in both tables occur for the period 1953–57. In the United States, our preferred method shows a 1 per cent decline, while the use of horsepower alone as an independent variable in place of its two components, D and M, produces a 4 per cent increase. The preferred equation is, however, clearly superior; its pooled variables (W, L, D, and M) have coefficients that are more than two times their standard errors and $\bar{R}^2$ is .912, while in the other equation the horsepower coefficient is smaller than its standard error and $\bar{R}^2$ is .890. Among the official indexes in Table 15.9, the U.S. wholesale price index produces a 12 per cent increase in prices between 1953 and 1957 while the consumers price index shows only a 5 per cent rise; the difference could be due to a narrowing of retail margins, but this seems improbable particularly in the light of the dealer margin data cited earlier.

It will be noted that for the period as a whole the NBER indexes show an 11 per cent increase in automobile prices in the United States while the official indexes show only a 9 per cent increase for the con-

Table 15.8

Price Relatives for Domestic Cars, Comparison of Various Regression
Estimates, 1953, 1957, 1961–64

Country	Variables	Mean $\bar{R}^{2a}$	$\dfrac{1957}{1953}$	$\dfrac{1961}{1957}$	$\dfrac{1962}{1961}$	$\dfrac{1963}{1962}$	$\dfrac{1964}{1963}$
U.S.[b]	*WLDM*	.879	99	105	107	100	100
	WLH	.861	104	105	106	100	98
	WLDM[c]	.873	99	105	107	100	100
U.K.	*WLDM*	.940	95	106	101	101	105
	WLH	.917	100	109	103	102	106
	WLDM[c]	.939	96	106	101	101	104
Germany	*WLDM*	.970	100	99	106	102	98
	WLH	.973	94	99	105	102	99
	WLDM[c]	.967	100	99	106	101	98
France	*WLDM*	.906	101	86	106	103	104
	WLH	.873	105	83	101	103	104
	WLDM[c]	.893	99	85	106	102	104
Italy	*WLDM*	.950	83	92	100	101	100
	WLH	.944	81	89	100	101	100
	WLDM[c]	.948	82	88	100	101	100
Japan	*WLDM*	.882		71	95	95	97
	WLH	.854		74	94	95	98
	WLDM[c]	.852		82	93	95	97

Note: The variables are weight (*W*), length (*L*), piston displacement (*D*), mean
effective pressure (*M*). The first two regressions in each set are based on flexible pooling
and in some cases therefore include slope dummies; the last, marked b, is based on
complete pooling. The *WLDM* regressions are those set out in Table 15.6.

[a]Average of $\bar{R}^2$ for five periods.
[b]All U.S. regressions include a dummy variable for automatic transmission.
[c]Based on complete pooling. See Note above.

Table 15.9

Time-to-time Changes in Domestic Car Prices, NBER vs. Other Indexes,
1953, 1957, 1961−64

Country	Source of Index	1957 / 1953	1961 / 1957	1962 / 1961	1963 / 1962	1964 / 1963
U.S.	NBER[a]	99	105	107	100	100
	WPI[b]	112	104	99	99	100
	CPI[b]	105	105	100	99	100
	F-G-K	83	100	NA	NA	NA
	Triplett	NA	NA	104	100	100
Germany	NBER[a]	100	99	106	102	98
	WPI[c]	88	105	103	101	100
	CPI[c]	NA	NA	101	101	101
	EPI[d]	99[e]	103	100	100	100
France	NBER[a]	101	86	106	103	104
	WPI[c]	103	77	102	102	101
	CPI[b]	NA	NA	102	102	102
Japan	NBER[a]	NA	71	95	95	97
	WPI[b]	73	82	99	99	97
	CPI[b]	NA	NA	100	96	94
	EPI	NA	NA	98	98	100

WPI = wholesale price indexes.

CPI = consumer price indexes.

EPI = export price indexes.

F-G-K = Calculated by applying data for average weight, length, and horsepower from our pooled samples to regression coefficients given by F. M. Fisher, Z. Griliches, and C. Kaysen, "The Costs of Automobile Model Changes since 1949," *Journal of Political Economy,* October 1962, p 436. Our estimate of the 1957/1953 relative was obtained by calculating the price in both years of a car with the average characteristics of the cars in our pooled sample for those two years, and the 1961/1957 relative by an analogous manner.

EPI = export price index.

Triplett = "Adjacent-year weights," "full model" estimates reported by Jack E. Triplett, "Automobiles and Hedonic Quality Measurement," *Journal of Political Economy,* May−June 1969, Table 3.

[a]As of beginning of each model year.

[b]December prior to each calendar year.

[c]Annual averages.

[d]June of each year.

[e]1957/1954.

sumers index and a 14 per cent increase for the wholesale index. How-ever, the NBER indexes are probably biased upward relative to the BLS indexes because the NBER did not, and the BLS did, make adjust-ments for changes from one model year to the next in accessories included as standard features. (Such changes were taken account of in the NBER indexes only to the degree to which they added to the weight of the car, and this understated their value.) If the changes shown for two impor-tant U.S. models in Tables 15.10 and 15.11 are typical of U.S. cars in general, the net additions of equipment, valued at list prices, would have amounted to about 11 per cent of the first year's price.[16] Only part of this net increase is taken into account by the weight variable in the regression. Thus it is clear that the rise in the NBER index would be less than the increases of 9 and 14 per cent shown by the BLS indexes if the additional equipment were fully accounted for. Incidentally, the inclusion of heaters in the price of standard cars in 1962 was the most important single change not taken into account in the NBER indexes; judging from the relationships for these two models only, the 1962/1961 price relative would have been 104 rather than 107 had allowance been made for the addition of heaters assuming that the NBER indexes had taken no account of their inclusion via the weight variable. (The addi-tion and deletion of automatic transmission in the Buick and other cars through the years were measured in our regressions, since we had a dummy variable for automatic transmission, although the estimates were not necessarily the same as those that would have been obtained from valuing the transmissions at list prices.)

We do not know to what extent European makers or even other U.S. manufacturers made net additions to the accessories included in the price of a standard car, but the trend has probably been in this direc-tion. If this is so, our time-to-time indexes for these countries are also biased upward, though not necessarily to the same degree as the United States or as each other.

The NBER indexes also differ from the BLS and other official indexes because of differences between the regression and conventional ap-proaches. In the conventional method efforts are usually made to match nearly comparable automobiles in two situations and to adjust prices (on a cost basis) for the differences between them not only in accessories

---

[16] Net additions were equivalent to 11.1 per cent of the 1953 price of the Chevrolet and to 10.1 per cent of the 1953 price of the Buick.

Table 15.10

Changes in Standard Items Included in List Price of Low-priced Four-door
Chevrolet Sedan, 1953, 1956–64

Model Year[a]	List Price[b]	Kind of Equipment	Value of Equipment Made Standard and Incl. in Price
1953	$1,575		
1956	1,705	Directional signals	$15.75
1957	1,857		
1958	1,955	Vacuum booster windshield wipers ($10.50), 30-amp generator ($7.00), junction block ($3.40)	20.90
1959	2,091	Electric windshield wiper	6.00
1960	2,106	Arm rests, right side sun shade, cigar lighter	15.00
1961	2,106		
1962	2,164[c]	Heater	69.00
		Oil filter	8.50
1963	2,164		
1964	2,202	Positive crankcase ventilation	10.00
		Rear seat arm rests	9.00
		Deluxe steering wheel	3.50
		Foam rubber rear seat cushion	4.35
		Front seat belts	10.00
		Deluxe floor covering	11.15
Total			183.15
Net			174.15

[a]There were no changes in standard equipment in the model years omitted from the table.

[b]For four-door Chevrolet Sedan: Model 150 from 1953–57, Del Ray in 1958, and Biscayne 1959–64; all six cylinder.

[c]Smaller tires, valued at $9.00, were made optional and excluded from the price.

Table 15.11

Changes in Standard Items Included in List Price of Regular Four-door
Buick Sedan, 1953, 1957, 1959–64

Model Year[a]	List Price[b]	Kind of Equipment	Value of Equipment Made Standard and Incl. in Price
1953	$2,064		
1957	2,412		
1959	2,545	Aluminum brake drum	$18.50
		Larger tires	16.00
1960	2,606	Instrument panel padding	15.00
		Custom trim (interior)	46.00
1961	2,826	Automatic transmission	205.00
1962	2,937	Heater	92.00
1963	2,732[c]	Positive crankcase ventilation	5.00
		Front seat belts	10.00
		Permanent coolant	6.50
1964	2,712		
Total			414.00
Net			209.00

[a]There were no changes in standard equipment in the model years omitted from the table.

[b]For regular four-door sedan: Buick Special 40, 1953–58; LeSabre from 1959–64. All eight-cylinder.

[c]Automatic transmission, valued at $205.00, was made optional and excluded from the price.

such as arm rests but also in such continuous characteristics as weight and horsepower. The adjusted prices are then compared to determine the price differences. This exercise may be carried out—often quite carefully and in consultation with the industry—for three, six, or a dozen or more models. The price change for automobiles is then taken as an average of these price comparisons. However, the bases for selecting the comparable pairs and, more important, the choices among alternative ways of making the price adjustments are *ad hoc* and are rarely described very fully.[17]

[17] The fullest account known to us is that by Margaret S. Stotz of the BLS, "Introductory Prices of 1966 Automobile Models," *Monthly Labor Review,* February 1966, pp. 178–181. See also O. A. Larsgaard and L. J. Mack, "Compact Cars in the Con-

The data below, referring to a standard six-cylinder, four-door, Chevrolet Biscayne sedan, illustrate the problem:

	1962	1963
Price (dollars)	$2,164	$2,164
Weight (pounds)	3,480	3,280
Length (inches)	209.6	210.4
Piston displacement (cubic inches)	235.5	230.0
Horsepower	135	140

The list price was the same in both years, but weight and piston displacement declined in 1963 while horsepower and length increased. How much should price be adjusted for the 6 per cent decline in weight and how much for the 4 per cent increase in horsepower? If interpolations are made in a systematic fashion in such cases, the method has never been described, to the best of our knowledge, by any producer of the important price indexes.[18]

The little that has been publicly said in the United States about the procedures in automobile price measurement in the official price indexes is consistent with a wide variety of practices at different times; quite possibly, no method has been consistently in use over the period covered by this study.

It is to be expected that the possibility for different answers to emerge from different methods will be greater the larger the changes in specifications between two periods. In our automobile data, as we mentioned, relatively large divergences in results were obtained from different methods during the period 1953–57, when the mix of specifications built into the average car was very greatly changed. In the United States in particular there was a sharp shift toward more powerful engines. Aver-

sumers Price Index," *Monthly Labor Review*, May 1961. Until the 1960 model year, quality adjustments were confined to changes in optional equipment made standard or vice versa (*The Consumer Price Index: Technical Notes, 1959–63*, BLS Bull. 1554, p. 5). The sample for the BLS consumer price index before 1961, Larsgaard and Mack report, was limited to standard Chevrolets, Fords, and Plymouths. In 1966, Stotz indicates, the CPI was based on eight models, of which four were sports cars or hardtops; and the wholesale price index, on eighteen models.

18 The Biscayne was not used in 1966, according to Stotz (*op. cit.*), but lists of models used for the earlier indexes have not, as far as we know, been published. The point made in the text applies, however, to the models that were used in 1966 unless the sample has been changed each year as a result of a systematic and successful search for models that were unchanged from the preceding year. Even if an adequate number of unchanged models could always be found among the volume sellers, a bias would be introduced if producers follow a policy of making larger price changes for models with altered specifications than for models with unchanged specifications.

Table 15.12
U.S. Price Competitiveness,[a] Cars, 1953, 1957, 1961–64
(1962 = 100)

	1953	1957	1961	1962	1963	1964
Relative to						
U.K.	110	104	106	100	101	106
Germany	108	108	101	100	102	100
France	122	124	102	100	103	108
Italy	138	122	108	100	101	101
Japan	NA	165	113	100	95	92

[a]Measured by the ratio of the foreign to the U.S. domestic price indexes in Table 15.7.

age horsepower of cars produced in the United States rose from 125 in 1953 to 233 in 1957; the peak of 260 came in 1958, and by our reference year 1961 it had dropped to 201, only to resume the climb back to 233 by our final year, 1964.[19] Judging from our samples, the same thing happened, at a lower horsepower level and to a smaller degree, abroad; in the United Kingdom and in Germany, average horsepower of the sedans in our sample rose by around 25 per cent between 1953 and 1957. No other pair of years saw such big changes in power or other specifications. Neither in the United States nor abroad was there any matching increase in size; indeed, the length of sedans tended to remain unchanged and weight declined somewhat.

The broad picture of changes in relative prices seems fairly clear. The price competitiveness of Japanese and Italian automobiles has improved substantially, and the positions of the United Kingdom and the United States have worsened. The details of these changes, as measured by our preferred price indexes, are shown in Table 15.12. The decline in U.S. price competitiveness was arrested in 1962; after that date, only Japan (which was, as we shall see, a high-priced producer) improved its price position vis-à-vis the United States. Some of the smaller changes shown in the table should be considered in the light of our earlier statements concerning our inability to allow for changes in the addition of accessories as standard features and the existence of a range of indeterminancy in price measurement. The underlying indexes represent the results of

[19] *Automotive Industries,* March 15, 1965, p. 122.

methods which we have described and which in our judgment are
preferable to others, but there is room for disagreement and further
improvement of methods in this area of statistical work.

International Comparisons of Automobile Prices, 1964

Home Market Comparisons

The regression methods used to derive time-to-time indexes of the
domestic prices of automobiles were also employed to make international
price comparisons for the last of our reference years, 1964. The situations paired this time were different countries for the same time period
rather than different times for the same country. Data for each of the
five foreign countries, in turn, were pooled with U.S. data.[20] For each
foreign-U.S. pair, prices were correlated with weight, length, displacement, and pressure, and with country and slope dummies which were
retained or discarded by the criteria set out above. The results are set
out in the first bank of figures in Table 15.13.

Two things are evident from a glance at the results. First, the domestic prices of foreign automobiles appear to be higher than the domestic
prices of U.S. automobiles. This outcome, it should be remembered, is
based on the assumption that the size and power of an automobile as
measured by weight, length, displacement, and pressure are adequate
measures of the relative amounts of automobile embodied in each particular model.

The second striking aspect of the figures is that it makes a great deal
of difference whether prices are compared for a U.S.- or foreign-type
car. When based on the specifications of the average U.S. car in our
sample, French prices, for example, are calculated to be more than four
times as great as U.S. prices; when, on the other hand, the comparison
is made in terms of the average French car, French prices are slightly
lower than U.S. prices. Intermediate results are obtained when the calculations are based on the midpoints of the U.S. and French averages—
i.e., the "median" car.

An alternative method is to limit the comparisons to ranges of cars
which are produced in both countries, as in the second bank of figures

[20] Since none of the foreign cars had automatic transmission as a standard feature,
the twelve U.S. cars with automatic transmission were deleted for the international
comparisons.

Table 15.13
International Comparisons of Domestic Car Price Levels,
Based on Regression Analysis, 1964
(U.S. = 100 for price relatives)

	U.K.	Germany	France	Italy	Japan
All cars pooled, each country paired with U.S.[a]					
$\bar{R}^2$	.917	.933	.902	.920	.895
Number of foreign cars[b]	67	40	17	17	50
Foreign-U.S. price relative for car with specifications of					
U.S. average car[c]	134	322	420	379	462
Foreign average car[c]	108	105	98	125	119
Median car[d]	120	183	203	218	235
Overlapping models (80–149 H.P.) pooled, each country paired with U.S.[a]					
$\bar{R}^2$	.848	.900		.907	.822
Number of foreign cars[e]	21	11		10	19
Foreign-U.S. price relative for car with specifications of median car[f]	125	143	NA	214	197
Individual country regressions[a, g]					
$\bar{R}^2$	.923	.967	.892	.957	.910
Foreign-U.S. price relative for car with specifications of					
U.S. average car[c]	140	332	437	342	459
Foreign average car[c]	108	105	99	125	119
Median car[d]	123	183	208	207	233

[a]All are pooled regressions based on the method of flexible pooling; all have log of price as the dependent variable and weight (W), length (L), piston displacement (D), and mean effective pressure (M) as independent variables. Twelve U.S. cars having automatic transmission as a standard feature are excluded.

[b]In each case, 195 U.S. cars.

[c]See Table 15.5 for specifications.

[d]Simple average of average specifications for the United States and the foreign country.

[e]In each case, 70 U.S. cars.

[f]The "median" cars here for each bilateral comparison are based on the average of the U.S. and foreign average specifications for models in the 80–149 horsepower range:

	U.S.	U.K.	Germany	Italy	Japan
Weight (lbs.)	2,843	2,780	2,442	2,626	2,764
Length (in.)	196	180	182	176	179
Displacement (cu. in.)	194	142	117	119	119
Pressure (H.P. x 100 ÷ D)	62	77	89	90	78

[g]Numbers of cars same as in pooled regression; $\bar{R}^2$ for U.S. = 0.845.

in Table 15.13, based on regressions that included only cars in the 80 to 149 horsepower range. France, with only two observations, was excluded,[21] and the number of observations for Italy and for Germany was reduced to less than a dozen. The new results are similar to the former ones for median cars for Italy and the United Kingdom but lower for Germany and Japan.

The final bank of figures in Table 15.13 shows the basic price comparisons derived from separate regressions for each of the countries. The results are not very different from those obtained by the method of flexible pooling which was used to derive the estimates in the first bank. The individual-country regressions are summarized in Table 15.14.

In view of the wide range of results presented in Table 15.13, the extent and consequences of the differences in the size and power of U.S. and foreign cars must be considered more closely. Our samples are comprehensive in the sense that they include almost every two- and four-door standard sedan produced in volumes of more than a few thousand in the United States or Europe. The sample averages in Table 15.5 and the distribution of sample cars by horsepower in Table 15.15 and by weight in Table 15.16 clearly reveal the larger size and greater power of U.S. cars relative to the others. Both the averages and the distributions suggest that the differences between the United States and the other countries are greater in power than in size; even the larger European cars tend to be less powerful than U.S. ones. The differences in size are large enough, however, to affect engine design; they may help explain the tendency abroad to produce engines that are smaller than American ones for a given horsepower output (i.e., have a smaller displacement and higher pressure).

There are differences among the other five countries also. Generally, however, the differences in prices and kinds of cars produced are small among the foreign countries relative to the differences between the United States and the rest. This is not surprising, since the five countries are more alike in the characteristics which determine the size and power of automobiles demanded on the domestic markets; the United States

---

[21] The actual prices of these two cars were 114 and 158 per cent, respectively, of the prices that cars with similar specifications sold for in the United States, the U.S. prices being estimated from a regression equation for seventy U.S. cars in the 80–149 horsepower range. Incidentally, in the French regression the predicted prices of these cars were 6 per cent and 15 per cent, respectively, less than the actual prices, lending support to the speculation that French prices for more powerful cars would be relatively high.

Table 15.14

Regressions of Domestic Prices of Cars on Selected Physical Characteristics, Six OECD Countries, 1964

(dependent variable, price, in logs; independent variables in arithmetic terms; figures in parentheses are *t*-ratios)

	U.S.[a]		U.K.	Germany	France	Italy	Japan
	(A)	(B)					
Weight (10^2 lbs.)	0.0150	0.0254	0.0413	.0143	-.0241	.0274	0.0005
	(6.25)	(7.70)	(6.66)	(3.49)	(-1.10)	(.72)	(.06)
Length (10 in.)	0.0139	-0.0019	0.0118	.0391	.1146	.0837	0.0259
	(1.78)	(-.02)	(1.07)	(2.40)	(3.26)	(.96)	(.80)
Displacement (cu. in.)	0.0004	0.0001	0.0009	.0065	.0084	.0042	0.0084
	(4.00)	(1.00)	(1.00)	(1.00)	(2.71)	(1.75)	(7.00)
Pressure ($10^2 H/D$)	0.0014	0.0022	0.0072	.0085	.0024	.0031	0.0063
	(2.00)	(2.20)	(7.20)	(9.44)	(1.41)	(1.15)	(4.50)
Constant	2.1328	2.1629	1.1677	.6949	.5594	.4300	1.3473
	(20.41)	(14.39)	(6.63)	(3.14)	(1.45)	(.63)	(3.90)
$\bar{R}^2$	.8451	.9042	.9233	.9674	.8922	.9570	.9100
S.E. of estimate	.0486	.0742	.1040	.0655	.0873	.1158	.1071
No. of observations	195	207	67	40	17	17	50

S.E. = standard error.

[a]A excludes cars with automatic transmissions as a standard feature. B includes them. The coefficient for the dummy variable for automatic transmission in the B equation was 0.0426, with *t*-ratio of 1.41.

Table 15.15

Number and Price per Horsepower Unit of Domestic Cars, by Horsepower Class, Six OECD Countries, 1964

Horsepower	U.S.	U.K.	Germany	France	Italy	Japan
		NUMBER OF CARS				
Under 50		9	7	7	3	13
50–74						
75–99	9	10	6	2	6	16
100–149	61	12	5		5	3
150–199	52		1			1
200–249	24	2				
250–299	23	1				
300 and over	26					
Total	195	67	40	17	17	50
		AVERAGE PRICE PER UNIT OF HORSEPOWER				
Under 50		$30.07	$30.73	$39.85	$34.03	$40.30
50–74		26.14	26.20	29.39	30.55	33.46
75–99	$20.75	25.08	24.72	29.61	28.20	29.16
100–149	16.26	26.40	25.54		31.83	34.98
150–199	12.24		31.97			29.57
200–249	10.48	17.35				
250–299	9.61	17.68				
300 and over	7.87					
All cars	11.57	25.19	26.58	32.17	30.45	32.50

is unique with respect to its per capita income, high-speed highways, distances traveled, and price of gasoline.

These generalizations based on our samples appear to be supported by the rough estimates that we have been able to make of the distribution of European and U.S. production by piston displacement, the variable with which we have been best able to obtain a look at the distribution of European output. When the percentage distributions of cars in our European samples are compared with those of production, as in Table 15.17, we see that because models with smaller engine sizes were produced in greater volume than those with large engines, our sample frequencies tend to underrepresent the importance of small cars, most seriously in the case of Italy. In the United States, there was no output below 2,360 cubic centimeters, and we estimate that only 13 per cent of 1964 production fell between that lower limit and 2,999, with another 6 per cent in the low 3,000's. Our sample frequencies correspond closely; 15 per cent of the observations are between 2,360 and 2,999 cubic centimeters.

The differences in the kinds of cars produced in each country affect our comparisons in two ways, one statistical and the other economic. Statistically, our regressions measure the relationship between price and the independent variables only within the range of observation provided by our sample. Prices for cars with specifications outside this range have

Table 15.16

Number and Price Per Pound of Domestic Cars, by Weight Class, Six OECD Countries, 1964

Weight (lbs.)	U.S.	U.K.	Germany	France	Italy	Japan
NUMBER OF CARS						
Under 1,200				2	2	2
1,200–1,599		9	6	3	1	6
1,600–1,999		25	17	4	1	7
2,000–2,399	3	9	9	6	5	12
2,400–2,799	49	11	2	2	5	9
2,800–3,199	60	4	5		2	14
3,200–3,599	52	7	1		1	
3,600–3,999	27	1				
4,000 and over	4	1				
Total	195	67	40	17	17	50
AVERAGE PRICE PER POUND						
Under 1,200				$0.95	$0.72	$1.25
1,200–1,599		$0.88	$0.84	0.91	0.79	0.92
1,600–1,999		0.88	0.84	0.91	0.82	0.96
2,000–2,399	$0.76	0.79	0.96	0.78	1.02	0.93
2,400–2,799	0.74	0.76	0.97	0.99	0.85	0.85
2,800–3,199	0.72	1.05	0.91		1.48	1.04
3,200–3,599	0.70	0.89	1.72		1.67	
3,600–3,999	0.69	1.19				
4,000 and over	0.73	1.41				
All cars	0.71	0.90	0.92	0.87	1.10	0.96

Table 15.17

Estimated Percentage Distribution of Car Production and NBER Sample,
by Piston Displacement, Four European Countries, 1964

Piston Displacement (cubic centimeters[a])	U.K.	Germany	France	Italy	Four Countries Combined
NUMBER PRODUCED					
Under 500		3	12	26	7
500–999	22	14	45	35	26
1,000–1,499	48	59	26	33	45
1,500–1,999	24	17	16	5	17
2,000–2,999	4	7	1	1	4
Over 3,000	2	b			1
Total	100	100	100	100	100
NUMBER IN SAMPLE					
Under 500			12	12	
500–999	7	15	35	6	
1,000–1,499	43	50	35	41	
1,500–1,999	24	23	18	18	
2,000–2,999	18	12		23	
Over 3,000	8				
Total	100	100	100	100	

[a]16.39 c.c. = 1 cubic inch. The class limits in the table convert to cubic inches as follows:

c.c.	cu. in.
500	30.5
1,000	61
1,500	92
2,000	122
3,000	183

[b]Less than 0.5 per cent.

to be estimated by extrapolation, and we cannot be sure that the relationship really would hold in this unobserved range. In an extreme case, we might find ourselves trying to compare prices for two countries which produced in completely different ranges of output so that extrapolation would be necessary if prices were to be compared. We are close to this situation in comparing France and the United States. If the matching criterion is displacement there is no overlap. With respect to horsepower, our French sample contains only 2 cars (out of a total of 17) with horsepower as great as 80 and none with horsepower over 90, whereas the U.S. sample includes no car with less than 80 horsepower and only 3 (out of 195) with less than 90 horsepower.

From an economic standpoint, the relationships between price and size and power in any country may be influenced by the scale of production in different ranges of size and power. As figures in the lower bank of Table 15.15 show, the prices of automobiles do not increase proportionately as horsepower rises. However, in the United States, where economies of scale are obtained for a wide range of horsepower, price per unit of horsepower is not only lower in each horsepower class but declines more sharply with increasing horsepower than in any other country. In other countries, the downward thrust of price per horsepower is lost as early as the 75–99 horsepower range, where the scale of production declines. Our rough estimates indicate that in France, for example, nearly two-thirds of 1964 output was concentrated in a range of horsepower from 18 to 50, and the scale of production even for leading makes was relatively small at horsepowers in the low 80's. Because of the greater economies of scale at the lower horsepower ranges, regressions for France and the other foreign countries will produce high prices relative to those of the United States for cars in the upper horsepower range observed abroad and very high prices indeed for the powerful cars which are in the middle of the U.S. distribution but well beyond the French or other distributions.

A similar set of influences can be seen at work with respect to weight in Table 15.16. In this case, however, the tendency is toward a U-shaped curve, with price per pound declining as the volume-produced middle range of each country's distribution is approached and then rising again as volume thins out with heavier cars. There appears to be less tendency for increasing weight per se to pull cost per pound down as does increasing horsepower with respect to cost per horsepower. But the effect upon the regressions is probably the same since the prices per pound for the heavier weights near the end of the distribution tend to be higher than for the very light cars at the beginning.

The reverse impact on the U.S. regressions—that is, the tendency for them to be tilted so as to produce very high prices when extrapolated to small cars with low-powered motors—is weaker. U.S. production is dispersed over a much wider horsepower range, and even at low horse-powers (80–100 units) and weights (2,000–2,399 pounds)—low, that is, for U.S. cars—cost per pound is not much higher than average, and the rise in cost per horsepower may be close to that inherent in engines of different size, scale of production being given. Even for these cars, the United States appears to have been able to obtain substantial economies of scale.[22]

These statistical and economic aspects of the regressions have a bearing upon their suitability for providing the answers we are seeking about international price competitiveness in automobiles. Our primary interest is in finding for comparison the prices in each producing country of the kinds of cars that enter international trade.[23] We do not have direct data on the characteristics of these cars but, bearing in mind both the country origins of exports (Table 15.3) and the type of cars produced in each country (Tables 15.5 and 15.15–15.17), we selected five cars of different sizes to represent the kinds of cars that are important in world trade.

The identity and specifications of these cars, and the share of OECD exports assigned to each are given in Table 15.18. The selection of the Italian Fiat and the German Volkswagen poses little question since each is not only representative of an important class of cars but important itself in its country's output and exports. French production, and probably exports as well, are concentrated in a less powerful range of cars than the Peugeot selected, but we needed a car in this range, and this one is at least well known both in its home market and abroad. Much the same is true of the English Zephyr. The U.S. Chevrolet is at the lower end of the U.S. horsepower distribution, but even so it already involves extrapolation beyond the observed horsepower range for France, and the U.S. production average (210 horsepower) would be beyond the ranges for all the other countries except the United Kingdom.

---

[22] A rough estimate based on data in *Ward's* indicates that more than 400,000 cars were produced in the United States in 1964 with horsepowers between 80 and 100. This number, though only a little more than 5 per cent of U.S. output, was equivalent to nearly one-third of total French production.

[23] Two questions still more difficult to answer on the basis of the regressions are: (1) What would be the price of an American-type car in Europe if it were produced in the same circumstances (particularly scale of production for individual firms and for the industry as a whole) as prevailed in 1964 for types actually produced, and (2) what would be the price of a European-type car in the United States if it were produced in the same circumstances as prevailed in 1964 for the types actually produced. Had we been able to develop a better indicator of the scale of production (see discussion of independent variables), it might have been possible to try to answer these questions.

Table 15.18

Specifications of Five Cars Taken as Representative of World Trade and
Shares of Trade Represented

	Shares of Trade Represented[a]	Weight (lbs.)	Length (in.)	Displacement		Horse-power
				C.C.	Cu. In.	
Fiat 600D (Italy)	20%	1,290	130.5	767	46.8	32
Volkswagen 1200 (Germany)	50	1,615	160.2	1,192	72.7	40
Peugeot 404 (France)	15	2,359	174.3	1,618	98.7	72
Zephyr 6 (U.K.)	5	2,618	180.9	2,553	155.8	106
Chevrolet Biscayne (U.S.)	10	3,300	209.9	3,770	230.0	140

[a]The starting point for estimates of the relative importance in OECD exports of cars best represented by each of these five was the share in OECD exports of each country. On this basis, we assigned 10 per cent (a little more than equivalent to U.S. and Canadian exports) to the Chevrolet Biscayne. The initial distribution for the other 90 per cent was based on the relative importance of different engine sizes in European production (the rightmost column of Table 15.17). However, an examination of exports by size classes for the one country (the United Kingdom) for which such data were available, and of unit values for the other European countries and Japan, suggested that very small cars (Fiat) were less important in trade than in production while the opposite was true for the next size class (Volkswagen). We therefore shifted ten percentage points from the initial estimates from the Fiat to the Volkswagen category, the amount of the shift being chosen to make our estimates of the net export prices approximate the unit values when the prices were weighted by the percentages in the distribution.

The price of each of these five cars in each foreign country was compared with the U.S. price by means of the regressions involving flexible pooling of all cars, pairing each country in turn with the United States. The results are set out in Table 15.19.

The comparisons for the Fiat and Volkswagen require extrapolations beyond the range of U.S. observations, but for reasons given above, we do not believe that the extrapolations lead to unreasonable results. Otherwise, aside from France, for which the observations do not cover even the Zephyr range of power, the comparisons are based in the main on cars actually produced—however uneconomically in some instances.

Table 15.19
Home-market Price Comparisons, Five Makes of Car, 1964
(U.S. price for each car = 100)

	Index: Ratio to United States of				
	U.K.	Germany	France	Italy	Japan
Fiat	79	71	72	72	92
Volkswagen	80	81	105	105	101
Peugeot	110	112	112	138	125
Zephyr	116	155	167	187	188
Chevrolet	134	247	307	337	305
Weighted mean	92	104	123	131	128
Addendum:					
$\bar{R}^2$	.92	.93	.90	.92	.89
Dummies retained[a]	WMC	LDMC	WLDC	LDMC	WDMC

[a]W = weight, L = length, D = piston displacement, M = mean effective pressure, C = country dummy.

Within the entire range of its actual production, the United States is the low-priced producer. The regressions tell us U.S. prices would be higher for Fiat- and Volkswagen-sized cars, if America produced them. It is possible that America could not beat European costs even if such cars were produced here in the same volume as current compacts and standard sedans; this might be the case if, for example, only small savings in labor costs were involved in shifting from production of a Zephyr- (or U.S. compact-) type to a Volkswagen- or Fiat-sized car.

Among the European producers the Continental countries are the low-priced producers of the smallest cars, but as we get to larger and more powerful models the United Kingdom emerges as the most price-competitive country. Germany, however, holds its own through the range that probably accounts for the great bulk of the export market. France becomes more and more expensive relative to the United Kingdom and Germany as car size increases, and Italy still more so. Japanese prices for very small cars are relatively high.

In the final row of the table we present a weighted average which indicates that overall the United Kingdom is about 8 per cent cheaper than the United States, Germany a little more expensive than the United States, and the other countries considerably higher priced. This outcome is highly sensitive to the weights we employed, as might be inferred from the substantial differences in the price relatives for the five cars. In any case, even a properly weighted overall average would throw much less light upon competition in the world motor market than the price relatives for the individual types of cars. The market is really a number of different markets for distinct types of cars with elasticities of substitution that are probably low between cars that differ widely in size and power. The relation between price levels and trade should be examined for each of these separate types, not for the aggregate of all automobiles. The influence of the low U.S. price for large cars, which may explain the U.S. market share for U.S.-type cars, is obscured in the world market where the demand for smaller cars predominates.

Comparisons in Selected Markets

All the estimates considered thus far are deficient for our purposes because they relate to the prices of each country's car in its home market, and thus may not provide reliable guides to international price competitiveness. The manufacturers in one country may follow a one-price policy for sales at home and abroad while those in another country may charge different prices in different markets. The general pricing policies of the different producers are difficult to ascertain, and even when it can be established that different prices are charged, it is extremely difficult to get the systematic information necessary for regression analysis.

In view of these difficulties, we sought another approach to the measurement of price competitiveness—viz., the comparison of cars from different competing countries in particular markets. Ideally, we should like to have such a comparison for several important automobile-consuming countries which import a wide range of cars from all six of our producing countries without any discriminatory import regulations and without the complication of having varying degrees of domestic assembly and parts manufacture. What we actually have falls far short of this, viz., prices and specifications for a list of imported and domestic cars on each of four markets—the United States, the United Kingdom, France, and Japan. Furthermore, except for the French market data the number of observations for individual producing countries is not very large—often less than 10 (see the notes to Table 15.20). While

Table 15.20
Regression Comparisons of Home Prices and Prices on Four Other
Markets, Five Makes of Car, 1964
(U.S. = 100 except in Japanese market, where Japan = 100)

	U.S.	U.K.	Germany	France	Italy
Home market prices					
Fiat	100[a]	79	71	72	72
Volkswagen	100[a]	80	81	105	105
Peugeot	100	110	112	112	138
Zephyr	100	116	155	167[a]	187
Chevrolet	100	134	247	307[a]	337
(No. of observations)	(195)	(67)	(40)	(17)	(17)
U.S. market					
Fiat	100[a]	98	99	81	80
Volkswagen	100[a]	102	105	91	86
Peugeot	100	120	136	142	115
Zephyr	100	142	178	228	159
Chevrolet	100	169	234[a]	366[a]	217
(No. of observations)	(129)	(11)	(7)	(6)	(3)
U.K. market					
Fiat	100[a]	33	38	39	40
Volkswagen	100[a]	38	49	48	52
Peugeot	100[a]	47	74	64	70
Zephyr	100	59	101	84[a]	117
Chevrolet	100	92	195	145[a]	236[a]
(No. of observations)	(110)	(50)	(11)	(8)	(12)
French market					
Fiat	100[a]	54	40	33	41
Volkswagen	100[a]	58	47	44	88
Peugeot	100[a]	63	65	48	79
Zephyr	100	77	65	59[a]	130
Chevrolet	100	95	76	90[a]	293
(No. of observations)	(33)	(54)	(32)	(33)	(20)

(continued)

Table 15.20 (concluded)

	U.S.	U.K.	Germany	France	Italy
Japanese market					
Fiat					202
Volkswagen		179	173	173	
Peugeot			212		
Zephyr	184		262		167
Chevrolet	112				
(No. of observations)	(2)	(3)	(7)	(1)	(2)

Note: In the description, below, of the regressions, C stands for a country dummy; D, piston displacement; H, horsepower; L, length; M, mean effective pressure, and W, weight.

Home markets: Each country pooled in turn with the United States. Independent variables: WLDM. Flexible pooling. See Table 15.19 and notes to Table 15.13.

U.S. market: Restricted to cars with 225 horsepower or less. All countries in one regression ($\bar{R}^2$ = .88). Independent variables: WH. Flexible pooling; country and H slope dummies retained for all four foreign countries.

U.K. market: Each country pooled in turn with the United States. Independent variables: WLDM. Flexible pooling. The dummies retained and $\bar{R}^2$ are, for the United States, DM and .91; for Germany, WC and .90; for France, W and .89; and for Italy, D and .87.

French market: Each country pooled in turn with the United Kingdom. (U.K. observations matched ranges of other countries better than French.) Independent variables: WLDM. Flexible pooling. The dummies retained and $\bar{R}^2$ are, for the United States, DMC and .93; for Germany, WLDC and .90; and for France, WLC and .92.

Japanese market: All countries in one regression ($\bar{R}^2$ = .98). Independent variable: H. Flexible pooling; country dummy retained for the United Kingdom and France, and H dummy for the United States, Germany, and Italy. There were 7 observations for Japanese cars.

Source: Home markets: See text discussion of Tables 15.1 and 15.2. U.S. market: U.S. cars as in home market; foreign cars from Automotive News, 1964 Almanac issue. U.K. market: Autocar Buyers Guide, October 11, 1963. French market: Argus, October 1963. Japanese market: Prices from Oriental Economist, May 1964; other data from source for home markets.

[a]Represents comparisons that fall outside the range of observed values of the country.

it is believed that all of the major imported models are included, the smaller the number of observations the more likely it is that the addition of another model could significantly affect the results.

The price comparisons for each of the four markets, derived by the methods applied to the home market data, are presented in Table 15.20 along with the Table 15.19 results. In France and the United Kingdom home-produced cars tended to be cheaper—usually by upward of 15 per cent—than the equivalent cars of the lowest-priced foreign supplier, while in the United States the same was true for the range of cars actually produced domestically. Whatever the country, transport costs, import duties and restrictions, and other cost elements encountered by foreign producers gave the domestic makes a substantial advantage in the home market. The results showed also that the pattern of comparative advantage tended to be similar in all the sets of price comparisons. The U.S. advantage, it is again shown, lay with large cars. Indeed, for the main part of its output, which was well beyond the Chevrolet Biscayne in size and power, the United States was the cheapest supplier. Even for the Chevrolet Biscayne range, only German exports destined for the French market were cheaper. France and Italy had a comparative advantage relative to the United Kingdom and Germany in very small cars.

Germany, the world's leading exporter, is rarely found to be the low-priced supplier. Only in the French market were its cars priced at or below the prices of other foreign countries. In the U.K. market, French prices were as low as the German or lower for cars through the Peugeot range, and the United States was cheaper for large cars. In the U.S. market, France and Italy were cheaper than Germany for small cars, and the United Kingdom was cheaper for large ones.

Since we were interested in comparative export prices, we attempted to estimate the various elements that constitute the difference between foreign retail and f.a.s. export prices. The estimates are rough and are based on information, supplied mainly by two manufacturers, about freight and insurance costs, duties and other (nonretail) taxes, and dealer discounts and other distributive costs. The results, it can be seen from Table 15.21, again show patterns similar to the earlier ones. As is to be expected from the adjustments, the foreigners in each market look more competitive relative to the local producer than they were before, and the United States looks more competitive vis-à-vis other foreigners, particularly in the French market where Germany and Italy have preferential tariff access and the high French taxes and slightly higher dealers' margins allowed by U.S. firms magnify the higher U.S. transport costs.

The results of Tables 15.20 and 15.21 are puzzling in two respects First, there is, as already mentioned, the absence of evidence of strong

Table 15.21
Export Price Level Comparisons Estimated from Regression
Equations, Four Markets, Five Makes of Car, 1964
(U.S. = 100)

Market and Type of Car	Producing Country				
	U.S.	U.K.	Germany	France	Italy
U.S. market					
Fiat	100[a]	65	66	54	53
Volkswagen	100[a]	68	70	61	57
Peugeot	100	80	91	95	77
Zephyr	100	95	119	152	106
Chevrolet	100	113	156	244[a]	145[a]
U.K. market					
Fiat	100[a]	58	40	41	42
Volkswagen	100[a]	66	52	51	55
Peugeot	100[a]	82	78	68	74
Zephyr	100	103	107	89[a]	124
Chevrolet	100	161	207	154[a]	250[a]
French market					
Fiat	100[a]	64	52	73	53
Volkswagen	100[a]	69	61	97	114
Peugeot	100[a]	75	84	106	102
Zephyr	100	92	84	130[a]	168
Chevrolet	100	113	98	198[a]	379

Note: The U.S. duty was 6.5 per cent, and a 10 per cent federal excise was levied on the duty-paid value; U.K. duties were 25.5 per cent; and French import levies (including a compensatory tax for internal excises) were 41 per cent for cars from EEC members and 58 per cent for cars from third countries (U.S. duty from F. K. Topping, *Comparative Tariffs and Trade*, Committee for Economic Development, March 1963; U.K., from *Her Majesty's Customs and Excise Tariffs of the United Kingdom, Great Britain and Northern Ireland;* and French, *Journal of Commerce,* December 1, 1964). Transport costs, dealer discounts, and distributive expenses borne by manufacturers have been estimated on the basis of data supplied by two automobile manufacturers. U.S. shipping costs to the U.K. and French markets have been taken at 15 per cent of the plant net price on the assumption that cars were shipped completely assembled; costs would be much lower—around 3 per cent—for knockdown shipments. All the estimates are rough, and no attempt was made to prepare separate estimates for cars of different sizes.

On the basis of these estimates export price comparisons were derived by dividing the figures in Table 15.17 by the following factors: U.S. market: 1.50 for all foreign countries; U.K. market: 1.75 for the United States, 1.65 for other foreign countries; French

(continued)

Notes to Table 15.21 (concluded)
market; 2.20 for the United States, 1.85 for the United Kingdom, and 1.70 for Germany and Italy. Data were reconverted to United States as 100 in the case of U.K. and French market adjustments.

The method used, it should be noted, involves the comparison in each foreign market of the home country's domestic prices with the export prices of the other countries. It is, therefore, the relationships among these "other" countries' prices that is most significant in evaluating export price competitiveness.

[a]Represents comparisons that fall outside the range of observed values of the country.

price competitiveness on the part of Germany. One possibility is that German prices really are lower but our methods do not reveal it. German cars might have superior qualities that are not reflected by our independent variables. For example, there is not much ground for choosing, solely on the basis of our size and power variables (W, L, D, M), between the German Mercedes Benz 190 and a U.S. Chevy II,[24] but the German car sold for twice the price of the American car in the U.S. market and for 40 per cent more than the U.S. home price in the German market and was clearly regarded as a higher-quality car. However, for this factor to explain our results, the average quality of German cars, holding size and power constant, would have to be superior to that of the other countries. But the United Kingdom and Italy also turn out expensive cars reputed to be high in quality that are no larger or more powerful than cheaper cars; in the United Kingdom, for example, the Daimler, Jaguar, and Rover probably fall into this category. A more thorough and more expert study than we have been able to make might be able to identify the physical characteristics that mark off these more prestigious cars from the others and include one or more of these qualities among the independent variables.

The second problem posed by the results of our price comparisons is that even after adjustment for transfer costs, U.S. price competitiveness in European markets is much weaker than is suggested by the comparisons of home market prices. If the adjustments had been correctly made and if all producers followed single-price policies, the figures in Table 15.21 for each of the three markets should approximate the

[24]

	Chevy II	Mercedes 190
Weight (lbs.)	2,495	2,591
Length (in.)	183	186
Piston displacement (cu. in.)	153	116
Horsepower	90	90

comparisons of home market prices in Table 15.19. In most cases, however, the foreign-to-U.S. export price ratios are lower than the home market price ratios.

The market price data tell us that wrong or incomplete adjustments are unlikely to be wholly responsible for the large price increases in U.S. cars when they are sold abroad as compared to those of European cars when they are sold outside of their home markets. In the U.K. market, for example, the costs of entry for German, French, and Italian cars should be moderately lower (probably in the range of 2 to 12 per cent lower owing to the difference in transport cost); [25] but they all cost less there compared to American cars than would be inferred from home market price comparisons among the four.

Another possibility is that the comparisons are not for the same models and that the differences in the samples produce the differences in results. This again seems improbable at least for the French and home market samples.

The remaining explanation is that the pricing policies of the U.S. producers differ from those of the European producers.

We have not found a way to sort out the relative roles of these factors very precisely, but some evidence may be found by comparing foreign and home prices for identical models. In the French market, for example, we were able to find seven U.S. cars in the 100–199 horsepower range which were in our U.S. sample. They were being offered at prices which ranged from 222 to 278 per cent of their U.S. prices (median, 253 per cent). The United Kingdom, which faces the same tariff and related obstacles in the French market and which has a transport advantage over the United States that probably does not exceed 12 or 13 per cent, had among its offerings in the same horsepower range five cars that were selling at prices varying from 111 to 169 per cent of their U.K. domestic prices (median, 153 per cent). In similar comparisons, summarized in Table 15.22, the foreign prices of U.S. cars consistently bear a higher ratio to home prices than do those of any of the other producing countries.

When the actual ratio of foreign to home prices is compared to the ratio that might be expected on the basis of entry and distribution costs,

---

[25] The actual difference is probably near the lower limit for U.S. cars shipped knocked down and near the upper limit for those shipped fully assembled. According to an industry source 60 per cent of U.S. exports were shipped assembled in 1964.

Table 15.22
Foreign-market as Percentage of Home-market Prices of Identical Cars, 1964
(range and median in percentages)

Producing Country and Horsepower Range	Foreign Market			
	U.S.	U.K.	France	Japan
U.S. cars				
Under 200 H.P.[a]				
No. of cars		3	7	2
Range of price relatives		147–252	222–278	316–333
Median		184	253	325
Over 200 H.P.				
No. of cars		2	5	
Range of price relatives		199–234	245–305	
Median		216	282	
U.K. cars				
Under 100 H.P.				
No. of cars	5		13	3
Range of price relatives	115–138		111–169	198–223
Median	135		153	208
100–199 H.P.				
No. of cars	2		5	
Range of price relatives	143–155		150–162	
Median	149		153	
200 and over				
No. of cars	1		3	
Range of price relatives	149		155–174	
Median			168	
German cars				
Under 100 H.P.				
No. of cars	5	4	11	6
Range of price relatives	126–145	116–147	108–138	188–247
Median	130	128	118	214
Over 100 H.P.				
No. of cars	3	2	3	1
Range of price relatives	120–150	147–150	139–168	266
Median	141	148	144	

(continued)

Table 15.22 (concluded)

| Producing Country | Foreign Market | | | |
and Horsepower Range	U.S.	U.K.	France	Japan
French cars				
Under 100 H.P.				
No. of cars	5	4		1
Range of price relatives	119–130	105–125		190
Median	124	118		
Italian cars				
Under 100 H.P.				
No. of cars	3	5	6	2
Range of price relatives	108–149	112–144	101–144	193–264
Median	123	112	113	228
Over 100 H.P.				
No. of cars	1		6	
Range of price relatives	114		124–141	
Median			139	

[a]No car with less than 100 H.P. was available for the comparisons in the French market and only one (95 H.P.) for the U.K. and Japanese markets.

as in Table 15.23, the contrast between foreign pricing by the United States and that by other countries again seems quite striking. The figures are subject to wide margins of error, since the adjustments are quite crude, but it seems clear that transport costs and tariffs cannot explain the relatively large gap between foreign and domestic prices of U.S. cars.

The explanation may lie in costs not included in our calculations, such as the need to maintain servicing and sales facilities; in view of the low volume of sales of U.S. cars in these markets, high prices may be necessary to recover these costs. But the other foreign countries are able to reach higher volume; why not the United States?

Perhaps U.S. firms already established in Europe do not find it economical to compete for the European market from so great a distance. This situation may be due in part, at least, to the European need for somewhat different design features—cars that are adapted to maneuverability in narrow city streets, driving on rough country roads, expensive

Table 15.23
Expected vs. Actual Foreign Market Prices of Cars, 1964
(prices as per cent of home market price)

	Foreign Market		
	U.S.	U.K.	France
U.S. cars			
Expected		140	176
Actual		199	266
U.K. cars			
Expected	120		148
Actual	137		155
German cars			
Expected	120	132	136
Actual	136	138	120
French cars			
Expected	120	132	
Actual	124	118	
Italian cars			
Expected	120	132	136
Actual	118	112	124

Note: Expected prices in foreign markets are those that would prevail if our estimates of entry and foreign distribution costs were correct and if producers did not discriminate between home and foreign markets in their price policies. The percentages of home prices that these expected prices represent were derived by dividing the adjustment factors given in the Note to Table 15.21 by 1.25 on the assumption that home retail list prices were 25 per cent higher than f.a.s. export prices.

Actual prices as a percentage of home prices for identical cars represent the median percentages of all the cars (without classification by horsepower) included in Table 15.22 for each producing country in each foreign market.

gasoline, and the investment of smaller amounts of capital to go with lower income levels.[26]

The variation of the ratios for individual producing countries in each market (in Table 15.22) clearly suggests that producers do not in general follow uniform pricing policies at home and abroad. As between markets also, there is some evidence (in Table 15.23) that a given producing country does not necessarily maintain the same export price or even the same (duty paid) price to dealers. German cars, for exam-

[26] At least in some European markets, U.S. exports consist mainly of expensive specialty-type models.

ple, are higher priced in the U.S. market and lower priced in France than one would expect solely on the basis of German home market prices and entry costs in those two markets. Similarly, French cars are cheaper than expected in the U.K. market. These differences, it may be noted, are consistent with the findings of the regression analysis (cf. Table 15.20). In some instances, such as some French cars in the U.K. market and Italian cars in France, the foreign car prices were only slightly above the home prices (Table 15.22), even though entry costs amounted to more than 30 per cent of the home price.

Summary of International Comparisons

In Table 15.24 we bring together the various means we have found to compare the prices of automobiles produced by different countries. The summary figures derived from the regressions (columns 3 to 6) represent weighted averages of the comparisons for the five types of cars presented earlier.

Despite some puzzling aspects, the results seem on the whole consist-

Table 15.24
Summary of Indicators of Relative Automobile Prices, 1964
(U.S. = 100)

	Domestic Price per			Foreign Market Data: Export Price per Car[d]		
				U.S. Market	U.K. Market	French Market
	H.P.[a]	Pound[b]	Car[c]			
	(1)	(2)	(3)	(4)	(5)	(6)
U.S.	100	100	100	100	100	100
U.K.	121	104	92	104	83	68
Germany	119	130	104	140	70	62
France	143	112	123	205	66	86
Italy	136	126	131	128	73	81
Japan	141	122	128			

[a]Cars with 75–99 H.P. (see Table 15.15).

[b]Cars weighing 2,000–2,799 pounds (see Table 15.16).

[c]Based on averages of price comparisons for five cars, each computed from regressions in which each country was paired with the United States (see Table 15.19).

[d]Data in Table 15.21 weighted as follows: U.K. and French market weights based on distribution of production shown in Table 15.17; U.S. market weights based on new-car registrations giving data for imported cars and breakdowns for all cars by cylinder (*Automotive Industries,* March 15, 1967, p. 102). In columns 4–6 the domestic prices of the home country's cars are compared with the export prices of the other countries.

ent with the trade flows. The price relationships in the French market in particular seem correctly to mirror the premier position of Germany in world exports and the runner-up place of the United Kingdom. German price competitiveness shows up less favorably in the other markets; the U.K. and U.S. foreign market data results may be discounted because they are based on a small number of observations, but this is not true of the home market data. It is possible, of course, and indeed even likely, that the relative price positions of different countries vary from one market to another and that our comparisons are correct for each market. It seems clear that the German price position is highly favorable to exports, but it is possible that German cars of a given size and horsepower tend in some markets to command premium prices relative to cars in a similar category produced by other countries.

The United States has the lowest home prices for the types of cars it actually produces, but its competitive position abroad is adversely affected by a number of factors, including foreign preferences for smaller and less powerful cars and higher markups in foreign markets over home prices than are found for cars produced by other countries.

PART FIVE

APPENDIXES

APPENDIX A

TRADE DATA FOR 1963

General Note

This appendix includes data on the origin and destination of exports of the countries of the OECD for the total of commodities covered and for two-digit SITC divisions in sections 6 and 7. Although the same data were collected for three-digit groups, we publish here, for these groups as well as for some four- and five-digit subgroups, only the value of total OECD exports and exports by the United States, the United Kingdom, Germany, Japan, and the Common Market countries as a group. Exports are also shown for any other country accounting for 10 per cent or more of the OECD total. The destinations listed include the United States, OECD Europe as a group, the United Kingdom, the EEC countries as a group, Germany, Canada, Japan, Latin America, and all other countries. In addition, any country that appears as an origin in an origin-destination table appears also as a destination.

The main source of information on the value of exports by the United States was a collection of unpublished tabulations by the U.S. Department of Commerce. These were used in preference to published OECD and UN reports based on earlier Department of Commerce tabulations. The published figures suffer from numerous misclassifications of the commodities in the attempt to translate the U.S. schedule into the Standard International Trade Classification.

Most of the data for other OECD countries except Japan were taken from *Trade by Commodities,* OECD Statistical Bulletin, Series C, Volume I, and the *Supplement,* 1963. Additional data for these countries on a five-digit SITC level and all the data for Japan were taken from the *1963 World Trade Annual* (Walker and Co. for the United Nations), Vol. IV, and some information was taken from the *Commodity Trade Statistics* of the United Nations.

In a few cases a finer breakdown of commodity classes than that provided by the OECD and UN was needed. For this purpose we used, for the United States, the unpublished tabulations already referred to and *United States Exports of Domestic and Foreign Merchandise; Commodity by Country of Destination,* 1963 Annual, Report FT 410, Part II (U.S. Dept. of Commerce, June 1964); and for the United Kingdom, *Accounts Relating to Trade and Navigation of the United Kingdom,* U.K. Board of Trade, December 1964. Occasionally, other sources of trade data were used, as is indicated in the notes to individual tables.

For many five-digit items, no export data were available for Canada or Austria. The five-digit breakdown of the four-digit export totals was estimated by assuming that exports were distributed among five-digit items in the same proportions as in imports from these countries by other OECD countries. The five-digit import data were for the most part taken from the *1963 World Trade Annual.*

Table A.1
Total OECD Exports, All Covered Commodities, by Country of Origin and Destination, 1963
(exports of metals and metal manufactures, machinery and transport equipment, and miscellaneous manufactured articles; sum of SITC groups 67–69, 71–73, 812, 861, 864, 891, and 894; millions of dollars)

Destination	Origin						
	Total OECD	U.S.	U.K.	EEC		Japan	Other
				Total	Germany		
Total, all destinations	44,560	10,224[a]	6,637	18,679	9,464	2,824	6,197
U.S.	3,948		489	1,370	801	799	1,290
OECD Europe	20,257	2,378	2,431	11,992	6,222	329	3,126
U.K.	1,674	390		674	313	59	551
EEC total	11,724	1,385	1,300	7,460	3,395	141	1,438
Germany	2,957	384	300	1,576		44	652
Canada	2,726	2,177	277	157	98	54	61
Japan	698	373	67	183	123		75
Latin America	3,563	1,669	280	1,009	462	229	377
Other	11,843	2,191	3,088	3,913	1,753	1,395	1,257
Unaccounted for by destination	1,525	1,436[b]	5	56	5	17	11

Notes to Table A.1

Note: The table below shows the sum of our special-category estimates vs. the distribution by country of destination of special-category items included in all U.S. export commodity groups as given by *Foreign Commerce and Navigation of the United States 1946–63* (FC&N). The *Foreign Commerce* figure for OECD Europe includes other countries in Europe not identified for security reasons ($52 million).

Destination	Special Category (millions of dollars)		Per Cent Distribution	
	NBER	FC&N	NBER	FC&N
Total special category	1,184	2,181	100	100
Total excluding unaccounted for	543	2,181		
OECD Europe	415	1,213	59	56
U.K.	57	47	8	2
EEC	279	907	40	42
Germany	67	460	10	21
Canada	160	128	22	6
Japan	80	129	8	6
Latin America	81	99	6	5
Other	71	611	6	28
Unaccounted for	641			

[a] U.S. Department of Commerce data have been adjusted to include missing exports for subgroups 681.1 and 682.23, estimated to be worth $44 million. See Table A.3.

[b] United States export data included special-category items amounting to $1,436 million which were not distributed by country of destination. The following groups included such items: SITC 711.4, 719.9, 724.9, 732, 733, 734, 735.1 and 861. In come cases we estimated the country distribution of these items.

Table A.2

OECD Exports of Iron and Steel (SITC 67), by Country of Origin and Destination, 1963
(millions of dollars)

Destination	Total OECD	U.S.	U.K.	Origin EEC Total	Germany	France	Belgium-Luxembourg	Japan
Total, all destinations	5,693	514	573	3,166	1,146	757	885	702
U.S.	631	87	52	232	67	48	113	213
OECD Europe	2,910	8	206	2,142	821	480	621	62
U.K.	148		8	68	9	14	16	2
EEC total	1,941	53	88	1,519	557	343	490	46
Germany	586	15	21	425		184	184	1
France	464	7	13	422	242		156	
Belgium-Luxembourg	148	10	11	112	48	38		a
Canada	188	114	25	30	13	5	12	14
Japan	14	4	1	6	5	a	a	
Latin America	364	93	30	143	42	28	29	62
Other	1,586	216	259	613	198	195	110	351

aLess than $500,000.

Table A.3

OECD Exports of Nonferrous Metals (SITC 68), by Country of Origin and Destination, 1963

(millions of dollars)

Destination	Total OECD	U.S.[a]	U.K.	Origin EEC Total	Germany	France	Belgium-Luxembourg	Canada	Japan
Total, all destinations	2,725	449	348	837	256	145	357	708	43
U.S.	587		38	98	35	21	36	372	15
OECD Europe	1,540	263	191	604	163	95	286	247	4
U.K.	314	69		28	9	3	12	173	1
EEC total	897	173	135	426	79	77	227	43	2
Germany	329	66	41	123		20	78	22	b
France	189	40	25	108	21		80	6	1
Belgium-Luxembourg	100	6	21	65	17	47		3	
Canada	84	59	21	2	1	b	1		b
Japan	47	18	9	7	2	1	4	12	
Latin America	84	33	5	16	7	4	3	23	2
Other	384	76	85	111	48	24	27	54	22

[a] The SITC 68 U.S. export data given by the Department of Commerce were adjusted as follows: U.S. exports of SITC 681.1 were not given, and we estimated these exports and incorporated them into this table. U.S. exports of 693.12 and 693.13 were included by the Department of Commerce in groups 682.21 and 684, respectively. These exports were estimated and removed from commodity group 68.

[b] Less than $500,000.

Table A.4

OECD Exports of Metal Manufactures, n.e.s. (SITC 69), by Country of Origin and Destination, 1963

(millions of dollars)

Destination	Origin					
	Total OECD	U.S.	U.K.	EEC		Japan
				Total	Germany	
Total, all destinations	2,519	500[b]	·371	1,146[a]	570	200
U.S.	252	97	23	96	40	94
OECD Europe	1,067	15	112	676	386	16
U.K.	71	15		30	19	3
EEC total	621	54	54	423	214	8
Germany	126	14	12	62		4
Canada	205	163	18	11	7	8
Japan	15	8	2	3	2	
Latin America	218	102	14	74	35	13
Other	762	130	204	285	100	69

[a]Of which, France $209 million.

[b]U.S. exports were adjusted to include exports of items 693.12 and 693.13 which, in the published 1963 data, were included in subgroup 684. We estimated the amount from 1965 data and transferred the estimated amount from subgroup 684 to subgroup 693.

Table A.5

OECD Exports of Machinery Other than Electric (SITC 71), by Country of Origin and Destination, 1963

(millions of dollars)

| | | | | Origin | | |
| | | | | | EEC | |
Destination	Total OECD	U.S.	U.K.	Total	Germany	Japan
Total, all destinations	14,164	4,046	2,404	5,492	3,299	351
U.S.	715		121	223	134	55
OECD Europe	6,502	1,113	927	3,465	2,210	33
U.K.	568	179		269	164	5
EEC total	3,739	650	541	2,005	1,201	18
Germany	822	170	138	294		7
Canada	1,044	866	112	40	24	4
Japan	432	227	37	129	92	
Latin America	1,299	653	115	380	199	24
Other	3,892	908	1,092	1,255	640	236
Unaccounted for by destination	280	279[a]				1

[a]These are special-category items for which country destination data are not available and of which $274 million are exports of aircraft engines and parts (SITC 711.4). However, some notion of the destinations of U.S. exports of aircraft engines and parts can be derived from information published for importing countries on their imports of aircraft engines from the United States and, for those countries not reporting imports, from the very incomplete export data by country of destination published by the United States (covering only $19 million out of $286 million of U.S. exports of aircraft engines). For those areas reporting imports—the OECD countries and Japan—the data should be fairly complete, although some engines imported for government use may be omitted. However, the figures must be very

much underestimated for Latin America, Asia (except Japan), and other countries, areas in which many countries did not report on imports. The table below shows the NBER estimates (in millions of dollars) of 711.4 exports and U.S. exports of 71 after these estimates have been incorporated into the Department of Commerce data:

Destination	NBER Estimate of U.S. 711.4 Exports	71 U.S. Exports Including NBER 711.4 Estimates
Total, all destinations	286	4,046
OECD Europe	96	1,206
U.K.	20	198
EEC	58	707
Germany	7	177
Canada	27	892
Japan	23	249
Latin America	15	663
Other	7	912
Unaccounted for by destination	118	124

The NBER estimate was made from import data of countries other than the United States and from incomplete U.S. export data covering piston engines only. For Latin America, $12.6 million is from import data and $2.2 from incomplete U.S. export data. The figures for other destinations comprise $5.8 million from import data and $1.4 million from incomplete U.S. export data. The data are from *Trade by Commodities*, OECD Statistical Bulletin, Series C, Vol. I, *Exports*, and Vol. II, *Imports*, the *1963 World Trade Annual*, Vol. IV, and the UN *Commodity Trade Statistics*, 1963.

Table A.6

OECD Exports of Electrical Machinery, Apparatus, and Appliances (SITC 72), by Country of Origin and Destination, 1963

(millions of dollars)

| Destination | Total OECD | Origin | | | | |
| | | U.S. | U.K. | EEC | | Japan |
				Total	Germany	
Total, all destinations	6,005	1,492	891	2,474	1,173	519
U.S.	397		42	88	46	187
OECD Europe	2,660	366	270	1,643	812	57
U.K.	173	58		79	30	5
EEC total	1,535	214	137	1,001	427	25
Germany	344	52	33	185		12
Canada	338	264	44	15	8	10
Japan	67	47	5	11	6	
Latin America	490	200	38	148	60	52
Other	1,708	272	492	570	241	213
Special category	344	344a				b

[a]The U.S. did not report distribution by destination for most U.S. exports of microphones, loudspeakers, amplifiers (SITC 724.92), other telecommunications equipment (SITC 724.99), automotive electrical equipment (SITC 729.4), and electrical machinery and apparatus n.e.s. (SITC 729.9). A rough estimate of the distribution by destination was made for these subgroups by using reported imports from the United States where they were available. The following table shows these estimates and U.S. exports of SITC 72 after incorporating the NBER estimates (in millions of dollars):

Destination	NBER Estimate of Special-category Items in U.S. Exports of SITC 724.9	SITC 729.4 and 729.9	SITC 72 U.S. Exports Including NBER Estimates
Total, all destinations	285	58	1,492
OECD Europe	73	4	443
U.K.	14		72
EEC total	47	2	263
Germany	2	2	56
Canada	35		299
Japan	9	3	59
Latin America		1	201
Other	4		276
Unaccounted for by destination	164	51	215

[b]Less than $500,000.

Table A.7

OECD Exports of Transport Equipment (SITC 73), by Country of Origin and Destination, 1963

(millions of dollars)

Destination	Origin					
	Total OECD	U.S.	U.K.	EEC Total	EEC Germany	Japan
Total, all destinations	10,496	2,704	1,764	4,472	2,345	626
U.S.	866		173	503	396	44
OECD Europe	4,233	299	618	2,781	1,379	81
U.K.	262	30		147	47	28
EEC total	2,186	157	277	1,667	664	4
Germany	529	40	37	418		2
Canada	690	598	41	41	34	1
Japan	73	47	8	16	9	
Latin America	946	526	73	211	92	64
Other	2,969	515	852	919	434	435
Unaccounted for	719	719				a

[a]Less than $500,000.

Note: Most of the U.S. exports of aircraft and parts (SITC 734) are special-category commodities, and the Department of Commerce reports country of destination for only a small portion of this group. Some notion of destinations can be derived from other countries' data on imports of group 734 from the United States. These fall far short of accounting for all U.S. exports in this group but do appear to cover over 60 per cent of them. However, it should be noted that the imports are c.i.f. values while exports are at f.a.s. values.

The following table shows the NBER 734 estimates and U.S. exports of 73 after these estimates have been incorporated into the Department of Commerce data (figures are in millions of dollars):

Destination	NBER Estimate of U.S. 734 Exports	73 U.S. Exports Including NBER 734 Estimates
Total, all destinations	817	2,704
OECD Europe	242[a]	449
U.K.	23[b]	38
EEC	172[c]	279
Germany	54[b]	86
Canada	98[c]	654
Japan	45[c]	57
Latin America	65[d]	546
Other	60[e]	538
Unaccounted for	308	460

[a]From *Trade by Commodities*, OECD Statistical Bulletin, Series C, 1963, except for Spain ($12.9 million), which is from U.S. export data.

[b]From *Commodity Trade Statistics*, United Nations.

[c]From *Trade by Commodities*.

[d]Colombia, Mexico, and Brazil from *Commodity Trade Statistics* ($43.7 million). Other countries are U.S. export figures from OECD *Trade by Commodities*. The U.S. export data give a total of $24.0 million for Colombia, Mexico, and Brazil.

[e]Consists of $27.6 million from import data, $32.6 million from U.S. export statistics, as in footnote d. The U.S. export figure for countries reporting imports was $5.0 million.

Table A.8

OECD Exports of Iron and Steel (SITC 67), Value by Origin and Subgroup, 1963

(millions of dollars)

SITC Number	Commodity Group	Total OECD	U.S.	U.K.	EEC Total	EEC Germany	EEC France[a]	EEC Belgium-Luxembourg[a]	Japan
67	Iron & steel	5,693	514	573	3,166	1,146	757	885	702
671	Pig iron, ferro-alloys, etc.	251[b]	9	10	109[c]	53	42		7
671.1	Spiegeleisen	2	d	d	2	1	1		
671.2	Pig iron incl. cast iron	101	4	4	50	37	7		
671.3	Iron & steel powders, shot, & sponge	14	1	2	4	2	2		
671.4	Ferromanganese	45	3		32	8	20		3
671.5	Other ferro-alloys	89	3	4	21	6	12		4
672	Ingots & other primary forms	415[e]	25	5	267	125		61	27
672.1 & 672.3	Puddled bars, pilings, etc., & ingots	47	1	1	24	12		4	d
672.5	Blooms, billets, slabs, etc.	216	24	4	130	79		30	4
672.7	Coils for rerolling	152		1	114	35		27	23
672.9	Blanks for tubes or pipes	d	d		d				
673	Bars, rods, angles, shapes, & sections	1,299	55	96	871	300	186	356	155
673.1	Wire rod	243	4	14	152	47	61	34	47
673.2 & 673.4	Bars & rods excl. wire rod	614	27	44	396	145	72	169	85
673.5	Angles, shapes, & sections	442	24	39	323	108	53	154	24

(continued)

SITC Number	Commodity Group	Total OECD	U.S.	U.K.	EEC Total	Germany	France[a]	Belgium-Luxembourg[a]	Japan
674	Universals, plates, & sheets	2,057	216	271	1,045	285	313	283	318
674.1 &									
674.2	———3mm. or more excl. tinned	447[f]	26	34	258	144	32	51	58
674.3	———less than 3mm., uncoated	1,036[f]	107	118	532	105	177	147	151
674.7	———Tinned	331[f]	53	87	152	22	72	30	38
674.8	———less than 3mm., coated excl. tinned	243	30	32	103	15	32	54	70
675	Hoop & strip	291[g]	29	31	177	66	32	68	13
675.01	———of other than high carbon or alloy steel	217	15	22	159	55	26	67	9
675.02	———of high carbon steel	22[h]		1	6	5	1	d	d
675.03	———of alloy steel	51	14	8	12	6	5	12	4
676	Rails & track construction material	111[i]	17	11	50	21	15	12	8
676.1	Rails	74	6	6	35	15	9	10	6
676.2	Sleepers & other track material	37	11	5	15	6	6	2	1
677	Iron & steel wire, excl. wire rod	233	15	28	119	43		53	43
677.01	———of other than high carbon or alloy steel	148[j]	10[k]	16	87	25		43	26
677.02	———of high carbon steel	50[j]	3[k]	7	20	10		8	14
677.03	———of alloy steel	34[j]	1	6	12	8		1	3
678	Tubes, pipes, & fittings	968[l]	129	115	503	244	116	132	132
678.1	Tubes & pipes of cast iron	57	14	12	27	10	16	3	3

(continued)

Table A.8 (concluded)

SITC Number	Commodity Group	Total OECD	U.S.	U.K.	EEC Total	Germany	France[a]	Belgium-Luxembourg[a]	Japan
678.2	Tubes & pipes excl. cast iron, seamless	361	66	53	156	111	9		48
678.3	Tubes & pipes excl. cast iron, welded, etc.	400	18	33	247	88	79		67
678.4	High-pressure conduits of steel	21	3	d	16	1	d		d
678.5	Tube & pipe fittings	129	29	18	57	34	13		12
679	Castings & forgings	61m	19	5	17	8		6	

[a] Only included if country's exports exceeded 10 per cent of total OECD exports.

[b] Of which Canada, $27 million; Norway, $51 million for SITC 671 ($9 million, 671.2; $8 million, 671.4; and $34 million, 671.5).

[c] Excluding Netherland exports of 671.2, estimated to be $8 million.

[d] Less than $500,000.

[e] Of which Austria, $40 million.

[f] Canada did not report exports of 674.2, 674.3 and 674.7. These exports were estimated from import data.

[g] Canadian exports were not available.

[h] Of which Sweden, $14 million.

[i] Of which Canada, $16 million.

[j] Four-digit breakdowns for Canada, Spain, Ireland, Portugal, and Austria were not available. The exports of all these countries, except Austria, amounted to less than $5 million. Austrian exports ($6.7 million) were broken down according to import data.

[k] U.S. exports of 677.01 and 677.02 were not available. Therefore, total 677 exports excluding 677.03, were broken down in the same proportion as total OECD exports excluding the United States.

[l] Four-digit breakdown for Ireland ($80 million) were broken down in the same

Table A.9

OECD Exports of Nonferrous Metals (SITC 68), by Origin and Subgroup, 1963

(millions of dollars)

SITC Number	Commodity Group	Total OECD	U.S.	U.K.	EEC Total	EEC Germany	EEC Belgium-Luxembourg[a]	Canada[a]	Japan
68	Nonferrous metals	2,725	449[b]	348	837	256[c]	357	708	43
681	Silver, platinum, etc.	226	44[b]	79	65	39		29	d
682	Copper	932	212[b]	104	373	120	207	155	15
682.1	——& alloys, unwrought	621	188	51	222	48	162	127	1
682.2	——& alloys, worked	312	24[b]	53	151	72	45	28	14
683	Nickel	327[e]	22	60	25	11		174	d
683.1	——& alloys, unwrought	279	17	42	10	d		168	d
683.2	——& alloys, worked	49	5	17	15	10		6	d
684	Aluminum	853[f,g]	121[b]	52	214[g]	60		281	17
684.1	——& alloys, unwrought	527	66	3	65	7		266	6
684.2	——& alloys, worked	326	55	48	149	54		15	11
685	Lead	60	1	10	28	6	14	15	d
685.1	——& alloys, unwrought	54	1	9	24	5	13	14	
685.2	——& alloys, worked	6	d	1	4	1	1	d	d
686	Zinc	120	11	4	51	8	32	39	1
686.1	——& alloys, unwrought	104	8	2	42	6	27	39	d

(continued)

Table A.9 (concluded)

SITC Number	Commodity Group	Total OECD	U.S.	U.K.	EEC Total	EEC Germany	EEC Belgium-Luxembourg[a]	Canada[a]	Japan
686.2	——& alloys, worked	17	4	2	9	2	5	1	d
687	Tin	67	5	27	33h	4	17		d
687.1	——& alloys, unwrought	64	4	26	31h	3	16		d
687.2	——& alloys, worked	4	1	1	2	d	1		d
689	Misc. nonferrous base metals	137i	33	12	48	8	26	14	9
689.3	Magnesium & beryllium	31	10	3	3	d		3	
689.4	Tungsten, molybdenum, & tantalum	18	4	1	7	2	1		1
689.5	Base metals, n.e.s.	86	18	8	37	6	25	11	8

[a] Included only if country's exports exceeded 10 per cent of total OECD exports.

[b] The SITC 68 U.S. export data given by the Department of Commerce were adjusted as follows: U.S. exports of 681.1 were not given, and we estimated these exports and incorporated them into this table; U.S. exports of 693.12 and 693.13 were included by the Department of Commerce in groups 682.21 and 684, respectively. These exports were estimated and removed from commodity group 68.

[c] Of which France, $145 million.

[d] Less than $500,000.

[e] Of which Norway, $42 million (683.1, $41 million).

[f] Of which Norway, $94 million (684.1, $91 million).

[g] Of which France, $85 million (684.1, $57 million; 684.2, $28 million).

[h] Of which the Netherlands, $12 million.

[i] Of which Norway, $14 million (689.3, $11 million; 689.5, $3 million).

Table A.10

OECD Exports of Metal Manufactures, n.e.s. (SITC 69), Value by Origin and Subgroup, 1963

(millions of dollars)

SITC Number	Commodity Group	Total OECD	U.S.	U.K.	EEC Total	EEC Germany	Japan
69	Metal manufactures, n.e.s.	2,519	500[a]	371	1,146[b]	570	200
691	Finished structural parts & structures, n.e.s.	317	77	47	147[c]	58	14
691.1	——of iron or steel	293	68	43	140	55	14
691.2	——of aluminum	24	10	4	8	3	[d]
692	Metal containers for storage & transport	176	39	27	87[e]	31	5
692.1	Tanks, vats, etc., for storage or manufacturing	61	12	9	34	11	3
692.2	Casks, drums, boxes, cans, etc., for transport	73	16	14	32	10	1
692.3	Compressed gas cylinders	42	10	4	22	10	1
693	Wire products, excl. electric, & fencing grills	205	19	32	115[f]	35	21
693.1	Wire cables, ropes, etc., not insulated	96[g]	10	20	44	13	14
693.2	Wire of iron or steel, of types used for fencing	33	4	1	22	3	3

(continued)

Table A.10 (continued)

SITC Number	Commodity Group	Total OECD	U.S.	U.K.	EEC Total	EEC Germany	Japan
693.3	Gauze, netting, grill, fencing, etc., of wire	72	4	9	47	18	4
693.4	Expanded metal	3	d	1	1	d	d
694	Nails, screws, nuts, bolts, etc., iron, steel or copper	214	31	21	84	40	49
694.1	Nails, tacks, staples, spikes, etc.	70	6	4	25	8	28
694.2	Nuts, bolts, screws, rivets, washers, etc.	144	26	16	59	32	21
695	Tools for use in the hand or in machines	505	114	74	203	137	27
695.1	Hand tools for agriculture or forestry	32	3	11	10	7	4
695.2	Other tools for use in hand or machines	474	111	63	193	130	23
696	Cutlery	160	8	36	69	45	33
697	Household equip. of base metals	235	32	25	133[h]	50	15
697.1	Domestic stoves, boilers, etc.	123	19	12	79	28	2
697.2	Domestic utensils of base metals	96	13	12	44	17	12
697.9	Other household equip. of base metals	16	d	2	10	4	2
698	Manufactures of metal, n.e.s.	707	180	110	307	174	36
698.1	Locksmiths' wares	162	40	19	81	59	8

(continued)

Table A.10 (concluded)

SITC Number	Commodity Group	Total OECD	U.S.	U.K.	EEC Total	Germany	Japan
698.2	Safes, strongrooms, etc.	7	2	2	2	1	d
698.3	Chain & parts of iron or steel	64	11	15	28	21	4
698.4	Anchors, grapnels & parts thereof	3		1	1	d	d
698.5	Pins & needles & base metal fittings, etc.	46	1	13	26	18	4
698.6	Springs & leaves for springs, iron, steel, or copper	28	1	4	16	10	2
698.8	Misc. articles of base metal	99	30	18	34	15	3
698.9	Articles of base metal, n.e.s.	293	95	38	115	51	16

aU.S. exports were adjusted to include exports of items 693.12 and 693.13 which, in the published 1963 data, were included in subgroup 684. We estimated the amount from 1965 data and transferred the estimated amount from subgroup 684 to subgroup 693.

bOf which, France $209 million.

cOf which, France $37 million.

dLess than $500,000.

eOf which, France $27 million (692.1, $13 million; 692.2, $10 million; and 692.3, $4 million).

fOf which, Belgium-Luxembourg, $48 million (693.1, $13 million; 693.2, $15 million; and 693.3, $20 million).

gIncluding wire cable, etc., of iron and steel (SITC 693.11), $68.6 million; of copper (SITC 693.12), $8.9 million; of aluminum (SITC 693.13), $15.4 million; not accounted for by type, $2.3 million. U.S. exports of items 693.12 and 693.13 were included in SITC subgroup 684 in the published statistics. We estimated the amount from 1965 data and transferred the estimated amount from subgroup 684 to these two items.

hOf which, France $27 million (697.1, $16 million; 697.2, $10 million; and 697.9, $1 million).

Table A.11

OECD Exports of Machinery Other than Electric (SITC 71), Value by Origin and Subgroup, 1963
(millions of dollars)

SITC Number	Commodity Group	Total OECD	U.S.	U.K.	EEC Total	EEC Germany	Japan
71	Machinery other than electric	14,164	4,046	2,404	5,492	3,299	351
711	Power generating mach. other than electric	2,024	661	483	593	300	41
711.1	Steam generating boilers	186	76	29	53	37	4
711.2	Boiler house plant	56	23	11	13	7	4
711.3	Steam engines	122	12	31	48	31	1
711.4	Aircraft engines incl. jet propulsion engines[a]	647	286	176	125	29	7
711.5	Internal combustion engines exc. for aircraft	900	225	225	319	181	22
711.6	Gas turbines exc. aircraft	27	14	3	4	1	
711.7	Nuclear reactors	8	1	5	2	b	
711.8	Engines, n.e.s.	77	23	4	28	14	2
712	Agricultural mach. & implements	1,398[c]	482	392	329	177	7
712.1	Soil preparation or cultivation mach.	125	26	21	34	20	4
712.2	Threshing, harvesting, sorting mach.	360	67	34	155	91	1
712.3	Dairy machinery	41	11	9	10	6	
712.5	Tractors[d]	770	299	322	118	57	2
712.9	Agricultural mach. & appliances, n.e.s.	103	80	6	12	3	b
714	Office machines	1,024	362	111	410[e]	164	8

(continued)

SITC Number	Commodity Group	Total OECD	U.S.	U.K.	EEC Total	EEC Germany	Japan
714.1	Typewriters, etc.	141	17	11	93	44	4
714.2	Calculating, accounting machines, etc., incl. electronic computers[f]	460	212	40	149	54	2
714.3	Statistical machines	162	14	28	85	33	1
714.9	Office machines, n.e.s.	260	119	32	83	33	1
715	Metalworking mach.	1,370	347	166	676	486	23
715.1	Metalworking machine tools[l]	1,016g,h	213	126	520	368	17
715.2	Metalworking mach. other than machine tools	354	134	40	156	117	6
717	Textile & leather mach.	1,296j	190	227	556k	356	119
717.1	Textile mach.	1,006	148	186	445	278	56
717.2	Leather mach.	46	6	9	26	19	b
717.3	Sewing machines	244	36	31	85	59	63
718	Mach. for special industries	2,015	708	332	715	494	36
718.1	Paper, pulp mill mach.	349	74	70	140	106	10
718.11	Mach. for making or finishing pulp, paper, etc.	218	46	58	73	50	9
718.12	Paper cutting & other paper mach.	131	28	12	67	56	1
718.2	Printing & bookbinding mach.	345g	75	48	180	146	2
718.21	Bookbinding mach.	25	8	2	9	8	b
718.22	Type making & setting mach.	68	18	20	26	19	1
718.29	Other printing mach.	252	50	27	145	120	1
718.3	Food processing mach.	197g,l	42	33	92	58	3
718.31	Grain-milling and related mach.	32	5	8	13	8	1

(continued)

Table A.11 (continued)

SITC Number	Commodity Group	Total OECD	U.S.	U.K.	EEC Total	EEC Germany	Japan
718.39	Other food processing mach.	164	37	25	79	50	2
718.4	Construction & mining mach.	819[g]	435	148	162	92	17
718.41	Road rollers, mechanically propelled	25[l,m]	6	5	11[n]	9	1
718.42	Excavating, leveling, boring, etc., mach.	794[l,m]	429	143	151[n,o]	83	16
718.5	Mineral crushing, etc., glassworking mach.	305[p]	81	33	140	92	4
718.51	Mineral crushing, sorting, etc., mach.	252[p]	65	28	120	88	3
718.52	Glassworking mach.	52[p]	16	5	20	4	1
719	Machinery & appliances, nonelect., & parts, n.e.s.	5,034	1,296	693	2,212	1,322	118
719.1	Heating & cooling equip.	819[q]	236	93	364[r]	187	8
719.11	Gas generators	10[s]	3	4	3	2	2
719.12	Air conditioners	66	45	4	12	4	2
719.13	Burners, stokers	54	16	8	19	10	b
719.14	Industrial furnaces	99	24	6	57	35	1
719.15	Refrigerators (nondomestic)	208	109	16	50	23	1
719.19	Heating & cooling equip., n.e.s.	382	39	56	223	114	4
719.2	Pumps & centrifuges	870	226	115	373	206	13
719.21	Pumps for liquids	338	101	51	140	82	5
719.22	Pumps for gases, etc.	344	75	47	146	65	6
719.23	Filtering & purifying mach., etc., for gases	188	51	16	87	59	2

SITC Number	Commodity Group	Total OECD	U.S.	U.K.	EEC Total	Germany	Japan
719.3	Mechanical handling equip.	810[t]	282	97	328	201	13
719.31	Lifting & loading mach.	688	238	78	282	176	12
719.32	Forklift & other industrial trucks	121	44	19	45	24	1
719.5	Powered tools other than metalworking	394[g,u]	93	44	182	124	6
719.51	Machine tools for working minerals	18	15	1	15	4	1
719.52	——for working wood, plastics, etc.	112	15	10	67	50	3
719.53	Motorized hand tools, nonelectric	101[v]	33	13	27	21	1
719.54	Parts & accessories of machine tools	163	46	20	72	49	2
719.6 & 719.8	Misc. nonelect. mach. & mechanical appliances	1,125	245	184	514	351	39
719.61 & 719.8	Rubber machinery	739[w]	31 }	30 }	344	235	35
	Plastics machinery		22				
	Other nonelectric machinery, mechanical appliances		71	107			
719.62	Mach. for cleaning & filling bottles, packaging mach., etc.	222	65	27	102	67	1
719.63	Weighing mach. & weights	52	11	7	29	21	b
719.64	Spraying mach.	99	42	12	32	23	3
719.65	Automatic vending machines	11	4	1	6	4	b
719.66	Railway & tramway track fittings, etc.	2		1	1	1	
719.7	Ball, roller or needle roller bearings	263[x]	65	27	79	47	28
719.9	Mach. parts & accessories	724	148[y]	131	351	191	11
719.91	Molding boxes & molds excl. ingot molds	34	z	2	24	10	1

(continued)

Table A.11 (concluded)

SITC Number	Commodity Group	Total OECD	U.S.	U.K.	EEC		Japan
					Total	Germany	
719.92	Taps, cocks, valves, similar appliances	325	77	56	148	79	6
719.93	Transmission shafts & cranks, pulleys, etc.	224	52	15	124	85	3
719.94	Metal-plastic joints (gaskets)	12	z	5	6	3	1
719.99	Mach. parts, nonelectrical, n.e.s.	129	19	53	50	14	1

Note: U.S. and U.K. exports by type of engine for SITC 711.5 (millions of dollars):

	U.S.	U.K.
Complete engines	126	126
Diesel	63	115
Automotive	11	53
Marine	20	20
Other	33	42
Other than diesel	62	8
Automotive	16	3
Marine	16	3
Other	30	3
Type not specified		4
Engine parts	98	99

U.S. and U.K. data, by type of engine, are from *Accounts Relating to the Trade and Navigation of the United Kingdom*, U.K. Board of Trade, December 1964, and from *United States Exports of Domestic and Foreign Merchandise; Commodity by Country of Destination*, 1963 Annual, U.S. Dept. of Commerce, Report FT 410, June 1964.

[a] The U.S. export data for aircraft engines published by the OECD covered only piston engines; $214 million in exports of engine parts were erroneously included under aircraft (SITC 734), as were more than $50 million in jet engine exports and many additional items belonging in other SITC classes.

The U.K. export data suffer from other deficiencies. They appear to cover aircraft engines which have been imported for repair and overhaul and then re-exported to the owners. "Aircraft imported temporarily for repair or modification and subsequent re-export" are excluded from the U.K. statistics (*Accounts Relating to Trade and Navigation of the United Kingdom*, U.K. Board of Trade, but U.K. exports as exports of "produce and manufactures of the U.K.,"

ᵃ...complete jet engines, of which only £16 million are newly constructed and the other £15 million are described simply as "other than newly constructed" (*ibid.*, p. 286). On the import side the U.K. data include such oddities as more than $19 million in imports of aircraft engines from African and Asian countries which have no production of these items, among them, for example, Lebanon ($4.2 million), Bahrain ($501,000), and the Sudan ($735,000).

The total for the subgroup excludes engines exported as part of complete aircraft. CAB data for U.S. airlines (Schedules B-7 and B-43) suggest that engines account for 15 per cent or more of the value of complete aircraft, or approximately $125 million.

ᵇLess than $500,000.

ᶜSweden did not report the 4-digit breakdown of its 712 total exports. Hence, the 3-digit Swedish total was broken down on the basis of reports of the importers of 712 Swedish products.

ᵈSee Chapter 12, footnote 11, for coverage.

ᵉOf which France, $78 million; and Italy, $120 million (714.1, $25 million; 714.2, $76 million; 714.3, $10 million; and 714.9, $9 million).

ᶠThere are serious inconsistencies among countries in reporting electronic computers. The clearest example is provided by the United Kingdom, which separates exports of electronic computers and related equipment into those designed to work with punched cards (£2,278,000 in 1964), listed under SITC 714.3, and those not designed to work with punched cards (£4,372,000 in 1964), listed under SITC 714.2. This distinction cannot be made in the U.S. data. As a result, U.S. exports appear higher than they really are relative to U.K. exports for SITC 714.2 and lower for SITC 714.3.

ᵍExcluding Ireland.

ʰOf which Switzerland, $88 million.

ⁱSITC 715.1 exports by type of machine:

Type of Machine	Total	U.S.	U.K.	EEC Total	Germany	Japan
Metal-cutting	716	132	87	389	274	12
Boring machines	70	11	11	35	22	3
Drilling machines	38	6	5	21	11	1
Gear-cutting machines	50	14	4	24	23	
Grinding machines	156	33	17	78	54	2
Lathes	194	26	31	108	76	4
Milling machines	90	11	11	54	34	2
Planers, broaching, & misc. cutting	119	30	8	68	53	1
Metal-forming	299	76	35	165	129	3
Hydraulic and pneumatic presses	43	9	8	24	18	1
Mechanical presses	74	21	7	42	31	1
Forming, except presses	182	46	20	100	80	2

(continued)

Notes to Table A.11 (continued)

The data by type of machine tool are from *World Trade in Machine Tools, 1955-1958*, and *World Trade in Machine Tools, 1961-1964*, U.S. Dept. of Commerce, Business and Defense Services Administration. The data are not precisely comparable with those above for several reasons. One is that they are based on unrevised tabulations of U.S. data. In addition, the coverage of these figures, as published, differs from the SITC definition. To improve comparability with the OECD tabulations we removed machine tool parts (Schedule B 74456 and 74468) from the published BDSA figures but we have not added in can-making machinery or certain minor military items recently declassified, because we were unable to make the corresponding adjustments in BDSA figures for other countries. Parts do not appear to be included in the U.K. total from the BDSA, but the story is not as clear for Germany. The BDSA figure for German exports of all machine tools is considerably above the OECD total instead of slightly below, as in most other countries.

Gear-cutting machinery exports from Japan were under $500,000.

jOf which Switzerland, $158 million (717.1, $145 million; and 717.3, $13 million).

kOf which Italy, $89 million (717.1, $66 million; 717.2, $5 million; 717.3, $18 million).

lAustria and Canada report only at the 4-digit level, and the 5-digit breakdown was estimated on the basis of OECD import data (for Austria) and U.S. import data, from *U.S. Imports of Merchandise for Consumption, 1963*, U.S. Dept. of Commerce, Report FT 110 (for Canada).

mBreakdown into 5-digit subgroups not available for Canada, Austria, and Greece. For Canada, assumed same as for the United States. For Austria and Greece, assumed same as OECD as a whole, other than these three countries.

nBelgium-Luxembourg and Netherlands reported only SITC 718.4 and SITC 718.42. Difference assumed to be SITC 718.41.

oDifference between UN and OECD figures for Italy ($105,000) assumed to belong in SITC 718.42.

pExcluding Canada and Ireland. Austria did not report 5-digit breakdown. Import data do not show any imports from Austria of 718.52; therefore, entire Austria 718.5 exports were assumed to be 718.51.

qOf which Sweden, $46 million. In the 5-digit breakdown, the United States reported exports only for SITC groups 719.11 to 719.15 and none for 719.19. Hence, it is assumed that the difference between the 719.1 grand total and the summation of 719.11 to 719.15 represents the 719.19 exports (heating and cooling equipment, n.e.s.).

rOf which Italy, $77 million; and France, $63 million.

sThese totals include estimated export figures of Canada and Austria which did not report at the 5-digit level. Austria's 5-digit 719.1 breakdown was estimated by inference from the reports of the importers of 719.1 commodities. Canada's was estimated by breaking up its 719.1 total export figure, weighting with the combined weights of the other OECD countries.

^tA major inconsistency between U.S. and U.K. classifications affects the measures of export shares in this group. The United States classifies "loaders, wheel or crawler mounted, self-propelled" (Schedule B 72015), which involved exports of about $110 million in 1963, in SITC 719.31, presumably on the ground that loading, rather than digging, is their main function. The United Kingdom, however, places "loading shovels, self-propelled," which includes, as a major item, the same front-end loaders classified under 719.31 by the United States, under construction and mining machinery (SITC 718.4), probably on the ground that they do at least a certain amount of digging. The group in question is important for the United Kingdom as well as the United States, with U.K. exports in 1963 at over $40 million. The U.K. method of classification does have one advantage, namely, that this type of machine, consisting essentially of a tractor and a loading attachment, is much more closely related to the other items in SITC 718.4 than to those in SITC 719.3.

It is not clear from the published statistics how the other OECD countries classify these machines.

^uOf which $34 million, Sweden. There is a strong possibility that the comparisons of export values are affected by differences in classification, particularly in subgroup 719.53. U.S. exports, as listed by the Department of Commerce, are composed of lubrication equipment (Schedule B 77545, $8.7 million), portable pneumatic metalworking tools (Schedule B 74570, $10.6 million), and woodworking chain saws and parts (Schedule B 76330, $13.3 million), but exclude pneumatic rock drills, mounted or unmounted (Schedule B 73227, $21.6 million). The revised U.S. export classification included portable pneumatic rock drills and their parts under SITC 715.3, and it is likely that some part of the pneumatic rock drills, excluded from the U.S. total, should have been included in 1963 for comparability with other countries.

^vOf which Sweden, $22 million.

^wU.S. and U.K. data for rubber and plastics machinery are from the sources cited in the Note to this table, above.

^xOf which Sweden, $44 million.

^yThe 5-digit U.S. data were taken from Report FT 410, using the commodity list underlying the revised Commerce Department data. The difference between the Commerce total and the sum of the individual commodities was assumed to represent parts and accessories, n.e.s. specifically fabricated for military watercraft (Schedule B 79560), formerly a special-category export.

^zNo exports reported by United States. However, other countries reported $9 million in imports from the United States (*1963 World Trade Annual*, Walker and Co. for the United Nations, Vol. IV) for 719.91 and 719.94 combined.

Table A.12
OECD Exports of Electrical Machinery, Apparatus, and Appliances (SITC 72), Value by Origin and
Subgroup, 1963
(millions of dollars)

SITC Number	Commodity Group	Total OECD	U.S.	U.K.	EEC		Japan
					Total	Germany	
72	Electrical mach., apparatus & appliances	6,005	1,492	891	2,474	1,173	519
722	Electric power mach. & switchgear	1,403	326	216	606[a]	316	57
722.1	Electric power mach.	803	200[b]	129[b]	323[a]	166	38
722.2	Switchgear	600	126	87	282[a]	150	19
723	Electricity distribution equip.	343	36	98	134[c]	60	39
723.1	Insulated wire & cable	283	26	89	113[c]	51	24
723.2	Electrical insulating equip.	61	10	10	21[c]	9	15
724	Telecommunications equip.	1,715	390	219	650	280	283
724.1	Television receivers	149	22	11	64[d]	43	41
724.2	Radio receivers	386	7	17	157[d]	69	189
724.9	Telecommunications equip., n.e.s.	1,180	361	191	429	168	52
724.91	Electric line telephone & telegraph equip.	358	34	80	139	81	9
724.92	Microphones, loudspeakers, amplifiers	67	21	5	25	9	13
724.99	Other telecommunications equip.	754	306	106	265	78	30

(continued)

Table A.12 (concluded)

SITC Number	Commodity Group	Total OECD	U.S.	U.K.	EEC Total	EEC Germany	Japan
725	Domestic electrical equip.	554	98	100	274[e]	133	20
725.01	Domestic refrigerators, electrical	168	42	14	90	34	4
725.02	Domestic washing machines	129	18	39	64	42	1
725.03	Electromechanical domestic appliances	110	16[f]	24	44	19	11
725.04	Electric shavers & hair clippers	43	5[f]	6	31	7	g
725.05	Other domestic electrical equipment	103	16	17	46	30	4
726 & 729	Misc. electrical mach. & apparatus	1,989[h]	643	258	811[i]	384	121
726.1	Electromedical apparatus	17	1	1	9	5	1
726.2	X-ray apparatus	73	12	4	47	25	1
729.1	Batteries & accumulators	116[j]	12	32	39	17	19
729.2	Electric lamps	144	26	16	84	25	14
729.3	Thermionic, etc., valves & tubes, transistors, etc.	339	88	34	177	34	28
729.4	Automotive electrical equip.	192[k]	74	25	78	49	9
729.5	Electrical measuring & controlling instruments & apparatus	456[l]	205	57	130	86	13
729.6	Electromechanical hand tools	64	18	10	27	21	1
729.7	Electron & proton accelerators	g	NA	NA	g	NA	NA
729.9	Electrical mach. & apparatus, n.e.s.	588[m]	207	78	219	123	35

Notes to Table A.12

^aOf which France, $126 million (722.1, $66 million; 722.2, $61 million).

^bU.S. exports of transformers, $30 million; generators, $105 million; electric motors, $52 million. For Britain, the figures are: transformers, $34 million; generators, $49 million; electric motors, $44 million. The data are from the sources cited in the Note to Table A.11.

^cOf which France, $33 million (723.1, $26 million; 723.2, $7 million).

^dExports of SITC 724.1 and 724.2 were not distinguished in the export data of the Netherlands and were all included by OECD in 724.2. By dividing these $54 million of exports in the same proportion as total imports from the Netherlands by OECD countries reporting a 4-digit breakdown the result for 724.1 for the Netherlands was $19 million; for the EEC, $83 million. The respective figures for 724.2 were $35 million and $138 million.

^eOf which Italy, $60 million (725.01, $42 million; 725.02, $11 million; 725.03, $4 million; 725.04, $1 million; and 725.05, $3 million).

^fU.S. Department of Commerce data showed a combined total for 725.03 and 725.04 which we divided between the two items by estimating exports of the latter as the sum of reported imports of this item as given in the *1963 World Trade Annual*, Walker & Co.for the United Nations, and in *Trade of Canada: Imports by Commodities*, Dominion Bureau of Statistics, December 1963.

^gLess than $500,000.

^hIn some cases the item breakdowns had to be estimated for particular exporters, from data on imports from them by other OECD countries. Such estimates were made for exports of Canada, Sweden, and Austria in SITC 729.1; the United States, Canada, and Austria in SITC 729.4; for Austria, Canada, and Sweden in SITC 729.5; and for the United States, Austria, and Canada in SITC 729.9.

ⁱOf which the Netherlands, $201 million.

^jOf which primary batteries and cells (SITC 729.11), $64 million; electric accumulators (storage batteries) (SITC 729.12), $56 million.

^kOf which electric starting and ignition equipment for internal combustion engines (SITC 729.41), $137 million; electric lighting, etc., equipment for vehicles (SITC 729.42), $55 million.

^lOf which electricity supply meters (SITC 729.51), $24 million; other electric measuring and controlling instruments and apparatus (SITC 729.52), $432 million.

^mOf which electromagnets, permanent magnets, and electromagnetic appliances (SITC 729.91), $32 million; electric furnaces, electric welding and cutting appliances (SITC 729.92), $142 million; electric traffic control equipment (SITC 729.93), $16 million; electric sound or visual signaling apparatus, n.e.s. (SITC 729.94), $13 million; electrical condensers (capacitors) (SITC 729.95), $88 million; electrical carbons (SITC 729.96), $70 million; electrical parts of machinery and appliances, n.e.s. (SITC 729.98), $62 million; other electrical goods and apparatus, n.e.s. (SITC 729.99), $164 million.

...ports of Transport Equipment (SITC 73), Value by Origin and Subgroup, 1963
(millions of dollars)

SITC Number	Commodity Group	Total OECD	U.S.	U.K.	EEC Total	EEC Germany	Japan
73	Transport equipment	10,496	2,704	1,764	4,472	2,345	626
731	Railway vehicles	459	140	58	163[a]	74	50
731.1	Railway locomotives, steam tenders	1		b	b	b	1
731.2	Railway locomotives, electric, not self-generating	24	2	b	18[c]	3	3
731.3	Railway locomotives, other	176[d]	102	12	27	6	2
731.4	Mechanically propelled cars	23	2	1	11	5	9
731.5	Passenger cars, not mechanically propelled	36	2	b	19	12	12
731.6	Freight & maintenance cars, not mechanically propelled	61	7	11	34	17	7
731.7	Parts of railway locomotives & rolling stock, n.e.s.	139	26	33	55	30	17
732 732.1 &	Road motor vehicles[e]	6,802	1,681	1,391	3,213[f]	1,910	214
732.6	Passenger cars	3,360	295	666	2,236[g]	1,324	40
732.2	Buses	90	26	19	41	19	4
732.3	Trucks	1,032	316	244	327	212	75
732.4	Special purpose trucks	155	113	13	21	10	3
732.5	Road tractors	18	NA	3	13	6	1
732.7	Other chassis	138	NA	79	35	27	14
732.8	Bodies, chassis, frames & other parts	1,842	931	351	462	291	19
732.9	Motorcycles & parts	166	1	18	79	22	59

(continued)

Table A.13 (concluded)

SITC Number	Commodity Group	Total OECD	U.S.	U.K.	EEC Total	EEC Germany	Japan
733	Road vehicles other than motor vehicles	221	25	67	95[h]	45	16
733.1	Bicycles & other cycles, not motorized, & parts	118	b	48	47	19	15
733.3	Trailers & other vehicles, not motorized, & parts	103	25	18	48	26	1
734	Aircraft & parts	1,543	817	130[i]	495	61	6
734.1	Aircraft heavier than air	847	474	57[j]	276	4	4
734.9	Airships, balloons & parts of aircraft	697	343	73	219	56	2
735	Ships & boats	1,467[k]	39	119	505[l]	255	340

[a] Of which France, $36 million; Italy, $30 million.

[b] Less than $500,000.

[c] Of which Italy, $7 million; France, $4 million; and Belgium, $4 million.

[d] Of which Canada, $24 million; Sweden, $4 million; and Austria, $4 million.

[e] Covers SITC 732, including parts.

[f] Of which Italy, $391 million; and France, $676 million.

[g] Of which France, $496 million.

[h] Of which France, $22 million.

[i] Source: *Accounts Relating to the Trade and Navigation of the United Kingdom*, U.K. Board of Trade.

[j] Includes SITC 734.91 (balloons and airships).

[k] Of which Sweden, $253 million. Division of total OECD exports of 735 is: warships (735.1), $20 million, of which United States, $15 million; ships and boats other than warships (735.2), $1,376 million; ships, boats, and other vessels for breaking up (735.8), $6 million; ships and boats, n.e.s. (735.9), $65 million.

Table A.14
OECD Exports of Miscellaneous Manufactured Articles (Selected Items from SITC 8), Value by
Origin and Subgroup, 1963
(millions of dollars)

SITC Number	Commodity Group	Total OECD	U.S.	U.K.	EEC Total	EEC Germany	Japan
812	Plumbing, heating, & lighting equip.	238	34	26	115	58	9
861	Scientific, medical, optical, measuring, & controlling instruments & apparatus	1,364[a]	336	144	550	388	151
864	Watches & clocks	477[b]	8	10	98	73	11
891	Musical instruments, sound recorders, & reproducers & parts	429	69	53	202	95	63
894	Perambulators, toys, games, & sporting goods	450	71	52	127	61	149

[a]Of which Switzerland, $70 million.
[b]Of which Switzerland, $347 million.

APPENDIX B

OECD EXPORTS, 1953–64

General Note

This appendix contains information on the value of exports by OECD countries in each of the SITC three-digit commodity groups covered in the study and some of the more important four-digit subgroups. The time span differs from one commodity to another, depending on the availability of data and the consistency of commodity classifications over time.

The U.S. export figures for 1962–64 were taken from the previously mentioned unpublished tabulations of the U.S. Department of Commerce (see Appendix A). Those for earlier years were calculated by adding up data for the Schedule B numbers included in the revised tabulations, matched as closely as possible with the 1962–64 classification, in an attempt to achieve comparability in coverage with later years. The earlier-year figures do not, however, represent revisions in the data for individual Schedule B categories, which were included in the later-year ones. The U.S. export data on a Schedule B classification were taken from *United States Exports of Domestic and Foreign Merchandise: Commodity by Country of Destination,* U.S. Dept. of Commerce, Report FT 410, Part II, for 1953, 1957, and 1961. In groups where the revised tabulations were little different from the published ones, some use was made of the sources cited below for other OECD countries.

Japanese data for 1964 were taken from *Trade by Commodities,* OECD Statistical Bulletin, Series C, 1964, Vol. I. Those for 1963 were from the sources mentioned in Appendix A and those for 1962, 1961 1957, and 1953 from *Commodity Trade Statistics,* United Nations.

For other OECD countries, the 1961–64 data were from variou annual volumes of *Trade by Commodities,* Series C, and the 195' figures were from the OEEC *Trade by Commodity,* Series III, 1957–58, and *Foreign Trade of Selected Commodities,* Series III, 1953, 1954. These figures were supplemented in some cases by information from various issues of *Commodity Trade Statistics,* United Nations.

The basic data for 1953 and 1957 were published in the old SITC classification. We translated these into the new classification but some incomparabilities could not be eliminated.

Table B.1

OECD Exports of Iron and Steel (SITC 67), by Country, 1953,
1957, 1961–64
(millions of dollars)

| | | | | | EEC | | | |
Year	Total OECD	U.S.	U.K.	Total	Ger-many	France	Belgium-Luxem-bourg	Japan
1964	6,680[a]	667	610	3,622	1,235	888	1,036	909
1963	5,693[a]	514	573	3,166	1,146	757	885	702
1962	5,471[a]	470	562	3,227	1,245	769	883	531
1961	5,528	485	594	3,360	1,288	884	853	380
1957	5,164[b]	1,111[c]	598	2,725	943	711	823	209
1953	2,717[b]	515[c]	378	1,401	335	478	498	140

[a]Excluding Canadian exports of 675, hoop and strip of iron or steel.
[b]Excluding Switzerland and Spain, $16 million and $35 million, respectively, in 1961.
[c]Unrevised. The old SITC classification corresponding to 67 was 681.

Table B.2

OECD Exports of Pig Iron, Ferro-alloys, etc. (SITC 671), by
Country, 1961–64
(millions of dollars)

Year	Total OECD	U.S.	U.K.	EEC Total	Germany	France	Norway	Canada	Japan
1964	285	21	9	115	47	49	61	33	5
1963	251	9	10	109	53	42	51	27	7
1962	265	14	15	118	60	48	43	29	11
1961	307	32	12	128	61	55	51	35	NA

Table B.3
OECD Exports of Ingots and Other Primary Forms of Iron and Steel
(SITC 672), by Country, 1961–64
(millions of dollars)

| Year | Total OECD | U.S. | U.K. | EEC | | | Japan |
				Total	Germany	Belgium-Luxem-bourg	
1964	599	65	20	348	128	95	59
1963	415	25	5	267	125	61	27
1962	367	21	9	241	120	68	9
1961	444	14	11	311	137	89	NA

Table B.4
OECD Exports of Iron and Steel Bars, Rods, Angles, Shapes, and Sections
(SITC 673), by Country, 1961–64
(millions of dollars)

| Year | Total OECD | U.S. | U.K. | EEC | | | | Japan |
				Total	Germany	France	Belgium-Luxem-bourg	
1964	1,485	82	101	994	313	206	402	160
1963	1,299	55	96	871	300	186	356	155
1962	1,286	52	97	912	315	197	368	104
1961	1,261	55	108	972	340	239	352	NA

Table B.5
OECD Exports of Universals, Plates, and Sheets of Iron or Steel
(SITC 674), by Country, 1961–64
(millions of dollars)

| Year | Total OECD | U.S. | U.K. | EEC | | | | Japan |
				Total	Germany	France	Belgium-Luxembourg	
1964	2,461	270	274	1,242	333	384	332	439
1963	2,057	216	271	1,045	285	313	283	318
1962	1,895	208	246	1,012	293	314	265	248
1961	1,634	206	236	1,014	296	344	241	NA

Table B.6
OECD Exports of Hoop and Strip of Iron or Steel
(SITC 675), by Country, 1961–64
(millions of dollars)

| Year | Total OECD | U.S. | U.K. | EEC | | | | Japan |
				Total	Germany	France	Belgium-Luxembourg	
1964	335[a]	42	23	207	78	32	83	16
1963	291[a]	29	31	177	66	32	68	13
1962	267[a]	24	24	172	67	28	66	13
1961	269	29	27	182	70	30	67	NA

[a]Excluding Canada.

Table B.7
OECD Exports of Rails and Railway Track Construction Material of Iron and
Steel (SITC 676), by Country, 1961–64
(millions of dollars)

	Total OECD	U.S.	U.K.	EEC				Canada	Japan
				Total	Germany	France	Belgium-Luxem-bourg		
1964	98	10	18	39	17	12	7	20	4
1963	111	17	11	50	21	15	12	16	8
1962	134	19	16	65	23	26	14	12	14
1961	116	17	22	65	26	24	12	8	NA

Table B.8
OECD Exports of Iron and Steel Wire, Excluding Wire Rod,
(SITC 677), by Country, 1961–64
(millions of dollars)

Year	Total OECD	U.S.	U.K.	EEC		Belgium-Luxem-bourg	Japan
				Total	Germany		
1964	270	20	30	133	47	59	55
1963	233	15	28	119	43	53	43
1962	219	10	29	115	45	51	40
1961	189	8	31	126	50	46	NA

Table B.9

OECD Exports of Tubes, Pipes, and Fittings of Iron or Steel
(SITC 678), by Country, 1961–64
(millions of dollars)

Year	Total OECD	U.S.	U.K.	EEC Total	EEC Germany	France	Japan
1964	1,066	129	127	527	265	115	171
1963	968	129	115	503	244	116	132
1962	981	104	125	574	316	115	94
1961	875	108	147	544	301	134	NA

Table B.10

OECD Exports of Nonferrous Metals (SITC 68), by Country, 1953, 1957,
1961–64
(millions of dollars)

Year	Total OECD	U.S.	U.K.	EEC Total	EEC Germany	EEC Belgium-Luxembourg	Canada	Japan
1964	3,232	498	387	1,057	296	421	799	58
1963[a]	2,685	410	348	837	256	357	708	43
1962	2,629	409	369	783	262	317	701	35
1961	2,625	432	341	804	263	312	698	28
1957[b]	2,142[c]	314[d]	347	587	194	227	634	42
1953[b]	1,425[c]	112[d]	213	504	128	205	440	23

[a]These figures differ from data given on the SITC 68 trade matrix, Table A.3, because the various classification adjustments of U.S. exports were not incorporated into this table. See notes to Table A.3.

[b]In 1953 and 1957 the 68 group included waste and sweepings of silver (285.02 in the new SITC grouping), copper matte (283.12), nickel matte and speiss, etc. (283.22), and zinc dust (284.08).

[c]Excluding Spain and Switzerland, $16 million and $35 million, respectively, in 1961.

[d]Unadjusted. The original classification of SITC 68 included 671 and 682–689 of the old SITC.

Table B.11
OECD Exports of Silver, Platinum, and Other Metals of the Platinum Group
(SITC 681), by Country, 1961—64
(millions of dollars)

Year	Total OECD	U.S.[a]	U.K.	EEC Total	EEC Germany	Japan	Canada
1964	209	11	85	69	41	1	33
1963	186	4	79	65	39	[b]	29
1962	148	2	60	53	29	1	25
1961	123	3	53	40	24	[b]	21

[a]U.S. data exclude exports of silver, unworked or partly worked (SITC 681.1) which
were not reported by the Department of Commerce. In 1963 these exports were
estimated to amount to $40 million.

[b]Less than $500,000.

Table B.12
OECD Exports of Copper (SITC 682), by Country, 1961—64
(millions of dollars)

Year	Total OECD[a]	U.S.[b]	U.K.	EEC Total	EEC Germany	EEC Belgium-Luxem-bourg	Canada	Japan
1964	1,113	228	113	474	151	237	177	23
1963	929	208	104	373	120	207	155	15
1962	986	222	155	368	143	179	154	14
1961	1,006	271	135	343	116	174	176	11

[a]Excluding Ireland.

[b]U.S. data exclude exports of copper foil (SITC 682.23), which in 1963 amounted to
approximately $5 million.

Appendix B

Table B.13
OECD Exports of Nickel (SITC 683), by Country, 1961–64
(millions of dollars)

Year	Total OECD[a]	U.S.	U.K.	EEC Total	Germany	Norway	Canada
1964	382	29	68	22	11	59	199
1963	327	22	60	25	11	42	174
1962	342	22	54	27	12	50	186
1961	342	20	56	21	11	52	189

[a]Exports by Japan were less than $500,000 in each year, and are therefore not shown separately.

Table B.14
OECD Exports of Aluminum (SITC 684), by Country, 1961–64
(millions of dollars)

Year	Total OECD	U.S.	U.K.	EEC Total	Germany	France	Norway	Canada	Japan
1964	990	159	49	260	62	98	124	295	21
1963	857	125[a]	52	214	60	85	94	281	17
1962	788	115	53	186	51	74	86	266	12
1961	707	93	49	185	46	82	76	239	8

[a]Adjustments made on Table A.9 were not incorporated in this table.

Table B.15
OECD Exports of Lead (SITC 685), by Country, 1961–64
(millions of dollars)

Year	Total OECD[a]	U.S.	U.K.	EEC Total	Germany	Belgium-Luxem-bourg	Canada
1964	79	4	13	34	9	16	21
1963	60	1	10	28	6	14	15
1962	57	1	8	21	6	12	17
1961	64	1	8	24	7	12	18

[a]Exports by Japan were less than $500,000 in each year, and are therefore not shown separately.

Table B.16
OECD Exports of Zinc (SITC 686), by Country, 1961–64
(millions of dollars)

Year	Total OECD	U.S.	U.K.	EEC Total	Germany	Belgium-Luxem-bourg	Canada	Japan
1964	169	14	5	69	9	47	58	2
1963	120	11	4	51	8	32	39	1
1962	111	12	4	43	7	29	39	a
1961	132	15	3	57	9	39	42	a

[a]Less than $500,000.

Table B.17
OECD Exports of Tin (SITC 687), by Country, 1961–64
(millions of dollars)

Year	Total OECD[a]	U.S.	U.K.	EEC Total	Germany	Belgium-Luxem-bourg	Netherlands
1964	115	10	29	70	4	15	49
1963	67	5	27	33	4	17	12
1962	64	1	24	35	4	18	12
1961	126	3	28	83	41	11	30

[a]Exports by Japan were less than $500,000 in each year, and are therefore not shown separately.

Table B.18
OECD Exports of Miscellaneous Nonferrous Base Metals Employed in
Metallurgy (SITC 689), by Country, 1961–64
(millions of dollars)

Year	Total OECD	U.S.	U.K.	EEC Total	Germany	Belgium-Luxem-bourg	Norway	Canada	Japan
1964	165	43	14	58	9	33	16	16	10
1963	137	33	12	48	8	26	14	14	9
1962	133	33	11	50	10	28	11	13	7
1961	124	26	9	52	9	32	10	13	8

Table B.19

OECD Exports of Manufactures of Metals, n.e.s. (SITC 69), by Country,
1953, 1957, 1961–64

(millions of dollars)

Year	Total OECD	U.S.	U.K.	EEC Total	EEC Germany	Japan
1964	2,828	539	403	1,289	643	236
1963	2,514	495	371	1,146	570	200
1962	2,358	481	380	1,061	534	177
1961	2,217	434	367	1,024	524	153
1957	1,747[a]	390[b]	360	753	391	72
1953	1,145[a]	263[b]	285	463	227	29

[a]Excluding Switzerland and Spain (1961 exports of $47 million and $4 million, respectively).

[b]Department of Commerce data were not adjusted to include exports of 693.12 and 693.13 as in Table A.10. The old SITC classification of 69 was 699.

Table B.20

OECD Exports of Finished Structural Parts and Structures, n.e.s. (SITC 691),
by Country, 1961–64

(millions of dollars)

Year	Total OECD	U.S.	U.K.	EEC Total	EEC Germany	France	Japan
1964	334	68	57	157	65	38	17
1963	317	77	47	147	58	37	14
1962	289	69	48	143	60	35	11
1961	263	50[a]	50	141	60	33	4

[a]Number 61907 of Schedule B could not be found for 1961. It was included in 1962–64 and was 8 per cent of the total in 1964.

Table B.21
OECD Exports of Metal Containers for Storage and Transport (SITC 692),
by Country, 1961–64
(millions of dollars)

Year	Total OECD	U.S.	U.K.	EEC Total	Germany	France	Japan
1964	194	40	28	99	37	28	6
1963	176	39	27	87	31	27	5
1962	164	40	28	80	29	22	3
1961	162	41	25	82	30	27	NA

Table B.22
OECD Exports of Wire Products (Excluding Electric) and Fencing Grills
(SITC 693), by Country, 1961–64
(millions of dollars)

Year	Total OECD	U.S.[a]	U.K.	EEC Total	Germany	Belgium-Luxem-bourg	Japan
1964	210	11	31	124	38	54	24
1963	200	14	32	115	35	48	21
1962	188	12	28	115	35	44	19
1961	161	9	27	109	36	41	NA

[a]U.S. data exclude exports of wire, cables, etc., not insulated, of copper and of aluminum (SITC groups 693.12 and 693.13), which were estimated to amount to $5 million in 1963. These exports were included in SITC group 684 in the published figures.

Table B.23
OECD Exports of Nails, Screws, Nuts, Bolts, Rivets, and Similar
Articles of Iron, Steel, or Copper (SITC 694),
by Country, 1961–64
(millions of dollars)

Year	Total OECD	U.S.	U.K.	EEC Total	Germany	Japan
1964	246	35	23	97	47	53
1963	214	31	21	84	40	49
1962	200	26	20	84	39	42
1961	157	23	22	83	39	NA

Table B.24
OECD Exports of Tools for Use in the Hand or in Machines (SITC 695),
by Country, 1961–64
(millions of dollars)

Year	Total OECD	U.S.	U.K.	EEC Total	EEC Germany	Japan
1964	563	130	78	220	144	32
1963	505	114	74	203	137	27
1962	503	119	89	189	130	25
1961	451	113	81	182	130	NA

Table B.25
OECD Exports of Cutlery (SITC 696), by Country, 1961–64
(millions of dollars)

Year	Total OECD	U.S.	U.K.	EEC Total	EEC Germany	Japan
1964	193	11	42	83	53	41
1963	160	8	36	69	45	33
1962	140	7	30	63	41	27
1961	107	7	27	61	41	NA

Table B.26
OECD Exports of Household Equipment of Base Metals (SITC 697),
by Country, 1961–64
(millions of dollars)

Year	Total OECD	U.S.	U.K.	EEC Total	EEC Germany	France	Japan
1964	274	37	28	155	58	29	19
1963	235	32	25	133	50	27	15
1962	190	32	22	99	34	21	15
1961	170	33	24	93	32	23	NA

Table B.27
OECD Exports of Manufactures of Metals, n.e.s. (SITC 698),
by Country, 1961–64
(millions of dollars)

Year	Total OECD	U.S.	U.K.	EEC Total	EEC Germany	Japan
1964	813	207	117	355	199	44
1963	707	180	110	307	174	36
1962	684	177	116	289	166	35
1961	597	157	111	272	157	NA

Table B.28
OECD Exports of Machinery Other than Electric (SITC 71),
· by Country, 1953, 1957, 1961–64
(millions of dollars)

Year	Total OECD	U.S.	U.K.	EEC Total	EEC Germany	Japan
1964	15,736	4,654	2,403	6,069	3,588	481
1963	14,164	4,046	2,404	5,492	3,299	351
1962	13,410	3,929	2,259	5,117	3,077	345
1961	12,088	3,487	2,172	4,573	2,833	319
1957	8,264[a]	3,245[b]	1,571	2,640	1,748	128
1953	5,234[a]	2,129[b]	1,112	1,537	968	57

[a]Excluding Switzerland and Spain (1961 exports of $477 million and $15 million, respectively).

[b]Unadjusted. The old SITC classification corresponding to 71 included 711 through 716.

Table B.29

OECD Exports of Internal Combustion Engines Other than for Aircraft
(SITC 711.5), by Country, 1953, 1957, 1961–64
(millions of dollars)

Year	Total OECD	U.S.	U.K.	EEC Total	EEC Germany	Japan
1964	1,027	277	244	349	204	28
1963	900	225	225	319	181	22
1962	847	220	208	296	175	21
1961	783[a]	188	217	279	167	NA
1957	626[b]	177	155	202	134	NA
1953	353[b]	122	87	105	78	NA

[a]Ireland not available.

[b]Excluding Switzerland and Spain (1961 exports of $28 million and $1 million, respectively).

Table B.30

OECD Exports of Agricultural Machinery and Implements (SITC 712),
by Country, 1961–64
(millions of dollars)

Year	Total OECD	U.S.	U.K.	EEC Total	EEC Germany	Canada	Japan
1964	1,624	620	378	384	209	138	10
1963	1,398	482	392	329	177	111	7
1962	1,185	400	337	283	159	90	6
1961	1,067	390	280	238	167	92	6

Table B.31
OECD Exports of Office Machines (SITC 714), by Country, 1953,
1957, 1961–64
(millions of dollars)

Year	Total OECD	U.S.	U.K.	EEC Total	EEC Germany	Italy	Japan
1964	1,153	434	112	445	197	114	15
1963	1,024	362	111	410[a]	164	120	8
1962	971	323	93	415	165	117	5
1961	896	310	82	359	145	103	25
1957	391[b]	138[c]	53	153	68	41	1
1953	205[b]	92[c]	31	59	26	15	1

[a]Of which France, $78 million.
[b]Excluding Spain ($2 million in 1961) and Switzerland ($23 million in 1961).
[c]Unrevised.

Table B.32
OECD Exports of Metalworking Machine Tools (SITC 715.1),
by Country, 1953, 1957, 1961–64
(millions of dollars)

Year	Total OECD[a]	U.S.	U.K.	EEC Total	EEC Germany	Switzerland	Japan
1964	1,093	291	129	502	346	94	24
1963	1,016	213	126	520	368	88	17
1962	1,060	304	106	502	350	87	11
1962	1,060[b]	304	106	502	350	87	11[b]
1961	942[b]	266	89	446	317	79	16[b]
1961	921[c]	266	89	446	317	79[c]	16[c]
1957	518[c]	149	79	207	157	58[c]	4[c]
1953	405[d]	159	65	163	106	NA	NA

[a]Excluding Ireland.
[b]Data for Japan from U.S. Business and Defense Services Administration (BDSA).
[c]Data for Japan and Switzerland from BDSA.
[d]Excluding Japan and Switzerland.

Table B.33
OECD Exports of Metalworking Machinery Other than Machine Tools
(SITC 715.2), by Country, 1961–64
(millions of dollars)

Year	Total OECD	U.S.	U.K.	EEC Total	EEC Germany	Japan
1964	343	117	51	137	94	11
1963	354	134	40	156	117	6
1962	343	131	44	145	110	5
1961	316	124	37	135	92	NA

Table B.34
OECD Exports of Textile and Leather Machinery (SITC 717),
by Country, 1961–64
(millions of dollars)

Year	Total OECD	U.S.	U.K.	EEC Total	EEC Germany	Switzerland	Japan
1964	1,504	228	231	656	413	172	162
1963	1,296	190	227	556	356	158	119
1962	1,278	200	225	531	334	144	133
1961	1,124	210	232	511	314	130	NA

Table B.35
OECD Exports of Machines for Special Industries (SITC 718),
by Country, 1961–64
(millions of dollars)

Year	Total OECD	U.S.	U.K.	EEC Total	EEC Germany	Japan
1964	2,269	809	325	825	543	60
1963	2,015	708	332	715	494	36
1962	1,929	704	324	648	441	52
1961	1,680	623	285	603	424	NA

Table B.36
OECD Exports of Paper Mill and Pulp Mill Machinery, etc.
(SITC 718.1), by Country, 1961–64
(millions of dollars)

Year	Total OECD	U.S.	U.K.	EEC Total	EEC Germany	Japan
1964	354	64	39	154	112	30
1963	349	74	70	140	106	10
1962	360	83	62	130	94	28
1961	278	67	45	118	90	NA

Table B.37
OECD Exports of Printing and Bookbinding Machinery (SITC 718.2),
by Country, 1961–64
(millions of dollars)

Year	Total OECD[a]	U.S.	U.K.	EEC Total	EEC Germany	Japan
1964	387	87	53	200	161	2
1963	345	75	48	180	146	2
1962	302	69	47	153	122	2
1961	263	58	37	142	115	NA

[a]Excluding Ireland.

Table B.38
OECD Exports of Food-processing Machinery (SITC 718.3),
by Country, 1961–64
(millions of dollars)

Year	Total OECD[a]	U.S.	U.K.	EEC Total	Germany	Japan
1964	238	57	44	108	69	4
1963	196	42	33	92	58	3
1962	208	38	42	98	60	4
1961	220	42	47	113	73	NA

[a]Excluding Ireland.

Table B.39
OECD Exports of Construction and Mining Machinery, n.e.s.
(SITC 718.4), by Country, 1961–64
(millions of dollars)

Year	Total OECD	U.S.	U.K.	EEC Total	Germany	Japan
1964	961[a]	512	155	208	106	19
1963	819[a]	435	148	162	92	17
1962	770	432	144	130	71	14
1961	667	384	131	113	69	NA

[a]Excluding Ireland.

Table B.40
OECD Exports of Mineral Crushing, Sorting, and Molding Machinery,
etc. (SITC 718.5), by Country, 1961–64
(millions of dollars)

Year	Total OECD	U.S.	U.K.	EEC Total	EEC Germany	Japan
1964	327[a]	89	33	154	95	4
1963	305[a]	81	33	140	92	4
1962	288[b]	83	28	137	93	3
1961	250[c]	73	25	118	76	NA

[a]Excluding Canada.

[b]Excluding Canada, Ireland, and Iceland.

[c]Excluding Canada, Ireland, and Japan.

Table B.41
OECD Exports of Pumps and Centrifuges (SITC 719.2), by
Country, 1961–64
(millions of dollars)

Year	Total OECD	U.S.	U.K.	EEC Total	EEC Germany	Japan
1964	963	243	126	418	234	14
1963	870	226	115	373	206	13
1962	798[a]	209	108	331	190	12
1961	671[b]	174	97	284	167	NA

[a]Excluding Iceland and Ireland.

[b]Excluding Iceland, Ireland, and Japan.

Table B.42
OECD Exports of Mechanical Handling Equipment (SITC 719.3),
by Country, 1961−64
(millions of dollars)

Year	Total OECD	U.S.	U.K.	EEC Total	Germany	Japan
1964	917	323	106	354	205	23
1963	810	282	97	328	201	13
1962	694[a]	233	78	296	184	10
1961	613[b]	226	73	251	157	NA

[a]Excluding Iceland and Ireland.
[b]Excluding Iceland, Ireland, and Japan.

Table B.43
OECD Exports of Power Tools, n.e.s. (SITC 719.5),
by Country, 1961−64
(millions of dollars)

Year	Total OECD[a]	U.S.	U.K.	EEC Total	Germany	Japan
1964	448	114	43	205	136	7
1963	394	93	44	182	124	6
1962	357	86	35	170	118	4
1961	293	77	29	129	88	NA

[a]Excluding Ireland.

Table B.44
OECD Exports of Other Nonelectrical Machines (SITC 719.6
and 719.8), by Country, 1962–64
(millions of dollars)

	Total			EEC		
Year	OECD	U.S.	U.K.	Total	Germany	Japan
1964	1,261	277	181	614	424	38
1963	1,125	245	184	514	351	39
1962	1,028[a]	234	240	456	304	28

[a]Excluding Switzerland.

Table B.45
OECD Exports of Electrical Machinery, Apparatus, and Appliances
(SITC 72), by Country, 1953, 1957, 1961–64
(millions of dollars)

	Total			EEC		
Year	OECD	U.S.	U.K.	Total	Germany	Japan
1964	6,836	1,666	882	2,915	1,311	638
1963	6,005	1,492	891	2,474	1,173	519
1962	5,312	1,361	804	2,164	1,085	429
1961	4,748	1,182	760	1,985	1,022	339
1957	3,063[a]	1,005[b]	636	1,148	642	78
1953	2,112[a]	853[b]	482	623	276	15

[a]Excluding Switzerland and Spain (1961 exports of $143 million and $6 million, respectively).

[b]Unrevised. The old SITC classification corresponding to 72 was 721.

Table B.46
OECD Exports of Electric Power Machinery and Switchgear
(SITC 722), by Country, 1953, 1957, 1961–64
(millions of dollars)

Year	Total OECD	U.S.	U.K.	EEC Total	Germany	Japan
ELECTRIC POWER MACHINERY AND SWITCHGEAR (SITC 722)						
1964	1,547	357	206	680	352	59
1963	1,403	326	216	606	316	57
1962	1,228	264	191	549	304	46
1961	1,096	245	191	500	288	NA
1957[a]	755	262	185	269	177	NA
1953[a]	555	189	166	171	95	NA
ELECTRIC POWER MACHINERY (SITC 722.1)						
1964	875	230	118	346	176	36
1963	803	200	129	323	166	38
1962	702	155	122	290	162	33
1961	635	149	117	279	157	NA
SWITCHGEAR (SITC 722.2)						
1964	672	127	88	334	177	22
1963	600	126	87	282	150	19
1962	526	109	69	259	143	13
1961	461	96	74	222	131	NA

[a]It was assumed that old SITC classification 721.01, electric generators, etc., is comparable to the present SITC 722 classification. Figures exclude Switzerland and Spain (1961 exports of $28 million and $1 million, respectively). Exports of Ireland not available; 1961 exports less than $500,000.

Table B.47
OECD Exports of Equipment for Distributing Electricity
(SITC 723), by Country, 1961–64
(millions of dollars)

Year	Total OECD	U.S.	U.K.	EEC Total	Germany	Japan
1964	377	34	99	149	66	53
1963	343	36	98	134	60	39
1962	320	30	80	145	62	25
1961	268	29	76	129	55	NA

Table B.48
OECD Exports of Telecommunications Equipment (SITC 724),
by Country, 1961—64
(millions of dollars)

Year	Total OECD	U.S.	U.K.	EEC Total	EEC Germany	Japan
TELECOMMUNICATIONS EQUIPMENT (SITC 724)						
1964	1,961	404	225	794	315	349
1963	1,715	390	219	650	280	283
1962	1,538	367	205	569	244	242
1961	1,106	274	186	525	246	NA
TELEVISION RECEIVERS (SITC 724.1)						
1964	198	34	10	80	53	58
1963	149	22	11	64	43	41
1962	111	28	10	50	37	17
1961	90	28	4	53	44	NA
RADIO RECEIVERS (SITC 724.2)						
1964	401	8	12	149	64	214
1963	386	7	17	157	69	189
1962	355	6	4	155	68	177
TELECOMMUNICATIONS EQUIPMENT N.E.S. (SITC 724.9)						
1964	1,362	363	202	565	198	77
1963	1,180	361	191	429	168	52
1962	1,072	333	192	364	138	48

Note: The data for the Netherlands reported by the OECD in 1961 and 1962 were apparently incomplete, and totals from *Commodity Trade Statistics* for these years were substituted for them. However, the subgroup breakdown for the Netherlands in *Commodity Trade Statistics* was inconsistent from year to year and reported incorrectly at least in 1962. It is clear from the Netherlands trade publications that SITC 724.1 and 724.2 cannot be separated; we have put the combination consistently under SITC 724.2 and left the rest of SITC 724 under 724.9 (*Maandstatistiek van de in-, uit- en doorvoer per goederensoort*, Centraal Bureau voor de Statistiek, 1962, 1963, 1964 annuals).

Table B.49
OECD Exports of Household Electrical Equipment (SITC 725),
by Country, 1961–64
(millions of dollars)

Year	Total OECD	U.S.	U.K.	EEC Total	Germany	Italy	Japan
1964	640	112	98	326	148	87	28
1963	554	98	100	274	133	60	20
1962	478	100	79	239	118	50	16
1961	452	106	76	230	114	40	NA

Table B.50
OECD Exports of Electrical Apparatus for Medical Purposes, etc.
(SITC 726 and 729), by Country, 1961–64
(millions of dollars)

Year	Total OECD	U.S.	U.K.	EEC Total	Germany	Netherlands	Japan
1964	2,311	759	254	966	430	253	149
1963	1,989	643	258	811	384	201	121
1962	1,799	598	247	715	358	172	101
1961	1,536	526	231	654	320	174	NA

Table B.51
OECD Exports of Transport Equipment (SITC 73),
by Country, 1953, 1957, 1961–64
(millions of dollars)

Year	Total OECD	U.S.	U.K.	EEC Total	Germany	Japan
1964	11,924	2,993	1,828	5,080	2,632	839
1963	10,496	2,704	1,764	4,472	2,345	626
1962	9,437	2,735	1,591	3,860	1,966	478
1961	8,882	2,480	1,621	3,633	1,890	476
1957	7,226[a]	2,630[b]	1,469	2,177	1,171	424
1953	4,720[a]	2,220[b]	1,043	1,020	429	117

[a]Excluding Switzerland and Spain (1961 exports of $13 million and $4 million, respectively).

[b]U.S. exports of 733 and 735 were unrevised.

Table B.52
OECD Exports of Railway Vehicles (SITC 731),
by Country, 1953, 1957, 1961–64
(millions of dollars)

Year	Total OECD	U.S.	U.K.	EEC Total	EEC Germany	Japan
ALL RAILWAY VEHICLES (SITC 731)						
1964	446	112	52	192	105	25
1963	459	140	58	163	74	50
1962	442	155	56	148	67	63
1961	404[a]	156	39	147	78	34
1957	478[b]	148	117	144	62	34
1953	426[b]	108	119	172	60	9
LOCOMOTIVES AND MECHANICALLY PROPELLED CARS						
(SITC 731.1–731.4)						
1964	183[c]	71	13	60	36	6
1963	224[c]	106	13	56	15	15
1962	219	119	14	50	23	26
1961	222	121	8	58	35	20[d]
1957	196	81	34	49	25	7[d]
OTHER RAILWAY VEHICLES AND PARTS (SITC 731.5–731.7)						
1964	257	38	39	132	70	19
1963	235	35	45	108	59	36
1962	222	36	42	97	43	37
1961	182	34	31	89	43	13
1957	282	67	83	95	37	26

[a]Excluding Iceland and Ireland.

[b]Excluding Switzerland and Spain (1961 exports of $47 million and $4 million, respectively).

[c]Including Canada: $25.2 million in 1964 and $24.0 million in 1963.

[d]*Annual Return of the Foreign Trade of Japan*, Ministry of Finance, Tokyo, 1961 and 1957.

Table B.53
OECD Exports of Road Motor Vehicles (SITC 732),
by Country, 1953, 1957, 1961–64
(millions of dollars)

Year	Total OECD	U.S.	U.K.	EEC Total	Germany	France	Italy	Japan
ROAD MOTOR VEHICLES (SITC 732)								
1964	7,792	1,918	1,508	3,658	2,198	644	456	299
1963	6,802	1,681	1,391	3,213	1,910	676	391	214
1962	6,040	1,522	1,259	2,840	1,639	587	395	160
1961	5,336	1,321	1,109	2,538	1,494	530	341	139
1957	3,929[a]	1,491	864	1,398	814	330	175	29
1953	2,367[a]	1,090	619	541	263	176	62	6
PASSENGER MOTOR CARS OTHER THAN BUSES OR SPECIAL VEHICLES (SITC 732.1 AND 732.6)[b]								
1964	3,795	326	721	2,497	1,514	442	281	77
1963	3,360	295	666	2,236	1,324	496	251	40
1962	2,936	273	603	1,930	1,080	429	268	30
1961	2,334	223	415	1,612	957	356	185	NA
1957	1,680[c]	307	443	872	497	222	100	NA
1953	911[c]	282	291	298	138	102	37	NA
BUSES, TRUCKS, SPECIAL PURPOSE VEHICLES, ETC. (SITC 732.2, 732.3, 732.4, 732.5, AND 732.7)[d]								
1964	1,587	489	367	520	319	83	62	104
1963	1,434	454	357	437	273	77	42	97
1962	1,337[e]	424	320	421	271	72	38	84
1961	1,265[e]	351	378	457	271	76	72	NA
1957	1,086[f]	503	241	288	192	68	16	NA
1953	676[f]	310	177	144	80	46	5	NA
BODIES, CHASSIS, FRAMES, AND OTHER PARTS OF MOTOR VEHICLES (SITC 732.8)								
1964	2,191	1,102	398	551	342	103	68	23
1963	1,841	931	351	462	291	89	59	19
1962	1,632	824	320	412	267	75	51	16
1961	1,536	682[g]	316	471	265	98	84	NA
1957	973[h]	615[g]	180	144	126	40	59	NA
1953	729[h]	451[g]	151	100	45	28	20	NA

Notes to Table B.53

[a]Excluding Switzerland and Spain (1961 exports of $5 million and $7 million, respectively).

[b]The data include SITC 732.1, passenger motor cars (other than buses or special vehicles) whether or not assembled, and 732.6 chassis for 732.1 vehicles with mounted engines. These two categories were combined because separate data for the United States were not available for SITC 732.6. The U.S. data for 1953 and 1957 are incomplete because numbers 79073 and 79078 of Schedule B were not available for these two years.

[c]Excluding Switzerland and Spain (1961 exports of $0.4 million and $0.5 million, respectively); Ireland not available.

[d]These categories were combined because separate data were not available for 732.2, 732.3, 732.4 and 732.5 before 1961 and because the United States reported chassis with engines mounted, other than for passenger cars (732.7), in the corresponding vehicle category.

[e]Switzerland, Iceland, and Ireland not available.

[f]Excluding Spain (1961 exports, $0.4 million) and Switzerland (1963 exports, $0.3 million).

[g]These figures are not completely comparable with those for later years because Schedule B, 79277, was not available.

[h]Includes SITC 732.9 except in the case of the United States.

Table B.54

OECD Exports of Road Vehicles Other than Motor Vehicles (SITC 733),
by Country, 1953, 1957, 1961—64
(millions of dollars)

Year	Total OECD	U.S.	U.K.	EEC Total	Germany	France	Japan
1964	263	33	63	123	60	26	20
1963	221	25	67	95	45	22	16
1962	202	26	59	87	41	20	15
1961	190	20[a]	60	85	40	21	14
1957	194[b]	31[c]	71	75	36	23	9
1953	160[b]	21[c]	76	52	18	17	7

[a]Excluding Schedule B, 79145.

[b]Excluding Switzerland and Spain (1961 exports of each less than $500,000).

[c]Unadjusted.

Table B.55
OECD Exports of Aircraft and Parts (SITC 734),
by Country, 1953, 1957, 1961–64
(millions of dollars)

Year	Total OECD	U.S.[a]	U.K.	EEC Total	EEC Germany	Japan
1964	1,764	854	121	560	41	4
1963	1,543	817	130	495	61	6
1962	1,507	979	115	280	10	4
1961	1,436	915	165	246	7	6
1957	1,125[b]	808	195	70	c	c
1953	975[b]	781	118	26	c	

[a]U.S. exports, 1962–64, are from unpublished tabulations of the U.S. Department of Commerce, and include corrections of major errors in previously published data (see Note to Table A.7). These corrections have been carried back, as far as possible, to 1953, using the detailed U.S. export statistics in the FT 410 series of the Department of Commerce. Engine parts were not distinguished in the 1953 figures, and we estimated them by assuming they bore the same ratio to total exports of aircraft and parts as in 1957.

[b]Excluding Switzerland (1961 exports, $3 million) and Spain (1961 exports negligible, $94,000).

[c]Less than $500,000.

Table B.56
OECD Exports of Ships and Boats (SITC 735),
by Country, 1953, 1957, 1961–64
(millions of dollars)

Year	Total OECD	U.S.	U.K.	EEC Total	EEC Germany	Sweden	Japan
1964	1,674	77	84	547	227	230	491
1963	1,467	39	119	505	255	253	340
1962	1,244	53	102	505	209	203	235
1961	1,512	68[a]	248	615	270	167	283
1957	1,500[b]	152[c]	222	489	258	155	352
1953	791[b]	219[c]	111	229	89	70	96

Notes to Table B.56

[a]The 1961 U.S. export data are not entirely comparable to those of later years because Schedule B, 79555, warships, was not available in the Department of Commerce FT 410 report. This item was taken from *Foreign Commerce and Navigation of the United States, 1946–1963*, U.S. Dept. of Commerce, 1965 (SITC 735, special categories).

[b]Excluding Switzerland (1961 exports, less than $0.5 million) and Spain (1961 exports, $2 million).

[c]Unadjusted.

Table B.57

OECD Exports of Sanitary, Plumbing, Heating, and Lighting
Fixtures and Fittings (SITC 812), by Country, 1962–64
(millions of dollars)

Year	Total OECD	U.S.	U.K.	EEC Total	EEC Germany	Japan
1964	292	41	31	140	70	13
1963	238	34	26	115	58	9
1962	215	34	27	102	50	8

APPENDIX C

INTERNATIONAL PRICE INDEXES

General Note

This appendix contains tables showing international price indexes for SITC two-digit commodity divisions, three-digit groups, four-digit subgroups, and in some cases, five-digit items. The indexes are given in the tables for all the subgroups and groups in which the amount and quality of the data were sufficient for publication. The notes that follow the tables cover all the subgroups including those not shown.

On the two-digit and three-digit levels two versions of the international price indexes are given. For each country, the four-digit indexes are aggregated, using the trade weights, to three-digit and two-digit averages. In addition, for countries other than the United States, we show three-digit and two-digit indexes extrapolated from the U.S. international price index by the U.S. index of international price competitiveness relative to that country. The notation following each country name indicates whether the index was aggregated (A) or extrapolated (E). The two versions may differ for two reasons, as was mentioned in Chapter 4. The aggregation of price competitiveness indexes gives results different from the aggregation of price indexes even if the basic price data are identical. Secondly, the price competitiveness index sometimes includes additional or different price data based on place-to-place comparisons. The notes to the tables refer only to the aggregated indexes, since the extrapolated version in each case is derived as explained above.

Table C.1

International Price Indexes, Iron and Steel, 1953, 1957, 1961–64
(1962 = 100)

SITC Number	Commodity Group, Country, and Index Type[a]	1953	1957	1961	1962	1963	1964
67	Iron and steel						
	U.S. (A)	84	101	102	100	99	100
	U.K. (A)	97	110	103	100	97	105
	U.K. (E)	99	110	102	100	96	104
	EEC (A)	100	119	105	100	96	105
	EEC (E)	101	118	104	100	96	104
	Germany (A)	95	111	104	100	96	105
	Germany (E)	94	111	104	100	96	104
	Japan (A)	NA	NA	111	100	101	101
	Japan (E)	NA	NA	110	100	99	100
671	Pig iron, ferro-alloys, etc.						
	U.K. (A)	99	120	104	100	94	95
	EEC (A)	121	143	111	100	88	88
	Germany (A)	111	134	106	100	90	90
673	Bars, rods, angles, shapes, and sections						
	U.S. (A)	NA	98	101	100	98	99
	U.K. (A)	NA	108	106	100	98	110
	U.K. (E)	NA	103	102	100	94	104
	EEC (A)	98	124	110	100	97	108
	EEC (E)	NA	124	110	100	99	108
	Germany (A)	89	115	107	100	97	106
	Germany (E)	NA	115	107	100	97	107
	Japan (A)	NA	NA	NA	100	105	108
	Japan (E)	NA	NA	116	100	102	104
673.1	Wire rod						
	EEC	99	118	114	100	96	108
	Germany	99	118	116	100	97	108
673.2	Bars and rods (excl. wire rod)						
	U.S.	NA	99	102	100	95	98
	U.K.	NA	NA	109	100	102	NA
	EEC	97	123	112	100	100	109
	Germany	87	116	107	100	98	104
673.4 & 673.5	Angles, shapes, and sections U.S.	NA	98	101	100	100	103

(continued)

Table C.1 (continued)

SITC Number	Commodity Group, Country, and Index Type[a]	1953	1957	1961	1962	1963	1964
673.4 & 673.5	Angles, shapes, and sections (continued)						
	U.K.	NA	NA	103	100	96	108
	EEC	98	129	106	100	94	106
	Germany	NA	NA	104	100	97	108
674	Universals, plates, and sheets						
	U.S. (A)	88	102	101	100	101	102
	U.K. (A)	113	118	104	100	92	103
	U.K. (E)	116	121	105	100	93	106
	EEC (A)	108	125	103	100	94	104
	EEC (E)	106	122	101	100	94	102
	Germany (A)	97	112	102	100	94	103
	Germany (E)	97	112	102	100	92	101
	Japan (A)	NA	NA	111	100	99	101
	Japan (E)	NA	NA	112	100	97	99
674.1 & 674.2	———3mm. or more (excl. tinned)						
	U.S.	NA	104	103	100	100	104
	U.K.	NA	NA	106	100	95	110
	EEC	101	136	107	100	93	114
	Germany	99	132	110	100	92	114
674.3	———less than 3mm., uncoated						
	U.S.	NA	103	100	100	102	101
	U.K.	108	114	104	100	89	NA
	EEC	114	122	100	100	94	98
	Germany	97	105	99	100	94	98
674.7	———tinned						
	U.S.	91	101	101	100	100	100
	U.K.	NA	105	103	100	102	104
675	Hoop and strip						
	EEC (A)	93	106	105	100	99	104
	Germany (A)	94	108	107	100	99	105
676	Rails and track construction material						
	EEC (A)	88	107	100	100	99	98
	Germany (A)	90	109	101	100	98	97
676.1	Rails						
	EEC	88	107	100	100	99	98
	Germany	90	109	101	100	98	97

(continued)

Table C.1 (concluded)

SITC Number	Commodity Group, Country, and Index Type[a]	1953	1957	1961	1962	1963	1964
677	Iron and steel wire (excl. wire rod)						
	U.S. (A)	NA	NA	100	100	100	98
	U.K. (A)	NA	NA	99	100	101	107
	EEC (A)	87	117	106	100	99	106
	EEC (E)	NA	117	106	100	99	104
	Germany (A)	97	115	103	100	100	107
	Germany (E)	NA	115	103	100	100	107
	Japan (A)	NA	NA	107	100	98	99
	Japan (E)	NA	NA	107	100	98	99
678	Tubes, pipes, and fittings						
	U.S. (A)	88	105	103	100	98	98
	U.K. (A)	NA	103	99	100	102	102
	U.K. (E)	90	102	98	100	100	102
	EEC (A)	97	108	102	100	99	105
	EEC (E)	95	108	100	100	99	103
	Germany (A)	100	104	102	100	100	106
	Germany (E)	96	103	101	100	99	102
	Japan (A)	NA	NA	101	100	100	89
	Japan (E)	NA	NA	103	100	102	92
678.1	Tubes and pipes of cast iron						
	EEC	92	99	99	100	100	100
	Germany	92	99	99	100	100	100
678.2	Tubes and pipes (excl. cast iron), seamless						
	U.S.	73	95	102	100	97	101
	U.K.	NA	98	98	100	101	102
	EEC	NA	110	104	100	101	108
	Germany	NA	110	105	100	100	110
	Japan	NA	NA	101	100	101	97
678.3	Tubes and pipes (excl. cast iron), welded, etc.						
	U.S.	NA	108	101	100	99	97
	U.K.	NA	NA	99	100	100	100
	EEC	100	116	99	100	99	106
	Germany	106	107	103	100	100	104
678.5	Tube and pipe fittings						
	U.S.	NA	NA	118	100	97	95
	U.K.	NA	NA	100	100	108	NA
	EEC	NA	93	103	100	95	94
	Germany	NA	86	96	100	97	99
	Japan	NA	NA	NA	100	87	NA

Notes to Table C.1

Note: **SITC 67:** The aggregated indexes are weighted averages of the 3-digit SITC groups for which we had data: the seven 3-digit groups listed in the table, plus group 672 (ingots and other primary forms of iron and steel). No data were available for group 679 (iron and steel castings and forgings, unworked, n.e.s.), which accounts for only 1 per cent of the total weight of group 67. The coverage of 3-digit groups varies by country. The *U.S.* index excludes 676 for all years, and 677 for 1953. The *U.K.* index excludes 675 and 676 for all years and 677 for 1953. The *EEC* and *German* indexes include all groups 671 through 678. The *Japanese* index, which covers only the period 1961—64, includes 673—678 for that period.

The data for group 672 were considered insufficient for publication as separate indexes but were included in the total calculation for 67. They were based on a small number of observations from foreign sources, supplemented in the case of the United Kingdom by domestic price data. (See below for notes on other 3-digit groups.)

671: The aggregated index for each country includes data for four of the five subgroups in 671. Excluded is 671.3 (iron and steel powders, shot, and sponge) which represents less than 6 per cent of the weight of 671. The *U.K.* index is based on between 20 and 30 observations, most of which were from the *Metal Bulletin*. The *EEC* and *German* indexes are based on from 5 to 10 observations from five sources. For 671.5 (ferro-alloys other than ferromanganese) we used import unit values based on U.S. imports from Germany and France. For the EEC these two were averaged with weights of 4 for France and 1 for Germany, estimated from 1963 U.S. imports of 671.5 from the two countries. The *U.S.* index for group 671 was considered too weak to publish separately. It was based on about 5 observations from two sources, supplemented by domestic price data.

673: The aggregated index for each country is a weighted average of indexes for the three 4-digit subgroups listed in the table. Subgroup indexes not shown were not sufficiently reliable to publish separately, but were included in the calculation of the 3-digit aggregate index (see below).

673.1: The *EEC* index is based on about 15 to 20 observations from six sources, including the official statistics on German export prices. The data were aggregated from a 5-digit level, with 673.11 (wire rod of other than high carbon or alloy steel) weighted 83 per cent and 673.12 and 673.13 combined (high carbon or alloy steel) weighted 17 per cent. The *German* index is based on about a dozen observations from four sources, and was calculated like the EEC index. The *U.S.* data, solely from domestic prices, and the *U.K.* data, from only one buyer source, were not sufficient to use separately. *Japanese* data were limited to a few observations on 673.11 for 1961 to 1964. They were from three sources including the official export price index.

673.2: The *U.S.* index is based on 5 observations in the earliest period (not published separately) and from 7 to 18 observations from eight buyer sources for the other periods. The data were aggregated from a 5-digit level, with 673.21 (bars and rods of other than high carbon or alloy steel) weighted 76 per cent and 673.22 and 673.23 combined (high carbon or alloy steel) weighted 24 per cent. The *U.K.* published index, for 1961—63, is based on 5 or 6 observations for each period from three buyer sources. The information for 1953—61 and for 1963 and 1964 (not published separately) consisted of only 1 to 3 observations. All of the U.K. data pertain to subgroup 673.21. For the *EEC* and *Germany* also we had data only on 673.21. There were between 10 and 20 observations, 9 of which were export price series from the German official statistics. In addition there were three buyer sources of German data, and a few buyer observations for France and Belgium including the German official index of import prices from France for the 1960s. The *Japanese* data, not published as a separate index, consisted of

(continued)

Notes to Table C.1 (continued)

the official export price index for 1961−64 and one buyer observation for the 1964/1963 link.

673.4 and 673.5: The price relatives for these two 4-digit groups were combined by weighting the average for each group by the number of observations. The *U.S.* index is based on 10 to 20 observations from three buyer sources. No data were available for the 1957/1953 link. The *U.K.* index is based on 10 to 20 observations from five buyer sources for the 1960s. For the earlier years we had a smaller number of observations from only two sources, not sufficient to publish separately. The *EEC* index is based on data for Germany, France, and Belgium for the period 1957−62 and for Germany and Belgium only for the other periods. The number of observations was between 5 and 10 for each period. Data were from five buyer sources. The *German* index was based on 5 observations for the period 1961−64. The earlier data consisted of fewer observations and were not sufficient to publish separately. The official export statistics were given a relatively small weight, since they referred to an atypical item within the subgroup. The *Japanese* data, not published separately, consisted of an official export price series for 1961−64, and a few buyer observations for the 1962/1961 and 1964/1963 links.

674: The aggregated index for each country except Japan is a weighted average of indexes for the three 4-digit groups listed in the table. No data were available on 674.8 (plates and sheets less than 3 mm., coated, except tinned plates) for these countries. The *U.K.* index also excludes 674.1 and 674.2 for 1953, the *EEC* index excludes 674.7 for 1953, and the *German* index excludes all periods except 1964 for 674.7. The *Japanese* index includes all four 4-digit groups for 1961−64 only. The Japanese data for 674.8 consisted of an official export price series, and were not considered sufficient to publish as a separate index.

674.1 and 674.2: The *U.S.* data were limited to 674.1 (universals, plates, and sheets over 4.75 mm.) but were given the total weight of 674.1 and 674.2. They came from two large U.S. producers and four buyer sources, including three large U.S. companies. There were about 10 observations for each period except the 1957/1953 link. For this earliest period only 2 observations from one of the buyers were available, and the published index was therefore not extended back to 1953. The *U.K.* index includes data for both 4-digit groups, weighted by the number of observations. Most of the observations were for the larger items (674.1) except for the 1964/1963 link where the reverse was true. There were from 7 to 12 observations for each period in the 1960s, only 2 for 1961/1957 (not published), and none for 1957/1953. There were four sources, and most of the data was from buyers. The *EEC* index is a weighted average of the German index described below, an index for Belgium, an official German import price index from France for the 1960s, and scattered observations for Holland. There were 16 observations for the earliest period, and between 20 and 30 for the later ones. There were three buyer sources in addition to the official German export and import statistics. The *German* index is based on from 15 to 20 observations from the official export statistics, and two buyer sources.

674.3: The *U.S.* index is based on 6 to 13 observations for each period from 1957 to 1964. The 1957/1953 link was based on only 4 observations, not sufficient to publish separately. The data were aggregated from a 5-digit level, with 674.31 (other than high carbon or alloy steel) weighted 77 per cent and 674.32 and 674.33 combined (high carbon or alloy steel) weighted 23 per cent. The sources of data were three U.S. buyer firms. We also used BLS wholesale price data for the high carbon and alloy steel subgroup. For the *U.K.* index we had data only on 674.31. There were about 10 observations for each period from 1953 to 1963 from three buyer sources. Only 2 observations from one source were available for the 1964/1963 link, which was therefore not included in the published index. The *EEC* index is a weighted average of indexes for Germany, France (1961 to 1963 only), Holland (1963/1962 link only) and Belgium; all available data pertained to 674.31. There were 13 observations in the early periods and 20 or more in the 1960s. The data on France came from one U.S. buyer and from German official import statistics; those for Holland and Belgium were from U.S. buyers. The *German* index is based on about 15 observations on 674.31 from German official export statistics and from three buyer sources. The *Japanese* data were not sufficient to publish as a separate index. They consisted of an official export series on 674.31, supplemented by buyer data from one source for 1964/1963; and one observation for each period from a U.S. buyer on 674.33.

   674.7: The *U.S.* index is based on 14 observations for the earliest period and between 5 and 10 for the later periods. The data were from four buyer sources. The *U.K.* index is based on 7 to 15 observations from four buyer sources for all but the 1957/1953 link. For the earliest period, not included in the published index, we had 2 observations from one buyer source. The *EEC* and *German* indexes were not based on sufficient data to publish. The data consisted of scattered observations from two buyer sources on France, the Netherlands, Belgium, and Germany. There were no data for the 1957/1953 link. Data for *Japan* were also too weak for a published index. They consisted of an official series for the 1960s and a few observations from three buyer sources covering the same period.

   675: The *U.S.* data were not sufficient to publish as a separate index. They consisted of less than 5 observations for each period, from four buyer sources. No data were available for the *U.K.* The *EEC* index is based on between 10 and 20 observations. The 1957/1953 and 1961/1957 links are based entirely on Germany. For the other periods we had data on Germany, France, and Belgium. Data on France were from official German import statistics. Those on Belgium were from a U.S. buyer. The data were aggregated from a 5-digit level with 675.01 (other than high carbon or alloy steel) weighted 75 per cent and 675.02 and 675.03 combined (high carbon or alloy steel) weighted 25 per cent. The *German* index is based on about a dozen observations for each period, including nine series from the official German export statistics, and data from two buyer sources. All German data pertained to 675.01.

   676: All data for this group pertained to 676.1. The indexes for 676.1 (see below) were assigned to 676 as a whole since 676.1 accounts for two-thirds of the 3-digit group. The remainder is made up of 676.2 (sleepers and other railway track material of iron or steel), for which no data were available.

   676.1: The *EEC* and *German* indexes are based primarily on five series from the German official export statistics. One additional source provided one observation for Germany for all periods and one for France for 1957–63. The French and German data were combined by weighting by the number of observations of each. *Japanese* data available but not published as a separate index consisted of an official price series on rails for 1961 to 1964.

   677: The *U.S.* index for 1961–64 was based on about a dozen observations for each period from five U.S. buyers. The data were aggregated from a 5-digit level with 677.01 (other than high carbon or alloy steel) weighted 64 per cent, 677.02 (higher carbon steel) weighted 21 per cent, and 677.03 (alloy steel) weighted 15 per cent. Not included in the published index were 2 buyer observations on 677.01 for the 1961/1957 link. The *U.K.* index covers 677.01 only. It is based on 6 or 7 observations for the 1960s, and 5 for the unpublished 1961/1957 link. Data were from four buyer sources. The *EEC* and

(continued)

Notes to Table C.1 (continued)

German indexes for the 1960s were aggregated from a 5-digit level with 677.01 weighted 64 per cent and 677.02 and 677.03 combined weighted 36 per cent. The earlier years are based only on 677.01. The *EEC* index includes data on Germany, France, Italy, and Belgium for the 677.01 component, but only German data for the 677.02 and 677.03 component. For the *EEC* index there were about 30 observations for the 1960s and about 15 for earlier years. Data were from seven buyer sources in addition to the German official export statistics. The *German* index is based on over 20 observations for the 1960s and over 10 for the earlier years. German data were from the official export statistics and two buyer sources. The *Japanese* index, covering the 1960s only, is based on 5 or 6 observations for each period from the official export index and two buyer sources. Data covered 677.01, weighted 81 per cent, and 677.03, weighted 19 per cent.

   678: The aggregated index for each country is a weighted average of the 4-digit groups for which we had data. In addition to the four 4-digit groups listed in the table, SITC 678 includes 678.4 (high-pressure hydroelectric conduits of steel), for which we had no data, but which accounts for only 2 per cent of the total 1963 OECD export weight of group 678. The coverage of 4-digit groups within 678 varies by country. The *U.S.* and *U.K.* indexes exclude 678.1; and the U.K., 678.3 before 1961. The *EEC* and *German* indexes include all four groups except 678.5 for 1953 for *Germany*. The *Japanese* data are limited to 678.2 for 1961–64 only, 678.3 for 1962–64 only, and 678.5 for 1962 and 1963 only.

   678.1: The *EEC* and *German* indexes are taken from the nine price series in the official German export statistics.

   678.2: This group was broken down into five categories of products with the following weights: oil country casing, 30 per cent; oil country tubing, 6 per cent; line pipe and standard pipe, 34 per cent; tubing other than for oil wells, not alloy, 20 per cent; tubing other than for oil wells, alloy, 10 per cent. (More detailed breakdowns of some categories were also made where differences in size or material appeared to be related to price movements. In these cases weights were assigned based on the best estimate of a product's relative importance in exports that could be made from the sample of observations.) The index for each country was then calculated as a weighted average of the average price relatives for each of the five categories. For the *U.S.* index a large volume of data was available from five U.S. oil companies and was supplemented by information from two other buyer sources. For the 1960s the index is based on over 50 observations, and for the earlier years, on between 20 and 30. The *U.K.* index also relies heavily on oil company data. There were five buyer sources in all. For the 1960s we had about 40 observations; for 1961/1957, only 7; and for 1957/1953 (not published), only 3. The *EEC* index is based on data for Germany, France, Belgium and Italy. Data for countries other than Germany were combined to form a separate index which was then averaged with the German index. Germany was given a weight of 70 per cent and other countries combined, 30 per cent. For the 1960s there were from 50 to 70 observations, for 1961/1957, 21 observations, and for 1957/1953 (not published), only 7. There were six buyer sources, primarily oil companies, in addition to the official German export statistics. The *German* index is based on about 30 observations for the 1960s, 12 for 1961/1957, and only 3 for 1957/1953 (not published). Data were from four buyer sources and from the official export statistics. The official statistics, based on 8 price series, were given a constant weight for all periods, derived from the ratio of the number of observations from this source to those from buyer sources in the period of maximum observations. The *Japanese* index is based on from 10 to over 20 observations from 4 oil company sources.

678.3: The *U.S.* index is based on about 15 observations for the 1960s, 7 observations for 1961/1957 and 4 for 1957/1953 (not published). Data were from four buyer sources. The *U.K.* index, which covers only 1961–64, is based on about a dozen observations from two buyers. The *EEC* index includes data for Germany and France for all periods, and for Italy for 1964/1963 only. There were from 12 to 24 observations from four buyer sources and the official German export statistics. The *German* index is based on 11 price series from the official export statistics and a few additional observations, for the two earliest periods and the last period, from two buyer sources. There were some *Japanese* data for 1962–64, which were not published as a separate index. They consisted of less than 10 observations from two buyers.

678.5: The *U.S.* index is based on data from six buyer sources. There were close to 100 observations for each of the links 1962/1961 and 1963/1962 and 10 for 1964/1963. For the earlier periods we had less than 10 observations, and we did not consider them reliable enough to extend the published index to these years. The *U.K.* index is based on data from four buyer sources. There were close to 90 observations for the links 1962/1961 and 1963/1962. For the other periods there were fewer than 5 observations, so that the published index is limited to 1961–63. The *EEC* index includes data on Germany, a few observations on France and Italy, and a large number of observations on Continental Europe as a whole. The data were combined by assigning the German data the weight of German exports, and the average of all other observations the weight of EEC exports excluding Germany. There were from over 10 to almost 70 observations for each of the periods except the earliest one. The 1957/1953 link contained only 2 observations and was not included in the published index. The data were from four buyer sources and the official German export statistics. The *German* index is based on 9 price series from the official export statistics and 2 or 3 observations for the 1960s from two buyer sources. The 1961/1958 relatives from the official statistics were used for the 1961/1957 link. The *Japanese* index covers only 1962 and 1963. The 47 observations are all buyer data.

[a]A in parentheses after country name indicates aggregated index; E, extrapolated index. See General Note to this appendix for a fuller explanation.

Table C.2

International Price Indexes, Nonferrous Metals, 1953, 1957, 1961–64

(1962 = 100)

SITC Number	Commodity Group, Country, and Index Type[a]	1953	1957	1961	1962	1963	1964
68	Nonferrous metals						
	U.S. (A)	96	100	101	100	100	108
	U.K. (A)	95	101	101	100	102	115
	U.K. (E)	95	101	101	100	102	115
	EEC (A)	100	102	101	100	101	117
	EEC (E)	100	102	101	100	101	117
	Germany (A)	100	105	101	100	100	116
	Germany (E)	100	105	101	100	100	115
682	Copper						
	U.S. (A)	98	95	100	100	100	107
	U.K. (A)	98	94	99	100	100	112
	U.K. (E)	98	94	99	100	100	112
	EEC (A)	100	96	101	100	100	119
	EEC (E)	100	96	101	100	100	119
684	Aluminum						
	U.S. (A)	99	108	103	100	97	103
	U.K. (A)	98	111	105	100	100	107
	U.K. (E)	98	111	105	100	100	108
	EEC (A)	107	109	103	100	97	104
	EEC (E)	107	109	103	100	97	104
684.1	Aluminum and aluminum alloys, unwrought						
	U.S.	104	109	103	100	94	103
684.2	Aluminum and aluminum alloys, worked						
	U.S.	92	107	102	100	101	103

Note: **SITC 68:** The aggregated index for each country is a weighted average of indexes for eight of the nine 3-digit groups which make up SITC 68. The two 3-digit groups shown in the table are the most important ones in world trade and the ones for which the amount and quality of data were sufficient for us to publish separate indexes (for description of these indexes see below). Data were also available and included in the 68 index for 681 (silver, platinum and other metals of the platinum group), 683 (nickel), 685 (lead), 686 (zinc), 687 (tin) and 689 (miscellaneous nonferrous base metals employed in metallurgy). For a discussion of the data on these "other nonferrous metals," see Chapter 10. The one group omitted was 688 (uranium and thorium and their alloys), which represents only 0.03 per cent of the weight of the total group. No data were available on SITC 68 for Japan.

682: As indicated in the text of Chapter 10, we had extensive data on producers' export prices of unwrought copper for the last few years of our study. For the earlier years, we had to rely on prices supplied by two very large purchasers in U.S. and European markets and by several smaller U.S. and foreign purchasers; these sources were also available for the later years. For worked copper, the sources were almost entirely buyers; the main exception was Germany, for which we had a number of index series of export prices. Counting the latter as a single source, we had a dozen sources of information on worked copper prices, only a minority from the United States.

As noted in the text, different price relationships seem to prevail for brass and copper. Trade statistics do not differentiate between copper and its alloys and we had to assume that about one-fourth of trade consisted of alloys because brass mills absorb one-third of copper refined in the United States and copper alloys take about one-fifth of U.K. copper (*Metal Statistics*, 1954–63, pp. 161 and 135). The method of handling premium-priced copper sales is given in the text; a similar technique was used for other years in which copper appeared to be available at prices other than those quoted by producers, although the discounts and premiums were much smaller than the 1964 premiums.

The indexes were computed separately for SITC groups 682.1 and 682.2. For worked copper at least, the more important 5-digit categories were weighted separately. These were bars, rods, shapes, and wire (682.21), 41 per cent of 682.2; plate, sheet, and strip (682.22), 23 per cent; and tubes and pipes (682.25), 26 per cent. For unwrought copper (682.1), since 96 per cent consisted of refined copper (682.12), no attempt was made to weight at the 5-digit level.

684: Information on aluminum prices comes from about a score of sources in addition to the various German exporters whose data contributed to the German price series. A little over half of the sources are American, and a large majority are purchasers. As noted in the text, our data include prices for a large fraction of U.S. exports.

Separate indexes were computed for SITC groups 684.1 (unwrought aluminum) and 684.2 (worked aluminum), and the figures in the table represent the combination of these two sets of indexes. Calculation of the EEC indexes was the same as for 682 (see above).

684.1 and 684.2: See 684.

[a]A in parentheses after country name indicates aggregated index; E, extrapolated index. See General Note to this appendix for fuller explanation.

Table C.3

International Price Indexes, Miscellaneous Metal Manufactures, n.e.s.,
1953, 1957, 1961–64

SITC Number	Commodity Group, Country, and Index Type[a]	1953	1957	1961	1962	1963	1964
69	Manufactures of metal, n.e.s.						
	U.S. (A)	86	98	98	100	100	102
	U.K. (A)	84	95	96	100	100	103
	U.K. (E)	90	101	103	100	99	103
	EEC (A)	88	94	98	100	100	101
	EEC (E)	87	99	100	100	97	98
	Germany (A)	86	93	98	100	100	101
	Germany (E)	84	93	98	100	99	101
	Japan (A)	NA	NA	108	100	86	90
	Japan (E)	NA	NA	98	100	93	101
691	Finished structural parts and structures, n.e.s.						
	U.K. (A)	NA	NA	98	100	100	104
	Germany (A)	NA	NA	95	100	100	102
692	Metal containers for storage and transport						
	U.S. (A)	86	99	100	100	100	101
	U.K. (A)	NA	NA	96	100	99	100
	U.K. (E)	NA	109	98	100	95	92
	EEC (A)	102	108	98	100	100	102
	EEC (E)	110	108	99	100	98	100
	Germany (A)	NA	92	99	100	100	100
	Germany (E)	NA	92	100	100	97	98
692.1	Tanks, vats, etc., for storage or manufacturing						
	U.S.	NA	97	100	100	96	NA
692.2	Casks, drums, boxes, cans, etc., for transport						
	U.S.	79	99	99	100	102	104
	U.K.	NA	NA	97	100	101	101
	EEC	102	108	98	100	100	102
	Germany	NA	92	99	100	100	100
693	Wire products (excl. electric) and fencing grills						
	U.S. (A)	97	105	97	100	101	106
	U.K. (A)	NA	100	98	100	98	102
	U.K. (E)	NA	105	102	100	95	99
	EEC (A)	84	101	101	100	100	103
	EEC (E)	82	98	99	100	95	104
	Germany (A)	84	101	101	100	100	103
	Germany (E)	84	101	102	100	95	108

(continued)

Table C.3 (continued)

SITC Number	Commodity Group, Country, and Index Type[a]	1953	1957	1961	1962	1963	1964
693	Wire products (excl. electric) and fencing grills (continued)						
	Japan (A)	NA	NA	104	100	95	94
	Japan (E)	NA	NA	101	100	92	94
693.1	Wire cables, ropes, etc., not insulated						
	U.K.	NA	NA	100	100	NA	NA
693.2	Wire of iron or steel, of types used for fencing						
	U.S.	NA	NA	101	100	100	104
	EEC	NA	NA	107	100	99	102
693.3	Gauze, netting, grill, fencing, etc., of wire						
	U.S.	NA	NA	102	100	98	97
	EEC	89	98	101	100	NA	NA
	Germany	89	98	101	100	100	101
694	Nails, screws, nuts, bolts, etc., iron, steel, or copper						
	U.S. (A)	90	97	98	100	101	104
	U.K. (A)	NA	NA	99	100	99	100
	U.K. (E)	NA	NA	98	100	98	92
	EEC (A)	100	97	99	100	97	98
	EEC (E)	99	97	99	100	97	98
	Germany (A)	94	96	100	100	95	95
	Germany (E)	NA	95	100	100	95	96
694.1	Nails, tacks, staples, spikes, etc.						
	U.S.	NA	NA	102	100	101	100
	EEC	97	99	102	100	97	99
	Germany	96	97	101	100	100	101
694.2	Nuts, bolts, screws, rivets, washers, etc.						
	U.S.	NA	NA	96	100	100	106
	EEC	103	96	98	100	97	97
	Germany	NA	95	99	100	93	93
695	Tools for use in the hand or in machines						
	U.S. (A)	85	97	98	100	101	103
	U.K. (A)	NA	NA	98	100	99	101
	U.K. (E)	NA	NA	98	100	99	101
	EEC (A)	78	85	95	100	100	103
	EEC (E)	78	85	95	100	100	103
	Germany (A)	78	85	96	100	100	103
	Germany (E)	78	85	96	100	100	103
696	Cutlery						
	U.S. (A)	NA	NA	99	100	101	101
	U.K. (A)	NA	NA	96	100	102	108

(continued)

Table C.3 (concluded)

SITC Number	Commodity Group, Country, and Index Type[a]	1953	1957	1961	1962	1963	1964
696	Cutlery (continued)						
	U.K. (E)	NA	NA	96	100	102	108
	Germany (A)	104	110	102	100	101	104
	Germany (E)	NA	NA	102	100	101	104
	Japan (A)	115	92	97	100	110	122
	Japan (E)	NA	NA	97	100	110	122
697	Household equipment of base metals						
	Germany (A)	87	99	98	100	100	101
698	Manufactures of metal, n.e.s.						
	U.S. (A)	75	91	99	100	98	101
	U.K. (A)	82	89	94	100	99	104
	U.K. (E)	NA	NA	94	100	99	104
	EEC (A)	88	94	99	100	100	99
	EEC (E)	80	96	99	100	100	99
	Germany (A)	87	92	99	100	100	99
	Germany (E)	80	96	99	100	100	99

Note: *United States*: Indexes for all groups were combined to form the aggregated index for the division as a whole. The group indexes were averages of 4-digit subgroup and, in some cases, 5-digit item indexes. The number of observations for the division ranged from 80 to almost 200, mainly from buyers. The index for SITC 698 is derived almost entirely from data for subgroup 698.3.

United Kingdom: Indexes for all groups for 1961–64, and for all except SITC 694 before that, were combined to form the division aggregated index. The total number of observations ranged from about 40 to over 100, mainly from buyers.

EEC: The coverage of groups in the EEC aggregated index is the same as that in the German index, described below, and the German series weigh heavily in the total. However, the EEC observations, of which there are about 300 in each year, include a higher proportion of observations from buyers.

Germany: The division aggregated index is a combination of group indexes for all groups. Most of the observations, which ranged in number from 250 to more than 300, are from export price reports by exporters to the Federal Statistical Office, but there are, in addition, many reports from buyers analogous to those included in the U.S. and U.K. indexes.

Japan: The aggregated index was constructed from only 20 to 30 observations for each year in groups 693, 695, 696, and 698, which together accounted for 63 per cent of trade in division 69. For 1963 the index also includes data for group 697, representing another 9 per cent of trade in division 69. Most of the reports were from buyers, but a few observations from the Japanese export price index were also included. The extrapolated index for division 69 differs considerably from the aggregated version because the extrapolator (the index of competitiveness) did not include data for group 698.

[a]A in parentheses after country name indicates aggregated index; E, extrapolated index. See General Note to this appendix for fuller explanation.

Table C.4

International Price Indexes, Machinery Other than Electric,
1953, 1957, 1961–64
(1962 = 100)

SITC Number	Commodity Group, Country, and Index Type[a]	1953	1957	1961	1962	1963	1964
71	Machinery other than electric						
	U.S. (A)	81	92	99	100	101	102
	U.K. (A)	81	92	98	100	100	102
	U.K. (E)	80	92	98	100	101	103
	EEC (A)	81	88	97	100	100	102
	EEC (E)	80	88	97	100	100	102
	Germany (A)	80	87	97	100	101	102
	Germany (E)	80	87	97	100	101	102
711	Power generating machinery, other than electric						
	U.S. (A)	83	93	98	100	104	106
	U.K. (A)	86	93	98	100	101	106
	U.K. (E)	NA	93	98	100	101	106
	EEC (A)	NA	91	97	100	102	100
	Germany (A)	82	88	96	100	102	99
	Germany (E)	84	87	94	100	103	101
711.4	Aircraft engines (incl. jet propulsion engines)						
	U.S.	85	92	95	100	105	110
	U.K.	NA	91	100	100	100	104
711.5	Internal combustion engines (exc. for aircraft)						
	U.S.	80	94	100	100	103	104
	Germany	85	89	97	100	102	98
712	Agricultural machinery and implements						
	U.S. (A)	83	89	98	100	102	103
	U.K. (A)	84	92	98	100	102	102
	U.K. (E)	85	93	99	100	102	102
	EEC (A)	84	90	98	100	102	102
	EEC (E)	84	90	98	100	102	102
	Germany (A)	84	91	99	100	101	101
	Germany (E)	84	91	99	100	101	101
712.5	Tractors, other than road tractors						
	U.S.	84	91	98	100	102	102
	U.K.	86	95	99	100	101	102
	EEC	86	92	98	100	103	104
	Germany	88	94	100	100	102	103

(continued)

Table C.4 (continued)

SITC Number	Commodity Group, Country, and Index Type[a]	1953	1957	1961	1962	1963	1964
714	Office machines						
	U.S. (A)	92	100	103	100	96	92
	U.K. (A)	90	96	100	100	93	89
	U.K. (E)	90	97	100	100	93	89
	EEC (A)	107	98	100	100	94	89
	EEC (E)	108	98	100	100	94	89
	Germany (A)	106	97	100	100	94	89
	Germany (E)	106	97	100	100	94	89
714.1	Typewriters and check-writing machines						
	U.S.	NA	99	101	100	99	99
	EEC	NA	98	101	100	99	98
	Germany	NA	NA	102	100	99	97
714.2	Calculating, accounting machines, etc. (incl. electronic computers)						
	U.S.	93	99	102	100	95	90
	U.K.	95	100	100	100	90	85
	EEC	109	97	99	100	92	86
	Germany	107	95	99	100	92	87
714.9	Office machines, n.e.s. (excl. statistical machines)						
	U.S.	90	100	104	100	96	92
	EEC	105	99	100	100	93	89
	Germany	104	99	100	100	93	89
715	Metalworking machinery						
	U.S. (A)	82	91	99	100	100	104
	U.K. (A)	75	85	95	100	101	107
	U.K. (E)	74	86	94	100	102	107
	EEC (A)	75	85	98	100	100	103
	EEC (E)	71	82	98	100	100	103
	Germany (A)	78	87	99	100	102	106
	Germany (E)	75	86	99	100	102	106
715.1	Machine tools for working metals						
	U.S.	81	90	98	100	101	105
	U.K.	75	85	95	100	101	107
	EEC	71	82	98	100	100	103
	Germany	75	85	98	100	103	107

(continued)

Table C.4 (continued)

SITC Number	Commodity Group, Country, and Index Type[a]	1953	1957	1961	1962	1963	1964
	Metal-cutting machine tools						
	U.S.	81	89	97	100	101	105
	U.K.	74	84	94	100	101	106
	EEC	72	81	98	100	97	102
	Germany	77	86	98	100	102	106
	Metal-forming machine tools						
	U.S.	NA	NA	101	100	100	105
	EEC	NA	NA	97	100	106	102
	Germany	NA	NA	98	100	106	108
715.2	Metalworking machinery other than machine tools						
	U.S.	NA	NA	101	100	100	102
	EEC	88	94	100	100	100	104
	Germany	88	94	100	100	100	104
717	Textile and leather machinery						
	U.S. (A)	81	92	98	100	100	101
	U.K. (A)	80	90	98	100	102	104
	U.K. (E)	80	90	98	100	102	104
	EEC (A)	82	90	97	100	100	102
	EEC (E)	82	90	97	100	100	102
	Germany (A)	82	90	97	100	100	103
	Germany (E)	82	90	97	100	100	103
	Japan (A)	NA	NA	100	100	101	102
	Japan (E)	NA	NA	100	100	101	102
717.1	Textile machinery						
	U.S.	80	91	98	100	100	101
	EEC	81	88	97	100	100	102
	Germany	81	88	97	100	101	103
717.2	Machinery (excl. sewing) for hides, skins, or leather						
	U.S.	NA	86	100	100	101	102
	U.K.	NA	NA	NA	100	101	93
	EEC	76	88	97	100	100	102
	Germany	76	88	97	100	100	102
717.3	Sewing machines						
	U.S.	88	100	99	100	99	103

(continued)

Table C.4 (continued)

SITC Number	Commodity Group, Country, and Index Type[a]	1953	1957	1961	1962	1963	1964
717.3	Sewing machines (continued)						
	Germany	88	99	97	100	98	102
	Japan	NA	NA	99	100	101	105
718	Machines for special industries						
	U.S. (A)	NA	88	98	100	102	104
	U.K. (A)	NA	91	101	100	101	103
	U.K. (E)	NA	89	99	100	100	101
	Germany (A)	73	81	96	100	100	103
	Germany (E)	NA	82	95	100	101	104
718.2	Printing and bookbinding machinery						
	U.S.	72	84	96	100	103	104
	U.K.	72	87	99	100	103	106
	Germany	72	80	97	100	102	108
718.3	Food-processing machines (excl. domestic)						
	U.S.	69	85	93	100	101	101
	EEC	75	82	92	100	103	105
	Germany	75	83	93	100	100	103
718.4	Construction and mining machinery, n.e.s.						
	U.S.	NA	90	100	100	102	104
	U.K.	NA	90	100	100	101	103
	Germany	74	83	95	100	101	104
	Japan	NA	NA	100	100	100	100
718.5	Mineral crushing, sorting, etc., and glass working machinery						
	Germany	76	83	97	100	99	99
719	Machinery and appliances (nonelect.) and parts, n.e.s.						
	U.S. (A)	83	94	100	100	100	101
	U.K. (A)	81	94	98	100	101	102
	U.K. (E)	82	93	99	100	102	104
	EEC (A)	80	88	97	100	101	103
	EEC (E)	77	88	96	100	101	102
	Germany (A)	78	86	96	100	101	103
	Germany (E)	77	85	96	100	101	103
719.1	Heating and cooling equipment						
	U.S.	89	98	100	100	100	103
	U.K.	NA	NA	100	100	100	102
	EEC	87	96	99	100	101	101
	Germany	75	84	96	100	102	104

(continued)

Table C.4 (continued)

SITC Number	Commodity Group, Country, and Index Type[a]	1953	1957	1961	1962	1963	1964
719.2	Pumps and centrifuges						
	U.S.	84	95	100	100	102	102
	U.K.	80	98	98	100	101	100
	EEC	79	89	97	100	101	102
	Germany	79	86	97	100	101	101
719.21	Pumps for liquids						
	U.S.	78	93	101	100	102	103
	Germany	80	84	95	100	102	102
719.22	Pumps for gases						
	U.S.	NA	98	98	100	100	100
	Germany	80	91	97	100	100	100
719.23	Centrifuges, and filtering and purifying machinery						
	Germany	74	83	99	100	101	102
719.3	Mechanical handling equipment						
	U.S.	NA	91	100	100	101	103
	U.K.	NA	101	99	100	100	103
	EEC	76	86	95	100	100	102
	Germany	75	85	95	100	100	102
719.31	Lifting and loading machinery						
	U.S.	NA	91	101	100	101	103
	EEC	74	86	95	100	100	102
	Germany	73	84	95	100	100	101
719.32	Forklift and other industrial trucks						
	U.S.	NA	89	97	100	101	106
	EEC	87	89	96	100	101	102
	Germany	87	88	96	100	101	102
719.5	Powered tools, n.e.s.						
	U.S.	78	90	98	100	102	99
	U.K.	81	88	100	100	103	102
	Germany	74	81	92	100	100	107
719.52	Machine tools for working wood, plastics, etc.						
	Germany	66	75	93	100	102	106
719.53	Motorized hand tools, nonelectric						
	Germany	81	79	90	100	100	102
719.54	Parts and accessories of machine tools						
	Germany	77	88	93	100	100	113

(continued)

Table C.4 (concluded)

SITC Number	Commodity Group, Country, and Index Type[a]	1953	1957	1961	1962	1963	1964
719.6 & 719.8	Nonelect. mach. and appliances, n.e.s. (excl. domestic appliances)						
	U.S.	84	91	98	100	102	102
	U.K.	NA	91	98	100	101	102
	EEC	76	84	96	100	103	108
	Germany	76	84	97	100	102	107
719.62, 719.63, & 719.64	Packaging, weighing, spraying machinery						
	Germany	75	87	98	100	101	103
719.61 & 719.8	Other nonelect. mach. (excl. rubber proc. mach.)						
	Germany	76	81	96	100	104	111
719.7	Ball, roller, or needle-roller bearings						
	U.S.	81	100	99	100	102	102
	Germany	92	92	99	100	100	98
719.9	Parts and accessories of machinery, n.e.s.						
	U.S.	80	95	102	100	96	97
	U.K.	NA	NA	96	100	100	102
	EEC	83	93	99	100	99	100
	Germany	81	91	99	100	100	100
719.92	Taps, cocks, valves, and similar appliances, n.e.s.						
	U.S.	80	95	103	100	96	96
	U.K.	NA	NA	100	100	100	102
	EEC	90	94	100	100	98	100
	Germany	87	91	100	100	100	101
719.93	Transmission shafts and cranks, pulleys, etc.						
	U.S.	NA	NA	NA	100	98	100
	Germany	74	91	97	100	100	99

Note: **SITC 71:** The aggregated index for each country is based on separate indexes for all the component 3-digit groups.

711: The aggregated index for the *U.S.* includes data for subgroup 711.1 (steam generating boilers) in addition to the indexes shown for 711.4 and 711.5. The *U.K.* aggregated index includes some data on 711.1, 711.2 (boiler house plant), 711.3 (steam engines) except 1953, and 711.5, in addition to the index shown for 711.4. For *EEC* and *Germany* the composition of the aggregated indexes is 711.1 (except 1953 EEC), 711.3 (1962–64 only), 711.5, and 711.8 (engines n.e.s.). The 4-digit indexes included in the aggregate 711 index, but not shown in the table, were not considered reliable enough to publish separately. Generally they were based on fewer than 10 observations for any one period.

711.4: The main sources of data on complete engines were reports filed by U.S. airlines with the Civil Aeronautics Board (CAB). These list all engines, of both domestic and foreign manufacture, placed in service and the prices paid for them, including prices of engines purchased as part of aircraft. The comparability of these prices from year to year was checked by the use of other data from U.S. manufacturers of aircraft and engines and from airlines.

Since none of the aircraft engines was produced for more than a few years, the index for complete engines was first calculated as a set of linked Laspeyres indexes (each year was compared to the preceding year, with the earlier year's purchases as weights). This index represented prices as of the date of delivery, and the indexes were converted to a date-of-order basis by assuming a two-year lag, which seemed closest to the lag indicated by the data from selling and purchasing companies. These indexes covered the period through 1962 on a date-ordered basis, and they were extended to 1964 by the use of prices reported by companies to the NBER. The U.K. indexes were constructed in the same manner as those for the United States, with a few exceptions. The U.K. sample is much smaller, and the CAB information was supplemented by company data before 1962. For later years CAB data on engines on order, instead of engines delivered, were used in the U.K. index.

Parts price indexes, which cover only 1961–64 for the United States and 1962–64 for the United Kingdom, were derived from data supplied by U.S. companies engaged in purchasing and selling engines. Parts were given a weight in the index equal to that of engines, for reasons indicated in the text.

711.5: The indexes were weighted (wherever there were enough price data) in accordance with very rough estimates of the relative importance of different components of 711.5. These weights were as follows: marine diesels, 1; other diesels, 4; outboard motors, 1; other gasoline engines, 2; and parts, 8. The *U.S.* index is based on price relatives varying in number from 7 for the 1957/1953 link to around 30 for the most recent links. The data were supplied by a dozen respondents, half of whom were large producers; the others were purchasers, mainly foreign. The *German* index is based on 18 diesel and 9 gasoline engine series from the export price index.

712: The aggregated indexes represent a combination of subgroup indexes. For the *U.S.* about a score of observations were available for the subgroups other than 712.5 (tractors), which is shown separately. These data come from more sources than the tractor information and did not thin out as much in the earlier years. Only one observation was available for 712.9 (agricultural machinery and appliances, n.e.s.) and this was averaged in with wholesale price changes for 7 to 14 products as reported by the Bureau of Labor Statistics. The amount of information available for the *United Kingdom* in the other categories was about the same as for tractors, but virtually all of it related to 712.1 (cultivating machines) and 712.2 (harvesting, threshing, and sorting machines). As a result, we were unable to make indexes for 712.3 (dairy-farming equipment) and 712.9, and their weights (10.4 per cent) were prorated over the other subgroups. For each *EEC* subgroup index the German index was combined with the indexes for other countries according to the relative importance of each country's exports. No data for 712.9 were available. *German* official series dominate the subgroups other than tractors, since we had only 6 to 11 observations to average in with indexes based on more than 40 German series.

712.5: The tractor index is subdivided to take account of the different price movements of farm and construction-type tractors. The *U.S.* index is based on more than a score of observations for the 1960s and for as few as 7 for the earlier links. They were

(continued)

Notes to Table C.4 (continued)

obtained from eight sources, of which six were producers. A regression analysis based on a total of 56 observations for the six reference years was used to derive a price index for construction-type tractors (see appendix to Chapter 12). The *U.K.* index is based on 7 to 14 observations from five sources. The *EEC* index is based on 4 tractor observations for France and Italy, averaged with the German index. The *German* index is based mainly on the index produced from 8 series in the German export price index. The additional observations we had (1 for 1953 and 1957, 3 for the other years) were averaged in but did not result in significant changes.

714: The aggregated index for the *United States* includes data for all periods for the subgroups shown separately (714.1, 714.2, and 714.9), as well as some data, except for 1953, for subgroup 714.3 (statistical machines). U.S. data are mostly export prices reported by U.S. companies, with some cost data as described in the text, and some purchase prices reported by foreign buyers. There were more than 40 observations for every link in the index. The *U.K.* aggregated index includes some data on 714.1 (except 1953), 714.3 (1962–64 only), and 714.9, in addition to the index shown separately for 714.2. U.K. data are mostly export prices reported by firms producing in both the United States and the United Kingdom. There are also some purchase price and cost data. The number of observations for each period was 20 or more. The EEC index was used for electronic computers because no U.K. time-to-time data were available. For the *EEC* and *Germany* the composition of the aggregated indexes is 714.1 (except 1953 Germany), 714.2, 714.3 (1962–64 only), and 714.9.

The EEC index includes German data as described below and indexes for other countries mainly derived from export price, cost, and some purchase price data reported to the National Bureau by companies operating both in the United States and in Common Market countries. The number of observations ranged from about 20 for 1957/1953 to almost three times as many in the later years.

German data are mainly export prices reported to the Federal Statistical Office with the addition of some selling, purchase price, and cost data reported to the National Bureau. The number of observations ranged from about 20 in the early years to almost twice that number for 1963/1962 and 1964/1963. The U.K. index was used for subgroup 714.3 because there were no German time-to-time data. For all countries the data for 714.3 were limited to punched-card equipment.

714.1: The index for each country is a combination of separate indexes for electric typewriters (weighted 1), standard typewriters (weighted 1), and portable typewriters (weighted 4). The weights, which are approximate, were estimated from data on U.S. exports and imports and interviews with industry sources. A more elaborate calculation from U.S. import data, using the assumption that each country's total exports were divided among the three types in the same proportions as their exports to the United States, yielded similar proportions, with a slightly higher weight for portable typewriters.

714.2: The index for each country is a combination of equally weighted indexes for electronic computers and for other calculating and accounting machines (excluding punched-card equipment). The data on computers cover only the period since 1961. The index for other calculating and accounting machines is composed of adding machines (weighted 1), calculating machines (weighted 2), bookkeeping and accounting machines (weighted 2), cash registers (weighted 1), and other calculating devices (weighted .1).

714.9: The index for each country is a combination of indexes for 714.91 (duplicating and addressing machinery), with a weight of slightly over 1 (estimated from U.S. export data), and 714.92 (parts of office machines), with a weight of almost 4. The index for the latter group was calculated by using for each type of machine part (such as typewriter parts, electronic computer parts, etc.), the index for the corresponding machine, with weights from U.S. exports.

715: The *U.S.* aggregated index for 1961–64 is a combination of subgroups 715.1 and 715.2, shown separately. For the earlier years it includes only 715.1. The *U.K.* aggregated index is based only on 715.1 for all years. The aggregated indexes for the *EEC* and *Germany* include both subgroups for all years.

715.1: Indexes for the 4-digit subgroup and two subdivisions thereof for the United States, the United Kingdom, and the EEC countries other than Germany were built up from subindexes for individual types of machine tools (see Table 12.24). There subindexes were weighted by the OECD export values given in that table.

U.S. data are a combination of prices supplied by both sellers and buyers of U.S. machine tools. The number of observations ranged from about 20 at the beginning to approximately 60 in most of the years. Buyer and seller data for each subgroup were compiled separately, and then combined, with equal weight given to each of the two.

The *U.K.* indexes were constructed from data supplied by buyers outside the United Kingdom and by U.K. sellers, who were mainly subsidiaries of U.S. machine tool manufacturers. The number of observations ranged approximately from 10 to 40. Buyer and seller data were compiled separately and then combined, with equal weight given to each.

The *German* and *EEC* indexes were extrapolated from the U.S. time-to-time index by the indexes of price competitiveness (see Appendix D). German and other EEC data on individual types of machine tools were mostly from buyers. Indexes of price competitiveness based primarily on buyer data for the United States and Germany (or the EEC) were therefore used to extrapolate from a U.S. price index which included seller as well as buyer data.

The official export price data for Germany give results that diverge widely from our other data. The direction of the difference is indicated by the following indexes calculated from official export price data (1962 = 100): *1953*, 63; *1957*, 78; *1961*, 94; *1962*, 100; *1963*, 101; *1964*, 104. The internal weighting for the official indexes of metal-cutting and metal-forming machinery is probably that of German exports rather than the OECD exports used elsewhere.

No index for 715.1 as a whole was constructed for *Japan*. However, a Japanese index for lathes is available from the *Export and Import Price Index Annual* of the Bank of Japan (see Table 12.24).

Because the number of observations in this group is fairly large it is possible to aggregate indexes for 715.1 solely from buyers' reports and solely from sellers' reports. Of course, each of these by itself is weaker than the combined index because the number of observations is reduced. The relationship between them, period by period, is as follows (buyers' price index as per cent of sellers' price index):

	1957/1953	1961/1957	1962/1961	1963/1962	1964/1963
U.S.	92	92	99	99	103
U.K.	103	98	97	101	99
EEC	86	94	96	100	98
Germany	87	92	95	101	97

715.2: All of the indexes are based on small samples of products, the U.S. data coming from buyers, mostly foreign, the German data mainly from sellers' reports used

(continued)

Notes to Table C.4 (continued)

in the official export price index, and the EEC index adding a few items from foreign buyers to the German data.

Since the U.S. index includes no data for SITC 715.23 we could compute a more complete version of the index by incorporating the wholesale price series for that subgroup. However, because the weight of SITC 715.22 is high, and because the index for 715.23 is not very different, the combined index would be the same as that shown.

717: The *U.S.* and *U.K.* aggregated indexes are each a combination of the three subgroups shown separately except that no data were available for the 1957/1953 link for the United States or the United Kingdom, nor for the 1962/1961 link for the United Kingdom. The *EEC* and *German* aggregated indexes cover all three subgroups for all periods. The aggregated index for *Japan* is based on only 717.1 and 717.3.

717.1: The indexes are weighted averages of separate indexes for four 5-digit groups, which accounted for all but 0.2 per cent of 1963 world trade in textile machinery: 717.11, spinning, extruding, etc., machines; 717.12, weaving, knitting, etc., machines; 717.13, machinery auxiliary to those in 717.12; 717.15, bleaching, washing, dressing, coating, printing, etc., machinery (excluding domestic washing machines). The number of *U.S.* price relatives available varied from less than a score for the 1957/1953 link to twice that number for the later years. More limited data were available for the other countries. The *EEC* index includes some observations for Italy and Belgium in addition to Germany.

717.2: We have data from several U.S. sources and 9 export price series for Germany. The data supplied by the U.S. firms, which include both producers and consumers of leather machinery, provide a fair amount of information on foreign prices as well. Thus we have time-to-time observations on 3 to 10 machines for France, Germany, and the United Kingdom, as well as on 13 U.S. machines. Except for the German time series data, however, we have no information in this category for the period prior to 1957, and the 1957 prices provide a reasonably adequate sample only for the United States.

717.3: The price information underlying the indexes came from more than a dozen sources, including several of the most important producers and several foreign purchasers. Each time-to-time link for the *United States* is based on 20 to 35 observations of price change obtained from these sources. The same respondents also provided some data about the movement of German export prices. The *EEC* and *German* indexes are derived in large part from German export price indexes based upon nine types of machines. (These data were not shown as a separate EEC index for 717.3 but were included in the calculation of the 3-digit EEC index.) The *Japanese* index is based in large measure upon official export price indexes for sewing machines.

718: The aggregated *U.S.* index is a combination of indexes for the four 4-digit groups shown separately. The *U.K.* aggregated index is based on subgroups 718.2, 718.4, and except for 1957, 718.5. The *German* aggregated index includes data for 718.1 (paper mill and pulp mill machinery, paper cutting and other machinery for the manufacture of paper articles), in addition to the four subgroups shown separately.

718.2: Each country's index is a combination of indexes for the three 5-digit subgroups. The *U.S.* indexes contain about 20 observations, mostly in the printing equipment area. Both sellers' and buyers' prices are included, but the latter predominate. The *U.K.* indexes are constructed from approximately 15 observations except in the last link when there were fewer than 10. Almost all were from buyers. The index for Germany was made up of 20 to 39 observations almost half of which were supplied by sellers of machinery. For printing machinery there were enough data to permit the computation of separate indexes from buyers' prices and sellers' prices, and the two were fairly close. The largest difference was in 1957–61, when the prices reported by sellers rose by over 17 per cent and those reported by buyers, by only 13 per cent.

718.3: *U.S.* data are prices supplied by American manufacturers for 70 or more individual items of food-processing equipment including accessories. The data are disproportionately concentrated in the area of baking machinery and do not cover SITC 718.31 at all. A small amount of information is taken from reports by importers of U.S. equipment. The *EEC* index includes the German data plus scattered observations for other countries, mainly for foreign subsidiaries of the U.S. companies. *German* data consist of export prices for more than 20 items of bakery and confectionary machinery. No information is available for SITC 718.31 or for other parts of SITC 718.32.

718.4: *U.S.* data are a combination of prices supplied by U.S. sellers and buyers of machinery and prices extracted from bids for the supply of machinery to several different countries in Latin America and Asia. Each link included more than 10 observations, and company-supplied data matched the movement of bid prices well whenever they could be compared. *U.K.* indexes are mainly from purchase prices, most of which are for domestic sales within the United Kingdom. The earliest links contained only 3 observations but all the others included 7 or more. *German* indexes are mainly official export price data. More than 10 observations are included. This index is a combination of separate indexes for construction machinery and for mining machinery, each of which included some items not properly classified under SITC 718.4. *Japanese* indexes are a combination of official data and purchasers' prices. The coverage is very weak, and the index therefore of very doubtful quality. However, the two sources agree closely in every year.

718.5: *U.S.* and *U.K.* indexes are very weak, being based on only 3 or 4 observations in each period. Most of the data are from buyers and refer to small parts of mineral processing machinery. *German* indexes are mainly from official export price series and include more than 10 items. They form a fairly reliable index.

719: The aggregated indexes for all countries are combinations of indexes for the seven subgroups shown separately, which account for over 99 per cent of the world trade weight of 719. Some data were available for each subgroup for all periods except for the 1957/1953 link for 719.3 for the United States and the United Kingdom and 719.6 and 719.8 combined for the United Kingdom.

719.1: The indexes were built up by weighting the indexes for the 5-digit categories shown in the text. We had no data for gas generators, and it was assumed that this category could be represented by the aggregate of the others.

The indexes are based mainly on reports from about a score of firms, of which about a third are foreign. All but a few were purchasers. The number of price relatives for the *U.S.* indexes ranged from less than a dozen for the 1957/1953 link to more than 40 for the 1964/1963 link. The *German* indexes are based on 40–55 series, most of them from the official export price index. The *U.K.* links shown in the table are based on about a dozen price relatives, while the number of observations for the EEC countries other than Germany varied from a dozen to a score.

719.2: The *U.S.* indexes for SITC 719.21 are based on 10 or 12 observations for the first two links (1957/1953 and 1961/1957) and about three times as many for the last three. A larger number of observations—over 50 for the last three links—were available for SITC 719.22. For SITC 719.23, however, only around a half dozen observations were available for the last two links and none for the earlier ones. The data were

(continued)

Notes to Table C.4 (continued)

obtained from more than a score of respondents, about one-fourth of whom were producers.

The *German* index for each subcategory is based on around 20 observations, mainly (and in SITC 719.23, exclusively) from the official export indexes.

We did not have enough data to publish separate indexes for the subcategories for the United Kingdom and the EEC. The United Kingdom index for SITC 719.2 as a whole is based on about a score (fewer in the early links and more in the later ones) of observations. Somewhat fewer observations were available for the EEC countries other than Germany.

719.21, 719.22, and **719.23:** See 719.2.

719.3: Indexes for total materials handling equipment are combinations of the two subgroup indexes.

U.S. indexes are averages for between a little more than 10 items in the worst year to more than 35 in the best. More than half of the observations were from buyers. In several of the years there were enough observations to permit the computation of separate indexes from buyers' reports and sellers' reports in subgroup 719.32, and in both 1961−62 and 1963−64 prices reported by sellers rose more rapidly by a substantial margin. In 1962−63 it was the buyers' reports that showed a greater price rise, but the difference was small, and the cumulative figures for 1962−64 showed a large gap, sellers' reports pointing to a rise of almost 15 per cent and buyers' reports to one of less than 5 per cent. In the much more important 719.31 category the two types of sources reported very similar changes, much closer to the buyers' reports in 719.32 than to the sellers'.

The *U.K.* index is the weakest of those shown, because it includes only 5 to 10 observations for each year. The data were too meager to permit the calculation of separate indexes for 719.31 and 719.32. Most of the data were from buyers, but there were some from sellers, and they told essentially the same story.

The *German* data are almost all sellers' prices reported to official agencies, but they contain a few additional observations from other sellers' reports and from buyers. About 25 to 30 observations are included in each index link.

The *EEC* indexes are the German indexes, combined with a scattering of information from both buyers and sellers for the other countries.

719.31, and **719.32:** See 719.3.

719.5: *U.S.* indexes are composed of 10 to 15 observations, about evenly divided between buyers' and sellers' reports. U.S. data for SITC 719.54 are not included. The *German* indexes, based mainly on official price data for approximately 60 items, but also including a few buyers' prices, cover all four subgroups. The *U.K.* indexes, weakest of the three, are based on only 5 to 10 observations in each period and cover only subgroups 719.52 and 719.53.

719.52, 719.53, and **719.54:** See 719.5.

719.6 and **719.8:** To calculate these indexes the group was divided into five 5-digit items, 719.62−719.66, and two additional subgroups: rubber processing machinery, and all other nonelectrical machinery and appliances (SITC 719.61 plus 719.8, minus rubber processing machinery).

U.S. data consisted of about 20 or more observations for each pair of years except the first, scattered over almost all the items in the group. Buyers' data predominated somewhat.

U.K. indexes were derived from only about 10 observations in most years and even fewer in the last year. Almost all were from buyers.

The indexes for *Germany* were developed from 60 or more observations throughout, mainly official export price data but including a considerable number of buyers' prices too. The *EEC* indexes consist of the German indexes, heavily weighted, plus a few prices, mainly supplied by buyers, from other countries.

719.62, 719.63, and **719.64:** See 719.6 and 719.8.

719.61 and **719.8** excluding rubber processing machinery: See 719.6 and 719.8.

719.7: The *U.S.* index is based on numbers of observations ranging from more than a dozen for the first link (1957/1953) to nearly three dozen for the last (1964/1963). The price comparisons came from ten sources of which two were producers; three of the sources were foreign firms, and the rest were domestic, most of them with overseas operations.

The *German* index is based on 4 series from two private purchasers and 8 series in the German export price index.

719.9: *U.S.* indexes are a combination of indexes for the five 5-digit items. The number of items ranges from 10 to 20 in the beginning of the period to more than 120 for the last three links. Most of the data were supplied by U.S. firms that were purchasers, but several sellers were also represented, and their reports did not differ substantially from the buyers' observations. In item 719.92 the individual observations were not treated as independent. Instead, averages for firms were combined to arrive at a country average. Treating each report as an individual observation we would have calculated that the U.S. international price indexes for SITC 719.92 and the total for the subgroup were as follows (1962 = 100):

	1953	1957	1961	1962	1963	1964
SITC 719.9	83	98	102	100	93	92
SITC 719.92	84	99	103	100	91	86

The international price indexes for the *U.K.* are a combination of item indexes for SITC 719.92, 719.93, and 719.94, mainly from buyers' data supplied by the same companies that provided the U.S. data. Approximately 100 observations or more were available for each of the indexes published here. The corresponding alternative indexes, averaging individual observations, would have been as follows (1962=100):

	1961	1962	1963	1964
SITC 719.9	95	100	100	99
SITC 719.92	96	100	99	98

The *German* and *EEC* indexes, the latter dominated by the former, were based on 40 to 60 observations, a large proportion of which were sellers' prices collected for the official German export price index.

719.92 and **719.93:** See 719.9

[a]A in parentheses after country name indicates aggregated index; E, extrapolated index. See General Note to this appendix for fuller explanation.

Table C.5
International Price Indexes, Electrical Machinery, Apparatus, and
Appliances, 1953, 1957, 1961–64
(1962 = 100)

SITC Number	Commodity Group, Country, and Index Type[a]	1953	1957	1961	1962	1963	1964
72	Electrical machinery, apparatus, and appliances						
	U.S. (A)	102	108	104	100	97	97
	U.K. (A)	94	102	102	100	101	100
	U.K. (E)	96	98	103	100	101	101
	EEC (A)	96	99	102	100	100	99
	EEC (E)	98	100	102	100	100	99
	Germany (A)	95	98	102	100	99	98
	Germany (E)	96	98	101	100	99	98
	Japan (A)	NA	119	107	100	95	100
	Japan (E)	NA	124	106	100	97	99
722	Electric power machinery and switchgear						
	U.S. (A)	NA	124	110	100	94	94
	U.K. (E)	NA	104	112	100	103	101
	EEC (E)	NA	107	105	100	99	99
	Germany (A)	NA	104	104	100	97	100
	Germany (E)	NA	102	104	100	97	100
	Japan (E)	NA	NA	106	100	96	106
722.1	Electric power machinery						
	U.S.	132	154	120	100	91	91
	U.K.	NA	116	110	100	100	92
	EEC	NA	125	111	100	98	99
	Germany	NA	117	108	100	96	100
722.2	Appar. for making, breaking, or protecting elect. circuits						
	U.S.	NA	NA	99	100	98	99
	EEC	88	90	100	100	99	99
	Germany	88	90	100	100	99	99
723	Equipment for distributing electricity						
	U.S. (A)	100	114	111	100	97	99
	U.K. (A)	81	91	99	100	100	102
	U.K. (E)	85	95	106	100	101	98
	EEC (A)	88	93	100	100	95	103
	EEC (E)	90	94	100	100	94	94

(continued)

Table C.5 (continued)

SITC Number	Commodity Group, Country, and Index Type[a]	1953	1957	1961	1962	1963	1964
723 Equipment for distributing electricity (continued)							
	Germany (A)	91	94	100	100	94	102
	Germany (E)	90	94	100	100	94	102
	Japan (E)	NA	NA	125	100	108	110
724	Telecommunications apparatus						
	U.S. (A)	NA	NA	101	100	95	96
	U.K. (E)	NA	NA	101	100	101	99
	EEC (A)	98	95	101	100	100	97
	EEC (E)	NA	NA	101	100	100	97
	Germany (A)	95	92	101	100	100	95
	Germany (E)	NA	NA	101	100	100	96
	Japan (E)	NA	NA	107	100	100	98
724.1 & 724.2	Television and radio broadcast receivers						
	U.S.	NA	NA	102	100	90	85
	EEC	125	113	103	100	96	94
	Germany	119	108	103	100	97	94
724.9	Telecommunications equipment, n.e.s.						
	U.S.	NA	NA	101	100	98	102
	U.K.	NA	90	100	100	106	107
	EEC	88	88	100	100	102	98
	Germany	86	86	100	100	102	95
725	Domestic electrical equipment						
	U.S. (A)	NA	102	98	100	102	102
	U.K. (A)	NA	111	106	100	98	100
	U.K. (E)	NA	NA	NA	100	98	102
	EEC (A)	104	102	100	100	99	99
	EEC (E)	NA	102	100	100	99	100
	Germany (A)	102	100	100	100	99	99
	Germany (E)	NA	101	100	100	99	99
725.01	Domestic refrigerators, electrical						
	EEC	140	118	101	100	97	96
	Germany	132	114	100	100	96	96
725.03	Electromechanical domestic appliances, n.e.s.						
	EEC	94	94	100	100	101	104
	Germany	92	93	100	100	101	104
725.05	Electric space heating equipment, etc.						
	EEC	NA	91	99	100	100	101

(continued)

Table C.5 (concluded)

SITC Number	Commodity Group, Country, and Index Type[a]	1953	1957	1961	1962	1963	1964
725.05	Electric space heating equipment, etc. (continued)						
	Germany	NA	91	99	100	101	101
726 & 729	Other elect. mach. and apparatus (incl. med. and radiol.)						
	U.S. (A)	97	106	104	100	98	98
	U.K. (A)	78	94	99	100	102	104
	U.K. (E)	83	94	97	100	101	101
	EEC (A)	89	98	101	100	102	101
	EEC (E)	93	97	100	100	101	100
	Germany (A)	90	98	101	100	100	99
	Germany (E)	93	97	100	100	100	98
	Japan (A)	NA	NA	104	100	90	90
	Japan (E)	NA	NA	104	100	92	92
729.1	Batteries and accumulators						
	U.S.	NA	NA	103	100	100	101
	EEC	NA	NA	101	100	102	107
	Germany	94	100	101	100	102	106
729.2	Electric lamps						
	U.S.	NA	116	108	100	100	104
	EEC	97	105	102	100	111	115
729.4	Automotive electrical equipment						
	U.S.	NA	NA	NA	100	100	106
	Germany	98	96	100	100	99	100
729.5	Elect. measuring and controlling instruments						
	U.S.	78	97	100	100	102	103
	U.K.	NA	83	95	100	97	97
	Germany	83	92	106	100	99	98
729.6	Electromechanical hand tools						
	U.S.	72	87	96	100	100	99
729.9	Electrical machinery and apparatus, n.e.s.						
	U.S.	89	98	100	100	101	102
	EEC	80	89	99	100	104	104
	Germany	84	92	99	100	105	104

Note: **SITC 72:** The aggregated indexes are based on separate indexes for the five 3-digit groups or combinations shown separately. The Japanese index excludes SITC 722 for 1953 and 1957, and 723 for all periods. The U.K. index excludes 722 for 1953. Indexes for other countries include all 3-digit groups throughout.

722: The *U.S.* index for SITC 722.1 is based mainly on a regression analysis of power transformer prices described in the appendix to Chapter 13 and, for electric motors, on a small number of time series observations, less than 10 in each link. The index used, from Table 13.28, equation 12, is extrapolated back to 1953 by a domestic price index adjusted for quality change and combined with another regression-based index for generators, calculated from domestic prices. Both of these indexes are discussed in the appendix to Chapter 13. For SITC 722.2 the *U.S.* index is derived from time-to-time price data for about 20 observations supplied by both buyers and sellers of equipment, principally the former. The calculations were carried back to 1957 for a smaller number of observations but the index for that year is not shown because the number of reporters was too small. It was used, however, in calculating the aggregated index for group 722.

The *U.K.* index for SITC 722.1 was calculated by multiplying the U.S. international price index by the index of U.S. price competitiveness relative to the United Kingdom (Table D.5), which included a small number of time-to-time observations for electric motors. No U.K. data were available for 722.2; therefore no U.K. 722 aggregated index is shown.

The *EEC* indexes were calculated in the same way as the U.K. index.

The *German* index for SITC 722.1 was calculated in the same way as that for the U.K. That for 722.2 was calculated from more than 20 time series observations based on sellers' reports to the Federal Statistical Office. The electric motors component of the index of price competitiveness for SITC 722.1 was from the same source as the data for SITC 722.2, but with 10 or fewer observations throughout.

The *Japanese* aggregated indexes were too weak to show in the table because of the small numbers of observations and because the price competitiveness index, except in the 1963–64 link, does not include electric motors. The results of the calculation, using the U.S. international price index for all of SITC 722.1 for 1963–64 and the U.S. price index for generators only in 1961–63, were as follows (1962 = 100): *1961*, 130; *1962*, 100; *1963*, 85; *1964*, 110.

An alternative index can be calculated from the official Japanese export price data for transformers, generators, and electric motors, as reported in various issues of the *Export and Import Price Index Annual*, Statistics Department, Bank of Japan (1962 = 100): *1961*, 101; *1962*, 100; *1963*, 100; *1964*, 100. In most commodity groups these data are used as part of the time-to-time index, but they are not used here because the resulting index would not be compatible with the index of price competitiveness.

722.1 and 722.2: See 722.

723: *U.S.* indexes are based on data from both buyers and sellers, with the number of observations ranging from about 10 to over 30, including some company price indexes composed of many individual observations.

U.K. data are mostly from buyers and range from only about 5 observations in the first link to about 15–25 in the later ones.

German and *EEC* indexes in this group are based on fewer than 10 observations throughout, mostly from sellers' prices reported to the German Federal Statistical Office.

724: Aggregated indexes for telecommunications equipment are weighted averages of indexes for television and radio receivers and for other telecommunications equipment. The former are weighted averages of indexes for television receivers and for radio

(continued)

Notes to Table C.5 (continued)

receivers, the latter of which are themselves weighted averages for portable transistor and other radio receivers. The weights are from the trade data of Table 14.14. No aggregated index for 724.1 and 724.2 or for 724 as a whole is shown for those countries for which data were missing on either transistor or nontransistor radios, because the differences in price movements were so great as to make the international price indexes for the group unreliable if either one were omitted. The indexes for each type of radio cannot be published separately because they are either too weak or depend on too few sources of data.

U.S. indexes are composed of observations for between 10 and 20 items, from both buyers and sellers. U.K. indexes for SITC 724.9 cover about 5 to 15 items throughout, while *German* and *EEC* indexes contain 20–40 observations, mainly from sellers' reports to the Federal Statistical Office. The only Japanese index shown is from the *Export and Import Price Index Annual* of the Bank of Japan.

The *German* and therefore also *EEC* data have one serious defect. The official German export price data are for a combination of SITC 724.1 and 724.2 without any breakdown between the two subgroups or within SITC 724.2 for portable transistors as opposed to other radios. Even if these were properly weighted to represent German exports, the weights would not be in accord with the world trade weights we have used. The main consequence of the incorrect (for our purpose) weighting would be an understatement of the price decline in SITC 724.2 due to the fact that portable transistor radios were not important in German exports.

724.1, 724.2, and **724.9:** See 724.

725: U.S. data are from reports of overseas buyers and U.S. producers. They cover all five subgroups in the later years but only three at the beginning. The indexes are based on from 5 to over 20 observations.

U.K. aggregated indexes are very weak, being based on only about 5–10 observations throughout and containing no data for 725.03 at all.

German and *EEC* aggregated indexes are mainly from sellers' reports to the Federal Statistical Office but also include some data from buyers. They cover all five subgroups and are based on approximately 30–60 observations throughout.

725.01, 725.03, and **725.05:** See 725.

726 and **729:** The U.S. index is an aggregate of 4-digit subgroup indexes covering all subgroups except SITC 729.7 (electron and proton accelerators). There were from almost 100 to more than 150 observations, from both buyers and sellers, with the former predominating in most groups. Some data on unit values of domestic shipments, which were subdivided in very fine detail, were added in subgroup 729.3 (thermionic, etc., valves and tubes, photocells, transistors, etc.) to provide coverage of transistors and other semiconductors.

The *U.K.* aggregated index is a combination of indexes for all subgroups except SITC 729.7 and, for 1953–57, SITC 729.3. The number of observations ranged from about 15 to more than 40, chiefly from buyers both within and outside the United Kingdom. The number of observations exaggerates the quality of the indexes because several groups, including the most heavily weighted, are represented by fewer than 5 observations for some links.

The *German* aggregated index is a combination of indexes for all subgroups except SITC 729.3 and 729.7. The index for other EEC countries was used for the former subgroup except in 1963–64 when some German prices were available. We had 60 to 80 observations, the greatest part from export price reports by sellers to the Federal Statistical Office but including some data from buyers as well.

The *EEC* aggregated index covers all subgroup indexes except SITC 729.7 and, for 1953–57, SITC 729.3. However, only German data were available for SITC 726 (electric apparatus for medical purposes and radiological apparatus), SITC 729.4 for 1953–62, SITC 729.5, and SITC 729.6. The number of observations ranged from about 85 to more than 100, almost all, other than the German data, being provided by buyers. The subgroup index for SITC 729.3 does not include any prices for semiconductors and is probably biased upward on that account.

For *Japan* no subgroup indexes could be calculated for SITC 726, 729.4, 729.6, or 729.7, and those that were computed for the remaining subgroups were weak. No subgroup index contained more than 5 observations, and the group as a whole was calculated from only 10 to 15 items, provided by both buyers and sellers. The subgroup index for SITC 729.3 does include semiconductors.

729.1, 729.2, 729.4, 729.5, 729.6, and **729.9:** See 726 and 729.

ªA in parentheses after country name indicates aggregated index; E, extrapolated index. See General Note to this appendix for fuller explanation.

Table C.6
International Price Indexes, Transport Equipment, 1953, 1957, 1961–64
(1962 = 100)

SITC Number	Commodity Group, Country, and Index Type[a]	1953	1957	1961	1962	1963	1964
73	Transport equipment						
	U.S. (A)	89	94	96	100	99	100
	U.K. (A)	87	93	99	100	102	106
	U.K. (E)	87	94	100	100	102	107
	EEC (A)	95	98	96	100	100	100
	EEC (E)	94	98	97	100	101	102
	Germany (A)	92	95	95	100	100	99
	Germany (E)	90	95	96	100	101	101
731	Railway vehicles						
	U.S. (A)	83	96	102	100	101	102
	U.K. (E)	NA	NA	103	100	104	NA
	EEC (A)	76	84	95	100	101	103
	EEC (E)	74	83	95	100	101	103
	Germany (A)	76	84	96	100	101	102
	Germany (E)	74	82	95	100	101	103
731.1, 731.2, & 731.3	Railway locomotives						
	U.S.	100	108	103	100	99	98
	U.K.	NA	NA	106	100	98	NA
	Germany	74	83	94	100	101	103
732	Road motor vehicles						
	U.S. (A)	89	91	94	100	99	98
	U.K. (A)	92	94	99	100	101	105
	U.K. (E)	92	95	100	100	101	106
	EEC (A)	95	94	95	100	102	102
	EEC (E)	95	95	96	100	102	103
	Germany (A)	91	91	94	100	101	100
	Germany (E)	90	92	95	100	102	101
732.1 & 732.6	Passenger motor cars; and chassis with engine mounted						
	U.S.	90	89	94	100	100	100
	U.K.	98	93	99	100	101	106
	EEC	102	100	95	100	102	102
	Germany	95	95	94	100	102	100
	France	109	110	95	100	103	108
	Italy	133	109	100	100	101	101
	Japan	NA	148	105	100	95	92

(continued)

Table C.6 (concluded)

SITC Number	Commodity Group Country, and Index Type[a]	1953	1957	1961	1962	1963	1964
732.2,	Buses, trucks, etc., and chassis with engines mounted						
732.3,	U.S.	86	92	93	100	97	93
732.4,	U.K.	81	95	98	100	100	102
732.5 &	EEC	81	84	94	100	101	102
732.7	Germany	81	84	94	100	100	100
734	Aircraft and parts						
	U.S. (A)	83	89	99	100	102	108
	U.K. (A)	NA	NA	NA	100	108	112
	U.K. (E)	NA	NA	NA	100	108	112
	France (A)	NA	76	93	100	102	104
	France (E)	NA	76	93	100	102	104
734.1	Aircraft, heavier than air						
	U.S.	80	86	95	100	103	104
	U.K.	NA	74	97	100	106	107
	France	NA	69	93	100	103	107
735	Ships and boats						
	U.S. (A)	98	116	101	100	96	97
	EEC (E)	111	130	99	100	91	90
	Germany (E)	108	124	95	100	93	92
	Japan (A)	112	140	99	100	86	87
	Japan (E)	112	140	99	100	86	87

Note: **SITC 73:** The *U.S.* aggregated index is a combination of separate indexes for the four 3-digit groups shown separately and SITC 733 (road vehicles other than motor vehicles). The *U.K.* aggregated index is based on the same five 3-digit groups except that data for SITC 731 are limited to 1961–63, and data for SITC 734 were not available for 1953. The *EEC* and *German* aggregated indexes are based on SITC 731, 732, 733, and 735 for all periods.

731: *U.S.* aggregated indexes for all railway vehicles are a combination of subgroup indexes for locomotives, for freight cars, and for railway vehicle parts. The locomotive price index is discussed below under 731.1, 731.2, and 731.3. The freight car price index, which was given a weight in the total to represent both freight and passenger cars, is derived from ICC and Association of American Railroads data on freight car purchases by U.S. railroads. This index was first compiled as a set of Laspeyres indexes for pairs of years, each year on the previous year as a base. This method was used because each type of freight car appeared in the list for only a short span of years, frequently only two or three. These indexes were then linked to form the longer spans from 1953 to 1957 and 1957 to 1961. The index for parts of railway vehicles is derived from export prices reported by both U.S. sellers and by foreign buyers. The number of observations is small and the index is therefore not shown separately.

(continued)

Notes to Table C.6 (continued)

German aggregated indexes for all railway vehicles are averages of separate subgroup indexes for locomotives and self-propelled cars (1954–64), for non-self-propelled freight and passenger cars (1958–64), and for railway vehicle parts (1955–64). The 1954 price level was taken to represent 1953. Approximately 15 to 20 observations, from both exporters and foreign purchasers, are included.

The *EEC* aggregated indexes include the German data, and a small number of French prices reported by purchasers.

731.1, 731.2, and **731.3:** The *U.S.* locomotive price index is composed of two parts. The first, covering 1953–61, is derived from ICC data on U.S. railroads' purchases of diesel locomotives, subdivided by horsepower and type of use. This index, like that for freight cars, was computed for pairs of years and then linked. The second part of the index, covering 1961–64, is an average of export price movements for locomotives reported by U.S. manufactureres. The indexes from ICC and company data were each computed, and can be compared, for the whole period from 1953 through 1964, and they can be compared also with several other indexes. For a further discussion of these alternative index comparisons see the appendix to Chapter 14.

The *U.K.* index for locomotives is from the appendix to Chapter 14.

The *German* index for locomotives includes self-propelled cars (SITC 731.4). The 1954 price level was taken to represent 1953.

732: The aggregated indexes are based on the two subgroups shown separately, as well as on indexes for parts (SITC 732.8), and in the case of Germany and the EEC for motorcycles (SITC 732.9).

732.1 and **732.6:** The indexes for passenger cars are based on regression analysis of domestic list prices (see Chapter 15). The index for the *EEC* was derived by combining indexes for Germany, France, and Italy with weights based on their 1963 exports.

732.2, 732.3, 732.4, 732.5, and **732.7:** The indexes for commercial vehicles are based on regression analysis for trucks for the *United States* and the *United Kingdom*. The features of the regressions are summarized below:

	1957/1953	1961/1957	1962/1961	1963/1962	1964/1963
United States					
$\bar{R}^2$	.98	.95	.93	.95	.94
Dummies retained	T	BD	WBD	T	T
United Kingdom					
$\bar{R}^2$	.91	.92	.95	.94	.95
Dummies retained	T	TB	TD	BD	WB

In the above table T = time dummy, W = slope dummy for gross vehicle weight, B = slope dummy for wheelbase, D = slope dummy for displacement. The basic independent variables were gross vehicle weight, wheelbase, displacement, and dummies kept in common for both years (i.e., for cowl, diesel, and, in the case of the United Kingdom, forward control). The basic independent variables were consistently more than two times their standard errors except for wheelbase, which was greater than its standard error in all the U.K. equations but only in two out of the five U.S. equations. For the United States only the last two regressions (for 1963/1962 and 1964/1963) included trucks with diesel engines. U.S. regressions restricted to gas engine trucks compared with the regressions used as follows (the retained dummy in each one is T):

	Gas Only		Gas and Diesel	
	$\dfrac{1963}{1962}$	$\dfrac{1964}{1963}$	$\dfrac{1963}{1962}$	$\dfrac{1964}{1963}$
$\bar{R}^2$	.92	.90	.95	.94
Price relative	96	94	97	96

The numbers of observation were:

	1953	1957	1961	1962	1963	1964
United States	22	35	53	55	49	50
United Kingdom	17	82	82	104	85	92

Eight diesel engine trucks were included in these observations in 1962 and 7 in the last two years.

For a description of the EEC and German indexes, see appendix to Chapter 14.

734: The indexes for complete aircraft (734.1 below), accounting for slightly more than half the weight of the whole group, were combined with aircraft parts price indexes. Data on parts were mainly prices for spare parts rather than for major sections of an aircraft, and were reported by buyers and sellers, that is, by aircraft companies and airlines. More than 100 individual parts were included in the index. Most of the index was composed of price relatives weighted by value of sales, but this weighted index was combined with an unweighted index for other parts prices, to give the final result which was incorporated in the aggregated indexes.

734.1: Prices are for civilian airline transport aircraft, excluding all military aircraft, helicopters, and civilian aircraft of the type sold as private or company planes. The prices are intended to refer to date of order rather than date of delivery.

The *U.S.* data on airframes are taken mainly from reports by airlines to the Civil Aeronautics Board on CAB Schedule B-7. These list all airframes delivered and the price paid for each, and cover all aircraft delivered to airlines in the United States. The reported prices were checked by correspondence with purchasers and by comparison with independent reports by both manufacturers and purchasers of aircraft, to eliminate spurious price movements resulting from leasing transactions and changes in specifications.

The price indexes for U.S. airframes were calculated by computing indexes for pairs of adjacent years, using the first year of each pair as a base, and then linking them. Because these prices referred to date of delivery, we back-dated them by two years to approximate date of order. The average lead time was actually larger than this, closer to three years, but the long leads were almost entirely for domestic sales. Foreign buyers tended to enter the market at a later stage in the development of each plane, and we therefore assumed a shorter lead time.

The price index for airframes was combined with one for aircraft engines, which is described in the appendix to Chapter 12. The airframes were given 85 per cent of the weight and engines 15 per cent. These weights were derived from the CAB data for 1963, which showed, for all aircraft purchased in that year, the cost of the airframe and the cost of the engines. The combination of these two indexes produced an index for complete aircraft.

An independent price index for complete aircraft can be derived from data, supplied

(continued)

Notes to Table C.6 (concluded)

by one of the cooperating companies, giving prices by date of order charged for all the leading types of commercial jet aircraft. Indexes for three subgroups of aircraft were computed from these prices, weighting each aircraft equally, and the three subgroup indexes were then combined with equal weights. The resulting index was as follows: *1957*, 90; *1961*, 97; *1962*, 100; *1963*, 103; *1964*, 107. Despite differences in the type of index, the weighting of individual aircraft, the timing of price reports, and the coverage of aircraft sales, the two indexes do not differ greatly over the period as a whole. One shows a 20 per cent price increase and the other a 19 per cent increase.

The indexes the the *United Kingdom* and *France* for complete aircraft are order price indexes from prices reported by an American company. The source is the same as for the alternative U.S. price index reported above.

735: The *U.S.* aggregated index is a combination of a Maritime Administration "new ship selling price index" and of an index of tanker prices we constructed mainly on the basis of information obtained from three U.S. oil companies which contracted for more than fifty tankers in the years covered by our study. The Maritime Administration index reflects the prices paid for ships constructed in its ship replacement program. Under this program, ship lines received a construction subsidy equal to the difference between the domestic and foreign construction costs up to a maximum of 55 per cent of the domestic cost (50 per cent before 1960). The agency was therefore obliged to keep careful track of ship prices at home and abroad. However, since the replacement program was concerned with cargo liners, the index does not cover tanker and dry bulk vessel prices. These types of ships accounted for roughly half of world ship exports. Our own index for tanker prices is based partly on actual prices and partly on curves drawn by engineers in two companies to show (for internal use) the relationships between prices and deadweight tonnage at each of the several dates. The price per ton declined sharply as size increased, though not in the same degree in every country; in 1964, for example, the price per ton in the United States for a 65,000 ton tanker was around two-thirds of the per ton price for a tanker half as large, while in Japan the per ton price of the larger size was over three-quarters that of the smaller one. Since the average size of tankers built for export increased sharply (from 12,300 gross tons in 1953 to 27,300 in 1964, according to *Lloyds Register*), we treated each of seven sizes of tankers (ranging from 27,500 to 90,000 deadweight tons) as a different product and used the 1963 estimated purchase pattern as weights. Data for only the two smallest sizes were available for the 1957/1953 link and for all seven sizes only for the 1964/1963 link. It may be further noted that prices since 1957 have tended to decline more for large tankers than for small ones; thus the price increase shown by our tanker index would have been about 10 per cent higher had it been based only on the two smallest sizes.

The tanker and Maritime Administration indexes were averaged together to obtain the indexes in the table.

Since only scattered data relating directly to temporal price changes were available for *Germany* and the *EEC* as a whole, no aggregated indexes were constructed.

The *Japanese* aggregated indexes are based upon official tabulations. The 1957/1953 link is based on the price of Japanese ships built for Japanese owners in the successive shipbuilding programs of the Japanese government. For 1957, 1961, 1962, 1963, and 1964 (fiscal years, beginning in April) we obtained complete tabulations of the vessels built in Japan for foreign owners with the price and physical characteristics of each. The indexes for 1957 on were derived from regressions fitted by methods described in the appendix to Chapter 14.

[a]A in parentheses after country name indicates aggregated index; E, extrapolated index. See General Note to this appendix for fuller explanation.

Table C.7
International Price Indexes, Miscellaneous Manufactured
Articles, 1953, 1957, 1961–64
(1962 = 100)

SITC Number	Commodity Group, Country, and Index Type[a]	1953	1957	1961	1962	1963	1964
861	Scientific, medical, etc., instruments and apparatus						
	U.K. (A)	76	92	100	100	100	106
	U.K. (E)	77	92	100	100	100	106
	Japan (A)	NA	NA	102	100	102	103
	Japan (E)	NA	NA	100	100	103	103
861.1, 861.2, & 861.3	Optical goods						
	EEC	NA	93	100	100	102	104
	Germany	NA	93	99	100	102	105
861.4, 861.5, & 861.6	Photographic and cinematographic apparatus and equipment, n.e.s.						
	U.S.	NA	NA	100	100	100	NA
	EEC	99	105	102	100	102	103
	Germany	100	107	103	100	102	104
861.7	Medical instruments, n.e.s.						
	U.S.	NA	NA	100	100	99	100
	EEC	78	84	94	100	101	101
	Germany	77	83	94	100	101	101
861.8	Meters and counters, nonelectric						
	EEC	NA	83	95	100	106	108
	Germany	NA	83	95	100	106	108
861.9	Measuring, controlling, and scientific instruments, n.e.s.						
	U.S.	86	93	98	100	102	104
	U.K.	NA	98	104	100	98	106
	EEC	85	92	98	100	100	102
	Germany	84	91	97	100	101	102
891	Musical instruments, recorders, etc., and parts and accessories						
	U.S. (A)	NA	96	97	100	100	103
	U.K. (A)	NA	NA	100	100	100	101
	U.K. (E)	NA	NA	100	100	100	101
	EEC (A)	78	87	93	100	104	108
	EEC (E)	NA	86	92	100	104	109
	Germany (A)	76	86	94	100	105	110
	Germany (E)	NA	84	93	100	105	111
	Japan (E)	NA	NA	100	100	99	101

(continued)

Table C.7 (concluded)

SITC Number	Commodity Group, Country, and Index Type[a]	1953	1957	1961	1962	1963	1964
891.1	Phonographs, tape recorders, etc.						
	U.S.	NA	NA	96	100	100	104
891.4	Pianos and other string musical instruments						
	U.S.	NA	NA	98	100	100	108
	EEC	79	89	98	100	105	107
	Germany	77	88	97	100	106	108
891.8	Musical instruments, n.e.s. (excl. records, tapes, etc.)						
	EEC	NA	88	95	100	99	104
	Germany	NA	86	96	100	99	101

Note: **SITC 861:** The *U.K.* aggregated index is based mainly on subgroup 861.9, which accounts for almost half the weight of the total 861 group (see 861.9 below). It also includes 861.7 for all periods, and some observations for each of the other subgroups for one or more periods. The *Japanese* aggregated index is based on between 10 and 20 observations from six different sources, covering each of the subgroups except 861.7.

861.1, 861.2, and **861.3:** The *EEC* index is based on the German index combined with few observations for France and Italy. The *German* index is based mainly on official export price indexes composed of 19 price series for 1957 to 1962 and 25 series for 1962 to 1964. In addition we had some buyer data on German prices.

861.4, 861.5, and **861.6:** The *U.S.* index is based on a small number of observations from 2 buyer and 2 seller sources. The *EEC* index is based on the German index combined with an official German import price index reflecting primarily French prices. The *German* index is based mainly on official export price indexes composed of 29 price series for 1957 to 1964; and 11 series for 1954–57, which were used for the 1957/1953 link. In addition we had scattered buyer data on German prices.

861.7: The *U.S.* index is based on from 8 to 13 observations from four buyer sources. The *EEC* index is based on the German index combined with some buyer data on French prices. The *German* index is based primarily on official export price indexes composed of 24 price series for 1954–62 and 29 series for 1962–64. The series in the later years include mechanotherapy appliances, while those for the earlier years do not. In addition we had some buyer data on German prices for the entire period.

861.8: The *EEC* and *German* indexes are based on official export price statistics for 12 series, combined with a small amount of buyer data on German prices for 1961–64. The official price index for 1958–61 was used for the 1961/1957 link.

861.9: The *U.S.* index was based on data from thirteen sources including both buyers and sellers. The number of observations varied from 12 in the first period to 50–60 in the later years. Individual indexes were constructed for the six 5-digit subgroups for which data were available, and these were then averaged with 1963 OECD export weights. The *U.K.* index also is a weighted average of individual indexes for 5-digit subgroups. Data were available on five or six subgroups for each period. About 20 to 30 observations were obtained from seven sources including both buyers and sellers.

The *EEC* index is a weighted average of seven individual 5-digit item indexes, all of which included German data, and three of which included a small amount of data from other EEC countries (France, Italy, Belgium, and the Netherlands). The *German* index was based mainly on official export price statistics for each of the seven subgroups, although data for the first link (1957/1953) were missing for two of these. We also had buyer and seller data from other sources for four of the subgroups. There were 30 to 50 observations in all for each period.

891: The aggregated index for each country is a weighted average of the 4-digit subgroups for which we had data. There are five subgroups in SITC 891. The two not listed in the table are 891.2 (phonograph records, recorded tapes, other recorded media, and prepared media for sound recording), and 891.9 (parts and accessories of musical instruments, other than strings). The *U.S.* index covers 891.4 and 891.9 for all years, 891.1 for all except the 1961/1957 link, 891.2 for 1962–64 only, and 891.8 for all years except 1953. The data for 891.2, 891.8, and 891.9 were not sufficient to publish separately, consisting of only a few observations for each group, all from one buyer source. The *U.K.* index covers 891.1 and 891.8 for all years, 891.2 for 1962–64 only, and 891.4 for 1961–64 only. The data for 4-digit groups were not sufficient to publish separately. In each group the number of observations was small. The sources included two foreign buyers and two U.S. manufacturers. The *EEC* index covers 891.4 and 891.9 for all years, 891.1 for 1963–64 only, 891.2 for 1962–64 only, and 891.8 for all years except 1953. The *German* index covers 891.4, 891.8, and 891.9 for all years, 891.1 for 1963–64 only, and 891.2 for 1962 and 1963 only. The EEC and German data on 891.1, 891.2, and 891.9 were not sufficient to publish separately. They consisted of a few buyer observations on Germany for each group, and a few on France for phonographs and records. The *Japanese* index covers 891.4 and 891.9 for all years, and 891.1 for 1961–64 only. The data for 4-digit groups were not sufficient to publish separately. They consisted of an export price index for tape recorders in the 1960s and a few observations from two buyer sources.

891.1: The *U.S.* index for the 1960s is based on 6 to 10 observations from two buyer sources and one U.S. manufacturer. For the earlier years we had only one observation, for the 1957/1953 link.

891.4: The *U.S.* index for the 1960s is based on about 10 observations from one buyer and one seller. For the earlier years the data were from only one source and not sufficient to publish separately. The *EEC* index is based on the German index combined with data on Italy and the Netherlands from one buyer and one seller. The number of observations was between 10 and 20 for each period. The *German* index is based on about 10 observations from the official export statistics and one buyer source.

891.8: The *EEC* index is based on 12 to 20 observations on accordions, saxophones, clarinets, flutes, and electric guitars from Germany, Italy, France, and the Netherlands. Data were from the official German export statistics and two buyer sources. The *German* index was based on accordions and similar instruments. There were 8 observations from the official export statistics and one buyer source.

[a]A in parentheses after country name indicates aggregated index; E, extrapolated index. See General Note to this appendix for fuller explanation.

APPENDIX D

INDEXES OF PRICE COMPETITIVENESS

General Note

The indexes of U.S. price competitiveness in the following tables are a measure of the movement of foreign relative to U.S. prices. A rise in the U.S. *price competitiveness* index occurs when the foreign price index rises relative to the U.S. price index. An index of U.S. price competitiveness for a commodity group is measured by (1) the ratio of foreign to U.S. price indexes (time-to-time relatives) or (2) the movement of the ratio of foreign to U.S. price levels (place-to-place data). For a more detailed description of price competitiveness indexes, see Chapter 1.

The indexes of price competitiveness were calculated on a four-digit, or in some cases five-digit, commodity group level. The two-digit and three-digit indexes are aggregations of these subgroup indexes, using 1963 OECD export weights. For each 4- or 5-digit group, the competitiveness index was calculated from time-to-time data, place-to-place data, or a combination of both, depending upon the amount and quality of each. The notes to the individual tables indicate the extent to which each type of data was used.

Indexes are given in the tables for all groups and subgroups for which the amount and quality of the data were sufficient for publication. The notes that follow the tables cover all the subgroups, including those not shown.

Table D.1

Indexes of U.S. Price Competitiveness, Iron and Steel, 1953, 1957, 1961–64
(1962 = 100)

SITC Number	Commodity Group and Country	1953	1957	1961	1962	1963	1964
67	Iron and steel						
	U.K.	117	108	101	100	97	104
	EEC	119	117	102	100	98	104
	Germany	112	110	102	100	97	104
	Japan	NA	NA	108	100	100	100
673	Bars, rods, angles, shapes, and sections						
	U.K.	NA	105	100	100	96	105
	EEC	127	126	109	100	102	110
	Germany	114	117	106	100	100	108
	Japan	NA	NA	115	100	104	106
673.2	Bars and rods (excl. wire rod)						
	U.K.	NA	NA	98	100	96	NA
	EEC	123	125	109	100	105	107
	Germany	NA	117	104	100	103	106
673.4 & 673.5	Angles, shapes, and sections						
	U.K.	NA	NA	102	100	98	103
	EEC	NA	132	105	100	100	108
	Germany	NA	NA	103	100	97	105
674	Universals, plates and sheets						
	U.K.	133	118	104	100	92	104
	EEC	121	119	100	100	93	100
	Germany	110	109	101	100	91	99
	Japan	NA	NA	110	100	96	98
674.1 & 674.2	———3mm. or more (excl. tinned)						
	U.K.	NA	NA	107	100	96	107
	EEC	NA	131	104	100	93	109
	Germany	NA	128	107	100	92	110
674.3	———less than 3mm., uncoated						
	U.K.	NA	111	104	100	NA	NA
	EEC	NA	119	100	100	92	97
	Germany	NA	102	99	100	93	97
674.7	———tinned						
	U.K.	NA	NA	NA	100	97	99

(continued)

Table D.1 (concluded)

SITC Number	Commodity Group and Country	1953	1957	1961	1962	1963	1964
676	Rails and track construction material						
	U.K.	NA	NA	98	100	100	NA
677	Iron and steel wire (excl. wire rod)						
	EEC	NA	122	105	100	99	106
	Germany	NA	120	103	100	99	108
	Japan	NA	NA	107	100	97	101
678	Tubes, pipes, and fittings						
	U.K.	102	98	95	100	102	104
	EEC	108	104	96	100	101	105
	Germany	109	99	98	100	102	104
	Japan	NA	NA	99	100	104	94
678.2	Tubes and pipes (excl. cast iron), seamless						
	U.K.	102	98	95	100	102	102
	EEC	129	105	96	100	102	102
	Germany	123	103	95	100	101	102
	Japan	NA	NA	99	100	109	104
678.3	Tubes and pipes (excl. cast iron), welded, etc.						
	U.K.	NA	NA	98	100	101	103
	EEC	NA	107	98	100	100	109
	Germany	NA	98	102	100	102	108
678.5	Tube and pipe fittings						
	U.K.	NA	NA	85	100	108	110
	EEC	NA	NA	93	100	103	99
	Japan	NA	NA	NA	100	94	NA

Note: **SITC 67**: The indexes are weighted averages of the 3-digit SITC groups for which we had data. These are the five 3-digit groups listed in the table, plus groups 671 (pig iron, spiegeleisen, sponge iron, iron and steel powders and shot, and ferro-alloys), 672 (ingots and other primary forms of iron and steel), and 675 (hoop and strip of iron and steel). No data were available for group 679 (iron and steel castings and forgings, unworked, n.e.s.), which accounts for only 1 per cent of the total weight of group 67. The coverage of the 3-digit groups varies by country. The *U.K.* index excludes 675 for all years, 676 for 1953 and 1957, and 677 for 1953. The *EEC* and *German* indexes exclude 676 for all years and 677 for 1953. The *Japanese* index, which covers only 1961−64, includes 673, 674, 675, 677, and 678 for that period.

The indexes for 671, 672, and 675 were based on time-to-time data, U.S. and foreign, either or both of which were considered insufficient to publish (see notes to Table C.1).

673: The indexes are weighted averages of the two 4-digit SITC groups listed in the table, plus SITC 673.1 (wire rod of iron or steel). For the United Kingdom, the EEC, and Germany, the coverage of the 4-digit subgroups is complete, except for 673.4 and 673.5 combined in 1953. The Japanese data for all subgroups are limited to the 1961—64 period.

The unpublished 673.1 indexes are based on time-to-time data, U.S. and foreign, either or both of which were considered insufficient to publish.

673.2: The *German* indexes are based on the time-to-time relatives underlying the international price indexes in Table C.1. The *U.K.* and *EEC* indexes are based on a combination of time-to-time and place-to-place data.

673.4, and 673.5: See 673.2.

674: The indexes are weighted averages of three of the four 4-digit subgroups. No data are available for 674.8 (plates and sheets less than 3 mm., coated, except tinned plates), representing about 12 per cent of the total weight of 674. In addition, 1953 data are lacking for U.K. 674.1 and 674.2 combined (universals, plates, and sheets 3 mm. and over); 1953 EEC data, 674.7 (tinned plates and sheets); 1953—62 German data, 674.7; and 1953—61 Japanese data, 674.3 (plates and sheets less than 3 mm.) and 674.7. The *U.K.* index is based on place-to-place data for 674.1 and 674.2 combined, and on a combination of time-to-time and place-to-place data for 674.3 and 674.7. The *EEC* and *German* indexes are based on time-to-time data for 674.1 and 674.2 combined, and 674.3, and on a combination of time-to-time and place-to-place data for 674.7. The *Japanese* index is based on both time- to-time and place-to-place data for 674.1 and 674.2 combined and 674.7. The 674.3 component is based on time-to-time data.

674.1, 674.2, 674.3, and 674.7: See 674.

676: The *U.K.* index, which covers only the 1960s, is a weighted average of 676.1 (rails) for 1961—64, and 676.2 (sleepers and other railway track material) for 1961—63. Both subgroup indexes are derived from place-to-place data.

677: The *German* and *Japanese* indexes are based on time-to-time data; the *U.K.* is based on place-to-place data; and the *EEC*, on a combination of both.

678: The indexes are weighted averages of the three 4-digit subgroups shown in the table. Data for 678.1 (tubes and pipes of cast iron) are not sufficient to construct indexes of competitiveness. No data are available for 678.4 (high-pressure hydroelectric conduits of steel).

678.2: Based on place-to-place data.

678.3: Based on time-to-time data; 1953 data for *EEC* and *Germany* were considered too weak to publish separately, but are included in the aggregation of the 678 index.

678.5: Based on place-to-place data. *EEC* indexes for 1953 and 1957 and *German* indexes for all years were considered too weak to publish separately, but are included in the aggregation of the 678 index.

Table D.2
Indexes of U.S. Price Competitiveness, Nonferrous Metals,
1953, 1957, 1961–64
(1962 = 100)

SITC Number	Commodity Group and Country	1953	1957	1961	1962	1963	1964
68	Nonferrous metals						
	U.K.	100	101	100	100	102	106
	EEC	105	102	100	100	101	108
	Germany	104	105	100	100	99	107
682	Copper						
	U.K.	100	99	99	100	100	105
	EEC	102	102	101	100	100	111
684	Aluminum						
	U.K.	99	103	102	100	104	104
	EEC	108	101	101	100	100	101

Note: **SITC 68:** The index for each country is a weighted average of indexes for eight of the nine 3-digit groups which make up SITC 68. The one group omitted is 688 (uranium and thorium and their alloys), which represents only 0.03 per cent of the weight of the total group. No data were available on SITC 68 for Japan. The subgroup indexes were all based on time-to-time data, except for the *U.K.* index for 687, which was based on place-to-place data. See notes to Tables C.2 and E.2 for description of underlying time-to-time and place-to-place data, respectively.

682 and **684:** These indexes are aggregates of the 4-digit subgroups, and are based on time-to-time data (see note to Table C.2).

Table D.3

Indexes of U.S. Price Competitiveness, Miscellaneous Metal Manufactures,
1953, 1957, 1961–64
(1962 = 100)

SITC Number	Commodity Group and Country	1953	1957	1961	1962	1963	1964
69	Manufactures of metal, n.e.s.						
	U.K.	105	103	105	100	100	100
	EEC	102	101	101	100	97	95
	Germany	99	95	100	100	99	98
	Japan	NA	NA	99	100	94	99
692	Metal containers for storage and transport						
	U.K.	NA	110	97	100	95	91
	EEC	128	109	98	100	98	99
	Germany	NA	93	100	100	97	96
692.1	Tanks, vats, etc., for storage or manufacturing						
	U.K.	NA	NA	97	100	91	89
692.2	Casks, drums, boxes, cans, etc., for transport						
	U.K.	NA	NA	98	100	98	92
	EEC	128	109	98	100	98	99
	Germany	NA	93	100	100	97	96
693	Wire products (excl. electric) and fencing grills						
	U.K.	NA	100	105	100	94	94
	EEC	84	94	102	100	94	99
	Germany	86	96	105	100	94	102
	Japan	NA	NA	104	100	91	89
693.1	Wire cables, ropes, etc., not insulated						
	U.K.	NA	106	111	100	95	NA
	EEC	NA	92	104	100	86	94
	Germany	NA	NA	111	100	86	100
	Japan	NA	NA	103	100	83	NA
693.2	Wire of iron or steel, of types used for fencing						
	EEC	NA	NA	105	100	99	98
693.3	Gauze, netting, grill, fencing, etc., of wire						
	EEC	NA	NA	99	100	101	104
	Germany	NA	NA	99	100	101	104
694	Nails, screws, nuts, bolts, etc., iron, steel or copper						
	U.K.	NA	NA	100	100	98	89

(continued)

Table D.3 (concluded)

SITC Number	Commodity Group and Country	1953	1957	1961	1962	1963	1964
694	Nails, screws, nuts, bolts, etc., iron, steel or copper (continued)						
	EEC	110	100	101	100	96	94
	Germany	NA	98	102	100	95	92
694.1	Nails, tacks, staples, spikes, etc.						
	EEC	NA	NA	99	100	96	99
	Germany	NA	NA	99	100	99	101
694.2	Nuts, bolts, screws, rivets, washers, etc.						
	EEC	NA	NA	102	100	96	92
	Germany	NA	NA	103	100	93	88
695	Tools for use in the hand or in machines						
	U.K.	NA	NA	100	100	98	98
	EEC	92	88	98	100	99	100
	Germany	92	88	98	100	99	100
696	Cutlery						
	U.K.	NA	NA	97	100	102	106
	Germany	NA	NA	103	100	100	102
	Japan	NA	NA	98	100	109	120
698	Manufactures of metal, n.e.s.						
	U.K.	103	92	94	100	101	103
	EEC	107	105	100	100	102	98
	Germany	107	105	100	100	102	98

Note: **SITC 69:** The indexes are weighted averages of the 3-digit SITC groups for which we had data. The *U.K.* index covers all 3-digit groups except 1953 and 1957 data for 691 and 694. The *EEC* index excludes 1953 and 1957 for 691. The *German* index covers all groups for all years. The *Japanese* index which covers only the 1960s, includes data for 693, 695, and 696 for all four years, and 692 and 697 for 1962–63 only.

The indexes for 3-digit groups are combinations of price competitiveness indexes for 4-digit subgroups. The majority of these were computed from the time series data underlying the international price indexes of Table C.3, but some were derived from the place-to-place price comparisons used to construct the price level indexes of Table E.3.

For the *United Kingdom*, the international price index data were used for SITC 696, 697, and 698, and price level data for SITC 691. For the other groups the price competitiveness indexes were a combination of the two types.

The *German* indexes, aside from those for SITC 691, for which we lacked adequate data, and 693, for which price level data were used, are based on time-to-time data. For SITC 698 the price competitiveness index is derived from data for subgroup 698.3 in both Germany and the United States, because the U.S. index contained almost no data for other subgroups.

For the *EEC,* international price index data for SITC groups 694–698 and price level data for SITC 691 were used. Indexes for SITC 692 and 693 are based on a combination of the two types of data. The EEC indexes for SITC 695–698 include only German data, as do a few of the links in the series for other groups.

The *Japanese* indexes for SITC 695 and 696 are derived from time series data; those for 692, from price level data; and for SITC 693, from a combination of the two types.

692: See SITC 69.

692.1: The *U.K.* index is based on place-to-place data.

692.2: The *U.K.* and *EEC* indexes are derived from a combination of time-to-time and place-to-place data. The *German* index is based on time-to-time data only.

693: See SITC 69.

693.1: The *Japanese* index is based on place-to-place data. For the *United Kingdom*, the *EEC*, and *Germany*, both time-to-time and place-to-place observations were used.

693.2: The *EEC* index is based on time-to-time data.

693.3: The *EEC* and *German* indexes are based on time-to-time data.

694: See SITC 69.

694.1 and **694.2:** The *EEC* and *German* indexes are based on time-to-time data.

695, 696, and **698:** See SITC 69.

Table D.4

Indexes of U.S. Price Competitiveness, Machinery Other than Electric,
1953, 1957, 1961–64

(1962 = 100)

SITC Number	Commodity Group and Country	1953	1957	1961	1962	1963	1964
71	Machinery other than electric						
	U.K.	99	99	99	100	100	101
	EEC	99	95	98	100	100	100
	Germany	99	94	98	100	100	100
711	Power generating machinery, other than electric						
	U.K.	106	101	100	100	97	100
	EEC	104	98	97	100	99	96
	Germany	102	94	96	100	99	94
711.4	Aircraft engines (incl. jet propulsion engines)						
	U.K.	NA	97	101	100	95	94
711.5	Internal combustion engines, excl. aircraft						
	Germany	106	95	97	100	99	94
712	Agricultural machinery and implements						
	U.K.	102	105	101	100	99	100
	EEC	101	102	100	100	100	100
	Germany	102	102	101	100	99	99
712.5	Tractors other than road tractors						
	U.K.	102	105	101	100	99	100
	EEC	103	102	100	100	101	102
	Germany	105	104	102	100	100	101
714	Office machines						
	U.K.	98	97	97	100	98	97
	EEC	118	98	97	100	98	97
	Germany	116	98	97	100	98	97
714.1	Typewriters and check-writing machines						
	EEC	NA	99	100	100	100	99
	Germany	NA	NA	101	100	100	98
714.2	Calculating, accounting machines, etc. (incl. electronic computers)						
	U.K.	102	101	99	100	95	94
	EEC	117	98	97	100	97	96
	Germany	115	96	97	100	98	96
714.9	Office machines, n.e.s. (excl. statistical machines)						
	EEC	117	100	96	100	97	96
	Germany	116	99	96	100	97	96

(continued)

Table D.4 (continued)

SITC Number	Commodity Group and Country	1953	1957	1961	1962	1963	1964
715	Metalworking machinery						
	U.K.	90	94	96	100	101	102
	EEC	87	90	100	100	100	99
	Germany	92	94	100	100	102	102
715.1	Machine tools for working metals						
	U.K.	90	94	96	100	101	102
	EEC	87	90	100	100	99	98
	Germany	92	94	100	100	103	101
	Metal-cutting machine tools						
	U.K.	92	95	96	100	100	102
	EEC	89	90	102	100	96	97
	Germany	95	96	102	100	101	101
	Metal-forming machine tools						
	U.K.	87	91	93	100	105	104
	EEC	83	91	96	100	106	97
	Germany	87	89	97	100	106	103
715.2	Metalworking machinery other than machine tools						
	EEC	NA	NA	99	100	100	102
	Germany	NA	NA	99	100	100	102
717	Textile and leather machinery						
	U.K.	98	97	99	100	102	102
	EEC	101	98	99	100	100	101
	Germany	101	98	99	100	101	101
	Japan	NA	NA	102	100	101	100
717.1	Textile machinery						
	EEC	102	97	99	100	100	101
	Germany	102	97	99	100	101	102
717.2	Machinery (excl. sewing machines) for hides, skins, or leather						
	U.K.	NA	NA	NA	100	100	91
	EEC	NA	102	97	100	99	100
	Germany	NA	102	97	100	99	100
717.3	Sewing machines						
	Germany	99	99	98	100	99	99
	Japan	NA	NA	100	100	102	102
718	Machines for special industries						
	U.K.	NA	102	102	100	98	98
	Germany	NA	94	98	100	99	100

(continued)

Table D.4 (continued)

SITC Number	Commodity Group and Country	1953	1957	1961	1962	1963	1964
718.2	Printing and bookbinding machinery						
	U.K.	99	104	103	100	100	101
	Germany	99	96	101	100	99	104
718.3	Food-processing machines (excl. domestic)						
	EEC	108	97	99	100	101	104
	Germany	108	98	100	100	99	102
718.4	Construction and mining machinery, n.e.s.						
	U.K.	NA	101	100	100	99	99
	Germany	NA	92	95	100	99	100
	Japan	NA	NA	101	100	98	95
718.5	Mineral crushing, sorting, etc., machinery; glassworking machinery						
	U.K.	NA	NA	102	100	91	NA
719	Machinery and appliances (nonelect.) and parts, n.e.s.						
	U.K.	99	99	99	100	102	102
	EEC	94	94	97	100	100	101
	Germany	93	91	97	100	101	101
719.1	Heating and cooling equipment						
	U.K.	NA	NA	100	100	100	99
	EEC	97	98	99	100	101	98
	Germany	84	86	96	100	102	101
719.2	Pumps and centrifuges						
	U.K.	96	104	99	100	99	98
	EEC	96	95	97	100	99	100
	Germany	95	92	97	100	99	99
719.21	Pumps for liquids						
	Germany	103	91	94	100	100	99
719.22	Pumps for gases						
	Germany	NA	93	99	100	100	100
719.3	Mechanical handling equipment						
	U.K.	NA	104	101	100	107	110
	EEC	84	94	95	100	99	99
	Germany	NA	94	95	100	99	98
719.31	Lifting and loading machinery						
	U.K.	NA	104	101	100	108	111
	EEC	NA	92	94	100	98	99
	Germany	NA	92	94	100	99	99

(continued)

Table D.4 (concluded)

SITC Number	Commodity Group and Country	1953	1957	1961	1962	1963	1964
719.32	Forklift and other industrial trucks						
	EEC	NA	99	99	100	100	96
	Germany	NA	99	99	100	100	96
719.5	Powered tools, n.e.s.						
	U.K.	105	99	103	100	102	99
	Germany	90	85	94	100	99	101
719.6 &	Nonelect. mach. and appliances, n.e.s. (excl. domestic appliances)						
719.8	U.K.	NA	98	100	100	99	103
	EEC	90	91	98	100	102	106
	Germany	90	92	99	100	101	105
719.7	Ball, roller, or needle-roller bearings						
	Germany	115	92	100	100	98	96
719.9	Parts and accessories of machinery, n.e.s.						
	U.K.	NA	NA	94	100	105	104
	EEC	103	97	97	100	104	102
	Germany	101	95	97	100	105	103
719.92	Taps, cocks, valves, and similar appliances, n.e.s.						
	U.K.	113	99	97	100	104	106
	EEC	113	99	97	100	103	104
	Germany	109	96	98	100	105	105
	Japan	NA	NA	NA	100	102	127
719.93	Transmission shafts and cranks, pulleys, etc.						
	Germany	NA	NA	NA	100	102	99

Note: **SITC 71:** The indexes are weighted averages of separate indexes for each of the seven 3-digit component groups.

711: The *U.K.* index is based on time-to-time data for 711.1 (steam generating boilers), 711.4 (see note below), and 711.5. The *EEC* and *German* indexes are based on time-to-time data for 711.1 and 711.5

711.4: The *U.K.* index was calculated by dividing its time-to-time price index by that for the U.S. The indexes are those of Table C.4 except for 1961 when the U.S. index for complete aircraft engines (excluding parts) was used to provide comparability with the U.K. index.

711.5: See 711.

712: The *U.K.* index is based on time-to-time data for 712.1 (cultivating machines), 712.2 (harvesting, threshing, and sorting machines), and 712.5. The *EEC* and *German* indexes are based on time-to-time data for 712.1, 712.2, 712.3 (dairy-farming equipment), and 712.5.

712.5: See 712.

(continued)

Notes to Table D.4 (continued)

714: The indexes are weighted averages of separate indexes for the three 4-digit groups listed in the table, and, for the 1962–64 period, 714.3 (statistical machines). The 4-digit indexes were derived by dividing the time-to-time index for each of the other countries by the U.S. index for the same period.

Changes in price competitiveness inferred from place-to-place indexes, although based on fewer and less reliable observations than the time-to-time calculations, are similar. The main difference between the two is that the place-to-place data show a deterioration in the position of the United States relative to the United Kingdom, which is not apparent in the time-to-time data.

714.1, 714.2, and **714.9:** See 714.

715: The *U.K.* index is based solely on time-to-time data for 715.1. The *EEC* and *German* indexes are based on time-to-time data and include 715.1 for all years and 715.2 for the 1960s (see below).

715.1: The indexes for the 4-digit group and its subdivisions are based on time-to-time price data and are aggregated from indexes for individual machine tools. In calculating the price competitiveness indexes for each subgroup the data were adjusted for differences between buyers' and sellers' reports. The *U.K.* index includes both buyers' and sellers' data for most products. The *German* and *EEC* indexes, on the other hand, are based almost exclusively on buyers' data.

715.2: Indexes for the *EEC* and *Germany* are based on time-to-time data. The following indexes for 1956–58 (1962 = 100) are based on a comparison of place-to-place data for those years with data for 1961–64: United States relative to the United Kingdom, 110; relative to the EEC, 86; relative to Germany, 85.

717: The *U.K., EEC,* and *German* indexes are based on the time-to-time data for the three 4-digit groups listed in the table. The *Japanese* index is also based on time-to-time data, but excludes 717.2.

717.1, 717.2, and **717.3:** See 717.

718: The *U.K.* index is a weighted average of the indexes shown for 718.2, 718.4, and 718.5, except that the 1953 figure for 718.5 was not included in the aggregation (see note below). The *German* index is a weighted average of the indexes shown for 718.2, 718.3, and 718.4, and time-to-time data for 718.5, which was not considered sufficient to publish as a separate index. An *EEC* index, covering the same groups as the German index, was constructed from time-to-time data and included in the aggregation of SITC 71, but was considered too weak to use separately. *Japanese* data were limited to 718.4 for the 1960s (see below).

718.2: The indexes are based on time-to-time data.

718.3: The indexes are based on time-to-time data. An alternative set of indexes, comparing prices for the same types of machinery in each country instead of comparing price movements for all items available, gives the following results:

	1953	1957	1961	1962	1963	1964
Relative to EEC	NA	98	99	100	102	104
Relative to Germany	NA	98	100	100	100	102

718.4: The indexes are based on time-to-time data.

718.5: The *U.K.* index was based on place-to-place data. The 1953 figure represents the U.K. price level relative to the United States in 1953, divided by this relative price level in 1962. However, since we did not have sufficient 1957 data, we had no 1957/1953 or 1961/1957 link for aggregating the index to the 3-digit level. Therefore the 1953 figure for 718.5 is not included in the 718 index. Although there are insufficient data for an index for 1957, a rough calculation for 1959 suggests an index of about 114, and 1957 would be only a little lower. There are too few observations for a 1964 index but those we have, and the U.S. wholesale price index, both suggest that there was little or no change between 1963 and 1964.

719: The indexes are weighted averages of separate indexes for the seven 4-digit groups shown separately, which account for over 99 per cent of the world trade weight of 719. Some data were available for each 4-digit group for all periods except for the 1957/1953 *U.K.* index links for 719.3 and for 719.6 and 719.8 combined.

719.1: The indexes are based on time-to-time data.

719.2: The indexes are derived from the time-to-time relatives underlying the international price indexes, aggregated from 5-digit subgroup indexes. For the links through 1961–62 the index of U.S. price competitiveness for SITC 719.2 is calculated from subgroup indexes for SITC 719.21 and 719.22. There are no U.S. price data for 719.23 (centrifuges) for the earlier links. The indexes from 1962 on include all three subgroups. Subgroup indexes of price competitiveness are weighted by the value of OECD exports, as given in Appendix A.

719.21 and **719.22:** See 719.2.

719.3: Indexes for total mechanical handling equipment are combinations of those for SITC 719.31 and 719.32. For lifting and loading machinery (SITC 719.31), the *U.K.* index is based on price level data. The *German* and *EEC* series, however, are derived mainly from the time-to-time data underlying Table C.3. For forklift and other industrial trucks (719.32) the *U.K.* index (not published) is based on price level data for 1964, and on the international price index time series data for earlier years. The index for *Germany* is derived from time series data and that for the *EEC* consists of the German series and some price level data for France.

A *U.K.* index derived from time-to-time data for SITC 719.31 was considered too weak to be published. Instead of the improvement in U.S. price competitiveness implied by the indexes in the table, it showed virtually no change from 1961 through 1964.

The *German* and *EEC* indexes of price competitiveness are dominated by German time series data, but the reported price level data can serve as something of an independent check. French data on price levels for 719.31, which are used in the index for 1962–64, confirm the slight decline in U.S. competitiveness over that period shown by the time series data. The German price level data, not used for the index, also suggest a decline in the U.S. competitive position. In the case of SITC 719.32, the price level data for *EEC* countires do not confirm the decline in U.S. price competitiveness shown by the time series data. For the most part they suggest either stability or a decline in 1963 followed by a rise in 1964, but in any case, not much difference between the 1962 and 1964 levels. Furthermore, some data for 1965 suggest a substantial improvement rather than a decline in U.S. competitiveness since 1962. The 1964 deterioration in U.S. price competitiveness therefore is somewhat questionable.

Some fragmentary price level comparisons with Japan in item 719.31 suggest an improvement in U.S. price competitiveness in 1964, but the opposite picture is conveyed by the domestic price indexes, which show a decline that year and every other year from 1961 to 1964.

719.31 and **719.32:** See 719.3.

719.5: The *U.K.* index is calculated from subgroup indexes for SITC 719.52 (except in 1964) and 719.53. There are no U.S. price data for 719.54 and no U.K. price data for 719.51 or 719.54. The index relative to Germany includes all subgroups except 719.54 except in 1964, when there was no U.S. price index for 719.51 either.

719.6 and **719.8:** The *U.K.* index was calculated from international price indexes for items 719.62–719.66. For rubber processing machinery and for miscellaneous

(continued)

Notes to Table D.4 (concluded)

machinery and mechanical appliances in items 719.61 and 719.8, the movement of the U.K./U.S. price level was used because it covers a larger number of observations. The *German* and *EEC* indexes are derived from international price indexes except for the rubber machinery index relative to Italy, which was calculated from price levels.

719.7: The index for *Germany* is based on time-to-time data.

719.9: The indexes shown in the table, with the exception of those for item 719.92 relative to the United Kingdom in 1953 and 1957, and those for Japan, are derived from time-to-time data as summarized in the international price indexes of Table C.4. The price competitiveness indexes for SITC 719.9 as a whole, with the same exceptions, are calculated from the corresponding international price indexes instead of being aggregations of item price competitiveness indexes as in other subgroups where the item indexes were stronger.

For item 719.92 the indexes used for the United Kingdom after 1957 and for the United States are the averages of company indexes described in the notes to Table C.4. If the international price indexes based on averages of individual observations had been used the price competitiveness indexes would have been as follows (1962 = 100):

	1953	1957	1961	1962	1963	1964
Machinery parts and accessories, n.e.s. (719.9)						
Relative to U.K.	NA	NA	92	100	107	108
Relative to EEC	99	95	97	100	106	108
Relative to Germany	97	93	97	100	108	109
Taps, cocks, valves, and similar appliances (719.92)						
Relative to U.K.	NA	NA	93	100	109	114
Relative to EEC	107	95	97	100	108	116
Relative to Germany	103	92	97	100	110	117

The indexes of price competitiveness relative to the *United Kingdom* for 1953 and 1957 and all those for *Japan* are based on place-to-place price comparisons. Both of these cover only item 719.92, with approximately 10 to 20 observations in each case. It is possible to construct, for all the years, an index of U.K. price competitiveness entirely from place-to-place comparisons of the type used in this table only for the early years. These data yield the following index for 719.92 (1962 = 100): *1953*, 121; *1957*, 107; *1961*, 104; *1962*, 100; *1963*, 113; *1964*, 125. The number of items used ranges from about 20 at the beginning to more than 100 in most of the years covered.

719.92 and 719.93: See 719.9.

Table D.5

Indexes of U.S. Price Competitiveness, Electrical Machinery,
Apparatus, and Appliances, 1953, 1957, 1961–64
(1962 = 100)

SITC Number	Commodity Group and Country	1953	1957	1961	1962	1963	1964
72	Electrical machinery, apparatus, and appliances						
	U.K.	94	91	99	100	105	103
	EEC	96	92	97	100	103	101
	Germany	94	91	97	100	102	101
	Japan	NA	115	102	100	100	102
722	Electric power machinery and switchgear						
	U.K.	NA	84	102	100	110	107
	EEC	NA	86	96	100	105	105
	Germany	NA	82	94	100	104	106
	Japan	NA	NA	97	100	102	113
722.1	Electric power machinery						
	U.K.	NA	75	91	100	109	101
	EEC	NA	81	92	100	108	109
	Germany	NA	76	90	100	105	111
	Japan	NA	NA	100	100	106	128
	Sweden	NA	NA	82	100	102	87
	Switzerland	NA	72	91	100	112	104
722.2	Apparatus for making, breaking, or protecting elect. circuits						
	EEC	NA	NA	101	100	101	100
	Germany	NA	NA	101	100	101	100
723	Equipment for distributing electricity						
	U.K.	85	84	96	100	103	99
	EEC	90	82	90	100	96	95
	Germany	90	82	90	100	97	103
	Japan	NA	NA	113	100	110	111
723.1	Insulated wire and cable						
	U.K.	NA	84	95	100	103	103
	Japan	NA	NA	115	100	113	114
723.2	Electrical insulating equipment						
	Japan	NA	NA	108	100	98	96
724	Telecommunications apparatus						
	U.K.	98	98	100	100	106	103

(continued)

Table D.5 (concluded)

SITC Number	Commodity Group and Country	1953	1957	1961	1962	1963	1964
724	Telecommunications apparatus (continued)						
	EEC	NA	NA	100	100	105	101
	Germany	NA	NA	100	100	105	99
	Japan	NA	121	106	100	105	102
724.1 & 724.2	Television and radio broadcast receivers						
	U.K.	100	94	102	100	99	98
	EEC	NA	NA	101	100	107	111
	Germany	NA	NA	101	100	108	111
	Japan	NA	151	124	100	110	110
724.9	Telecommunications equipment, n.e.s.						
	U.K.	97	100	99	100	109	105
	EEC	96	97	99	100	104	96
	Germany	94	95	99	100	104	94
	Japan	NA	110	99	100	102	98
725	Domestic electrical equipment						
	U.K.	NA	NA	NA	100	97	100
	EEC	NA	100	102	100	98	98
	Germany	NA	99	102	100	97	97
726 & 729	Other elect. mach. and apparatus (incl. med. and radiol.)						
	U.K.	86	89	94	100	103	102
	EEC	96	92	96	100	103	101
	Germany	95	92	96	100	102	100
	Japan	NA	NA	100	100	93	93
729.1	Batteries and accumulators						
	EEC	NA	NA	98	100	101	106
	Germany	NA	NA	98	100	101	105
729.2	Electric lamps						
	EEC	NA	90	94	100	111	110
729.4	Automotive electrical equipment						
	Germany	NA	NA	NA	100	99	95
729.5	Elect. measuring and controlling instruments						
	U.K.	NA	86	95	100	96	94
	Germany	107	95	106	100	97	94
729.9	Electrical machinery and apparatus, n.e.s.						
	EEC	80	81	95	100	104	102
	Germany	81	83	95	100	104	101

Notes to Table D.5

Note: **SITC 72:** The index for each country is a weighted average of separate indexes for the five 3-digit groups or combinations listed in the table. The *EEC* and *German* indexes exclude 722 for 1953, and the *Japanese* index excludes 722, 723, and 725 for 1953 and 1957.

722: Indexes relative to the *United Kingdom* for SITC 722.1 are derived from place-to-place data for power transformers, instrument transformers, and generators, and a combination of place-to-place and time-to-time data for electric motors. The transformers and generators are weighted at 65 per cent and the electric motors at 35 per cent. Most of the data are from competitive bidding covering projects in the United States and many foreign countries. The indexes for SITC 722.2 are from a small number of place-to-place comparisons, not sufficient for publication.

The *German* indexes were derived from similar data, except that only time-to-time observations were used for electric motors in SITC 722.1 and for SITC 722.2 as a whole, as described in the note to Table C.5. The indexes for other *EEC* countries, which cover only SITC 722.1, were derived entirely from place-to-place comparisons for power transformers, generators, and electric motors, largely from bidding data. Both the Swiss and Swedish indexes were derived from place-to-place data for power transformers, instrument transformers, and generators, with the weight of instrument transformers held constant relative to that of power transformers and generators. Constant weights, based on the number of observations for each type in all years combined, were used because the instrument transformer price relatives were regularly lower than those of other products and it was important to eliminate fluctuations in the average due solely to fluctuation in the relative number of observations in the two groups.

The *Japanese* data are weakest of all, with each link based on fewer observations, all from place-to-place comparisons of power transformers, instrument transformers, generators, electric motors, and circuit breakers. The weight of electric motors was set at 35 per cent of SITC 722.1 in the years for which data were available. An alternative index of U.S. price competitiveness relative to *Japan* for SITC 722.1, calculated from time-to-time data for the two countries and using the U.S. international price index and the official Japanese export price indexes (see notes to Table C.5), is as follows (1962 = 100): *1961*, 84; *1962*, 100; *1963*, 110; *1964*, 110. In most groups this index from time series data would be the preferred one. Here, however, we use place-to-place data because of the weakness of the U.S. international price index.

Most of the bidding data for generators and power transformers was adjusted for differences in quality among offers, as reported by the purchasing agencies. In some cases, especially for instrument transformers, where there were no adjusted data or where the difference between adjusted and unadjusted data appeared to be due mainly to the limited coverage of the former, rather than to the adjustments, we used the unadjusted price comparisons.

For further discussion of bidding data see notes to Table E.5.

722.1 and **722.2:** See 722.

723: *U.K.* indexes are a combination of price competitiveness indexes for subgroups 723.1 and 723.2. The former are based on place-to-place data for 1957–64, and on weak time-to-time data for 1953–57; the latter are based on place-to-place data for 1961–64 and on time-to-time data for 1953–61. The *EEC* index is based on place-to-place comparisons for countries other than Germany, 1962–64, and on time-to-time data for Germany, 1953–64. *Japanese* indexes are derived entirely from place-to-place price comparisons.

(continued)

Notes to Table D.5 (concluded)

723.1 and **723.2:** See 723.

724:   The indexes of price competitiveness are built up entirely from time-to-time data using the price series underlying Table C.5. The price competitiveness table is more complete than Table C.5, however, since it makes use of subgroup indexes based on small numbers of series for which the comparison of two countries was considered more representative than either country's international price index. The *U.K.* index is a combination of price competitiveness indexes for SITC 724.1, portable transistor radios in SITC 724.2, and SITC 724.9. The *German* index is a combination of a price competitiveness index for SITC 724.1 and 724.2 combined, and one for SITC 724.9. Data are mostly from official export price data, and the relative weights of television and radio receivers in the German series are German export rather than world trade weights. The *EEC* index is mainly derived from German data with a few additional observations for other countries. The *Japanese* index is a combination of price competitiveness indexes for SITC 724.1, portable transistor radios in SITC 724.2, and SITC 724.9. The Japanese export price indexes used for 1957–61 actually refer to the period January 1960 to June–July 1961, and probably understate the fall in Japanese prices and in U.S. price competitiveness.

The indexes for Germany and the EEC are not strictly comparable to those for the United Kingdom and Japan because they include both portable transistor and other radios in SITC 724.2. A more comparable, but less complete, set of calculations using only transistor radios in SITC 724.2 and giving 724.2 only the weight of the transistor radio portion results in the following indexes of U.S. price competitiveness (1962 = 100):

	1953	1957	1961	1962	1963	1964
Telecommunications equipment (SITC 724)						
Relative to U.K.	98	99	100	100	107	104
Relative to EEC	97	102	100	100	102	98
Relative to Germany	96	100	100	100	102	97
Relative to Japan	NA	115	103	100	103	100
Television and radio receivers (SITC 724.1 and 724.2)						
Relative to U.K.	98	96	101	100	100	100
Relative to EEC	119	110	102	100	96	102
Relative to Germany	122	122	102	100	96	102
Relative to Japan	NA	137	117	100	106	107

All these indexes are based on small numbers of observations, considerably smaller, in the case of the EEC countries, than those used in Table D.5. Indexes for 1953 and 1957, omitted there, are shown here because, although the number of observations is smaller, we have more assurance of comparability between countries.

724.1, 724.2, and **724.9:** See 724.

725: Indexes are weighted averages of U.S. price competitiveness indexes for subgroups, each calculated from time-to-time data underlying the indexes of Table C.5.

726 and **729:** Data are from time-to-time indexes underlying Table C.5. Price competitiveness indexes were calculated for each 4-digit subgroup, and these were aggregated to total group price competitiveness indexes.

729.1, 729.2, 729.4, 729.5, and **729.9:** See 726 and 729.

Table D.6
Indexes of U.S. Price Competitiveness, Transport Equipment,
1953, 1957, 1961–64
(1962 = 100)

SITC Number	Commodity Group and Country	1953	1957	1961	1962	1963	1964
73	Transport equipment						
	U.K.	98	100	104	100	103	107
	EEC	107	105	101	100	101	102
	Germany	102	101	100	100	102	101
731	Railway vehicles						
	U.K.	NA	NA	102	100	103	NA
	EEC	89	86	94	100	100	102
	Germany	88	85	94	100	100	101
731.1,	Railway locomotives						
731.2, &	U.K.	NA	NA	102	100	102	NA
731.3	Germany	74	77	91	100	102	105
732	Road motor vehicles						
	U.K.	104	105	106	100	102	107
	EEC	107	105	102	100	103	104
	Germany	102	102	101	100	102	102
732.1 &	Passenger motor cars and chassis with engines mounted						
732.6	U.K.	109	105	106	100	101	106
	EEC	114	113	102	100	102	102
	Germany	106	107	101	100	102	100
	France	122	124	102	100	103	108
	Italy	138	122	108	100	101	101
	Japan	NA	167	113	100	95	92
732.2,	Buses, trucks, etc., and chassis with engines mounted						
732.3,	U.K.	94	104	106	100	103	110
732.4,	EEC	95	91	102	100	104	110
732.5, &	Germany	95	91	102	100	103	107
732.7							
734	Aircraft and parts						
	U.K.	NA	NA	NA	100	106	103
	France	NA	85	94	100	100	96
734.1	Aircraft, heavier than air						
	U.K.	NA	86	102	100	103	103
	France	NA	80	98	100	101	103

(continued)

Table D.6 (concluded)

SITC Number	Commodity Group and Country	1953	1957	1961	1962	1963	1964
735	Ships and boats						
	EEC	114	112	98	100	95	93
	Germany	110	106	94	100	97	95
	Japan	114	120	98	100	90	90

Note: SITC 73: The *U.K.* index is a weighted average of indexes for 731 (1961–1963 only), 732, 733 (road vehicles other than motor vehicles), 734 (except in 1953), and 735. The *EEC* and *German* indexes cover 731, 732, 733, and 735 for all years. *Japanese* data are limited to 735 (shown separately), and some data for the 1960s for 731 and 733 (not published). This is not sufficient to construct a Japan index for 73 as a whole.

731: The *U.K.* index is based on separate price competitiveness indexes for (1) 731.1, 731.2, and 731.3 combined (see note below), and (2) 731.7 (based on place-to-place data for parts of railway vehicles). The former was assigned the OECD export weight of 731.1–731.4, as given in Appendix A. The *EEC* index is a combination of a German index for 731.1 through 731.4 (see note below), and EEC competitiveness indexes for 731.5 and 731.6 combined and for 731.7, both based on time-to-time data. The *German* index is a combination of indexes derived from time-to-time data for 731.1 through 731.4 (see note below, 731.5 and 731.6 combined, and 731.7).

731.1, 731.2, and 731.3: The *U.K.* index is based on time-to-time indexes derived from selected bidding data. (See appendix to Chapter 14.) The *German* index covers 731.4 (self-propelled cars), as well as locomotives. It is based on time-to-time data underlying the international price indexes of Appendix C.

732: The indexes for the *United Kingdom,* the *EEC* and *Germany* are based on the two 4-digit combination subgroups, and on 732.8 (parts). Figures show ratios of foreign to U.S. international price indexes. International price indexes comparable to each other in coverage and method were used in each foreign-U.S. comparison in this table, whereas those in Table C.6 are the best estimates that could be made for each country, regardless of comparability. The differences, however, are slight.

732.1 and 732.6: The indexes for *France, Italy,* and *Japan* are based on time-to-time data. For other countries, see 732.

732.2, 732.3, 732.4, 732.5, and 732.7: See 732.

734: Indexes are derived entirely from the time-to-time indexes given in Table C.6. These were based on Civil Aeronautics Board data for U.S. airframes and engines and on company data for other aircraft and for all aircraft parts. Several alternative indexes were available but were considered less reliable. However, they may be interesting as indicators of the range of possibilities using other measurements. The results are as follows:

Aircraft and parts, relative to the United Kingdom: A U.K.-U.S. price competitiveness index based on CAB data for U.K. aircraft declined to 99 in 1964. However, this index covers only short-range aircraft, in which the U.K. position was most favorable. Substitution of U.S. company data completely independent of the CAB reports but comparable to the company data used in the U.K. index yields an index of 102.

Aircraft and parts, relative to France: Substitution of company reports for CAB data in the U.S. price index results in an index of U.S. price competitiveness of 95 instead of 96 in 1964, and one of 82 instead of 85 in 1957.

Complete aircraft, relative to the United Kingdom: Use of CAB data for U.K. aircraft prices indicates a decline in U.S. price competitiveness, but this comparison, as mentioned above, is confined to short-range aircraft. Substitution of company for CAB data on U.S. aircraft results in a 1964 price competitiveness index of 100.

Complete aircraft, relative to France: If company data are used for both the U.S. and France, the price competitiveness index for 1961 through 1963 shows no change, instead of a slight rise, but a somewhat larger gain in U.S. price competitiveness from 1957 through 1962.

734.1: See 734.

735: These indexes are derived from the international price indexes in Table C.6. The U.K. index given in the text produces the following index of price competitiveness relative to the United States: *1953*, 97; *1957*, 97; *1961*, 100; *1962*, 100; *1963*, 105; *1964*, 110.

Table D.7

Indexes of U.S. Price Competitiveness, Miscellaneous Manufactured
Articles, 1953, 1957, 1961–64

(1962 = 100)

SITC Number	Commodity Group and Country	1953	1957	1961	1962	1963	1964
861	Scientific, medical, etc., instruments and apparatus						
	U.K.	87	97	101	100	99	104
	Japan	NA	NA	101	100	102	100
861.4,	Photographic and cinematographic equipment, n.e.s.						
861.5, &	EEC	NA	NA	102	100	102	101
861.6	Germany	NA	NA	103	100	102	101
861.7	Medical instruments, n.e.s.						
	EEC	NA	NA	94	100	104	109
	Germany	NA	NA	94	100	104	109
861.9	Measuring, controlling, and scientific instruments, n.e.s.						
	U.K.	NA	105	107	100	97	102
	EEC	99	98	100	100	99	98
	Germany	98	98	100	100	99	98
891	Musical instruments, recorders, etc., and parts and accessories						
	U.K.	NA	NA	103	100	100	98
	EEC	NA	89	95	100	105	106
	Germany	NA	88	96	100	106	107
891.4	Pianos and other string musical instruments						
	EEC	NA	NA	99	100	106	102
	Germany	NA	NA	99	100	106	100

Note: **SITC 861:** The *U.K.* index is a combination of (1) price competitiveness indexes based on time-to-time data for 861.1, 861.2, and 861.3 combined (optical goods) 1957–64; 861.4, 861.5, and 861.6 combined, 1961–62; 861.7; and 861.9; and (2) an index based on a combination of time-to-time and place-to-place data for 861.8 (meters and counters, nonelectric). The *Japanese* index is based on time-to-time data and covers 861.1, 861.2, and 861.3 combined; 861.4, 861.5, and 861.6 combined; and 861.9.

    861.4, 861.5, and **861.6:** See 861 and 864.

    861.7: See 861 and 864.

    861.9: For the *United Kingdom*, see 861. For the *EEC* and *Germany*, see 861 and 864.

    891: The *U.K.* index for the 1960s is based on time-to-time data and covers 891.1 (phonographs, tape recorders, etc.); 891.2 (phonograph records, recorded tape, etc.), except 1961; 891.4; and 891.9 (parts and accessories of musical instruments). The *EEC* and *German* indexes for 1957–64 are based on time-to-time data and cover 891.1, 1964 only; 891.2, 1963 and 1964 only; 891.4; 891.8; and 891.9.

    891.4: See 891.

APPENDIX E

PRICE LEVEL INDEXES

General Note

This appendix contains tables showing price level indexes for SITC 2-digit commodity divisions, 3-digit groups, 4-digit subgroups, and in some cases, 5-digit items. The indexes are given in the tables for the subgroups and groups in which the amount and quality of the data were sufficient for publication. The notes that follow the table cover all the subgroups, including those not shown.

The indexes represent country-to-country comparisons of price levels of internationally traded goods at a given point in time. They are expressed as the ratio of a foreign country's price level to that of the United States for a single year.

These place-to-place indexes are aggregated from a 4-digit level. For each 4-digit subgroup a benchmark year was selected for which the best place-to-place data were available, and an index was calculated for that year. Place-to-place indexes for other years were then extrapolated from the benchmark index by the 4-digit index of price competitiveness (which, as explained in Appendix D, may be based in whole or in part on place-to-place data). Weighted averages for 3-digit groups were calculated for 1962, which was in general the year for which we had the best data. The resulting 3-digit 1962 averages were extrapolated to other years by the 3-digit indexes of price competitiveness.

Aggregation to the 2-digit level was done in the same manner, using 1962 as the benchmark and the 2-digit index of price competitiveness as the extrapolator.

For an explanation of 5-digit indexes, where they appear, see notes to the individual tables.

Table E.1
Price Level Indexes, Iron and Steel, 1953, 1957, 1961—64
(U.S. for each year = 100)

SITC Number	Commodity Group and Country	1953	1957	1961	1962	1963	1964
67	Iron and steel						
	U.K.	92	85	79	78	76	82
	EEC	88	87	76	74	72	78
	Germany	85	83	77	76	73	78
	Japan	NA	NA	75	70	70	70
673	Bars, rods, angles, shapes, and sections						
	U.K.	NA	84	80	79	76	84
	EEC	84	84	72	66	67	72
	Germany	78	80	72	68	68	74
	Japan	NA	NA	73	63	66	67
673.2	Bars and rods (excl. wire rod)						
	U.K.	NA	NA	79	81	78	NA
	EEC	73	74	64	59	62	63
	Germany	NA	70	62	60	62	64
	Japan	NA	NA	70	NA	NA	NA
673.4 & 673.5	Angles, shapes, and sections						
	U.K.	NA	NA	78	76	75	79
	EEC	NA	104	82	79	78	85
	Germany	NA	NA	82	80	77	84
	Japan	NA	NA	79	NA	NA	NA
674	Universals, plates, and sheets						
	U.K.	98	87	77	74	68	77
	EEC	92	91	76	76	70	76
	Germany	87	86	80	79	72	78
	Japan	NA	NA	80	73	70	71
674.1 & 674.2	——3mm. or more (excl. tinned)						
	U.K.	NA	NA	84	78	75	84
	EEC	NA	105	83	80	75	88
	Germany	NA	102	86	80	74	88
	Japan	NA	NA	NA	NA	NA	81
674.3	——less than 3 mm., uncoated						
	U.K.	NA	74	69	66	NA	NA
	EEC	NA	82	68	68	63	66

(continued)

Table E.1 (concluded)

SITC Number	Commodity Group and Country	1953	1957	1961	1962	1963	1964
674.3	—less than 3 mm., uncoated (continued)						
	Germany	NA	73	70	71	66	69
	Japan	NA	NA	NA	64	NA	NA
674.7	——Tinned						
	U.K.	NA	NA	NA	90	88	90
	EEC	NA	NA	90	NA	NA	NA
	Japan	NA	NA	NA	90	NA	NA
674.8	——less than 3 mm., coated (excl. tinned)						
	EEC	NA	NA	NA	79	NA	NA
	Germany	NA	NA	NA	79	NA	NA
675	Hoop and strip						
	EEC	NA	NA	NA	77	NA	NA
	Germany	NA	NA	NA	76	NA	NA
677	Iron and steel wire (excl. wire rod)						
	EEC	NA	81	69	66	65	70
	Japan	NA	NA	60	57	55	57
678	Tubes, pipes, and fittings						
	U.K.	86	82	80	84	86	87
	EEC	86	82	76	79	80	83
	Germany	86	78	76	78	80	82
	Japan	NA	NA	73	74	76	69
678.2	Tubes and pipes (excl. cast iron), seamless						
	U.K.	91	87	84	89	91	90
	EEC	111	90	82	86	87	87
	Germany	107	89	83	87	88	88
	Japan	NA	NA	70	70	76	73
678.3	Tubes and pipes (excl. cast iron) welded, etc.						
	U.K.	NA	NA	85	86	87	89
	EEC	NA	83	76	78	78	85
	Germany	NA	75	78	77	78	83
	Japan	NA	NA	NA	NA	NA	71
678.5	Tube and pipe fittings						
	U.K.	NA	NA	54	64	69	71
	EEC	NA	NA	61	65	67	65
	Germany	NA	NA	55	60	61	59
	Japan	NA	NA	NA	64	60	NA

Notes to Table E.1

Note: **SITC 67:** The 1962 price level index for each country is a weighted average of the 3-digit groups for which we had place-to-place data. For the *United Kingdom* all 3-digit groups are included except 679. In addition to the published indexes for 673, 674, and 678, described below, there are approximately 25 price level observations for the 3-digit groups which are not published separately. The *EEC* index excludes 676 and 679; and the *German* index, 671, 676, and 679. In addition to the 3-digit indexes shown in the table, there are a dozen observations in each case covering the unpublished groups. The *Japanese* index covers only 673, 674, 677, and 678, all of which are described below.

673: The 1962 price level indexes for the *United Kingdom* and *Germany* are each based on the 1962 weighted average of 673.2, and 673.4, and 673.5 combined, described below. The 1962 *EEC* and *Japanese* indexes are derived in the same way except that in each case one or two observations for 673.1 are also included in the average. In the case of Japan, the extrapolation to 1962 of 673.2 and of 673.4 and 673.5 combined is not shown in the table, since the indexes of price competitiveness for these two groups are not reliable enough to publish separately.

673.2: The benchmark year is 1961 for all countries. There were 22 place-to-place observations for that year for the *United Kingdom*, 26 for the *EEC*, 12 for *Germany*, and 16 for *Japan*.

673.4 and 673.5: The price level in 1964, based on 36 observations, is the benchmark for the *U.K.* index. For the *EEC* and *Germany* the benchmark is the 1962 level, with 66 EEC observations, 52 of which were for Germany. The *Japanese* price level index is shown only for 1961, for which we had 13 observations.

674: The 1962 price level index for the *United Kingdom* is the weighted average of the 1962 indexes for 674.1 and 674.2 combined, 674.3, and 674.7, described below. The *EEC* and *German* 1962 price level indexes are the weighted averages of 1962 indexes for all four 4-digit groups. The 1962 *EEC* price level for 674.7 is not shown in the table, since the index of price competitiveness for this group is not reliable enough to publish separately. The extrapolated index for 1962, however, is included in the 674 average. For *Germany* the 674.7 index, not shown in the table but included in the aggregation, is based on two place-to-place observations for 1962. The 1962 *Japanese* price level index is a weighted average of 1962 indexes for 674.1 and 674.2 combined, 674.3, and 674.7. The 1962 Japanese price level for 674.1 and 674.2 combined is not shown in the table, since the index of price competitiveness used as an extrapolator is not reliable enough to publish separately.

674.1 and 674.2: The benchmark year for the *U.K.*, the *EEC*, and *Germany* is 1962, with 44 observations for the United Kingdom, and 100 for the EEC, 83 of which are for Germany. The *Japanese* index is based on 32 place-to-place observations for 1964.

674.3: The benchmark year for the *U.K.* and *Japan* is 1962, with from 10 to 15 observations for each country. For the *EEC* and *Germany* the benchmark year is 1963, with 24 observations, half of which are for Germany.

674.7: The benchmark year for the *United Kingdom* and *Japan* is 1962, with between 5 and 10 observations for each. The *EEC* benchmark is 1961, based on 10 observations.

674.8: The benchmark for both *EEC* and German indexes is 1962, based on 71 German observations.

675: The benchmark year is 1962 for both the *EEC* and *Germany*. The EEC index for that year is based on 19 place-to-place observations, 16 of which are for *Germany*.

677: The *EEC* benchmark is 1962, with 47 observations. For *Japan,* 1964 is the benchmark year, for which we had 10 observations.

678: The 1962 price level index for each country is the weighted average of the 1962 indexes for 678.2, 678.3, and 678.5, described below. The 1962 *Japanese* price level for 678.3 is not shown in the table, since the index of competitiveness for this group is not reliable enough to publish separately. The extrapolated index for 1962, however, is included in the 678 average.

678.2: The benchmark year is 1964 for the *United Kingdom,* the *EEC,* and *Germany.* The indexes for that year are based on 91 U.K. observations and 128 EEC observations, 71 of which are for *Germany.* The *Japanese* benchmark year is 1963, with 73 observations.

678.3: The benchmark year is 1962 for the *United Kingdom,* the *EEC,* and *Germany.* The indexes for that year are based on 13 U.K. observations, and 51 EEC observations, 18 of which are for *Germany.* The *Japanese* benchmark year is 1964, with 31 observations.

678.5: The benchmark year for each country is 1962. For that year we have between 100 and 150 place-to-place observations for the *United Kingdom* and the *EEC* and between 40 and 50 for *Germany* and *Japan.*

Table E.2
Price Level Indexes, Nonferrous Metals, 1953, 1957, 1961–64
(U.S. for each year = 100)

SITC Number	Commodity Group and Country	1953	1957	1961	1962	1963	1964
68	Nonferrous metals						
	U.K.	92	93	93	92	94	98
	EEC	96	93	91	91	92	99
	Germany	98	98	93	94	93	100
682	Copper						
	U.K.	94	93	93	94	94	99
	EEC	96	96	95	94	94	105
682.2	Copper and alloys, worked						
	U.K.	NA	NA	NA	88	NA	NA
684	Aluminum						
	U.K.	90	94	94	92	95	95
	EEC	96	90	90	89	90	90
	Germany	NA	NA	NA	94	NA	NA
684.1	Aluminum and aluminum alloys, unwrought						
	U.K.	NA	NA	NA	95	NA	NA
	EEC	NA	NA	NA	95	NA	NA
	Germany	NA	NA	NA	101	NA	NA
684.2	Aluminum and aluminum alloys, worked						
	U.K.	NA	NA	NA	86	NA	NA
	EEC	NA	NA	NA	80	NA	NA
	Germany	NA	NA	NA	82	NA	NA

Note: **SITC 68:** The 1962 price level index for each country is a weighted average of the indexes for eight of the nine 3-digit groups which make up SITC 68. The one group omitted was 688 (uranium and thorium and their alloys), which represents only 0.03 per cent of the weight of the total group. No Japanese data were available for SITC 68. For 682 (copper) and 684 (aluminum), see notes below. For a discussion of the data on other nonferrous metals in the 68 group, see Chapter 10.

682: For the *U.K.* index the best data available for both 682.1 (unwrought copper) and 682.2 (worked copper) were for 1962. The 682 index for 1962 is, therefore, a weighted average of direct 1962 place-to-place observations for both 4-digit groups. For the *EEC* the benchmarks are 1962 for 682.1 and 1961 for 682.2. The 682 index for 1962 is therefore a combination of direct observations for 682.1 and an extrapolated index for 682.2.

682.2: See 682.

684: The 1962 indexes are weighted averages of direct observations of 1962 price levels for 684.1 and 684.2. The number of observations is substantial for that year, in some cases numbering several hundred.

684.1 and 684.2: See 684.

Table E.3
Price Level Indexes, Miscellaneous Metal Manufactures, 1953, 1957, 1961–64
(U.S. for each year = 100)

SITC Number	Commodity Group and Country	1953	1957	1961	1962	1963	1964
69	Manufactures of metal, n.e.s.						
	U.K.	97	95	97	92	92	92
	EEC	97	96	97	96	93	91
	Germany	90	87	92	92	91	90
	Japan	NA	NA	74	74	69	73
691	Finished structural parts and structures, n.e.s.						
	U.K.	NA	NA	NA	NA	93	NA
	EEC	NA	NA	144	NA	NA	NA
692	Metal containers for storage and transport						
	U.K.	NA	103	91	93	88	85
	EEC	125	107	96	98	95	96
	Japan	NA	NA	NA	95	89	NA
692.1	Tanks, vats, etc., for storage or manufacturing						
	U.K.	NA	NA	86	90	81	80
	EEC	NA	NA	NA	NA	84	NA
692.2	Casks, drums, boxes, cans, etc., for transport						
	U.K.	NA	NA	94	96	94	89
	EEC	127	108	98	99	97	98
693	Wire products (excl. electric) and fencing grills						
	U.K.	NA	95	100	95	89	89
	EEC	65	72	78	77	72	76
	Germany	74	82	90	85	80	87
	Japan	NA	NA	89	86	78	76
693.1	Wire cables, ropes, etc., not insulated						
	U.S.	NA	103	108	97	92	NA
	EEC	NA	70	80	77	66	72
	Germany	NA	NA	87	78	68	79
	Japan	NA	NA	88	86	71	NA
693.3	Gauze, netting, grill, fencing, etc., of wire						
	EEC	NA	NA	75	76	77	80
694	Nails, screws, nuts, bolts, etc., iron, steel, or copper						
	U.K.	NA	NA	89	89	87	79
	EEC	97	88	89	88	85	83

(continued)

Table E.3 (concluded)

SITC Number	Commodity Group and Country	1953	1957	1961	1962	1963	1964
694.1	Nails, tacks, staples, spikes, etc.						
	U.K.	NA	NA	80	NA	NA	NA
	EEC	NA	NA	69	70	67	69
694.2	Nuts, bolts, screws, rivets, washers, etc.						
	U.K.	NA	NA	NA	91	NA	NA
	EEC	NA	NA	99	97	94	89
695	Tools for use in the hand or in machines						
	U.K.	NA	NA	101	100	99	99
	Germany	75	71	79	81	80	81
696	Cutlery						
	Japan	NA	NA	74	76	82	91
698	Manufactures of metal, n.e.s.						
	U.K.	87	77	80	84	85	87
	EEC	97	96	91	91	93	89
	Germany	96	94	89	89	91	87
	Japan	NA	NA	NA	NA	NA	73

Note: **SITC 69:** The 1962 benchmark indexes are weighted averages of the 1962 indexes for the 3-digit groups for which we have data. All eight 3-digit groups are included in the *U.K.* and *EEC* indexes for 69. The *German* index excludes 691. The *Japanese* index is based only on 692, 693, 695, and 696. Benchmark levels estimated at the 3- or 4-digit level are based on a total of over 400 observations for the United Kingdom, about the same number for EEC, approximately 150 for Germany, and about 170 for Japan. Indexes for 697, not shown separately, are based on 1963 benchmark data.

691: This group was treated as a whole since data are not detailed enough for a 4-digit breakdown. The benchmark year for the *United Kingdom* is 1963; and for the *EEC*, 1961. Extrapolation to other years is not shown, since the indexes of competitiveness are not sufficiently reliable to publish separately.

692: The 1962 *U.K.* benchmark is a weighted average of 692.1 and 692.2, shown separately and described below. The 1962 *EEC* benchmark is a weighted average of 692.1, 692.2, and 692.3. The first two of these components are described below. For 692.3 we had a 1964 benchmark level based on nine observations and extrapolated to 1962 by the index of competitiveness for 692 as a whole. The *Japanese* index is based on a few 1963 place-to-place observations for 692.1 (extrapolated to 1962 by a competitiveness index for that group), and for 692.2 (extrapolated to 1962 by the competitiveness index for 692 as a whole). The *German* index, not good enough to publish separately, covers 692.2 only.

692.1: For both the *United Kingdom* and the *EEC* the benchmark year is 1963. There were 12 place-to-place observations in each case.

692.2: For both the *United Kingdom* and the *EEC* the benchmark year is 1964. There were 23 observations for the United Kingdom and 31 for the EEC.

693: For the *United Kingdom,* the *EEC,* and *Germany* the 1962 benchmarks are weighted averages of 693.1, 693.2, and 693.3, representing over 98 per cent of the total weight of 693. For the United Kingdom the benchmark year is 1962 for all subgroups. For the EEC the benchmark year is 1962 for 693.1, 1964 for 693.2, and 1963 for 693.3. For Germany the benchmark year is 1962 for 693.1 and 693.2 and 1963 for 693.3. The *Japanese* benchmark level for 1962 is based solely on 693.1.

693.1 and **693.3:** See 693.

694: For both the *United Kingdom* and the *EEC* the 1962 benchmark is a weighted average of 694.1 and 694.2 (see notes below). A *German* index was also constructed, based on 1961 place-to-place data and indexes of competitiveness for both 694.1 and 694.2. This *German* index is included in the 69 aggregate but is not based on sufficient data to show separately.

694.1: For both the *United Kingdom* and the *EEC* the benchmark year is 1961. Extrapolation to other years is not shown for the United Kingdom, since the index of competitiveness is not sufficiently reliable to publish separately.

694.2: The benchmark year for the *United Kingdom* is 1962, and for the *EEC,* 1961.

695, 696, and **698:** These groups are each treated on the 3-digit level, since data were not detailed enough for a 4-digit breakdown. The benchmark year for all countries is 1962 for 695, and 1963 for 696. For 698 the benchmark year is 1963 for the *United Kingdom,* 1962 for the *EEC* and *Germany,* and 1964 for *Japan.*

Table E.4

Price Level Indexes, Machinery Other than Electric, 1953, 1957, 1961—64
(U.S. for each year = 100)

SITC Number	Commodity Group and Country	1953	1957	1961	1962	1963	1964
71	Machinery other than electric						
	U.K.	89	90	90	90	90	91
	EEC	92	89	91	93	93	92
	Germany	92	88	91	93	93	93
711	Power generating machinery other than electric						
	U.K.	99	94	93	93	91	93
	EEC	100	94	93	96	95	92
	Germany	96	89	91	94	94	89
711.4	Aircraft engines (incl. jet propulsion engines)						
	U.K.	NA	94	98	97	92	91
711.5	Internal combustion engines exc. for aircraft						
	U.K.	97	95	90	90	88	94
	EEC	101	95	94	96	95	92
	Germany	100	90	91	94	93	88
712	Agricultural machinery and implements						
	U.K.	88	90	86	86	86	86
	EEC	92	92	91	91	90	90
712.5	Tractors, other than road tractors						
	U.K.	80	82	79	78	77	78
	EEC	87	86	84	84	85	86
714	Office machines						
	U.K.	98	97	97	100	97	97
	EEC	117	98	97	99	98	96
	Germany	115	96	96	99	97	96
714.2	Calculating, accounting machines, etc. (incl. electronic computers)						
	U.K.	104	103	100	102	97	96
	EEC	120	100	100	103	100	98
715	Metalworking machinery						
	U.K.	77	80	81	85	86	87
	EEC	77	80	88	88	88	87
715.1	Machine tools for working metals						
	U.K.	77	80	81	85	86	87
	EEC	75	78	86	86	85	84
	Germany	80	82	87	87	89	88

(continued)

Table E.4 (continued)

SITC Number	Commodity Group and Country	1953	1957	1961	1962	1963	1964
	Metal-cutting machine tools						
	U.K.	73	76	77	80	80	81
	EEC	72	73	82	80	78	78
	Germany	76	78	82	81	82	81
	Metal-forming machine tools						
	U.K.	84	88	90	97	101	100
	EEC	82	90	96	99	105	97
	Germany	88	90	99	101	108	104
715.2	Metalworking machinery other than machine tools						
	EEC	NA	NA	94	95	95	97
	Germany	NA	NA	93	94	94	96
717	Textile and leather machinery						
	U.K.	83	83	84	85	86	87
	EEC	89	86	87	88	88	88
	Germany	89	86	87	88	88	89
717.1	Textile machinery						
	EEC	88	84	85	86	86	87
	Germany	88	84	86	86	87	88
717.2	Machinery (excl. sewing) for hides, skins, or leather						
	U.K.	NA	NA	NA	71	71	65
	EEC	NA	77	74	76	75	76
717.3	Sewing machines						
	EEC	95	95	94	96	95	95
	Germany	96	96	95	97	96	96
718	Machines for special industries						
	U.K.	NA	106	106	104	102	102
	Germany	NA	99	103	106	104	106
718.2	Printing and bookbinding machinery						
	U.K.	92	97	96	93	93	94
	Germany	92	89	94	93	91	96
718.3	Food-processing machines (excl. domestic)						
	U.K.	NA	NA	NA	NA	NA	134
	EEC	99	89	91	92	93	95
	Germany	101	91	94	94	93	95
718.4	Construction and mining machinery, n.e.s.						
	U.K.	NA	109	109	108	107	107
	EEC	NA	NA	NA	NA	111	NA
	Germany	NA	106	110	115	114	114

(continued)

Table E.4 (continued)

SITC Number	Commodity Group and Country	1953	1957	1961	1962	1963	1964
718.4	Construction and mining machinery, n.e.s. (continued)						
	Japan	NA	NA	103	102	100	97
718.5	Mineral crushing, sorting, etc., machinery; glassworking machinery						
	U.K.	NA	NA	90	88	80	NA
	Germany	NA	NA	NA	NA	100	NA
719	Machinery and appliances (nonelect.) and parts, n.e.s.						
	U.K.	85	85	85	86	87	88
	EEC	84	84	88	90	91	91
	Germany	84	82	87	90	91	91
719.1	Heating and cooling equipment						
	U.K.	NA	NA	94	94	94	93
	EEC	101	102	103	104	105	102
	Germany	85	87	97	101	103	102
719.2	Pumps and centrifuges						
	U.K.	92	100	96	97	96	95
	EEC	97	95	98	101	100	100
	Germany	95	91	96	100	99	99
719.3	Mechanical handling equipment						
	U.K.	NA	86	84	83	89	91
	EEC	72	80	81	86	85	85
	Germany	NA	73	74	78	78	77
719.31	Lifting and loading machinery						
	U.K.	NA	83	81	80	86	89
	EEC	NA	76	77	82	81	82
	Germany	NA	69	70	75	74	74
	France	NA	NA	NA	106	102	106
	Italy	NA	NA	NA	NA	81	NA
	Japan	NA	NA	NA	NA	73	80
719.32	Forklift and other industrial trucks						
	U.K.	NA	NA	NA	NA	101	103
	EEC	NA	105	105	106	106	102
719.5	Powered tools, n.e.s.						
	U.K.	95	90	93	90	92	89
	Germany	89	83	92	98	97	99
719.6 & 719.8	Nonelect. mach. and appliances, n.e.s. (excl. household appliances)						
	U.K.	NA	82	84	84	83	86
	EEC	82	82	89	91	92	96
	Germany	84	86	92	93	94	98

(continued)

Table E.4 (concluded)

SITC Number	Commodity Group and Country	1953	1957	1961	1962	1963	1964
719.9	Parts and accessories of machinery, n.e.s.						
	U.K.	NA	NA	63	66	70	69
	EEC	74	70	70	72	75	74
	Germany	73	69	70	72	75	74
719.92	Taps, cocks, valves, and similar appliances, n.e.s.						
	U.K.	78	69	67	69	72	74
	EEC	87	76	75	77	79	79
	Germany	80	70	71	73	77	77
	Japan	NA	NA	NA	70	71	89

Note: **SITC 71:** The 1962 index for each country is a weighted average of the seven 3-digit component groups.

711: The 1962 *U.K.* index is a weighted average of 1962 indexes for all component 4-digit groups except 711.6 and 711.7, which were relatively insignificant in OECD exports. For 711.2 and 711.8 we had 1961 benchmark levels, and for 711.3 a 1963 benchmark level. Since we did not have indexes of competitiveness for these three subgroups, the price level indexes were extrapolated to 1962 by the 3-digit competitiveness index. For 711.1 the benchmark is 1962 (see notes below for 711.4 and 711.5). The 1962 *EEC* and *German* indexes are weighted averages of the 1962 indexes for all component 4-digit groups except 711.4 and 711.7. For 711.2 we had a 1961 benchmark level; and for 711.3, a 1963 one. Since we did not have indexes of competitiveness for these two subgroups, the price level indexes were extrapolated to 1962 by the 3-digit competitiveness index (see notes below for 711.5).

711.4: The basis for the place-to-place indexes for complete aircraft engines is a multiple correlation between engine price, power (thrust), and weight, for 20 U.S. and British aircraft engines available in 1962. For a detailed description of the derivation of this equation, and comparisons with alternative measures, see the appendix to Chapter 12. The average ratio of British prices to those calculated from the regression line was divided by the average ratio for American prices to give the place-to-place index for complete aircraft engines (excluding parts) in 1962, and this ratio was extrapolated to other years by the competitiveness index for complete aircraft engines, based on time-to-time data.

A place-to-place index for aircraft engine parts for 1964 was calculated from company price data, and extrapolated back to 1962 by the competitiveness index for parts. This was combined with the 1962 index for complete engines, assuming equal weights for parts and engines.

711.5: This group was further subdivided by type of engine, and 1962 price levels were estimated separately for three types, as follows:

	U.K.	EEC	Germany
Automotive diesel engines	70	NA	85
Outboard motors	94	100	NA
Parts of internal combustion engines	87	95	90

(continued)

Notes to Table E.4 (continued)

The 1962 indexes for automotive diesel engines are mainly from Chapter 5. The indexes for outboard motors are from the appendix to Chapter 12, and those for engine parts are based on nearly 200 price comparisons by purchasers of parts, mainly engine manufacturers. The above indexes were combined with other data for gasoline engines and automotive and marine diesels, mainly from U.S. and foreign buyers, using the following weights: diesel, 4; outboard, 1; gasoline, 2; parts, 8.

712: The indexes were built up from indexes for each subgroup, but only 712.5 (tractors) is reliable enough to publish separately. Within the latter subgroup the *U.K.-U.S.* tractor comparisons are based on nearly a score of observations for 1964, obtained from 10 different sources, mostly producers. The *EEC* comparison with the United States is based on a dozen tractors; half of the comparisons were between German and U.S. prices. In some cases, where prices of tractors that were reported to be similar and competitive differed in horsepower and weight, we compared the extent and direction of the deviations of actual foreign and U.S. prices from the prices estimated by the logarithmic regression equation (based on 61 observations and including weight and horsepower) described in the appendix to Chapter 12. The comparisons for the subgroups other than tractors are based on 8 to 10 observations for 1963.

712.5: See 712.

714: The 1962 index for each country is a weighted average of the four 4-digit subgroups. Data for subgroup 714.1 are mainly price comparisons by purchasers and cost data from international companies producing in several countries. There are also some export comparisons from companies operating in several countries. The benchmark year for this subgroup is 1962 for the *United Kingdom* and 1964 for the *EEC* and *Germany*. Indexes for subgroups 714.2 and 714.3 are mainly from export price reports of international companies and cost data. Benchmark years are 1962 for 714.2, 1963 for 714.3 for the United Kingdom, and 1961 for 714.3 for the EEC and Germany. Price levels for 714.9 are a combination of data for item 714.91, from company export price comparisons, with estimates for machine parts based on the corresponding machine indexes. The benchmark year is 1962 for all countries for 714.9.

The place-to-place comparisons for benchmark years are based on over 35 observations from eight sources for the *United Kingdom,* on from 10 to 15 observations from six sources for *Germany,* and on more than 40 observations from eleven sources for the *EEC* as a whole.

714.2: See 714.

715: The *U.K.* index is based on 715.1 only. The 1962 indexes for the *EEC* and *Germany* are weighted averages of 715.1 and 715.2.

715.1: Benchmark levels were calculated for 1962. The *U.K.* relative price level estimate for 1962 is based on more than 50 comparisons with U.S. prices, covering all but one of the machine tool categories. About two-thirds of the data were supplied by sellers of machine tools, including U.S. companies with U.K. subsidiaries. The *EEC* estimate is composed of about 70 observations with all categories of tools included, but only about 30 observations were available for the *German* index.

For three types of machine tools there are enough observations to permit the publication of separate indexes, shown below:

	U.S.	U.K.	EEC
Drilling machines	100	NA	83
Lathes	100	NA	87
Milling machines	100	70	85

A completely independent source of machine tool price comparisons is provided by a survey of distributors of U.S. machine tools in thirty-six foreign countries taken by the National Tool Builders' Association in 1963. The results were published in *Survey of Foreign Machine Tool Markets*, National Machine Tool Builders' Association, Washington (no date, but probably 1963). These foreign distributors were asked to estimate both the price differential and the quality differential between U.S. and foreign machine tools in their countries. For each importing country we computed a quality-adjusted place-to-place comparison among the exporters' prices from these two estimates by dividing the price ratio by the quality ratio, and further adjusted it for differences in tariffs levied on tools from different sources of supply. We then averaged these across the list of purchasing countries, weighting each purchasing country's observations equally. The results follow, for the indexes unadjusted and adjusted for quality differences:

Country of Origin of Tools	Unadjusted	Adjusted
U.S.	100	100
U.K.	72	87
EEC	68	85
Germany	70	84
France	71	90
Italy	62	90
Switzerland	82	86
Japan	57	94

Both sets of indexes have been adjusted for tariff differences to place sellers' prices on an f.a.s. basis.

715.2: Relative price levels for 1961–64 as a whole were estimated from place-to-place comparisons for the *United Kingdom,* the *EEC,* and *Germany.* The years were combined because of the scarcity of place-to-place data in this group. More than 10 individual price comparisons were used for the United Kingdom and German price levels and approximately 30 for the EEC level.

These price level estimates for Germany and the EEC countries were then extrapolated to individual years by the indexes of price competitiveness. For the United Kingdom no extrapolation was possible since we did not have an index of price competitiveness.

Data for 1956 and 1957, insufficient for calculation of reliable indexes, suggest that the *German* and *EEC* price levels, particularly the former, were considerably lower relative to the United States, at about 80, while the *U.K.* relative price level was substantially higher than in 1961–64 and probably a bit above the U.S. level.

717: The 1962 indexes are weighted averages of the three 4-digit subgroups.

717.1: The benchmark year for the *EEC* and *Germany* is 1963. For the *United Kingdom* an index was constructed based on 1962 benchmark data. This 1962 index is included in the 3-digit aggregate, but is not sufficiently reliable to publish separately. For information on type and quantity of data for all countries see Chapter 12.

717.2: The benchmark year for the *United Kingdom* was 1964 and for the *EEC* 1963. A German index, not published separately, was constructed based on a 1963 benchmark, and the 1962 extrapolated figure is included in the 3-digit aggregate. For information on type and quantity of data for all countries, see Chapter 12.

717.3: The benchmark year for the *EEC* is 1964; and for Germany, 1963. A *U.K.*

(continued)

Notes to Table E.4 (continued)

index, not published separately, is based on a 1964 benchmark, and the 1962 extra-polated figure is included in the 3-digit aggregate. For information on type and quantity of data for all countries see Chapter 12.

718: The 1962 *U.K.* index is a weighted average of the five 4-digit subgroups. For 718.1 a 1963 benchmark index was extrapolated to 1962 by the 3-digit index of price competitiveness. For other 4-digit subgroups, see notes below. The 1962 *German* index covers all 4-digit subgroups except 718.1 (see notes below). An *EEC* index covering all five subgroups was constructed and included in the aggregation for SITC 71, but was not sufficiently reliable to publish separately.

718.2 The benchmark year is 1962 for both the *United Kingdom* and *Germany* as well as for the unpublished *EEC* index. The 1962 indexes are composed mainly of place-to-place comparisons for that year by buyers, including about 15–20 observations for both the *U.K.*-to-*U.S.* and the *German*-to-*U.S.* comparisons. The great bulk of the data is for printing equipment, which is weighted at almost three-quarters of the total.

Another set of price level estimates can be calculated using place-to-place data for all years, which we consider to be less reliable in this group than the time-to-time data. These give the following results:

	1953	1957	1961	1962	1963	1964
U.K.	83	90	95	93	95	98
Germany	90	90	92	93	94	103

These comparisons for years other than 1962 are from the same sources as the 1962 index used above. The 1961–63 indexes for both Germany and the United Kingdom should be about as reliable as those for 1962, but the earlier and later ones cover a narrower range of products and include fewer observations.

718.3: The benchmark year for the *United Kingdom*, the *EEC*, and *Germany* is 1964. Indexes for 1964 were derived from approximately 20 place-to-place observations, about evenly divided between relatives for the United Kingdom and relatives for the EEC. A 1961 *U.K.* index of 123 was also calculated from place-to-place data. For aggregating, the U.K. index was extrapolated to 1962 by the 718 index of price competi-tiveness, since we did not have a 4-digit price competitiveness index. Some remarks in one of the sources used suggest that the 1964 ratio for EEC countries other than Germany may be understated because quality differences were not taken into account. Independent data for 1963 suggest that German and other EEC prices in that year were both slightly higher than U.S. prices.

718.4: The benchmark year for all countries is 1963. The 1963 indexes combine buyers' and sellers' observations. Most are bid data from buyers, covering a wide variety of construction equipment, but only a few observations involve mining or oil-well dril-ling equipment. The *U.K., EEC,* and *German* indexes each include 15–20 observations, and the *Japanese* index includes about 10. The indexes for other years are derived from indexes of price competitiveness based on time-to-time data, and thus do not represent an independent check on them, but there are a few independent observations. An aver-age of *U.K.* price relatives for 1964, composed of fewer items and different ones from the 1963 index, is 105. A smaller set of relatives, roughly comparable in coverage in the two years, shows averages of 105 in 1963 and 104 in 1964. For *Japan*, a very small set of place-to-place observations confirms the indication of a fall in Japanese prices relative to U.S. ones. In a few cases we could compare prices offered by U.S. companies with those offered by their subsidiaries in the United Kingdom for the same model of a machine. In all of these cases the U.K. price was lower than the U.S. one, and the average ratios for 1963 and 1964 were 93 and 96 per cent. These comparisons are likely to involve machines more similar from one country to another than those usually compared. However, their production by U.S. subsidiaries suggests that they may not have been a random sample of either U.K. or U.S. export items.

718.5: The benchmark year is 1963 for both the *United Kingdom* and *Germany,* as well as for the unpublished *EEC* index.

The U.K. price level for 1963 is based on the average of more than ten items including both complete machines and machine parts.

Approximately two-thirds of the items were parts; and one-third, complete machines. If the ratios are reweighted to give equal weights to parts and complete machines, the 1963 average is about 87, and if complete machines are given twice the weight of parts, it is about 93. There are no world trade weights distinguishing parts from complete machines, but U.S. export data for some of the machines and their parts suggest that the complete machines should have between one-half and two-thirds of the total weight. Such a weighting of the two groups would give an index of 90 instead of the 80 per cent shown here.

The *German* price level for 1963 is an average ratio for more than five items, all but one of which were complete machines.

719: The 1962 index for each country is a weighted average of all 4-digit components except 719.4 (domestic appliances, nonelectric). For 719.7, not shown separately, the indexes are based on 1962 benchmark data. For other subgroups, see notes below.

719.1: The benchmark year is 1962 for the *United Kingdom,* the *EEC,* and *Germany.* The place-to-place comparisons are based on reports from about thirty-five sources. The basic procedure was to adjust individual reports to 1962 through the use of the appropriate 5-digit time-to-time indexes. Each of the basic foreign-U.S. comparisons was computed from more than a score of observations.

719.2: The benchmark year was 1963 for the *United Kingdom,* the *EEC,* and *Germany.* Each benchmark is a weighted average of place-to-place price relatives for 1963 for each of the three subcategories. In some cases the underlying 5-digit relatives were simple averages for 1963, but more often advantage was taken of the stability of the international price relationships in 1962–64 to pool data for these years. For 719.21 and 719.22, the 1963 estimates are based on from around 35 to 125 comparisons, but for 719.23 only around a dozen observations were available.

719.3, 719.31, and 719.32: The 719.3 benchmark year is 1963 for the *United Kingdom,* the *EEC,* and *Germany.* For the *United Kingdom,* the index of price competitiveness used for extrapolation to other years was derived from place-to-place observations ranging from 5 in 1953 to 15–20 or more in later years. Most of these were in 719.31, and for that reason the index for 719.32 was strong enough to publish only for 1963 and 1964. Almost all of the data were supplied by buyers of equipment, excepting mainly loaders in SITC 719.31 and forklift trucks in 719.32. All the indexes contain wide ranges of price ratios, partly, but not completely, associated with identifiable groups of commodities, and therefore exhibit considerable erratic fluctuation. Comparisons for forklift trucks, loaders, and complex conveying systems tended to be more favorable to the United States than those for cranes and hoists. Among the latter group were a fair number of bids at prices over 40 and even over 50 per cent below U.S. prices, without any clear U.S. quality margin, according to the purchasers.

(continued)

Notes to Table E.4 (continued)

The *German* index for 1963 is derived from approximately 15 place-to-place observations, mainly supplied by purchasers from bid data. The data for 719.32, too thin to produce a publishable index, show German prices at approximately the level of U.S. ones. The German price level for 719.31 may be affected by the lack of German price data for loaders, an item for which U.S. prices tended to be much more competitive than for the cranes and hoists which make up the rest of the subgroup. The U.K. index for 1963, for example, would have been almost five percentage points lower if loaders had been excluded. Separate *French* and *Italian* indexes could be calculated only for SITC 719.31, and only for 1962–64 for France and 1963 for Italy. Even these indexes are based on only 5 to 10 place-to-place observations, mainly from bids reported by purchasers. The comparisons do not cover loaders, and the indexes probably have some downward bias on that account. The *EEC* index for SITC 719.31 is a combination of the German, French, and Italian indexes (weighted by the importance of each country in exports of this subgroup). The French and Italian indexes were extrapolated by the German index to years not covered by their data.

The EEC index for SITC 719.32 is an unweighted average of about 5 observations for 1962–64, extrapolated to individual years by the index for Germany. For 1963 the two subgroup indexes are combined using world trade weights. The *Japanese* data for 719.31 are entirely from almost 20 place-to-place observations for the two years, supplied by purchasers. The movement from one year to the next is not reliable, because of the small number of observations and the wide range of the ratios.

719.5: The benchmark year is 1963 for the *United Kingdom* and *Germany*, and 1962 for the unpublished EEC index. The 1963 price levels for both the United Kingdom and Germany are averages of place-to-place price relatives for that year. The U.K. index is an average of about 15 observations from buyers in subgroups 719.52 and 719.53, with subgroup indexes averaged to calculate the total index. The German index is a similar average, but containing only about 10 observations, also from buyers.

In subgroup 719.53 we have data on a series of bids in 1963 in which several countries participated. These provide a set of comparisons for essentially identical specifications in this group. The average ratios for these bids follow (per cent of United States):

	U.K.	Germany	Sweden
All available bids (11,7, and 10 items)	87	95	87
Items on which all those countries bid (7 items)	82	95	75
Items on which U.K. and Sweden bid (9 items)	89		86

The U.K. level for 719.53 used in the computations for the group as a whole was 85, and that for Germany was 95.

It was possible in subgroup 719.53 to make a number of comparisons between prices offered by American companies in 1963 and those offered by their foreign subsidiaries to the same buyers, and to compare these with offers by other U.S. and foreign companies. The results suggested that, in this group at least, the comparison with subsidiaries was not equivalent to a comparison of the lowest prices offered by each country and might, in fact, be seriously biased against the United States. In every case the ratio of lowest prices was more favorable to the United States than the ratio of subsidiary to parent company prices and the averages, for four items, were: foreign subsidiary price to parent company price (8 pairs), 50 per cent; lowest price in foreign country to lowest

U.S. price, 82 per cent. The very low ratio between parent companies and their subsidiaries was confirmed by completely independent data provided by U.S. producers. We decided that parent-subsidiary comparisons in this subgroup did not provide the comparisons among lowest offers from each country called for by the design of our study and therefore excluded them from the place-to-place averages. The reason for the large difference between the two types of place-to-place information is made clear by the following data: Ratio, U.S. parent company price to lowest U.S. price, 194 per cent; foreign subsidiary price to lowest foreign price, 108 per cent. The U.S. parent companies were very high bidders in all four cases while their foreign subsidiaries were low bidders in some cases and close to the low in others.

719.6 and 719.8: The benchmark year, from which the total index was extrapolated, was 1964 for the *United Kingdom*, the *EEC*, and *Germany*. The benchmark levels were derived from separate indexes for three component groups. For the *United Kingdom*, for items 719.62–719.66, the 1963 price level was estimated from place-to-place observations for 1963 and 1964 and extrapolated to other years by the indexes of price competitiveness. The U.K. price level for 1964 was used in the two other groups. The benchmark price level estimates were based on over 30 observations. The German benchmark years were 1963 and 1964 for items 719.62–719.66, 1961 for rubber processing machinery, and 1964 for other machinery; and over 30 observations were included. For the *EEC*, for items 719.62–719.66 and for miscellaneous machinery other than rubber processing machines, benchmark price levels for 1964 were used. The 1964 price level for rubber processing machinery was extrapolated from a 1963 benchmark. More than 60 observations made up the benchmark estimates for the *EEC* as a whole.

719.9 and 719.92: The 719.9 benchmark year is 1964 for the *United Kingdom*, *EEC*, and *Germany*. This group was further subdivided into 5-digit categories. For the United Kingdom, for each of the 5-digit items on which we had place-to-place data, the best year was selected as a benchmark. These were 1964 for 719.92, 1962 for 719.93, and 1963 for 719.94. More than 150 individual price comparisons went into the calculation of the benchmark price levels. Each of these benchmark price levels was extrapolated to 1964 by means of indexes of price competitiveness from time-to-time data, and the 1964 item price levels were aggregated to estimate a price level for the whole subgroup. For item 719.92, for which place-to-place data are plentiful, two alternative price level indexes can be constructed entirely on this basis. The changes in their level are independent of those in the table, but the 1964 level is not. One of the two is an unweighted index of all the available observations for each year, without adjustment for changes in the composition of the sample. The second is constructed by comparing only identical products from year to year, keeping company weights constant because there are differences among companies in both product composition and in reported price level relationships. The two indexes are:

	1953	1957	1961	1962	1963	1964
Unweighted	72	75	64	67	68	74
Weighted: comparable items only	72	63	62	59	66	74

For *Germany* and the *EEC*, price levels for benchmark years in each item were extrapolated to 1964 in the few cases where that was not the benchmark year, and averaged into a price level for the subgroup as a whole. The extrapolation was by the index of price competitiveness for 719.92. Only 20 to 40 observations were available for

(continued)

Notes to Table E.4 (concluded)

estimating the benchmark levels, and the level for 719.92 is the only one that can be considered as at all solidly based. Even this is inferior to most of the price level measures used in other subgroups. For *Japan*, data were available only for item 719.92, and there were about 10 to 40 observations.

For a fair number of products in item 719.92 there are comparisons between *Swiss* and U.S. prices. However, these are confined to certain types of products, and it is therefore safer to consider only the relation of Swiss to U.K. prices for the same products, since the U.K. comparison with the United States is much more broadly based. The results, which cover only 1961–64, suggest that Swiss prices were, on the average, very similar to those of the United Kingdom. The differences favored the United Kingdom slightly for the 20 or so items covered, and the trend, if any, was in the direction of improving the relative position of the United Kingdom. Even at the end of the period, however, Swiss prices remained lower on many items.

Table E.5
Price Level Indexes, Electrical Machinery, Apparatus, and Appliances,
1953, 1957, 1961–64
(U.S. for each year = 100)

SITC Number	Commodity Group and Country	1953	1957	1961	1962	1963	1964
72	Electrical machinery, apparatus, and appliances						
	U.K.	97	94	102	103	108	106
	EEC	90	86	91	94	97	95
	Germany	90	87	93	96	98	97
	Japan	NA	103	91	89	90	91
722	Electric power machinery and switchgear						
	U.K.	NA	79	96	94	103	101
	EEC	NA	77	86	90	94	94
	Germany	NA	79	90	95	99	101
	Japan	NA	NA	85	88	90	99
722.1	Electric power machinery						
	U.K.	NA	74	90	99	108	100
	EEC	NA	64	73	79	85	86
	Germany	NA	60	71	79	83	87
	Japan	NA	NA	73	73	77	93
	Sweden	NA	NA	67	82	83	71
	Switzerland	NA	59	76	83	93	87
722.2	Appar. for making, breaking, or protecting elect. circuits						
	U.K.	NA	NA	NA	NA	NA	102
	EEC	NA	NA	106	105	106	105
	Germany	NA	NA	118	117	119	117
	Japan	NA	NA	NA	NA	NA	101
723	Equipment for distributing electricity						
	U.K.	73	73	83	87	90	86
	EEC	68	62	68	76	73	72
	Japan	NA	NA	79	69	77	77
723.1	Insulated wire and cable						
	U.K.	NA	70	80	84	87	87
	Japan	NA	NA	79	69	78	78
723.2	Electrical insulating equipment						
	Japan	NA	NA	77	72	70	69
724	Telecommunications apparatus						
	U.K.	113	112	115	115	122	118

(continued)

Table E.5 (concluded)

SITC Number	Commodity Group and Country	1953	1957	1961	1962	1963	1964
724	Telecommunications apparatus (continued)						
	EEC	NA	NA	89	89	93	89
	Germany	NA	NA	88	88	93	87
	Japan	NA	104	91	86	90	88
724.1 & 724.2	Television and radio broadcast receivers						
	U.K.	111	104	113	111	109	108
	EEC	NA	NA	83	82	88	91
	Germany	NA	NA	85	84	90	92
	Japan	NA	135	111	89	98	98
724.9	Telecommunications equipment, n.e.s.						
	U.K.	114	116	116	.117	127	123
	EEC	88	89	91	92	96	88
	Germany	85	86	90	90	94	85
	Japan	NA	93	84	84	87	83
725	Domestic electrical equipment						
	U.K.	NA	NA	NA	92	90	93
	EEC	NA	93	95	93	90	90
726 & 729	Other elect. mach. and apparatus (incl. med. and radiol.)						
	U.K.	89	93	98	104	107	107
	EEC	99	95	100	104	107	105
	Germany	102	98	103	107	109	107
729.2	Electric lamps						
	EEC	NA	89	92	98	109	108
729.4	Automotive electrical equipment						
	EEC	NA	NA	104	NA	NA	NA
729.5	Elect. measuring and controlling instruments						
	EEC	NA	NA	NA	NA	93[a]	
	Germany	109	97	108	102	99	96
729.9	Electrical machinery and apparatus, n.e.s.						
	EEC	88	90	105	111	115	113
	Germany	92	94	107	113	118	115

Note: **SITC 72:** The 1962 price level index for each country is a weighted average of the five 3-digit groups or 3-digit combinations listed in the table, except that the *German* index excludes 725.

722: The 1962 index for each country is a weighted average of 722.1 and 722.2 (see below).

722.1 and 722.2: For the *United Kingdom* a 1962 price level benchmark for 722.1

was estimated from approximately 70 price comparisons for that year, mainly from international bidding on power and instrument transformers and on generators, and from company data on electric motors. The *German* price level for 1963 was estimated from more than 30 place-to-place observations for generators, power and instrument transformers, and electric motors. The 1963 figure was extrapolated to other years by the index of price competitiveness. The price level for *EEC* countries other than Germany was estimated from about 80 place-to-place observations for 1963, combined with the German price level for that year, and extrapolated to other years by the index of price competitiveness for the EEC as a whole.

For 722.2 the *U.K.* price level benchmark is 1964, based on about 30 observations. To aggregate to the 3-digit level, a 1962 figure for 722.2 was estimated from a small number of place-to-place observations for that year. However, the year-to-year movement was not reliable enough to publish as a separate index. The 1964 *German* price level for 722.2, based on about 20 observations, was extrapolated back by an index of price competitiveness based on time-to-time data. For the *EEC*, the procedure was the same as for 722.1 except that the 1964 price levels were used and the index of price competitiveness used for extrapolation applied only to Germany. There were about 50 observations for the EEC countries other than Germany.

Japanese price level indexes for 1963 for 722.1 (from over 20 observations) and for 1964 for 722.2 (also from more than 20 observations) were extrapolated to other years by indexes of price competitiveness.

For *Sweden* and *Switzerland* the 722.1 indexes are averages of between 10 and 30 place-to-place comparisons each year on generators and power transformers.

723: The 1962 indexes for the *United Kingdom* and *Japan* are weighted averages of 723.1 and 723.2 (see below). For the *EEC* the 1964 German price level was calculated for 723 as a whole and combined with an estimate for other than EEC countries calculated separately for 723.1 and 723.2. This 1964 price level for the EEC as a whole was then extrapolated to other years using an EEC index of price competitiveness as described in the notes to Table D.5. Almost 60 observations went into the 1964 price level index. The price level data for *Germany* are too weak to be shown separately.

723.1 and 723.2: The *U.K.* benchmark year for both subgroups is 1961. A total of almost 40 buyer observations was used for 723.1, but data for 723.2 were too weak to publish separately. The *Japanese* benchmark year for both subgroups is 1962. There were close to 20 observations for 723.1 and over 50 for 723.2, based in both cases on buyers' bidding records.

724: The 1962 price level index for each country is a weighted average of 724.1 and 724.2 combined, and 724.9 (see below). For an alternative set of indexes, see Chapter 13.

724.1 and 724.2: The 1962 index for each country is a weighted average of three components: 724.1 (television receivers), nontransistor radios of 724.2, and transistor radios of 724.2. Nontransistor radios were assigned 55 per cent of the world trade weight of 724.2; and transistor radios, 45 per cent. For the *United Kingdom*, the benchmark years were 1962 for 724.1, and 1964 for both components of 724.2. For the *EEC* and *Germany* the benchmark year was 1964 for all three items. Extrapolation to earlier years for all three items was by a combined index of price competitiveness for 724.1 and 724.2, since more detailed data were not available. For *Japan*, the benchmark year was 1962 for television sets, 1964 for nontransistor radios, and 1961 for transistor radios. For an alternative set of indexes, see Chapter 13.

724.9: The benchmark level for each country was estimated by combining observa-

(continued)

Notes to Table E.5 (concluded)

tions for 1962, 1963, and 1964, to calculate an average for the three years. Levels for individual years were then estimated using the index of price competitiveness.

725: The benchmark year was 1964 for the *United Kingdom* and the *EEC*. Price level estimates for that year were based on only 5 to 10 observations. The *Japanese* data were too weak to publish.

726 and **729**: The 1962 index for each country is a weighted average of 726 as a whole and the eight 4-digit subgroups of 729, to the extent that we had data for each of these subgroups. A price level benchmark was established for each subgroup, using a single year, or in some cases an average for a two- to four-year period. Indexes for single years were extrapolated from these benchmarks by indexes of price competitiveness based on time-to-time data. The composition of the combined indexes and the benchmarks used are as follows. *U.K.:* 726, 1961 through 1964; 729.1, 1961 through 1963; 729.2, 1963; 729.4, 1961; 729.5, 1962; 729.9, 1962 through 1964. *EEC:* 726, 1961 through 1964; 729.1, 1962; 729.2, 1962; 729.4, 1961; 729.5, 1963 and 1964; 729.6, 1964; 729.9, 1961 through 1964. *Germany:* 726, 1961 through 1964; 729.1, 1962; 729.2, 1962; 729.4, 1961; 729.5, 1963 and 1964; 729.6, 1964; 729.9, 1961 and 1964. *Japan* (not shown in table): 729.2, 1962; 729.9, 1961 and 1964.

729.2, 729.4, 729.5, and **729.9**: See 726 and 729.

[a]Average of 1963 and 1964.

Table E.6
Price Level Indexes, Transport Equipment, 1953, 1957, 1961–64
(U.S. for each year = 100)

SITC Number	Commodity Group and Country	1953	1957	1961	1962	1963	1964
73	Transport equipment						
	U.K.	85	87	90	87	89	93
	EEC	102	100	96	96	97	98
	Germany	94	94	92	93	94	93
731	Railway vehicles						
	U.K.	NA	NA	103	102	105	NA
	EEC	109	105	115	122	123	125
731.3	Diesel locomotives						
	U.K.	NA	NA	112	110	112	NA
	EEC	NA	NA	114	NA	NA	NA
	Japan	NA	NA	104	NA	NA	NA
732	Road motor vehicles						
	U.K.	91	91	92	87	89	93
	EEC	109	107	103	101	104	106
	Germany	100	99	99	98	100	100
732.1 & 732.6	Passenger motor cars and chassis with engines mounted						
	U.K.	87	83	84	79	80	84
	EEC	108	107	97	95	97	97
	Germany	94	95	90	89	91	89
	France	129	131	108	106	109	114
	Italy	139	123	109	101	102	102
732.2, 732.3, 732.4, 732.5, & 732.7	Buses, trucks, etc., and chassis with engines mounted						
	U.K.	86	95	97	91	94	100
	EEC	92	89	100	98	102	107
	Germany	92	89	100	98	101	105
734.1	Aircraft, heavier than air						
	U.K.	NA	93	110	107	111	110
735	Ships and boats						
	EEC	68	66	58	59	56	55
	Germany	62	60	53	56	54	53
	Japan	59	62	50	51	46	46

Notes to Table E.6

Note: **SITC 73**: The 1962 price level index for the *United Kingdom* is a weighted average of the five component 3-digit groups. The 1962 indexes for the *EEC* and *Germany* excludes 734 (aircraft). *Japanese* data were limited to 731 and 735, and were not sufficient to construct an index for group 73 as a whole.

731: The 1962 index for the *United Kingdom* is a combination of the index for 731.3 (see below), which was assigned the OECD export weight of 731.1–731.4; and direct place-to-place data for 731.7 (parts of railway locomotives and rolling stock, n.e.s.). The 1962 index for the *EEC* is a combination of the 1961 index for 731.3 (see below), extrapolated to 1962 by the German index of competitiveness for 731.1–731.3 and assigned the weight of 731.1–731.4; and direct place-to-place data for 731.5 and 731.6 combined (railway cars not mechanically propelled), consisting mainly of about 20 price comparisons by purchasers of various types of railway cars for use outside the United States. The composition of the *German* index is the same as that for the *EEC*, but the data were too weak to publish separately. The *Japanese* data for this group were limited to 731.3 (see below).

731.3: The 1961 benchmark price levels for diesel locomotives were derived from bidding data. These were offers on locomotives of prescribed specifications made under circumstances which permitted worldwide bidding. For each bidding only the lowest offer from a country was used for the index. More than 30 individual comparisons with U.S. offers make up the 1961 averages shown here. The EEC index for 1961 is a weighted average of indexes for Germany, France, and Belgium, using 1963 export values as weights.

732: The 1962 index for each country is a weighted average of three subgroups: passenger cars (732.1 and 732.6), commercial vehicles (732.2–732.5 and 732.7), and motor vehicle parts (732.8). No data were available for motorcycles and parts (732.9). The benchmark year for each component was 1964. For further discussion of the benchmark data, see Chapters 14 and 15.

732.1, 732.6, 732.2, 732.3, 732.4, 732.5 and **732.7**: See 732.

734.1: The 1964 benchmark index was computed from press comment, manufacturers' brochures, and other company data comparing the VC-10 and Super VC-10 with the Boeing 707 and the Douglas DC-8, the Trident with the Boeing 727, and the BAC-111 with the Douglas DC-9. Only in the last case was an adjustment made for seating capacity. For long-range aircraft, separate computations were made for sales to the United Kingdom and other sales. The indexes for the several types of aircraft were combined by weighting them in proportion to estimated orders for long-, medium-, and short-range aircraft, 1961–63, as reported by one of the cooperating companies.

735: The indexes represent a combination of separate comparisons for tankers and dry cargo vessels with equal weights. The tanker comparisons were based primarily on the oil company data referred to in the Note to Table C.6. There were, in addition, bid price comparisons, for about a dozen other tankers, scattered throughout our period, usually involving bids from several countries. The dry cargo comparisons were based largely on Maritime Administration findings of price differentials made in order to determine ship construction subsidies. We also had bid data for another score of ships, usually involving bids from several countries. The benchmark years were 1963 for the *United Kingdom* (not shown), 1961 for the *EEC* and *Germany*, and 1964 for *Japan*.

Table E.7
Price Level Indexes, Miscellaneous Manufactured Articles, 1953, 1957, 1961–64
(U.S. for each year = 100)

SITC Number	Commodity Group and Country	1953	1957	1961	1962	1963	1964
861	Scientific, medical, etc., instruments and apparatus						
	U.K.	76	85	89	88	87	91
	Germany	86	86	87	88	88	88
	Japan	NA	NA	83	82	84	83
861.7	Medical instruments, n.e.s.						
	EEC	NA	NA	80	86	89	93
	Germany	NA	NA	78	83	87	91
861.8	Meters and counters, nonelectric						
	EEC	NA	NA	NA	68	NA	NA
	Germany	NA	NA	NA	68	NA	NA
861.9	Measuring, controlling, and scientific instruments, n.e.s.						
	U.K.	NA	91	92	87	84	89
	EEC	87	86	88	88	87	86
	Germany	86	86	88	88	87	86
	Japan	NA	NA	NA	NA	90	NA
891	Musical instruments, recorders, etc., and parts and accessories						
	U.K.	NA	NA	93	91	91	89
	EEC	NA	78	83	87	92	92
	Germany	NA	77	84	88	94	94
891.4	Pianos and other string musical instruments						
	EEC	NA	NA	87	88	93	87

Note: **SITC 861:** The 1962 price level index for the *United Kingdom* is a weighted average of separate indexes for 861.7, 861.8, and 861.9. The benchmark years were 1963 for 861.7 and 1964 for the other two subgroups. The 1962 indexes for the *EEC* and *Germany* are based on separate indexes for 861.7, 861.8, and 861.9 (see below) and direct place-to-place data for 861.1, 861.2, and 861.3 combined (optical goods). The 1962 *Japanese* index is a weighted average of indexes for 861.1, 861.2, and 861.3 combined; 861.4, 861.5, and 861.6 combined (photographic equipment); and 861.9 (see below). The benchmark year was 1963 for all three components.

861.7: The benchmark year for the *German* index was 1964. The price level for that year is based on 60 observations from U.S. and foreign manufacturers, U.S. government bidding data, and foreign buyers. The *EEC* price level is based on a 1963 benchmark calculated by combining 1963 data on France and Italy (weighted 7.2) and a German index extrapolated from 1964 by the index of price competitiveness in Table D.7 (weighted 38.1).

(continued)

Notes to Table E.7 (concluded)

861.8: The *German* index for 1962 is based on 11 observations, mostly from bidding data. The 1962 *EEC* index is a combination of 17 observations for Italy, Netherlands, and Belgium (weighted 2.6) and the 1962 German data (weighted 15.3).

861.9: This subgroup was further subdivided into 5-digit items. The *U.K.* index is based on a 1964 benchmark which covers 861.93 (drawing, measuring, calculating instruments, etc.), 861.96 (hydrometers, thermometers, etc.), 861.97 (instruments for measuring or controlling the flow, depth, pressure, etc., of liquids or gases), 861.98 (instruments, other than mechanical, for physical or chemical analysis, etc.), and 861.9 (parts and accessories of articles in 729.5, 861.8, 861.96, and 861.97). A total of 30 observations, from both buyers and sellers, was used for the 4-digit index. The *EEC* and *German* indexes were based on 1963 benchmark levels covering 861.93, 861.96, and 861.97. There were a total of 35 observations, 24 for Germany. The 1963 *Japanese* index was based on 33 observations for that year, covering 861.93 and 861.96.

891: The 1962 *U.K.* index is a weighted average of indexes for 891.1 (phonographs, tape recorders, etc.), 891.2 (phonograph records, recorded tape, etc.), and 891.4, all of which were based on 1964 benchmark data. The *EEC* index is a weighted average of indexes for all five 4-digit subgroups, all of which were based on 1964 benchmark data. The *German* index was derived in the same way as the EEC index, except that it excludes 891.2.

891.4: See 891.

APPENDIX F

INDEXES FROM WHOLESALE PRICES AND RELATED DATA

General Note

This appendix contains price indexes and indexes of U.S. price competitiveness computed from domestic wholesale price series for SITC 2-digit commodity divisions, 3-digit groups, and 4-digit subgroups. The foreign countries included in this appendix are the United Kingdom, Germany, France, and Japan. There were insufficient data for the computation of indexes for the EEC. Some additional series on German producers' prices are shown, in addition to the wholesale price data.

The indexes were collected in as great a commodity detail as possible, and each series was classified by the SITC coding system. The SITC groups and subgroups listed are all those for which wholesale price series are available, even if only a single commodity is covered.

The foreign wholesale price indexes are, in most cases, annual averages for the years 1953, 1957, 1961, and 1962, and midyears for 1963 and 1964. U.S. wholesale price indexes are midyears (June–July averages) for all the years included. For all the indexes, 1962 equals 100. Changes in German prices between 1957 and 1961 were adjusted to take account of a 5 per cent appreciation of the German mark, and French price series were adjusted for the 29 per cent depreciation of the French franc in 1961.

For each country the 4-digit wholesale price indexes, when available, were aggregated to 3-digit averages, and then to 2-digit averages, using international trade weights. The indexes of U.S. price competitiveness computed from wholesale price indexes were calculated at the most detailed level available and aggregated using international weights.

The sources for the official wholesale price series used for each country are listed below:

United States: *Wholesale Prices and Price Indexes,* Bureau of Labor Statistics, U.S. Dept. of Labor, July issues, and unpublished data of the BLS.

United Kingdom: *Annual Abstract of Statistics,* Central Statistical Office, No. 95, 1958, and No. 100, 1963; *Board of Trade Journal,* October 16, 1964, and August 14, 1968; and correspondence with Statistics Division, Board of Trade.

Germany: *Statistisches Jahrbuch für die Bundesrepublik Deutschland,* 1959 and 1963, Section XX, Table V; and correspondence with IFO Institute.

France: *Bulletin Mensuel de Statistique,* Institut National de la Statistique et des Études Économiques, various issues; and correspondence with the Institut National.

Japan: *Wholesale Price Index Annual,* Statistics Department, Bank of Japan.

Table F.1

Indexes from Wholesale Prices, Iron and Steel (SITC 67), 1953, 1957, 1961–64
(1962 = 100)

SITC Number and Country	Number of Series	1953	1957	1961	1962	1963	1964
67							
U.S.	49–54	77	98	100	100	100	100
U.K.	23–24	74	95	97	100	100	100
Germany[a]	5	85	90	99	100	98	98
France	5	88	106	98	100	102	102
Japan	47–48	89	110	108	100	100	100
671							
U.S.	8	89	101	101	100	90	85
Japan	3–7	90	116	103	100	97	97
671.2							
U.S.	5	85	99	100	100	95	95
U.K.	2–3	66	95	99	100	100	100
Germany	1	94	104	108	100	92	90
France	2	88	113	100	100	100	100
671.4							
U.S.	1	105	134	116	100	90	79
671.5							
U.S.	2	87	91	95	100	84	78
672							
U.K.	2–5	76	97	98	100	100	100
France	1	NA	106	97	100	101	NA
672.1 & 672.3							
U.K.	2	66	94	98	100	NA	NA
672.5							
U.S.	3–4	77	97	100	100	100	104
U.K.	1–2	79	97	98	100	100	100
Germany	1	86	93	100	100	100	100
Japan	2	92	115	113	100	107	105
672.9							
U.K.	1	NA	94	96	100	100	100
673							
U.S.	9–12	74	97	100	100	99	100
U.K.	2–5	77	96	98	100	100	100

(continued)

Table F.1 (continued)

SITC Number and Country	Number of Series	1953	1957	1961	1962	1963	1964
673 (continued)							
Germany	1	84	87	98	100	99	99
Japan	4–13	90	123	109	100	101	101
673.1							
U.S.	1	71	96	100	100	100	98
U.K.	1	76	99	98	100	100	100
Japan	1–3	100	123	106	100	96	96
673.2							
U.S.	7–11	76	98	101	100	97	99
U.K.	1–3	77	94	98	100	100	100
Japan	3–6	86	122	109	100	100	103
673.4 & 673.5							
U.S.	1	71	96	100	100	100	103
U.K.	1	NA	96	96	100	NA	NA
Japan	4	NA	NA	110	100	106	101
674							
U.S.	9	78	97	100	100	101	101
U.K.	3–5	76	96	97	100	100	100
Japan	3–10	93	109	109	100	100	102
674.1 & 674.2							
U.S.	2	73	97	100	100	102	104
U.K.	1	72	96	97	100	NA	NA
Japan	2–4	81	120	112	100	96	105
674.3							
U.S.	4	80	97	100	100	101	100
U.K.	1–2	75	95	96	100	100	100
Japan	1–2	102	107	109	100	99	99
674.7							
U.S.	2	81	96	100	100	100	100
U.K.	1	81	97	96	100	100	100
Japan	2	NA	NA	102	100	101	101
674.8							
U.S.	1	80	94	100	100	104	104
U.K.	1	NA	98	98	100	100	99
Japan	2	NA	NA	108	100	109	109
675							
U.S.	3	79	101	100	100	102	102

(continued)

Table F.1 (concluded)

SITC Number and Country	Number of Series	1953	1957	1961	1962	1963	1964
675 (continued)							
U.K.	1–2	76	94	98	100	100	100
Japan	2–3	94	110	104	100	100	100
676							
U.S.	3	76	96	100	100	100	100
Germany	1	71	78	94	100	100	100
France	1	89	102	97	100	105	105
676.1							
U.S.	2	77	96	100	100	100	100
U.K.	1	NA	NA	98	100	102	NA
Japan	2	NA	NA	99	100	99	99
676.2							
U.S.	1	74	96	100	100	100	100
677							
U.S.	2	75	97	100	100	100	100
France	1	88	102	98	100	104	104
Japan	2–4	92	114	111	100	104	102
678							
U.S.	10–11	76	101	100	100	99	101
U.K.	2	71	89	97	100	101	102
Japan	3	82	96	107	100	95	94
678.1							
U.S.	2–3	90	104	101	100	98	100
678.2 & 678.3							
U.S.	8	75	100	100	100	99	101
U.K.	2	71	89	97	100	101	102
678.2 & 678.4							
Japan	2	86	97	109	100	94	92
678.5							
Japan	1	74	96	102	100	97	102
679							
U.S.	2–3	71	90	100	100	100	101
U.K.	1	70	89	98	100	101	103
Germany	1	80	88	97	100	100	102

[a]The 3-digit groups included in the German wholesale price index cover only 32 per cent of OECD exports of the 2-digit SITC division 67.

Table F.2
Indexes from Wholesale Prices, Nonferrous Metals (SITC 68),
1953, 1957, 1961–64
(1962 = 100)

SITC Number and Country	Number of Series	1953	1957	1961	1962	1963	1964
68							
U.S.[a]	15–27	86	97	103	100	98	103
U.K.[a]	6	82	94	102	100	101	112
Germany[a]	4	103	100	104	100	98	107
France	11–15	119	127	102	100	102	112
Japan	15–26	100	101	103	100	100	106
681							
Japan	1	105	116	86	100	117	121
682							
U.S.	5–11	96	96	101	100	99	104
U.K.	5	86	96	103	100	98	115
Germany	1	100	93	100	100	99	110
France	2–3	111	116	102	100	104	116
Japan	8–12	95	92	103	100	97	102
683							
U.S.	1	76	94	103	100	100	100
France	1	NA	172	102	100	99	99
Japan	1	109	119	108	100	96	96
684							
U.S.	5–8	80	100	105	100	94	98
U.K.	1	78	92	100	100	105	109
Germany	1	105	105	110	100	98	104
France	2–4	123	131	99	100	101	103
Japan	2–4	102	103	104	100	100	106
685							
U.S.	1	142	147	116	100	116	137
Germany	1	131	138	104	100	102	127
France	2–3	123	148	115	100	106	151
Japan	1–4	120	128	115	100	94	116
686							
U.S.	1	99	88	100	100	104	116
Germany	1	99	101	100	100	100	105

(continued)

Table F.2 (concluded)

SITC Number and Country	Number of Series	1953	1957	1961	1962	1963	1964
686 (continued)							
France	2	103	128	107	100	104	160
Japan	1	116	95	114	100	94	123
687							
U.S.	2	73	86	104	100	104	142
France	1	81	93	104	100	100	140
Japan	1–2	115	111	98	100	98	118
689							
U.S.	2	NA	NA	100	100	97	97
France	1	NA	131	100	100	100	98

[a]Indexes obtained by adding trade journal prices to official series:

	1953	1957	1961	1962	1963	1964
U.S.	88	98	101	100	99	105
U.K.	91	100	101	100	103	115
Germany	104	100	105	100	100	111

Table F.3
Indexes from Wholesale Prices, Manufactures of Metal, n.e.s. (SITC 69),
1953, 1957, 1961–64
(1962 = 100)

SITC Number and Country	Number of Series	1953	1957	1961	1962	1963	1964
69							
U.S.	63–91	78	95	99	100	101	104
U.K.	15	75	88	97	100	102	107
Germany	5–7	82	88	96	100	100	101
France	5	79	81	93	100	105	107
Japan	6–36	89	102	103	100	98	101
691							
U.S.	1–21	79	103	102	100	101	102
U.K.	1	74	88	99	100	103	106
Japan	4	NA	NA	106	100	97	100
692							
U.S.	11–13	85	101	100	100	101	106
U.K.	1	65	84	92	100	105	110
Japan	1–3	94	120	104	100	95	94
692.1							
U.S.	5–7	81	97	99	100	104	106
France	1	94	86	92	100	99	99
692.2							
U.S.	4	84	104	100	100	100	113
Japan	1–2	91	116	101	100	97	97
692.3							
U.S.	2–3	93	103	101	100	98	96
Japan	1	NA	NA	110	100	90	89
693							
U.S.	4–9	96	105	102	100	98	99
France	2	NA	NA	97	100	102	102
Japan	2	93	102	105	100	94	105
693.1							
U.S.	1–4	100	101	100	100	98	104
France	1	NA	NA	100	100	100	100
Japan	1	122	135	99	100	89	103
693.2							
U.S.	1	82	104	100	100	100	100

(continued)

Table F.3 (concluded)

SITC Number and Country	Number of Series	1953	1957	1961	1962	1963	1964
693.3							
U.S.	2–4	98	111	107	100	95	93
France	1	NA	NA	94	100	105	103
Japan	1	74	79	114	100	100	107
694							
Japan	2–5	78	107	105	100	99	98
694.1							
Japan	1–2	91	116	106	100	101	102
694.2							
U.S.	7–8	65	82	90	100	103	104
Germany	2	NA	NA	98	100	99	104
Japan	1–3	73	103	105	100	98	97
695							
U.S.	16–18	74	90	100	100	102	105
U.K.	6	68	85	95	100	102	107
Germany	1	75	86	95	100	100	98
France	1	NA	NA	96	100	103	104
Japan	1–7	90	94	99	100	98	99
696							
U.S.	2	81	91	98	100	100	100
U.K.	2	80	94	98	100	103	105
Germany	1	83	87	95	100	102	105
Japan	2	NA	NA	100	100	100	115
697							
U.S.	4	82	95	100	100	102	102
U.K.	3	81	90	98	100	100	104
Germany	2	82	87	96	100	101	103
Japan	4	NA	NA	99	100	102	108
698							
U.S.	15–18	78	95	100	100	100	106
U.K.	2	82	91	98	100	103	108
Germany	1	88	88	97	100	99	100
France	1	73	77	90	100	108	114
Japan	9	NA	NA	105	100	98	99

Table F.4
Indexes from Wholesale Prices, Machinery Other than Electric
(SITC 71), 1953, 1957, 1961–64
(1962 = 100)

SITC Number and Country	Number of Series	1953	1957	1961	1962	1963	1964
71							
U.S.	175–195	78	93	99	100	101	102
Germany	13–17	76	83	95	100	101	104
France	9–18	120	114	99	100	102	102
Japan	10–18	92	103	100	100	100	99
711							
Japan	1–5	105	100	100	100	99	98
711.1							
Germany	1	78	85	96	100	103	105
Japan	1	NA	NA	98	100	102	100
711.5[a]							
U.S.	8–9	80	94	99	100	100	102
France	1	124	113	100	100	101	101
Japan	1–4	106	100	100	100	98	97
712							
U.S.	35–48	81	88	99	100	101	103
Germany	2	79	85	96	100	100	101
France	4–9	114	115	97	100	104	104
Japan	1–5	86[b]	101[b]	101	100	101	99
712.1							
U.S.	8–15	76	83	97	100	102	104
France	1	NA	NA	96	100	104	105
Japan	3	NA	NA	98	100	100	100
712.2							
U.S.	11–14	78	86	98	100	102	103
France	1–5	99	114	97	100	106	107
Japan	1	NA	NA	101	100	104	105
712.3							
U.S.	1–2	91	94	98	100	100	99
712.5							
U.S.	7–8	83	90	99	100	101	103
Germany	1	82	85	96	100	100	101
France	1	125	116	98	100	102	101

(continued)

Table F.4 (continued)

SITC Number and Country	Number of Series	1953	1957	1961	1962	1963	1964
712.5 (continued)							
Japan	1	86	102	102	100	100	96
712.9							
U.S.	7–12	85	94	99	100	101	102
France	1	102	111	92	100	107	109
714[c]							
U.S.	9–10	88	99	101	100	101	101
Japan	2	NA	NA	100	100	100	100
714.1							
U.S.	3	83	99	101	100	101	101
714.2[d]							
U.S.	3–4	91	99	101	100	101	101
Japan	1	NA	NA	100	100	100	100
714.9							
U.S.	3	86	98	100	100	101	102
Japan	1	NA	NA	100	100	100	100
715							
U.S.	8	73	89	97	100	100	102
Japan	3–4	NA	NA	102	100	96	96
715.1							
U.S.[e]	1	70	89	97	100	100	103
Germany	1	68	78	93	100	101	103
Japan	6	NA	NA	103	100	95	95
715.2							
U.S.[f]	7	80	92	97	100	100	102
Japan[g]	1	NA	NA	100	100	100	100
717							
Germany	1	74	81	95	100	101	105
Japan	3–4	84	102	96	100	102	103
717.1							
U.S.	1	NA	NA	99	100	101	102
Japan	2	81	102	96	100	103	104
717.3							
Japan	1–2	100	100	100	100	100	100
718							
U.S.	14–19	73	90	98	100	101	103
Germany	3–6	74	83	96	100	102	104

(continued)

Table F.4 (continued)

SITC Number and Country	Number of Series	1953	1957	1961	1962	1963	1964
718 (continued)							
Japan	3	NA	NA	97	100	100	99
718.2							
U.S.	1	NA	NA	97	100	100	103
Japan	1	NA	NA	90	100	101	101
718.3							
U.S.	1	NA	NA	99	100	102	104
Germany[h]	3	NA	NA	99	100	103	106
718.4							
U.S.	2	76	91	99	100	101	103
Germany	1	78	85	97	100	101	102
Japan	2	NA	NA	100	100	99	98
718.5							
U.S.	10–15	66	88	98	100	101	103
Germany[i]	1	76	82	95	100	101	104
719							
U.S.	97–101	79	94	99	100	101	102
Germany	5–6	77	84	95	100	100	103
Japan	5–18	93	106	100	100	100	98
719.1							
U.S.	3–7	92	101	98	100	102	102
Germany	1	NA	NA	93	100	98	101
Japan	1–2	113	109	100	100	99	93
719.2							
U.S.	12–14	77	92	100	100	100	100
Japan	2–5	82	103	99	100	102	101
719.3							
U.S.	22–23	74	92	99	100	100	102
Germany	1	75	80	94	100	102	104
Japan[j]	5	NA	NA	101	100	97	93
719.5							
U.S.	15–17	74	88	97	100	100	100
Germany[k]	2	70	82	95	100	101	104
Japan	1	NA	NA	100	100	96	96
719.6							
U.S.[l]	12–15	81	96	100	100	102	103
Japan[m]	1	86	108	100	100	105	107

(continued)

Table F.4 (concluded)

SITC Number and Country	Number of Series	1953	1957	1961	1962	1963	1964
719.7							
U.S.	6–7	83	99	100	100	100	100
Japan	1	114	98	106	100	93	86
719.9[n]							
U.S.	18–20	70	92	101	100	102	102
Germany	2	85	91	96	100	100	104
Japan	3	NA	NA	99	100	99	99

[a]The series in this group are not entirely comparable. U.S. series cover diesels, outboard motors, and other gasoline engines, while data for France refer solely to gasoline engines. Japan has diesel series for the entire period, and beginning in 1961 series also for gasoline engines, kerosene engines, and marine diesels.

[b]Only the tractor series was available for 1953 and 1957.

[c]Excluding 714.3, statistical machines.

[d]Excluding electronic computers.

[e]This is an index for "other metalworking machinery" and covers not only SITC 715.1, but also hand tools and accessories and parts for tools.

[f]Covers 715.23 only.

[g]Covers 715.21 only.

[h]Covers meat processing machinery only.

[i]This is the Wholesale Price Index for mining machinery and includes items classified by the SITC in 718.4 and other groups.

[j]The series cover SITC 719.31 only.

[k]The series cover SITC 719.52 only.

[l]The U.S. series cover SITC subgroups 719.63, 719.64 and 719.65 only.

[m]The series cover SITC 719.64 only.

[n]These series cover only two main items, SITC 719.92 and 719.93.

Table F.5
Indexes from Wholesale Prices, Electrical Machinery, Apparatus, and
Appliances (SITC 72), 1953, 1957, 1961–64
(1962 = 100)

SITC Number and Country	Number of Series	1953	1957	1961	1962	1963	1964
72							
U.S.	84–105	94	103	103	100	99	98
Germany	20–21	NA	NA	99	100	99	100
Japan	25–45	99	104	103	100	97	96
722							
U.S.	36–42	83	103	103	100	99	99
Germany	5	NA	NA	98	100	99	99
Japan	8–9	82	102	103	100	97	97
722.1							
U.S.	17–19	89	108	105	100	99	97
Germany	2	NA	NA	98	100	99	100
France	1	114	110	97	100	104	106
Japan	5	79	100	102	100	97	97
722.2							
U.S.	19–23	77	96	100	100	100	101
Germany	3	NA	NA	100	100	98	98
Japan	3–4	86	105	104	100	97	97
723.1[a]							
U.S.	4	112	106	101	100	100	104
Germany	2	NA	NA	102	100	96	104
Japan	5–7	82	94	106	100	89	94
724							
U.S.[b,c]	5–6	118	113	105	100	98	96
Germany	3	NA	NA	98	100	99	99
Japan[b]	3–6	111	106	102	100	100	99
724.1							
U.S.	1–2	113	106	103	100	99	97
Japan	1	NA	NA	105	100	100	98
724.21							
U.S.[b]	4	122	118	106	100	97	96
Japan[b]	1–2	206	150	111	100	100	97
724.9							
Germany	2	NA	NA	98	100	101	101
Japan	2–3	100	100	100	100	100	100

(continued)

Table F.5 (continued)

SITC Number and Country	Number of Series	1953	1957	1961	1962	1963	1964
725							
U.S.	8–15	113	108	102	100	96	95
U.K.	3–8	105	103	102	100	102	108
Germany	8	NA	NA	99	100	98	98
Japan	9	NA	NA	103	100	98	96
726 & 729							
U.S.[d]	29–39	79	95	103	100	99	100
Germany[d]	2–3	NA	NA	98	100	101	101
Japan	9–4	106	105	105	100	95	92
726							
Japan	1	87	101	93	100	102	102
729.1							
U.S.	4–6	80	99	105	100	99	102
Japan	2	95	98	106	100	93	94
729.2							
U.S.	3–5	84	93	101	100	100	100
Germany	1	NA	NA	98	100	100	97
Japan	1–3	118	93	102	100	96	96
729.3							
Japan	1–3	99	83	110	100	89	88
729.4							
U.S.	1	NA	NA	120	100	100	95
729.5							
U.S.	6	66	83	98	100	100	102
Germany	1	NA	NA	98	100	101	102
Japan	1	120	110	100	100	100	100
729.6							
U.S.	8	84	92	96	100	99	98
Japan	1	96	98	103	100	98	96
729.9							
U.S.	8–13	85	101	102	100	99	99
Germany	1	NA	NA	99	100	NA	NA
Japan	2–3	113	129	108	100	92	84

[a]Subgroup SITC 723.1 accounts for 82 per cent of OECD exports of SITC 723.

[b]The U.S. series do not include portable transistor radios, while Japanese 724.2 series include only portable transistor radios, and are therefore presumably biased downward relative to other countries' indexes.

[c]The 4-digit groups included in the U.S. SITC 724 index comprise only 21 per cent of OECD exports of the 3-digit groups.

[d]These series do not cover SITC 729.

Table F.6
Indexes from Wholesale Prices, Transport Equipment (SITC 73),
1953, 1957, 1961–64
(1962 = 100)

SITC Number and Country	Number of Series	1953	1957	1961	1962	1963	1964
73							
U.S.	6–9	85	96	100	100	100	99
Germany	8	97	91	98	100	101	101
France	4–7	117	123	98	100	102	104
Japan	6–15	124	114	101	100	99	98
731							
U.S.	1	NA	NA	100	100	100	100
Japan	2–4	98	103	100	100	99	99
731.5 & 731.6							
Germany[a]	2	73	81	94	100	102	104
Japan	2	99	103	101	100	98	98
731.7							
Japan	1	NA	NA	100	100	99	99
732							
U.S.	3–4	85	96	100	100	100	99
Germany	4	99	92	98	100	101	101
France	3–5	117	123	98	100	102	104
Japan	3–10	128	115	101	100	99	98
732.1 & 732.6							
U.S.	1	86	96	101	100	99	99
Germany	1	104	92	97	100	101	101
France	1	123	127	98	100	102	103
Japan	1–2	168	124	101	100	99	95
732.2–732.5 & 732.7							
U.S.	2	83	94	100	100	99	99
Germany	1	92	89	98	100	101	101
France	1–3	103	113	97	100	103	107
Japan	1–4	105	110	101	100	99	99
732.8							
U.S.	1	NA	NA	NA	100	104	100
Germany	1	95	94	101	100	100	101
Japan	1	96	105	100	100	100	100

(continued)

Table F.6 (concluded)

SITC Number and Country	Number of Series	1953	1957	1961	1962	1963	1964
732.9							
Germany	1	95	89	100	100	101	103
France	1	136	135	99	100	103	104
Japan	3	NA	NA	101	100	100	100
733							
U.S.	3–4	93	98	100	100	101	100
Germany	2	85	86	97	100	102	102
733.1							
U.S.	1	98	101	100	100	100	98
Germany	1	87	88	97	100	103	105
Japan	1	93	101	96	100	101	102
733.3							
U.S.	3	88	95	99	100	102	103
Germany	1	82	84	97	100	100	99

[a]Includes SITC 731.62 only.

Table F.7
Indexes from Wholesale Prices, Miscellaneous Manufactured Articles
(SITC 812, 861, 864, 891, and 894), 1953, 1957, 1961–64
(1962 = 100)

SITC Number and Country	Number of Series	1953	1957	1961	1962	1963	1964
812							
U.S.	28–48	90	101	103	100	101	101
812.1							
U.S.	17–25	90	99	101	100	100	100
812.2							
U.S.	2	94	112	115	100	105	105
812.3							
U.S.	9–11	90	99	101	100	102	101
812.4							
U.S.	14–15	NA	NA	102	100	100	101
861							
U.S.	10–15	77	90	98	100	101	104
U.K.[a]	3	82	88	97	100	103	106
Germany	5	77	82	95	100	101	103
Japan[a]	1–7	136	122	102	100	103	101
861.1–861.3							
U.K.	1	81	87	95	100	103	105
Germany	1	75	79	95	100	101	102
Japan	1	NA	NA	99	100	110	106
861.4–861.6							
U.S.	1	85	90	96	100	101	99
U.K.	1	84	89	99	100	104	105
Germany	1	88	85	98	100	100	102
Japan	1–4	138	124	104	100	98	98
861.7							
U.K.	1	78	86	97	100	103	108
Germany	1	70	74	91	100	101	109
861.9							
U.S.	9–14	74	90	99	100	100	106
Germany	2	74	82	94	100	101	103
864							
U.S.	4–5	92	96	100	100	100	97
Germany	1	85	88	96	100	100	99

(continued)

Table F.7 (concluded)

SITC Number and Country	Number of Series	1953	1957	1961	1962	1963	1964
864.1							
U.S.	2–3	92	98	100	100	100	97
864.2							
U.S.	2	90	91	100	100	100	97
Japan	1	100	100	100	100	100	100
891							
U.S.	6–8	103	105	106	100	99	97
Germany	1	78	82	94	100	103	106
891.1							
U.S.	1	109	114	109	100	99	96
Japan[b]	1	NA	NA	102	100	100	95
891.2							
U.S.	2–3	101	84	100	100	99	98
891.4							
U.S.	2	75	91	97	100	103	104
891.8							
U.S.	1–2	97	97	98	100	99	99
894							
U.S.	26–29	97	99	100	100	100	100
U.K.	3	83	96	98	100	102	104
Germany	2	84	85	97	100	102	104
894.1							
U.S.	1–2	92	97	100	100	101	103
U.K.	1	81	92	97	100	102	104
894.2							
U.S.	8–10	101	99	100	100	99	99
U.K.	1	85	98	98	100	102	105
Germany	1	84	85	97	100	103	105
894.3							
U.S.	9	82	94	99	100	101	102
894.4							
U.S.	8	90	98	100	100	102	102
U.K.	1	76	90	97	100	104	104

[a]OECD exports of the subgroups covered by the United Kingdom and Japan represent 37 per cent and 30 per cent, respectively, of total OECD exports of SITC 861.

[b]OECD exports of 891.1 represent 66 per cent of OECD exports of 891.

Table F.8
Indexes of U.S. Price Competitiveness Computed from Domestic Wholesale
Price Series, Iron and Steel (SITC 67), 1953, 1957, 1961–64
(1962 = 100)

SITC Number and Country	1953	1957	1961	1962	1963	1964
67						
U.K.	97	97	97	100	100	100
Germany	112	93	99	100	100	98
Japan	117	112	108	100	100	100
671						
Japan	100	113	102	100	108	114
671.2						
U.K.	78	97	99	100	105	105
Germany	111	106	108	100	97	94
France	104	115	100	100	105	105
672						
France	NA	109	97	100	101	NA
672.5						
U.K.	102	100	98	100	100	96
Germany	112	96	100	100	100	96
Japan	120	118	113	100	107	101
673						
U.K.	103	99	97	100	102	102
Germany	115	90	97	100	100	99
Japan	120	126	108	100	103	101
673.1						
U.K.	108	103	98	100	100	102
Japan	142	128	106	100	96	97
673.2						
U.K.	101	96	97	100	103	101
Japan	112	125	108	100	103	104
673.4 & 673.5						
U.K.	NA	100	96	100	NA	NA
Japan	NA	NA	110	100	106	98
674						
U.K.	97	99	97	100	99	100
Japan	120	112	108	100	99	101

(continued)

Table F.8 (concluded)

SITC Number and Country	1953	1957	1961	1962	1963	1964
674.1 & 674.2						
U.K.	98	99	97	100	NA	NA
Japan	110	123	112	100	94	101
674.3						
U.K.	95	98	96	100	99	100
Japan	128	111	109	100	98	100
674.7						
U.K.	100	101	96	100	100	100
Japan	NA	NA	102	100	101	101
674.8						
U.K.	NA	104	98	100	96	95
Japan	NA	NA	108	100	105	105
675						
U.K.	96	94	98	100	99	98
Japan	118	109	104	100	98	99
676						
Germany	93	81	94	100	100	100
France	116	106	97	100	105	105
676.1						
U.K.	NA	NA	98	100	102	NA
Japan	NA	NA	99	100	99	99
677						
France	117	105	98	100	104	104
Japan	122	117	111	100	104	102
678						
U.K.	94	89	97	100	102	101
Japan	114	96	109	100	95	91
678.2 & 678.3						
U.K.	94	89	97	100	102	101
679						
U.K.	98	100	99	100	100	101
Germany	112	98	98	100	99	101

Appendix F

Table F.9

Indexes of U.S. Price Competitiveness Computed from Domestic Wholesale
Price Series, Nonferrous Metals (SITC 68), 1953, 1957, 1961–64
(1962 = 100)

SITC Number and Country	1953	1957	1961	1962	1963	1964
68						
U.K.	93	96	98	100	105	111
Germany	114	101	101	100	101	104
France	133	130	98	100	104	108
Japan	115	102	101	100	100	101
682						
U.K.	90	99	102	100	99	111
Germany	104	96	99	100	100	105
France	116	120	101	100	104	112
Japan	99	95	102	100	98	98
683						
France	NA	184	99	100	99	99
Japan	143	127	105	100	96	96
684						
U.K.	98	92	95	100	112	111
Germany	132	105	105	100	104	106
France	154	130	94	100	107	106
Japan	128	103	99	100	107	109
685						
Germany	92	94	89	100	88	93
France	87	101	99	100	92	111
Japan	84	87	99	100	81	85
686						
Germany	100	115	100	100	96	90
France	105	146	107	100	100	137
Japan	118	108	114	100	90	106
687						
France	111	108	100	100	96	98
Japan	158	128	94	100	94	83
689						
France	NA	NA	100	100	103	101

Table F.10
Indexes of U.S. Price Competitiveness Computed from Domestic Wholesale
Price Series, Manufactures of Metal, n.e.s. (SITC 69),
1953, 1957, 1961–64
(1962 = 100)

SITC Number and Country	1953	1957	1961	1962	1963	1964
69						
U.K.	96	93	97	100	101	102
Germany	107	95	98	100	98	97
France	100	85	93	100	104	103
Japan	112	108	104	100	97	97
691						
U.K.	94	85	98	100	102	104
Japan	NA	NA	105	100	97	98
692						
U.K.	76	82	93	100	105	103
Japan	111	114	104	100	95	89
692.1						
France	116	89	92	100	95	93
692.2						
Japan	108	111	101	100	97	86
692.3						
Japan	NA	NA	108	100	92	93
693						
France	NA	NA	94	100	106	103
Japan	93	96	102	100	97	106
693.1						
France	NA	NA	100	100	102	96
Japan	122	134	99	100	90	99
693.3						
France	NA	NA	87	100	110	111
Japan	76	72	106	100	105	115
694						
Japan	114	126	117	100	95	93
694.2						
Germany	NA	NA	109	100	96	100
Japan	114	126	117	100	95	93

(continued)

Table F.10 (concluded)

SITC Number and Country	1953	1957	1961	1962	1963	1964
695						
U.K.	93	94	96	100	100	102
Germany	102	95	96	100	98	94
France	NA	NA	97	100	101	100
Japan	122	104	99	100	96	95
696						
U.K.	99	103	100	100	103	105
Germany	102	95	97	100	102	105
Japan	NA	NA	103	100	100	115
697						
U.K.	99	95	98	100	98	101
Germany	100	92	96	100	99	101
Japan	NA	NA	99	100	99	105
698						
U.K.	105	96	98	100	102	102
Germany	112	94	97	100	99	94
France	94	82	90	100	108	108
Japan	NA	NA	105	100	97	93

Table F.11
Indexes of U.S. Price Competitiveness Computed from Domestic
Wholesale Price Series, Machinery Other than Electric (SITC 71),
1953, 1957, 1961−64
(1962 = 100)

SITC Number and Country	1953	1957	1961	1962	1963	1964
71						
Germany	98	90	96	100	100	101
France	149	124	100	100	102	100
Japan	114	109	101	100	99	97
711.5[a]						
France	157	120	101	100	101	99
Japan	133	106	101	100	99	95
712						
Germany	98	96	98	100	99	98
France	140	129	99	100	102	100
Japan	104[b]	114[b]	102	100	99	96
712.1						
France	NA	NA	99	100	102	100
Japan	NA	NA	101	100	98	96
712.2						
France	127	132	98	100	105	103
Japan	NA	NA	102	100	102	102
712.5						
Germany	99	94	97	100	99	98
France	151	130	99	100	101	98
Japan	104	114	103	100	98	93
712.9						
France	119	118	94	100	106	108
714						
Japan[c]	NA	NA	99	100	99	99
714.2						
Japan[c]	NA	NA	99	100	99	99
714.9						
Japan	NA	NA	100	100	99	98
715						
Japan	NA	NA	106	100	96	94

(continued)

Table F.11 (continued)

SITC Number and Country	1953	1957	1961	1962	1963	1964
715.1						
Germany[d]	96	88	96	100	101	100
Japan[d]	NA	NA	106	100	95	92
715.2						
Japan[e]	NA	NA	103	100	100	98
717						
Germany	NA	NA	97	100	100	103
717.1						
Japan	NA	NA	97	100	102	102
718						
Germany	103	92	98	100	100	100
Japan	NA	NA	98	100	98	96
718.2						
Japan	NA	NA	92	100	101	98
718.3						
Germany[f]	NA	NA	100	100	101	102
718.4						
Germany	103	93	98	100	99	99
Japan	NA	NA	101	100	98	95
718.5						
Germany[g]	114	93	96	100	100	101
719						
Germany	97	89	95	100	99	101
Japan	112	110	101	100	99	96
719.1						
Germany	NA	NA	95	100	97	99
Japan	122	108	101	100	97	91
719.2						
Japan	107	111	99	100	103	100
719.3						
Germany	100	87	95	100	101	102
Japan[h]	NA	NA	103	100	97	91
719.5[i]						
Germany	94	93	98	100	101	104
Japan	NA	NA	103	100	96	96

(continued)

Table F.11 (concluded)

SITC Number and Country	1953	1957	1961	1962	1963	1964
719.6						
Japan[j]	106	112	100	100	103	104
719.7						
Japan	137	100	106	100	93	86
719.9						
Germany	121	99	95	100	98	101
Japan	NA	NA	98	100	97	97

[a]See footnote a to Table F.4.
[b]Japanese data for these two years covered only tractor series.
[c]Data exclude electronic computers.
[d]See footnote e to Table F.4.
[e]U.S. data cover 715.23 only; and Japanese data, 715.21.
[f]Meat processing machinery only.
[g]See footnote h to Table F.4.
[h]Japanese data cover SITC 719.31 only.
[i]German and Japanese data cover SITC 719.52 only.
[j]See footnotes l and m to Table F.4.

Table F.12
Indexes of U.S. Price Competitiveness Computed from Domestic
Wholesale Price Series, Electrical Machinery, Apparatus,
and Appliances (SITC 72), 1953, 1957, 1961–64
(1962 = 100)

SITC Number and Country	1953	1957	1961	1962	1963	1964
72						
Germany	NA	NA	96	100	100	100
Japan	129	113	102	100	98	97
722						
Germany	NA	NA	96	100	99	101
Japan	98	99	100	100	98	99
722.1						
Germany	NA	NA	93	100	100	103
France	129	102	92	100	106	110
Japan	89	92	97	100	98	101
722.2						
Germany	NA	NA	99	100	99	97
Japan	112	108	103	100	97	96
723.1						
Germany	NA	NA	101	100	96	100
Japan	73	89	105	100	89	90
724						
Germany	NA	NA	94	100	98	98
Japan[a]	168	126	103	100	102	101
724.1						
Japan	NA	NA	102	100	101	101
724.21						
Japan[a]	169	127	104	100	103	101
725						
U.K.	93	96	100	100	106	114
Germany	NA	NA	98	100	102	103
Japan	NA	NA	102	100	102	101
729						
Germany	NA	NA	98	100	101	99
Japan	144	122	104	100	96	92
729.1						
Japan	119	99	101	100	94	93

(continued)

Table F.12 (concluded)

SITC Number and Country	1953	1957	1961	1962	1963	1964
729.2						
Germany	NA	NA	97	100	100	97
Japan	141	100	101	100	97	96
729.5						
Germany	NA	NA	100	100	101	100
Japan	183	133	102	100	100	98
729.6						
Japan	115	105	108	100	98	98
729.9						
Germany	NA	NA	97	100	NA	NA
Japan	133	128	106	100	93	85

[a]See footnote b to Table F.5.

Table F.13

Indexes of U.S. Price Competitiveness Computed from Domestic Wholesale
Price Series, Transport Equipment (SITC 73), 1953, 1957, 1961−64
(1962 = 100)

SITC Number and Country	1953	1957	1961	1962	1963	1964
73						
Germany	117	95	97	100	100	102
France	137	128	98	100	103	105
Japan	166	124	101	100	99	98
731						
Germany	NA	NA	95	100	102	104
Japan	NA	NA	101	100	99	99
732						
Germany	118	95	97	100	100	102
France	137	128	98	100	103	105
Japan	169	124	101	100	99	98
732.1 & 732.6						
Germany	121	95	96	100	102	102
France	143	132	97	100	103	104
Japan	196	128	101	100	100	96
732.2−732.5 & 732.7						
Germany	111	95	98	100	102	102
France	124	120	98	100	104	108
Japan	126	117	101	100	100	100
732.8						
Germany	NA	NA	NA	100	96	100
Japan	NA	NA	NA	100	96	100
733						
Germany	91	88	97	100	101	103
733.1						
Germany	89	87	97	100	103	108
Japan	95	100	95	100	102	104
733.3						
Germany	94	89	98	100	98	97

Table F.14

Indexes of U.S. Price Competitiveness Computed from Domestic Wholesale Price Series, Miscellaneous Manufactured Articles (SITC 861, 864, 891, and 894), 1953, 1957, 1961–64

(1962 = 100)

SITC Number and Country	1953	1957	1961	1962	1963	1964
861 & 864						
Germany	104	94	102	100	99	103
861						
U.K.	100	99	103	100	103	106
Germany	101	92	97	100	100	99
Japan	163	137	108	100	98	98
861.4–861.6						
U.K.	100	98	103	100	103	106
Germany	104	94	102	100	99	103
Japan	163	137	108	100	98	98
861.9						
Germany	100	91	95	100	100	97
864						
Germany	93	91	97	100	100	102
864.2						
Japan	111	109	100	100	100	103
891						
Germany	86	87	93	100	103	107
891.1						
Japan	NA	NA	94	100	101	99
894						
U.K.	85	97	98	100	103	104
Germany	87	86	97	100	103	104
894.1						
U.K.	89	95	97	100	101	101
894.2						
U.K.	85	99	98	100	103	105
Germany	83	86	97	100	104	105
894.4						
U.K.	85	92	97	100	102	102

Table F.15
German Producers' Price Indexes, 1957, 1961–64
(1962 = 100)

SITC Number and Commodity Group	1957	1961	1962	1963	1964
696					
Cutlery	90	94	100	101	104
712					
Tractors (712.5)	90	96	100	100	100
Other agricultural machinery	92	96	100	100	101
714					
Office machines	105	100	100	100	99
715.1					
Metalworking machines					
Plane type	84	92	100	101	103
Except plane type	82	91	100	100	102
717					
Textile & leather mach.	86	95	100	100	105
718.1 & 718.2					
Paper mach.	85	92	100	102	105
718.4					
Construction mach.	91	117	100	122	123
Mining mach.	90	93	100	100	104
719.52					
Machine tools for working wood, plastics, etc.	87	95	100	101	102
719.93					
Transmission shafts, cranks, pulleys, etc.	90	94	100	101	102
722					
Elect. power mach. & switchgear	93	97	100	98	99
723					
Elect. distributing equip.	104	101	100	97	101
724					
Telecommunications apparatus	100	99	100	99	98
725					
Domestic elect. equip.	102	97	100	99	97

(continued)

Table F.15 (concluded)

SITC Number and Commodity Group	1957	1961	1962	1963	1964
729.5					
Elect. measuring & controlling instruments	91	97	100	101	101
732.1					
Passenger motor cars	98	96	100	100	100
723.3					
Lorries & trucks (incl. ambulances, etc.)	94	97	100	100	101
861 & 864					
Precision tools, optical instruments, clocks, watches	90	95	100	100	101
Optical manufactures	88	95	100	100	101
Photographic, projection, and cinematic equip.	89	97	100	99	98
Clocks & watches (864)	93	97	100	100	99

APPENDIX G

INDEXES FROM
U.S. EXPORT UNIT VALUE DATA

General Note

This appendix contains U.S. price indexes computed from the export unit value data used for the Department of Commerce export unit value indexes. They were classified here by the SITC coding system and combined by international trade weights at the 4- or 5-digit level, instead of the U.S. export weights used by the Commerce Department. The unit value indexes in this appendix differ from those published by the Department of Commerce not only in their weighting but also in the index number formulas used.[1]

Sources

The U.S. Department of Commerce made available the worksheets it used to compute its U.S. unit value indexes for 1953 through 1962. These worksheets list commodities used in its indexes, classified according to its Schedule B numbers.

We also used *United States Exports of Domestic and Foreign Merchandise; Commodity by Country of Destination,* 1963 Annual, U.S. Dept. of Commerce, Report FT 410, June 1964, and *ibid.,* 1964 Annual, June 1965.

[1] For a description of U.S. export price indexes, see *The Price Statistics of the Federal Government* prepared by the Price Statistics Review Committee of the NBER (New York, 1961), Appendix A.

Table G.1
Indexes from U.S. Export Unit Value Data, 1953, 1957, 1961–64
(1962 = 100)

SITC Number	Number of Series	1953	1957	1961	1962	1963	1964
		IRON AND STEEL					
67	26–35	75	95	99	100	99	100
671[a]	1	NA	NA	86	100	119	109
673	2–4	76	98	99	100	103	101
674	9–10	81	98	99	100	96	95
675	1	89	123	104	100	96	112
676[b]	1	78	95	96	100	104	100
677	2	70	90	106	100	92	128
678	10–16	63	83	99	100	96	94
		NONFERROUS METALS					
68[c]	6–7	90	110	99	100	98	99
682	4	92	102	97	100	101	104
684	2–3	89	120	101	100	94	94
		MANUFACTURES OF METALS, N.E.S.					
69[d]	3–5	84	98	102	100	103	109
692[e]	1	NA	NA	89	100	103	109
693[f]	1	86	102	106	100	98	107
694[g]	1	NA	NA	103	100	90	96
695	2	86	100	104	100	111	114
		MACHINERY OTHER THEN ELECTRIC					
71	14–28	76	89	100	100	104	108
711[h]	1–2	74	96	98	100	100	100
712	7–15	62	81	94	100	102	113
714[i]	3–4	72	76	95	100	91	98
717[j]	1–2	88	86	120	100	144	149
718[k]	1–2	85	93	106	100	92	99
719[l]	1–2	NA	91	97	100	103	105

(continued)

Table G.1 (concluded)

SITC Number	Number of Series	1953	1957	1961	1962	1963	1964
ELECTRICAL MACHINERY, APPARATUS, AND APPLIANCES							
72	13–19	96	100	101	100	104	100
722	1–3	76	77	97	100	108	107
724	2–3	113	112	105	100	101	89
725	2–4	111	111	102	100	104	112
729	7–9	97	107	101	100	103	102
TRANSPORT EQUIPMENT[m]							
732	8–10	84	96	103	100	94	88
MISCELLANEOUS MANUFACTURED ARTICLES							
812[n]	1	NA	NA	110	100	131	104
861	1	NA	NA	98	100	99	92
891[o]	1	NA	NA	97	100	100	101

[a]671.2 only.

[b]676.1 only.

[c]Unit value data for 68 are confined to copper and aluminum and represent only two out of nine 3-digit groups, which account for 65 per cent of the total 68 OECD exports.

[d]The 3-digit groups included in this index represent only 44 per cent of total 69 OECD exports.

[e]692.2 only.

[f]693.1 only.

[g]694.2 only.

[h]711.5 only; OECD exports of 711.5 account for 8 per cent of 711 OECD exports.

[i]Excluding 714.3, 714.9, and electronic computers in 714.2.

[j]717.3 only; OECD exports of 717.3 account for 19 per cent of 717 OECD exports.

[k]718.4 only; OECD exports of 718.4 account for 41 per cent of 718 OECD exports.

[l]719.1 and 719.3 only; these two subgroups account for 32 per cent of 719 OECD exports.

[m]Only SITC 732 has been covered by the Department of Commerce. It accounts for 65 per cent of OECD exports of 73.

[n]812.2 only.

[o]891.1 only.

Index

(References to appendixes are by table number rather than by page, e.g., A.1, B.1.)

Adams, Walter, 207n, 221
Adelman, Irma, 96–97
Aggregation, methods of, 79–89
Agricultural machinery and implements, 299–307
  errors or inconsistencies in trade statistics, 299n
  export unit values, G.1
  international price index, 304–306, C.4
  price competitiveness, 304–306, D.4, F.11
  price levels, 306–307, E.4
  regression analysis of price, 120–121, 357–361
  tractors, 75, 120–121, 303–306, 357–361
  trade patterns, 299–303, A.11, B.30
  wholesale price index, 303, 306, F.4, F.11
Aid tying. See Government intervention
Aircraft, 45, 453–463
  errors or inconsistencies in trade statistics, 287, A.7n, B.55n
  international price index, 459–461, C.6
  nonprice influences on trade, 456–458
  price competitiveness, 462–463, D.6
  price levels, 460–462
  trade patterns, 453–458, A.13, B.55
Aircraft engines and parts, 285–292
  errors or inconsistencies in trade statistics, A.5n, A.11n
  international price index, 289t, C.4
  military, 287
  parts prices and trade, 287–289, 291–292
  price competitiveness, 290–292, D.4
  price levels, 292t, 347–352, E.4
  regression analysis of price, 97, 120, 347–352
  trade patterns, 285–289, A.11
Aluminum, 239–240, 241, 248–252
  export unit values, G.1

international price index, 251t, C.2
price competitiveness, 251t, D.2, F.9
price levels, 252, E.2
trade and production, 239–240, 248–249, A.9, B.14
wholesale price index, F.2, F.9
See also Nonferrous metals
Automobiles, 451, 484–530
  consumer price index, 500, 502t
  data sources, 487–492
  engines. See Automotive diesel engines; Internal combustion engines
  international price index, 447–450, 499–508, C.6
  intracompany transfers of, 79
  list prices, 487–492, 504–506
  price competitiveness, 449–450, 507–508, D.6, F.13
  price levels, 449–451, 508–530, E.6
  regression analysis of price, 95, 96, 123, 493–498, 500, 508–516
  trade and production, 484–486, 510–518, A.13, B.53
  wholesale price index, 447–450, 500–508, F.6, F.13, F.15
  See also Motor vehicles
Automotive diesel engines
  price levels, 113–117, 297–299
  product differentiation among, 115, 297–299
  regression analysis of price, 105–119
  trade, 295

Balassa, Bela, 11n, 53n, 54t, 169n
Baldwin, Robert E., 56n
Ball, R. J., 158n, 324n, 328n, 329
Becker, Gary S., 78n
Ben-David, S., 101n
Bhagwati, J., 57n, 144–145
Bidding data, 76–78
  See also Electric power machinery and switchgear; Electricity distribution equipment; Railway vehicles

Boats. *See* Ships and boats

Brown, Murray, 33*n*

Brussels Tariff Nomenclature (BTN), 129

Business machines. *See* Office machines

Buy American. *See* Buy-domestic policies

Buy-domestic policies
 effect on international trade, 48, 56, 67–68, 392
 effect on price differences, 48, 56, 66
 of governments, 48, 56, 67, 371, 378, 456–457

Buyers' and sellers' prices compared, 15–16, 73, 76, 325*n*–326*n*, 327*n*, 343, 384–385, 408

Canada
 aircraft, 453–456
 nonelectrical machinery, 285, 299–302
 nonferrous metals, 227, 235, 238, 240, 248–250, 252–253

Capacity utilization, 160*t*, 161–163

Cars. *See* Automobiles; Railway vehicles

Chender, J. L., 246*n*, 248*n*

Cheng, Hang Sheng, 211*n*, 217*n*, 221*n*, 222

Chow, Gregory C., 311*n*

C.i.f. (cost, insurance, and freight), 53

Computers. *See* Office machines

Consumer price index
 automobiles, 500, 502*t*
 and international competition, 6

Copper, 240–248
 international price index, 246–247, C.2
 price competitiveness, 246*t*, D.2, F.9
 price levels, 246–248, E.2
 trade and production, 240–243, A.9, B.12
 wholesale prices, F.2, F.9

Cost
 as measure of competitiveness, 42–43
 as substitute for price data, 309–310, 312–313

Court, Andrew, 95, 96

Credit-tying. *See* Government intervention

Cross-exporting
 aluminum, 73, 250
 metalworking machine tools, 321
 and product differences, 34–35, 73

Cutler, Frederick, 79*n*

Data sources, 63–69, App. A–G
 aircraft, 459–460
 automobiles, 487–492
 automotive diesel engines, 105–106
 Civil Aeronautics Board, 347, 352*t*
 Fortune directory, 63–64
 Hebrew University of Jerusalem, 66
 IFO-Institut für Wirtschaftsforschung, 66, 154, 156*t*
 individual firms, 64–66, 89–93, 105, 151–154, 165–168
 Interstate Commerce Commission, 473–475
 National Association of Business Economists, 151, 168
 public bidding, 10, 15, 76–78, 161, 162*t*, 377, 438, 473, 477–478
 railway vehicles, 433*n*, 434*n*
 trade flows, App. A and B
 trade journals, 211–213, 230–232, 239
 United Kingdom Iron and Steel Board, 212*t*–213*t*, 215
 United States Department of Commerce, 212–214, 233, 311, 381, App. G

Dean, Charles R., 409*n*, 415, 418*c*, 419*t*, 420–421

De Podwin, Horace J., 409*n*, 415, 418*c*, 419*t*, 420–421

Delivery time
 effect on measurement of quantity-price relations, 328, 374, 471–472
 as element in international competition, 35, 59, 158–165, 321–324, 472

Dhrymes, Phoebus J., 105*n*

Diesel engines. *See* Automotive diesel engines; Internal combustion engines; Railway vehicles

Dirlam, Joel B., 207*n*, 221
Domestic electrical equipment. *See*
Household electrical equipment
Domestic prices, 6–7, 157–158
methods of studying, 75–76, 94
use in international price index, 75–
76
See also Automobiles; Consumer
price index; Producers' price indexes; Railway vehicles; Wholesale price indexes
Dowley, M., 145*t*
Dumping, 206–207, 217, 250, 277–278
See also Price discrimination among
markets

Eaton, J. R., 158*n*, 324*n*, 328*n*, 329
Economies of scale, 33, 370, 457–458,
516
Elasticity
price, 132–144
of substitution, 29–31, 42–43, 131–
148, 191–194, 297
of supply, 128, 137
Electric power machinery and switchgear, 367–382, 408–421
data sources, 76, 381–382, G.1
generators, 367–370, 376–377, 386
government intervention in, 370–372,
374
international price index, 379–382,
418–421, C.5
monopolistic practices, 372, 374
nonprice influence on trade, 370–372
price competitiveness, 372–375, 379,
D.5, F.12
price levels, 375–379, E.5
regression analysis of price, 121, 378–
380, 408–421
trade patterns, 367–370, A.12, B.46
transformers, 367–370, 376–380, 408–
421
wholesale price index, 381, 415, 418–
421, F.6, F.12, F.15
Electrical machinery, apparatus, and
appliances, 362–421
errors or inconsistencies in trade statistics, A.6*n*, A.12*n*, B.48*n*

export unit values, 187*t*, 188, 190*t*,
G.1
international price index, 172*t*, 174*t*–
176*t*, 178, 181*t*, 185*t*, 187*t*, 188,
190*t*, 365–366, C.5
price competitiveness, 20–22, 183*t*–
184*t*, 185*t*, 365–366, D.5, F.12
price levels, 22, 365–366, E.5
shipment delays on, 158–163
trade patterns, 362–365, A.6, A.12,
B.45–B.50
wholesale price index, 172*t*, 174*t*–
176*t*, 178, 181*t*, F.5, F.12
See also Electric power machinery
and switchgear; Electricity distribution equipment; Household
electrical equipment; Telecommunications equipment.
Electricity distribution equipment, 382–
388
international price index, 384–385,
C.5
price competitiveness, 387–388, D.5
price levels, 385–387, E.5
trade patterns, 382–383, A.12, B.47
wholesale prices, F.5, F.12, F.15
Engines. *See* Aircraft engines and parts;
Automotive engines and parts;
Internal combustion engines;
Railway vehicles
European Economic Community
(EEC), effects of, 53–54
European Free Trade Association
(EFTA), effects of, 53–54
Export and domestic prices compared.
See Export unit value indexes;
Wholesale price indexes
Export price indexes
Germany, 66
iron and steel, 211–214
relation to international price indexes,
5, 43–47
See also Export unit value indexes;
International price indexes
Export unit value indexes, App. G
coverage on, 189–191
domestic electrical equipment, 405
and domestic price index compared,
212*t*–213*t*, 216–217, 219

Export unit value indexes, App. G (cont.)
electric power machinery and switchgear, 381–382
electrical machinery, apparatus, and appliances, 187
and international price index compared, 4–7, 16–17, 186–191, 195–196, 212–215, 219, 231t, 233, 311t
iron and steel, 4–5, 186, 187t, 212–215
locomotives, 434–435
mechanical handling equipment, 343n
metal manufactures, n.e.s., 187t, 188t
motor vehicles, 4
nonelectrical machinery, 187t, 189, 190t, 311t, 343n
nonferrous metals, 187t, 188t, 189, 231–233, 265–266
office machines, 311–313, 320
telecommunications equipment, 394
transport equipment, 187t, 188
United Nations, 190–191
and wholesale price index compared, 230–233, 311t

F.a.s. (free alongside ship), 91, 93
adjustment of domestic prices to, 75n
as basis for price comparisons, 47–48, 68, 77
defined, 47n
Fettig, Lyle P., 358n
Fisher, F., 97n, 502t
F.o.b. (free on board), 91, 93, 161
defined, 47n
Foreign affiliates, effect on prices and trade, 68, 150, 285, 307, 309, 319, 341, 344–345, 436, 440, 445, 484–485
as source of price data, 68, 78–80
Fox, P., 145t
France
aircraft, 453–455, 458–459, 461–463
automobiles, 440–443, 447–451, 484–489, 491–493, 498–502, 508–515, 517–529
automotive diesel engines, 106, 114, 117n

electric power machinery and switchgear, 367–370
metal manufactures, n.e.s., 267, 273
nonelectrical machinery, 287–288, 339, 344–345
wholesale prices, App. F
Freight rates. See Transport costs
Friedlander, K., 262n

General Agreement on Tariffs and Trade (GATT), 55, 279
Generators. See Electric power machinery and switchgear
Germany. See individual product and subject entries
Ginsburg, Alan L., 141–143, 147n
Government intervention
on aircraft, 56–57, 456–458
credit tying, 60, 69, 153t, 155t, 371, 431–432, 436, 457
on electric power machinery and switchgear, 370–372
by European Coal and Steel community, 206, 209, 216–217
in iron and steel trade, 204–206, 209
on metal manufactures, n.e.s., 277, 279
by NATO, 205–206
on nonferrous metals, 236–238, 255, 257, 265
ships and boats, 467
through stockpile purchases and sales, 237–238, 253, 257–258, 261–262
by tariffs and quotas, 6, 47–48, 53–55, 236, 255, 257–258, 279
See also Buy-domestic policies; Tariffs
Grant aid to less developed countries. See Government intervention
Great Britain. See United Kingdom
Griliches, Zvi, 95, 96–97, 140, 502t
Grubel, Herbert G., 35n
Grunfeld, Y., 140

Haitovsky, Yoel, 112n
ul Haq, Mahbub, 57n
Harberger, Arnold C., 131
Hedonic price indexes. See Regression analysis of prices

Hirsch, Seev, 150*n*
Hitchner, Steven, 478*n*
Home prices. *See* Domestic prices
Household electrical equipment, 400–408
  export unit value index, G.1
  international price index, 402–405, C.5
  price competitiveness, 405–406, D.5, F.12
  price levels, 406–408, E.5
  trade patterns, 400–403, A.12, B.49
  wholesale prices, F.12, F.15

Internal combustion engines (other than for aircraft), 292–299
  international price index, 296–297, C.4
  price competitiveness, 296–297, D.4, F.11
  price levels, 297–299, 352–357, E.4
  regression analysis of price, 352–357
  trade patterns, 292–296, A.11, B.29
  wholesale prices, F.4, F.11
  See also Aircraft engines and parts; Automotive diesel engines
International price indexes, App. C
  aggregation of, 83–89
  comparison with export unit value and wholesale price indexes. *See* Export unit value indexes; Wholesale price indexes
  defined, 8
  extrapolation of, 87–88
  new measures of, 7–11
  weighting, 7–9, 27–29
Intracompany transfers. *See* Foreign affiliates
Iron and steel, 199–223, C.1, E.1, F.1, F.8, G.1
  Brussels Convention, 217
  export price data, 211–214
  export unit value index, 4–5, 186, 187*t*, 212–215, G.1
  international price index, 20–21, 172*t*, 174*t*–176*t*, 178, 181*t*, 185*t*, 186, 187*t*, 188*t*, 208*t*, 212–214, C.1

  nonprice influences on trade in, 203–207
  price competitiveness, 20–23, 183*t*–184*t*, 185*t*, 218–221, D.1, F.8
  price flexibility, 209–211
  price levels, 22–23, 221–222, E.1
  shipment delays on, 158–159, 160*t*, 162*t*, 163
  tariffs on, 205
  trade patterns, 14, 199–203, A.3, A.8, B.1–B.9
  wholesale prices, 172*t*, 174*t*–176*t*, 178, 181*t*, 208, 212*t*–213*t*, 215–217, F.1, F.8
Italy
  automobiles, 440–443, 451, 484–489, 491, 493, 498–502, 509–514, 516–525, 529
  household electrical equipment, 400–403, 407
  motor vehicles, 440–445
  telecommunications equipment, 391–392

Japan. *See* individual product and subject entries
Jeffrey, F. R., 258*n*
Jennings, B. H., 107*n*
Jets. *See* Aircraft
Jung, A. F., 490*n*
Junz, Helen B., 4*n*, 169*n*
Juster, F. Thomas, 60*n*

Kain, John F., 78*n*
Kaysen, C., 97*n*, 502*t*
Kindahl, James K., 6*n*, 178, 217, 232*n*, 325*n*
Korean War, effect on world trade, 253, 256, 257
Krause, Lawrence B., 54*n*, 207*n*
Kravis, Irving B., 33*n*, 55*n*, 74*n*, 165–168, 231*t*
Kubinski, Z., 142*n*
Kuhlman, John M., 415–421

Lancaster, K., 95*n*
Larsgaard, O. A., 505*n*
Lary, Hal B., 7*n*, 169*n*
Lead. *See* Nonferrous metals

Leather machinery. *See* Textile and leather machinery
Lewis, Cleona, 60n
Linneman, Hans, 41n
Lipkowitz, Irving, 250n
Lipsey, Robert E., 5n, 57n, 89n, 136n, 165–168, 231t
List prices vs. transaction prices. *See* Buyers' and sellers' prices compared; Export price indexes; Wholesale price indexes
Loans
  by Agency for International Development, 371–372, 432
  by Export-Import Bank, 371–372, 432
  International Bank, 371, 432
  See also Government intervention
Locomotives. *See* Railway vehicles

MacDougall, G. D. A., 31, 131n, 144–147
Machinery. *See* entries for individual types
Mack, L. J., 505n
Mechanical handling equipment, 339–346
  errors or inconsistencies in trade statistics, 299n, 345, A.11n
  export unit value index, 343n
  international price index, 342–343, C.4
  price competitiveness, 345–346, D.4
  price levels, 343–345, E.4
  trade patterns, 339–342, A.11, B.42
Metal Bulletin, as source of price data, 211–214, 247
Metal manufactures, n.e.s., 267–280
  errors or inconsistencies in trade statistics, A.4n, A.10n
  export unit value index, 187t, 188t, G.1
  international price index, 20–23, 172t, 174t–176t, 181t, 185t, 187t, 188t, 274t, C.3
  nonprice influences on trade, 273–274
  price competitiveness, 21–23, 183t–184t, 185t, 275–276, D.3, F.10
  price levels, 22–23, 276–279, E.3
  shipment delays on, 158–163
  trade and production, 267–274, A.4, A.10, B.19–B.27
  wholesale price index, 172t, 174t–176t, 181t, 276t, F.3, F.10
Metals. *See* Aluminum; Copper; Iron and steel; Nonferrous metals
Metalworking machine tools, 320–331
  delivery time for, 321, 325, 328
  international price index, 325–326, C.4
  for metal-cutting, 323t, 325t, 326–329
  for metal-forming, 323t, 325t, 326–329
  price competitiveness, 326–328, D.4, F.11
  price levels, 328–331, E.1
  trade patterns, 320–325, A.11, B.32
  wholesale price index, 326, F.4, F.11
Military shipments, 287, 388, 454–457
Mincer, Jacob, 78n
Modigliani, Franco, 169n
Monopolistic practices, 55–56, 206–207, 239, 245, 372, 374
Morgan, James N., 98n
Moses, Leon N., 78n
Motor vehicles, 439–453
  commercial, 440–453
  errors or inconsistencies in trade statistics, B.53n
  export price index, 447–449, 451–453, G.1
  export unit values, 4, G.1
  international price index, 446–450, C.6
  motorcycles, 442t, 444–445
  passenger. *See* Automobiles
  price competitiveness, 449–450, D.6, F.13
  price levels, 449–453, E.6
  regression analysis of truck prices, 122, 445–447, 451–452
  trade and production, 439–445, A.13, B.53
  trucks, 122, 442t, 444–453
  wholesale price index, 447–450, F.6, F.13
  See also Automobiles; Automotive diesel engines; Internal combustion engines

NATO (North Atlantic Treaty Organization), effect on trade, 205–206
Neisser, Hans, 169*n*
Netherlands, the
  aircraft, 453–455, 463
  telecommunications equipment, 388, 391–392
Nicholson, R. J., 144–145, 147*n*
Nickel. *See* Nonferrous metals
Nonelectrical machinery, 281–361
  errors or inconsistencies in trade statistics, 299*n*, 317, 345, A.5*n*, A.11*n*
  export unit value index, 187*t*, 190*t*, G.1
  international price index, 20–23, 172*t*, 174*t*–176*t*, 178, 181*t*, 185*t*, 187*t*, 188*t*, 190*t*, 285*t*, C.4
  price competitiveness, 20–23, 183*t*–184*t*, 185*t*, 285*t*, D.4, F.11
  price levels, 22–23, 285*t*, E.4
  shipment delays on, 158–162
  trade patterns, 13–14, 281–284, A.5, A.11, B.28–B.44
  wholesale price index, 172*t*, 174*t*–176*t*, 178, 181*t*, F.4, F.11
  See also Agricultural machinery and implements; Aircraft engines and parts; Automotive diesel engines; Internal combustion engines; Mechanical handling equipment; Metalworking machine tools; Office machines; Textile and leather machinery
Nonferrous metals
  errors or inconsistencies in trade statistics, A.3*n*, A.9*n*
  export unit value indexes, 187*t*, 188*t*, 189, 231–233, 265–266, G.1
  international price indexes, 20–22, 172*t*, 174*t*–176*t*, 178, 181*t*, 185*t*, 186, 187*t*, 188*t*, 227, 229, 231*t*, 246–248, 250–251, 255, 262, C.2
  International Tin Agreement, 261
  lead, 257–260
  London Metal Exchange, 236, 243–245, 258, 262
  nickel, 235, 238, 239, 252–254
  nonprice influences on trade, 233–242

  platinum, 255–256
  price competitiveness, 20–22, 183*t*–184*t*, 229, 246–248, 250–251, 256, 258–259, D.2, F.9
  price flexibility, 227, 238–239, 244–245, 247, 264–265
  price levels, 22–23, 229–231, 247–248, 250–252, 254, 258–259, 263–265, E.2
  shipment delays on, 158–163
  silver, 238, 254–255
  stockpiling, 237–238, 253, 257–258, 261–262
  tin, 235, 260–262
  trade and production, 13–14, 224–227, 234–236, 240, 242–243, 248–250, 252–257, 259–261, A.3, A.9, B.10–B.18
  wholesale price index, 231–232, 265, F.2, F.9
  zinc, 256–259, 260
  See also Aluminum; Copper
Nonprice influences on trade, 31–33, 132–133, 135
  in aircraft, 456–458
  compatibility with existing equipment, 392–393, 430–432, 457–458
  credit terms, 15, 59–60, 92, 153*t*, 155*t*, 432, 457
  delivery speed, 15, 35, 59, 92, 153*t*, 155*t*, 156*t*, 158–165, 321–324, 328
  in electric power machinery and switchgear, 370–372
  and international price measures, 59–61
  in iron and steel, 203–207
  on metal manufactures, n.e.s., 273–274
  price and, 151–157
  product quality, 33–35, 59, 72, 78, 153*t*, 154, 155*t*, 156*t*, 330–331, 377–378
  in railway vehicles, 429–432
  reliability of supplier, 76, 153*t*, 155*t*, 430
  safety regulations, 273–274

Nonprice influences on trade (cont.)
service, 59, 92, 153–156, 430, 458, 527
in ships and boats, 466–468
technological leadership, 32–33, 321, 323, 370
telecommunications equipment, 392
transport costs, 6, 47–55, 59, 522, 523
in transport equipment, 429–432, 456–458, 466–468
and U.S. competitive position, 31–35, 45, 59, 92, 153t, 155t
See also Product differentiation
Norway, nonferrous metals, 235, 249, 253

Obert, E. F., 107n
Offer prices. See Buyers' and sellers' prices compared; Price flexibility
Office machines, 307–320
computers, 75, 307–309, 311, 312n, 314–317, 320
cost data, 309–310, 312–313
errors and inconsistencies in trade statistics, 317, A.11n
export unit values, 311–313, G.1
international price index, 309–312, C.4
price competitiveness, 312–313, D.4, F.11
price levels, 313–315, E.4
trade patterns, 307–309, A.11, B.31
typewriters, 44–45, 307–309, 314–317, 320
wholesale price index, 311t, F.4, F.11, F.15
Orcutt, Guy H., 131n
Outboard motors. See Internal combustion engines

Parts prices and trade, 287–289, 445, 455–456
Passenger motor cars. See Automobiles
Pennock, Robert S., 333n
Pizer, Samuel, 79n
Platinum. See Nonferrous metals
Price competitiveness
aggregation of indexes of, 82–89

comparison of measures from international and wholesale prices, 182–194
in all covered commodities, 19–21
definition and measurement, 8–10, 43–47
diffusion of changes in, 22–25
relation to trade, 29–31, 39–42, 127–144, 191–194
in aircraft engines, 292
in domestic electrical equipment, 406
in electric power machinery and switchgear, 374–375
in electrical machinery and appliances, 365
in electricity distribution equipment, 388
in internal combustion engines, 296–297
in iron and steel, 220–221
in locomotives, 437–439
in metalworking machine tools, 327–328
in office machinery, 318–319
in ships and boats, 470–473
in telecommunications equipment, 397
in transport equipment, 423–424
Price discrimination among markets, 68, 157–158, 246, 250, 264–265, 378–379, 386–387, 524–530
Price flexibility, 209–211, 227, 238–239, 244–245, 247, 264–265
See also Buyers' and sellers' prices compared
Price indexes. See Consumer price index; Domestic prices; Export unit value indexes; International price indexes; Price competitiveness; Price level indexes; Producers' price indexes, Germany; Regression analysis of prices; Wholesale price indexes
Price level indexes
for all covered commodities, 19–21
defined, 9–10
relation to trade
in automobiles, 529–530

in electricity distribution equipment, 386
in internal combustion engines, 298–299
in locomotives, 439
in mechanical handling equipment, 345
in metal manufactures, n.e.s., 279
in metalworking machine tools, 329–330
in nonferrous metals, 265
in office machinery, 315–318
in telecommunications equipment, 399–400
Producers' price indexes, Germany, F.15
Product differentiation, 34–35, 57–59, 152–157
in agricultural machinery, 302–303
in automobiles, 510–518, 522–530
in automotive diesel engines, 115
in cutlery, 279
in domestic appliances, 407–408
in internal combustion engines, 297–298
in mechanical handling equipment, 339, 341
in metalworking machine tools, 321
in office machinery, 314–315
in railway locomotives, 426
in textile machinery, 34, 331, 333, 336
See also Nonprice influences on trade
Pugh, S., 145t
Purchasing power parity theory, 11

Radio receivers. See Telecommunications equipment
Railway vehicles, 425–439, 473–478
bidding data on, 435–437, 476–478
export unit values, 434–435
freight cars, 426, 430, 436, 439
ICC data, 433n, 434n, 473–477
international price index, 432–435, C.6
locomotives, 45, 77, 97, 121, 426–439, 473–478
nonprice influences on trade, 429–432

price competitiveness, 437–439, D.6, F.13
price levels, 435–437, E.6
regression analysis of price, 97, 121, 433n–434n, 473–478
trade patterns, 425–429, A.13, B.52
wholesale prices, 434, F.13
Reciprocity agreements. See Nonprice influences on trade
Refrigerators. See Household electrical equipment
Regression analysis of prices, 16, 94–124
agricultural machinery and implements, 120–121, 357–361
aircraft engines and parts, 97, 120, 347–352
automobiles, 95, 96, 122–123, 486–530
automotive engines, 105–119
computers, 311
electric power machinery and switchgear, 378–380, 408–421
internal combustion engines, 353–357
methods of, 16
motor vehicles, road, 122, 445n–446n, 452n
outboard motors, 120
pooled, 100, 103, 110–116, 118–119
power transformers, 121
railway locomotives, 97, 121, 433n–434n, 473–478
ships, 121–122, 478–483
tractors, 120–121
trucks, 122
Rhomberg, Rudolf R., 4n, 169n
Rogowski, A. R., 107n, 494n
Romanis, Anne, 39n
Rosenberg, Nathan, 33n
Ryan, J. P., 254n

Salant, Walter S., 169n
Schroeder, H. J., 257n
Sellers' prices. See Buyers' and sellers' prices compared
Shay, Robert, 60n
Shipment delay. See Nonprice influences on trade, delivery speed; Strikes

Ships and boats, 463–473, 479–483
errors or inconsistencies in trade statistics, B.56n
international price index, 468–469, C.6
nonprice influences on trade, 466–468
price competitiveness, 469–471, D.6
price levels, 471–472, E.6
regression analysis of price, 121–122, 478–483
tankers, 465, 479–480, 482
trade patterns, 463–466, A.13, B.56
Silver. See Nonferrous metals
Smith, Richard Austin, 420n
Sonquist, John A., 98n
Standard Industrial Trade Classification (SITC), 134–141
changes in, 129
defined, 11–12
See also individual product entries
Steel. See Iron and steel
Stern, Robert M., 42n, 137n, 141–143, 147n
Steuer, M. D., 158n, 324n, 328n, 329
Stigler, George J., 4n, 6n, 95n, 96n, 178, 217, 232n, 325n
Stone, Richard, 95
Stotz, Margaret S., 505n
Strikes, effect on international trade, 159, 163, 203–205
Sturmey, S. G., 465n
Subsidiaries, foreign. See Foreign affiliates
Suez crisis, effect on international trade, 173, 208, 215, 216, 218, 220, 222, 468, 472
Suits, D. B., 103n
Sweden
electric power machinery and switchgear, 367, 373, 376–377, 381
ships and boats, 45, 463–467
Switchgear. See Electric power machinery and switchgear
Switzerland, metalworking machine tools, 330
textile machinery, 331, 333, 335

Tariffs, 6, 47–48, 53–55, 91, 98, 250, 265, 392, 522

Telecommunications equipment, 388–400
errors or inconsistencies in trade statistics, A.12n, B.48n
export unit value index, 394, G.1
international price index, 393–394, C.5
Italy, 391–392
the Netherlands, 388, 391–392
nonprice influences on trade, 392
price competitiveness, 395–397, D.5, F.12
price levels, 397–400, E.5
radio receivers, 75, 392–400
telephone systems, 392–394
television, 75, 388–399
trade patterns, 388–393, A.12, B.48
wholesale price index, 394, F.5, F.12, F.15
Telephone systems. See Telecommunications equipment
Television. See Telecommunications equipment
Terms-of-trade index, 44
Textile and leather machinery, 331–339, A.11, B.34, C.4, D.4, E.4, F.4, F.11, F.15, G.1
international price index, 332–334, 336–337, 338t, C.4
price competitiveness index, 334t, 337t, 338t, D.4, F.11
price level index, 334–335, 336–339, E.4
sewing machines, 332t, 336–338
Switzerland, 331–335
trade patterns, 331–333, 335–337
Tin. See Nonferrous metals
Tinbergen, Jan, 141
Tomek, W. G., 101n
Topping, F. K., 523t
Tractors. See Agricultural machinery and implements
Trade statistics, errors and inconsistencies in
agricultural machinery, 299n
aircraft, 287, A.7n, B.55n
aircraft engines and parts, A.5n, A.11n
computers, 317, A.11n

construction machinery, 299*n*, 345, A.11*n*
electrical machinery, A.6*n*
metal manufactures, n.e.s., A.4*n*, A.10*n*
motor vehicles, B.53*n*
nonferrous metals, A.3*n*, A.9*n*
pneumatic tools, A.11*n*
ships and boats, B.56*n*
sources of, App. A and B
telecommunications equipment, A.12*n*, B.48*n*
Transaction prices. *See* Buyers' and sellers' prices compared; Price flexibility
Transfer costs. *See* Transport costs
Transport costs, 6, 47–55, 59, 98, 147*n*, 148, 250, 255
Transport equipment
errors or inconsistencies in trade statistics, 287, A.7*n*, B.53*n*, B.55*n*, B.56*n*
export unit value index, 187*t*, 188, G.1
international price index, 21–22, 172*t*, 174*t*–176*t*, 181*t*, 185*t*, 187*t*, 188, 422, C.6
price competitiveness, 21–22, 183*t*–184*t*, 185*t*, 423–424, D.6, F.13
price levels, 22–23, 424–425, E.6
shipment delays on, 158–163
trade patterns, 14, 422, A.7, A.13, B.51–B.56
wholesale price index, 172*t*, 174*t*–176*t*, 181*t*, F.6, F.13
See also Aircraft; Motor vehicles; Railway vehicles; Ships and boats
Triplett, Jack E., 502*t*
Trucks. *See* Motor vehicles
Typewriters. *See* Office machines

Union of Soviet Socialist Republics
nonferrous metals, 248, 250, 252, 253*n*, 255–256, 262
steel, 205–206
Unique products, 74–75, 153*t*, 154–156
See also Product differentiation

Unit values. *See* Export unit value indexes
United Kingdom. *See* entries for individual products
United States. *See* entries for individual products

Vernon, Raymond, 33*n*, 150*n*

Ware, G. C., 255*n*
Washing machines. *See* Household electrical equipment
Weighting of price and price competitiveness indexes
differences between beginning- and end-of-period weights, 136–137
individual country vs. common weights, 27–29
use of world trade weights, 3, 5, 7–8, 11, 80–82
Wholesale price indexes, App. F
agricultural machinery and implements, 303, 306, F.4, F.11
automobiles, 447–450, 500–503, F.6, F.13
electric power machinery and switchgear, 381, 415, 418–421, F.5, F.12
electrical machinery, apparatus, and appliances, 172*t*, 174*t*–176*t*, 178, 181*t*, F.5, F.12
and export unit value index compared, 311*t*
and international price index compared, 16–17, 171–182, 194–195, 212*t*–213*t*, 219*t*, 230–232, 274–275, 306*t*, 311*t*, 447–450
iron and steel, 172*t*, 174*t*–176*t*, 178, 181*t*, F.1, F.8
as a measure of domestic prices, 170
metal manufactures, n.e.s., 172*t*, 174*t*–176*t*, 181*t*, 274–276, F.3, F.10
metalworking machine tools, 326, F.4, F.11
motor vehicles, road, 447–450, F.6, F.13

Wholesale price indexes, App. F (cont.)
  nonelectrical machinery, 172*t*, 174*t*–
    176*t*, 178, 181*t*, 303, 306, 311*t*,
    326, F.4, F.11
  nonferrous metals, 172*t*, 174*t*–176*t*,
    178, 181*t*, 231*t*, F.2, F.9
  office machines, 311*t*, F.4, F.11
  and price competitiveness index com-
    pared, 17, 306*t*
  railway vehicles, F.6, F.13
  regression analysis of price from,
    191–194
  telecommunications equipment, 394,
    F.5, F.12
  transport equipment, 172*t*, 174*t*–176*t*,
    181*t*, F.6, F.13

  and unit value index compared, 230–
    233
  weighting, 7, 178
  See also Consumer price index; Do-
    mestic prices; Producers' price
    indexes
Wideman, F. L., 242*n*
Williamson, Harold F., Jr., 78*n*
Wood, Harleston R., 208*n*

Zarnowitz, Victor, 164*n*
Zelder, Raymond E., 131*n*, 141–143
Zimmerman, J., 244*n*, 245*n*
Zinc. *See* Nonferrous metals
Zupnick, Elliot, 42*n*, 137*n*